Handbook of
Global Supply Chain Management

Handbook of
Global Supply Chain Management

John T. Mentzer
University of Tennessee

Matthew B. Myers
University of Tennessee

Theodore P. Stank
University of Tennessee

Editors

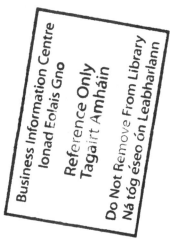

SAGE Publications
Thousand Oaks ▪ London ▪ New Delhi

For information:

Sage Publications, Inc.
2455 Teller Road
Thousand Oaks, California 91320
E-mail: order@sagepub.com

Sage Publications Ltd.
1 Oliver's Yard
55 City Road
London EC1Y 1SP
United Kingdom

Sage Publications India Pvt. Ltd.
B-42, Panchsheel Enclave
Post Box 4109
New Delhi 110 017 India

Printed in the United States of America

Library of Congress Cataloging-in-Publication Data

Handbook of global supply chain management / editors, John T. Mentzer, Matthew B. Myers, Theodore P. Stank.
    p. cm.
Includes bibliographical references and index.
ISBN 1-4129-1805-7 (cloth)
    1. Business logistics. 2. Delivery of goods—Management. I. Mentzer, John T. II. Myers, Matthew B. III. Stank, Theodore P. IV. Title.
HD38.5.H353 2007
658.5—dc22   2006002917

This book is printed on acid-free paper.

06 07 08 09 10 9 8 7 6 5 4 3 2 1

Acquisitions Editor:	Al Bruckner
Editorial Assistant:	MaryAnn Vail
Production Editor:	Diane S. Foster
Copy Editor:	QuADS and Linda Gray
Typesetter:	C&M Digitals (P) Ltd.
Proofreader:	Scott Oney
Indexer:	Will Ragsdale
Cover Designer:	Glenn Vogel

Contents

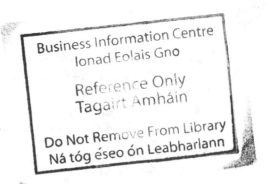

Preface   **xiii**

1. Why Global Supply Chain Management?   **1**
John T. Mentzer, Theodore P. Stank, and Matthew B. Myers
   About Global Supply Chain Management   2
   About the Handbook   5
   Understanding Global Supply Chains   5
   Managing the Functions   7
   Resource Management   10
   Managing the Relations   11
   Making It Happen   14
   Conclusions   15

PART I: UNDERSTANDING GLOBAL SUPPLY CHAINS

2. Global Supply Chain Management Strategy   **19**
John T. Mentzer, Theodore P. Stank, and Matthew B. Myers
   Background   20
   Global SCM Strategy   22
   Impacts on Strategic Orientation   22
   Capabilities and Structural Elements of GSCMS   25
   Performance Implications   32
   Integration of GSCMS Into Firm Strategy   33

3. Assessing the Global Environment   **39**
Matthew B. Myers, Antonio Borghesi, and Ivan Russo
   Yesterday's Supply Chains in Today's Global Environment   40
   Cross-Cultural Influences and the Global Supply Chain   41
   Foreign Currency Volatility   43
   Political Economies   44
   Two Sets of Rules   45
   The New Environment of Hypersecurity   47
   Conclusions   47

4. Value and Customer Service Management   **51**
Daniel J. Flint and Britta Gammelgaard
    Value Management   52
    Customer Service   59
    Customer Service and Value Management   61

5. Demand Management   **65**
John T. Mentzer, Mark A. Moon,
Dominique Estampe, and Glen Margolis
    Derived Versus Independent Demand   66
    A Model of Supply Chain Demand Management   69
    Forecasts Versus Plans Versus Targets   69
    Sales and Operations Planning   70
    Why Is a Sales Forecast Needed?   72
    The Tools of Sales Forecasting Management   73
    Sales Forecasting Management Questions   77
    Demand Management: An Iterative Process   84

6. Knowledge Management   **87**
Donna F. Davis and Didier Chenneveau
    From Data to Knowledge   88
    Building Knowledge Management Competence   90
    Challenges to Building Knowledge
       Management Competence   101

7. Process Orientation   **103**
Everth Larsson and Anders Ljungberg
    Introductory Views on SCM and Processes   103
    The Heritage of the Function-Oriented Organization   103
    Different Processes   106
    A Business Viewed as a System   107
    Elements in a Process-Oriented Organization   109
    Designing the Process-Oriented Organization   110
    Is SCM Possible in Function-Oriented Organizations?   112
    Should Processes Be Company-Specific or Standard?   113
    How to Make SCM Work   113
    Measurement, Analysis, and Development   114
    Conclusions   116

PART II: MANAGING THE FUNCTIONS

8. Marketing and Sales Management   **119**
Thomas E. DeCarlo and William L. Cron
    Marketing Strategy   120
    Strategic Implementation Decisions   122
    Sales Force Program Decisions   129
    Summary   134

9. Product Management   **135**
Margaret Bruce, Lucy Daly, and Kenneth B. Kahn

    The Role of Product Management   136
    Global Product Launch   137
    Launch Strategy Influencers   139
    Global Launch Strategy Considerations   140
    Company One   140
    Company Two   143
    Summary   145

10. Operations Management   **149**
E. Powell Robinson, Jr., and Funda Sahin

    What Is Operations Management?   150
    Operations Management Decision Problems   151
    Evolution of Operations Management   152
    Different Perspectives of Operations Management   155
    Operations Management in the New Economy   162
    Synchronizing the Marketplace and Operations Through Agility   165
    Implications and Conclusions   167

11. Integrated Logistics Management   **169**
Abré Pienaar

    Logistics in the Context of Supply Chain Management   169
    Business Process Integration   171
    The Business Process Framework   173
    Methods and Techniques   174
    Organization and People   174
    Systems and Data   174
    Designing Integrated Logistics Business Processes   176
    Implementing Integrated Logistics Management   178
    Global Pharmaceuticals   181
    Summary   182

12. Inventory Management   **185**
Funda Sahin and E. Powell Robinson, Jr.

    Inventory Basics   186
    Independent Versus Dependent Demand Inventory   186
    Reasons for Inventory   186
    Reasons Against Inventory   187
    Types of Inventory   188
    Inventory Control Systems   188
    Single-Period Inventory Systems   189
    Multiperiod Inventory Systems   189
    Implications and New Strategies in Inventory Management   195
    Postponement   196
    Reducing Seasonal and Short-Life-Cycle Inventory
        Costs With Quick Response (QR)   197

Supply Chain Partnerships and Vendor-Managed Inventory   198
Conclusions   200

13. Transportation Management   **203**
Thomas J. Goldsby, Michael R. Crum, and Joel Sutherland
Transportation Decision Making   204
Transportation Cost Behavior   207
Collaborative Transportation Management   210
Global Transportation Issues   214
Conclusions   219

14. Warehouse Management   **223**
Thomas W. Speh
The Role of Warehousing in Global Supply Chains   226
Product Type and Warehousing Operations   227
Why Have a Warehouse?   230
The Location of Warehouses   232
Warehouse Design and Operations   232
The Role of Information in Warehouse Management   245
Technology and Warehouse Operations   246
Future Trends for Warehousing   249
Suggested Readings   251

15. Supply Management   **253**
Lisa M. Ellram and Paul Cousins
The Strategic Supply Management Process   255
Trends in Supply Management   266
Concluding Thoughts   271

16. Personnel   **273**
Scott Keller
The Changing Nature of the Workplace   274
Creating a Customer-Focused Logistics Workforce   274
Fundamental Information Exchange   275
Knowledge Development   277
Assistance to Employees   278
Performance Feedback   279
Workplace Affirmation   280
Implementing a Customer-Focused Employee Plan   281

PART III: RESOURCE MANAGEMENT

17. The Lean Supply Chain: The Path to Excellence   **285**
Mandyam M. Srinivasan and James M. Reeve
Conventional Supply Chain Management   285
It Is More Than "Just-in-Time"   288
Lean Supply Chain Basics: Flow and Pull Replenishment   288
Work Flow Characterization: V, A, and T Configurations   290

Fulfillment Characterization: Build-to-Stock,
    Assemble-to-Order, Build-to-Order, and Engineer-to-Order   293
Applying Lean Principles to a BTS V-Type Process   294
Conclusions   297

18. Financial Management   **299**
Stephen G. Timme
  Key Drivers of Financial Performance   300
  Measuring Financial Performance   305
  Making the Financial-SCM Connection:
    A Top-Down Approach   307
  Conclusions   315
  Appendix   316

19. Risk Management   **319**
Ila Manuj, J. Paul Dittmann, and Barbara Gaudenzi
  What Is Risk?   320
  Types of Risks in Global Supply Chains   321
  A Risk Management Process Model   324
  Step 1: Identifying and Profiling Risks   325
  Step 2: Risk Assessment and Evaluation   326
  Step 3: Managing Risks and Risk Management Strategies   329
  Step 4: Supply Chain Risk Management
    Strategy Implementation   333
  Step 5: Mitigating Supply Chain Risks   335
  Conclusions   335

**20. Interpretation Systems: Knowledge,
Strategy, and Performance**   **337**
*G. Tomas M. Hult, David J. Ketchen, Jr., S. Tamer Cavusgil,
and Roger J. Calantone*
  Recent Research on Information Management Within
    Supply Chains   338
  The Next Step: Fitting Supply Chain Knowledge and Strategy   340
  Identification of Ideal Profiles   342
  Implications   347
  Conclusions   350
  Appendix   350

PART IV: MANAGING THE RELATIONS

21. Relationship Management   **361**
Jagdish N. Sheth and Arun Sharma
  Shift in Organizational Strategy   361
  Relationship With Suppliers   362
  Examples of Benefiting From Supplier Relationships   363
  Establishing and Maintaining Supplier Relationships   366
  Organizational Changes to Establish Supplier Relationships   368

| | Emerging Issues in Relationship Management | 370 |
| | Summary | 370 |

22. Logistics Outsourcing — 373
Clifford F. Lynch, Theodore P. Stank, and Shay Scott

	Logistics Outsourcing History	374
	Why Outsource Logistics Activities?	376
	The Challenges of Global Logistics Outsourcing	385
	Some Concluding Examples	389

23. International Sourcing: Redressing the Balance — 393
Masaaki Kotabe and Michael J. Mol

	The International Sourcing Phenomenon	393
	Wave After Wave	394
	The Performance Rationale	395
	On Balance	397
	Redressing the Balance	399
	Riding the Waves	403

24. Negotiating Throughout the Supply Chain — 407
Lloyd M. Rinehart

	Relationship Types Resulting From Supplier-Customer Negotiations	408
	Following the Negotiation Process in a Global Supply Chain Context	414
	Conclusions	425

25. Interfunctional Coordination — 427
Susan L. Golicic and Kate Vitasek

	What Is Interfunctional Coordination?	428
	Axes of Effective Interfunctional Coordination	431
	Mechanisms to Drive Coordination	432
	Common Goals and Measures	435
	Achieving Interfunctional Coordination	438
	Interfunctional Coordination: A Collaborative Climate for Success	441

26. Intercorporate Coordination — 443
Terry L. Esper

	The Managerial Behaviors of Interorganizational Coordination	445
	Environmental Characteristics for Effective Interorganizational Coordination	451
	Conclusions	454

27. Global Supply Chain Control — 455
Daniel C. Bello and Meng Zhu

| | Characteristics of the Controller's Strategy | 456 |
| | Magnitude and Scope of Control Requirements | 462 |

Implementation Effectiveness From
    Institutional Arrangements   466
The Moderator Role of Institutional
    Environmental Differences   468
Conclusion   470

PART V: MAKING IT HAPPEN

28. Supply Chain Innovation   475
Daniel J. Flint and Everth Larsson
  Innovation as Strategy   477
  Supply Chain Innovation   477
  Innovation Processes   480
  The Importance of Organizational Culture and Processes   484
  Ramifications of Global Supply Chains   485
  Summary   485

29. Global Supply Chain Security   487
Omar Keith Helferich and Robert Lorin Cook
  Disaster Classification and Vulnerability Assessment   487
  Disaster Management Process   490
  Disaster Preparedness: Current Status   500
  Recent and Emerging Developments   501
  Conclusions   504

30. Diagnosing the Supply Chain   507
James H. Foggin, Paola Signori, and Carol L. Monroe
  Diagnosis   508
  Benchmarking Approaches   508
  Mapping Approaches   512
  Means-Ends Approaches and Cause-and-Effect Diagrams   515
  Curing Problems and Eliminating the Pain Points   519
  Summary   520

31. Change Management   523
J. Paul Dittmann and John E. Mello
  What Is Change Management?   524
  Developing the Change Management Strategy   525
  The Change Management Plan   526
  People and Organizational Issues   527
  Organizational Readiness for Change:
    The Change Management Survey   528
  Change Management Organizational Roles   528
  The Initial Response to an Announced Change   530
  Complacency   532
  Resistance to Change   533
  Resistance to Different Types of Change   533

Change Management Myths and Realities   534
Launching the Change   535
Summary of Key Success Factors: The Change Equation   536
Change Management in a Global Environment   537
Summary   540

Name Index   **543**

Subject Index   **549**

About the Editors   **567**

About the Contributors   **569**

Preface

This book is the work of many people besides the authors, and they all deserve recognition. First, the many scholars who went before us and thought and wrote about global supply chain management provided invaluable insights for this book. In fact, the original idea for writing this book came from a recognition that so much was being written on the subject that it was time for an all-encompassing handbook of global supply chain management. To these supply chain scholars, we are most grateful.

No one person could have written this handbook. We wanted the top expert in the area of each topic, and no one qualifies for that distinction in all the areas of global supply chain management. Thus, a handbook where each chapter is written by the people most qualified and the overall handbook is edited by a team was the best approach. In keeping with the global theme and the goal of a handbook, we tried, in as many chapters as possible, to have international scholars and practitioners involved. We hope the result is a handbook that addresses, for each topic, the global extant theory needed by scholars who teach and research in this area and the specifics needed by practitioners.

We hope this book brings clarity and comprehensive insight to the phenomenon of global supply chains and their management. For students, we hope this handbook aids in understanding the scope and specifics. For practitioners, we hope this handbook provides additional insights into the nuances of managing global supply chains. For researchers, we hope this book generates additional questions, the answers to which will continue to enrich our understanding of and ability to manage global supply chains.

1

Why Global Supply Chain Management?

John T. Mentzer

Theodore P. Stank

Matthew B. Myers

T he term *supply chain management* (SCM) has risen to prominence over the past 15 years, becoming such a "hot topic" that it is difficult to pick up a periodical on manufacturing, distribution, marketing, customer management, or transportation without seeing an article about SCM-related topics. Logistics, one central element of SCM, has long been an area of concern for both practitioners and academics. In fact, the professional association for logistics and SCM professionals—the Council of Logistics Management, which changed its name in 2005 to the Council of Supply Chain Management Professionals (CSCMP) to encompass the broader management area of SCM—holds an annual conference that often draws more than 4,000 participants. Furthermore, every company today either sources globally, sells globally, or competes with some company that does. Thus, global supply chain management (GSCM) represents a central area of focus for many businesses and business schools today.

Although the extraordinary growth of GSCM attests to its robustness and practical importance, the field is diffuse and complex. Many methods and perspectives on GSCM have emerged from logistics, operations, marketing, management, economics, sociology, personnel, information systems, and international relations. Their diversity and rapid growth make it hard to keep abreast of significant developments. Moreover, many of these approaches have evolved with relative independence, paying little attention to how they relate to existing methods or interrelate with each other. This makes it difficult to accumulate wisdom in the field and to develop a coherent knowledge base to guide research and practice.

Thus, this handbook is aimed at providing a comprehensive understanding and assessment of the field of GSCM. In each chapter, the authors describe and critically examine the key perspectives guiding GSCM, taking stock of what we know (and do not know) about them. They identify emerging developments and delineate their significance to the practice of GSCM. The chapters are not intended to be exhaustive summaries of all the relevant literature and research, but emphasize basic knowledge and understanding of the field. They pay particular attention to identifying connections among methods and perspectives and exploring how they contribute to integration of knowledge in GSCM.

The handbook maps the broad terrain of GSCM from multiple viewpoints seeking to explain what is already known, what new developments are occurring, and how different methods and approaches are interrelated. For each chapter, we tried to select the most knowledgeable and prominent practitioners and scholars in the global arena to represent the key perspectives in the field. These contributors share their unique perspectives and insights within the broad parameters of this handbook. The result, we believe, is a handbook that offers a comprehensive, yet in-depth, examination of GSCM. Thus, it is intended for all relevant audiences in GSCM. For researchers, the handbook provides a broad inventory of what is currently known about GSCM and identifies significant knowledge gaps and issues that need to be addressed. It provides a fertile ground for future research. Advanced students should use the handbook to gain a solid foundation in GSCM. It will help them understand and appreciate the multiple perspectives that guide the field and show them where GSCM is likely headed. For thoughtful practitioners, the handbook provides a valuable reference and source of ideas and methods for developing organizations. It also provides them with conceptual frameworks for understanding GSCM practice and for creating new methods and techniques.

About Global Supply Chain Management

The current trend toward the globalization of supply chains renders many managers confused as to what *globalization* really means. Often, the term is little more than a battlefield of semantics, of little value to the individual tasked with managing value creation and cost reduction processes in the movement of goods. Clearly, globalization infers the cross-border movement of goods and the emergence of global competitors and opportunities across competing supply chains within an industry. Managers, however, often question the differences between a global market and a single market, in that many of the same conditions exist in both. Although this may be true, the complexities of cross-border operations are exponentially greater than in a single country, and the ability to compete in the global environment often depends on understanding the subtleties that emerge only in cross-border trade—that is, in GSCM.

Why do so many people spend so much time thinking, writing, and doing GSCM? The answer is that it is a considerable source of competitive advantage in the global marketplace. The fierce competition in today's markets is led by advances in industrial technology, increased globalization of demand and supply sources, tremendous improvements in information availability, plentiful venture capital, and creative business designs (Bovet and Sheffi 1998). In highly competitive markets, the simple pursuit of market share is no longer sufficient to ensure profitability, and thus, companies focus on redefining their competitive space or profit zone (Bovet and Sheffi 1998). For example, companies pursue cooperative relationships to capture lifetime customer share (as opposed to mass market share) through systematic development and management of cooperative and collaborative partnerships (Gruen 1997). Markets have been changed by factors such as power shifts from corporate buyers to end users, the requirement for mass customization, emergence of global consumer segments, time- and quality-based competition, improvements in communications and information technology, increasing knowledge intensity, and changing government policies.

Power in a broad spectrum of supply chains has shifted downstream toward the customer or end user (LaLonde 1997), and as a result, customer satisfaction becomes the ultimate goal of a company. As the customer increasingly is in charge in the marketplace, interfirm cooperation is critical to satisfy customers. Manufacturers and their intermediaries must be nimble and quick or face the prospect of losing market share, and thus, relationships and predictable performance become very important in a supply chain (LaLonde 1997).

Mass customization provides a tremendous increase in variety without sacrificing efficiency, effectiveness, or low costs (Pine 1993). In other words, customers want low cost with high levels of service and customization with availability (Bovet and Sheffi 1998). Pine (1993), therefore, argues that mass customization can be achieved only through the committed involvement of employees, suppliers, distributors, retailers, and end customers.

Firms are competing in a global economy, and thus, the unit of business analysis is the world, not just a country or region. The communications revolution and globalization of consumer culture will not tolerate hand-me-down designs or excessive delivery times (Bovet and Sheffi 1998). In this context, Kotler (1997) states, "As firms globalize, they realize that no matter how large they are, they lack the total resources and requisites for success. Viewing the complete supply chain for producing value, they recognize the necessity of partnering with other organizations" (p. 72).

Time- and quality-based competition focuses on eliminating waste in the form of time, effort, defective units, and inventory in manufacturing-distribution systems (Larson and Lusch 1990; Schonberger and El-Ansary 1984; Schultz 1985). In addition, there has been a significant trend to emphasize quality, not only in the production of products or services but also throughout all areas in a company (Coyle, Bardi, and Langley 1996).

LaLonde and Powers (1993) suggest that the most profound and influential changes that directly affect companies are information technology and communications. With the advent of modern computers and communications, monolithic companies, which had become highly bureaucratic, started eroding. Fast communication that links all members of a company decreased the need for multiple layers of people who were once the information channel and control mechanism. The decreased cost and ready availability of information resources allow easy linkages and eliminate time delays in the network (LaLonde and Powers 1993).

In the new competitive landscape, knowledge (information, intelligence, and expertise) is a critical organizational resource and is increasingly a valuable source of competitive advantage (Hitt, Ireland, and Hoskisson 1999). Similarly, LaLonde and Powers (1993) characterized the 1990s as the era of reassembly or reintegration after that of disintegration. Current reintegration is based not on position or prescribed roles in a hierarchy; it is based on knowledge and competence (LaLonde and Powers 1993). Bringing together the knowledge and skills to effectively serve the market requires coordination (Malone and Rockart 1991).

Finally, government policy may encourage cooperative strategies among firms. The U.S. 1996 Telecommunications Act and subsequent court battles have created significant uncertainty for the firms involved; consequently, a significant number of alliances have emerged (Hitt et al. 1999). The enactment of the U.S. National Cooperative Research Act of 1984, as amended in 1993, eased the U.S. government's antitrust policy to encourage firms to cooperate with each other to foster increased competitiveness of American industries (Bowersox and Closs 1996; Barlow 1994).

Today's business environment puts stress on both relations with customers and the service provided to such customers (Hitt et al. 1999). Kotler (1997) argued, "Customers are scarce; without them, the company ceases to exist. Plans must be laid to acquire and keep customers" (p. 109). The level of competition to capture customers in both domestic and international markets demands that organizations be quick, agile, and flexible to compete effectively (LaLonde 1997; Fliedner and Vokurka 1997). This level of flexibility cannot be obtained without coordination of the companies in the global supply chain.

Arguably, SCM has risen to prominence from its beginnings in the logistics management literature (Cooper, Lambert, and Pagh 1997). The CSCMP (2005) defines logistics management as

> that part of Supply Chain Management that plans, implements, and controls the efficient, effective forward and reverse flow and storage of goods, services and related information between the point of origin and the point of consumption in order to meet customers' requirements. (para. 3)

This definition tells us that logistics management involves all the movement and storage activities that are associated with product and service flows. It is focused on what we call the "focal organization," that is, on managing that organization's inbound and outbound flows of goods, services, and related information. We can imagine that "related information" encompassing inventory quantities and locations, order status, shipment status and location, transportation status and vehicle location, and so on. But what about information that flows up and down a supply chain that is not related to the flow of goods and services? Information on marketing plans, advertising effectiveness, pricing structure, product management status, ownership and title, and financial status do not seem to be within the realm of logistics. For that matter, what about actual financial flows?

There are clearly flows up and down the global supply chain that are not part of the CSCMP definition of logistics management. CSCMP acknowledges that SCM is something more than logistics management by stating that "Logistics Management is that part of Supply Chain Management that . . ." So, SCM must encompass logistics management and these other flows mentioned above.

It was this realization that led the Supply Chain Research Group at the University of Tennessee (Mentzer 2004) to define SCM as

> the systemic, strategic coordination of the traditional business functions within a particular company and across businesses within the supply chain, for the purposes of improving the long-term performance of the individual companies and the supply chain as a whole. (p. 22)

Unlike logistics management, which focuses on the inbound and outbound flow of products, services, and related information from a focal organization's perspective, this definition leads us to the conclusion that SCM is a management process that deals with inbound and outbound flows, from the perspective of the focal organization, its suppliers, and its customers. This means a fundamental aspect of GSCM is the consideration of not just the cost and profit goals of one company (the focal organization) but of all the companies involved in managing the global supply chain.

About the Handbook

Given these definitions of the scope of GSCM, this handbook is divided into five major parts: (1) "Understanding Global Supply Chains," (2) "Managing the Functions," (3) "Resource Management," (4) "Managing the Relations," and (5) "Making It Happen." Each part is summarized in the following pages.

Understanding Global Supply Chains

Understanding the environment in which the firm will operate is critical to strategy development and implementation. Nowhere is this truer than in the global environment. The chapters in this part address the following areas essential to understanding global supply chains: global supply chain management strategy, assessing the global environment, value and customer service management, demand management, knowledge management, and process orientation.

Chapter 2: Global Supply Chain Management Strategy

In this chapter, the strategic management literature is reviewed to provide an underpinning for GSCM strategy (GSCMS). In addition, literature from logistics, operations management, purchasing/procurement, and marketing are reviewed to specify external environmental characteristics and internal processes and capabilities that are critical to establishing a sustainable competitive advantage through GSCMS.

Chapter 3: Assessing the Global Environment

Since 9/11, the pressures on supply chain managers have intensified, given new security concerns and the ensuing transportation delays that come with increased customs scrutiny. This—coupled with previously existing political, cultural, and economic variance across markets—has contributed to the stress supply chains feel when trying to meet delivery and service expectations, both at home and abroad. Perhaps not coincidentally, security crises arrived simultaneously with increased access to overseas labor, materials, and consumers. This dramatic exposure to both risk and return opportunities leads firms to face environmental challenges outside the realm of previously developed capabilities in SCM.

In this chapter, the authors discuss the environmental conditions influencing global supply chain decisions and effectiveness—that is, those conditions that need continuous assessment by managers. Most important, this discussion takes place in the context of a post-9/11 marketplace, where GSCM depends on effective manipulation of, and preparation for, increasingly volatile environmental conditions.

Chapter 4: Value and Customer Service Management

The concept of value management in global logistics and SCM is closely connected to the idea of value chains (Porter 1985). In the relatively narrow logistics discipline, the idea was then far from new even though it was not common to use the exact term *value chain* but rather the term *supply chain*. The basic thinking about the two concepts was, and is, however, the same—namely, that the fundamental understanding of the company is closely linked to its relations to other actors contributing to the transformation of raw materials to final products required by the ultimate customer or end user. The concept of customer service is fundamental and essential to logistics thinking, as well as to value management. In this chapter, the authors take a closer look into value management based on the idea of value chains. After that, what customer service means to value creation is discussed.

Chapter 5: Demand Management

Demand management activities in any global supply chain consist of three activities: demand management, demand planning, and sales forecasting management. In this chapter, the authors discuss how it is important to note that only one company in any given supply chain is directly affected by independent demand. The rest are affected by derived or dependent demand or both. Equally important, the techniques, systems, and processes necessary to deal with derived and dependent demand are quite different from those of independent demand. Recognizing the differences between independent, dependent, and derived demand; recognizing which type of demand affects a particular company; and developing techniques, systems, and processes to deal with that company's particular type of demand can have a profound impact on global logistics and supply chain costs and customer service levels. The authors first explore the implications of independent and derived demands, followed by a model of the demand management function in GSCM, and then move on to the role of sales forecasting management within demand management.

Chapter 6: Knowledge Management

A key reason for the failure of knowledge management initiatives is that few managers understand either the nature of knowledge or how to manage it. Many managers mistake information processing for knowledge management. As a result, they narrowly focus efforts on improving information management by carrying out a series of disjointed projects. A fundamental insight of companies that excel in knowledge management is that a firm is not an assembly of interchangeable machine parts. Firms are made up of human beings. Like people, firms develop knowledge by learning. Learning includes not only acquiring "hard" (i.e., quantifiable explicit) information but also mastering "soft" skills (i.e., tacit know-how). A firm cannot build knowledge management competence project by project; rather, this task must be approached holistically. Building knowledge management competence requires engaging the whole organization in a commitment to learning.

Effective knowledge management strategies ensure a holistic approach by developing knowledge management as a core competence of the firm. Building knowledge management competence is like constructing a three-legged stool that rests equally on the *climate, processes,* and *infrastructure* for knowledge management. The tendency to focus on one leg while ignoring the other two can produce unfortunate effects. In this chapter, the authors discuss the components of knowledge management competence and provide real-world examples of how these components work in global supply chains.

Chapter 7: Process Orientation

In Chapter 7, the authors argue that core processes decide the competitiveness of the firm, and they differentiate between successful and less successful organizations. Core processes should be targeted to the unique features of different business strategies, environments, and customers. Uniquely designed core supply chain processes enable firms to reach "next best practice" ahead of what could be reached using standardized processes and subprocesses that do not account for the specific features, strategies, or success factors of different companies or supply chains. On the other hand, certain noncore processes might very well be standardized, at least within the same organization.

Managing the Functions

The traditional business and logistics functions must be coordinated and managed within the context of the global supply chain. Thus, the chapters in this part address the following topics: marketing and sales management, product management and global product launch, operations management, integrated logistics management, inventory management, transportation management, warehouse management, supply management, and personnel.

Chapter 8: Marketing and Sales Management

Many organizations are finding that sales force changes are needed to match the needs of more demanding customers in an increasingly competitive world. Global supply chain innovations have necessitated changes in the way sales forces are organized, compensated, developed, and measured. The goal of this chapter is to explain how to make effective sales force and sales program decisions for maximum marketing efficiency and effectiveness in a global supply chain environment.

Chapter 9: Product Management

Product management focuses on both new and current products, where new product encompasses conceptualizing, developing, producing, and testing efforts and current product management encompasses sustaining and eventual disposal considerations. The processes of commercializing and launching overlap the domains of new versus current products and pose unique and pressing issues stemming from an oversimplifying presumption that there is a clean break between activities related to managing new versus current products. Often, product launch is assumed to be a stopping point for product development—something that is not really true. During and after launch, product managers continue to critique the new product to possibly broaden the brand or product line, as well as delineate market trends and customer needs that future offerings should serve. Launch is, therefore, a focal topic requiring keen attention. As companies expand beyond their domestic markets toward establishing a global presence, global product launch is emerging as a preeminent contemporary topic for product management. Accordingly, in this chapter the authors detail the role of product management, with particular emphasis on managing the global product launch.

Chapter 10: Operations Management

Globalization of supply bases and marketplaces, advances in information technology software and hardware, and the widespread recognition and acceptance of supply chain concepts are enabling managers to redefine their operational strategies at the enterprise and network levels, thereby providing significant opportunities for innovation and threats for those locked into the traditional functional perspective of operations management. In this chapter, the authors examine the current perspectives of operations management and provide projections for its future development in the global economy. Toward this end, operations management is defined, its decision-making scope discussed, significant points in its historical development are used to differentiate between the functional and process perspective of operations management, factors that are rapidly changing the role of the operations manager are identified, and several key operations management success factors for the future are proposed.

Chapter 11: Integrated Logistics Management

The objective of integrated logistics is the coordinated flow and storage of materials across the supply chain. Integrated logistics management is achieved by integrating the logistics business processes of the partners in a supply chain. The very essence of GSCM depends on the ability to coordinate the flow and storage of materials across multiple partners using integrated business processes. It is the glue that holds a supply chain together. In this chapter, the author examines logistics in the context of GSCM, explores the benefits of integrated business processes, and presents a framework and guidelines for the design and implementation of integrated logistics management.

Chapter 12: Inventory Management

Effective inventory management is a critical concern for firms in all industries and plays a major role in determining a firm's success. Striking a balance between the economic benefits and costs of inventory investment is a central success element for any company. The authors review the most widely applied models for planning and controlling independent demand inventory, identify the environmental parameters driving each one, indicate the appropriate application of each, and discuss a variety of emerging supply chain inventory strategies that are being implemented by leading firms to tackle the complexities associated with increased product variety, demand for higher levels of customer service, and the globally expanding marketplace.

Chapter 13: Transportation Management

In this chapter, the authors explore the global environment for transportation management, surveying the cost and service aspects of transportation operations, opportunities for collaboration among shippers and carriers, and key global transportation issues, and they review the decision scope of transportation-related decisions in logistics and SCM.

Chapter 14: Warehouse Management

Warehousing functions play a vital role in the overall supply chain process. In the past, the warehouse was generally regarded as simply a place to store goods. As supply chains have evolved, the warehouse has assumed a larger role in the global supply chain process because of the ability to reduce overall supply chain costs and improve service to the ultimate customer through the performance of many functions. In this chapter, the author provides an overview of the role of the warehouse in the global supply chain process, describing the rationale for warehousing, activities performed in the warehouse, the relationship of warehousing to other supply chain functions, the technology applicable to warehousing operations, and key warehousing business issues.

Chapter 15: Supply Management

With the professionalization of supply management, standard processes have been developed that are used by many organizations to guide their global procurement endeavors. In this chapter, the authors introduce the standardized, step-by-step approach to strategic supply management. As part of this process, a classic approach to commodity segmentation is also presented. The chapter ends with a presentation of cutting-edge supply management trends.

Chapter 16: Personnel

The goal of this chapter is to identify and discuss the core principles for developing and supporting employees in the new and dynamically competitive global supply chain environment, with the ultimate goal of leveraging human resources for their tangible and intangible supply chain value.

Resource Management

To remain competitive, companies in global supply chains must efficiently and effectively manage their resources. Thus, the topics addressed in this part are lean supply chains, financial management, risk management, and interpretation systems.

Chapter 17: The Lean Supply Chain

The lean supply chain involves more than just-in-time or doing more, faster. Rather, there are a number of basic principles applied in any supply chain configuration: begin with customer requirements, deliver what is demanded, build what is sold, supply what is consumed, and balance the flow. However, these basic principles must fit within the basic product and process supply chain structure. In addition, the basic principles must be applied within the strategic configuration required by the customer. Thus, two configuration dimensions give rise to a variety of design combinations, none of which can be thought of as necessarily dominant. The authors identify the importance of matching the time interval for demanding the product mix with all upstream execution time intervals. Once this is accomplished, capacity rates and boundaries are established for all elements of the supply chain. The actual execution of flow fits within these planned capacities and flexes with short-term variation. With these principles in place, certain supply chains are able to exhibit stable, repetitive, and predictive performance.

Chapter 18: Financial Management

All companies compete against each other in the financial markets. Those companies offering a competitive return tend to prosper and grow. Those that do not are limited in their ability to grow and many times cease to exist. Providing a competitive return is becoming more complex because of increasingly demanding customers, heightened competition, and ever-changing technologies. SCM has the potential to provide solutions. There are three common impediments to companies making the financial-SCM connection. First, many executives view SCM as a tactical backroom cost-center activity and not a key tool for managing overall financial performance. Fortunately, this view appears to be changing. Second, most SCM professionals do not speak the language of finance. Hence, they lack the ability to link SCM to key financial metrics and articulate how SCM drives financial performance. Third, SCM drives performance throughout the enterprise. Therefore, SCM strategic and tactical decisions cannot be made in a vacuum. Yet most SCM scorecards and analysis of SCM initiatives are incomplete because they are not from an enterprisewide perspective. In this chapter, the author explores the connection between financial performance and SCM with a three-step top-down approach.

Chapter 19: Risk Management

There is little debate that global supply chains are sources of considerable competitive advantage. The global configurations of firms provide access to cheap labor and raw materials, subsidized financing opportunities, larger product markets, arbitrage opportunities, and additional incentives such as tax rebates offered by foreign governments to attract foreign capital. These benefits are available to firms today because of (1) unprecedented transnational mobility of capital, information, people, products, and services; (2) tremendous leaps in information and communications technology; and (3) increased opportunities and willingness to engage in e-commerce. However, along with these benefits are the challenges that businesses need to overcome when operating globally. These challenges are related to foreign national economies, logistics, cultures, competition, and infrastructure. These challenges give rise to several risks in global supply chains. In this chapter, the authors explore these global supply chain risks and how to manage them.

Chapter 20: Interpretation Systems

The authors of this chapter suggest that managers can benefit from viewing supply chains as interpretation systems. Specifically, managers need to recognize that creating and maintaining fit across knowledge elements and strategy can help ensure supply chain success.

Managing the Relations

Much of the emphasis of GSCM centers on the relationships between supply chain partners and between functions within a given company. Thus, the topics addressed in this part are relationship management, logistics outsourcing, international sourcing, negotiating throughout the supply chain, interfunctional coordination, intercorporate coordination, and global supply chain control.

Chapter 21: Relationship Management

Relationship management is becoming a strategic function and a key factor in competitive positioning. In this chapter, the authors suggest that next-generation competitive advantage may come from effective relationships with supply chain partners. The primary reasons for the emphasis on supply chain partners are changes in most market spaces that have witnessed consolidation of firms within industries, continuous product evolution, and constant pressure on costs. Although relationship management is of strategic importance to a firm, good relationships between customers and suppliers are elusive. Firms realize that collaborative business relationships improve their ability to respond to the new business environment by allowing them to focus on their core businesses and to reduce costs in business processes. Firms, therefore, need to emphasize aspects that enhance supply chain partner relationships. The authors discuss the emergence of supply chain relationships and how this shift has changed and will continue to change the role, processes, and strategies of firms.

Chapter 22: Logistics Outsourcing

Although increased logistics outsourcing has been beneficial for logistics service providers, it has not come without its costs, mostly due to heightened expectations that logistics outsourcing clients have for the value delivered by service providers. Logistics service contracts have become more sophisticated and place more pressure on service providers to continually invest in process and cost improvements and to share these benefits with clients. Although success stories in this new environment are plentiful, logistics outsourcing has also been a victim of poor planning, lack of understanding, inadequate performance, and in some cases, abject failure. There are a number of reasons for this, but lack of understanding on the part of both client and provider often is the major cause of difficulty and failure in logistics outsourcing relationships. This comment is even more poignant when made in relation to global logistics outsourcing. Until recently, although any number of firms had operations in foreign countries, in most cases their logistics activities were confined to the countries in which they were located and those in close proximity. Today, products are routinely moved back and forth throughout the world. To many firms, global logistics outsourcing has become more important than it is in their domestic markets. In this chapter, the authors highlight the business case for global logistics outsourcing and provide a guide for the outsourcing process. The specific case of global logistics outsourcing is considered, and keys and barriers to success are identified.

Chapter 23: International Sourcing

This chapter expressly focuses on international sourcing (or offshoring) as it adds many more complexities that do not apply in domestic sourcing strategy. In developing viable international sourcing strategies, companies must consider not only manufacturing and delivery costs, the costs of various resources, and exchange rate fluctuations but also availability of infrastructure (including transportation, communications, and energy), industrial and cultural environments, the ease of working with foreign host governments, and so on. Furthermore, the complex nature of sourcing strategy on a global scale spawns many barriers to its successful execution. In particular, logistics, inventory management, distance, nationalism, and lack of working knowledge about foreign business practices, among others, are major operational problems identified by both U.S. and foreign multinational companies engaging in international sourcing. From a contractual point of view, the international sourcing of intermediate products such as components and services by companies takes place in two ways: (1) from the parents or their foreign subsidiaries on an "intrafirm" basis (i.e., internal sourcing) and (2) from independent suppliers on a "contractual" basis (i.e., external sourcing). The authors propose that there is a negative curvilinear relationship between the extent of international sourcing and the performance of the firm, such that firms should neither keep all their activities at home nor outsource everything to faraway locations. With this model in hand, the authors discuss the variables that predict the extent of international sourcing firms ought to engage in, and examine some practical implications of the model.

Chapter 24: Negotiating Throughout the Supply Chain

The elements of the negotiation process include the environments that surround the parties to the negotiation (negotiation environmental factors), the nature of the relative relationship between the parties (negotiation potential), the activities of preparation that take place to ensure that necessary information is available for decision making during the interactions between the parties (negotiation preparation), the actual discussions that take place between the parties (bargaining), and the interpretation of the outcomes of the negotiation process (negotiation outcome). All of these elements are critical to creating successful negotiation outcomes and are discussed in this chapter, along with seven types of supplier and customer relationships.

Chapter 25: Interfunctional Coordination

In this chapter, the authors define interfunctional coordination and its essential elements: communication, collaboration, and an organizational climate that supports the two. Once the groundwork has been laid, the authors explore important dimensions for effective interfunctional coordination within the company. The mechanisms that can be used to drive coordination within a company are then discussed. Finally, the authors offer some examples of interfunctional coordination and the state of the art in business today.

Chapter 26: Intercorporate Coordination

Many firms have turned to coordination with supply chain partners as a way of facing the challenges of operating in the rapidly changing marketplace. Supply chain relationships have moved from adversarial exchanges toward more collaborative ventures. Thus, instead of relationships based on opportunism and competition, many supply chain exchanges now put a greater emphasis on trust, interdependency, and coordination solutions to operational issues that benefit all parties involved. In this chapter, the author highlights the various strategic behaviors involved in global supply chain coordination efforts and environmental issues that support more effective global supply chain coordination.

Chapter 27: Global Supply Chain Control

The purpose of this chapter is to specify the control processes associated with implementing a supply chain strategy across institutional arrangements and environments in a global context. The authors introduce a model detailing the connections between the characteristics of the supply chain strategy developed by a multinational corporation, the magnitude and scope of the control requirements inherent in the strategy, and the impact of a foreign market's institutional environment on implementation effectiveness. The authors analyze the characteristics of the controller's strategy, the dimensions of the strategy's control requirements, and the implications for implementation effectiveness from institutional arrangements and environments.

Making It Happen

Strategy means little if it cannot be implemented. Thus, this part is about how companies make global logistics and SCM happen and, as a result, create competitive advantage. The specific topics addressed are supply chain innovation, global supply chain security, diagnosing the supply chain, and change management.

Chapter 28: Supply Chain Innovation

In this chapter, the authors discuss the notion of innovation as strategy, innovation in supply chains, what constitutes supply chain innovations, and processes for being innovative. They then discuss these concepts and implications within a global context.

Chapter 29: Global Supply Chain Security

Lengthy, complex global supply chains are especially vulnerable to disruptions caused by a myriad of major disasters such as terrorist attacks, electric power blackouts, and hurricanes. Such disruptions have significant negative impacts on supply chain effectiveness and efficiency that, in turn, devastate corporate performance and profitability. Consequently, global supply chain managers must have a basic understanding of disasters and their likely effects on the supply chain, plus knowledge regarding the process of disaster preparedness.

Chapter 30: Diagnosing the Supply Chain

In this chapter, a variety of tools for diagnosing potential problems in a supply chain are reviewed and discussed. These diagnostic tools vary in terms of format, complexity, and cost. Quantitative approaches as well as some qualitative diagnostic tools are described. Some of these tools require less data gathering than others and are, therefore, less time-consuming. Discussion as to when one tool versus another might be used is also included. The tools listed are suitable either for self-assessment or for assessment employing a small team of facilitators.

Chapter 31: Change Management

Change management is defined as those strategies and action plans that support and maintain transition from the current state to a new outcome. Maintaining the transition is often more difficult than implementing initial change. Change management involves two very different critical processes: training and the buy-in process. Once an organization accepts the change, a well-designed and executed training plan is essential. Prior to that, the process of organizational buy-in sets the organization up for change and is arguably the most challenging aspect of any new initiative. The coming change must be embraced not only cross-functionally but also at all organizational levels. Achieving organizational support for change is thus critical to achieving the goals set forth in any change management initiative.

Conclusions

The editors' intention in producing this handbook is to facilitate the evolution of a thought process among both academic researchers and practicing managers that recognizes at once the complexities of a global, cross-functional, cross-enterprise view of business and fosters an appreciation for key dimensions that contribute to success within this new environment. The layout of the book, as highlighted above, is designed to guide the reader through five distinct "layers" of thought regarding GSCM.

The first part, "Understanding Global Supply Chains," provides a broad perspective on GSCM that can be used to frame and scope the phenomenon, as well as provide general insights into the issues that managers and researchers engaged in GSCM must confront. The second part, "Managing the Functions," is designed to provide in-depth insight into how specific functional areas must change to conform to a GSCM perspective. The third part, "Resource Management," highlights the critical need to link functional activity management to strategic resource allocation and provides guidance as to how to approach this complex task. Part IV, "Managing the Relations," illuminates issues related to the management of the essential enablers of effective GSCM—internal functional and external organizational relationships. Finally, Part V, "Making It Happen," provides guidance on four key processes that are vital to implementing GSCM strategy.

We hope this handbook becomes a tool to which readers can refer frequently along their journeys toward a better understanding of the business world of the 21st century.

References

Barlow, Jim (1994), "What Sparks Cooperation?" *Houston Chronicle,* September 25, Sunday, 2 Star Edition, Business Section, 1.

Bovet, David and Yossi Sheffi (1998), "The Brave New World of Supply Chain Management," *Supply Chain Management Review,* 2 (Spring), 14–22.

Bowersox, Donald J. and David C. Closs (1996), *Logistical Management: The Integrated Supply Chain Process.* New York: McGraw-Hill.

Cooper, M. C., Douglas M. Lambert, and Janus D. Pagh (1997), "Supply Chain Management: More Than a New Name for Logistics," *International Journal of Logistics Management,* 8 (1), 1–14.

Council of Supply Chain Management Professionals (2005), *Supply Chain Management/ Logistics Management Definitions.* Retrieved January 20, 2006, from http://cscmp.org/ Website/AboutCSCMP/Definitions/Definitions.asp

Coyle, John J., Edward J. Bardi, and C. John Langley, Jr. (1996), *The Management of Business Logistics,* 6th ed. St. Paul, MN: West Publishing.

Fliedner, G. and R. J. Vokurka (1997), "Agility: Competitive Weapon of the 1990's and Beyond," *Production and Inventory Management Journal,* 38 (3), 19–24.

Gruen, Thomas W. (1997), "Relationship Marketing: The Route to Marketing Efficiency and Effectiveness," *Business Horizons,* 6 (40), 32.

Hitt, Michael A., Duane R. Ireland, and Robert E. Hoskisson (1999), *Strategic Management.* Cincinnati, OH: Southwestern College Publishing.

Kotler, Philip (1997), *Marketing Management,* 9th ed. Englewood Cliffs, NJ: Prentice Hall.

LaLonde, Bernard J. (1997), "Supply Chain Management: Myth or Reality?" *Supply Chain Management Review,* 1 (Spring), 6–7.

LaLonde, Bernard J. and Richard F. Powers (1993), "Disintegration and Reintegration: Logistics of the 21st Century," *International Journal of Logistics Management,* 4 (2), 1–12.

Larson, Paul D. and Robert F. Lusch (1990), "Quick Response Retail Technology: Integration and Performance Measurement," *International Review of Retail, Distribution and Consumer Research,* 1 (1), 17–35.

Malone, Thomas W. and John F. Rockart (1991), "Computers, Networks and the Corporation," *Scientific American,* 265 (3), 128.

Mentzer, John T. (2004), *Supply Chain Management.* Thousand Oaks, CA: Sage.

Pine, B. Joseph, Jr. (1993), *Mass Customization: The New Frontier in Business Competition.* Boston: Harvard Business School Press.

Porter, Michael E. (1985), *Competitive Advantage: Creating and Sustaining Superior Performance.* New York: Free Press.

Schonberger, Richard J. and Adel El-Ansary (1984), "Just-in-Time Purchasing Can Improve Quality," *Journal of Purchasing and Materials Management,* 20 (Spring), 1–7.

Schultz, David P. (1985), "Just-In-Time Systems," *Stores,* 67 (April), 28–31.

PART I

Understanding Global Supply Chains

2

Global Supply Chain Management Strategy

John T. Mentzer

Theodore P. Stank

Matthew B. Myers

A s we had mentioned in Chapter 1, the Supply Chain Research Group at the University of Tennessee (Mentzer 2004) defines supply chain management (SCM) as

> the systemic, strategic coordination of the traditional business functions within a particular company and across businesses within the supply chain, for the purposes of improving the long-term performance of the individual companies and the supply chain as a whole. (p. 22)

Inherent in this view of SCM is an acceptance that traditional functional areas represent components of a strategic firm orientation. Further, the definition highlights the perspective that the enterprise (or *we*) encompasses more than just the focal firm; it is also concerned with the entire set of organizations engaged in delivering end value to the customer. To global SCM-oriented firms, *we* refers to all the firms collectively within the supply chain network, versus *we* meaning one's own firm. Highly SCM-oriented firms think in terms of the overall global system when considering most critical processes. This perspective on how an organization defines who *we* stands for is central to understanding the relationship between firm strategy and behavior and SCM.

The following sections review research from the strategic management literature that provides an underpinning for global SCM strategy (GSCMS). In addition, literature from logistics, operations management, purchasing/procurement, and marketing are reviewed to specify external environmental characteristics and internal processes and capabilities that are critical to establishing a sustainable competitive advantage through GSCMS.

Background

Determining how organizations invest scarce resources to achieve objectives that establish and maintain a superior competitive position or advantage is at the heart of strategy development (Porter 1985; Day 1994). Traditionally, the key to competitive advantage involved the choice of where to compete and defending market share in these segments using price and product performance attributes. Contemporary strategic thought, however, considers competition a "war of movement" that depends on anticipating market trends and changes in customer needs (Stalk, Evans, and Schulman 1992, p. 62). Competitive advantage results from implementing value-creating strategies that are not currently implemented by competitors (Barney 1991). Such strategies involve leveraging superior competencies to create customer value and achieve cost and/or differentiation advantages, resulting in market share and profitability performance (Day and Wensley 1988; Prahalad and Hamel 1990). The advantage becomes sustainable when other firms are unable to duplicate benefits that are perceived and valued by customers (Coyne 1986; Day and Wensley 1988). Firms may set up barriers that make imitation difficult by continually investing to sustain or improve the advantage.

The strategy-structure-performance (SSP) paradigm provides a way of viewing the nature of strategic planning (Galunic and Eisenhardt 1994). The underlying premise of the SSP paradigm is that a firm's strategy, created in consideration of external environmental factors, drives the development of internal structures within which resources, capabilities, and competencies can be brought to bear (Galbraith and Nathanson 1978; Miles and Snow 1978). Firms that have properly aligned strategy with structure are expected to perform better than competitors that lack the same degree of strategic fit (Child 1972; Galbraith and Kazanjian 1986; Galunic and Eisenhardt 1994; Habib and Victor 1991; Hoskisson 1987; Lubatkin and Rogers 1989; Miles and Snow 1978, 1984; Rumelt 1974; Wolf and Egelhoff 2002).

The SSP paradigm views strategic choice as emerging from an enterprise's assessment of externally based opportunities. Strategic planning, therefore, focuses on identification of the nature of the external environment, including domestic and global markets, government and regulatory conditions, characteristics related to global supply chain and industry, the nature of competition, and firm-related characteristics such as management style, shared values, and culture. Structure refers to the way the enterprise organizes its resources, including formal organizational lines of authority; communication systems and information flows; coordination techniques and processes; development, reward, and compensation systems; and performance evaluation systems (Chandler 1962; Galbraith and Kazanjian 1986; Miles and Snow 1978).

SSP relates the need for fit between externally driven strategic choice and the structural components used to operationalize that choice. It is relatively silent, however, regarding how resources can be invested to create the core competencies through which competitive advantage is derived (Hofer and Schendel 1978; Van Hoek, Commandeur, and Vos 1998; Varadarajan and Jayachandran 1999; Walker and Ruekert 1987; Webster 1992). The resource-based paradigm or view (RBV) presents an alternative to strategic planning that finds competitive advantage in a firm's internal capabilities and resources (Barney 1991; Wernerfelt 1984). The objective is to view firms in terms of their resources rather than their products. In the RBV, a firm seeks to create situations in which the positioning of its internal resources directly or indirectly makes it more difficult for other firms to "catch up" (Wernerfelt 1984, p. 173). RBV, therefore, centers on leveraging internal firm resources and capabilities to gain competitive advantage. From a decision-making standpoint, RBV requires firms to identify the skills and resources that exert the most leverage on positional advantages and future performance and then allocate resources toward those with the highest potential leverage to improve performance with the least expenditure (Day and Wensley 1988).

The RBV views a firm as a bundle of resources that can be used to influence performance, where resources include anything that can be thought of as a strength or weakness of a firm and consist of both tangible and intangible assets that are tied semipermanently to a firm. Examples include brand names, in-house knowledge of technology, skilled personnel, machinery, trade contracts, and efficient procedures (Wernerfelt 1984). On their own, resources are rarely productive; productivity requires the coordination and cooperation of teams of resources (Morgan, Strong, and McGuinness 2003). Resources joined in strategically advantageous combinations create capabilities (Day 1994; Day and Nedungadi 1994). Capabilities are defined sets of processes (Stalk et al. 1992) or dynamic routines (Lowson 2003) that reflect the way resources have been deployed (Dutta, Narasimhan, and Rajiv 1999) and applied to the environment (Chetty and Patterson 2002). It is a firm's capabilities, not simply the resources that they possess, that give it competitive advantage (Chetty and Patterson 2002, p. 70).

The integration of SSP and RBV facilitates understanding of how strategic planning results in a firm choosing one of several different strategic alternatives (see, e.g., Miles and Snow 1978; Porter 1985). Treacy and Wiersema (1995) emphasized the power of an organization that narrows down its focus to one of three different strategies: operational efficiency (low cost), product leadership (innovation), or customer intimacy (niche). The authors argued that firms needed to be competent in all three areas but should intensely focus on only one. Literature and practice, however, have been limited in their perspective on implementing these strategic choices. In particular, the implementation of one or more of these strategic choices has typically centered on the focal firm and not on the broader supply chain. An organization with a high level of GSCMS orientation is posited as viewing implementation of strategic choice from the perspective of how it might align multiple firms to complement each other and work toward overall strategic goals that apply to the entire global supply chain network and not only to the focal firm.

Global SCM Strategy

The SSP concept of strategic fit is directly transferable to the management of individual enterprises within a broader global supply chain (Galbraith and Nathanson 1978; Miles and Snow 1978, 1984). The premise is that the degree or level to which an enterprise subscribes to a GSCMS orientation depends on an astute sense of environmental characteristics and conditions, including those of the global markets in which the enterprise competes and the internal characteristics of the enterprise itself.

The RBV paradigm is manifested across core capabilities in which a firm engages in executing its responsibilities as part of an integrated global supply chain. The capabilities encompass the coordinated efforts of all activities engaged in planning, implementing, and controlling demand, sourcing, operations, and delivery processes for products, services, information, and finances from the point of material origin to the point of ultimate consumption (Bowersox, Closs, and Cooper 2002; Mentzer et al. 2001). Resource investment to develop each capability in accordance with the organization's GSCMS orientation is made across the structural elements identified within SSP (i.e., formal organizational hierarchy, coordination processes, information and communication systems, human resource systems, and measurement systems) (Chandler 1962; Galbraith and Kazanjian 1986; Miles and Snow 1978).

Performance measures must be integrated across firms and take both a holistic, end-to-end view and a between-firm, dyadic view to ensure that the linkages at each step in the global supply chain are actively monitored and tuned (Antia and Frazier 2001; Christopher and Ryals 1999; Lambert and Pohlen 2001). Lambert and Pohlen (2001) proposed an approach to integrated global supply chain performance measurement that assesses the economic value added (EVA) of combined effort to demonstrate that the benefits of GSCMS occur across the extended firms engaged in the global supply chain. Specifically, they demonstrate that when overall value is created, each individual firm in the global supply chain also benefits by improving shareholder value in one or more of four distinct areas: revenue enhancement, operating expense reduction, and working capital and fixed capital efficiency.

The key to GSCMS success lies in the ability of managers to assess the global market and internal enterprise environmental characteristics to develop appropriate capabilities (value, product and service, demand, relationship, and resource management) using SSP structural elements of formal organizational hierarchies, coordination processes, information and communication systems, human resource systems, and measurement systems.

Impacts on Strategic Orientation

In the following sections, the impact of the global market and internal enterprise characteristics on the strategic decision regarding the degree to which the organization seeks to develop a GSCMS orientation decision is explored.

Global Market Characteristics

Research has identified key global market characteristics to include capacity and dynamism (Achrol and Stern 1988), munificence and complexity (Dess and Beard 1984), regulatory changes to specific industries (Forte et al. 2000), and degree of segmentation (Choi and Rajan 1997).

Environmental capacity refers to the perceived global economic and demand conditions characterizing the market's capacity to absorb resources of the global supply chain, whereas dynamism is the perceived frequency of change and turnover in global marketing forces in the environment. "Environments that are dynamic or shifting present greater contingencies to the organization . . . and therefore increase the relevant uncertainty faced by decision makers" (Achrol and Stern 1988, p. 38). Changing marketing practices and competitor strategies, as well as dynamic customer preferences, are likely to place increased pressure on inventory, long-range planning, coordination, and product mix decisions within the global supply chain (Leblebici and Salancik 1981). Similarly, the capacity represented by opportunities and resources provided by the global environment is likely to be a key factor affecting interorganizational relationships in global supply chains (Achrol and Stern 1988). The need for resources is an important factor behind forming interorganizational relations across borders. Global environments, "rich" in particular resources, including demand levels, generally result in fewer global supply chain strategies aimed at controlling or integrating processes within the firm (Dwyer and Welsh 1985), leading to less complex value chain configurations across borders.

The concept of munificence in the global environment is similar to that of capacity, in that it addresses the extent to which the environment can sustain growth within the organization or global supply chain (Dess and Beard 1984). However, munificence refers more specifically to complex external social relationships with institutional gatekeepers (e.g., local governments and thought leaders) who ensure flows of resources and opportunities. Current examples include political economies that provide capital, labor, and information flows across borders. The complexity, or heterogeneity, of the environment refers to the number and diversity of competing global supply chains with which the organization must interact in its competitive efforts (Dess and Beard 1984).

Forte et al. (2000) indicate that dynamic industry regulations influence organizational forms. Extrapolating from this finding, it is clear that changing or incongruent regulations across borders influence global supply chain characteristics and designs. Regulations addressing both the tangible (i.e., components and finished products) and the service (e.g., logistics) offerings within global supply chains change consistently and are often driven by protectionist measures of local markets. As a result, global supply chain designs are influenced by local content and labor requirements, import and export regulations, and safety provisions, which often dictate the location of specific global supply chain activities and increase the difficulty in standardizing global supply chain efforts across multiple markets.

Finally, how markets are segmented relative to customer preferences influences global supply chains (Choi and Rajan 1997). For example, business-to-business provisions of products and services may need to be specialized for buyers in a single market (vertical segments) or can often be standardized across multiple markets. This is due to similarities in buyer preferences (horizontal segments) (Bolton and Myers 2003), enabling cost efficiencies at multiple points within the global supply chain. By identifying specific customer segments, some of which may transcend national borders, global supply chain managers can benefit from reduced costs, enhanced revenue, and the ability to differentiate their offering from the highly competitive marketplace (Mentzer, Myers, and Cheung 2004). However, in a global context, the ability of managers to serve specific segments effectively can be limited by regulations and political economies that restrict the ability to standardize the offerings and processes needed to do so. These, often dichotomous, environmental conditions (segment preferences and market regulations) alone account for the often exponentially more difficult management conditions faced by global, rather than single-market, supply chain managers.

In the rush to expand globally, firms have adopted different strategies in response to these key global market characteristics. Some firms adopt a market replication or transaction cost reduction approach by entering foreign market environments that display characteristics similar to domestic ones (i.e., high similarity/low deviation between exchange partners' market environmental characteristics) (Rosenzweig and Singh 1991). Transaction cost analysis predicts this behavior due to a firm's ability to both specialize in a foreign market environment and benefit from economies of scale based on existing skills, knowledge, and assets developed in the primary market (Klein, Frazier, and Roth 1990). Matching foreign to home market environmental characteristics allows the firm to take advantage of extant competencies, tacit knowledge, routines, and standard operating procedures through replication in the new market.

There is no agreement, however, on the robustness of the transaction cost approach. Research has shown that maximization of environmental similarity can be counterproductive if organizational change is needed or if the firm has adopted conflicting goals to correspond to a complex competitive environment (Lengnick-Hall and Lengnick-Hall 1988). Environmental diversification offers flexibility to shift market penetration efforts and the location of global supply chain activities according to environmental conditions across countries (Kogut 1985; 1991; Kogut and Kulatilaka 1994).

Internal Enterprise Characteristics

The characteristics of the internal enterprise create the organizational environment within which firm strategies, structures, and performance exist. An orientation toward GSCMS must be predicated on an organizational culture and management philosophy that recognizes the importance and complexities associated with managing the risks, relationships, and trade-offs of global supply chain exchange (Trent 2004). Deshpande and Webster (1989, p. 4) define organizational culture as "the pattern of shared values and beliefs that help individuals understand organizational functioning and thus provide them norms for behavior in the organization." Schein (1985) introduced a model that demonstrates how an organizational culture can influence the behavior of the members. At the surface level, visible artifacts of the organization include rules of conduct, dress codes, records, physical layout, stories, and rituals (Marcoulides and Heck 1993). These represent the overt behaviors and other physical manifestations of the organization (Gordon 1991). A second, less visible, level of culture consists of the organization's values. Values in a cultural sense represent the way things "ought to be." They serve as normative or moral guides for how group members deal with such issues as how people should relate to each other or exercise power (Schein 1985). At an even deeper level are the underlying assumptions, such as beliefs, habits of perception, thoughts, and feelings, that are the ultimate source of values and action.

Organizational culture is central to the determination of the level of GSCMS orientation. The culture of the firm is its "personality," which can be used by other organizations within the global supply chain, as well as its own employees, to determine the focal firm's appreciation for exchange in the value chain (McAfee, Glassman, and Honeycutt 2002). One of the key components of culture that influences GSCMS orientation is top management support. The upper echelon of the firm plays a critical role in shaping the organization's strategic orientation and direction (Hambrick and Mason 1984; Marcoulides and Heck 1993). Hence, firms in which top management is supportive of and committed to behaviors consistent with high levels of GSCMS orientation will potentially be more successful at managing their respective global supply chain (Cooper, Lambert, and Pagh 1997). Key to this success, however, is how thoroughly acculturated a company is to the GSCMS concept. When GSCMS orientation extends to all levels of a firm, it is more likely to be executed in a uniform and effective manner. This can become especially critical at the boundary-spanning level of the organization, where employees interface with, and make decisions relating to, other members of the global supply chain.

The internal enterprise environment is critical to the determination of GSCMS orientation. The culture of the firm not only indicates how it interacts with the external environment (Bucklin and Sengupta 1993; Cooper et al. 1997); it also governs the manner in which firms manage the capabilities associated with GSCMS.

Capabilities and Structural Elements of GSCMS

SSP and RBV support the notion that strategic orientation, adopted in response to external environmental characteristics, is implemented through the development of core capabilities. The management of value, products and services, demand, relationships, and rewards are core capabilities associated with high levels of GSCMS. Development of these core GSCMS capabilities is predicated on resource investment to align structure with strategic orientation.

The following subsections center on discussions regarding the nature of core capabilities associated with GSCMS, defining each capability and relating high capability levels to key structural elements of formal organizational hierarchy, coordination processes, information and communication systems, human resource systems, and measurement systems.

Value Management

Value management, in the context of an integrated global supply chain, refers to two important and related concepts: value creation and value appropriation. Value creation addresses the global supply chain's ability to offer a better value proposition to customers than that offered by competitors (Gale 1994; Woodruff 1997). Value appropriation addresses firms' abilities to extract value from the marketplace at a sufficient level to meet earnings and profitability targets (Mizik and Jacobson 2004).

Value creation involves the generation of market intelligence and using it to guide operational execution (Gale 1994; Woodruff 1997; Woodruff and Gardial 1996). Market intelligence generation enables an organization to understand what customers value and why, anticipate what they will value and why in the future, and understand customers' satisfaction levels with value created by their interactions or experiences with products, services, and processes. Operational execution guidance refers to the management of processes that help create the value customers want, ensuring that every stage from product and service conceptualization through product and service development, manufacturing, distribution, and communication contributes to the value proposition that customers experience.

Both business customers and consumers think of value in at least five different ways. First, they think in terms of the trade-offs they make between benefits received and sacrifices made, the simplest form being the trade-off between quality and price (e.g., Hauser and Urban 1986; Lapierre 2000; Slater and Narver 2000; Teas and Agarwal 2000; Woodruff 1997; Zeithaml 1988). Second, customers think in terms of linkages between product and service attributes and the consequences created by using these product and service attributes. The linkages between product and service attributes and the consequences they create and the reverse (i.e., the linkages between consequences desired and attributes sought) are known as value hierarchies or means-end chains (e.g., Gutman 1982; Holbrook 1994; Lai 1995; Woodruff 1997; Zeithaml 1988). Third, customers often categorize value in terms of the functional, relational, and service benefits they receive in light of the monetary and nonmonetary sacrifices they must make to obtain them (Gassenheimer, Houston, and Davis 1998; Lapierre 2000; Sheth, Newman, and Gross 1991). Fourth, customers view products and services within specific use situations and in light of their core values, goals, and objectives (Woodruff 1997; Woodruff and Gardial 1996). Fifth, the customer value concept is hedonic value, the emotional component (e.g., enjoyment or pleasure) that customers derive from using products and services (e.g., Holbrook 1994).

Value management captures the voice of the customer from many sources throughout the integrated global supply chain, bringing customer-relevant information together into a central location, regularly discussing and making sense out of customer data and acting on insights before competitors do or in a superior way (Flint et al. 2005). Structures created to support value management, therefore, must enable the organization to tune in to market demands. For example, firms often utilize cross-functional account management teams and colocation with customers to both capture complex aspects of customers' businesses and create superior value for these customers (Flint et al. 2005). Customer-value-focused firms communicate far down the integrated global supply chain to end-use customers, as well as immediate customers, to develop holistic images of the marketplace. They formally manage critical data such as customer-derived value assessments, projections of future desired value, satisfaction levels, and competitive customer value maps, using this information within internal processes as well as within integrated global supply chain relationships to develop value propositions that direct process design, research and development efforts, and manufacturing expertise. Firms with high levels of value management also communicate the value their system brings to the marketplace, enabling other firms within their integrated global supply chain to extract value from the relationship. This integrated marketing communication ties together advertising, account management, promotion, and public relations messages and media in consistent and complementary ways to build and solidify brand, product, and firm images within targeted market segments. Extended to a GSCMS perspective, the planning and execution of integrated marketing communications is shared, coordinated, and possibly collaborated on across multiple firms in the global supply chain.

Value appropriation directs the firm to pursue the best means of extracting value from the marketplace (Mizik and Jacobson 2004). Value management measurement systems, therefore, provide firms with insight regarding when to pursue pricing or volume strategies. In cases where market prices are dropping at the end-use customer level, as is the case in the digital consumer electronics market, improvements in profitability often come from reducing costs at a faster rate than the falling market price. Value management can also be leveraged in the marketplace in ways that translate into higher prices relative to competition. These higher prices come from such areas as more efficient interorganizational processes, more consistent and higher-quality products, more customized value propositions that include better order processing, better product availability, and more informed customer service representatives due to information systems, better product visibility, better product condition on arrival, and better product timeliness.

Product and Service Management

Product and service management involves those processes and activities concerned with the flow of goods and services, including planning, management, and execution of sourcing and procurement, conversion, and logistics. Two important concepts in product and service management include cycle time management and integration (Daugherty and Pittman 1995; Lowson 2003; McGinnis and Kohn 1993; Mentzer, Min, and Zacharia 2000; Srivastava, Shervani, and Fahey 1999).

Cycle time management involves managing the time required to capture actual or forecast orders and schedule procurement and/or production. Postponement and speculation represent opposite ends of a cycle time management continuum, with the appropriate location along the continuum dependent on unique product and demand characteristics. Postponement involves delaying the finishing and/or forward movement of goods as long as possible. Raw materials or finished goods can be stored in central locations within the global supply chain, waiting for downstream demand cues to signal the requirement to finish or move the order (Van Hoek et al. 1998). Once demand signals are known, acceleration speeds up order transmittal, processing, preparation, and transit so that a firm can translate orders into finished products quickly, eliminating wasted capital while capturing time-sensitive buyers better than competitors (McGinnis and Kohn 1993; Murphy and Farris 1993). Reducing the time required for order fulfillment activities allows businesses to respond to demand fluctuations with less distortion of the order cycle process (Daugherty and Pittman 1995; McGinnis and Kohn 1990). Speculation involves procuring, manufacturing, and positioning finished goods in large volumes in anticipation of demand, enabling a firm to take advantage of economies of scale and market positioning of products.

Integration is a state existing among organizational elements that is necessary to achieve unity of effort to meet global supply chain goals such as improved service and lower total cost (Bowersox, Closs, and Stank 2003). Integration comprises two fundamental components, interaction and collaboration (Kahn and Mentzer 1996). Interaction represents the communication aspects associated with interdepartmental and organizational activities. Integration commits each department or organization to perform the roles that best focus their core competencies on creating value for the end customer, leveraging competency while reducing duplication and waste. Collaboration represents the willingness of departments and organizations to work together. It is characterized as the attitudinal aspect of interdepartmental and organizational relationships, representing an affective, volitional, mutual/shared process that achieves greater customer-relevant performance than that attainable by working independently. Another aspect of integration involves the integration of processes (Achrol and Kotler 1999; Srivastava et al. 1999).

Structural elements must be developed to facilitate product and service management. In particular, process coordination and information and communication systems, supported by appropriate organizational hierarchy, and human resource and measurement systems, facilitate product and service management capability. Process modularization and/or standardization creates "a focused expertise with materials and processes to a point where it is much easier to identify sources of delay, unnecessary steps," and redundancies (Jayaram, Vickery, and Droge 2000, p. 530). Improved coordination of global supply chain operations requires expertise that ensures use of common, standardized policies and procedures to facilitate day-to-day market fulfillment operations, freeing resources to focus on emergent or exception conditions (Schonberger 1990, 1992). Standardization identifies the best operating practices across an organization and applies the methods and technologies across the entire product and service supraprocess. Adherence to common application of these best standards, methods, and procedures becomes the means to reduce operating variance. Product and service management is further enhanced by reducing working capital and capital investments (Srivastava et al. 1999) through developing expertise in simplification of processes. Doing so eliminates waste and redundancy resulting from poorly designed and disintegrated work routines and processes as well as overly complex operations and facility networks (Schonberger 1990, 1992).

Investment in communication systems to facilitate information exchange has been recognized as a way for firms to enhance product and service capability

(Daugherty, Myers, and Richey 2002; Deeter-Schmelz 1997; Glazer 1991; Mabert and Venkataramanan 1998; Parsons 1983; Porter 1980; Porter and Millar 1985; Rayport and Sviokla 1995; Whipple, Frankel, and Daugherty 2002). At least three dimensions of communications systems exist: (1) information technology, which is the hardware, software, and network investment and design to facilitate processing and exchange across internal and external global supply chain entities; (2) information sharing, which is the willingness to exchange key technical, financial, operational, and strategic data; and (3) connectivity, or the expertise to exchange data in a timely, responsive, and usable format. Many different approaches can be employed to utilize these dimensions of information exchange, but the key is to accelerate the speed of information, which then can be substituted for physical inventories (Achrol and Kotler 1999; Day 1994; Slater and Narver 1995).

Demand Management

Demand management is the capability of an organization to synchronize two primary global supply chain functions: demand generation and supply. Demand is primarily the responsibility of sales and marketing. In many companies, the sales organization is responsible for generating and maintaining demand from large end-use customers or from wholesale or retail partners. Marketing is responsible for generating and maintaining demand from end consumers. Supply is the responsibility of a number of functions, including manufacturing, procurement, logistics, related human resources, and finance. It is also the responsibility of the suppliers who provide raw materials, component parts, and packaging. The sales and operating plan (S&OP) process provides the "junction box" of demand management, where information can flow between the demand side and the supply side of a firm.

The sales forecast, a projection into the future of expected demand given a set of environmental assumptions, is the critical input to the S&OP process (Mentzer and Moon 2004). The sales forecast should originate on the demand side of the enterprise, since it encompasses the activities of the enterprise (i.e., sales and marketing) and entities of the global supply chain (i.e., demand side global supply chain partners) responsible for generating demand and with the best perspective on future demand. In addition to the sales forecast, which originates in the demand side of the company, another critical input to the S&OP process is a capacity plan. A capacity plan is a projection into the future of what supply capabilities will be given a set of environmental assumptions (Mentzer and Moon 2004). This input is provided by the supply side of the enterprise and the global supply chain and documents both long- and short-term supply capabilities. The process that occurs inside the S&OP process is the matching of future demand projections (the sales forecast) with future supply projections (the capacity plan).

The S&OP process creates two critical plans: the operational plan and the demand plan (Lapide 2002). The operational plan consists of manufacturing, procurement, distribution, finance, and related human resource plans. Operational plans include items such as monthly production schedules, extended contracts for raw materials with global supply chain partners, or even plans to expand manufacturing capacity internally and/or with partners. The other critical plan that emerges from the S&OP process is the demand plan, where sales and marketing make plans about what should be sold and marketed, and when, given the supply capabilities of the firm and the integrated global supply chain. Demand plans may involve suppressing demand for products or services that are capacity constrained or shifting demand from low- to high-margin items.

The role of demand management is dependent on the firm's position in the global supply chain. Any global supply chain has only one point of independent demand—or the amount of product demanded (by time and location) by the end-use customer of the global supply chain. The company in the global supply chain that directly serves this end-use customer experiences this independent demand. All subsequent companies in the global supply chain experience a demand that is tempered by the order fulfillment and purchasing policies of other companies in the global supply chain. This second type of global supply chain demand is called derived demand because it is demand that is derived from what other companies in the global supply chain do to meet their demand from their immediate customer (i.e., the company that orders from them) (Mentzer and Moon 2004). It is important to note that only one company in any given global supply chain is directly influenced by independent demand. The rest are influenced by derived demand. Equally important, the formal organizational hierarchy, coordination processes, information and communication systems, human resource systems, and measurement systems necessary to deal with derived demand are quite different from those of independent demand. Recognizing these differences can have a profound impact on integrated global supply chain costs and customer service levels.

Relationship Management

Relationship management covers the management of dynamic interactions between suppliers, customers, investors, government, media, community, and industry groups, recognizing the need to understand the behavioral interpretations from the perspective of both parties to a relationship. It acknowledges that entities that have interacted for a long time may view their relationship very differently from those that have little experience with each other. Therefore, understanding relationships requires time-based assessments by both parties of dimensions that are critical to many relationships.

One dimension central to relationship management capability is the level of trust that exists between the entities in a relationship (Ganesan 1994). Through trust, each party gains a level of confidence that the other party will do what the former expects. This confidence is gained through the honesty and integrity of the parties who are involved in the relationship. Structural elements that affect organizational-level dimensions of trust influence the capability of one organization to meet the needs of the other through their offerings. Trust at this level implies that a firm has the organizational hierarchy in place and resources available and is capable of implementing these resources for the benefit of the relationship. For example, a firm's assignment of specific human or capital resources to a relationship can affect the other party's interpretation of that firm's willingness to pursue or continue the relationship. In other words, the commitment of resources to the relationship plays a major role in cultivating trust.

Communication or information sharing is another fundamental dimension of business relationships. Therefore, as relationship managers exchange information, this information provides cues to the other party as to what the relationship managers consider important to their organizations and the relationship. For relationship managers to react appropriately, they must be able to interpret the information and determine its value to their organizations.

Commitment to the relationship is a dimension that reflects the dependence that exists when one party does not entirely control all the conditions necessary for achievement of a desired outcome (Cadotte and Stern 1979; Emerson 1962). Three critical factors that affect the degree of perceived dependence of one party on the other are the importance of the product or service exchanged, the extent to which each of the parties has discretion over the exchange, and the extent to which the parties have alternatives to the current relationship. Commitment to a relationship is also demonstrated by the commitment of resources to the relationship (Heide 1994). Therefore, longer-term relationships tend to be characterized by a willingness of both parties to commit a variety of different resources to a set of future transactions.

The measurement system used to assess the contribution to value of a relationship is another critical dimension of relationship management. One barrier to successful long-term relationships is the inability of multiple organizations to measure jointly created and shared value as well as to develop ways to allocate shared risk.

Resource Management

Resource management capability facilitates the development and management of human capital, information technology and knowledge, financial resources, and property. The complex configurations of an integrated global supply chain, often globally dispersed, provide access to resources such as cheap labor and raw materials, subsidized financing opportunities, and larger product markets. For global value chains, the resources of a company are subject to greater uncertainties and risks in the system. Harland, Brenchley, and Walker (2003) provide a comprehensive list of risks facing an organization: strategic risk, operations risk, supply risk, customer risk, asset impairment risk, competitive risk, reputation risk, financial risk, fiscal risk, regulatory risk, and legal risk. In particular, the risks faced by a global integrated global supply chain can be classified into macroeconomic risks associated with significant economic shifts in wage rates, interest rates, exchange rates, and prices; policy risks associated with the unexpected actions of national governments; competitive risks associated with uncertainty about competitor activities in foreign markets; resource risks associated with unanticipated changes in resource requirements or availability in foreign markets (Ghoshal 1987); and global supply chain supply and demand risks.

The realization of these risks could lead to outcomes such as the inability of the focal firm to meet customer demand within anticipated costs, threats to customer life and safety, impairment of a firm's internal ability to produce goods and services, inadequate quality of finished goods, decreased profitability of the company, chaos in the system (such as the bullwhip effect), and lower likelihood of a customer placing an order with the organization (Simons 1999; Wilding 1998; Zsidisin et al. 2004). To prevent or reduce the potential damages and losses to resources, resource management capability must provide the ability to manage risks.

Risk management is the process of minimizing the potential damage to the available resources and mitigating the consequences if a risk is realized. Risk management processes include identifying risks and their sources, evaluating risks, selecting and implementing risk management strategies (reducing the probabilities of adverse occurrences), and developing risk mitigation strategies (reducing the impact of adverse occurrences). Thus, the organizational hierarchies, coordination processes, and information and communications, human resource, and measurement systems necessary to implement risk management techniques are central to resource management capability.

Performance Implications

SSP portrays performance as resulting from the fit of structure to the chosen strategy of the firm. Strategic determination is equated with establishing goals, whereas performance is the evaluation of how well the goals are met (Chandler 1962; Hofer and Schendel 1978; Mentzer and Konrad 1991). Atkinson, Waterhouse, and Wells (1997) define three roles for performance measurement: (1) *coordination*, which focuses decision making on the most important objectives; (2) *monitoring*, or the actual measurement and reporting of performance; and (3) *diagnostic*, which is used to evaluate performance, identify the improvements needed, and tie the non-financial metrics to financial measurement criteria and goals. Goals established in strategy formulation are eventually translated into performance measures that are evaluated periodically and ultimately drive adjustments to goals and strategies. Performance, therefore, is the measurable outcome of strategy execution and structural implementation. Thus, the shared goals identified in global supply chain strategy formulation are used to derive performance measures for the global supply chain. Failure to link performance to strategy may lead to the inability of the global supply chain to achieve goals and meet customer expectations and will not provide the vision necessary to influence individual goal-directed behaviors.

Mentzer and Konrad (1991) break traditional performance down into measures of efficiency and effectiveness and state that both elements are necessary. Efficiency measures how well the resources expended were utilized, whereas effectiveness assesses the degree to which goals are accomplished. Unfortunately, assessment of overall global supply chain performance has been limited as the metrics employed have often been measures of internal operations as opposed to measures of GSCMS. Lambert and Pohlen (2001) proposed an approach to GSCMS performance measurement that assesses the EVA of combined global supply chain effort to demonstrate that the benefits of GSCMS occur across the extended firms. Specifically, the Lambert and Pohlen model demonstrates that overall system value benefits each firm in the global supply chain by improving shareholder value in one or more distinct areas: revenue enhancement, operating expense reduction, and working capital and fixed capital efficiency.

Overall revenue enhancement is accrued by improving the effectiveness of operations, for example, availability of products and services that prove most important to the global supply chain's revenue and profit generation, as well as by creating proper information flows and metrics to provide an incentive for global supply chain firms to sell these products and services. Operating expense reduction is realized by streamlining processes, reducing redundancy and duplication, and improving productivity and operating asset utilization. Working capital efficiency translates to inventory elimination. Improving flow-through and inventory turnover by enhancing forecast accuracy, streamlining flow processes, and speeding up cycle times serves to reduce cycle inventory considerably and improve the global supply chain's ability to respond to actual demand without huge investment in pipeline inventory. Fixed asset efficiency results indirectly from reductions in operating expenses and working capital. Specifically, global supply chain work performed more efficiently with operating assets and inventory utilized with higher productivity enables firms to reduce facilities, equipment, and labor invested (Christopher and Ryals 1999).

Integration of GSCMS Into Firm Strategy

Managers involved in strategic decision making should find this framework useful as a means of clarifying the nature of GSCMS and how it fits within and across organizations. In particular, managers may assess critical aspects of the global market and internal enterprise characteristics to determine the GSCMS level their organization should seek and the degree of alignment global supply chain partners should have with a similar GSCMS perspective. It also provides guidance on how to employ structural elements within the five core GSCMS capabilities to achieve global supply chain performance improvement.

References

Achrol, Ravi S. and P. Kotler (1999), "Marketing and the Network Economy," *Journal of Marketing,* 63 (4), 146–163.

Achrol, Ravi S. and Louis W. Stern (1988), "Environmental Determinants of Decision Making Uncertainty in Marketing Channels," *Journal of Marketing Research,* 25 (February), 36–50.

Anita, K. D. and G. L. Frazier (2001), "The Severity of Contract Enforcement in Interfirm Channel Relationships," *Journal of Marketing,* 65 (4), 67–81.

Atkinson, A. A., J. H. Waterhouse, and R. B. Wells (1997), "A Stakeholder Approach to Strategic Performance Management," *Sloan Management Review,* 19 (2), 25–37.

Barney, Jay (1991), "Firm Resources and Sustained Competitive Advantage," *Journal of Management,* 17 (1), 99–120.

Bolton, R. N. and M. B. Myers (2003), "Price-Based Global Segmentation for Services," *Journal of Marketing,* 67 (July), 108–129.

Bowersox, Donald J., David J. Closs, and M. Bixby Cooper (2002), *Supply Chain Logistics Management.* Boston: McGraw-Hill/Irwin.

Bowersox, Donald J., David J. Closs, and T. P. Stank (2003), "How to Master Cross-Enterprise Collaboration," *Supply Chain Management Review,* 7 (4), 18–26.

Bucklin, L. P. and S. Sengupta (1993), "Organizing Successful Co-marketing Alliances," *Journal of Marketing,* 57 (2), 32–46.

Cadotte, Ernest R. and Louis Stern (1979), "A Process Model of Interorganizational Relations in Marketing Channels," *Research in Marketing,* 2, 127–158.

Chandler, Alfred D., Jr. (1962), *Strategy and Structure.* Cambridge: MIT Press.

Chetty, Sylvie and Andrea Patterson (2002), "Developing Internationalization Capability Through Industry Groups: The Experience of a Telecommunications Joint Action Group," *Journal of Strategic Marketing,* 10 (1), 69–90.

Child, John (1972), "Organization Structure, Environment and Performance: The Role of Strategic Choice," *Sociology,* 6 (1), 1–22.

Choi, J. and M. Rajan (1997), "A Joint Test of Market Segmentation and Exchange Risk Factor in International Capital Markets," *Journal of International Business Studies,* 28 (1), 29.

Christopher, M. and L. Ryals (1999), "Supply Chain Strategy: Its Impact on Shareholder Value," *International Journal of Logistics Management,* 10 (1), 1–10.

Cooper, Martha C., Douglas M. Lambert, and Janus D. Pagh (1997), "Supply Chain Management: More Than a New Name for Logistics," *International Journal of Logistics Management,* 8 (1), 1–14.

Coyne, Kevin P. (1986), "Sustainable Competitive Advantage: What It Is, What It Isn't," *Business Horizons,* 29 (1), 54–62.

Daugherty, P. J., M. B. Myers, and R. G. Richey (2002), "Information Support for Reverse Logistics: The Influence of Relationship Commitment," *Journal of Business Logistics,* 23 (1), 85–106.

Daugherty, P. J. and P. H. Pittman (1995), "Utilization of Time-Based Strategies: Creating Distribution Flexibility/Responsiveness," *International Journal of Operations & Production Management,* 15 (2), 54–60.

Day, George S. (1994), "The Capabilities of Market-Driven Organizations," *Journal of Marketing,* 58 (4), 37–52.

Day, George S. and Prakash Nedungadi (1994), "Managerial Representations of Competitive Advantage," *Journal of Marketing,* 58 (2), 31–44.

Day, George S. and Robin Wensley (1988), "Assessing Advantage: A Framework for Diagnosing Competitive Superiority," *Journal of Marketing,* 52 (2), 1–20.

Deeter-Schmelz, D. R. (1997), "Applying Teams in Logistics Processes: Information Acquisition and the Impact of Team Role Clarity and Norms," *Journal of Business Logistics,* 18 (1), 159–178.

Deshpande, Rohit and Frederick E. Webster, Jr. (1989), "Organizational Culture and Marketing: Defining the Research Agenda," *Journal of Marketing,* 53 (1), 3–15.

Dess, G. G. and D. W. Beard (1984), "Dimensions of Organization Task Environments," *Administrative Science Quarterly,* 29 (1), 52–73.

Dutta, Shantanu, Om Narasimhan, and Surendra Rajiv (1999), "Success in High-Technology Markets: Is Marketing Capability Critical," *Marketing Science,* 18 (4), 547–568.

Dwyer, F. R. and M. A. Welsh (1985), "Environmental Relationships of the Internal Political Economy of Marketing Channels," *Journal of Marketing Research,* 22 (November), 397–414.

Emerson, Richard (1962), "Power-Dependence Relations," *American Sociological Review,* February, 31–41.

Flint, Daniel J., Everth Larsson, Britta Gammelgaard, and John T. Mentzer (2005), "Logistics Innovation: A Customer Value-Oriented Social Process," *Journal of Business Logistics*, 26 (1), 113–147.

Forte, M., J. J. Hoffman, B. Lamont, and E. N. Brockmann (2000), "Organizational Form and Environment: An Analysis of Between-Form and Within-Form Responses to Environmental Change," *Strategic Management Journal*, 21 (7), 753–773.

Galbraith, Jay R. and Robert K. Kazanjian (1986), *Strategy Implementation: Structure, Systems, and Process*. St. Paul, MN: West Publishing.

Galbraith, Jay R. and Daniel A. Nathanson (1978), *Strategy Implementation: The Role of Structure and Process*. St. Paul, MN: West Publishing.

Gale, Bradely T. (1994), *Managing Customer Value*. New York: Free Press.

Galunic, D. Charles and Kathleen M. Eisenhardt (1994), "Renewing the Strategy-Structure-Performance Paradigm," *Research in Organizational Behavior*, 16, 215–255.

Ganesan, Shankar (1994), "Determinants of Long-Term Orientation in Buyer-Seller Relationships," *Journal of Marketing*, 58 (April), 1–19.

Gassenheimer, Jule B., Franklin S. Houston, and J. Charlene Davis (1998), "The Role of Economic Value, Social Value, and Perceptions of Fairness in Inter-organizational Relationship Retention Decisions," *Journal of the Academy of Marketing Science*, 26 (Fall), 322–337.

Ghoshal, Sumantra (1987), "Global Strategy: An Organizing Framework," *Strategic Management Journal*, 8 (5), 425–440.

Glazer, R. (1991), "Marketing Is an Information-Intensive Environment: Strategic Implications of Knowledge as an Asset," *Journal of Marketing*, 55 (4), 1–19.

Gordon, G. G. (1991), "Industry Determinants of Organizational Culture," *The Academy of Management Review*, 16 (2), 396–415.

Gutman, Jonathan (1982), "A Means-End Chain Model Based on Consumer Categorization Processes," *Journal of Marketing*, 46 (Spring), 60–72.

Habib, Mohammed M. and Bart Victor (1991), "Strategy, Structure, and Performance of U.S. Manufacturing and Service MNCs: A Comparative Analysis," *Strategic Management Journal*, 12 (8), 589–606.

Hambrick, D. C. and P. A. Mason (1984), "Upper Echelons: An Organization as a Reflection of Its Top Managers," *Academy of Management Review*, 9 (2), 193–206.

Harland, Christine, Richard Brenchley, and Helen Walker (2003), "Risk in Supply Networks," *Journal of Purchasing & Supply Management*, 9 (2), 51–62.

Hauser, John R. and Glen Urban (1986), "The Value Priority Hypotheses for Consumer Budget Plans," *Journal of Consumer Research*, 12 (March), 446–462.

Heide, Jan (1994), "Interorganizational Governance in Marketing Channels," *Journal of Marketing*, 58 (January), 71–85.

Hofer, Charles and Dan Schendel (1978), *Strategy Formulation: Analytical Concepts*. St. Paul, MN: West Publishing.

Holbrook, Morris B. (1994), "The Nature of Consumer Value," in *Service Quality: New Directions in Theory and Practice*, Roland T. Rust and Richard L. Oliver, eds. Newbury Park, CA: Sage, pp. 21–71.

Hoskisson, Robert E. (1987), "Multidivisional Structure and Performance: The Contingency of Diversification Strategy," *Academy of Management Journal*, 30 (4), 625–644.

Jayaram, J., S. K. Vickery, and C. Droge (2000), "The Effects of Information System Infrastructure and the Process Improvements on Supply-Chain Time Performance," *International Journal of Physical Distribution & Logistics Management*, 21, 523–539.

Kahn, K. B. and J. T. Mentzer (1996), "Logistics and Interdepartmental Integration," *International Journal of Physical Distribution & Logistics Management*, 26 (8), 6–14.

Klein, Saul, Gary L. Frazier, and Victor J. Roth (1990), "A Transaction Cost Analysis Model of Channel Integration in International Markets," *Journal of Marketing Research,* 27 (2), 196–208.

Kogut, B. (1985), "Designing Global Strategies: Comparative and Competitive Value-Added Chains," *Sloan Management Review,* Summer, 15–28.

Kogut, B. and N. Kulatilaka (1994), "Operating Flexibility, Global Manufacturing, and the Option Value of a Multinational Network," *Management Science,* 40 (1), 123–149.

Lai, Albert W. (1995), "Consumer Values, Product Benefits, and Customer Value: A Consumption Behavior Approach," in *Advances in Consumer Research,* Frank R. Kardes and Mita Sujan, eds. Provo, UT: Association for Consumer Research, pp. 381–388.

Lambert, D. M. and T. L. Pohlen (2001), "Supply Chain Metrics," *International Journal of Logistics Management,* 12 (1), 1–19.

Lapide, Larry (2002), "You Need Sales and Operations Planning," *Journal of Business Forecasting,* Summer, 11–14.

Lapierre, Jozée (2000), "Customer-Perceived Value in Industrial Contexts," *Journal of Business and Industrial Marketing,* 15 (2/3), 122–140.

Leblebici, H. and G. S. Salancik (1981), "Effects of Environmental Uncertainty on Information Decision Processes in Banks," *Administrative Science Quarterly,* 26 (December), 578–596.

Lengnick-Hall, C. A. and M. L. Lengnick-Hall (1988), "Strategic Human Resource Management: A Review of the Literature and Proposed Typology," *Academy of Management Review,* 13, 454–470.

Lowson, Robert H. (2003), "The Nature of an Operations Strategy: Combining Strategic Decisions From the Resource-Based and Market-Driven Viewpoints," *Management Decision,* 41 (6), 538–549.

Lubatkin, Michael and Ronald C. Rogers (1989), "Diversification, Systematic Risk, and Shareholder Return: A Capital Market Extension of Rumelt's 1974 Study," *Academy of Management Journal,* 32 (2), 454–465.

Mabert, V. A. and M. A. Venkataramanan (1998), "Special Research Focuses on Supply Chain Linkages: Challenges for Design and Management in the 21st Century," *Decision Sciences,* 29, 537–552.

Marcoulides, G. A. and R. H. Heck (1993), "Organizational Culture and Performance: Proposing and Testing a Model," *Organization Science,* 4 (2), 209–225.

McAfee, R. B., M. Glassman, and E. D. Honeycutt (2002), "The Effects of Culture and Human Resource Management Policies on Supply Chain Management," *Journal of Business Logistics,* 23 (1), 1–18.

McGinnis, M. A. and J. W. Kohn (1990), "A Factor Analytic Study of Logistics Strategy," *Journal of Business Logistics,* 11 (2), 41–63.

McGinnis, M. A. and J. W. Kohn (1993), "Logistics Strategy, Organizational Environment, and Time Competitiveness," *Journal of Business Logistics,* 14 (2), 1–23.

Mentzer, John T. (2004), *Supply Chain Management.* Thousand Oaks, CA: Sage.

Mentzer, John T., William DeWitt, James S. Keebler, Soonhoong Min, Nancy W. Nix, Carlo D. Smith, and Zach G. Zacharia (2001), "Defining Supply Chain Management," *Journal of Business Logistics,* 22 (2), 1–25.

Mentzer, John T. and B. P. Konrad (1991), "An Efficiency/Effectiveness Approach to Logistics Performance Analysis," *Journal of Business Logistics,* 12 (1), 33–61.

Mentzer, John T., S. Min, and Z. G. Zacharia (2000), "The Nature of Interfirm Partnering in Supply Chain Management," *Journal of Retailing,* 76, 549–568.

Mentzer, John T. and Mark A. Moon (2004), "Understanding Demand," *Supply Chain Management Review,* 8 (May/June), 38–45.

Mentzer, John T., M. B. Myers, and M. S. Cheung (2004), "Global Market Segmentation for Logistics Services," *Industrial Marketing Management*, 33 (1), 15–21.

Miles, Raymond E. and Charles C. Snow (1978), *Organizational Strategy, Structure and Process*. New York: McGraw-Hill.

Miles, Raymond E. and Charles C. Snow (1984), "Fit, Failure and the Hall of Fame," *California Management Review*, 26 (3), 10–28.

Mizik, Natalie and Robert Jacobson (2004), "Trading Off Between Value Creation and Value Appropriation: The Financial Implications of Shifts in Strategic Emphasis," *Journal of Marketing*, 67 (1), 63–76.

Morgan, Robert E., Carolyn A. Strong, and Tony McGuinness (2003), "Product-Market Positioning and Prospector Strategy," *European Journal of Marketing*, 37 (10), 1409–1439.

Murphy, D. J. and M. T. Farris (1993), "Time-Based Strategy and Carrier Selection," *Journal of Business Logistics*, 14 (2), 25–40.

Parsons, G. L. (1983), "Information Technology: A New Competitive Weapon," *Sloan Management Review*, 25 (1), 3–14.

Porter, Michael (1980), *Competitive Strategy*. New York: Free Press.

Porter, Michael (1985), *Competitive Advantage*. New York: Free Press.

Porter, Michael and V. E. Millar (1985), "How Information Gives You Competitive Advantage," *Harvard Business Review*, 63 (4), 149–161.

Prahalad, C. K. and Gary Hamel (1990), "The Core Competence of the Corporation," *Harvard Business Review*, 68 (3), 79–93.

Rayport, J. F. and J. J. Sviokla (1995), "Exploiting the Virtual Value Chain," *Harvard Business Review*, 73 (6), 75–85.

Rosenzweig, P. M. and J. V. Singh (1991), "Organizational Environments and the Multinational Enterprise," *Academy of Management Review*, 16 (2), 340–361.

Rumelt, Richard P. (1974), *Strategy, Structure, and Economic Performance*. Cambridge, MA: Harvard University Press.

Schein, E. H. (1985), *Organizational Culture and Leadership*. San Francisco: Jossey-Bass.

Schonberger, R. (1990), *Building a Chain of Customers: Linking Business Functions to Create the World Class Company*. New York: Free Press.

Schonberger, R. (1992), "Is Strategy Strategic? Impact of Total Quality Management on Strategy," *Academy of Management Executive*, 6 (3), 80–87.

Sheth, Jagdish N., Bruce I. Newman, and Barbara L. Gross (1991), *Consumption Values and Market Choices: Theory and Applications*. Cincinnati, OH: Southwest Publishing.

Simons, Robert (1999), "How Risky Is Your Company?" *Harvard Business Review*, 77 (3), 85–94.

Slater, Stanley F. and John C. Narver (1995), "Market Orientation and the Learning Organization," *Journal of Marketing*, 59 (3), 63–74.

Slater, Stanley F. and John C. Narver (2000), "Intelligence Generation and Superior Customer Value," *Journal of the Academy of Marketing Science*, 28 (Winter), 120–127.

Srivastava, Rajendra K., Tasadduq A. Shervani, and Liam Fahey (1999), "Marketing, Business Processes, and Shareholder Value: An Organizationally Embedded View of Marketing Activities and the Discipline of Marketing," *Journal of Marketing*, 63 (Special Issue), 168–179.

Stalk, George, Philip Evans, and Lawrence E. Schulman (1992), "Competing on Capabilities: The New Rules of Corporate Strategy," *Harvard Business Review*, March–April, 57–69.

Teas, R. Kenneth and Sanjeev Agarwal (2000), "The Effects of Extrinsic Product Cues on Consumers' Perceptions of Quality, Sacrifice, and Value," *Journal of the Academy of Marketing Science*, 28 (Spring), 278–291.

Treacy, M. and F. Wiersema (1995), *The Discipline of Market Leaders*. Reading, MA: Addison Wesley.

Trent, R. J. (2004), "The Use of Organizational Design Features in Purchasing and Supply Management," *Journal of Supply Chain Management*, 40 (3), 4–18.

Van Hoek, Remko I., Harry R. Commandeur, and Bart Vos (1998), "Reconfiguring Logistics Systems Through Postponement Strategies," *Journal of Business Logistics*, 19 (1), 33–55.

Varadarajan, P. Rajan and Satish Jayachandran (1999), "Marketing Strategy: An Assessment of the State of the Field and Outlook," *Journal of the Academy of Marketing Science*, 27 (2), 120–144.

Walker, Orville C. and Robert W. Ruekert (1987), "Marketing's Role in the Implementation of Business Strategies: A Critical Review and Conceptual Framework," *Journal of Marketing*, 51 (3), 15–34.

Webster, Frederick E., Jr. (1992), "The Changing Role of Marketing in the Corporation," *Journal of Marketing*, 56 (4), 1–18.

Wernerfelt, Birger (1984), "A Resource-Based View of the Firm," *Strategic Management Journal*, 5 (2), 171–180.

Whipple, J. M., R. Frankel, and P. J. Daugherty (2002), "Information Support for Alliances: Performance Implications," *Journal of Business Logistics*, 23 (2), 67–82.

Wilding, Richard (1998), "The Supply Chain Complexity Triangle," *International Journal of Physical Distribution & Logistics Management*, 28 (8), 599–616.

Wolf, Joachim and William G. Egelhoff (2002), "A Reexamination and Extension of International Strategy-Structure Theory," *Strategic Management Journal*, 23 (2), 181–189.

Woodruff, Robert B. (1997), "Customer Value: The Next Source for Competitive Advantage," *Journal of the Academy of Marketing Science*, 25 (2), 139–153.

Woodruff, Robert B. and Sarah Fisher Gardial (1996), *Know Your Customer: New Approaches to Customer Value and Satisfaction*. Cambridge, MA: Blackwell.

Zeithaml, Valerie (1988), "Consumer Perceptions of Price, Quality, and Value: A Means-End Model and Synthesis of Evidence," *Journal of Marketing*, 52 (July), 2–22.

Zsidisin, George A., Lisa M. Ellram, Joseph R. Carter, and Joseph L. Cavinato (2004), "An Analysis of Supply Risk Assessment Techniques," *International Journal of Physical Distribution & Logistics Management*, 34 (5), 397–413.

3

Assessing the Global Environment

Matthew B. Myers

Antonio Borghesi

Ivan Russo

The current trend toward the *globalization* of supply chains renders many managers confused as to what globalization really means. Often, the term is little more than a battleground of semantics, of little value to the individual tasked with managing value creation and cost reduction processes in the movement of goods. Clearly, globalization infers the cross-border movement of goods and the emergence of competitors and opportunities across competing supply chains within an industry. Managers, however, often question the differences between a global market and a single market, in that many of the same conditions exist in both. Although this may be true, the complexities of cross-border operations are exponentially greater than in a single country and the ability to compete in the global environment is often dependent on understanding the subtleties that emerge only in cross-border trade.

Descriptions of the global environment faced by supply chain managers have been frequent, including an excellent summary by Nix (2001). Yet since 9/11, the pressures on supply chain managers have intensified, given new security concerns and the ensuing transportation delays that come with increased customs scrutiny, coupled with previously existing political, cultural, and economic variance across markets. This situation has contributed to the stress supply chains feel when trying to meet delivery and service expectations, both at home and abroad. Perhaps not coincidentally, the security crises arrived simultaneously with increased access to overseas labor, materials, and consumers. This dramatic exposure to both risk and return opportunities leads firms to face environmental challenges outside the realm of previously developed capabilities in supply chain management.

In this chapter, we discuss the environmental conditions influencing global supply chain decisions and effectiveness—for example, those conditions that need continuous assessment by managers. Most important, this discussion takes place in the context of a post-9/11 marketplace, where global supply chain management depends on effective manipulation of, and preparation for, increasingly volatile environmental conditions.

Yesterday's Supply Chains in Today's Global Environment

Given the enormous attention paid to supply chain activities over the past 15 years, it is not surprising that supply chain efficiencies, and even service offerings, have developed in multinational corporations. Unfortunately, the very characteristics that make supply chains cost-effective also make them vulnerable to the volatile global environment in which they exist. Both academics and consultants, such as A. T. Kearney (Monahan, Laudicina, and Attis 2005), note that just-in-time (JIT), automatic replenishment programs (ARP), and vendor-managed inventory (VMI) have reduced inventory levels to the bare minimum, with little or no safety stock. As a result, the recent outbreak of severe acute respiratory syndrome (SARS) in East Asia and the resultant disruptions in production in China caused auto manufacturing plants and computer assembly operations in the United States to shut down because of lack of parts and microchips. Sourcing from abroad means longer channels and lead times, as well as exposure to economic and political risks in the sourcing market. The current trend in outsourcing also leads to longer lead times and more middlemen, exposing firms to risk across multiple markets, as well as a loss of control over suppliers and third-party functionaries. Finally, the popularity of consolidating supply chain functions, by reducing the number of production and assembly facilities, suppliers, and middlemen, also exposes firms to increased risk from a less than diversified portfolio of partners. Although all these approaches have been effective in cost reductions, and are taught consistently in business schools, their application in a global context needs significant modification.

Although outside the control of managers, global supply chains are exposed to an increased number of technological and natural disasters that affect efficiencies and disrupt supply chain functions. For example, the Centre for Research on the Epidemiology of Disasters (2004) notes that technological disasters (those defined as industrial or transportation accidents) have increased exponentially worldwide over the past 30 years (see Figure 3.1). This should influence managers toward greater safety stock and other contingency efforts. But this has not been the case for most operations.

As a result of these "efficiency deficiencies," it is critical that the supply chain manager assess several aspects of the global environment capable of influencing

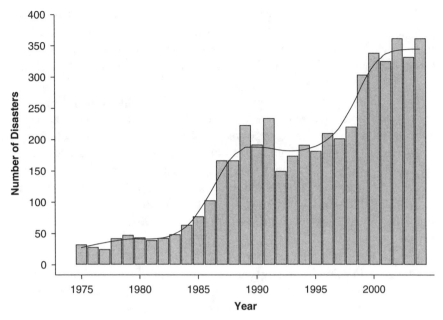

EM-DAT: The OFDA/CRED International Disaster Database: www.em-dat.net
Université Catholique de Louvain, Brussels, Belgium

Figure 3.1   Total Number of Technological Disasters Reported Worldwide: 1975
to 2004

profitability and effectiveness. These variables, namely, the cross-cultural nature of supply chain management, foreign currency risk, security, and the political economy of markets, are specific to the global supply chain and often act to detrimentally affect an otherwise efficient operational strategy.

Cross-Cultural Influences and the Global Supply Chain

In today's supply chains, geographical distances between the partners are longer than in the past owing to firms seeking to take advantage of labor, raw materials, and tax differentials. These opportunities stimulate the organizations to expand and enlarge their supply chain across different countries. At the same time, competition demands a reactive and fast supply chain. Yet "globalization requires a highly coordinated flow of goods, information, and cash within and across national boundaries" (Bowersox and Calantone 1998, p. 86). For these reasons, many firms have decided to outsource their supply chain tasks abroad, where the cost of labor and raw materials is lower than in their home market. To globalize the supply chain is often ineluctable and requires the development of good relationships across multiple cultures. To choose a partner or a country solely based on labor cost is problematic as the best country for labor or raw materials could be the worst cultural match. The damages could be very serious if, for instance, a supplier or distributor will not share information, is apathetic regarding on-time delivery, or has significantly different ethical standards.

Each country has its specific elements of originality and peculiarity, and matching supply chain strategies with the different cultural imperatives is a challenge for every organization that decides to go abroad to do business. It is possible to develop an effective global supply chain design in every detail, yet a fit or match between culture and strategy is essential for strategy implementation and good performance. This means every firm should consider specific cultural aspects, such as ethnic, racial, political, and religious characteristics, for both supply chain partners and other entities within the market (Griffith and Myers 2005; Christie and Marshall 2001).

"Design and management of supply chain activities must consider the influence of differences in culture, industry structure, legal requirements, and infrastructure in different countries on customers, suppliers, competitors, and supply chain partners" (Zacharia 2001, p. 28). Culture, or the "collective programming of the mind which distinguishes the members of one group or category of people from another" (Hofstede 1991, p. 5), provides a society's characteristic profile with respect to norms, values, script, or sequences of appropriate social action, which affords an understanding of how societies manage relations (Schank and Abelson 1977; Triandis 1988; Bhawuk 2001; Hofstede 2001). Individuals operate based on their cultural orientation when engaging in business practice, for example, in negotiations (e.g., Brett and Okumura 1998).

One of the relevant issues in global supply chain relationships is how culturally founded norm expectations are embedded in bilaterally established relational norm governance strategies. Griffith and Myers (2005) developed a theoretical foundation for the influence of cultural norm expectations on relational strategies and focused on the cultural norm expectations driven by cultural theory and their implication and role in global supply chain management. The findings suggest that with the limited resources available to supply chain managers (time, manpower, etc.), firm performance is enhanced when supply chain processes such as information sharing and commitment levels are fit to culture-based norm expectations across culturally diverse relationships. In short, understanding the implications of the cultural variables affecting supply chain relationships results in better management of the global supply chain and the relationships between the partners.

Compatible corporate culture and management techniques of each organization in a supply chain are necessary for successful supply chain management (e.g., Cooper, Lambert, and Pagh 1997; Lambert, Stock, and Ellram 1998), and organizational compatibility is a prerequisite for creating a supply chain orientation in every firm of the network (Mentzer, Myers, and Cheung 2004). Thus, supply chain managers must focus on two important, yet related, aspects of culture: national and organizational. Pothukuchi et al. (2002) showed that differences in organizational culture are more significant in causing problems than differences in national culture and are more difficult to manage.

A relational strategy incorporating intercultural issues encourages identification of supply chain partners that share a common vision and are pursuing parallel objectives to create structures and processes that improve cross-organizational behavior (Rodrigues, Stank, and Lynch 2004). "It can be argued that in today's challenging global markets, the route to sustainable advantage lies in being able to leverage the respective strengths and competencies of network partners to achieve greater responsiveness to market needs" (Christopher and Peck 2003, p. 121). Often, these strengths are in managing cross-cultural relationships.

Foreign Currency Volatility

Despite the consolidation of a number of currencies in recent decades, foreign currency volatility remains an important problem for supply chain managers (Christie and Marshall 2001). Failure to properly account for foreign currency changes the costs of businesses by hundreds of millions of dollars per year. Exchange risk is the change in the dollar, yen, or euro value of exposed assets or liabilities resulting from changes in the spot rate during a given period. Often, supply chain managers fail to realize their exposure to foreign currency swings when remittances are due in 90, 120, or 180 days. Depending on the size of the contract, a 1% change in currency value can lead to thousands of dollars (or euros, yen, etc.) in losses. Furthermore, the value of inventory held in foreign warehouses must be restated each reporting period when fluctuating exchange rates result in the recognition of an unrealized gain or loss. Adjustments for these gains and losses must be considered when restating data in foreign currencies.

Although it is a somewhat dramatic example, Table 3.1 indicates foreign currency fluctuations relative to the U.S. dollar for the week after September 11, 2001. In this instance, the tumble in the dollar value had significant effects on any outstanding contracts. For a firm that owed $100,000 on September 17, 2001, at the end of a 30-day contract, the value of that payment fell precipitously against the major European and Japanese currencies.

Table 3.1 Foreign Currency Volatility and Supply Chain Exposure: Changes From 10 September – 17 September 2001

Currency	% Change in U.S. Dollar Value
French franc	−2.52
German mark	−2.64
Euro	−2.63
Yen	−2.70
Swiss franc	−4.85
British pound	−0.41

NOTE: At the time, both the euro and the individual country currencies were in circulation.

In reality, the financial and accounting complexities of foreign exchange (FX) rates go beyond the understanding, or responsibility, of global supply chain managers. Instead, it is the task of managers to reduce FX risk in global supply chain transactions. The simplest method is to conduct transactions in the firm's home currency. Samiee and Anckar (1998) note that choice of foreign currency is often an important negotiating point in global supply chains. Interestingly, the use of foreign currencies was found to be positively related to sales volume and transaction value but negatively related to profitability. This is very likely due to an inability, or unwillingness, on the part of supply chain managers to hedge against possible FX changes while catering to partner desires regarding currency use. As a result, competitive supply chains have become adept at using hedging techniques or, at the very least, negotiating profitable terms relative to potential fluctuations.

Political Economies

Global supply chain designs must take into account changing political economy infrastructures to remain competitive. Political economies, in the form of regional economic integration, are agreements among countries in a geographic region to reduce, and ultimately remove, tariff and nontariff barriers to the free flow of goods, services, and factors of production among each other. Supply chain optimization mandates that firms take advantage of these trade arrangements to meet multiple market needs, or benefit from multiple market offerings, while reducing the overall costs associated with taxes, tariffs, and other trade barriers. Economic integrations run from the simple free flow of goods (free trade areas) to full political and economic integration (political unions), and their influence on supply chain operations varies as regulations change across types (see Table 3.2). Proper assessment of the political economy scenario often facilitates considerable savings in tariffs, as well as market opportunities. It is essential to evaluate political risk, credit risk, social risk, and market risk and minimize their effects through awareness of their impact and cost across global supply chains.

Often, the political economy forces firms to alter their supply chain designs. For example, China, by understanding the need of U.S. and Western European firms to have access to its enormous market, can leverage this to force multinationals to comply with strict local content and local labor requirements. As a result, instead of exporting directly to China, firms must enter joint venture relationships with Chinese businesses or locate their own wholly owned subsidiaries inside the Chinese market. This enables the use of Chinese labor and components, yet forces the firm to modify its supply chain significantly. The rationale behind this policy is more than simply a desire by local governments to increase employment and local business sales; it is also seen as an opportunity to absorb the process technologies of Western firms. As a result, maintaining barriers to private processes and technologies is often difficult, and many multinationals find themselves creating competitors in overseas markets. Yet the trade-off is difficult, because the increased emphasis on sales volume to combat compressed margins mandates access to large markets such as India and China.

Table 3.2   Regional Integration and Supply Chain Options

Type of Regional Integration	Regulations	Supply Chain Perspectives
FTA[a]	All barriers to trade of goods and services are removed; each country can determine its own trade policies relative to nonmembers	Potential benefit of importing into low-tax market, distributing across all affiliated markets in FTA Local production and warehouse facilities serving multiple markets tariff free
Customs Union	Same as FTA, except with common external trade policy	Potential benefits from lowest-tax import closed Local production and warehouse facilities serving multiple markets tariff free
Common Market	Similar to Customs Union, but factors of production can move freely across borders	Labor and capital can be used in multiple markets without penalty
Economic Union	Similar to Common Market, but now using one currency, with harmonization of tax rates among members, common monetary and fiscal policy	Reduced translation exposure to currency fluctuations Often, greater demand for use of local content and local labor when accessing these markets; increased call for local production and assembly
Political Union	Full integration both economically and politically	Same as Economic Union

a. Free Trade Area.

Two Sets of Rules

A frequent assertion among managers in Western Europe and the United States is that unfair trade practices make it difficult for firms from developed nations to compete with products from lower-cost developing markets. In fact, this is the case, in that the organizations that set trade regulations develop two sets of trade rules, one for developed and one for developing markets. The rationale behind the discrepancy between markets is that with the massive disequilibrium in wealth levels between the market categories, a method of enabling developing markets to compete on the world stage is to slacken the tax, tariff, and subsidy regulations for developing markets relative to their developed competitors. In this way, developing

Table 3.3   Two Sets of Rules: GATT[a]–Uruguay Round Regulations for Agricultural Products, Developed Versus Developing Economies

Tariffs	Developed Countries: 1996–2001	Developing Countries: 1996–2004
Average cut for all agricultural products (%)	−36	−24
Minimum cut per product (%)	−15	−10
Domestic support		
Total AMS[b] cuts per sector (from 1988 baseline) (%)	−20	−13
Exports		
Value of subsidies (%)	−36	−24
Subsidized quantities (%)	−21	−14

a. General Agreement on Tariffs and Trade.

b. Aggregate measure of support.

nations can protect their own markets while at the same time shipping to higher-paying developed markets at a reduced tax and tariff. Using agricultural products as an example, it is evident that the World Trade Organization, in the General Agreement on Tariffs and Trade (GATT) talks of the Uruguay round, has set different regulations for developed versus developing economies (see Table 3.3). Not only are developing economies mandated to reduce taxes and subsidies to a significantly lower level than developed markets, they also have three more years to accomplish the task. In this manner, low-cost products from overseas often enter developed markets with ease, meaning that local producers have trouble competing.

From a global supply chain perspective, however, managers should see opportunities in these discrepancies. Besides offering developing economies an opportunity to benefit from reduced regulatory pressures, the system is designed to provide incentives to multinational firms to select suitable developing locations and conduct specific supply chain tasks in those locales. By conducting manufacturing, assembly and subassembly, distribution and warehousing, and other functions in these markets, developing economies can benefit from increased labor levels, technology transfer, and foreign direct investment. Simultaneously, global supply chain managers benefit from operating in countries with reduced tax burdens, gaining access to those markets as well as shipping from reduced-tax ports. Often, survival of firms within supply chains depends on the ability, or willingness, of supply chain managers to consider moving critical tasks abroad.

The New Environment of Hypersecurity

Today's global supply chain environment is highly security conscious. Concerns have arisen over potential product tampering, manifest integrity, and the actual contents of containers and units moving through supply chain facilities around the world (Rinehart, Myers, and Eckert 2005). Global supply chain managers focus on security for two very good reasons: (1) fear of improper products being introduced into the supply chain and (2) concerns that not meeting security requirements will mean longer delays in customs processes. Longer delays could mean disruptions in customer production schedules, added costs, and, ultimately, higher prices on finished products. One of the more interesting tools to solve this problem is radio-frequency identification (RFID). Through the use of RFID, it is possible to have visibility of supply chain flows from the first manufacturer to the last customer.

The assessment of personal and organizational relationship characteristics that exist between global supply chain partners can help improve the efficiency and effectiveness of security efforts around the world. In fact, managers are more frequently demanding that their supply chain partners take significant steps to ensure security precautions are taken and that these partners have the capability to meet the strengthened security requirements (Mentzer et al. 2004). Often, partner choices are dictated by the ability to meet these new environmental conditions.

Conclusions

Research on the organization of multinational corporations has projected the emergence of complex, internally differentiated structures (Malnight 2001). Largely, these complex structures are the result of organizations, including supply chains, operating in increasingly complex external environments. The shift of the firm's strategic focus is outside its home market, with emphasis on emergent strategic opportunities associated with managing a network of dispersed worldwide operations (Malnight 2001; Kogut 1984).

Similar to the focus on the multinational company, investigating emerging global supply chain patterns and managerial techniques mandates an understanding of the discrepancies across markets and the environmental variables that influence, or should influence, strategic decisions. Effective management of supply chain relationships depends on the ability of managers to appropriately fit, or align, organizational elements with environmental opportunities and threats (Griffith and Myers 2005). Largely, these opportunities and threats to global supply chains result from cross-cultural, political, economic, and security-oriented phenomena.

Typically, operationally oriented supply chain managers see culture as an intangible, more relevant to marketers than to themselves. The lack of inclusion of culture in strategic designs is a noteworthy limitation given the demonstrated influence of culture on global supply chain management issues (Wacker and Sprague 1998). Unfortunately, little, if any, cross-cultural research has empirically examined relational and knowledge development resources in global supply chain settings. As a result, managers are left with little guidance in the applicability of cultural research to this domain.

> Further, and more importantly for global supply chain management, while some inter-cultural supply chain research . . . has been conducted, this research tends to consist of single country studies primarily conducted in the U.S., thus providing researchers little understanding of how firms from different cultures perceive the relational and knowledge development resources when operating in inter-cultural, global supply chain relationships. (Griffith, Myers, and Harvey 2005, p. 17)

It is abundantly clear that a clash of cultures can detrimentally affect supply chain performance (Christie and Marshall 2001).

To a far greater extent, management's ability to factor political and economic environmental conditions into their global supply chain models has been supported by meaningful research in these areas, particularly relative to handling foreign currency volatility, managing complex political economy arrangements, security issues, and trade law. However, these issues continue to be enormous challenges to supply chain managers. Often, regional trade groupings, tax and tariff regulations, and even currencies themselves may change during the development of a global supply chain design or strategy. Nonetheless, these environmental conditions must be considered when developing strategies. Yet these environmental conditions will continue to influence the effectiveness and profitability of supply chains and their entities as the number of multinationals grows.

Increasingly, firms have reduced options relative to manufacturing, supplying, assembling, and selling in their home markets. Raw material prices, wage rates, trade regulations, and market access mandate that to survive, firms and their supply chain partners must pursue opportunities overseas. The larger the portfolio of markets in which the supply chain operates, the greater the opportunities and, simultaneously, the greater the complexities and risks resulting from turbulent environmental conditions.

References

Bhawuk, Dharm P. S. (2001), "Evolution of Cultural Assimilators: Toward Theory-Based Assimilators," *International Journal of Intercultural Relations,* 25 (2), 141–163.

Bowersox, Donald J. and Roger J. Calantone (1998), "Executive Insight: Global Logistics," *Journal of International Marketing,* 6 (4), 83–93.

Brett, M. Jeanne and Tetsushi Okumura (1998), "Inter- and Intracultural Negotiation: U.S. and Japanese Negotiators," *Academy of Management Journal,* 41 (5), 495–510.

Centre for Research on the Epidemiology of Disasters (2004), *EM-DAT: The OFDA/CRED International Disaster Database.* Brussels, Belgium: Université Catholique de Louvain.

Christie, Eilidh and Andrew Marshall (2001), "The Impact of the Introduction of the Euro on Foreign Exchange Risk Management in UK Multinational Companies," *European Financial Management,* 7 (3), 11–15.

Christopher, Martin and Helen Peck (2003), *Marketing Logistics*. Amsterdam: Butterworth-Heineman.

Cooper, Martha C., Douglas M. Lambert, and Janus D. Pagh (1997), "Supply Chain Management: More Than a New Name for Logistics," *The International Journal of Logistics Management*, 8 (1), 1–14.

Griffith, David A. and Matthew B. Myers (2005), "The Performance Implications of Strategic Fit of Relational Norm Governance Strategies in Global Supply Chain Relationships," *Journal of International Business Studies*, 36 (3), 254–269.

Griffith, David A., Matthew B. Myers, and Michael A. Harvey (2005), "Global Supply Chain Management: Intra- and Inter-Cultural Influences on Relationship and Knowledge Development Resources," Working paper.

Hofstede, Geert (1991), *Cultures and Organizations: Software of the Mind*. London: McGraw-Hill.

Hofstede, Geert (2001), *Culture's Consequences*. Thousand Oaks, CA: Sage.

Kogut, Bruce (1984), "Normative Observations on the International Value-Added Chain and Strategic Groups," *Journal of International Business Studies*, 15 (2), 151–167.

Lambert, Douglas M., James R. Stock, and Lisa M. Ellram (1998), *Fundamentals of Logistics Management*. Boston: Irwin/McGraw-Hill.

Malnight, Thomas W. (2001), "Emerging Structural Patterns Within Multinational Corporations: Toward Process-Based Structures," *Academy of Management Journal*, 44 (6), 1187–1210.

Mentzer, John T., Matthew B. Myers, and Mee Shew Cheung (2004), "Global Market Segmentation for Logistics Services," *Industrial Marketing Management*, 33 (1), 15–21.

Monahan, Sean, Paul Laudicina, and David Attis (2005), "Supply Chains in a Vulnerable, Volatile World," *Executive Agenda*, 6 (3).

Pothukuchi, Vijay, Damanpour Fariborz, Choi Jaepil, Chen C. Chao, and Ho Seung Park (2002), "National and Organizational Culture Differences and International Joint Venture Performance," *Journal of International Business Studies*, 33 (2), 243–265.

Rinehart, Lloyd M., Matthew B. Myers, and James A. Eckert (2005), "Using Supply Chain Relationship Characteristics as a Basis for Setting Global Logistics Strategy in a Security Driven Environment," *Supply Chain Management Review*, 8 (6), 52–63.

Rodrigues, Alexandre M., Theodore P. Stank, and Daniel F. Lynch (2004), "Linking Strategy, Structure, Process, and Performance in Integrated Logistics," *Journal of Business Logistics*, 25 (2), 65–94.

Samiee, Saeed and Patrik Anckar (1998), "Currency Choice in Industrial Pricing: A Cross National Evaluation," *Journal of Marketing*, 62 (July), 112–127.

Schank, Roger and Robert Abelson (1977), *Script, Plans, Goals and Understanding: An Inquiry Into Human Knowledge Structure*. Hillsdale, NJ: Earlbaum.

Triandis, Harry C. (1988), "Collectivism vs. Individualism: A Reconceptualization of a Basic Concept in Cross-Cultural Social Psychology," in *Cross-Cultural Studies of Personality, Attitudes and Cognition*, G. K. Verma and C. Bagley, eds. London: Macmillan, pp. 60–95.

Wacker, J. G. and L. G. Sprague (1998), "Forecasting Accuracy: Comparing the Relative Effectiveness of Practices Between Seven Developed Countries," *Journal of Operations Management*, 16 (2/3), 271–290.

Zacharia, Z. G. (2001), "What Is Supply Chain Management?" in *Supply Chain Management*, John T. Mentzer, ed. Thousand Oaks, CA: Sage, pp. 1–25.

4

Value and Customer Service Management

Daniel J. Flint

Britta Gammelgaard

A call center for the U.S.-based computer and consumer electronics firm Dell, operated in India, responds to a Danish customer's product requests. A U.S. L.L. Bean customer discusses the performance of the climbing boots he recently purchased from L.L. Bean while on his last hiking trip to Mt. Katahdin in Maine with L.L. Bean's customer service representative before discussing inventory availability of additional hiking gear for his next trip. A Ford transportation manager discusses automobile to railcar loading operations with a Norfolk Southern operations manager. Each of these interactions and thousands more like them that occur every day represent variants of customer service and value management, concepts explored in this chapter.

The concept of value management in global logistics and supply chain management is closely connected to the idea of value chains (Porter 1985). In the relatively narrow logistics discipline, the idea was then far from new even though it was not common to use the exact term *value chain*; rather, the term *supply chain* was used. The basic thinking about the two concepts was, and is, however, the same—namely, that the fundamental understanding of the company is closely linked to its relations to other actors contributing to the transformation of raw materials to the final products required by the ultimate customer or end user. The major contribution of Michael Porter's book from a logistics perspective was, however, that it put logistics and this particular view of the company onto the broader management agenda. The importance of global logistics and supply chain management became visible to top management. And what it did further for the logistics discipline was to emphasize the value concept rather than merely the cost concept. The task of every single operation or process in the value chain was, and is, to contribute to the creation of value for the ultimate customer. In doing this, the necessity of eliminating all kinds of waste became obvious, and this aspect is especially closely linked to another well-known management term, namely, *lean production* (Womack, Jones, and Roos 1990).

Besides the value chain perspective, the concept of customer service is fundamental and essential to logistics thinking as well as to value management. Of course, customer service is also a basic concept in marketing theory, but in contrast to a marketing approach, the benefit of the whole chain must be taken into consideration in supply chain management. If, for example, customer service from the customer's viewpoint requires day-to-day deliveries based on day-to-day orders with no forecasted demand, which means the supplier must have large stocks, this may be a disadvantage for the supply chain as a whole.

In this chapter, we take a closer look at value management based on the idea of value chains. After that, we discuss what customer service means to value creation.

Value Management

Before we can discuss value management within a global supply chain context, we must first explain what is meant by the term *value*. Value perceptions are in the eyes of the beholder, in this case the individual customers. To be specific, value is not inherent in a product or service. In fact, marketing thought leaders are recognizing that the service components of value propositions have become the dominant differentiator for business enterprises. This is due in part to the value that supply chain management, in addition to other service aspects, can help create for customers. Customer value is created only when customers perceive that suppliers' products and services help them achieve their goals at an acceptable expense; that is, supply chain management creates value only when customers perceive worth in supply chain management processes and services. For example, customers of Best Buy, a major consumer electronics retailer in the United States, become quite displeased when they find that Best Buy is out of the latest Sony television they came in to buy after viewing a Sony advertising campaign. If the customer is ready to make the purchase, he or she will, in all likelihood, go to a competitor such as Circuit City. Sony's and Best Buy's joint inventory management efforts, which include forecasting down to the stock-keeping-unit level, negotiated delivery lot sizes and timing, product placement decisions within the store, and communication about promotional initiatives each plans to run, all affect the level of customer service the end-use consumer receives and, as a result, the value that consumer perceives in buying from Best Buy or Sony products. (An alternative reaction for the consumer in this example would be to buy an alternative brand television from Best Buy.) Balancing the costs of customer service levels with the costs of lost sales is a constant and critical global supply chain issue across industries.

There are many supply chain initiatives that focus on cost reduction or even process improvement that may not be recognized by customers and as such create value for the firms concerned but not necessarily customer value. However, if these cost efforts result in lower prices or improved service levels to customers, then customers do recognize the efforts and *customer* value is created. In this section, we discuss the concepts of customer value, value appropriation (i.e., extracting value from customers), and then value management.

The Concept of Customer Value

A fair amount of research has been conducted on customer value (Woodruff 1997). The concepts apply equally well to internal customers and external customers, and even to upstream supply chain relationships if one thinks broadly and considers suppliers as a form of customer as well. For example, Norfolk Southern, one of the four largest U.S.-based railroad companies, has a complex network of operations. The product planning group "serves" the operations group, and vice versa. Each can be seen as a "customer" to the other. Scanning the landscape of customer value research reveals that customers, regardless of what served group or individual you wish to consider, think of value in at least five distinct, but related, ways:

1. As a trade-off between what is gained and what is given up

2. As a hierarchy of links between supplier attributes and experienced benefits and sacrifices

3. As an interaction of products or services, use situations, and goals

4. As categorized by functional and relational benefits, and monetary and non-monetary costs

5. As compared with other options

First, customers think in terms of trade-offs, that is, what they get for what they must give up. In its most basic sense, this may be a given quality level for a given price. For example, some customers are willing to pay significantly more money for high-quality handling or rapid delivery with little variation from one service episode to another. Many medical, pharmaceuticals, and consumer electronics customers of FedEx pay for consistent, high-quality transportation and warehouse services due to the critical and time-sensitive nature of the products in the medical industry or the high unit value and fragility in the consumer electronics industry. The large medical firm Medtronics values the speed and precision of delivery FedEx offers for its stent implant devices. Similarly, Tech Data, a large "white box" computer assembler and distributor, values the security and damage control procedures FedEx uses to support transport of their products. Customers recognize that certain attributes or features come at a cost. But customers rarely stop at the quality-price trade-off. They examine bundles of product and service features alongside the costs required to obtain them. It is important to recognize this trade-off notion so that firms do not get overly fixated on the positively perceived features of a product or service, effectively ignoring what customers are willing (or not willing) to pay for those features. Customers often evaluate supply chain solutions by examining value propositions in terms of the trade-offs in each.

The second way customers perceive value is in terms of a means-end chain, or value hierarchy. Customers do not think of supply chain service features in isolation but rather because of the benefits or sacrifices they create. Benefits and sacrifices are consequences experienced or desired by customers as a result of contracting with a particular supplier. These consequences reflect the customer's operations, that is, the customer's world. For example, timely, consistent order delivery is valued because it helps customers schedule their operations, helps them forecast, and reduces their inventory levels, all of which help customers manage their labor and reduce their costs. Tesco, a U.K. retailer, expects these kinds of consequences from Nestlé, one of its suppliers of confectionary products. These are but a few consequences customers experience. Value is created because these benefits are realized. Customer value is reduced when these benefits are not realized. Figure 4.1 provides a view of the value hierarchy concept. Figure 4.2 is an example of a basic value hierarchy linking supplier services to customer benefits. Remember, this entire hierarchy is an image of what is in an individual customer's mind; it reflects only the attributes the customer perceives and the linkages the customer makes between those attributes and the benefits the customer experiences. The horizontal lines represent the distinction between attributes, the consequences of using those attributes, and the high-order goals or desired end states. Note the links to each concept. These are important because they show the customer's perception of relationships between various aspects of a supplier relationship.

Sacrifices represent what the customer gives up to obtain the benefits he or she receives. These are created by supplier features or attributes that are undesirable, such as processes and systems that make it difficult for customers to do business with a supplier (e.g., difficult to reach people, excessive paperwork, or lack of

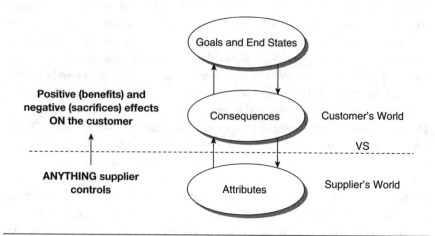

Figure 4.1   Value Hierarchy Concept

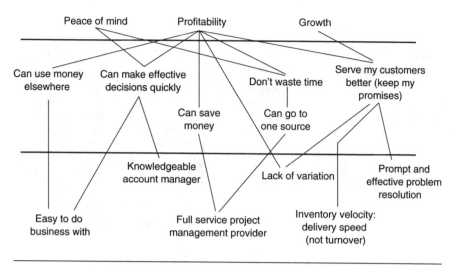

Figure 4.2   Example of a Customer Benefits Value Hierarchy

responsiveness). For example, when plastic bottle producers find it difficult to resolve invoicing problems from their polyethylenterephthalate (PET) suppliers, they experience monetary costs due to the time involved and emotional costs due to the frustration. In essence, many business customers will state broadly that some suppliers are just too difficult to do business with. Figure 4.3 is an example of a basic, hypothetical sacrifice value hierarchy.

The third way customers view value is in terms of use situations. This means that customers value specific products and services because they facilitate goal achievement *within* certain kinds of situations that occur in their operations. For example, in situations where business is slow, some customers might value suppliers who relax contractual buying constraints as well as hold back order shipment and retain it in inventory. Conversely, when customers' businesses are strong, they might value more frequent deliveries, higher inventory levels generally, greater flexibility, and preferential treatment in terms of capacity dedicated to their specific products.

Customers tend to categorize what they value as well. This fourth conceptualization of value stipulates that customers categorize the benefits and sacrifices they receive from suppliers in terms of their functional, relational, service, monetary, and nonmonetary significance. Customers often make distinctions between what they want functionally and what they want from relationships with suppliers. For example, Home Depot, the large home improvement retailer, makes distinctions between the functionally related condition of water pumps delivered from Grundfos, a Danish pump manufacturer, and the training services the company offers for Home Depot sales employees to sell the pumps more efficiently to consumers.

Finally, customers' value perceptions are comparative. Specifically, customers see greater or lesser value in supplier propositions based on how the value propositions compare with alternative offers by other suppliers or compared with what they

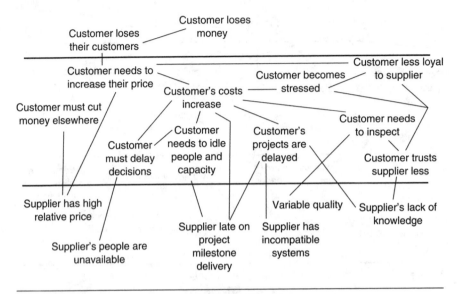

Figure 4.3   Example of a Sacrifice Experiences Value Hierarchy

expected. In many cases, suppliers' value propositions are compared with internal sourcing of the same services. The make or buy analysis is a fundamental aspect of third-party logistics business. Firms whose core competency does not lie with global supply chain management, logistics, or even certain components of logistics, operations such as transportation or warehousing, will consider outsourcing these operations to third parties who can execute them more effectively and efficiently. However, some firms may feel that the monetary and nonmonetary costs, that is, relinquishment of control and visibility, outweigh the benefits that might be achieved and decide to maintain logistics operations in-house. The bottom line is that customers value supply chain services to a greater or lesser extent depending on how they compare with the services offered by others.

Within a supply chain management context, value is often cocreated between customers and suppliers (see Vargo and Lusch 2004). By this, we mean that supply chain partners often work together to develop services and products that create value for the multiple organizations involved as well as downstream customers. We also mean that services are both produced and consumed simultaneously and, as such, customers are part of the value creation process.

This all means that customers vary significantly in what they value from suppliers. The supply chain services critical to one customer are not critical to another. The more globally diverse the markets are that a supplier serves, the more diversity in value perceptions that supplier's customers will exhibit.

Value Appropriation

The other side of the value concept is the value that suppliers and marketers extract from their customers in the marketplace. Simply maximizing value for customers, responding to every customer's request, will not help enterprises grow and profit—a key objective of most firms. Obviously, managers must clearly select what markets to target with what products and services. Even within target markets, most firms come to realize that some customers are more valuable than others. Recent research has placed a spotlight on the importance of considering the lifetime value of specific customers to determine which customers are truly important to a firm's long-term success. Some customers are clearly more profitable over the life of their relationships with suppliers than others, and they are often not simply those customers who place the largest contracts. What this means is that market segments and customers within those segments must be carefully chosen based on well-thought-out criteria, some of which ought to be cost-to-serve related. Supply chain management processes can account for a significant portion of the costs to serve customers. Some of these costs will exceed the value they create for the supplying firm. For example, many of the young "dot-com" firms discovered very quickly that by possessing a Web site, they were potentially global and, as such, took on significant distribution and inventory costs that they did not expect.

Managing Value

So what does it mean to "manage value"? In a global supply chain context, it means to develop formal processes that uncover what customers around the globe value and create products and services that help to create value for carefully targeted customers where and when desired while at the same time creating value for one's own firm—extracting value from the marketplace. Doing so means integrating global market intelligence processes and systems and linking voice-of-the-customer data to interorganizational service creation and delivery. A value management strategy might look like the one shown in Figure 4.4, where firms engage in processes aimed at understanding what customers value, choose from what they know about the voice of the customer those pieces that they do well, create and deliver their propositions, communicate to customers the value they are helping to create for customers, and then assess how well they are doing in actually creating that value for customers (i.e., customer satisfaction monitoring processes). Thus, three important aspects of value management are capturing the voice of the customer, information sharing, and evaluating customer lifetime value.

Capturing the Voice of the Customer

Globally, successful firms analyze market opportunities carefully and target customer segments and specific customers within those markets. They have a solid understanding of what supply chain services are valued, by whom, and why. World class firms create processes that regularly capture voice-of-the-customer data and incorporate that voice into formal customer value management (Flint et al. 2005; Gale 1994; Woodruff and Gardial 1996). Most firms have many pieces of voice-of-the-customer data scattered around their organizations. These data take the form of sales call reports, call center records, customer council meetings, customer satisfaction survey results, secondary market analysis reports, point-of-sale data, and many

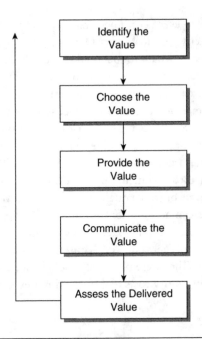

Figure 4.4   General Value Management Strategy

others. Many firms are finding that capturing customers' supply-chain-specific desires can partly be accomplished by including logisticians on account management teams (Flint and Mentzer 2000; Flint et al. 2005). Nestle, Sony, and Norfolk Southern are a few companies following this account management strategy. These logisticians are able to gain insights directly from the marketplace without the possibility of the information being filtered through sales, marketing, or market researchers. In fact, for firms with many customers, vast and diverse voice-of-the-customer data may take two years or more to gather and convert into a common format usable by many functions throughout the organization. This was the case for both Harrah's, one of the largest casino operators in the world, and Continental Airlines, where such efforts eventually paid off significantly in helping to both create and extract greater value in their supply chains (Gulati and Oldroyd 2005).

Sharing Information

Creating superior value only begins with voice-of-the-customer data. Successful firms regularly share and make available on demand customer insights with appropriate functions and supply chain partners in a timely manner. This involves ensuring that supply chain managers are fully aware of service requirements and how they vary by market segment, customer, and customers' use situations. Timely market knowledge provides valuable lead time for supply chain managers to respond to opportunities and threats ahead of competitors. Sharing of customer information helps organizations link customer value knowledge to product development and supply chain resource assignment.

Assessing Customer Lifetime Value

Finally, customer- and supply-chain-oriented firms do not attempt to create superior value for every customer. Some customers are more important than others. The firms that recognize this *examine* the lifetime value of their customers, homing in on the most profitable ones over the lifetime of their relationships with them. Customers with high customer lifetime value (CLV) are often not those customers who buy most frequently or the largest quantities of products and services. In short, not all customers are created equal (Mentzer 2004).

Customer value management significantly relates to the management of customer service, a critical component of global supply chain management, and specifically to the kinds of services developed for certain kinds of customers.

Customer Service

Customer service can be a key link between marketing and logistics as well as a key component of differentiation strategies (Langley and Holcomb 1992; Innis and LaLonde 1994). Customer service has been viewed both very broadly and quite narrowly over the years and is the focus of a great deal of supply chain and logistics research. It can be thought of as both a process and an attitude of providing valued support for a seller's products that facilitates the customer's purchase, use, and disposal of products and strengthens the relationship between both parties. This view is quite broad. A constant goal of many organizations is to balance customer service levels with cost containment efforts. Maintaining high levels of customer service requires significant resources.

Elements of Customer Service

Many activities make up what we term *customer service*. For example, physical distribution service has been positioned as a component of customer service. As few as 12 and as many as 61 elements have been positioned as components of physical distribution services alone by logistics researchers over the years. However, a number of these customer service elements were consistently identified by managers as critical over the last two decades, such as delivery time, service quality, after-sales service, information about delivery, pricing processes, and technical support. In an extension of some of this work, logistics service quality research combined customer service insights with service quality research in service industries to study the effects of logistics service quality on customer satisfaction (Mentzer, Flint, and Hult 2001). It seems that creating superior logistics service quality involves managing at least 9 service-related elements that pertain to either order placement or order receipt:

- Personnel contact quality
- Order availability
- Information quality

- Ordering procedures
- Order accuracy
- Order condition
- Order quality
- Order timeliness
- Order discrepancy handling

Personnel contact quality refers to the level of customer orientation of the supplier's customer service people. Customers judge entire firms largely through the lens of their interactions with supplier contact personnel as they place orders or try to resolve product and delivery issues. Order availability concerns inventory management and forecasting. When customers make contact to place orders, they fully expect that the desired products will be in stock. Information quality refers to customer's perceptions of the information provided by the supplier regarding products, their availability, and the procedures for placing and receiving orders. Ordering procedures refer to the effectiveness and ease of placing orders. Order accuracy reflects the customer's perception of how closely shipments match the orders placed. Order condition refers to the lack of damage to delivered goods. Order quality refers to how well products work as compared with expectations. Order timeliness refers to customers' perceptions that orders arrived when they were expected to arrive. Order discrepancy handling implies that often orders are not accurate, in good condition, of high quality, or timely. The procedures used by suppliers to address these discrepancies affect customer satisfaction levels. Many times, suppliers see discrepancies as problems to simply "get through" or survive rather than as opportunities to influence customers' perceptions of value. Sometimes, customers who have a current crisis situation resolved beyond expectations are more loyal than customers who never had a problem to begin with.

Customers appear to pay attention to these nine aspects of customer service when they place and receive orders, and as such their satisfaction levels with firms' products and services are dependent in part on their perceptions of these nine customer service elements. However, all market segments do not weight each of these aspects equally. For example, textile customers of the U.S. Defense Logistics Agency (DLA) value different aspects of customer service than do electronics customers of DLA (Mentzer et al. 2001). These elements can be leveraged to increase market share, enable mass customization, complement marketing and product development efforts, and essentially create differential advantage in the marketplace.

One way firms have attempted to address a few of these customer service elements is through customer relationship management (CRM) systems. These systems help customer service personnel capture, recall, and use customer-specific data to improve the effectiveness and efficiency of their customer contacts. Many firms have had mixed results with CRM software because they fail to see the CRM system as merely one piece in a larger customer-oriented enterprise. When executed well, CRM systems can provide significant improvements in customer-supplier interactions by improving information quality, responsiveness, visibility, and general communication by enabling suppliers to retain and leverage customer-specific data.

The Internet has had a significant impact on customer service operations and customers' service expectations. Customer service, and specifically logistics customer service, has become a critical aspect of online consumer interactions (Dadzie, Chelariu, and Winston 2005). As with logistics service quality research, this research shows that consumers expect value to be created through both the online purchase experience and the actual product delivery. The former addresses the ease of use of the information on the relevant Web site, the accuracy and completeness of the information available, and the appearance of the Web site. The products then must arrive in a timely manner and in good condition. These online shopping experiences place a great deal of emphasis on ensuring product delivery in a more timely, as well as precise, manner and in a superior condition, both of which create superior value for customers. The standards are quite high. Yet firms must continue to maintain control over their costs and retailers' costs, which demands sound forecasting, demand management, inventory management, distribution, and information systems (Rabinovich and Evers 2003).

Another aspect of product availability concerns availability at store locations. For example, researchers have studied customers' reactions to stock-outs at stores and are finding that customers are able to isolate single incidents of stock-outs from other factors that affect their overall image of the store, but customers' situational variables, such as urgency of their need for the product, do affect the likelihood of their going to another store (Zinn and Liu 2001). Recall from our value concept discussion earlier that customers view products and services in light of their current use situations. Clearly, product availability continues to be a key aspect of customer service to which customers pay close attention. In short, customer service involves both interpersonal and operational support services that help create value for customers as customers place orders, receive orders, resolve discrepancies, and use products.

Customer Service and Value Management

If value management is about identifying the most valuable customers and suppliers, understanding what those customers and suppliers value, and creating and communicating that value for them, then customer service creates value for customers when services are designed based on voice-of-the-customer data and executed in a fashion that will help customers obtain and use the products they want at the right time in the right place in the right condition at the right price with a reasonable level of sacrifices along the way. Creating superior customer services requires accurate, timely, and deep knowledge about what customers value. Executing these superior customer service processes will then actually help create a differential advantage for the supplier firm, leading to increased customer satisfaction and loyalty. Customer service is an extremely critical and visible aspect of value management. It requires the close coordination and collaboration of supply chain partners.

What do value and customer service management mean within a global supply chain context? They mean more complexity. Understanding what customers around the globe value and comparing those perceptions across multiple market segments is a complex undertaking requiring extremely formalized processes to regularly capture voice-of-the-customer data and then feed that intelligence to appropriate parties within and outside of the firm to develop the necessary products and services to serve diverse audiences.

Global supply chain management is largely about processes and relationships because it involves managing the flow of goods and information through multiple organizations. As a result, processes must be designed in such a way as to create value for upstream suppliers and downstream customers through to end-use customers. Similarly, supply chain partners must be chosen carefully based on their ability to contribute to value creation activities and to embrace similar customer-oriented visions.

As firms consider the global supply chain, they must take diverse customer service requirements as well as varying marketing strategies into account. What works for one region of the world or one market segment within one nation may not work elsewhere. This diversity of expectations, as well as costs to serve, demands a formal approach to uncovering customer service expectations and designing supply systems that create the right amount of value for the right customers.

Additionally, the global marketplace brings with it complex and varying infrastructures, regulations, monetary issues, and security issues, not to mention various cultural backgrounds, that impinge on customer service requirements. Being able to deal with this complexity and variation requires investments in knowledge about and processes to serve a more complex environment than traditional domestic operations.

References

Dadzie, Kofi Q., Cristian Chelariu, and Evelyn Winston (2005), "Customer Service in the Internet-Enabled Logistics Supply Chain: Website Design Antecedent and Loyalty Effects," *Journal of Business Logistics*, 26 (1), 53–78.

Flint, Daniel J., Everth Larsson, Britta Gammelgaard, and John T. Mentzer (2005), "Logistics Innovation: A Customer Value-Oriented Social Process," *Journal of Business Logistics*, 26 (1), 113–148.

Flint, Daniel J. and John T. Mentzer (2000), "Logisticians as Marketers: Their Role When Customers' Desired Value Changes," *Journal of Business Logistics*, 21 (2), 19–45.

Gale, Bradley T. (1994), *Managing Customer Value*. New York: Free Press.

Gulati, Ranjay and James B. Oldroyd (2005), "The Quest for Customer Focus," *Harvard Business Review*, April, 92–101.

Innis, Daniel E. and Bernard J. LaLonde (1994), "Customer Service: The Key to Customer Satisfaction, Customer Loyalty and Market Share," *Journal of Business Logistics*, 15 (1), 1–27.

Langley, John C. and Mary C. Holcomb (1992), "Creating Logistics Customer Value," *Journal of Business Logistics*, 13 (2), 1–28.

Mentzer, John T. (2004), *Fundamentals of Supply Chain Management*. Thousand Oaks, CA: Sage.

Mentzer, John T., Daniel J. Flint, and G. Tomas M. Hult (2001), "Logistics Service Quality as a Segment-Customized Process," *Journal of Marketing,* 65 (4), 82–104.

Porter, Michael E. (1985), *Competitive Advantage: Creating and Sustaining Superior Performance.* New York: Free Press.

Rabinovich, Elliot and Philip T. Evers (2003), "Product Fulfillment in Supply Chains Supporting Internet-Retailing Operations," *Journal of Business Logistics,* 24 (2), 205–236.

Vargo, Stephen L. and Robert F. Lusch (2004), "Evolving to a New Dominant Logic for Marketing," *Journal of Marketing,* 68 (1), 1–17.

Womack, James P., Daniel T. Jones, and Daniel Roos (1990), *The Machine That Changed the World.* New York: Rawson/Macmillan.

Woodruff, Robert B. (1997), "Customer Value: The Next Source for Competitive Advantage," *Journal of the Academy of Marketing Science,* 25 (2), 139–153.

Woodruff, Robert B. and Sarah Fisher Gardial (1996), *Know Your Customer: New Approaches to Customer Value and Satisfaction.* Cambridge, MA: Blackwell.

Zinn, Walter and Peter C. Liu (2001), "Consumer Response to a Retail Stockout," *Journal of Business Logistics,* 22(1), 49–72.

5

Demand Management

John T. Mentzer

Mark A. Moon

Dominique Estampe

Glen Margolis

D emand management activities in any global supply chain consist of three activities: demand management, demand planning, and sales forecasting management (Mentzer and Moon 2004b). The role of sales forecasting changes depending on the position in the supply chain that a company occupies. Any supply chain has only one point of **independent demand**—or *the amount of product demanded (by time and location) by the end-use customer of the supply chain*. Whether this end-use customer is a consumer shopping in a retail establishment or online (B2C), or a business buying products for consumption in the process of conducting their business operations (B2B), these end-use customers determine the true demand for the product that will flow through the supply chain.

The company in the supply chain that directly serves this end-use customer directly experiences this independent demand. All subsequent companies in the supply chain experience a demand that is tempered by the order fulfillment and purchasing policies of other companies in the supply chain. This second type of supply chain demand is called **derived demand** because it is not the independent demand of the end-use customer but rather a *demand that is derived from what other companies in the supply chain do to meet their demand from their immediate customer (i.e., the company that orders from them)*.

The derived demand for one company is often the dependent demand of their customers. **Dependent demand** is the *demand for the component parts that go into a* *product.* Often called bill of materials (BOM) forecasting, this is usually demand that is dependent on the demand for the product in which it is a component. The exception is when different amounts of a component part go into different versions of the product; this requires a special kind of forecasting, called statistical BOM forecasting. For example, the manufacturer of a large telecommunications switch may have 50 different component parts that can go in each switch, with the number of each component included varying from 0 to 5, depending on the customer order. Thus, the independent demand of customers for the switch, and the independent demand of customers for various switch configurations (and their resulting BOM), must be forecast to determine the dependent demand for each component part.

It is important to note that only one company in any given supply chain is directly affected by independent demand. The rest are affected by derived or dependent demand (or both). Equally important, the techniques, systems, and processes necessary to deal with derived and dependent demand are quite different from those of independent demand.

Recognizing the differences between independent, dependent, and derived demand, recognizing which type of demand affects a particular company, and developing techniques, systems, and processes to deal with that company's particular type of demand can have a profound impact on global logistics, supply chain costs, and customer service levels. We first explore the implications of independent and derived demand, followed by a model of the demand management function in global supply chain management. We will then move on to the role of sales forecasting management within demand management.

Derived Versus Independent Demand

Figure 5.1 depicts a traditional supply chain, with a retailer serving the end-use customer, a wholesaler supplying the retailer, a manufacturer supplying the wholesaler, and a supplier providing raw materials to the manufacturer. The source of independent demand for this supply chain is 1,000 units for the planning period. However, the retailer (as is typically the case) does not know this with certainty. In fact, the retailer has a reasonably good forecasting process and forecasts end-use customer demand to be 1,000 units for the planning period. Since the forecast has typically experienced ±10% error in the past, the retailer places an order to his or her supplier (the wholesaler) for 1,100 units (i.e., 1,000 units for expected demand and 100 units for safety stock to meet expected forecasting error). It is critical to note in this simple example of a typical, *unmanaged* supply chain that the demand the wholesaler experiences is 1,100 units, not 1,000.

The wholesaler, in turn, has a reasonable forecasting system (note that the wholesaler is not forecasting end-use customer independent demand but is inadvertently forecasting retailer derived demand) and forecasts the demand affecting the wholesaler at 1,100 units. Again, the wholesaler believes forecasting error to be approximately ±10%, so the wholesaler orders 1,100 plus 10% (or 1,210 units) from the manufacturer. If the manufacturer and the supplier both assume the same ±10% forecasting error, then they will each add 10% to their orders to their

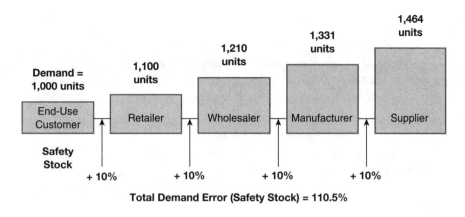

Total Demand Error (Safety Stock) = 110.5%

Figure 5.1   Demand Error in a Traditional Supply Chain

suppliers. Note that we are assuming here, for simplicity's sake, that there is no BOM. If there were, the logic would still hold, but the illustration would become unnecessarily complicated.

As Figure 5.1 illustrates, simple failure to recognize the difference between independent demand (which needs to be forecast) and derived demand (which can be derived and planned)—even in a supply chain where forecasting error is only ±10%—adds greatly to the safety stock carried in the supply chain. In fact, since each member of the supply chain only needed 1,000 units to meet the actual demand, plus 100 units for the potential forecasting error, this particular supply chain is carrying 705 too much inventory ((210 − 100) + (331 − 100) + (464 −100) = 705), or a 16.0% supply-chain-wide inventory overstock ((705/4,400) = 16.0%) for the actual end-use customer demand. Inventory carried for total demand error (safety stock) in this supply chain is 1,105 (100 + 210 + 331 + 464), or 110.5% of actual end-use customer demand!

This example allows us to introduce the supply chain concept of **demand planning**, which is *the coordinated flow of derived and dependent demand through companies in the supply chain*. Demand planning is illustrated in the supply chain shown in Figure 5.2. End-use customer demand is the same as in Figure 5.1, and the retailers' faith in their forecast (±10%) is unchanged. What has changed, however, is that the other companies in the supply chain are no longer even attempting to forecast the demand of their customers. Rather, each member of the supply chain receives point-of-sale (POS) demand information from the retailer, and the retailer's planned ordering based on this demand. Combined with knowledge of the time-related order flows through this supply chain, each company can plan its processes (including orders to their suppliers). The result is that each member of the supply chain carries 1,100 units in inventory—a systemwide reduction in inventory of 13.81% from 5,105 (i.e., 1,100 for the retailer, 1,210 for the wholesaler, 1,331 for the manufacturer, and 1,464 for the supplier) to 4,400 (i.e., 1,100 each for the retailer, wholesaler, manufacturer, and supplier). More important, the inventory carried for forecasting error (safety stock) drops from 1,105 to 400 (from total

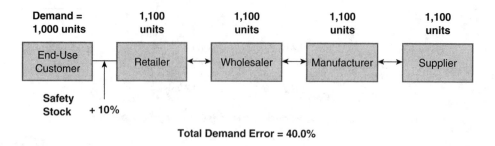

Figure 5.2   Demand Error in a Demand Planning Supply Chain

demand error of 110.5% to 40.0%)—for a reduction of total demand error inventory (safety stock) of 63.8% ((1,105 – 400)/1,105).

Note, however, that the inventory reductions are not uniform across the supply chain. Whereas the supplier has a reduction in safety stock of 78.4% (from 464 to 100), the retailer experiences no reduction. In fact, the farther up the supply chain, the greater the safety stock reduction. This illustrates a paradox of demand planning in any supply chain—the very companies that are most needed to implement supply chain demand planning (i.e., implementation of systems to share with suppliers real-time POS information held by retailers) have the least economic motivation (i.e., inventory reduction) to cooperate. This leads us to the concept of demand management.

Demand management is *the creation across the supply chain and its markets of a coordinated flow of demand.* Much is implied in this seemingly simple definition. First, the traditional function of marketing creates demand for various products but often does not share these demand-creating plans (such as promotional programs) with other functions within the company (forecasting, in particular), much less with other companies in the supply chain.

Second, the role of demand management is often to decrease demand. This may sound counterintuitive, but demand often exists for company products at a level management cannot realistically (or profitably) fulfill. Demand management implies an assessment of the profit contribution of various products and customers (all with capacity constraints in mind—including the capacity of all components in the BOM), emphasizing demand for the profitable ones, and decreasing demand (by lessening marketing efforts) for the unprofitable ones.

Finally, as we mentioned earlier, considerable supply chain savings can result from demand planning, but the rewards are not always consistent with the need to obtain collaboration from all companies in the supply chain. Thus, an aspect of demand management is **supply chain relationship management,** which is *the management of relationships with supply chain partners to match performance with measurements and rewards so that all companies in the supply chain are fairly rewarded for overall supply success (measured as cost reduction and increased customer satisfaction).*

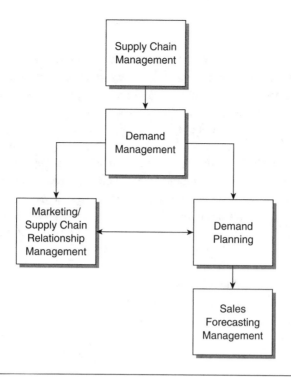

Figure 5.3   Demand Management in Supply Chain Management

A Model of Supply Chain Demand Management

This leads us to an overall model of the role of demand management, demand planning, and sales forecasting management in the supply chain. Figure 5.3 illustrates these roles. Global supply chain management has many aspects, only one of which is demand management. As previously illustrated, demand management encompasses the traditional marketing functions, along with the coordination of marketing activities with other functions in the company and the supply chain. However, the traditional demand creation role of marketing is tempered in demand management by a desire to coordinate the flow of demand across the supply chain (demand planning) and to create incentives for supply chain partners to help manage these flows (supply chain relationship management). Demand planning is concerned with the coordination across the global supply chain of derived and dependent demand. Sales forecasting management is concerned with the independent demand that occurs in any global supply chain.

Forecasts Versus Plans Versus Targets

We define a **sales forecast** as a projection into the future of expected demand, given a stated set of environmental conditions. This should be distinguished from *plans,* which we define as a set of specified managerial actions to be undertaken to meet or exceed the sales forecast. Examples of plans include production plans, procurement plans, distribution plans, and financial plans. Both the sales forecast and the plans should be distinguished from the *sales target*, which we define as sales goals that are established to provide motivation for sales and marketing personnel.

Note that our definition of a sales forecast does not specify the technique (quantitative or qualitative), does not specify who develops the forecast within the company, nor does it include managerial plans. The reason for this is that *many companies confuse the functions of forecasting, planning, and target-setting*. Plans for the level of sales to be achieved should be based on the forecast of demand, but the two management functions should be kept separate. Similarly, target-setting should be done with a realistic assessment of expected future demand in mind, and this assessment comes from the sales forecast. In other words, the functions of planning and target-setting should be informed by forecasts of demand, but should not be confused with sales forecasting.

Note that these definitions imply different performance measures for sales forecasts than for plans. Since the purpose of sales forecasting is to make projections of demand given a set of specified environmental assumptions, one of the key measures of sales forecasting performance is accuracy of the forecast, and one of the key methods to explain variances in accuracy is how the environment varied from the one defined. This explanation is not intended to excuse forecast inaccuracy; rather it helps us understand the business environment and forecast more accurately in the future.

In contrast, the goal of plans is not accuracy but rather to effectively and efficiently meet forecasted demand. In addition, whereas forecasts are meant to be accurate, targets are meant to be met or exceeded. A mistake made by many companies is to confuse the sales forecast, where the objective is accuracy, with the sales target, where the objective is to at least meet—and, ideally, exceed—the goal or quota. In other words, companies should never be guilty of confusing forecasting with the firm's motivational strategy.

Sales and Operations Planning

In many companies, sales forecasting is an integral part of a critical process for matching global demand and supply that is sometimes referred to as sales and operations planning or S&OP (Mentzer and Moon 2004a). Figure 5.4 offers a simplified picture of how sales forecasting contributes to the S&OP process. As seen in Figure 5.4, an enterprise can be thought of as consisting of two primary functions: a demand function and a supply function. Demand is the responsibility of sales and marketing. In many companies, the sales organization is responsible for generating and maintaining demand from large end-use customers, or from wholesale or retail channel partners. Marketing is usually responsible for generating and maintaining demand from end consumers. Supply is the responsibility of a number of functions, including manufacturing, procurement, logistics or distribution, human resources, and finance. It is also the responsibility of a variety of suppliers, who

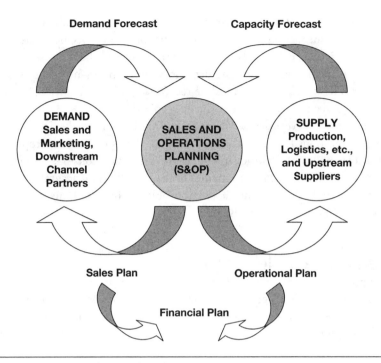

Figure 5.4   S&OP: The Junction Box

must provide raw materials, component parts, and packaging. The S&OP process provides a "junction box" where information can flow between the demand side and the supply side of an enterprise.

As shown in Figure 5.4, critical input to the S&OP process is the sales forecast, which is, as defined above, the projection into the future of expected demand. The sales forecast should originate in the demand side of the enterprise, since it is the demand side of the enterprise (i.e., sales and marketing) that is responsible for generating demand, and who should have the best perspective on what future demand will be. In addition to the sales forecast, which originates in the demand side of the company, another critical input to the S&OP process is a **capacity plan**. A capacity plan is a projection into the future about what supply capabilities will be, given a set of environmental assumptions. This input is provided by the supply side of the enterprise, and documents both long- and short-term supply capabilities. The process that occurs inside the S&OP process—the junction box—is the matching of future demand projections (i.e., the sales forecast) with future supply projections (i.e., the capacity plan).

Out of the S&OP process come three critical plans—the operational plan, the demand plan, and the financial plan. As discussed above, the operational plan consists of manufacturing plans, procurement plans, distribution plans, and human resource plans. These various operational plans can be short-term in nature, such as a monthly production schedule. They can be long-term in nature, such as extended contracts for raw materials, or even plans to expand manufacturing capacity. The second critical plan that emerges from the S&OP process is the demand plan, where sales and marketing make plans about what should be sold and marketed, and when, given the supply capabilities of the firm. As mentioned above, demand plans may involve suppressing demand for products or services that are capacity constrained, or shifting demand away from low-margin products to high-margin items. These plans must be reconciled with the financial plan, which manages resource costs against performance projections.

Other authors have discussed how to effectively manage the S&OP process within organizations (see, e.g., Lapide 2002), but this is beyond the scope of this chapter. It is important, however, to understand the critical role that sales forecasting plays in the overall planning activities of the firm. Without accurate and credible estimates of future demand, it is impossible for organizations to effectively manage their global supply chains.

Why Is a Sales Forecast Needed?

If we can simply set a sales goal and expect marketing and sales to exceed it, why do we even need a sales forecast in the first place? This is a question many managers ask and often answer incorrectly (i.e., we do not need a forecast), to their eventual sorrow.

The correct answer is that every time we develop a plan of any kind, we first make a forecast. This is true of individuals, as well as profit and nonprofit companies, government organizations, and in fact, any entity that makes a plan. It can be as simple as planning what we will wear tomorrow. When we decide to lay out wool slacks and a sweater for the next day, we are forecasting it will be cool. If we add an umbrella to our ensemble, we are forecasting rain. The plan was predicated on the forecast, whether we consciously thought about it or not.

This is not much different from a company making financial plans based on expected sales and the costs of meeting those sales. The trick is to not get caught in the trap of making "inadvertent sales forecasts." Inadvertent sales forecasts are made when we are so intent on developing the plan that we simply assume what sales will be, rather than giving any concentrated thought to and analyzing the market conditions that will be necessary to create this level of sales.

One great example of such an inadvertent forecast came from a manufacturer in the grocery products industry. The owner of the company explained to us that the sales plan called for an increase in sales of 5% for the next year. However, we had also been told that this industry in this country was not growing and that any attempt to grab market share from the competition was only met by countermoves that caused greater promotional expenditures, but no shift in market share. "Wait a minute," we said to the owner. "How can industry size not change, market share not change, but sales grow? It does not take a math major to figure out that this is not going to work." The answer was that management would simply have to motivate everyone to work harder to achieve the (mathematically impossible) plan. Of course, it is obvious what happened—no amount of motivation is going to overcome an impossible situation, and the sales plan was not achieved. It was not achieved because it was based on an inadvertent and uninformed forecast. This is also a classic example of management confusing forecasting, planning, and target-setting. In this case, no reasonable *forecast* would predict a 5% increase in sales. The 5% increase should have been seen for what it was—a stretch *goal*.

Let's look at one more example. A large regional distributor of food products to restaurants develops an elaborate annual profit plan. Hundreds of person-days go into the development of this plan, but it always starts with such comments as, "We need profits to increase next year by 6%. Let's figure out how much sales have to be to achieve that goal." Note that the term *goal* sneaked into that quotation. Where these executives should have started was to ask about market and environmental conditions facing the company during the planning horizon, and what levels of sales could be expected based on these conditions. The plan then becomes one of determining what marketing and sales efforts will be necessary to meet and exceed these projections to a level necessary to achieve the profit plan. The plan cannot drive the forecast; it has to be the other way around.

The *sales forecasting level* is the focal point in the corporate hierarchy where the forecast is needed. A corporate forecast, for instance, is a forecast of overall sales for the corporation. The *sales forecasting time horizon* generally coincides with the time frame of the plan for which it was developed. If, for instance, we continue the example just given, a corporate plan may be for the next two years and, thus, we need a sales forecast for that two-year time horizon. The *sales forecasting time interval* generally coincides with how often the plan is updated. If our two-year corporate sales plan must be updated every three months (not an unusual scenario), we can say the level is corporate, the horizon is two years, and the interval is quarterly. The *sales forecasting form* is what needs to be forecast or planned. Some functions need to know what physical units are to be produced and shipped, whereas other functions need to know the dollar equivalents of these units, and still other functions need to plan based on total weight or volume. These constitute the *forms* a sales forecast (and a plan) can take.

The Tools of Sales Forecasting Management

Just as any modern management function must make use of the state of the art in techniques to get the job done, the information systems available to it, the latest in managerial processes and approaches to managing the function, and methods of measuring and rewarding performance, so must sales forecasting management.

Sales Forecasting Techniques

A myriad of forecasting techniques exist and are available to the sales forecasting manager. In fact, it often seems that too many techniques are available, and the choice decision can border on information overload (at last count, there were over 70 different time-series techniques alone). Such a scenario often causes decision makers to give up any hope of understanding the full field of techniques; they consistently use only one or two with which they are familiar, whether these techniques are appropriate for the forecasting situation or not.

Fortunately, this scenario can be considerably simplified. To understand the sales forecasting technique selection process, the sales forecasting manager needs to understand the characteristics of a relatively small set of groups of techniques, and to realize in what situations each group of techniques works best. Once the technique group has been chosen, selection of the specific technique to use is a much more straightforward decision, which can be influenced by a great deal of research that has looked at which techniques are most often used and when they work best (McCarthy et al. forthcoming).

The common categories for sales forecasting techniques are based on whether the technique uses subjective or statistical analysis, whether endogenous data (a forecasting term that means only using the history of sales and not any other factors, which may explain changes in sales) or exogenous data (a forecasting term meaning the use of other data, such as price or promotional changes, competitive actions, or economic measures, to explain the changes in sales) are analyzed, and whether these data are actually analyzed by the forecaster or simply input to a technique for calculation of the forecast. These characteristics lead to three broad categories of sales forecasting techniques: time-series, regression (also called correlation, and incorrectly called causal, techniques), and judgmental (also called qualitative or subjective techniques).

Time-Series Techniques

Time-series techniques are based on the interrelationship of four data patterns: level, trend, seasonality, and noise. *Level* is a horizontal sales history, or what sales patterns would be if there was no trend, seasonality, or noise. *Trend* is a continuing pattern of a sales increase or decrease, and that pattern can be a straight line or a curve. *Seasonality* is a repeating pattern of sales increases and decreases such as high sales every summer for air conditioners, high sales of agricultural chemicals in the spring, or high sales of toys in the fall. The point is that the pattern of high sales in certain periods and low sales in other periods repeats itself every year. *Noise* is random fluctuation—that part of the sales history that a time-series technique cannot explain. This does not mean the fluctuation could not be explained by regression analysis or judgment; it means the pattern has not happened consistently in the past, so the time-series technique cannot pick it up and forecast it.

Time-series techniques arrive at a forecast by assuming one or more of these patterns exist in a previous sales history and projecting these patterns into the future. Exponential smoothing is a common time-series technique.

Time-series techniques are often simple and inexpensive to use and require little data storage. Many of the techniques also adjust very quickly to changes in sales conditions and, thus, are appropriate for short-term forecasting. Time-series techniques, however, will probably be less accurate than correlation analysis if the forecaster utilizes a time-series technique that assumes data patterns do not exist but are, in fact, in the sales history. Simple exponential smoothing assumes, for example, that the sales history consists of only level and noise. If trend and seasonality exist in the sales history, simple exponential smoothing will consistently err in its forecast.

Regression (Correlation) Analysis

Correlation analysis is a statistical approach to forecasting that seeks to establish a relationship between sales and exogenous variables that affect sales, such as advertising, product quality, price, logistics service quality, and/or the economy. Past data on exogenous variables and sales data are analyzed to determine the strength of their relationship (e.g., every time the price goes up, sales of the product go down is a strong negative relationship). If a strong relationship is found, the exogenous variables can then be used to forecast future sales. Corporate, competitive, and economic variables can be used together in a correlation analysis forecast, thus giving it a broad environmental perspective. Correlation analysis can also provide statistical value estimates of each variable. Thus, variables contributing little to the forecast can be dropped.

Correlation analysis is potentially one of the most accurate forecasting techniques available, but it requires a large amount of data. These large data demands also make correlation analysis slow to respond to changing conditions. Understanding the advantages and disadvantages of correlation analysis helps clarify when it is more useful—as in longer-range (greater than six-month time horizon) corporate-level forecasts for which a large amount of data on exogenous variables is readily available.

Qualitative (Subjective) Techniques

The previously discussed techniques (time-series and correlation analysis) are based on the idea that historical demand may follow some patterns, and the goal of the techniques is to identify and numerically document these patterns, then project these patterns into the future. However, it is often the case that the future will not look exactly like the past. For example, there may be no historical demand data available, as is the case with new products. There may also be new conditions that arise, such as a changing competitive landscape or changes in distribution patterns, that make previous demand patterns less relevant. Thus, there is a need for qualitative, or subjective, forecasting techniques. Subjective techniques are procedures that turn the opinions of experienced personnel (e.g., marketing planners, salespeople, corporate executives, and outside experts) into formal forecasts. An advantage of subjective techniques is that they take into account the full wealth of key personnel experience and require little formal data. They are also valuable when little or no historical data is available, such as in new product introductions.

Subjective forecasting, however, takes a considerable amount of key personnel time. Because of this drawback, subjective techniques are typically used as a part of long-range, corporate-level forecasting, or for adjustment purposes in short-range product forecasting. For example, the forecast committee of one auto parts manufacturer with whom we have worked meets once a quarter to subjectively generate a three-year forecast and once a month to subjectively adjust the product forecasts by product line (e.g., all product forecasts in a particular product line may be raised by 3%). Individual product forecasts by inventory location, however, are left to an appropriate time-series technique determined by the forecast managers. Individual product forecasts by the forecast committee would be a waste of valuable executive time.

Sales Forecasting Systems

Many companies with which we have worked have asked us to advise them on the sales forecasting system they should use. Invariably, when we are asked this question, we ask them to describe the management process by which the sales forecasts are developed. Often, there is no answer—the company is trying to develop a systems solution without an understanding of the management process! This is a backward approach to sales forecasting management.

In many companies, there is no one person who understands the entire sales forecasting process. Many individuals understand bits and pieces of the process, but few understand the *entire* process. Without such an understanding, it is not possible to design and implement a system to augment this process. In fact, the sales forecasting system should be a communication and analysis framework (template) that can be laid over the sales forecasting management process. The company has to define the process first. An example should help illustrate this concept.

One global manufacturer of industrial products with which we worked has multiple product lines sold all over the world by a direct sales force. Many of these products are sold to customers in numerous industries. Thus, we may have a product that is sold by one salesperson in Australia to a particular industry and another salesperson in Europe who sells the same product for a different use in another industry. This has led to a worldwide sales force that specializes in certain products, in certain industries, and in certain geographic areas.

Given this multifaceted complexity of the sales forecasting environment, the company wanted a system that allowed development of a quantitative forecast, with qualitative adjustment by geographic territory by industry by the sales force, with adjustment by product line by marketing managers, and with overall planning adjustments by upper management. This led to a definition of their sales forecasting process that is illustrated in Figure 5.5. The process starts with a computer-model-generated forecast. These sales forecasts are broken down by product, industry, and geographic territory and sent electronically to the sales force. Each salesperson is provided with a quarterly report of economic and market trends in his or her industry and asked to make adjustments to the quantitative forecasts. When adjustments are made, the salesperson is asked to electronically record the logic behind his or her adjustments.

The total of all sales force adjustments are electronically transmitted back to the forecasting group, where they are combined. Marketing managers then receive the adjusted forecasts for the product lines in their markets. Again, the marketing managers are asked to qualitatively adjust these forecasts and record their logic.

These forecast adjustments are received and compiled by the forecasting group and transmitted to management for adjustment at the division level. Once the upper management adjustments are received, the forecasts are broken down to the level and horizon appropriate for each functional planning area and transmitted electronically for use in planning.

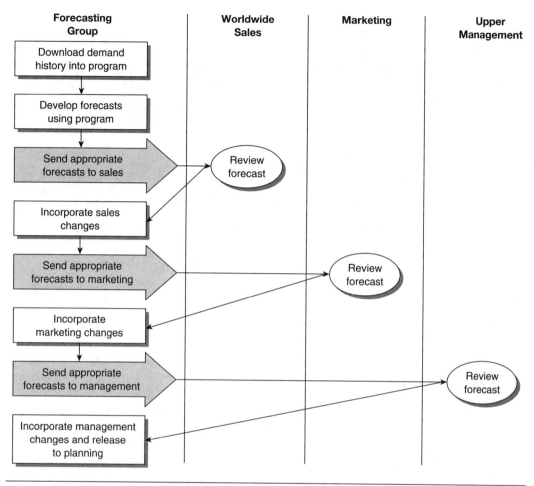

Figure 5.5   Example of a Sales Forecasting Process

Note that this process has laid over it the systems template to transmit all information electronically, pull information necessary for the computer model forecasts from appropriate data sources within the company and the supply chain, aggregate and disaggregate to the level and horizon needed at each step, and compare each forecast and adjustment with the actual demand once it is received.

Sales Forecasting Management Questions

There are a number of questions (listed in Table 5.1) you should ask yourself about your company. They must be answered for each company in their unique way, and should be constantly reexamined. The answers to these questions should tell you much about how the sales forecasting function should operate to efficiently and effectively help your company conduct the business of demand management.

Table 5.1   Sales Forecasting Management Questions

1. Customer base narrow or broad?

2. Data characteristics (shipments, sales, and demand, age, detail, external data, quality)?

3. Number of forecasts (horizons and intervals, products, channels, locations)?

4. Number of new products?

5. Regional differences?

6. Seasonality?

7. Sophistication of personnel (systems and forecasting) and systems?

8. Sales forecasting budget?

9. Accuracy needed?

Narrow or Broad Customer Base

The first question to ask is, Is your company's customer base narrow or broad? A narrow customer base simply means the sales of the company (regardless of the unit or dollar volume) go to a relatively small number of customers. An example of a broad customer base is the consumer markets served by packaged goods manufacturers, whereas an example of a narrow customer base is one served by a manufacturer of specialized industrial components. One company with which we have worked produces a product that is only sold directly to automobile assembly plants in North America. Thus, even though this is a company with annual dollar sales in excess of $50 million, its customer base is only 56 customers (the number of automobile assembly plants in North America).

The narrower the customer base, the more likely a company can rely on direct customer contact information to produce more qualitatively oriented sales forecasts. In the example just given, the sales forecasting function calls the production scheduling department of each of its 56 customers each month and asks for the schedule of car production, which is sent by electronic data interchange (EDI). From this information, a very accurate, qualitative sales forecast can be derived.

Contrast this example with a large manufacturer of consumer products that sells to all the 45 million households in the United States. Such a broad customer base makes any appreciable customer contact impossible (even if we surveyed 1 million homes, we would still have only contacted about 2% of our customers!) and causes more reliance on quantitative forecasting (i.e., time-series and regression) techniques. Thus, the narrower the customer base, the more a company can rely on direct customer contact qualitative techniques, and the broader the customer base, the more reliance will be placed on quantitative techniques (time-series and regression), with qualitative adjustments.

Data Characteristics

The second set of questions concerns the type, availability, and quality of data:

1. What data are available to your company for use in the forecasting function? Specifically, do you have data available on shipment history, order history, and/or end-consumer demand (e.g., POS data)?

2. How old are the data (i.e., how many weeks, months, or years are contained in the data)?

3. At what level of detail are the data?

4. What data external to your company can you obtain to facilitate sales forecasting (i.e., external factors that might affect product demand for use in a regression model)?

5. How accurate are the available data?

Sales, Shipments, and Demand

The answer to the first question determines what we will forecast. It is important to distinguish between sales, shipments, and demand. Although called sales forecasting, this function is really about forecasting demand. *Demand* is what our customers would buy from us if they could; *sales* is our ability to accept orders from our customers; and *shipments* is what our operations system can actually deliver to our customers. Suppose, for example, that demand for one of our products next month is 10,000, but our salespeople (due to uncertainty about delivery time commitments) can only confirm 9,000 units in actual sales. Suppose, further, that our production/logistics system can only produce and deliver 7,500 units of those ordered (sold). If our information system only collects and records shipments, our historical record of this month will show shipments of 7,500 units, *and nothing else!* What will be lost is the fact that we actually sold 1,500 units more, and could have sold 2,500 units more, if the capacity to produce and deliver had been available. With only this shipments history available to the forecasting function, we will continue to forecast "demand" to be 7,500 units per month, never recognize the lost sales each month, and never increase capacity to capture this extra true demand. However, if the only data we have are a history of what we have shipped in the past, these are the data we will have to use until more meaningful demand data can be gathered—but the commitment should be immediately made to begin gathering this more accurate sales and demand data.

Data Age

How much historical data is available largely defines the sales forecasting techniques that can be used. If less than one year of data is available, only the more simplistic fixed model time-series techniques (TIME SERIES) are going to work—any time-series technique that considers seasonality needs at least two years of data (so it can identify two complete seasonal patterns) to begin forecasting effectively. Open model time-series (OMTS) techniques typically need at least four years of data, whereas regression typically needs at least five periods of data for each variable in the regression equation (so if we had sales as one variable and advertising, price, and trade promotions as the three independent variables, we would need at least 4 variables times 5, or 20 periods of data). Of course, many companies have such a short life cycle for their products that many of these techniques are simply never practical.

Data Level

The level of detail of the data refers to the planning detail required. If we are forecasting annual dollar sales by product line for a marketing plan, data at the same level and time horizon are fine. However, if we also need weekly unit forecasts by stock-keeping unit by location (SKUL), annual product line data will be of little help. Since we need sales forecasts for a number of different functional plans, data at the level of detail corresponding to each of these planning needs are necessary.

This level of detail is called the **forecasting hierarchy** and is defined as all the planning levels and time horizons and intervals at which forecasts are needed. Figure 5.6 illustrates one such forecasting hierarchy for a company with which we have worked. In this company, the logistics function needs forecasts by week, by SKUL (SKU); the production and purchasing functions need forecasts biweekly, by stock-keeping unit; the sales function needs dollar sales by product by quarter; the marketing function needs annual dollar sales for the next year by product line and for the next five years by division; and finance needs annual dollar sales for the next five years by strategic business unit (SBU) and for the overall corporation. The data detail required for developing a forecast for each of these functions must match each planning level, horizon, and interval. The figure is drawn as a triangle to represent the number of forecasts that are required at each level of the hierarchy. Many more forecasts are required at the SKUL level than at the SKU level, more at the SKU than at the product level, and so on.

External Data Availability

Finally, the availability of data on factors external to the actual sales history determines whether or not regression analysis can be used. If the only data available are concerned with sales, shipments, or demand history, there is no information on which to build a regression model. Historical data on factors such as price, advertising, trade and consumer promotions, economic activity, and competitive actions (for just a few examples) must be available.

Data Quality

Corporate records are not always as trustworthy as we would like them to be. Invoices sometimes do not get entered, when they are entered they are entered with errors, or demand is recorded in the wrong period. All these are examples of data quality problems.

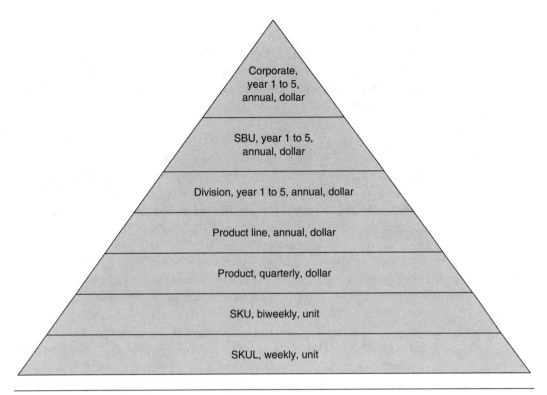

Figure 5.6   Example of a Forecasting Hierarchy

One company with which we worked was quite proud of their EDI system of recording their distributors' POS demand. However, when we interviewed distributors for this company, we found that these POS orders were actually taken and filled by a paper system and entered into the electronic system later. During high-demand months, distributors "simply do not have the time to keep the system up-to-date—we are too busy selling." The result was that many orders did not get entered into the system until the month after the demand occurred. Of course, this resulted in inaccurate data on monthly demand patterns.

Number of Forecasts

The third set of questions concerns how many forecasts you need, and this is a function of the following:

1. At what levels, time horizons, and intervals are forecasts required?

2. How many products, that is, product lines and product items (SKUs), must be forecast?

3. In how many distribution channels are your products marketed?

4. How many product/location combinations (e.g., by sales regions, distribution centers, individual customers) must be forecast?

Levels, Horizons, and Intervals

As discussed earlier, different functional areas require forecasts at different levels, time horizons, intervals, and forms. How the various functions answer these questions of how many forecasts are required and how often they are required will begin to define the forecasting hierarchy.

Number of Products

To understand the impact of forecasting different numbers of products, contrast the forecasting process for a company that manufactures a group of specialized industrial components with the forecasting process for an apparel manufacturing company that must forecast the numerous SKUs generated by multiple size, color, style, and fabric combinations. Limited product line companies can devote considerably greater attention to any one forecast than broad line companies that have literally thousands of products to forecast for each of the levels, horizons, and intervals mentioned in the previous question. For example, one telephone company we worked with in the 1980s had essentially only one product to forecast—new phone installations. With no local competition, this was the only forecast relevant to all the planning functions, and thus, a team of three people devoted their full attention to developing one forecast each month. This team could put considerably greater time into using sophisticated OMTS and regression analysis than a company like Brake Parts, Inc., which has several hundred thousand products to forecast each month (Mentzer and Schroeter 1993).

Distribution Channels

The third question in this set considers companies that have multiple channels for the same product. For example, an automotive parts manufacturer may market a certain product directly to original equipment manufacturers, through a separate channel under its own brand name, and through a large retailer channel under the brand name of that retailer. Thus, this one product is now marketed through three separate channels, each with its own demand patterns and, therefore, forecasting needs.

Product and Location Combinations

Similarly, the difference between the number of SKUs and SKULs can dramatically change the number of forecasts that are required. The number of forecasts needed to meet the planning needs of all business functions is determined by the number of products we produce *and* the number of locations where they are shipped or sold.

New Products

Similarly, the number of new products introduced in a given planning horizon affects how we will forecast. Are these variations on existing products or truly new products? Not surprisingly, we have found that the forecasting of genuinely new products is cited by many companies as one of the most difficult forecasting problems they face. At its best, new product forecasting is a leap into the future with little or no historical information to tell us which way to leap. New product forecasting can take a great deal of sales forecasting personnel time, can hurt the credibility of the forecasting group through poor new product forecasting accuracy, and can reduce the morale of the forecasting group. It is, however, a necessary function in the competitive environment of most global supply chains.

Regional Differences

Regional differences in demand for products increase the number of forecasts to be made and the analysis required. For example, manufacturers of agricultural chemicals have a very different market in the United States than in Canada. The much shorter growing season in Canada creates entirely different market behaviors that must be forecast differently.

Seasonality

Similarly, the degree of seasonality of the products we market affects the techniques used to forecast. Many time-series techniques and regression do not consider seasonality and, thus, either should not be used in highly seasonal situations or should be used in conjunction with techniques that do consider seasonality.

Personnel and Systems Sophistication

How sophisticated are the personnel involved in the sales forecasting function? Do they have educational backgrounds in statistics or econometrics? What is their level of experience and knowledge regarding the industry in which your company does business? If the answers to these questions are on the lower side, additional training of sales forecasting personnel is probably in order (statistical/quantitative analysis training for those with business experience, and business experience/qualitative analysis training for those with statistical backgrounds), and the sophistication of the techniques used should be limited until such training is obtained.

How sophisticated are the hardware and software systems available for use in forecasting? Are there electronic interfaces among the systems (hardware and software applications) in use by producers and users of the sales forecasts? Without such interconnectivity, many of the benefits that accrue from sales forecasting systems cannot be realized.

Budget

Similarly, without a commitment to the sales forecasting budget, these training and systems problems will probably not get fixed. Interestingly, in our studies of hundreds of companies, few felt their sales forecasting budget was adequate.

Accuracy Needed

Finally, what level of accuracy is required for the various forecasts? That is, what are the consequences of forecasting error at various levels (e.g., SKULL), time horizons, and time intervals? We have found that forecasting accuracy is often considered to be like customer service—the more the better. However, true analysis of sales forecasting management often produces the conclusion that the benefit of improved accuracy is not worth the cost. The costs of training, new systems, and improved techniques should all be weighed against the improvements in supply chain costs, planning costs, and customer service levels. In most cases, the return on investment (ROI) on such investments is dramatic, but it should still be evaluated to determine what is an acceptable level of sales forecasting accuracy for each business function in each level, horizon, and interval.

Demand Management: An Iterative Process

An integral part of any demand management process is an implementation of an iterative process of sales forecasting and planning. Many companies use the business plan to drive the sales forecast—a naive approach, as the forecast should be driven by the realities of the marketplace, not the financial needs of the corporation. More sophisticated companies develop the sales forecast independently of the business plan, but when the forecast and the plan diverge, the forecast is made to "fit" the plan.

In fact, companies that are effective at sales forecasting and business planning start with the sales forecasting process. Remember our definition of a sales forecast: *a projection into the future of expected demand, given a stated set of environmental conditions.* Given expected economic and competitive conditions *and* initial marketing, sales, production, and logistics plans, we make a projection of future expected demand. From this base, the business plan can be developed. When the resultant business plan does not meet the financial needs and goals of the company, we iterate back to the sales forecast and examine what additional efforts in marketing or sales can be undertaken to increase the demand forecast and what additional efforts can be undertaken by production or logistics to increase capacity to the level necessary to meet the business plan. It is this iterative process of sales forecast to business plan back to sales forecast to business plan, and so, on that ensures a business plan that is based on the financial *and* marketplace realities facing the company, its production and logistics capacities, and its global supply chain.

References

Lapide, Larry (2002), "You Need Sales and Operations Planning," *Journal of Business Forecasting*, Summer, 11–14.

McCarthy, Teresa M., Donna F. Davis, Susan L. Golicic, and John T. Mentzer (forthcoming), "The Evolution of Sales Forecasting Management: A 20-Year Longitudinal Study of Forecasting Practices," *Journal of Forecasting.*

Mentzer, John T. and Mark A. Moon (2004a), *Sales Forecasting Management: A Demand Management Approach.* Thousand Oaks, CA: Sage.

Mentzer, John T. and Mark A. Moon (2004b), "Understanding Demand," *Supply Chain Management Review,* 8 (May/June), 38–45.

Mentzer, John T. and Jon Schroeter (1993), "Multiple Forecasting System at Brake Parts, Inc.," *Journal of Business Forecasting,* 12 (Fall), 5–9.

6

Knowledge Management

Donna F. Davis

Didier Chenneveau

F irms around the world are entering a new era of business competition. Globalization of supply chains and the escalating pace of technological change have set the stage for the emergence of global network competition. In network competition, firms must not only compete with other firms for favorable positions within a trading network but also collaborate with trading partners to secure competitive advantage for their global supply chains. The ability to win in network competition hinges on competent management of knowledge resources. Indeed, knowledge management is rapidly becoming a critical core competence for achieving a sustainable competitive advantage. However, the efforts of many firms to develop knowledge management competence have been disappointing.

A key reason for the failure of knowledge management initiatives is that few managers understand either the nature of knowledge or how to manage it. Many managers mistake information processing for knowledge management. As a result, they narrowly focus efforts on improving information management by carrying out a series of disjointed projects. For example, a firm may undertake projects to enhance information infrastructure (e.g., integrate multiple databases in a data warehouse), improve information processes (e.g., implement collaborative planning, forecasting, and replenishment [CPFR]), or engage workers in developing a climate supportive of information sharing (e.g., a change management initiative). Nonaka (1991) proposes that this piecemeal approach grows primarily out of the tradition of Western management, which is based on the view of the firm as a machine for information processing. Naturally, improving a machine's performance involves a sequence of tune-ups or replacement of parts. A fundamental insight of companies that excel in knowledge management is that a firm is not an

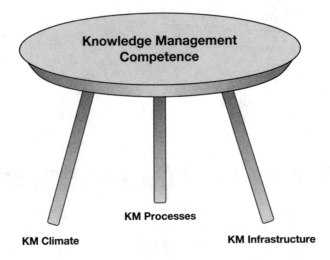

Figure 6.1   Components of Knowledge Management (KM) Competence

assembly of interchangeable machine parts. Firms are made up of human beings. Therefore, a firm is more like a living organism than a machine. Like people, firms can have a collective identity, purpose, and intelligence. Like people, firms develop knowledge by learning. Learning includes not only acquiring "hard" (i.e., quantifiably explicit) information but also mastering "soft" skills (i.e., tacit know-how). A firm cannot build knowledge management competence project by project; rather, the acquisition of such competence must be approached holistically. Building knowledge management competence requires engaging the whole organization in a commitment to learning.

Effective knowledge management strategies ensure a holistic approach by developing knowledge management as a core competence of the firm. Building knowledge management competence is like constructing a three-legged stool that rests equally on the *climate, processes,* and *infrastructure* for knowledge management (Figure 6.1). The tendency to focus on one leg while ignoring the other two can produce unfortunate effects. For example, focusing solely on infrastructure by adopting the latest technology can rob a firm of rich knowledge gained in processes that promote social interactions, both across functions within a firm and between firms in a supply chain. Similarly, investing time and money in new knowledge-sharing processes will fail if the climate encourages counterproductive behavior, such as knowledge hoarding. In this chapter, we discuss the components of knowledge management competence and provide real-world examples of how these components work in global supply chains.

From Data to Knowledge

For a productive discussion of knowledge management competence, we must first define what we mean by knowledge and knowledge management. As a starting point, it is useful to distinguish data and information from knowledge. **Data** are *raw facts,* such as point-of-sale data from retailers. **Information** is *data that have been organized for use.* For example, a sales trend analysis extracted from point-of-sale data is information that can be used in collaborative forecasting. Although data and information are the essential building blocks of knowledge, knowledge management involves much more than bulking up a data warehouse or producing well-designed reports. **Knowledge** is the *understanding gained through human reasoning and learning that results in increased capacity for decision making and action to improve performance.*

As it is with individuals, learning is integral to knowledge development in firms. Firms learn through a cyclical process in which a firm interacts with the environment, the environment responds, and the firm updates knowledge about cause-effect relationships. For example, a national brand apparel manufacturer faced a downward sales trend for an item that retailed for $19.99. Based on past experience, management knew that periodically offering this item for the promotional price of two for $40 resulted in a 20% lift in sales (note that the pricing is unchanged in the promotional scheme). The manufacturer collaborated with a key retail trading partner to offer the modified pricing scheme and, once again, reversed a downward trend. The manufacturer in this example interacted with the environment (i.e., offered a promotional pricing scheme), the environment responded (i.e., sales volume increased), and the response was interpreted through a learning routine by which the manufacturer updated knowledge about a cause-effect (i.e., action-response) relationship. In this example, consumers of this national brand continued to respond favorably to periodic promotional pricing.

There are two types of knowledge to be managed: explicit and tacit. **Explicit knowledge** is *what we know that can be articulated.* Because it can be codified (i.e., captured in words, numbers, or symbols), explicit knowledge can be separated from an individual worker for the benefit of the firm. Explicit knowledge can be shared across a firm through communication channels (e.g., meetings, reports) or by adopting rules and practices that embed knowledge in organizational routines. In the previous example, a rule was written into reporting software to flag any item that experienced three consecutive weeks of declining sales. Thus, the knowledge that a downward trend requires intervention was embedded in an organizational routine of exception reporting.

In contrast, **tacit knowledge** is *what we know but cannot explain.* Because we cannot explain it, tacit knowledge is difficult to communicate or codify in organizational routines. Tacit knowledge is located in the minds of individual workers and shared through person-to-person interactions. For example, after years of experience, a master craftsman develops a wealth of knowledge, captured in the term *know-how.* This highly personal knowledge can be passed on to an apprentice, who learns by observation, imitation, and practice. Knowledge that results from working together, such as the relationship between a manufacturer's sales representative and a retail merchandise manager, is largely tacit. In our example, knowing how to persuade a particular merchandise manager to participate in a two-for-$40 campaign is an example of a sales manager's tacit knowledge.

We define **knowledge management** as a business process that promotes organizational learning by integrating a firm's approach to creating, sharing, and using knowledge resources. **Knowledge resources** make up a firm's intellectual capital. Although they include intellectual property such as patents and trademarks, knowledge resources are more than just intellectual property. Knowledge resources reflect the knowledge and experience of a workforce that allow a firm to produce a market offering that has value. They include the explicit and tacit knowledge of individual workers and workgroups as well as knowledge incorporated into organizational routines. For example, competitive intelligence gathered by the sales force is a knowledge resource. A manufacturer's production processes and the skill of production workers are knowledge resources. The ability of a purchasing department to manage a global sourcing program is a knowledge resource. When knowledge resources are carefully managed, they have the potential to create a sustainable competitive advantage in the global marketplace.

Building Knowledge Management Competence

Knowledge management competence is a firm's ability to deploy tangible and intangible resources to develop knowledge management in a way that helps the firm compete in its marketplace. Competences are difficult to accurately describe because they are deeply rooted in experience in a specific context. Building a competence requires learning by doing. Thus, a firm's knowledge management competence is largely tacit, complex, and firm specific, making it difficult—if not impossible—to imitate. When a critical resource is difficult to imitate and has no ready substitutes, it can secure sustainable competitive advantage for the firm that possesses the resource. Building knowledge management competence requires synchronized development of three components: (1) knowledge management climate, (2) knowledge management processes, and (3) knowledge management infrastructure. Each of these components has three facets, which we describe in the following sections (Figure 6.2).

Knowledge Management Climate

Perhaps the most difficult, and most vital, aspect of building knowledge management competence is creating a favorable knowledge management climate. Climate is closely related to organizational culture. Climate is the visible behavior that is rooted in cultural values, which are deeper and less consciously held. It is "what happens around here" and can be managed through the implementation of policies and practices that shape behavior. A firm's **knowledge management climate** is *the shared perception of how the work setting either encourages or hinders knowledge management.* Maintaining a climate that embraces and rewards knowledge management is the responsibility of executive leadership.

It is important for executives to recognize that the climate for knowledge management may vary within the firm by function, management level, or geographic region. Varying climates often lead groups to define knowledge management in

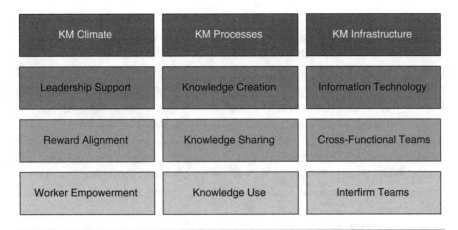

Figure 6.2   Facets of Knowledge Management (KM) Competence Components

ways that work at cross-purposes. Knowledge management in the marketing department may focus on decreasing the cycle time for new product introductions to the detriment of operation's objective of learning how to manage inventory levels better. Senior management may experiment with projects to learn how to improve future bottom-line profitability, whereas regional sales managers view such projects as interfering with their primary learning objective—how to increase today's levels of customer satisfaction to boost sales. Operations in the Asian region may push for higher levels of standardization to improve production efficiency, whereas the South American region works to increase customization in order to build relationships that influence retailers' brand preferences.

The climate for knowledge management also varies between firms in a global supply chain. For example, the knowledge management climate of a consumer electronics retailer focuses on innovation. All knowledge management efforts are harnessed to the goal of maintaining their image as a cutting-edge retailer. They encourage action-oriented experimentation that calls for frequent, informal interactions with trading partners. Believing that knowledge development requires flexibility and risk taking, they resist attempts to codify knowledge in standard reports and processes. In contrast, the knowledge management climate of a key vendor is anchored in systematic, formal procedures and practices. It is important to the vendor to be able to leverage knowledge management investments across multiple trade relationships. This involves thoughtful development and thorough documentation of knowledge management processes. As a result, these trading partners are often at odds with each other. They must spend time identifying and reconciling differences in their knowledge management climates in order to work together to create and share knowledge that can improve performance.

Differing climates for knowledge management often lead to miscommunication and misunderstandings among workgroups in a firm and between trading partners. Identifying and managing these differences is critical to effective knowledge management. Within a firm, managers of units should examine the extent to which differences in knowledge management climates are generating unproductive tension and take action to reconcile those differences. With trading partners, managers are well-advised to strive for harmony between their firm's and their customer's knowledge management climates. They should be realistic about expectations of new behaviors by trading partners. Is it realistic to expect the ready-fire-aim retailer in our example to engage in a vendor's formal, procedurally oriented knowledge management practices? Can the vendor's practices be modified to adapt to the retailer's freewheeling knowledge management climate? Or should managers of both firms invest in change management to align knowledge management climates better? Changing a knowledge management climate involves managing three facets of climate: leadership support, reward alignment, and worker empowerment.

Leadership support is *the shared perception of executive commitment to knowledge management.* Executives must demonstrate their commitment by creating and communicating a clear vision of knowledge management (see Table 6.1). The vision statement provides employees with a sense of purpose that motivates participation in and commitment to knowledge management. In the absence of guidance by executive leadership, a firm's knowledge management efforts will flounder due to a lack of commitment and focus. Creating an effective vision statement is a necessary first step. However, executives must also "walk the talk" to demonstrate their commitment to knowledge management.

Table 6.1   Knowledge Management Vision in Korea

In his 1999 New Year message to the nation, President Kim Dae-Jung unveiled a nationwide plan to develop and manage knowledge resources in Korea. The thrust of President Kim's vision and subsequent legislation was to manage information and knowledge as national resources in order to position Korea as a viable participant in a knowledge-based global economy.

Based on Cyber Korea 2000 and the 2000 Act of Knowledge and Information Resources Management, US$550 million was dedicated to accomplishing the following objectives:

- To digitize all valuable and useful knowledge and information in order to preserve and use them at the national level and build national knowledge bases or repositories,·
- To develop a National Knowledge and Information Portal System (NK&IPS) in order to integrate all knowledge and information, and
- To enable everyone to easily get the right knowledge and information at the right time through a high-speed internet.

The benefits are expected to be immense. In addition to more reliable access to and improved sharing of knowledge and information resources, Korea expects knowledge management to enhance the quality of people's lives and to ultimately build a national competency to use knowledge assets.

SOURCE: Gangtak (2000).

A firm's reward structure is the strongest signal executives send to workers about the relative value of various activities. Managers have long recognized the link between rewards and behavior as reflected in the old saying, "What gets measured gets rewarded, and what gets rewarded gets done." **Reward alignment** is *the degree to which reward systems recognize behaviors that strengthen knowledge management while penalizing behaviors that weaken knowledge management.* In other words, managers must ensure that rewards and incentives related to knowledge management encourage constructive behavior and discourage destructive behavior. Although this may sound rather straightforward, rewards and incentives in most companies do the exact opposite. For example, there is a long-standing tradition in many firms of dispensing individual rewards and incentives linked with preset targets. This often has the unintended consequence of undermining knowledge management by encouraging individuals to hoard or distort information to earn rewards.

Jensen (2001) offers a useful discussion of how individual rewards and incentives work in most firms. Incentive plans are typically based on achieving some percentage of a target over a specified period of time (Figure 6.3). Exceeding the agreed-upon bonus hurdle (Point A) results in additional financial rewards, up to some maximum cap on earnings (Point B). For example, account executives may earn 100% of their bonuses if they cross the hurdle and up to 110% if they exceed the target by at least 5%. This type of compensation plan can produce disastrous effects for knowledge management. When the minimum target is out of reach for the current period, the wise course of action is to hold back to ensure a bonus in the next period. Giving up the current period as a lost cause and pushing results forward (e.g., a salesperson pushing orders forward) ensures the best possible chance for achieving the target in the next period. On the other hand, one executive reported it was common for sales managers at his firm to book 105% of their quotas in the last five days of the quarter to maximize their bonuses. Of course, this was routinely followed by a sharp drop in orders, which wreaked havoc in production planning the following quarter. Individual incentive plans tied to preset targets encourage people to distort critical information, seriously limiting a firm's ability to build knowledge management competence.

Despite overwhelming evidence that most individual-performance-based financial incentives provide little value to firms, executives continue to believe they are a necessary ingredient for business success. Today's knowledge-based organizations are designed around interdependent parts, so setting targets and incentives for each part does not make much sense. In fact, estimating the marginal contribution of an individual is believed to be impossible in today's business environment. Rewards that support knowledge management competence should motivate workers to focus on meaningful contributions to group performance. Successfully shifting rewards from individual performance to group performance requires fortitude and finesse. However, companies that develop the right mix of incentives to reward workers for creating and sharing knowledge go a long way toward developing knowledge management competence.

Although rewards and incentives are important to motivate workers to engage in knowledge management, research shows that worker empowerment is the single

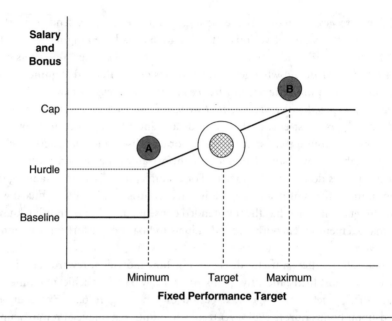

Figure 6.3   Effect of Individual Merit-Based Compensation Plans

SOURCE: Adapted from Jensen (2001).

most important job characteristic to knowledge workers. Knowledge workers invest a great deal of time and money honing their skills. As a result, they thrive in a climate that strikes the proper balance between independence and support. A climate characterized by **worker empowerment** allows *a high level of autonomy in work design.* Autonomy includes responsibility for scheduling work, assigning group members to tasks, and monitoring progress as well as the freedom to experiment and take reasonable risks. Within the context of knowledge management, autonomy encourages workers to take responsibility for organizing their own communication networks to create and share knowledge. These self-organizing networks promote knowledge management by building mutual trust among members, which contributes to cooperative learning.

Worker empowerment establishes an expectation of social interaction that structures the environment within which people communicate. For example, a climate that promotes interaction and collaboration allows relationships to develop and perspectives to be shared by those who are not working side by side. This type of interaction is essential to transmission of knowledge across functions in a firm. In contrast, there may be functional areas within a firm where workers are not expected to continually share knowledge and collaborate with people in other departments. In fact, time spent in meetings outside the area is thought of as time away from the "real" job. Therefore, these workers do not develop routine practices for collaboration and knowledge sharing. When workers are not in the habit of sharing knowledge, introducing knowledge-sharing tools such as a data warehouse or cross-functional work processes will have a limited impact on improving knowledge management. These workers wear functional blinders that restrict their context for interpreting or using knowledge. They may use knowledge-sharing tools to access and distribute explicit knowledge, but their ability to contribute to improved knowledge management is limited by their narrow view of what is important to the firm.

The ground rules for social interaction have a powerful effect on knowledge management not only across functions within a firm but also between firms in a supply chain. Workers who routinely collaborate and share knowledge within their own firms are better prepared to engage in collaborative relationships with trading partners. They have repeatedly experienced the positive benefits of collaborative problem solving. Therefore, they are accustomed to taking responsibility for seeking out ways to work with others to solve problems or create knowledge that benefits the partnership.

Knowledge Management Processes

Knowledge management processes are *organizational routines that facilitate knowledge creation, knowledge sharing, and knowledge use.* These processes are interdependent; that is, the value of each depends on the merits of the other two. For example, knowledge creation is exciting, but it is not of much use to a firm if it is not shared. On the other hand, knowledge sharing is a waste of time if the knowledge created is worthless. Ultimately, the value of knowledge depends on the frequency of its use.

Organizational processes do not, in themselves, create knowledge. **Knowledge creation** is carried out by individuals. However, an organization can influence knowledge creation by implementing processes that encourage and support individuals who create knowledge. Knowledge is created for a firm when an individual's knowledge is integrated into the knowledge network of the organization. Nonaka (1994) describes a dynamic relationship among four types of processes that explain knowledge creation in firms (Figure 6.4).

The first two forms of knowledge creation involve a combination of similar types of knowledge. First, knowledge can be created for a firm when tacit knowledge is transferred from one worker to another through *socialization* (i.e., *tacit-to-tacit* in Cell 1). Tacit knowledge is acquired through observation, imitation, and practice. Within a firm, person-to-person interactions such as on-the-job training and mentoring allow tacit knowledge to be transferred. For example, managers at a global tire manufacturer recognized junior forecast analysts needed to "learn the business" to better understand and incorporate factors that affected demand in their analyses. To foster cross-functional communication, the analysts were relocated from a central forecasting office to the sales divisions for which they were responsible. As the junior analysts worked alongside senior sales representatives, they came to understand issues with particular products or customers that affected demand. This knowledge was inaccessible to them when their offices were located in the forecasting division. Between firms in a global supply chain, colocation or interfirm teams (i.e., teams made up of people from two or more trading partners) accomplish tacit-to-tacit knowledge creation and transfer. Although this type of

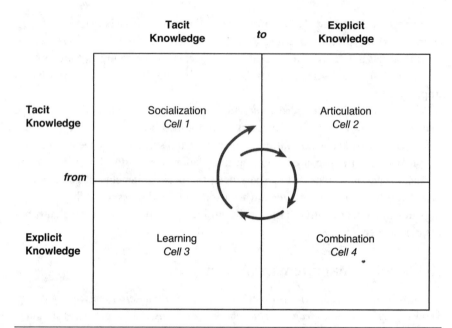

Figure 6.4   Spiral of Knowledge Creation

SOURCE: Adapted from Nonaka (1994).

knowledge creation is valuable, it is limited due to the amount of time it takes for the personal interaction required to create and transfer tacit knowledge.

The second type of knowledge creation is the *combination* of different sources of explicit information to form new knowledge (i.e., *explicit-to-explicit* in Cell 4). When explicit knowledge is combined, it can be reconfigured through sorting, recombination, and analysis to create new knowledge. For example, think about a firm that adopts optimization software and combines it with the existing database of distribution center statistics and transportation routes. The software provides new (to the firm) explicit information that allows existing explicit information to be sorted and reconfigured in a way that gives the firm new knowledge about opportunities to optimize transportation routes and the location of distribution centers. Firms also use the social process for combining explicit information. Individuals exchange explicit information in informal conversations and formal meetings. For example, an account executive may have an informal hallway conversation with a brand manager. The account executive's knowledge of a customer's plans for new stores can be combined with a brand manager's knowledge of market trends to create new knowledge of future sales trends. Or trading partners may establish a joint product development team that allows a manufacturer's knowledge of new technologies to be combined with a retailer's knowledge of consumers' needs to create new markets.

The engine of knowledge creation for firms resides in the third and fourth types of knowledge creation. A firm's knowledge grows over time as explicit and tacit knowledge interact in an expanding spiral of knowledge creation. The creation of explicit knowledge from tacit knowledge (i.e., *explicit-from-tacit* in Cell 2) is called *articulation*. For example, a manufacturer that has a great deal of experience with quality control may offer assistance by sending engineers to observe a trading partner's production processes. Owing to their long-time experience in quality control, these engineers instinctively know what to look for as they walk the production lines. Drawing on their tacit knowledge, they are able to articulate changes to improve product quality in the form of engineering specifications for modifications in production processes.

When tacit knowledge is created from explicit knowledge (i.e., *tacit-from-explicit* in Cell 3), it is internalized through a *learning* process. The engineers in the previous example first acquired explicit knowledge by studying engineering textbooks and manuals. As they applied this explicit knowledge in a work setting, they gained understanding of how abstract engineering principles work in real-world production lines. Thus, their explicit knowledge was transformed into tacit knowledge through learning by doing.

The power of knowledge creation is realized by managing a continuous cycle of shifts from one mode of knowledge creation to another. First, socialization typically begins when a team is formed to allow workers to share experiences and perspectives. Second, the articulation mode is triggered as team members hammer out a common understanding through rounds of dialogue. In this dialogue, team members reveal tacit knowledge as they articulate their viewpoints of the issue at hand. Third, new concepts are formed by combining different types of explicit data, from either team members' own knowledge or searches for knowledge outside the team. Through repeated trial and error, concepts finally emerge in concrete form. The give-and-take among team members as they try out various combinations of explicit knowledge triggers the fourth mode of knowledge creation—internalization of understanding by team members who are engaged in learning by doing. Interactions between tacit and explicit knowledge become larger in scale and faster as more people in the organization become involved. Thus, knowledge creation can be seen as an upward spiral that begins at the individual level, moves up to teams, and then expands to the level of the entire firm, ultimately reaching outside the firm by extending to knowledge creation between trading partners in a supply chain.

Knowledge sharing is fundamental to knowledge management. Knowledge must be shared in order to create value; however, knowledge sharing is often sacrificed at the altar of a climate that reinforces the superiority of individual knowledge over group knowledge. When knowledge is power, engaging in knowledge sharing can be risky. As long as people benefit from hoarding knowledge, a firm's ability to develop knowledge management competency will be severely constrained.

In many firms, knowledge sharing is limited by a long-held practice of providing information only on a "need-to-know" basis. This practice is often embedded in password security levels that were originally set to restrict access to a firm's confidential or proprietary information. But the implied message of withholding knowledge from some workers or functions is, "We don't trust you." The level of trust greatly influences the amount of knowledge that flows both laterally between individuals and functions and vertically, up to senior management. A lack of trust has a negative effect on workers' willingness to share their knowledge by depositing it in the firm's databases, sharing it in meetings, or incorporating it into organizational routines. Another unfortunate interpretation of the need-to-know rule is that some people or functions are less valuable than others. In other words, you do not need to know because you are not important enough to know. This perception is also likely to choke out knowledge sharing, reinforcing a silo mentality as functions jealously protect their knowledge to increase their importance to the firm.

Firms rely on both formal and informal processes to encourage knowledge sharing. Formal processes include routine dissemination of knowledge through reports, meetings, and training. Firms that value knowledge sharing are conscientious about ensuring that critical knowledge is widely distributed on a timely basis. Some firms encourage knowledge sharing by asking employees to teach what they know about the business to others, both in on-the-job training of new employees and in formal classroom settings in a corporate university. In addition to formal processes, knowledge is shared in informal interactions in hallways and company cafeterias and at social functions. Providing space and time for informal interactions, such as a common break room that provides coffee or soft drinks, supports a higher level of informal knowledge sharing.

Information technology (IT) is both a key facilitator and a major limitation to knowledge sharing within firms and between trading partners. Advances in IT promote knowledge sharing by allowing on-demand access to knowledge in a firm's data warehouse as well as instant communication of knowledge through intranets, extranets, e-mail, messaging, bulletin boards, and chat rooms. However, technology has not yet provided efficient tools for capturing and sharing complex, evolving ideas represented in multiple formats, such as text with diagrams and photos. Searchable Web logs (also called "blogs") are a step in this direction. A Web log is a user-friendly tool that allows an individual to instantly publish chronological postings with links to multiple, relevant pieces of information. But the scarcity of software tools beyond Web logs is an impediment to knowledge sharing. The creation of new software tools (i.e., the ability to "Google" information sitting on individual desktops) will lead to better knowledge access and sharing throughout a firm and beyond to trading partners.

Ironically, **knowledge use** typically receives less attention than knowledge creation and knowledge sharing. The presumption is once knowledge is created and shared, it will be put to use by the firm. Processes that ensure the application of knowledge to business problems are essential to harness knowledge resources to the goal of achieving a sustainable competitive advantage. It is widely understood that performance improvement depends more on a firm's ability to turn knowledge into action than on the knowledge itself. For example, many retailers recognized that the lifting of import quotas would have an effect on their supply chains. But one major retailer acted on this knowledge by restructuring merchandising teams in a way that would allow them to centrally manage import relationships in order to take advantage of this knowledge. Previously, store managers were allowed to determine the quantity and mix of national brands and private label brands sold in their stores. Foreseeing potential growth in direct imports due to the lifting of quotas, the retailer centralized decision making at the corporate headquarters. This change allowed the retailer to build stronger relationships with offshore manufacturers to support growth in their private label brands. As illustrated in this case, turning knowledge into action requires determining which information is relevant and then deciding how this knowledge fits within the context of a particular firm.

Another important aspect of knowledge use is the way a firm handles mistakes or the "lessons learned" through painful failures. Mistakes can be leveraged to create new knowledge, or they can be ignored, explained away, and covered up. In global supply chain competition, the ability to uncover and learn from mistakes is critical to success. For example, Hewlett-Packard's (HP's) first attempt at collaborative planning in the Inkjet Printing Group actually had a detrimental effect on operations (Culbertson, Harris, and Radosevich 2005). A small army of engineers worked with customers to generate collaborative 12-week forecasts with key customers, but no linkage was made between this information and HP's upstream supply processes with contract manufacturers based in Asia. When the new demand signal from the collaborative forecast was added, with no guidance on how the information should be applied, the result was chaos. The collaborative forecast generated valuable knowledge, but it was lost because there was no linkage to internal actions that would interpret this information and transfer it to upstream contract manufacturers. HP evaluated the gaps between the process that produced the collaborative demand signal and the process that generated the contract manufacturer's build plan. They closed the gaps in a new, integrated process called Demand-Supply Management Program (DSMP). DSMP closed the loop by defining the specific steps and timing for incorporating knowledge from collaborative forecasts into supply planning. In other words, DSMP provided a road map that ensured the application of knowledge gained through collaborative forecasting to performance improvement. Following implementation of DSMP, the inventory levels across the supply chain dropped by an average of 20%. Ship-to-plan performance ability to meet the forecast at a four-week horizon increased from 70% to 97%, reducing by half the incidence of insufficient product to support on-shelf availability. DSMP allowed HP to use knowledge generated by collaborative forecasting to streamline their contract manufacturer's production runs and reduce costs for inbound supplies. At the same time, retailers could rely on having the right mix of products available for planning advertisements and promotions.

Knowledge Management Infrastructure

The **knowledge management infrastructure** is composed of *communication channels that enable knowledge creation, knowledge sharing, and knowledge use.* Communication channels are connections through which knowledge flows. There are two basic types of connections that open up communication channels among functions within a firm or between trading partners in a supply chain: IT links and social structures.

IT often takes center stage in discussions of knowledge management. Many managers were first introduced to knowledge management by consultants who were promoting adoption of knowledge management software. The belief was that implementation of new technology would enforce process reengineering. However, many companies quickly learned that IT adoption did not necessarily translate into process improvement. Certainly, IT opens essential communication channels for creation, sharing, and use of knowledge in global trading networks. A wide variety of communication tools provided by an IT infrastructure enables timely distribution of information as well as circulation of interpretations of the information's meaning. IT opens communication channels, but it does not fill them with relevant knowledge.

For IT to be an efficient communication channel, a firm must have standards for collecting, storing, and sharing information using compatible platforms and centralized databases. In firms that do not have an integrated IT infrastructure, workers routinely manipulate data as it passes between functions. Data are downloaded from one database, reformatted, and uploaded into the next application. This not only takes up valuable time; it also raises the risk of introducing errors, thereby reducing the credibility of the information. As a result, departments resort to collecting and storing their own versions of critical information, isolating it on fragmented systems or "islands of information." A user-friendly, integrated IT infrastructure ensures the standardization, compatibility, and interoperability of systems and data required to build knowledge management competence.

IT holds the promise of allowing global supply chains to realize significant gains through end-to-end knowledge sharing. For example, the introduction of radio-frequency identification (RFID) technology allows an incredible amount of knowledge to be captured and shared across a global supply chain. A Brazilian division of a consumer electronics firm has a sole-source arrangement with a contract manufacturer. In the production process, an RFID chip is imprinted with rich information about each individual unit (e.g., source of components, the line on which the product was built, quality control information) and is attached to the unit. This information is extremely helpful to the manufacturer in diagnosing production and rework issues. In addition, the same RFID provides tracking information that gives retailers real-time visibility of the precise composition and location of shipments.

Social structures are the second type of communication channel in the knowledge management infrastructure. An organizational chart is a map of a firm's formal social structure. In most firms, people doing similar work are grouped together within functions to optimize knowledge creation, sharing, and use in a particular area of expertise. However, functional social structures often have the unintended consequence of isolating knowledge within functional boundaries. In fact, structures that optimize knowledge management within a function can suboptimize knowledge management for a firm by limiting knowledge sharing across functions. Learning organizations handle this problem by setting up social structures that encourage cross-functional transfer of knowledge and skills.

Cross-functional teams ensure systematic cross-functional communication of essential information and allow multiple perspectives to be considered in interpreting information. Cross-functional knowledge transfer improves knowledge management efficiency and effectiveness by ensuring *redundancy*—the conscious overlapping of information and activities that promotes common understanding. To most managers, the idea of redundancy sounds inefficient and wasteful. However, redundancy improves knowledge management by creating a common ground for knowledge creation, sharing, and use. In most organizations, there can be significant barriers to critical, contradictory information. Yet this is often precisely the information needed to enhance organizational learning. Cross-functional teams provide a vehicle for reconciling contradictory information by challenging conventional wisdom as new points of view are brought to bear on issues.

Interfirm teams are essential conduits of knowledge between trading partners in a global supply chain. They allow firms to align expectations and provide a mechanism for quickly identifying and resolving issues. In recognition of the importance of interfirm teams, many companies have reorganized themselves around key customers to ensure the timely exchange of meaningful information. Joint product development teams are a prime example of the use of interfirm teams to improve knowledge management. These teams establish social connections between firms that support knowledge creation, sharing, and use. Through frequent interactions, joint product development teams allow trading partners to develop a common understanding of each other's processes and business requirements.

Challenges to Building Knowledge Management Competence

Firms face different challenges as they attempt to build knowledge management competence, depending on their organizational culture, the nature of their business, and factors in the business environment. Various studies of knowledge management in firms across multiple industries and in several countries show that managers believe building a supportive climate for knowledge management is the most difficult challenge. A supportive climate is built on the deeply held belief that the firm's future depends on its knowledge management competence. This is the driving force for embracing knowledge management as a core competence rather than a one-off project. Without this perspective, knowledge management is likely to be viewed as a set of "extra" activities that must be accommodated by an already overburdened workforce.

Changing the mind-set from "knowledge is power" to "knowledge sharing is power" is essential for knowledge management. Firms that successfully implement knowledge management reward participation in group processes to ensure knowledge creation, sharing, and use. This builds an expectation of collaborative problem solving within the firm and with trading partners. It also favors putting hard-earned knowledge to use instead of reinventing the wheel each time an issue is encountered. Changing the mind-set requires identifying and rooting out formal and informal practices that encourage dysfunctional behavior, such as distorting or hoarding knowledge.

Firms are confronted with varying levels of diversity in the types of knowledge they must manage, depending on the type of business. For example, manufacturers of national brands must manage knowledge about the needs of trading partners as well as individual consumers. Manufacturers further from end consumers, such as chemical companies, have products that are used in a wide range of finished goods.

Thus, they must manage an extremely diverse set of industrial customer expectations. In both situations, the nature of the business determines the complexity of knowledge that must be managed.

Factors in the business environment also affect a firm's knowledge management efforts. Some industries have a higher proportion of firms that are on the leading edge of business process and technology adoption, making it much easier to manage knowledge with trading partners. Others are made up of companies that lack the business expertise or technological sophistication to productively engage in collaborative activities. In some cases, this is due to a lack of financial resources for hiring people with the necessary expertise. In other cases, it is due to a lack of willingness to engage in collaboration with trading partners.

Building knowledge management competence is not an easy task. It is far easier for managers to focus on projects that promise short-term results than to take on the mission of positioning a firm to compete over the long term in a global supply chain. It is a complex, never-ending process. There is no one-size-fits-all solution. Each firm must evaluate its needs and chart its own path to knowledge management competence. Even the best-laid plans are full of potential pitfalls, and there will be failures along the way. Companies that learn equally from both failures and successes attain higher levels of knowledge management competence than those that give up when mistakes are made. Many firms will not have the commitment or willpower to stay the course. This is precisely why firms that successfully cultivate knowledge management as a core competence will achieve a sustainable competitive advantage in global supply chain competition.

References

Culbertson, Scott, Ike Harris, and Steve Radosevich (2005), "Synchronization—HP Style," *Supply Chain Management Review*, March, 24–31.

Gangtak, O. (2000), "Knowledge Management Vision in Korea," *Korea-US Joint Workshop on Digital Libraries*, August.

Jensen, Michael C. (2001), "Corporate Budgeting Is Broken—Let's Fix It," *Harvard Business Review*, November, 95–101.

Nonaka, Ikujiro (1991), "The Knowledge Creating Company," *Harvard Business Review*, November–December, 96–104.

Nonaka, Ikujiro (1994), "A Dynamic Theory of Organizational Knowledge Creation," *Organization Science*, 5 (1), 14–37.

7

Process Orientation

Everth Larsson

Anders Ljungberg

Introductory Views on SCM and Processes

Most definitions of supply chain management (SCM) are characterized by Phrases such as "a chain of processes," "a network of processes," "a set of management processes," or "integrating and managing processes across the supply chain." Thus, it is safe to say that there are close relations between process orientation and SCM and supply chain orientation (SCO). The concepts of SCM and SCO are very much about coordination, cooperation, and integration, as are process management and process orientation. In books and papers treating SCM, processes are often mentioned or even play a main role—but without any definition or anything written that can contribute to the knowledge and understanding of the concept of processes. In this chapter, a **process** is defined as *a repetitively used network of activities linked in an orderly manner using information and resources for transforming "object in" into "object out," extending from the point of identification to that of the satisfaction of a customer's needs.*

The Heritage of the Function-Oriented Organization

To contribute to the understanding of what "process orientation" and a "process oriented organization" are, and to a certain extent also what each entails, it is of value to look at the aim of an organization and at traditional organizational forms. One of the most important tasks for top management is to create conditions for the organization to realize its objectives. If an organization resembles a large ship, what corresponds to the CEO? The traditional answer is probably the captain, but what role does the designer of the ship play? If the ship is 200 meters long and the rudder only 25 centimeters, what possibility does the captain have to turn the ship when needed? Of course, it also depends on the engine and other things, but the possibilities to turn the ship are more or less zero. The ship has not been *designed to fit its purpose*. In the same way, an organization must have an appropriate design in order to successfully and efficiently realize its objectives. It is the task of the management to design, establish, and develop a suitable infrastructure. The management is the designer of the organization.

An organization is, from the point of view of structure and functioning capability, to a large extent a result and a reflection of the surrounding world. The function-oriented and hierarchical organization was well fitted to its purpose, environment, and prevailing values when it was created 200 years ago or more, and it has also been successful in its different variants. But it is easy to be somewhat hesitant to extend this organizational model into the 21st century when one considers the following assumptions, which were the original basis for it:

- It is possible to identify small, specialized work assignments.
- Improvement of each assignment leads to improvement of the whole.
- There is always *one* best way to perform each assignment.
- Employees lack or have very little education.
- It is the task of the bosses to think.

The assumptions have very little to do with the realities of today. However, they are in accordance with the building stones of bureaucracy:

- Impersonal relations
- Management by rules of the work
- Functional specialization
- Hierarchical order
- Promotion according to technical competence

Assumptions and prerequisites like these have led to function-oriented and hierarchical organizations, where specialized divisions take care of their respective parts of the business. A number of transfers are done between areas of responsibility before a task is completed. The fragmented way of working requires bosses to coordinate and integrate.

To improve the function-oriented organization, a number of variants have been developed, like divisions, partial division organizations, matrix organizations, and project organizations. The differences are, however, not fundamental since they are all built on the same organizational paradigm. A common denominator for the types of organizations mentioned above can be described as the *function-based silo*, depending on the manner of working and acting. Another commonly used picture is one of walls, which illustrate the borders between an organization's

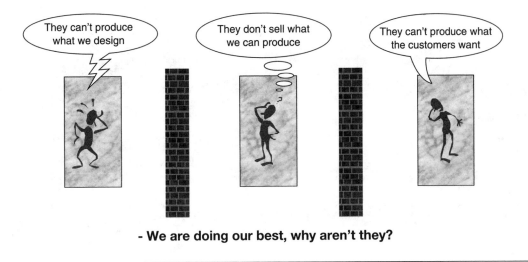

- **We are doing our best, why aren't they?**

Figure 7.1   Attitudes in a Function-Oriented Organization

divisions, functions, or equivalent factors. The picture might be perceived as over-explicit, but the walls really exist in a function-oriented organization (Figure 7.1). Cooperation requires border crossing, which makes cooperation artificial and unnatural.

In a function-oriented organization, the internal organization is a vertical one, and managers tend to focus on their own silo. This is in itself not surprising because they have been appointed specifically to take responsibility for their own silo. The business is managed, measured, and developed vertically. This also gives certain characteristics to the employees regarding both their values and their actions. In a function-oriented organization, the borders of responsibility are crossed too seldom, simply because there is nothing that encourages doing so. Instead, there are obstacles not only in the form of mental barriers but also in the form of accounting systems, division budgets, awarding systems, lack of information, measurement systems, quality systems, information flow, and even career paths. Outside the organization, there is the customer with a horizontal view of what he or she wants in the form of product or service, and this does not harmonize with the vertical view of the supplier. The customer is fully dependent on how well the supplier functions and the effectiveness and efficiency from a horizontal point of view.

Process Treatment in the Function-Oriented Organization

Managers in a function-oriented organization are normally only responsible for part of a process, with the next manager in the chain responsible for another part of the process and so on (Figure 7.2). Limits or borders to the responsibility of a

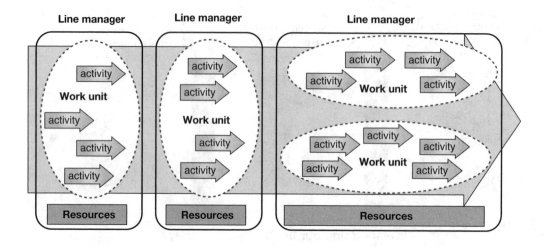

Figure 7.2   Split of Responsibility in a Function-Oriented Organization

certain manager can be quite illogical in relation to the overall process. It is also evident that the respective manager is expected to be competent in relatively different areas (management of processes, resources, and work). This may require essentially different skills than what was originally the basis of promotion of a manager to his current position.

It should be evident that the type of organization described above strikes a discordant note with processes and process orientation—not the least of which regards the demands of a comprehensive view, a customer focus, and cooperation across borders. This is especially the case in global SCM, where cooperation is needed not only across company borders internal to a company but also across different corporate cultures, different legal systems, different languages, different business ideas, and different strategies in a global supply chain.

There is ample reason to say that everybody in a function-oriented organization does his work—and that is the problem! The work is defined in a manner that in reality does not favor the organization itself, its objectives, its employees, or its customers.

Different Processes

Processes should mirror and be adapted to the specific organization's business strategies, purpose, environment, and customers. Processes are perhaps the main differentiator between competing organizations. They are hard to copy in their entirety. Physical products, for instance, are normally easy to copy. Industrial facilities, equipment, and manpower can be bought. Even if there is a lot to learn by comparing the similarities between organizations, there is also a lot to gain by emphasizing the differences between organizations in a more and more global marketplace.

Processes can be divided into three different types, depending on purpose and level of detail: **core processes, support processes,** and **management processes.** *Core processes* can be described as follows:

- Processes whose activities enable goods and services to reach an external customer
- Processes that realize the business goal
- Processes that together constitute the foundation of the business (if one process is taken away the business falls)

The task of identifying or deciding on the core processes of an organization is partly subjective. The combination of core processes can furthermore vary over time depending on situation and needs.

It may also be fitting to discuss what a core process does *not* constitute. A core process is not another name for a function. A process satisfies a *need*, whereas the aim of functions is mainly to take care of a special *competence,* which is then used in one or more processes. Most core processes need several different types of competence, which means they are normally cross-functional. The process "satisfy customer's future demands" (develop new products) is cross-functional because it makes use of design competence, production competence, market competence, and procurement competence.

Furthermore, core processes ought to be separated from support and management processes, respectively. *Support processes* are needed to make the core processes work as well as possible, but they are not critical to the success of the company. *Management processes* are used to control and coordinate the core and support processes. Examples of support processes could include invoicing customers, creating forecasts, planning production, and budgeting. Management processes could include establishing directions for the organization, showing the direction, creating conditions, and follow-up and correction.

A core process map can be an important complement or even alternative to the traditional organizational chart, because it gives much more information about what the business is all about and how it creates value.

A Business Viewed as a System

A general and system-oriented model of the overall structure of process-based business development takes its origin in the following dimensions:

- Business idea
- Processes
- Organizational structure
- Leadership and work management
- Competency and resources
- Supporting systems and structures
- Organizational culture and values

Business Idea. Before processes are focused, the foundations of the business need illuminating. Examples of questions are these: What is the business idea? Who are the customers? How do we create value for them? If attention is not paid to the business idea, there is a risk of building "straight roads between the wrong points," meaning that the processes will only be improved from an internal perspective.

Processes. The business idea is realized first of all via a combination of core processes. When the business idea is defined and understood, there are prerequisites of identifying and focusing the core processes. It is the system of core processes that creates value for customers and stakeholders, that creates deliverables to be invoiced, and that to a high degree determines the effectiveness and consumption of resources. The core processes should, therefore, serve as a starting point for the design and development of the organizational structure, competence and resources, leadership and work management, supporting systems and structures, and organizational culture and values.

Organizational Structure. The organization should be designed so that the whole will be fully process-supporting regarding boundaries, roles and positions, responsibilities, and authorities. The organizational structure should facilitate an efficient use of the processes.

Leadership and Work Management. This dimension deals with how people are managed, how they work, and how they work together. Even if the design and structure of the processes are well thought through and the organizational structure supports the processes, there can still be obstructions to an efficient execution. The leadership and related degree of empowerment should also be process oriented as these have a major impact on the performance. It takes a process-oriented way of both leading and performing the work to liberate the full potential of processes and coworkers.

Competency and Resources. Processes and organization must harmonize with the competency of the persons carrying through the work in the processes. Important issues at hand are which competency is accessible, how best to take care of this in the business, and how to maintain and develop it. Furthermore, one might need to ask which competencies are needed now and in the future. Competence-based resource allocation is also a key feature for increasing the value of a process-oriented enterprise.

Supporting Systems and Structures. Supporting systems and structures mean different types of information technology (IT) systems, management systems (including ISO 9000 and ISO 14000), organizational measurement systems (such as Balanced Scorecard), reward systems, career paths, and calculation systems.

Organizational Culture and Values. The last step in process-based business development is by no means the least important or the one that takes the shortest time. This last step might very well be, regarding time, the largest. It might seem wrong to make such extensive changes as the earlier steps imply, without having created the mental maturity needed in the organization. There are, of course, no impediments to begin to affect the values at an earlier stage; in fact, it is desirable to do so. Waiting with the implementation of larger changes until the mental maturity has appeared in the whole organization may involve too great a risk. Besides, it can be the changes themselves that, in the end, convince people of the value of the underlying ideas.

All dimensions must be in harmony with each other for the enterprise to function satisfactorily in its entirety. One of the major challenges when developing an enterprise is to understand these dimensions, and the relations between them, and to be able to coordinate their development.

During a transition period, the business will be between "the old" function-oriented organization and "the new" process organization. Some systems, structures, and values will harmonize with the former organization and some with the new. To introduce the new but still keep the old, which quite a few organizations aim at or do in practice, implies that instability and disharmony are made permanent. As long as the harmony is not regained, there is a large risk that the change will fail.

Elements in a Process-Oriented Organization

In the process organization, processes are the natural basis for how the business is viewed, designed, managed, carried out, and developed.

How the Business Is Viewed. The process organization is built on a new organizational paradigm, which encompasses the organization and its employees as well as the business environment. The business is first of all viewed as a system of value-adding processes. The change of paradigm can be described by some major transformations as follows:

- From functions to processes (This does not mean that the tasks of the functions disappear but that they are done in a different manner.)
- From profit to performance
- From products to customers
- From inventory to information
- From transactions to relationships (Christopher 2004)

The Design of the Business. Processes are the basis for how the organization as a whole is designed. Functions do not retain their previous form. The power to lead and develop the business has been taken away from them. On the other hand, they still develop competent staff and resources. The functions have been transformed to competence and resource centers. As providing competence is a matter of survival, their status is high, probably higher than in a function-oriented organization.

The Management of the Business. The leadership presupposed in the process organization is unfortunately an area that has still not been sufficiently researched.

A "modern" cooperative leadership is necessary. It is important to establish that there is a **process owner** who is responsible for each process, including structure, suitability, effectiveness and efficiency, development, and strategy. **Resource owners** are responsible for the different resources or competence centers and their development. **Team leaders** leading cross-functional teams are responsible for the work.

If we use a road as a metaphor for a process, the process owner is the one with responsibility that the road is straight, fit for use, without hindrances, in good condition, permitting the required speed. The resource owner is responsible for the vehicles, drivers, and other forms of equipment and people using the road. Each journey is taken care of by the team leader. Sometimes, the journeys can be divided into groups (segmentation according to customers, products, geographical area, etc.), where you can talk about a business owner responsible for each group.

The Carrying Out of the Business. As mentioned earlier, cross-functional teams carry out the operational work.

The Development of the Business. Development takes place from a comprehensive perspective on both the short- and the long-term perspective.

Designing the Process-Oriented Organization

A process can be compared to a *road,* a structure that can be used repetitively. As a process can start with a customer need and end with customer satisfaction, the road starts at "Needville" and ends at "Satisfactionville." Seeing processes as value-adding structures is the number one key to successful process development and process orientation.

To better understand the process concept and the drivers behind it, let us first see what it looks like in a *function-oriented* organization. Being responsible for a typical function in a function-oriented organization also means being responsible for a certain part of the process (road). A manager of a function is rarely responsible for an entire core process from customer need to customer satisfaction.

To sum up, each functional manager is responsible for a part of the road, a part of the journey, and the related resources. If we relate to the image discribed above but clear out all the details, we could end up with an image as seen below.

Before possible ways of dividing this work load are discussed, it is beneficial to reflect on some principles for organizational design. The purpose of all organizational designs, expressed in the form of organizational charts, is to do the following:

- **Differentiate**—to separate and give attention to various roles and areas of responsibility and authority. Each area on an organizational chart can be seen as an expression that "this is a key area for our business well worth a dedicated manager, measurements, goals, budgets, etc." Also related to an area of responsibility are measurements and rewards to secure that the area is given full attention.

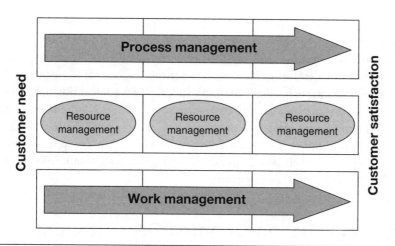

Figure 7.3   The Process-Oriented Organization, Horizontal Approach

- **Integrate**—to make the organizational design complete by combining and relating the differentiated parts into a suitable totality. The end result can be seen as an expression of the attitude that "this is the way we like to relate our preferred managerial areas."

A typical function-oriented organization has found that a key entity to differentiate in the organizational chart is the functions. Each function manager gets his or her share of the process, resources, and work execution. The dominating perspective is vertical rather than horizontal. An alternative way of dividing the workload is found if a horizontal and process-oriented perspective is applied. A horizontal perspective provides for three management areas (Figure 7.3): *process management, resource management,* and *work management.*

The person responsible for management of a certain process has already been discussed as the *process owner* and is by far the most well-known role in a process organization. *Resource owners* work at liberating, developing, and distributing the brainpower that exists in the different parts of the organization. To take care of and continuously develop competence for continuous competitiveness and development is important, as is also allocating the right competence at the right quantity to the right place at the right time at the right cost. The work of the resource owners has a strategic role that is not second to that of the process owners.

The resource owner is the manager of a *competence center.* The competence center can be regarded as a pool of talents or a knowledge bank from which personnel are distributed to the different processes. Thus, no operative work is performed in the center. This is performed in full in the processes. In the centers, personnel are educated, supported, and developed to make possible efficient work in the processes. Resource owners have three different and major areas of responsibility: competence development, competence allocation, and personnel administration.

Work managers (team leaders) are, as described earlier, the people who combine the process structure provided by the process owners and the resources provided by the resource owners to create the result of the process. The work managers are basically each responsible for a single "journey" along the process.

In a large organization there can be a complex structure of "process users" in the form of order owners, project leaders, and persons responsible for segments. Note that the work manager normally has a title specific for the actual situation. The title often reflects a way of segmenting customers, products, or a combination of them.

Depending on the situation, the number of people involved in managing a process can be significant. The work of these people and the group they represent cannot, in turn, be unmanaged. The person responsible for a number of work managers is often called the *business owner*.

Is SCM Possible in Function-Oriented Organizations?

A prerequisite to be able to see SCM as an application of the process view is knowledge and understanding not only of SCM but also of the process concept. Throughout history, industrial and organizational improvement activities have mostly been concentrated on single and isolated tasks, activities, departments, functions, or companies. The approach has been strongly oriented to the organization chart and the concept of division of labor, a concept—as mentioned earlier—developed more than 200 years ago under circumstances fundamentally different from the situation of today. The organization chart and its related roles is the natural starting point for the manager's improvement efforts. This means that the way areas of responsibility are defined determines the type and magnitude of changes within the area.

What, then, does an organization chart look like for a global supply chain with at least three different companies or other types of organizational units, each function oriented? This is not only a matter of structure description—the employees are hired to fit well in such a functional "silo-oriented" organization, and their rewards, career possibilities, objectives and targets, education, and working experiences are all adapted to the hierarchical and function-oriented paradigm. People working in a function-oriented organization are used to having a "vertical focus," which is quite different from the "horizontal focus" in a global supply chain.

Even in a single company, the integration or cooperation across department borders is difficult. How difficult would it then be with three or more units that are different not only from an organizational point of view but also maybe from geographical, cultural, industry, and size perspectives? It is further complicated by the fact that the same company normally is a member of several supply chains; probably with different commitments, strategies, objectives, roles, importance, risk, and reward agreements.

How should the areas of responsibility and authority be defined and distributed in the chain? Can and should the responsibility for development and practical operations be separated? Does it look principally different at the strategic, tactical, and operational levels? What about the information and communication systems? Even in the same company, there are often a large number of IT systems.

Who manages and controls the supply chain? The question about who is in charge of respective global supply chain processes is often left unanswered. In the process concept, a process owner is responsible for each of the processes, and there are also resource owners responsible for their respective resource or competence centers.

Should Processes Be Company-Specific or Standard?

One advantage of beginning with standardized processes on a company level is that they can be compared with or benchmarked against the corresponding processes at another company or organization. On the other hand, you do not really have to understand the concept of process to do this. It is much more difficult to develop the process, and the lack of understanding might affect those in the organization who are employed to work in the process. Lack of understanding decreases motivation, and there is a risk of people making more mistakes.

The most well-known standardized model is probably the SCOR (Supply Chain Operations Reference) model developed by the Supply Chain Council. It works with five different types of processes: Plan, Source, Make, Deliver, and Return. It is a tool mainly intended to study physical flows like the order process.

Why, then, concentrate on company- or organization-specific processes? The main reason is that what really determines a company's competitive power is the main or core processes, so it is important to identify, map, understand, and develop these core processes. Using a simplified, standardized "one size fits all" process model of the company's relatively few, but most important, core processes can hardly give many competitive advantages.

There are, however, cases where standardized processes are appropriate. This is true for certain management processes in a company that are not core. For instance, department-specific processes for invoicing may not give any competitive advantage to the company. Even if certain department heads might argue that their own business is different from others, it is probably not worthwhile to have a department-specific support process for such processes as invoicing or recruitment of personnel. Then it is probably better to try to design standard processes and, if needed, change working habits to fit the processes.

How to Make SCM Work

First of all, it is not sufficient to talk about management at a general level; *somebody* has to be in charge. If we suppose that no other changes are made, each core process over the whole supply chain must have a process owner assigned to it. The process owner is responsible for development and management of the process from a comprehensive point of view and for optimizing the total result of the process in the long run. The overall objectives of the process owner are to confirm the relevance of the process, optimize the efficiency of the process, and create prerequisites for a flexible process. The process owner has responsibility for tasks like formulating the strategy of the process, development of the process, designing a measurement system, mapping and analysis, and implementation of improvements.

More or less in parallel with the appointment of process owner, the process in question must be identified and mapped. Mapping normally takes its point of origin in the products or services created and then shows what this network looks like and what happens from beginning to end. Remember that mapping can be carried through either from a transaction point of view (e.g., by following the flow of material in a manufacturing process) or from a value chain point of view (e.g., by following how customer value is created). Unfortunately, these two perspectives will give completely different maps.

Mapping can be done at different levels of detail. It is important, but sometimes difficult, to decide at which level of detail. The actual mapping work can also be time-consuming and difficult because the people involved may not agree on reality! It is important to involve people from various organizational levels in the mapping work to support reliability and to facilitate understanding and later implementation.

There are different ways to collect information aimed at forming a basis for the process map. A "walk-through" means that one or more people literally walk through the process, make observations, conduct interviews, and document the process graphically. Figure 7.4 is an example of a simple, yet relevant, map.

Measurement, Analysis, and Development

When the processes are identified and mapped, it is time for *measurement*. A popular saying is "what is measured gets done." Looking at what is often measured in companies, one is tempted to say, "Can it really be this bad!" Shortages in traditional measurement include the following:

- Too much focus is on financial issues.
- Measures are too internally focused.
- Measures are too historical and give too little information about the future.
- Measures are structured according to the organization's functional needs.
- The focus is on input instead of output.

What is important is to develop a measurement system aimed at creating knowledge. A process-oriented measurement system is different from a function-oriented one in design as well as in implementation. Process-oriented measures are much more interrelated and customer focused, and they give a more comprehensive view.

When analyzing and developing processes, it is necessary to prioritize the processes that are most important and add most economic value. There are a number of relatively simple but efficient methods for process analysis:

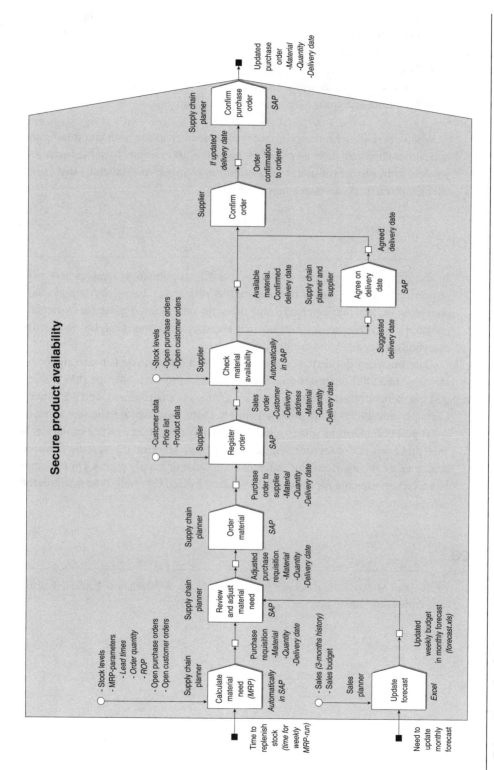

Figure 7.4 Example of a Process Map

115

- Value analysis, where the activities can be divided into value-adding activities, non-value-adding activities, and waste
- Bottleneck analysis
- Process map analysis
- Process structure analysis
- Lead time analysis

When developing processes, on must to remember to use both continuous and radical development. Take a certain car model as an example. In some years, it is possible to implement minor, but continuous, changes. After a while, that is not enough; you have to develop a new model.

Conclusions

In the process concept, you also have specially appointed process owners with responsibility to take care of the cross-border operations. In a global supply chain consisting of function-oriented companies, no one is responsible for horizontal cooperation. Of course, you can say that everybody is responsible, but in practice everybody is normally the same as nobody.

Core processes decide the competitiveness and differentiate between successful and less successful organizations. Should the core processes then be standardized and independent of strategy, business idea, business environment, and customers? Certainly not. Individually designed supply chain processes are the way to reach "next practice" ahead of what could be reached by using best practice in standardized processes and subprocesses, not taking into account the specific features, strategies, or success factors of different companies or supply chains. On the other hand, certain noncore processes might be standardized very well, at least within the same organization.

Reference

Christopher, M. (2004), *Logistics and Supply Chain Management.* Harlow, England: Pearson Professional Education.

PART II

Managing the Functions

8

Marketing and Sales Management

Thomas E. DeCarlo

William L. Cron

Many organizations are finding that sales force changes are needed to match the needs of more demanding customers in an increasingly competitive world. Giant retailers such as Wal-Mart are leveraging electronic data technology and are requiring manufacturer sales forces to assume responsibility for *just-in-time* inventory control, ordering, billing, sales, and promotion. Other companies have found that renting an office in a key customer's headquarters building and stationing an account manager there helps to enhance the relationship and increase customer profitability. These types of innovations have necessitated changes in the way sales forces are organized, compensated, developed, and measured. Our goal in this chapter is to explain how to make effective sales force and sales program decisions for maximum marketing efficiency and effectiveness. Figure 8.1 illustrates the sequence of marketing, sales force, and sales program decision making.

As depicted in Figure 8.1, Level 1 decisions—business and marketing strategies—are made by top management along with the participation of the top sales executive. Level 2 decisions focus on implementing a firm's business and marketing strategy. Given that strategy implementation is likely to be cross-functional, top sales executives along with managers from other functional areas in the firm are typically involved in these decisions. Level 3 decisions are largely under the control of the sales management team.

Figure 8.1 also shows that business and marketing strategy and implementation decisions affect sales force program decisions. That is, strategy and implementation

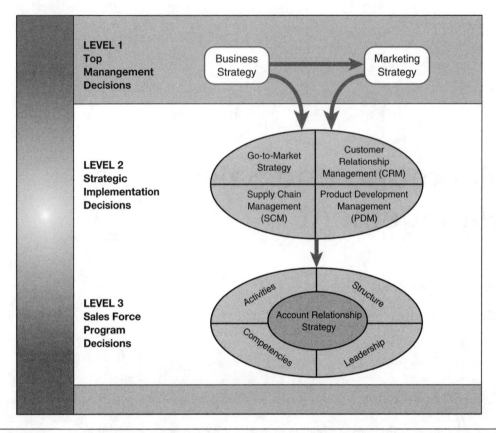

Figure 8.1   The Sales Force Decision Sequence

decisions provide the context within which sales program decisions are made and implemented. Our intent is not to fully explain business strategy. Instead, we offer an overview of marketing strategy, while focusing on four-strategy implementation decisions (see the "Strategic Implementation Decisions section") because they influence a firm's sales force program more directly (Dalrymple, Cron, and DeCarlo 2004).

Marketing Strategy

Marketing strategy is the set of integrated decisions and actions a business undertakes to achieve its marketing objectives by addressing the value requirements of its customers. As such, marketing strategy is concerned with decisions related to market segmentation and target marketing, as well as the development and communication of a positioning strategy.

Effective marketing programs necessitate a customer focus that requires companies to segment and target selected markets (or customers, or both) to maximize the returns on their marketing efforts. Market segmentation is generally defined as aggregating customers into groups that (1) have one or more common characteristics,

(2) have similar needs, and (3) will respond similarly to a marketing program. Target marketing refers to the selection and prioritizing of segments or specific customers on which the company will focus its marketing efforts.

These marketing decisions have important implications for how salespeople should set priorities and allocate their time among different customers. Sometimes the sales force must even be restructured to effectively implement a target market program. Hewlett-Packard (HP), for example, decided to target companies with three characteristics: significant worldwide presence, large size, and high growth potential. These accounts were selected for the Global Accounts Program and were staffed with a separate technical and selling team to provide added attention and sales support.

Positioning Strategy

Having settled on specific marketing goals and identified the target market(s), the next step in the planning process is to develop and implement a positioning strategy based on product, price, distribution, and promotion decisions. Positioning occurs in the mind of the consumer and refers to how the consumer perceives the product, brand, and company vis-à-vis competitors. Some of the fundamental questions customers ask about brands are (1) Who are you? (brand identity); (2) What are you? (brand meaning); (3) What do I think or feel about you? (brand responses); and (4) What kind, and how much, of a connection would I like to have with you? (brand relationships).

Achieving a clear and unique brand position in the customer's mind is accomplished by designing the proper marketing mix (i.e., product, promotion, distribution, and price). A significant change in any of these elements usually has ramifications for the sales force program. It was found in a recent study, for instance, that when a company chooses to introduce a new product, the most likely sales program changes are a change in sales quotas, the compensation plan, and the sales support material the sales force has at its disposal (Wotruba and Rochford 1995).

In some cases, repositioning involves helping supply chain partners reposition themselves as well. As network-related physical products such as switches and routers have become increasingly commoditized, margins for suppliers and resellers of such products have declined. In this environment, Cisco Systems, a leading provider of such products, found it necessary to reposition itself as a company selling network-related solutions for leveraging voice-, video-, and data-based applications. To accomplish this repositioning, Cisco needed not only to redefine itself but also to help its more than 36,000 resellers redefine their business as providers of value-added network-based solutions. Resellers had to change from a transactional to a consultative selling approach. Cisco now helps each reseller partner identify its strengths so they can select appropriate target markets and then provides the reseller with the appropriate training, tools, and support to succeed in those target markets (Mitchell 2001).

Up to this point we have outlined Level 1 decisions and business and marketing strategy and discussed how these decisions affect the sales force. Although sales executives have a voice in Level 1 decisions, they have a much greater voice in Level 2 decisions, which focus on the implementation of an organization's strategy. Strategic implementation, or Level 2, decisions require cross-functional cooperation and coordination. Sales executives will likely work with top executives from finance, operations, logistics, engineering, customer service, and other areas of the organization in making these decisions. We now turn our attention to these critical Level 2 decisions.

Strategic Implementation Decisions

Strategic implementation decisions refer to a set of processes that organizations develop to create customer value and achieve a competitive advantage. Some of the fundamental decisions that most companies make with respect to these Level 2 processes involve (1) how customers are accessed (*go-to-market strategy*), (2) how new offerings are developed and existing products improved (*product development management*), (3) how physical products are created and delivered to the customer (*supply chain management* [SCM]), and (4) how customer relationships are enhanced and leveraged (*customer relationship management*). Although we discuss each of these decisions in sequence, it is important to realize that decisions in one area often have an impact on the other areas.

Go-to-Market Strategy

A world-class sales force is a powerful resource for any company, but the sales force is only one of the options companies have for going to market. In addition to a direct sales force, advertising and promotions, value-added resellers, the Internet, and telemarketing can all play a role in connecting a supplier with its customer base. For many companies, all these activities must be performed to attract and retain customers. A go-to-market strategy defines who performs these activities and for which customers. The process for determining a go-to-market strategy consists of answering four major questions:

1. What is the best way to segment the market?

2. What are the essential activities required by each segment?

3. What non-*face-to-face* selling methods should perform these activities?

4. What face-to-face selling participants should be used?

Segmenting the Market

An important first step in any go-to-market strategy is to identify market segments. As described earlier when discussing marketing strategy, market segmentation involves identifying different groups of customers with similar characteristics, product needs, and responsiveness to marketing efforts. Since segments are identified in developing an overall marketing strategy, the relationship between overall marketing strategy and go-to-market strategy becomes fairly evident.

Customer segments and go-to-market strategies vary depending on the product sold. Adult diapers and baby diapers are very similar in how they are manufactured but have very different go-to-market strategies. Most adult diapers are sold in bulk to nursing homes via distributors and with very little advertising. Most baby diapers are sold at retail with massive advertising support.

A number of factors can be used to segment a market. Some of the typical factors used in developing a go-to-market strategy include the industry (What business is the customer in?), customer potential (What are the potential revenues of the prospect?), buying process (Who is in the buying center? Do we have access to the decision makers?), and geography (Where is the customer located? Can we adequately service this customer?).

For purposes of developing a go-to-market strategy, it is important to generate groups of customers whose members require similar customer attraction and retention activities. For example, some segments require significant prospecting and attraction activities because the customers are still learning about the offering, whereas other segments require considerable servicing activities because they are already current customers.

Essential Activities

From the first time a prospect is identified to the first time a customer hears about a product, to the first sale, to the last service and system upgrade call, many activities must successfully take place. The activities considered essential to serve a customer properly can be divided into four groups: interest creation, prepurchase, purchase, and postpurchase. These activities roughly mirror the typical selling cycle. It is important to note that these activities are recursive, as good postpurchase activities and support can lead to interest creation, building a continuing relationship with the customer.

Interest creation activities include all the ways customers can learn about the benefits of the product and the company. After all, only customers who want to buy will buy. Specific selling activities involved in interest creation include prospecting, generating leads, creating awareness and interest, and providing information about the company's products and services. The prepurchase phase is different from interest creation in that customers are actively considering and evaluating competitive product offerings. Essential activities in the prepurchase phase include explaining features and benefits, qualifying prospects, assessing customer needs, cooperating in problem solving, and demonstrating company and product capabilities. The purchasing phase includes the set of activities culminating in a purchase. As such, it is the set of activities most likely to involve direct salespeople. Activities in this phase include negotiating, bidding, finalizing terms and conditions, and writing proposals. It is important to note that the essential work does not conclude with the purchase. The postpurchase activities may include delivery, installation, servicing of products, addressing customer questions that need answering, providing information about new features, and collecting payment.

Go-to-Market Options

Once the set of essential activities has been identified, the next question is who should participate in performing these activities. Figure 8.2 provides several go-to-market participants, including the Internet, telemarketing, advertising, promotion, direct mail, and face-to-face selling (including a direct sales force, independent agents, distributors, integrators, and alliances). Most large companies access their markets using more than one touch point. To successfully defend their customer base, expand market coverage, and control costs, companies are adopting multiple methods for reaching different target markets.

The combination of go-to-market participants that is most appropriate for each customer segment and type of essential activity depends on a number of factors, including efficiency and effectiveness. The efficiency of a marketing instrument refers to its ability to generate customer contacts for the money spent. On the other hand, the more results created from the number of customers contacted, the more effective the marketing instrument. The following is a brief discussion of the major non-sales-force go-to-market options: advertising and promotion, telemarketing, and the Internet.

Advertising and Promotion. Advertising and promotion consists of instruments such as broadcast media, magazines, trade publications, newspapers, and direct mail. These strategies are typically very efficient in that they are inexpensive per customer contact. Some estimates indicate that it costs around 32 cents per contact to reach business markets through specialized business publications (Penton Media 1997). Direct mail is estimated to cost only $1.68 per business contact. Although advertising and direct mail are efficient, they are not always very effective. This is why companies generally use these marketing tools to raise awareness and interest

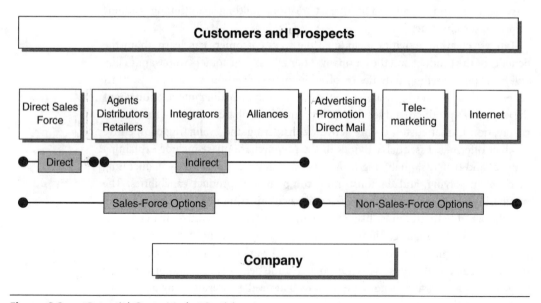

Figure 8.2   Potential Go-to-Market Participants

and then use other means to drive purchase behavior. Consider HP's go-to-market efforts in the introduction of a new printer. First, HP sent sales kits to customers and dealers, followed by a mailing program and telemarketing. The company then sent its sales reps to the dealerships to make follow-up calls and provide management briefings. This marketing program highlights the importance of having a coordinated effort among advertising, sales promotions, channels of distribution, and the sales force.

Telemarketing. Telemarketing refers to customer contacts using telecommunications technology for personal selling without direct, face-to-face contact. Business-to-business telemarketing is estimated to cost $31.16 per qualified contact. Given that U.S. firms are generating sales in excess of $100 billion yearly and the average sale is approximately $1,000, it is not surprising that business-to-business telemarketing is growing at a rate of 30% to 40% a year (Direct Marketing Educational Foundation 1995). Corporations such as IBM, Procter & Gamble, Chase Manhattan Bank, and Union Pacific Railroad have all developed effective telemarketing systems.

Companies are also using telemarketing to perform a variety of essential activities. Firms such as IBM are using telemarketing to handle the prepurchase and purchase activities for their smaller customers. Other companies are using telemarketing to perform the early activities in the selling process. One leading supplier of computer data storage equipment uses telemarketing to generate and qualify leads targeting larger customers, and a special technical support group handles post-sales-service activities for these large customers.

The Internet. Extensive use of the Internet to gather information and make purchases is a key business go-to-market development. The Internet can be used in all phases of essential activities that need to be performed. Its advertising and streaming qualities can be used on a company's Web site to create interest. Prepurchasing and purchasing activities are accomplished on e-commerce buying sites. Automated reordering, tracking of transactions, billing information, and other posttransaction activities are also efficiently and effectively executed on the Internet. Although the Internet costs a little more per contact than direct mail, overall it is more effective at generating the desired customer behaviors. With continued technological advances, the Internet's effectiveness is likely to continue to increase.

Many companies have found that the Internet is able to increase the effectiveness of their sales forces. HP, for example, has aggressively pursued electronic channels with HP Shopping Village (for consumers), HP Commerce Center (for businesses buying from authorized resellers), and Electronic Solutions (for contract customers). Thanks to a tight integration between HP's own intranet and resellers' home pages, HP takes the customer's order and kicks the order over to the reseller's home page. The reseller completes the order, ships the product, and gets the commission. In this way, HP helps to alleviate the conflict that often arises when selling through multiple channels.

Even companies that are 100% committed to the Internet are finding that they need to understand their customers better. An executive at Intel noted, "Today we notice that trying to get our customers to purchase through the Web has not worked. But we do know that buyers will make their purchasing decisions because of the Internet. They continue to want to talk to our salespeople about price— maybe if we had a 'haggle' button on the Web, they'd use it" (Strout 2001, p. 39).

Face-to-Face Selling Alternatives

After deciding that a face-to-face sales force should perform some of the essential activities, a company must still address another question. Should the selling be performed by a direct company sales force, a selling partner, or some combination? The main outsourcing options available to most companies are agents, resellers, integrators, and alliances.

Independent Sales Agents. An important alternative to the direct sales force is to hire independent sales agents (sometimes referred to as manufacturer's reps, reps, or brokers) to perform the selling function. Independent sales agents are not employees but rather independent businesses given exclusive contracts to perform the selling function within specified geographic areas. Unlike distributors, they take neither ownership nor physical possession of the products they sell and are always compensated by commission. Agents are often used to develop new markets through a combination of persuasive selling skills and technical competence. This technical competence exists in part because agents typically handle five to eight noncompeting but related product lines they know fairly well and sell to similar types of buyers. In certain situations, independent sales agents represent a cost-effective alternative to a direct sales force.

Resellers. Resellers are channel members, retailers, and distributors, who take title to the offerings they sell to end users. They perform many functions within the channel, including warehousing, breaking bulk, extending credit, and providing information, but one of their primary functions is to market their suppliers' offerings to their own customers. It is in this capacity that they function as a possible substitute in performing the activities of a supplier's sales force by calling directly on the end user. Distributors have many, even hundreds, of salespeople calling on thousands of customers, in effect multiplying the efforts of the supplier's salesperson.

Integrators. In a number of industries, new channel members, called integrators, have arisen. An integrator is a service supplier unaffiliated with specific products, whose advice the end customer has sought regarding a complex choice. Examples of integrators are personal financial advisers, building contractors, and systems integrators. Because they typically do not take possession of the supplier's offering, as do distributors, and are not under contractual agreement with a supplier, integrators represent a new and complex situation. Since the end user seeks out the integrator's advice, a supplier must sell to the integrator as well as to the end customer. On the other hand, integrators are also considered competitors to the extent that they may advise clients to purchase a competing offering. At a minimum, they have changed the role of the supplier's salesperson in that they represent a new and powerful buying influence.

Alliances. An increasingly popular alternative for accessing markets is to establish an alliance with another organization in a joint venture to sell products to specific markets. Although this strategy has often been used to expand globally, it is also used in situations where there is an enormous profit potential but a limited time period in which to capture the profits. For example, there is often pressure in the pharmaceutical industry to fully penetrate the market as soon as possible. Physicians have consistently rated Pfizer as one of the best sales forces in the industry. When Parke-Davis launched its blockbuster cholesterol-lowering drug, Lipitor, it entered into an alliance for Pfizer's sales force to perform many of the essential sales activities. Soon after, Searle sought Pfizer's assistance in selling its arthritis medication, Celebrex.

The number of different go-to-market arrangements continues to mushroom. The net effect has been extremely important to the sales force and sales management. First, many large firms have reduced the size of their field sales forces by focusing them on only certain essential activities and on medium- and large-size accounts. Second, efforts to coordinate the various participants have affected the sales force. IBM, for example, attempts to limit the direct competition between its value-added resellers and its direct sales force by crediting 85% of the volume generated by resellers in the salesperson's territory against the salesperson's annual sales quota. Third, valuable company resources must be allocated to the various channel partners. In the commercial airline industry, for example, one of the biggest challenges is allocation of passenger seat inventory to Internet sellers, travel agencies, and bulk buyers, such as corporate customers. Airlines are finding that their *distressed* inventory is a valuable commodity to resellers because of the market draw potential. Depending on one's view, this may be a marketing decision, but this sort of channel allocation has huge ramifications for the sales organization as well.

When designing a sales force program, management also needs to consider the interactions and relationships that the sales force should have with other functional areas within the organization. The nature of these interactions depends on the business processes that an organization develops to create customer value. The three core processes that successful firms leverage to create customer value—SCM, product development management, and customer relationship management—are illustrated in Figure 8.1. Given the focus on global supply chain issues in this book, we limit our discussion to the role of the sales force in the SCM process.

Supply Chain Management

In recent times, many companies have experienced the whiplash of too much or too little inventory to satisfy demand, missed production schedules, and ineffectual transportation and delivery schedules. To get a handle on the problem, companies are turning to SCM to make sure the products are available at the right time, at the right place, and in the right form and condition. Fundamental to this perspective is recognizing that a supply chain is not a linked series of one-on-one relationships between buyers and sellers but a synchronized network or ecosystem involving a supplier's own suppliers as well as downstream customers and their distributors, brokers, carriers, and final customers. The magnitude of the opportunity in SCM is suggested by U.S. statistics indicating that companies spend annually over $500 billion transporting raw materials and finished goods and another $375 billion on material handling, warehousing, storage, and holding inventory ("U.S. Logistics Closing on Trillion Dollar Mark," 1998).

How is the sales force involved in SCM? Historically, the sales force's involvement has been largely focused on issues dealing with ordering services, pricing, and terms management. These activities are typically at the tail end of the process when interfacing with the customer and channel members. However, the role of the sales force is undergoing an important shift as companies adopt more of a market-driven focus in SCM. This focus entails a change from sourcing inputs at the cheapest possible prices to designing, managing, and integrating the entire supply chain. The benefits to the end customer are becoming the driving objective, as opposed to internal goals such as delivery cycles, production schedules, and operating costs. The following paragraphs detail some of the important implications of SCM for the evolution of the sales force.

Knowledge of the Entire Upstream and Downstream Supply Chain. The experience of a leading consumer foods processor is a good example of the opportunity that is available to firms. This company makes a perishable product with no more than a 12-month shelf life. As a consequence, it was shipping the product 2 to 4 days after its manufacturing. What it did not know was that the distribution chain was exceptionally sluggish. It took anywhere from 2 to 12 months for the item to reach grocery shelves. Had there been trust and shared knowledge, the sales force would have conveyed this information to the home office.

Thinking Strategically About Partnering. Consider again the case of the food processor. The most important "success item" for this company's sales force should not have been generating more orders but working with distributors and retailers to decrease the time it took for the product to get to the grocery shelf. This necessitates talking to people other than the purchasing agents and merchandisers for their product, the traditional customer targets for this sales force. The sales force also needs to develop skills in process analysis and logistics operations.

Establishing Good Lines of Communications and Influence With Senior Corporate Management. In a benchmark study by consultants, Meritus-IBM, suppliers, and customers all recognized and emphasized the importance of openness, honesty, good communications, and mutual strategy creation. But the study found that in reality, suppliers and customers did not achieve openness and often did not even try. To understand why this is the case, consider the example of the retailer who planned a special promotion but refused to tell the beverage bottler which of its products was involved. Why would the retailer not share this information? Because they were afraid that details would leak out to other retail competitors. Probably every grocery retailer can readily recall an instance in which a competitor sabotaged a special promotion after finding out about it ahead of time. So the bottler had to build up inventory levels of several possible products and be prepared to incur the extra costs of fulfilling late-breaking orders. Naturally, after the promotion was launched, the bottler ended up with excess inventory for several weeks, or even months, in those products not selected for the promotion.

Although the sales force has been mostly involved in the downstream processes of the supply chain, high-performance global supply chains are not likely to come into existence without a fundamental change in the role and style of the sales force. Some companies have made such a commitment to SCM that they organized a separate specialized sales function, a customer general manager to address supply chain issues for specific customers. Although this organization may not be right for all companies, it does suggest the critical role the sales force can play in executing an SCM program.

Summary

Much of today's business literature focuses on Level 2 strategic implementation decisions that companies make to fully implement their overall strategies. It is not an exaggeration to suggest that these are the most important decisions a firm makes and are instrumental in determining the financial and competitive success of most organizations. As the previous discussion suggests, the sales force has an important stake in the success of a firm's global SCM process. Although top sales executives are likely to have an important voice in these decisions, these processes are cross-functional in nature and are likely to involve executives from across the organization. In other words, they are not likely to be solely or even largely under the control of a firm's sales management team.

We now turn our attention to the sales force program, or Level 3, decisions. There are two distinctions between Level 3 decisions and Level 2 decisions. First, the Level 3 sales force program is developed within the context of previous strategic decisions. That is, the various elements of the sales program are based on an understanding of the role of the sales force in the Level 2 decisions and the firm's overall objectives and strategies. For instance, a decision to emphasize global SCM usually necessitates a certain type of customer relationship that will also affect almost every element of the sales force program. Second, unlike in Level 2 decisions, the sales management team is largely responsible for developing and executing the sales program, although the sales force must still coordinate its decisions and actions with the other functional areas of the firm.

Sales Force Program Decisions

A sales force program is a tool for planning how the sales force will perform its role in achieving the firm's objectives. The major elements of the sales force program and how they are related are illustrated in Figure 8.3. The process begins with a careful consideration of the objectives and target markets specified in the marketing plan and estimates of the sales potential and forecast for various market segments. The next step in the process is deciding on an account relationship strategy, which involves determining the kinds of relationships the organization wants to build with its target markets. This decision is critical in that it influences and frames decisions with respect to the remaining four elements of the sales program. This is why the account relationship strategies are discussed next. The other elements of the sales force program—selling actions and behaviors, organizational structure, competency development, and leadership system—although important, are beyond the scope of this chapter.

Account Relationship Strategy

A firm's account relationship strategy refers to the type of relationship it intends to develop with its customers. This decision is the basis for how a firm acquires, maintains, and develops its customers. Most important, this decision determines which customers will be profitable because it calls for very different levels of investment into customer relationships. Some firms, for instance, take a transactional approach to customers because customers can quite easily switch their business from one supplier to another, depending on which one offers the lowest price. Other firms may establish relationships with their key customers involving a close integration of their operating processes. To further complicate the situation, many firms have decided to establish one type of relationship with certain customers and a different type of relationship with other customer groups. Selection of the right customers for the right type of relationship is strategic for both the customer and the supplier.

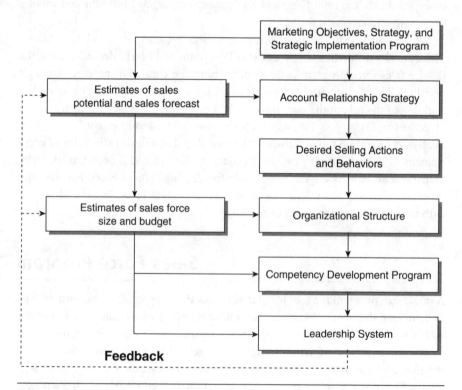

Figure 8.3   Sales Force Program

Account relationships may take a variety of forms, each having major implications for the sales force with respect to recruitment and selection, compensation, necessary competencies, and behaviors. Although many types of relationships are feasible and successful, for illustrative purposes we confine our discussion to three general types of account relationships: transactional, consultative, and enterprise.

Transactional Relationships

Most business-to-business transactions take place as part of an ongoing relationship between supplier and customer. A transactional relationship is one that is based on the need for a product of acceptable quality that is competitively priced with a convenient buying process for the customer. Often, a good transactional relationship involves a personal relationship between the buyer and the seller; this distinguishes it from other kinds of relationships. As a Scandinavian executive remarked, "You know, I personally have never bought anything from someone I didn't like." This is at the heart of a transactional relationship. This type of relationship, like all relationships, is based on a history of building trust, creating value, and meeting or exceeding the customer's expectations.

What types of firms are likely to emphasize a transactional-type customer relationship? A recent study sheds some light on this question. Based on a sample of companies from four countries, the study concluded that 68% of all firms focus on a transactional relationship with at least some of their customers. Consumer goods firms and large organizations are most likely to emphasize transactional-type relationships with their customers. Business-to-business firms are likely to employ different types of customer relationships, depending on customer needs and characteristics (Coviello et al. 2002). These alternative types of relationships are discussed next.

Consultative Relationships

A consultative relationship, a quite common relationship in industrial markets, is based on the customer's demand and willingness to pay for a sales effort that creates new value and provides additional benefits outside the product itself. Although suppliers may want to establish a consultative relationship with their customers, the success of consultative relationships rests on the ability of the salesperson or sales team to get very close to the customer and to intimately grasp the customer's business issues. In these relationships, the sales force attempts to create value for the customers by helping them understand their problems and opportunities in a new or different way. For example, in consultative relationships salespeople might help customers develop better solutions to problems than they would have discovered on their own. Other types of activities might include acting as the customer's advocate inside the supplier's organization and ensuring the timely allocation of resources to deliver customized or unique solutions to meet the customer's special needs.

The role of salespeople in consultative relationships is quite different from their role in transactional relationships. Much more time is spent learning the special needs of the individual customer and marshaling resources inside the supplier's company to meet those needs. The additional customer value resides in the nonproduct resources the salesperson brings to the relationship. This type of relationship also puts a premium on gathering and analyzing information about customers and their business issues. As a result, the selling process is usually longer, so the value of the customer to the supplier must be great enough to cover the higher selling costs. Thus, the relationship must usually be long term in nature for the customer equity to justify the investment in the customer. Note also that the salesperson must have a great deal of skill in gathering customer information, business acumen, and technical competency.

It is critical to choose the right situations in which to invest in consultative relationships. Experience indicates that a consultative relationship is most appropriate when one or more of the following conditions are present:

- The product or service can be differentiated from competitive alternatives.
- The product or service can be adapted or customized to the needs of the customer.
- The customer is not completely clear about how the product or service provides solutions or adds value.
- The delivery, installation, or use of the product or service requires coordinated support from the selling organization.
- The benefits of the product or service justify the relatively high cost of consultative relationships.

When these conditions are present, the sales force may have an opportunity to create customer value through consultative selling.

Enterprise Relationships

In recent years, customers have been downsizing their supplier base and replacing their myriad vendors with a very small number of possibly long-term relationships offered only to a select few suppliers. A widely quoted figure is that customers are working today with one-third fewer suppliers than they did 10 years ago. Combined with merger mania and market consolidation, the trend toward purchasing from fewer suppliers has resulted in customers capable of leveraging the volume of their purchases for enhanced services and cost-cutting opportunities. The response of many sellers to the emergence of very large and powerful customers has been to develop a system of enterprise relationships to meet the needs of their major customers better.

An enterprise relationship is one in which the primary function is to leverage any and all corporate assets of the supplier to contribute to the customer's strategic success. In such a situation, both the product and the sales force are secondary, and the customer must be of strategic importance to the selling organization. Adjectives to describe this category of relationships abound and include major, strategic, national, global, corporate, and key account programs. To achieve successful enterprise relationships, the supplier must deliver exceptional customer value while also extracting sufficient value from the relationship. This is always challenging, especially when the customer has worldwide needs. Thus, in enterprise relationships, there is an unusually high degree of intimacy resulting in immediate responsiveness from suppliers, sharing of information, radical empowerment of suppliers, and termination of the relationship as a remote and difficult option.

The activities of the sales force, the structure of the sales force, compensation, and even the sales philosophy differ for each type of relationship. For instance, as the buyer-seller relationship becomes more sophisticated and complex, the sales force's role as the primary point of contact between customer and supplier often diminishes. The focus also shifts from sales volume generation to management and maintenance of the relationship and the conflicts that are likely to arise over time. Studies have shown that enterprise type business-to-business relationships tend to focus on lowering the customer's overall operating costs. Industrial salespeople are typically trained in selling behavior and in how to present technical product features, not process and cost analysis. Salespeople are needed who can develop a thorough understanding of the customer's operations and the way costs are influenced by the supplier's products and customer interactions. Suppliers may also have to analyze whether their sales compensation system rewards salespeople for lowering customer costs, which usually requires a long-term perspective or short-term volume gains.

Cautionary Notes

In today's business world, strategic decisions can be quite complex. At IBM, for example, American Airlines is viewed as both a customer and a supplier; that is, American sells airline seats to IBM, but IBM is also a primary supplier of computer equipment and software to American. This type of relationship requires that the supplier's account manager navigate within his or her own procurement area as well as that of the customer.

A critical mistake is to assume that more investment in the customer relationship will automatically create a better relationship with improved results. The experience of a packaging materials manufacturer provides a typical example of this mistake. Because the manufacturer's costs were slightly higher than competitors' costs, they were losing business. This manufacturer decided that the best way to halt this decline was to upgrade their sales force. Their *packaging consultants* were charged with adding value to their products through providing customers with help and advice. The investment in upgrading the sales force, including retraining and recruiting, together with the development of a new marketing strategy, was in excess of $10 million. The average cost of each sales call increased to $890, and the average sales cost to acquire a new account was $112,000. It turned out, however, that most customers simply did not want advice or help. They needed packaging material, pure and simple, and that is all they were prepared to pay for. The company was soon taken over at a fire-sale price. Studies suggest that this case is not unusual. In fact, one study found that more than half the companies offering enterprise level relationships to their strategic customers rated the performance of these programs as "poor." Although the challenges of these programs are significant, the risks of revenue and profit loss associated with losing these accounts to competitors are often of even greater significance.

Summary

The sales force strategy and management structure should be planned and designed within the context of an organization's overall business and marketing strategy. Competitive advantage resides in the firm's ability to develop and perform a set of basic business processes for implementing a firm's business strategy. As the primary customer contact, the sales force and sales management are likely to play an important role in these processes. This chapter has given numerous examples of how sales force decisions are subject to and contribute to the overall strategy of the company and its marketing strategy within a global supply chain environment.

References

Coviello, Nicole, Roderick Brodie, Peter Danaher, and Wesley Johnston (2002), "How Firms Relate to Their Markets: An Empirical Examination of Contemporary Marketing Practices," *Journal of Marketing*, 66 (July), 33–46.

Dalrymple, Douglas J., William L. Cron, and Thomas E. DeCarlo (2004), *Sales Management*, 8th ed. Hoboken, NJ: Wiley.

Direct Marketing Educational Foundation (1995), *Economic Impact: U.S. Direct Marketing Today*. New York: Direct Marketing Educational Foundation.

Mitchell, Thomas (2001), "Cisco Resellers Add Value," *Industrial Marketing Management*, July/August, 15.

Penton Media (1997), *PRO Reports No. 303A*. Cleveland, OH: Penton Research Services.

Strout, Erin (2001), "Fast Forward," *Sales & Marketing Management*, December, 39.

"U.S. Logistics Closing on Trillion Dollar Mark," (1998), *Business Week*, December 28, 78.

Wotruba, Thomas and Linda Rochford (1995), "The Impact of New Product Introductions on Sales Management Strategy," *Journal of Personal Selling and Sales Management*, Winter, 35–51.

9

Product Management

Margaret Bruce

Lucy Daly

Kenneth B. Kahn

P roduct management oversees the product planning process, which encompasses conceptualizing, developing, finalizing, testing, commercializing, launching, sustaining, and eventually disposing company offerings to satisfy marketplace needs and achieve company objectives (Kahn 2000). Given the diversity of these activities, product management is inherently a broad and complex endeavor that mandates a boundary-spanning, cross-functional perspective toward product planning.

Traditionally focused on a company's existing products, product management focuses on both new and current products, where new products encompass conceptualizing, developing, producing, and testing efforts, and current products encompass sustaining and eventual disposal considerations. The remaining two processes of commercializing and launching cover the domains of both new and current products (Figure 9.1) and pose unique and pressing issues. These stem from an oversimplifying presumption that portrays a clean break between activities for new and current products and implies a stopping point for product development—something that is not really true. During and after launch, product managers continue to critique the new product to possibly broaden the brand or product line, as well as to delineate market trends and customer needs that future offerings should serve. Launch is, therefore, a focal topic requiring keen attention. As companies

AUTHORS' NOTE: The authors wish to thank the companies participating in the study as well as the Centre for Business Research, MBS, and EPSRC for their support.

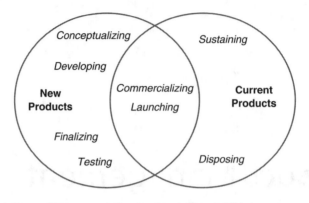

Figure 9.1   The Product Planning Process

expand beyond their domestic markets toward establishing a global presence, global product launch is emerging as a preeminent contemporary topic for product management. Accordingly, the present chapter details the role of product management, with particular emphasis on managing the global product launch. Two company case studies assist in illustrating these details and reinforcing key implications.

The Role of Product Management

Broadly speaking, product management has two broad responsibilities. First, product management is responsible for the planning activities related to the product or product line. Second, product management must get organizational support for marketing programs recommended in the product marketing plan. Product management thus represents a cross-functional, integrative function that links operations, supply chain, sales, and marketing, for example, into a strategically focused whole. Resource allocation is a critical component in these two responsibilities, as product management must determine and prioritize the resources needed to be successful. Naturally, not all products deserve the same resources, so partitioning of company resources across products is required. This leads to product mix coordination, which is the effort to balance the various products that the company offers to ensure that a particular type of product is not overwhelming the company's offerings or diluting customer interest. Product management should provide a product mix that provides the strongest market presence possible and where some or all the products in the mix are complementary in nature (thereby minimizing the potential for sales cannibalization among company products).

Marketing program support is also an important responsibility of product management. Working with market research and conducting its own analyses, product management should provide customer and market information to enlighten company management about competition and customer needs. With the driving objective to better focus and meet the intended target market(s) and refine current marketing programs, appraisal of company offerings (the product and its marketing program) is ongoing. Such appraisal evaluates the performance of current products (and services) to reveal their impact on the business, often in terms of cash flow. Decisions regarding product continuation, modification, or termination are the outcomes.

Note that although the term product is used in conjunction with product management, the term service could be easily substituted. This is because products and services have specifically become innately intertwined in today's global markets. For example, when buying a car, the product components of the car include chassis, engine, tires, and windows, but one also receives warranties on various components of the car and may receive special financing, be given a customer service telephone number for complaints, be offered in a special car servicing program (e.g., free oil changes and tire rotation). Together these items serve as the total package of what one would consider *buying a car*. Truly distinguishing between product and service elements is rather purposeless and in some instances misleading. Henceforth, the term *product* is used, but should be interpreted in the broadest sense as the company's offering to the marketplace.

Global Product Launch

Both normative and empirical research studies emphasize that the manner in which the product launch is managed predisposes the ultimate success or failure of the new product. Yet even with such understanding, many companies still mishandle, or even overlook, the necessary launch decisions. The issue of properly constructing, executing, and sustaining product launch strategy is particularly acute in light of the fact that launch spending can account for a significant, if not the major, proportion of overall product development costs. For example, the 1994 launch of the mobile network Orange was £7 million, reportedly three times the cost of developing the service (Baker and Hart 1999). As companies expand their markets globally and undertake more global product launch campaigns, cost and the need for meticulous planning are exacerbated. Global launch still encompasses those considerations associated with all product launches, but global product launch forces the product management function to now consider the compounding issues of language, cultural, and other issues.

Product Launch Strategy

An effective launch strategy clearly articulates product advantages to the target market (Hultink and Hart 1998) in the course of delineating price, distribution, market entry timing, marketing communications, and the launch budget (Garrido-Rubio and Polo-Redondo 2005). An effective launch strategy specifically requires product managers to ask a number of questions to focus on what, when, where, how, and why to launch. A main consideration during global launch is global logistics, with product managers needing to ensure that the product is available at the point of sale (POS) and in sufficient quantities to deliver on the expectations raised in the supporting promotional activities. Otherwise, the product could be in short supply at the crucial launch time.

Decisions that define the product objectives with regard to the organization, technologies, target markets, and competitive position, and thereby serve as benchmarks for evaluating the development process (Hultink and Hart 1998), are preeminent considerations. Decisions referring to innovativeness, producing at lower costs, erecting competitive barriers, increasing penetration, capitalizing on an existing market, and expanding the product range are important as well. The focus on manufacturing and advertising planning also offers a higher propensity for the firm to achieve high returns and market share gains while timing the launch (Di Benedetto 1999).

The most critical consideration is identification of the target market, which should be considered early in the product development process (Hultink and Hart 1998; Hart and Tzokas 2000), well in advance of the launch planning process. The target market then drives decisions related to product positioning and pricing while achieving the expected financial performance during launch. Pricing should include not only the launch price but also the long-term decision between penetration pricing and price skimming (Hart and Tzokas 2000). Price skimming proves to be more successful than penetration pricing in product launch of consumer products (Garrido-Rubio and Polo-Redondo 2005), even though the pricing decision is more often based on the scale of entry, with skimming advised for small-scale entry and penetration advised for large-scale entry (Hultink and Hart 1998).

Identification of the target market underlies the company's ability to create *marketing hype*, which refers to the collection of prelaunch activities that create a receptive market environment (Wind and Mahajan 1987). Target market identification also better hones market-testing initiatives. Keenly identifying the target market better enables the marketing communications program to inform those parties that must be informed to drive adoption of the new product such as in the case of lead users (von Hippel 1988) and the use of preannouncements and announcements (Biemans and Setz 1995).

It is remiss to not attend to global supply chain issues as a component of effective product launch strategy. Consideration of logistics and inventory flow of materials from manufacturer to end user is an important, but often overlooked, aspect of product launch strategy (Stryker 1996; Chryssochoidis and Wong 1998). Global supply chains play an important role in ensuring customer acceptance of a new product through availability (Hart and Tzokas 2000), and distributors play a crucial role in the positioning of the product and communicating the product benefits to the end consumer. Availability, capability, and quality stem from aspects of accurate order processing, delivery, invoicing, and backup services (Hultink and Hart 1998), and prompt delivery remains an important aspect of brand differentiation (Oakley 1997). Not only do lead times between order and delivery affect the customer's perceptions of the brand, but reduced lead times enable the organization to manage any changes in demand for the product (Oakley 1997). As part of the global launch strategy, investment may be needed in manufacturing close to the region to be served. *Store-ready* products, with all the relevant POS material, may be required by the manufacturer to speed up the distribution process.

Cross-functional integration is the mechanism for constructing, enabling, and sustaining an effective launch strategy. Studies reveal that product launches involving cross-functional teams result in success across all measures—overall profitability, competitive profitability, competitive sales, and competitive market share. Product management teams, therefore, should comprise marketing, engineering, and manufacturing skill sets, where marketing provides linkages to commercialization needs related to branding, promotion, and distribution channels; engineering provides linkages to science and technical issues; and manufacturing can enable production cost efficiencies to create a competitive advantage (Garrido-Rubio and Polo-Redondo 2005). In addition, integrating logistics with marketing, manufacturing, and operations allows companies to manage around pending demand uncertainty to achieve a more successful product launch, and focus particular attention on after-sales service planning, which requires logistics expertise (Di Benedetto 1999).

Launch Strategy Influencers

The organization decision on whether to be a *first-mover, fast-follower, early me-too,* or *late entrant* influences a general launch strategy (Hultink and Hart 1998; Hart and Tzokas 2000). First-movers set the parameters for how the market views the new product. Accordingly, first-movers must pay keen attention to the market knowledge that they wish consumers to gain. First-movers also have potential advantages in adopting a premium pricing strategy, creating barriers to entry for competitors, and establishing an enhanced market image for the product (Oakley 1997; Hultink and Hart 1998; Hart and Tzokas 2000). Fast-followers tend to come into the market with relatively lower marketing expenditures (Lambkin 1988, cited in Hart and Tzokas 2000). Later entrants to the market attempt to learn from the mistakes of first-movers and fast-followers to develop superior skills, enabling a competitive advantage over others in the market (Hultink and Hart 1998; Hart and Tzokas 2000).

The type of new product innovation also has a potential influence on launch strategy. Gatignon and Robertson (1989) note that incentives, as well as the presence of technical expertise in sales support technological innovation in the business-to-business arena. This said, Gatignon and Robertson (1989) reinforce the crucial role of investment in marketing, and Hultink et al. (1998) stress the role of the promotional mix and the investment required in marketing communications spending.

Timing is another launch strategy influencer. Companies need to ensure that aspects including service policies and channel or trade promotions are defined well in advance of launch to ensure that the launch is on time (Di Benedetto 1999). Global logistics needs to be included early in planning the launch to ensure that the timing of the launch is achievable across the global supply chain. Related to the timing issue, speed—getting the product to the market—can be important in responding to and driving market receptiveness of the new product, especially in the case of traditional consumer market products (Oakley 1997).

Global Launch Strategy Considerations

For the most part, the focus of product launch strategy has not taken account of the global nature of product launches, which many multinational companies face. The company managing a global launch naturally contends with the complexities faced at the domestic level, but other issues come to light. Identification and recruitment of supply chain owners is a crucial consideration to achieve the required market reach in each region. Global logistics also has to be managed to deliver demand expectations in each region. Checking the language and cultural references so that the promotional mix properly underpins the global launch is crucial. Brand names appropriate in one region may have negative connotations in another. Colors have different associations across cultures. For example, white is associated with cleanliness in the United Kingdom and death in Asia.

To illustrate the nuances and salient drivers of global product launches, two case studies are presented. The two companies discussed are based in Europe, with one predominantly focused on business-to-business markets for domestic appliance components and the other predominantly a flooring specialist already located in multiple countries. Interviews were held with senior executives representing R&D, marketing, finance, and production and the agencies responsible for implementation of the promotional mix.

Company One

Company One is a world leader in kettle control manufacturing. Their range of products includes kettle controls, thermostats, and water-boiling elements, which account for 40% of the total cost of a kettle. The Company produces both immersed and underfloor (concealed) products and currently holds 70% of the market share in its core business area.

Company One made the decision to diversify into water filters for hot water. This technology underpins the development of kettles, forms a new consumer appliance, and paves the way for growth in the market for filtration. Currently, cold-water filtration accounts for 90% of the water filtration market, but hot-water filtration is a new area. There is only one main supplier, and one competitor has been operating in the water filter market for over 20 years and is the global market leader. Hot-water filtration gives a benefit of *clean water* for hot drinks, which is particularly important in areas of the world where the water quality is poor, and also offers possible health benefits for countries with a high standard of clean water.

Company One provides an enabling platform to the hot-water appliance industry and operates in a business-to-business setting—it is not a consumer brand. The company's strength and reputation reside in technology, system design, manufacturing, and quality management for brand owners of kettles and appliances. Engineering drives company growth, and ideas tend to be pushed by technology rather than pulled by the market.

To sustain its market position, Company One has patented technology for hot-water filtration and produced an appliance based on this patented technology. This appliance is targeted for the final consumer market. To use the appliance, cartridges are required, and these, in themselves, are a new product and brand for the consumer market. The appliance and cartridge were to be launched globally with the focus on Europe and the Far East. The United States was to be a secondary launch, as electrical appliance standards differ across these two regions, and so, further technical work was required prior to this launch.

Global Supply Chain Partners

Company One was breaking into markets through collaboration with brand owners of domestic appliances positioned at the *top end* of the market in each country. This means that separate agreements needed to be reached in Germany, Russia, and the United Kingdom as the brand owners differ across Europe. Regional sales teams, being key to the recruitment of brand owners, were cultivating different sets of relationships within these companies other than their normal relationships. Traditionally, Company One supplied components to these brand owners but was working with their technical and marketing functions to develop a new appliance for a new market.

The brand owners benefit from new technology, financial incentives with profit sharing in the initial stages of market development, investment in manufacture, and support for design of the appliance, and they retain their own brand name. Through existing relationships with the brand owners and also with their reputation for innovation, Company One was able to recruit brand owners in each country. Behind the initial product was a family of products that would eventually be brought into the market for filtration of beverages.

In addition, Company One was forging links with retailers and distributors for the cartridges, which are needed with the appliance. One of the main problems in defining the category for this new product was the question, "Is it a grocery purchase or an electrical/hardware purchase?" This affected the type of retailer to which Company One needed to sell its product in each country. In the United Kingdom, the specialist electrical retailers were targeted, as these would maintain the premium price of the product, whereas the grocery retailers would supply at a lower price than Company One wanted at the introductory stage of market entry and also required a larger slice of the margin.

At the time of recruitment of global supply chain partners, the main competitor in the market was also signing up deals with brand owners. The competitor was a well-established global brand and was willing to cobrand appliances and so attract brand owners. It was aware of Company One's product developments and so announced advanced products to *steal* the market and undermine Company One. Company One had to adapt its product and pricing and consider significant incentives to offer to brand owners to withstand the competitive pressure it was facing at the time of its global launch.

Promotional Mix

Company One found managing the global launch to be a complex endeavor, as reflected through the challenges for the promotional mix. For the appliance, the brand owners had their own outlets for the new kettle, and their reputation gave confidence to the consumer. However, the brand owners would neither take a lead in communicating the benefits of the water filtration to the consumers nor promote the cartridge. Company One had to produce a launch pack for the trade so that brand owners could understand the product benefits and their sales force could properly present the new product to their distributors and retailers.

For the retailers and distributors, store managers and shop floor staff needed to understand what the product does and be able to communicate these benefits to the consumer. Because retailers had existing relationships with brands and also stock their own brands, incentives to stock and promote a new product were needed. Retailers needed logistics support and launch material to be sorted out by the supplier to reduce inertia and resistance to the new product. To do this, Company One developed POS material to be used in stores to attract consumers and persuaded them to try and purchase the product. Leaflets, labels, packaging, and the product design had to be presented to the consumer in such a way that the product had appeal and motivated purchase.

The design of the product also varied from country to country—for example, blue plastic in Russia, stainless steel and wood in the United Kingdom. Accordingly, the packaging had to communicate the product values and give the appearance of high quality. Because the product was priced at the top end of the kettle market, the product design and packaging had to reinforce the status of the product.

Along with the appliance, Company One had to create awareness of the cartridge. They achieved this through *tie-in* with the brand owners of the appliances, so the appliance has a label to remind consumers of the cartridge. Company One also had to retail and distribute the cartridge globally. This required building a brand around the cartridge and ensuring that the name of the brand worked globally, the packaging of the cartridge was recognizable in all regions, and the cartridge use instructions were understandable. Company One launched the brand in China and discovered that the brand name did not work well, so they gave the cartridge different names in the different regions in which it is available. The packaging is generic, but the local language is used.

The Internet was a direct channel to market for Company One and was employed to explain the benefits of the filtration system, how to use the cartridge, and how the cartridge can be ordered on the Web. This was launched globally.

In each region, promotional activities and events were held to support the launch. For example, demonstrations in the store, discounts, trade and the local press, and local celebrities to endorse the product were all used.

Logistics

The senior executives of Company One worked together to plan the activities for product development and global market launch. This multidisciplinary approach meant that each area knew where potential problems resided: for example, technical issues with the material for the kettles, tooling-up delays, and shorter times to market to work with retailers' calendars for product launch in different regions (Russia prior to Germany and Germany prior to the United Kingdom). Where activities had not been covered, such as Internet support, they were given priority and resources.

All the manufacturing base was undertaken in China, and the manufacturer had to be able to make different variants for the local markets and package these so that they were *store ready* when shipped. Ticketing and presentation for the store is, in itself, a complex activity for global product launch. To provide demand fulfillment for the cartridges bought online, warehousing facilities were found locally to service different regions. The competence of manufacturing gave Company One an advantage in terms of the cost of production and the resultant margins. The willingness to share these margins with supply chain partners provided a lead into the market for hot-water filtration compared with the major competitor in this field.

Company Two

The laminate flooring industry is traditionally a builders' industry. In recent years, home interiors have become more fashionable, and consumers regard flooring as a feature that reflects their lifestyle and tastes. With this change, Company Two has made investment in product design, whereas previously, product development was a cost-saving exercise.

Company Two is a leading company in the sector, with strong brand recognition and commitment to product development. Markets include the end-consumer market, intermediaries (e.g., interior designers, contractors, builders, and architects), and the retail industry. The development and launch of new products is a key feature in Company Two's strategies for future growth, and substantial investments have been undertaken—for example, for directly laminated flooring and glue-free joining systems.

Initially, the company had one range of products, which were sold worldwide. The company now has a European range and a North American (mostly the United States) range to account for differences in taste between the two continents. As a result, there is a European design team and a U.S.-based design manager. There is a very strong brand presence and recognition in the United States, and Company Two is seen as a commonplace name for laminate flooring in the U.S. markets.

Definition of the brand message is seen as key. Generally, customer experience is missing from many areas of the laminate flooring industry, and the product is viewed functionally rather than as a lifestyle choice. New products have been developed with finishes of tiles, papyrus, birch bark, and so on, rather than beech laminates, and with new surface treatments to ensure durability and ease of aftercare. Company Two recognized the opportunity to offer customers aspects of design and to provide a design and installation service, as well as advice and inspiration. They wanted to tempt customers with new ideas and encourage people to purchase. An *ideas book* was created to show room sets of different flooring designs and flooring matched with paints, to provide residential customers and contractors with inspiration. A number of themes that reflect different tastes have been identified:

- Natural Touch—chalky, organic, linens
- Vintage—romantic, texture, *cottagy*

- Exotic—funky, eclectic, Asian
- Original—Scandinavian, classic, timeless

Within these global styles, some products have been customized to reflect the distinct tastes and experiences of particular markets. For example, the U.S. market has Pecan and Hickory, and a stronger Oak wood-grain flooring than is common for European markets. Leading-edge designers and architects are used in the trend forecasting process and to increase the profile of the brand. *Signature* brands created by well-known designers in specific global markets are another facet of this focus on design for the customer experience.

Technology is used to lock out competitors, and Company Two constantly reviews products to ensure that the offering is leading edge and effectively satisfies customer requirements. New technologies are integrated with design to create new features. For example, a high gloss finish was used with the new Exotic design to create a new and innovative product for the marketplace. The company uses patents to cover new technologies and also tries to protect any new designs.

Global Supply Chain Partners

Target markets for the company in Europe include residential, Ikea, and contract markets. Each does not currently have information on the profile of a typical Company Two residential customer, and Company Two produces 80% of Ikea flooring. Contract customers include builders, who choose a basic product; interior designers, who are often looking for a more innovative product; and large companies such as Marks and Spencer and Christian Dior, who often purchase high-performance, signature products. In the United States, target markets are residential and mass merchandising retailers, such as Home Depot. Company Two has different relationships with contract customers and retail customers, and it often works closely with contract clients to develop a product to meet specific requirements. Past projects have included a red flooring product for Vodafone and the Formula 1 winning flag floor that is used in Seat showrooms.

Products are launched globally, but particular styles are used for certain regions. For example, Europe is a key market, but there are clear differences between Northern and Southern Europe, with Northern Europe showing a preference for a pale, clean style and Southern Europe (such as Spain and Italy) preferring the darker, richer colors.

Marketing Communications

The company works with its regional sales and marketing teams to identify key styles within regions. Workshops are held with design, sales and marketing, and country managers to discuss customer requirements. Retailers are also involved, to identify their focus and direction. For example, in the United States, Home Depot has a do-it-yourself focus, whereas Lowe's focuses much more on interior design. Store managers are presented with the collections and trained to understand the key selling points and how to implement POS material in stores.

POS presentation is fundamental and is launched globally, but with regional variations of language. Company Two has developed a *platform for promotion* based on enhancing the customer experience. Essentially, this is a style book designed for in-store use and is split into style groups of Vintage, Exotic, Modern Tile, Natural Touch, and Original.

POS material enables Company Two to organize the collection in a way that is meaningful to the consumer, by providing a cohesive story and enabling different regions to recognize and embrace a particular look. The book gives consumers interior design ideas for each of the product groups and also advice on planning interiors, such as increasing the perception of space in the room and addressing issues such as poor light levels. This enhances the whole product experience by focusing on the entire service and not just the product.

Logistics

Retailers are involved to ensure the timing of the product launch. Company Two conducts research to identify trends emerging over the next four to five years, and it is important to optimize the timing of each product launch. In particular, retailers have different launches, based on their seasonal calendar, and it is important to ensure that Company Two products fit with these launch periods. For example, in the United States, Home Depot launches new products in February, whereas Lowe's launches new products in July.

Manufacturing is carried out in Sweden and the United States. Recent investment has been made in the United States to bring on a new plant to service the U.S. region and to meet demand expectations. For some technical applications (i.e., printing and engraving), the company carries out third-party sourcing. Often in these cases, the company invests financially in the supplier or develops exclusivity agreements to ensure the protection of its technology and designs.

Summary

The product management function's ability to enact a successful, effective global product launch strategy is predicated on a number of investments in financial, human, and time resources. Marketing communications investments make customers aware of the product and its benefits. Logistics ensures that demand expectations are met. Timing is necessary for the synchronization of decisions in the company and through the global supply chain. Sales force incentives provide the motivation to sell the product and focus on customer needs rather than product functionality. The requirements of the product; promotional mix; involvement of regional distributors, intermediaries, and retailers to reach the market; and regional versus single-source manufacturing make global product launch a complex endeavor.

In addition to these, the case studies presented here portray the need for product management considerations of design, marketing communications, logistics, and participation of *supply chain partners* within the global product launch setting.

Design aspects of the product may be needed to differentiate and appeal to the needs, preferences, and tastes of different regions. Marketing communications have to consider issues of brand name, color, imagery, packaging, and POS materials affected by language and culture. And as the Internet has a global reach, the nature of Internet use and reception in a particular country and global region must be assessed.

To meet logistics challenges, Company Two invested substantially in new manufacturing plants to serve a new global market. There was also recognition that retailers have different calendars for product launch per country and that the supplier has to work with these to underpin global launch. In addition, recruitment of channel owners has to be dealt with. Company One was in an intensively competitive situation and this drove it to speed up the participation of channel owners in the regions where the global launch was due to take place. The channel owners, in this case, included brand owners of domestic appliances and retailers, predicated on the issue of finding the appropriate category for the cartridge and ease of use of the product to facilitate final consumer acceptance.

The reputation of the supplier does endorse the product and serves to motivate channel owners to assess and adopt the product, as shown in both case studies. Company One had to go much further in persuading the channel owners to adopt its products and reduce the perceived risks associated with doing so. Investment in tooling up, sharing of profits, provision of promotional material, and development of a family of products to introduce new products into the market over a period of time was considerable. Channel owner relationships can help to speed up adoption, and because Company One had established relationships with channel owners, it was able to build on these to encourage adoption.

In sum, as companies expand to markets across different global regions, the need to understand and better manage global launches becomes acute, especially in light of distinct language and cultural issues. Such considerations and investment during a global launch affect the likely adoption and corresponding commercial success of the product (Garrido-Rubio and Polo-Redondo 2005). It is, therefore, imperative that companies give more careful thought and visibility to global launch considerations as part of their product management thinking. This is because the manner in which the global launch is managed can heavily predispose—even more so than inherent product attributes—the ultimate success or failure of the company's new product and, consequently, affect the company's global market financial viability.

References

Baker, M. and S. Hart (1999), *Product Strategy and Management*. London: Prentice Hall.

Biemans, W. and H. J. Setz (1995), "Managing New Product Announcements in the Dutch Telecommunications Industry," in *Product Development: Meeting the Challenge of the Design-Marketing Interface*, M. Bruce and W. Biemans, eds. Chichester, UK: Wiley, pp. 207–229.

Chryssochoidis, G. and V. Wong (1998), "Rolling Out New Products Across Country Markets: An Empirical Study of Causes of Delays," *Journal of Product Innovation Management*, 15, 16–41.

Di Benedetto, A. (1999), "Success Factors in New Product Launch," *Journal of Product Innovation Management,* 16 (6), 530–544.

Garrido-Rubio, A. and Y. Polo-Redondo (2005), "Tactical Launch Decisions: Influence on Innovation Success/Failure," *Journal of Product and Brand Management,* 1 (4), 29–38.

Gatignon, H. and T. Robertson (1989), "Technology Diffusion: An Empirical Test of Competitive Effects," *Journal of Marketing,* 53 (January), 35–49.

Hart, S. and N. Tzokas (2000), "New Product Launch 'Mix' in Growth and Mature Product Markets," *Benchmarking: An International Journal,* 7 (5), 389–405.

Hultink, E., A. Griffin, H. Robben, and S. Hart (1998), "In Search of Generic Launch Strategies for New Products," *International Journal of Research in Marketing,* 15 (3), 269–285.

Hultink, E. and S. Hart (1998), "The World's Path to the Better Mousetrap: Myth or Reality? An Empirical Investigation Into the Launch Strategies of High and Low Advantage New Products," *European Journal of Innovation Management,* 1 (3), 106–122.

Kahn, Kenneth B. (2000), *Product Planning Essentials.* Thousand Oaks, CA: Sage.

Oakley, P. (1997), "High-Tech NPD Success Through Faster Overseas Launch," *Journal of Product and Brand Management,* 6 (4), 260–274.

Stryker, J. (1996), "Launching a New Business-to-Business Product," in *The PDMA Handbook of New Product Development,* M. D. Rosenau, A. Griffin, G. A. Castellion, and N. F. Anschuetz, eds. New York: Wiley, pp. 363–380.

Von Hippel, E. (1988), *The Sources of Innovation.* New York: Oxford University Press.

Wind, Y. and V. Mahajan (1987), "Marketing Hype: A New Perspective for New Product Research and Introduction," *Journal of Product Innovation Management,* 4 (1), 43–49.

10

Operations Management

E. Powell Robinson, Jr.

Funda Sahin

O perations management (OM), which considers the design and management of transformation processes in manufacturing and service organizations, is undergoing a sweeping transition reflecting the expanding boundaries of the OM function. Whereas in the past, the operations manager often assumed a functional role focused on improving efficiency within the four walls of the factory or service organization, today's operations manager faces a complex task in which success often hinges on securing and maintaining a value-added position within one or more global supply chains.

This new era of OM philosophy and practice is precipitated by the globalization of supply bases and marketplaces, advances in information technology (IT) software and hardware, and the widespread recognition and acceptance of supply chain concepts. These alterations of the business environment are enabling managers to redefine their operational strategies at the enterprise and network level, thereby providing significant opportunities for innovation and threats for those locked into the traditional functional perspective of OM.

The objectives of this chapter are to examine the current perspectives of OM and provide projections for its future development in the global economy. Toward this end, we define OM, discuss its decision-making scope, recap significant points in its historical development, differentiate between the functional and process perspectives of OM, identify the factors that are rapidly changing the role of the operations manager, and propose several key OM success factors for the future.

What Is Operations Management?

The term **operations management** refers to *the planning, control, execution, and improvement of the processes that transform inputs into the products and services that the firm provides to its internal and external customers.* At the most fundamental level, OM is about designing and consistently executing processes that get the work done in an efficient manner, quickly, and without errors. A vital characteristic of OM is helping companies improve their customer service levels and reduce cost over time.

Transformation processes are used in all public and private organizations to provide both manufactured products and services. In general, they create value by transforming the following:[1]

- Product form (as in manufacturing and education)
- Location (as in transportation)
- Time availability (as in inventory storage)
- Exchange (as in retailing)
- Physiological aspect (as in health care)
- Information (as in telecommunications)

These transformation processes are not mutually exclusive within an organization. For example, a hospital may provide medical treatment (physiological aspect), ambulance service (changing location), maintenance of medical supply inventory (time availability), insurance processing (exchange), and e-mail reminders of upcoming appointments (information).

There are several misconceptions about OM. First, owing to its close ties to industrial engineering, OM is frequently considered synonymous with manufacturing. However, OM is equally relevant in service businesses, such as hotels, hospitals, retailers, transportation systems, and schools, where issues of capacity planning, facility design, inventory control, manpower scheduling, and customer service are equally critical to the firm's success. The unique demands and operational characteristics of service industries often provide a more challenging environment for the operations manager. Some of the special characteristics that differentiate service from manufacturing operations include the simultaneous production and consumption of the firm's product, the inability to inventory final output, and the presence of the customer during the provision of the firm's product. These differences place special requirements on workforce scheduling, facility location, design, layout and capacity, inventory management, and product design, among other factors. Levitt (1972) examines several of these issues and how developments in the manufacturing sector can be applied in a service context. McDonalds, Wal-Mart, and Federal Express are sterling examples of service firms that derive competitive advantage from operational excellence.

A second misconception is that OM is an engineering discipline. OM is a functional area of business, such as accounting, finance, human resources, logistics, and marketing, with clear-cut management responsibilities. Hence, there is usually a vice president in charge of operations or a chief operations officer (COO). Below them are directors, managers, staff, and operational personnel. As a business management function, the OM focuses on the strategic planning, positioning, and execution of the transformation processes from a managerial context, which involves coordination with the other business functions. On the other hand, industrial engineering is an engineering function responsible for the design of transformation processes as specified by managerial decisions. As such, industrial engineering is more concerned with the technical development and design of transformation processes than with their managerial planning and execution.

Finally, OM is often confused with operations research (OR) or management science (MS), which is the development of quantitative methods for general problem solution. The field of OR or MS began its development during World War II to support the efficient allocation of scarce resources associated with the war effort, often in the areas of production and logistics management. Many of these mathematical developments are applicable for solving OM problems. However, whereas OR or MS techniques are part of the operations manager's tool kit, OM is a functional area that should not be confused with the development of mathematical procedures or quantitative techniques.

Operations Management Decision Problems

The operations manager addresses a wide variety of decision problems in providing products and services to customers. These can be classified into three broad categories: strategic, tactical, and operational. *Strategic decisions* are broadly defined and specify the long-term competitive priorities the firm employs to satisfy its target markets and achieve its financial objectives. Included within the strategic decisions are plans detailing resource requirements and their alignment for achieving strategic objectives. Strategic OM decisions must be coordinated with the other functional areas to ensure a consistent overall business strategy for the firm. The strategic planning horizon is typically three to eight years, which is reviewed annually or when a major shift in the business environment occurs. Examples for strategic decisions requiring OM input include (1) planning the location of manufacturing, distribution, and service facilities; (2) determining the appropriate transformation processing strategies (e.g., make-to-stock, assemble-to-order, or make-to-order), capacities, and product family assignments to facilities; (3) developing new products including issues associated with manufacturability; (4) setting target customer service levels for order fill rate and delivery lead time; and (5) defining order fulfillment policy. The outputs of the strategic plan include projected annual production by facility; capacity levels stated in terms of labor, equipment, and storage; and financial projections for investments (inventory, facility, etc.) and cash flow.

The strategic plan provides guidelines and constraints for tactical (also known as aggregate and seasonal) planning, which establish plans for utilizing strategic resources in the intermediate term. The tactical planning horizon is typically from 12 to 24 months, covering at least one complete seasonal cycle. The tactical plan is updated quarterly. Planning units are in generic product family units, where a product family is a set of items sharing common production or distribution resources. The tactical plan specifies monthly production rates and inventory levels for the product families. In doing so, it determines the monthly activity levels of manufacturing and distribution facilities, inventory storage, transportation, and labor and provides the foundation for determining the firm's annual operating budget. Examples of two *pure* tactical (seasonal) plans are as follows:

1. *Level production plan.* The level production plan maintains a constant production rate, building up seasonal inventories during low demand periods when the production rate exceeds the demand rate and then drawing down inventories when the demand rate exceeds the production rate. This plan reaps efficiencies associated with maintaining a stable production rate at the cost of maintaining seasonal inventories.

2. *Chase demand plan.* The chase demand plan adjusts production capacity to match demand requirements by utilizing alternate production routings, overtime, hiring or firing seasonal workers, subcontracting, and slack capacity during nonpeak demand periods. This plan maintains minimal seasonal inventories at the expense of capacity adjustment costs.

In most cases, the tactical plan employs a combination of the two pure planning approaches. The clothing industry provides an example where *speculative* seasonal inventories are built up prior to the demand season. During the peak sales season, regular and overtime production and distribution capacity are allocated to replenish the hottest selling items and balance inventories.

The operational plan, not to be confused with OM, executes the daily and weekly activities of the firm. Where the tactical plan provides production and inventory buildup rates for product families, the operational plan *disaggregates* the tactical plan into production schedules for specific end items. Some of these items may be produced for seasonal inventory buildup, whereas others fill immediate demand. The operational plan balances short-term demand fluctuations for specific end items against available capacity. Setting production priorities, scheduling work orders on specific machines, input and output control, determining weekly work schedules, and quality control are examples of operational activities in a manufacturing environment. Hourly, daily, and weekly manpower planning, customer order processing, administering medical treatment, reordering medical supplies, monitoring customer satisfaction, quality inspection, and claims processing are examples of operational activities in service industries.

Evolution of Operations Management

Developing a solid understanding of OM and its trends requires understanding its evolution. The introduction of division of labor concepts in the 1700s and early 1800s marks the beginning of the industrial revolution and OM. During this era, skilled craftsmen, organized in guilds according to specialization, produced high-quality products with each end item possessing a unique individuality reflecting its maker. The custom nature of craft work prevented the development of mass production techniques and resulted in regionally oriented marketplaces. This began to change in the early 1800s, when Eli Whitney, after securing a contract to supply 10,000 muskets, showed that machine tools could make standardized parts to exact specifications, which could be interchanged among end items. This opened the door for large-scale production and introduced several OM issues relating to specialization of labor, process capability, quality control, and worker training.

During the late 1880s, Frederic Taylor proposed *scientific management,* as a systematic approach to productivity improvement based on the idea that each task can be defined and the best way to perform the task can be determined scientifically using efficiency principles. Hence, management's job is to determine the most efficient methods for completing the work, standardize these *best practices*, provide the proper tools, train labor in the proper work methods, and establish incentive systems to ensure the scientific practices are followed. The scientific approach increases productivity, which benefits the firm through increased profits, workers through higher wages, and society through less expensive and more plentiful products.

Several other studies were built on Taylor's concepts including Henry Gantt's efficiency studies of the textile industry and introduction of Gantt charts, Frank and Lillian Gilbreth's further development of efficiency methods, and Walter Shewhart's pioneering work on statistical quality management methods. By the early 1900s, several prominent industries had adopted scientific management principles and mass production concepts, but none more wholeheartedly than the meatpacking industry. The meatpacking industry utilized a fast-paced mechanized process, specialized by animal type, to move the animals through a specialized *disassembly line* in which each worker performed only a small set of tasks as the work flowed through his or her workstation.[2] Henry Ford credits the meatpacking industry's highly efficient process with planting the seeds that later evolved in 1913 into the first integrated and scientifically managed assembly line for making the Model T automobiles. Specialized equipment, standardized work tasks, on-time delivery, and constant product flow were critical considerations of Ford's assembly line concept.

Scientific management continued to fuel the mass production concepts that dominated U.S. manufacturing through World War II and into the 1960s, where the economic environment was one of increasing market demand and scarce capacity. Consequently, maximizing output at minimum cost was often the operations manager's objective. In an effort to efficiently allocate scarce resources, management applied quantitative models to *optimize* production and logistics processes. MS tools such as mathematical programming, simulation, waiting-line theory, inventory modeling, and decision theory continue to provide important decision-making tools to support OM. The late 1950s also saw the development of project management techniques, including DuPont's critical path method and the Navy's program evaluation and review technique, for assisting managers with the planning and controlling of large-scale and complex programs.

The mid-1960s ushered in the material resource planning (MRP) crusade, which launched the American Production and Inventory Control Society (APICS).

Pioneered by visionaries such as Joseph Orlicky and George Plossel, MRP represents the first large-scale application of the data processing capabilities of computers to the production planning and inventory control problems facing manufacturing firms. IBM, an early vendor of production planning and control software, provided an integrated suite of product modules consisting of forecasting, inventory planning, bills of material, MRP, and capacity planning, all of which shared a common database. MRP eventually evolved into MRPII, which integrates engineering, financial, marketing, and human resource systems with production planning. The enterprise resource planning (ERP) systems of today have their roots deeply grounded in MRP.

During the 1970s and 1980s, manufacturing strategy concepts were developed by a team of researchers at Harvard Business School and found application in industry. Building on W. Skinner's (1974) focused factory concepts, several researchers (such as William Abernathy, Kim Clark, and Robert Hayes) proposed utilizing the firm's operational capabilities to gain strategic competitive advantage. Recognizing that a single factory cannot be equally successful on all performance measures (e.g., cost, quality, speed), the competitive advantage model suggests that to gain strategic advantage, the firm should identify the limited set of performance dimensions that drive sales in the marketplace and focus its competitive priorities accordingly.

Issues of quality management rose to the forefront in the United States in the 1980s as numerous industries came to be dominated by Japanese firms offering superior quality products. Although E. Edwards Deming, Joseph Juran, and Philip Crosby found receptive ears for the quality message during the post-World War II restructuring efforts in Japan, the message was not well received in the United States until after significant market share had been lost. With a renewed interest in quality, many firms adopted the total quality control (TQC) philosophy that aggressively tries to eliminate the causes of production defects. The U.S. government also noted the strategic importance of improving the quality of U.S.-made products and instituted the Baldrige National Quality Award in 1987, which launched the total quality management (TQM) movement. Several quality certification standards, such as the ISO 9000 standards created by the International Organization for Standardization (ISO), gained popularity at this time. Today, ISO 9000 certification status is a requirement for conducting business with many European and U.S. firms.

In addition to TQC, Japanese manufacturers introduced the Toyota Production System (TPS) and other just-in-time (JIT) approaches to U.S. manufacturers. JIT, originally adopted as a manufacturing philosophy that targeted high-volume production, focuses on eliminating waste by removing all activities that do not add value. The primary focus has been on inventory reduction through continual process improvement and the elimination of quality problems. It is worth noting that the JIT process must extend to suppliers as well, since in the absence of inventory buffers, any disruption in supply caused by poor vendor quality or unreliable delivery cascades throughout the system, eventually shutting it down. JIT concepts are ingrained in modern OM philosophy yielding lower costs, higher quality, and increased customer service levels.

The 1980s also saw an explosion in factory automation through the application of advanced computer technology. Computer-integrated manufacturing (CIM) targeted the complete integration of production planning and control processes, shop floor execution, and business management. Integral components of shop floor management included the application of computer numerically controlled (CNC) machines, computer-aided design/computer-aided manufacturing (CAD/CAM), and flexible manufacturing systems (FMS), which theoretically could handle the complex production and routings of products through the workplace. Statements such as "Will the last person to leave the factory turn out the lights?" signified the potential of automation to revolutionize the workplace.

Advances in manufacturing productivity extend to services as well. Since the 1980s, the U.S. economy has become more service oriented with an increased outsourcing of manufacturing to utilize cheaper offshore labor. McDonald's consistently demonstrates the successful application of scientific management and OM practices to the service industry. Their Hamburger University ensures that best practices are understood by all restaurant employees and serves as a research avenue for developing innovative methods for improving operational efficiency. Service industries ranging from health care to airlines continue to benefit from OM concepts first developed for application in manufacturing.

The global economic recession of the 1990s put additional pressure on companies to eliminate waste in their processes and adopt lean manufacturing practices. The lean approach rests heavily on business process reengineering (BPR), in which firms critically evaluate existing processes and radically alter them to eliminate the non-value-added activities. In contrast to the continuous improvement approach of JIT, BPR is a monolithic approach to revamping business processes.

By the mid-1990s, businesses began to recognize the potential benefits associated with coordinating their transformation processes with supply chain partners through the application of advanced IT. Wal-Mart's retail link program provides an early example of supply chain coordination in which the retailer collects point-of-sales data during customer checkout and shares them with vendors. The vendors, in turn, manage retailer inventories based on mutually agreed upon product availability and storage space constraints. Providing real-time demand data and empowering vendors to manage inventory (VMI) enables more efficient production and transportation processes for the supply chain. Based on Wal-Mart's success, other industries followed suit by investigating other approaches for coordinated supply chain management in an attempt to also lower costs and improve customer service. The continued advances in information technology and e-business practice further accelerated the widespread acceptance of supply chain concepts and broadened the focus of the operations manager beyond the four walls of the enterprise.

Different Perspectives of Operations Management

The evolution of OM from focusing on manufacturing efficiency to supply chain management in both manufacturing and service industries raises questions about the proper positioning and potential evolution of OM within the firm's organizational structure. To provide insight into this issue, the following two sections examine the functional and process perspectives of OM.

Functional Perspective of Operations Management

The value chain concept, introduced by Michael Porter (1985), highlights the critical role of the OM function in achieving the firm's goals. Porter classifies the firm's efforts into primary and support activities, where primary activities add direct value for the customer and support activities provide infrastructure for accomplishing the primary activities. Figure 10.1 provides Porter's value chain model, where inbound logistics, OM, outbound logistics (distribution), marketing and sales, and service represent *natural* categories of primary activities.

Porter's definitions of the primary activities are as follows:

- Inbound logistics includes the activities associated with receiving, storing, and providing the direct materials[3] to the point of usage, for example, material handling, inbound quality control, warehousing, inventory control, vehicle scheduling, and returns to suppliers.
- Operations activities are associated with transforming inputs into the final product or service form, such as machining, cooking, serving customers, packaging, assembly, equipment maintenance, testing, printing, and facility operations.
- Outbound logistics includes activities that are associated with collecting, storing, and physically distributing the product to buyers, such as finished goods warehousing, material handling, delivery vehicle operations, order processing, and scheduling.
- Marketing and sales activities are associated with identifying, attracting, and providing a means for customers to buy the firm's products, such as advertising, promotion, sales force management, channel selection, and pricing.

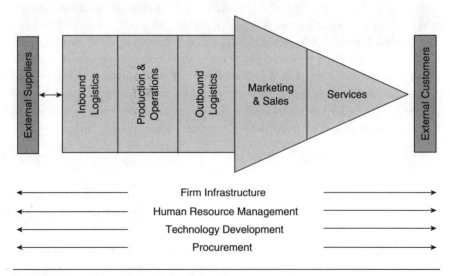

Figure 10.1 Value Chain of the Enterprise

- Service activities are associated with providing customer support to enhance or maintain the value of the firm's product or service, such as technical support, installation, repair, and training.

Porter stresses the need to focus on value-adding activities since they are major cost drivers and directly affect customer satisfaction. Consequently, their design and execution may be vital to competitive advantage, depending on the industry. For example, outbound logistics may be a critical activity for a distributor but inconsequential for a service firm providing services on its premises.

Support activities include procurement, technology development, human resource management, and firm infrastructure:

- Procurement refers to the function of purchasing both direct and indirect materials. Although procurement may be carried out throughout the firm, it is typically associated with a purchasing department.
- Technology development consists of a range of activities carried out to improve the product or processes. This includes improvements in operating procedures, software, equipment, order entry systems, and servicing procedures, among others.
- Human resource management activities are associated with recruiting, hiring, training, developing, and compensating personnel.
- Firm infrastructure consists of activities that support the entire value chain, including general management, finance, accounting, and legal.

Although the value chain model illustrates the importance of the operations function in providing customer value, it portrays a functional orientation, as commonly applied in industry, suggesting that OM decisions can be locally optimized and carried out in relative isolation from the other functional areas. However, this silo approach to management, as noted by Porter, fails to consider the impact that functional decisions may have on other areas of the firm, which can lead to suboptimal performance.

Setting production lot-size quantities provides a simple illustration of the shortcomings of functional silo management. Under a functional orientation, operations managers are typically evaluated based on productivity measures, such as the number of units of output per labor hour input. Hence, in an effort to maximize productivity, the operations manager is encouraged to schedule large production lot sizes in order to spread equipment setup costs over as many product units as possible. However, producing large infrequent lot sizes may disrupt supply chain efficiencies by increasing the variability of orders and thereby making the supplier's operations and inbound logistics activities less efficient. In addition, when the large production lot size is transferred to distribution, it causes a spike in storage requirements, significant inventory holding costs are incurred, and the item may become obsolete while awaiting customer demand. Hence, in an effort to maximize productivity, the operations manager may compromise the overall effectiveness and efficiency of the firm and channel. This example highlights the importance of coordinating functional activities. This lack of coordination occurs when a decision

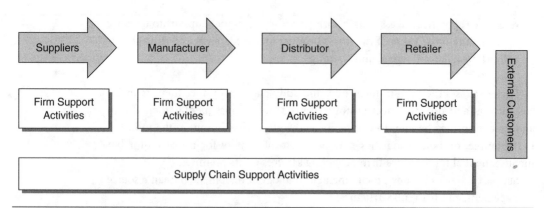

Figure 10.2 Value Chain System, or Supply Chain

maker does not have full system information, the decision maker does not consider all relevant costs in the decision-making process, or the decision maker's incentive system is not aligned with system objectives (see Sahin and Robinson 2002, for a discussion of flow coordination in supply chains).

The lot-size example illustrates that OM decisions can seldom be made from a purely functional perspective. Instead, the impact on inbound and outbound logistics, marketing, and other functional areas must also be coordinated as the firm seeks to maximize its performance. This requires that the firm's infrastructure, particularly its information systems, supports enterprisewide decision making.[4]

The task of considering all the relevant issues when making decisions is further exacerbated by the fact that multiple firms often participate in the value-adding process. Figure 10.2 illustrates a simple value chain system, or what is commonly known as a supply chain. In this scenario, the value-added activities are spread among multiple firms, where traditionally each firm attempts to maximize its own operations given the demand placed on it by its immediate downstream customer. However, because of each supply chain member's isolated view of the supply chain and frequently conflicting goals, what seems to be a rational attempt to optimize their link in the supply chain may actually compromise the effectiveness of the system.

Motorola's supply chain for cell phones in the late 1990s illustrates the difficulties of coordinating OM decisions across supply chain members. Forecasting a rapid growth in demand for cell phones, particularly in China, Motorola ramped up capacity in marketing, final assembly, and distribution. However, they were unable to induce their suppliers to follow suit by expanding component production capacity. Hence, the supply chain's production capacity remained unbalanced, which compromised the capability of the supply chain to respond to the strong sales growth potential.

Process Perspective of Operations Management

The managerial difficulties associated with functional and interorganizational coordination call for a broader perspective of OM than provided by the traditional functional approach. The process model of OM provides such a perspective. The process model recognizes that some processes may be wholly contained within the OM function and can be functionally managed, whereas others span multiple functions and require functional coordination.[5] This provides substantial justification for organizing around operating processes instead of functions. Returning to the lot-size scheduling decision, although selecting the best machine on which to run the job may only affect operations performance, the lot-size quantity decision needs to consider the impact on other functional areas.

Processes are the essential activities organizations use to add customer value and achieve their goals. Processes often require several steps, may receive input from multiple participants, and are hierarchically or horizontally linked to other processes. Consider Dell Computer's order fulfillment process (OFP),[6] which is composed of smaller processes such as receiving, acknowledging order receipt, and entering customer orders into the order management system from the Web site; scheduling customer orders into a production time slot; selecting and shipping the proper components from vendor supply hubs to assembly operations; assembling the computer; machine burn-in and testing; packaging the computer and other purchased components; order shipping; billing; and providing after-sales support service. These linked processes span several functional areas within Dell and their supply chain partners, but all support the mission of adding value for the customer. Although we can think of each of these processes independently, it is their unique design and integration into a highly responsive and focused OFP that provides a distinct competitive advantage for Dell Computer, but these processes must be continually improved to maintain competitive advantage.

Generic Process Model

Figure 10.3 provides a general process model that can be used to design and control processes over time. Inputs into the process come from internal or external suppliers in the form of information, materials, capital, and knowledge. The transformation process applies land, equipment, labor, and technology to change the form, time, or location of inputs. Process outputs either go to internal customers as inputs into their processes or to external customers who are final end-item users or intermediaries such as distributors and retailers. The arc spanning the top of the process represents process planning and design, which ensures that the inputs and transformation steps of the process efficiently and effectively meet the customers' desired output in terms of quality, cost, service, and other critical dimensions. The feedback loop below the transformation process provides a mechanism for comparing the intended and actual outputs of the transformation process. If the output deviates from the plan, corrective actions are taken to bring either the inputs or the transformation process back into control. Changes in supply, demand, or transformation technology may require process redesign to better satisfy customer needs.

Value Chain Process Model

Returning to Porter's value chain model, we can remove the functional activity categories and replace them with business processes, where a business process may contain activities associated with multiple functions. We can then classify the

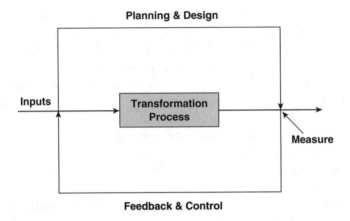

Figure 10.3   Generic Transformation Process Model

processes as either core or supporting processes. Core processes, such as developing new products or services, deliver value to external customers interacting with external suppliers and customers and producing the product or service. Examples include designing a new clothing line, e-purchasing, product delivery, order processing, and assembling a computer to order. Support processes are the infrastructure that provides inputs and enables the execution of core processes. Providing accounting, financial, legal, and purchasing services are examples of support processes.

Figure 10.4 provides a high level process view of an enterprise's value chain, indicating relationships and information flows between core and support processes.[7] Each of the processes includes layers of nested and horizontally linked subprocesses. The four core processes identified in the figure are described as follows:

- Customer relationship management (CRM) is the process that identifies, attracts, and builds relationships with customers, and facilitates customer interactions with the firm in areas such as order placement, customer service, product and service evaluation, and product tracking.
- Supplier relationship management (SRM) identifies, selects, develops, and manages suppliers of materials and services to the firm. Supplier certification, contract negotiation, and spending analysis are examples of activities of supplier relationship management.
- OFP includes the activities required to produce and deliver the product or service to the customer. Many of these activities are spread across the traditional functional areas of inbound and outbound logistics and OM. OFP includes receiving inbound materials from suppliers, producing the product or service, order picking, packaging, and delivery.
- New product development (NPD) ensures a steady flow of new and updated products that satisfy evolving customer requirements. Process inputs come from a variety of sources, including suppliers for identification of new

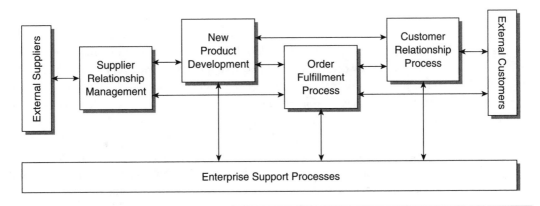

Figure 10.4   Enterprise Process Model Showing Major Linkages

product technologies and potential applications, customers for desired capabilities and product specifications, and OFP for potential design improvements in product manufacturability, distribution, and quality.

As illustrated in Figure 10.4, core processes interface with external customers, other core processes, and support processes. Some of the characteristics of the model are as follows:

- The organizational structure in Figure 10.4 focuses on business processes and not business functions. Hence, the internal logistics, OM, and outbound logistics activities are not explicitly represented in the figure. Instead, many of their traditional activities are integrated into the OFP, ensuring a proper alignment of managerial attention and incentives on the OFP instead of functional objectives. This facilitates total cost analysis and the accomplishment of system versus functional goals.
- OFP and SRM interfaces address strategic aspects of supplier management such as the introduction of new and improved products and services, technology trends, and capacity planning, among others.
- OFP and CRM interfaces include information exchange about upcoming promotions, early market feedback on sales of new products, changes in geographical markets, customer feedback on product quality, and order tracking, among others.
- OFP and NPD share information concerning product development and life cycle management, which includes OFP capabilities and process design considerations, rollout strategies for new products, manufacturing and distribution capacity ramp up, startup provisioning of spare parts for new product introductions, and technical support.

Figure 10.5 expands the enterprise process model to the supply chain level. A major distinguishing characteristic about the supply chain process model is that the OFP must be planned and executed as an integrated seamless process spanning all supply chain participants and all functional areas of each supply chain member.

This includes both core and support processes. Although some support processes span only their individual firm, such as human resource management, others may span multiple supply chain members. For example, information processing systems and technology development support supply-chain-wide OFP infrastructure by (1) capturing external customer demand information and sharing it with appropriate supply chain members, (2) enabling OFP to access order tracking information throughout the supply chain, and (3) providing real-time information describing inventory and capacity availabilities in the system.

Similarly, NPD processes must also span multiple supply chain members to receive customer performance requirements from external customers and input concerning manufacturability, current and emerging technology options, and resource availability from upstream supply chain members.

When compared with the traditional functional perspective of OM, the process model of the value chain provides a radically different perspective. Under the process model, the focus is on the core processes that add direct value to the customer and the requisite support processes. As such, the primary organizational focus of the enterprise is on process teams, which are not hindered by functional boundaries. A similar perspective holds for the value chain, where the focus is on supply chain, not individual firm, performance. This process orientation facilitates breaking down the traditional organizational silos created by the functional perspective of OM within the firm and the myopic tendency of firms to attain local optimization of their organizational goals instead of seeking to optimize the supply chain as a whole. As such, taking a process perspective to operations design enables management to design a value chain more closely attuned to the customer's needs.

Operations Management in the New Economy

Hayes et al. (2005) describe several factors that are ushering in the *new economy*: the globalization of the marketplace and supply bases, a greater tendency for firms to outsource and offshore operational processes, and advances in information technology. Each of these factors will have a profound effect on OM in the future.

Today's customer is becoming better educated and more globally diverse with rapidly developing markets in China, Russia, and India. Customers are demanding increasingly wider product variety, higher service levels, and a constant stream of new products. The impact of these changes is reducing the size of the market for individual products, causing more widely fluctuating demand, geographically stretching the supply chain, and shortening product life cycles. These changes can have a negative effect on operational and logistic efficiencies.

The globalization of supply is also significantly altering the business environment. To respond more effectively, firms are placing greater emphasis on developing their strategic competencies and outsourcing or offshoring nonstrategic activities to third-party logistics providers, low-cost offshore producers, and contract manufacturers. The trend toward globalization of operations is accelerating as management becomes more comfortable with its ability to virtually integrate operations

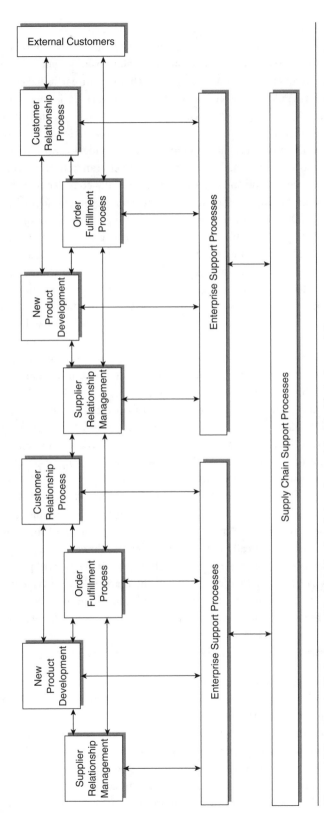

Figure 10.5 Supply Chain Process Model Indicating Enterprise and Supply Chain Support Processes

using the e-business technologies. However, outsourcing or offshoring places greater importance on the firm's ability to manage complex and geographically dispersed facility networks and organizational relationships. These complexities include more frequent shocks to the supply chain from earthquakes and other natural disasters, political instability, exchange rate variation, energy prices and availability, delays associated with customs clearance, terrorism, and other factors.

Advances in IT will continue to evolve in the future, offering improved tools for solving many OM problems. ERP systems, which provide a central point for data storage and retrieval and facilitate enterprise level transaction processing, will expand their scope beyond the enterprise to more fully consider *inter-prise* transaction processing linking multiple trading partners. Automatic identification and data capture (AIDC) technologies, such as bar coding and radio-frequency identification, will see greater application as the technologies mature and firms gain experience in their application. AIDC's capability to efficiently and accurately collect vast amounts of data and automatically transmit them to computers for processing will enable real-time management of dispersed operations such as product tracking through operations and logistics processes. The standardization of data communication and transaction formats, such as XML and EDI, will facilitate the interoperability of information systems among supply chain members, speeding the flow of data over the Internet and enabling greater *plug and play* capability, which lowers hurdle costs for adding or deleting supply chain members. Informatics technology, which extracts operating and physical flow data, processes it on the fly, and provides real-time visibility of operational status, will also continue to evolve, allowing management to pinpoint potential operational problems and take corrective action before they occur. Finally, advanced planning systems, based on state-of-the-art MS models, will witness increasing application as the input data for analysis becomes more readily available.

Although these environmental changes pose many challenges for the firm and operations manager, they also provide opportunities for gaining competitive advantage. However, the firm must lay aside its tendency toward functional management and instead critically evaluate its order fulfillment, NPD, supplier relationship management, and customer relationship management processes and realign them as necessary to effectively serve the marketplace's diverse needs. This requires closing the loop on information and coordination, synchronizing the heartbeat of the marketplace and operations, and creating adaptable processes.

Closing the Loop on Information and Coordination

It is well accepted that timely information can reduce uncertainty and thereby substitute for inventory, capacity, lead time, and customer service. Information helps to monitor the market in real time, which facilitates demand management and the refocusing of assets in the short, intermediate, and long terms. However, even though the technology for sharing information may be in place, the functional orientation of many firms prohibits this from happening. Management's failure to provide operations with advance warning of an impending promotional campaign provides an all too familiar example. The promotional campaign may be planned months ahead of time, but the proper processes are often not in place to ensure operations managers are informed sufficiently ahead of time to adequately handle the upcoming spike in demand. Furthermore, the performance evaluation metrics for the marketing and operations managers may not be properly aligned to ensure coordinated processes and maximum system performance. Thorough analysis of the promotional campaign may reveal that the loss in order fulfillment efficiency caused by the promotion's self-induced seasonal demand exceeds the promotion's benefit. Procter & Gamble, HEB grocery stores, Wal-Mart, and other consumer product manufacturers and retailers reached this conclusion for their supply chains, opting for an everyday low price strategy versus one based on promotions. Closing the loop on information, incentive alignments, and decision making, coordination among functional areas and supply chain partners is a critical success factor for the future.

Synchronizing the Marketplace and Operations Through Agility

A key component of JIT philosophy is to smooth product flows and promote efficiency by synchronizing the heartbeat of operations with that of the customer. However, small and rapidly changing marketplaces, as are projected in the future, make it difficult to synchronize demand and supply. Hence, during new product introductions or under shifting demand patterns, stock-outs and overstocks occur due to insufficient flexibility to change production and distribution schedules to meet changes in demand. The end result is poor financial performance and lost customer goodwill. The approach for handling this problem is to improve process agility or the ability to respond quickly and efficiently to unexpected shifts in demand.

Lee (2004) provides six rules of thumb for promoting agility in supply chains that all relate to altering basic OFPs and often require bridging functional and organizational boundaries as follows:

1. Provide data on changes in supply and demand to partners continuously, so that they can respond quickly.

2. Develop collaborative relationships with suppliers and customers so that companies work together to design or redesign processes, components, and products as well as prepare backup plans.

3. Design products so that they share common parts and processes initially and differ substantially only by the end of the production process. This permits the postponement of product variety until late in the supply chain when the firm has more complete information concerning expected demand.

4. Keep a small inventory of inexpensive nonbulky components that are often the cause of bottlenecks.

5. Build a dependable logistics system that can enable your company to regroup quickly in response to unexpected needs.

6. Put together a team that knows how to invoke contingency plans.

Zara, a Spanish retailer of fashion clothing, provides a novel example of building a marketing niche in the high-fashion clothing industry by developing highly flexible product development and OFPs. A common problem for every seasonal or short-life-cycle supply chain is how to forecast demand for specific end items months before the sales season begins. A poor forecast yields either an understock situation with lost potential sales or an overstock situation requiring markdowns to clear out unsold items at the season's end.

Zara's innovative operations processes provide a distinct competitive advantage by altering the heartbeat of both the marketplace and operations. The strategy is based on developing efficient small lot-size production capability through the use of standardized components, quick changeover equipment, and buffer capacity. Next, product development lead times are shortened by using focused multifunctional design teams composed of designers, marketing analysts, and operations mangers. These teams ensure the marketability and short-lead-time manufacturability of the designs. Finally, instead of attempting to forecast and maintain inventory of specific stock-keeping units, Zara produces in small batch sizes and continually introduces new updated designs replacing older ones. With its short product development cycle, Zara can quickly provide the latest fashion trends while small lot-size production minimizes the risk of overstocking. Because of the short product life cycles, the customers experience a wide and ever-changing assortment of current styles from which to choose. However, they had better buy an item they like when they find it, because availability is limited and it most likely will not be there if they come back for it later. This short-life-cycle strategy works in Zara's favor to increase sales and keep customers coming back frequently to check up on new product offerings. Zara's innovative product development and OFPs provide the supply chain with a unique competitive advantage in the marketplace.

Creating Adaptable Processes

Successful operations in the future will be adaptable such that they can be reconfigured to reflect changes in the marketplace or supplier base. The key is to monitor the environment, quickly spot trends, and develop the capability to modify the supply base. Demand changes are frequently associated with progression through the product life cycle, demographic changes, opening of new sales regions, altering of a target market, and new technology developments.

Setting up McDonalds restaurants in Russia provides one example, where McDonalds established local suppliers for its food components to ensure product consistency prior to entering the market. Similarly, setting up production in China may require establishing new suppliers in the region to support production processes.

Fender Musical Instruments provides an example of adapting to the market and stages of the product life cycle. Founded in 1946, Fender initially produced high-end guitars for the U.S. market. In 1982, an American-Japanese joint venture was established to produce and market vintage reissues and scaled-down versions of the Fender U.S. models in Japan. At first, these Fender made-in-Japan models were not intended for the U.S. market. However, intense price competition in the U.S. market for budget-priced guitars led to establishing distribution channels in the United States to handle the made-in-Japan Squier series. Today, for the world guitar market, Fender-Korea provides the lower-priced models reflecting their lower wage rates, Fender-Japan produces middle level models reflecting an increase in quality, Fender-Mexico supplies the upper-middle price range by completing wood finishing and assembly operations of U.S. parts, and Fender-USA provides the higher-end standard models and custom shop guitars. By adapting to the evolving marketplace and supply base, Fender remains a leader of the industry whereas most others have failed.

The lessons for managing the capability to adapt include the following: outsource so you can change suppliers or add capacity quickly, develop multiple suppliers with different process and product capabilities, utilize modular design and common components across the product line, and develop partners with the potential and willingness to adapt.

Implications and Conclusions

The field of OM is constantly evolving. From their initial focus on manufacturing efficiency, operations managers now face the complex problem of managing globally dispersed facility networks to effectively and efficiently supply products and services worldwide. In the past, a functional orientation to OM seemed logical because the majority of the operations manager's tasks were assumed to be contained in the manufacturing silo. However, the complexity of today's marketplace and supply base suggests that a process orientation will be more effective in the future. The process orientation is better equipped to span functional and organizational boundaries, promotes creativity, invites radical redesign of operational processes, and provides the greatest opportunity for developing competitive advantage.

The process model perspective places new requirements on the operations manager; most important is assuming a broader perspective on the firm's operations and system integration. This includes, in addition to a solid OM background, more in-depth knowledge about inbound and outbound logistics, marketing, information systems, and finance. Only with a well-rounded background can the manager understand the opportunities and benefits associated with better system integration. As such, the new job title of the higher-level operations manager might be better denoted as the supply chain or order fulfillment manager, which is more reflective of the broadening perspective of OM.

It must be clearly understood that the top level operations managers will refocus from being functional managers to process managers. As such, they must develop process management skill sets including competencies in team and consensus building, project management, process charting and analysis, communication, negotiation, and risk and contingency management. Finally, next-generation successful operations managers must be creative, agile, and willing to adapt to the changing environment, like the processes they manage.

Notes

1. Adapted from Chase, Jacobs, and Aquilano (2006).

2. Upton Sinclair, in his novel *The Jungle* (1906), provides an in-depth description of the meat packing industry's processes, along with a commentary on some of the possible societal consequences of an unbridled pursuit of efficiency.

3. Direct materials are raw materials, components, and assemblies that are procured for input into a manufactured product or held for resale.

4. Current ERP software is making strides in this direction with respect to data acquisition, storage, and transaction processing. However, the execution of many OM decisions, such as setting lot-size quantities, remains a manual process in which the linkages among functional areas are not explicitly considered by the software.

5. The process view of the organization is taken by ERP systems where the software orientation is on executing business transaction processes and not on the functional areas that use the software. In this manner, the relevant functional considerations are coordinated as required by the process *best practices*.

6. This process is the set of activities required to produce and deliver the product or service to the external customer.

7. Adapted from Krajewski and Ritzman (2005).

References

Chase, R. B., F. R. Jacobs, and N. J. Aquilano (2006), *Operations Management for Competitive Advantage*. Homewood, IL: McGraw-Hill-Irwin.

Hayes, R., G. Pisano, D. Upton, and S. Wheelwright (2005), *Operations, Strategy, and Technology: Pursuing the Competitive Edge*. New York: Wiley.

Krajewski, L. J. and L. P. Ritzman (2005), *Operations Management: Processes and Value Chains*. Upper Saddle River, NJ: Prentice Hall.

Lee, H. (2004), "The Triple-A Supply Chain," *Harvard Business Review*, October, 102–112.

Levitt, T. (1972), "Production-Line Approach to Service," *Harvard Business Review*, September–October, 41–52.

Porter, M. E. (1985), *Competitive Advantage: Creating and Sustaining Superior Performance*. New York: Free Press.

Sahin, F. and E. P. Robinson (2002), "Flow Coordination and Information Sharing in Supply Chains: Review, Implications, and Directions for Future Research," *Decision Sciences*, 33 (4), 505–536.

Skinner, W. (1974), "The Focused Factory," *Harvard Business Review*, May–June, 113–121.

11

Integrated Logistics Management

Abré Pienaar

he objective of integrated logistics is the coordinated flow and storage of materials across the supply chain. Integrated logistics management is achieved by integrating the logistics business processes of the partners in a supply chain. The very essence of global supply chain management depends on the ability to coordinate the flow and storage of materials across multiple partners using integrated business processes. It is the glue that holds a supply chain together.

In the following sections of this chapter, I first view logistics in the context of global supply chain management and then explore the benefits of integrated business processes. Subsequently, I introduce a framework and guidelines for the design and implementation of integrated logistics management. Finally, I present some examples of integrated logistics management in global supply chains.

Logistics in the Context of Supply Chain Management

To deliver product to final customers, multiple organizations—usually business entities—hold inventory and add value to the product as it moves along the supply chain (Figure 11.1).

Every organization or business within the supply chain manages its activities with business processes. As far as logistics is concerned, it is useful to understand that there is a sequential relationship. First, the organization quantifies the demand that is likely to be placed on it from downstream in the supply chain using a forecasting business process. Subsequently, managers plan their activities in response to

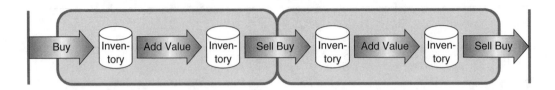

Figure 11.1 The Logistics Supply Chain Model

this demand with a planning process or processes. Next, they execute these plans with purchasing, operations, and selling processes. Finally, they monitor and review planned versus actual performance to determine if, when, and where to restart this cycle. These high-level logistics business processes are illustrated in Figure 11.2.

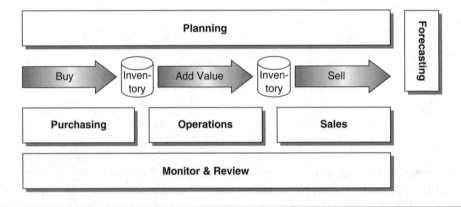

Figure 11.2 Logistics Business Processes

Many businesses focus all their attention on their own activities without much regard for what happens upstream and downstream in the supply chain. The design of their logistics business processes reflects this strategy. Forecasting only quantifies the expected demand from their immediate downstream customer. The planning processes may aim to satisfy only some of the forecast demand since the organization's strategy may call for culling less profitable or problematic demand. It may even plan quantities in excess of the forecast demand with the intention of launching initiatives to find additional customers. Logistics-intensive value-adding activities such as movement of materials may be designed on a lowest-cost basis for each activity if the impact of late deliveries for this organization is small.

In marked contrast stands the promise of supply chain management: multiple organizations collaborating to deliver a product to the end customer at the lowest total cost for the whole supply chain. This global optimization objective requires that inventory be kept where it serves the supply chain best, and inventory movements are planned and executed to support the overall supply chain requirements. Thus, logistics business processes in the context of supply chain management are designed and implemented differently. Forecasting becomes a conduit for anticipating demand from the whole downstream supply chain. Planning what, when, and how many items to move and store in an individual organization depends on the overreaching supply chain strategy. It becomes imperative that execution control business processes in purchasing, operations, and sales provide transparency to upstream and downstream supply chain partners. Monitoring and reviewing processes measure performance and trigger corrective action in terms of compliance to overall supply chain management objectives. Logistics business processes that function in this manner are what we mean by integrated logistics management.

Business Process Integration

Fundamentally, inventory exists in a supply chain because of the time it takes for a product to flow through the "pipeline" to the end consumer. On top of that, a supply chain carries inventory because of technical or commercial inabilities to match batch size demand with the same batch size supply. Inventory is also held to protect against uncertainty in the demand coming from the downstream customers, the supply from the upstream suppliers, or both.

This is just the planned inventory. Organizations also end up frequently with unplanned inventory because of differences between expected and actual demand from the end customer and unforeseeable events disrupting activities. Sometimes, the unplanned inventory and attendant additional costs result from the way organizations conduct their business—the business process design. Consider the logistics business processes in an "unmanaged" supply chain such as the one depicted in Figure 11.3. Following the sequence of business processes described in the previous section, the downstream organization in this supply chain forecasts the independent demand of the end consumer. Subsequently, using their planning process, they may elect to plan their logistics in a way that is designed to satisfy some of, all of, or more than this demand depending on the strategic intent of this organization.

Independently, the upstream organization has a forecasting business process that quantifies what they believe the demand of the downstream organization on

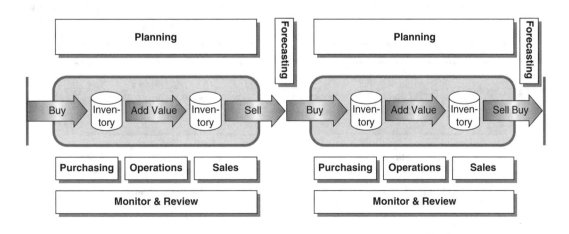

Figure 11.3   An Unmanaged Supply Chain

them will be in future time periods. They then proceed to plan their logistics in a way that is designed to satisfy some, all, or more of this demand depending on the strategic intent of this organization.

The execution processes of both organizations now swing into action to purchase materials, perform value-adding activities, and sell product with the plans they made. What the upstream organization is trying to sell in accordance with its plans will, in general, not be exactly the same as what the downstream organization is trying to buy in accordance with its plans. Any mismatch between what the two organizations are trying to do results in too much inventory of some materials and too little of others—often both simultaneously—as well as additional costs incurred to deal with the mismatches. The effect of unforeseen events in the upstream organization on the activities of the downstream organization may not be immediately apparent but then may require emergency action—with attendant costs—to resolve.

Supply chain management, on the other hand, calls for the collaboration of partnering organizations to deliver products to the end customer at the lowest cost. To do this, each organization should be planning and executing its activities with knowledge of what the other partner is doing. In other words, they should integrate their planning and execution control business processes (Figure 11.4).

Under a supply chain management regime, forecasting the independent demand of the end consumer is performed only once by the downstream organization. The planning processes of both organizations—linked together—plan the supply chain response to this demand. They may still elect to plan their respective logistics activities in a way that is designed to satisfy some of, all of, or more than this demand, but the two organizations now follow a common supply chain strategy in doing so and end up with plans that are synchronized with each other.

The execution control processes of both organizations next purchase materials, perform value-adding activities, and sell product in accordance with the common

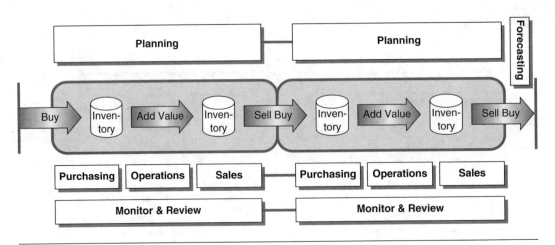

Figure 11.4   Integrated Business Processes

plans. At a minimum, the purchasing process of the downstream organization is linked with the sales process of the upstream organization so that any unforeseen events become known up and down the supply chain. Corrective action is coordinated by linking the monitoring and review of actual versus planned performance of both organizations to common measures of performance.

Supply chain management, thus, clearly requires effective and efficient integration between the logistics business processes of the partners in a supply chain. Since the degree to which this is possible and the effort required to do so depend on the nature of the business processes in the partnering organizations, much effort in supply chain management is spent designing appropriately integrated logistics business processes.

The Business Process Framework

Design and implementation of business processes—especially on a global scale— imply much more than deciding how the activities should follow one after another. The organizational structures and the people inside and outside the organization responsible for each aspect of the business process must receive due consideration. Furthermore, technology is an indispensable part of every business process design. Most important, all the different aspects of the business process have to be in balance if it is to work in a practical supply chain. The key is the balance, not the parts. Figure 11.5 illustrates this balancing act.

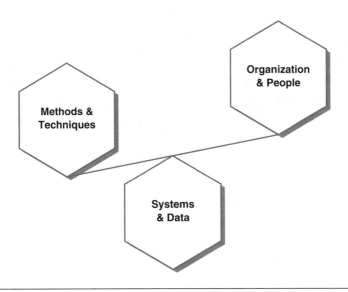

Figure 11.5   Business Process Framework

Methods and Techniques

A business process is a set of logically related tasks or activities performed to achieve a defined business outcome (Cox, Stone, and Spencer 1995). Of the many different ways in which one may elect to organize activities to achieve the desired outcome of the business process, some have proved, over the years, to work better than others. In the last decade or so, these have been standardized as "best practices." Most organizations are better served by following these best practices than by "re-inventing the wheel" by designing their own business processes from start to finish. A best practice business process selected in this way is a template to adapt and modify to the particular requirements of a particular organization and supply chain—in other words, business process design. This "design" includes adding or eliminating event sequences, documenting procedures, developing one or more performance measurements, and selecting techniques to perform calculations if required. Figure 11.6 illustrates, in the form of a flowchart, a typical logistics business process design with the activities in sequential order.

Organization and People

The organization and people aspect of business process design are more extensive than just deciding who should perform each process activity. Business process design cements roles and responsibilities as well as decision-making authority in place and should be carefully considered.

An example of how *not* to do business process design is the case of a business whose culture paid lip service to decentralized decision making. Business processes to establish appropriate inventory levels for *A* items in this organization were accordingly designed for localized decision making. In practice, though, the chief executive officer insisted on "reviewing" such decisions before they were implemented. The business process as implemented did not make provision for authorization by a central authority and so many decisions just ended up "waiting" while chaos reigned in the operational area.

Similar examples abound where a business process is designed on the premise that a person or persons with a specific skill set are responsible for a particular activity, although the organization does not have anybody with that skill set and has no intention of either training someone to the required level or hiring a person with such skills. When implemented, the business process will fail.

The organization and people aspects of business process design are commonly codified in policies stating decision-making authorities and in work flows specifying the sequence and the hold points in which individuals work together to achieve a business process objective.

Systems and Data

In principle, systems and data refer to any technology that supports business process activities, including paper-based systems and verbal data. In practice,

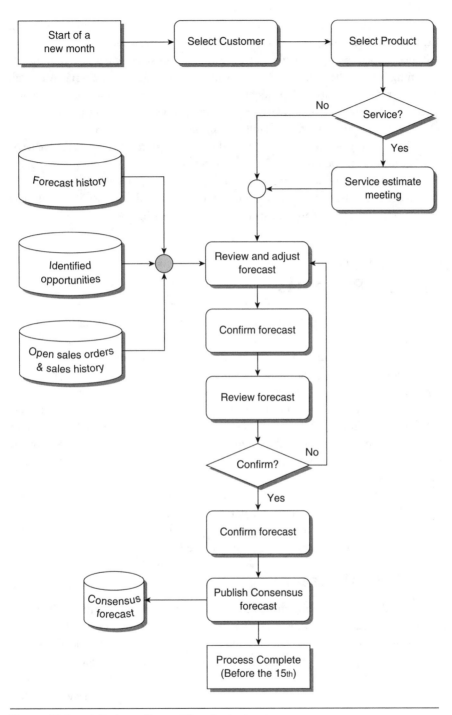

Figure 11.6   A Business Process Flowchart

systems and data mean computerized databases managed by computer-based business systems. Systems and data perform two roles: they automate certain aspects of individual business processes and integrate different business processes.

In both roles, the revolution in computer systems in the last few decades of the 20th century drastically altered business processes in general and—even more so—logistics business processes in particular. As an example, consider material requirements planning (MRP), the technique used to plan dependent demand material. Although it is clearly superior (for dependent demand) to the order-point technique also used for material planning, MRP only came into widespread use in the last few decades as computer systems became ubiquitous in manufacturing.

It is difficult to understate the effect of computer systems and connective technology in the integration of business processes across functions in a single organization and across multiple organizations in a supply chain. We consider this in more detail in the next section, where the generalized discussion of business processes given above is applied specifically to logistics business processes.

Designing Integrated Logistics Business Processes

Unfortunately, in integrated logistics management—as in other areas—there is no "master list" of best practices valid for all times, in all cases, and in all places. Best practices vary from industry to industry and from country to country. Within industries, one of the many alternative best practices may often be employed. Furthermore, best practices change over time. As noted in the previous section, computer technology has, over the last decade, made practical a whole array of best practices that simply did not exist previously. As another example, a large number of business process designs that were in widespread use in the United States prior to 9/11 are no longer considered best practices because of inherent security deficiencies.

So, how should a person tasked with the design and implementation of an integrated logistics business process in a global supply chain go about it? In this section, we suggest guidelines in the form of a few key questions. In the next section, some examples from global supply chains are presented.

Who Takes the Lead?

As per definition, the objective of integrated logistics management is to integrate logistics business processes with other organizations across the supply chain. It stands to reason then that collaboration across the supply chain should also be the driving motivation in the design of the business processes that specify how this should come about. It should be a team effort involving the functional personnel (in planning, inventory control, supply management, demand management, etc.) of each organization and business in the supply chain.

In practice, there has to be a leader. Where different business units working together in a supply chain form part of one corporate entity, a corporate logistics function is best placed to take that leadership role.

Where the supply chain is dominated by one powerful organization, the logistics function of that organization usually takes the lead even though there may be no corporate relationship with its supply chain partners. The integrated supply chain that Toyota built between its assembly plants and its first- and even second-tier suppliers in Japan is an excellent example. The Toyota assembly plant dictates how things will be done.

The situation is much more difficult in supply chains consisting of multiple, independent organizations with no clear dominant entity. Examples of integrated logistics management in such supply chains are less common. In those examples that do exist, the supply chain partners usually transfer the authority to design integrated logistics business processes to a separate entity. The collaboration of industry-specific business processes in online marketplaces can be seen as examples of this leadership structure.

Who Owns the Inventory?

A simplified view of the difference between moving and storing inventory and integrated logistics management is that in the latter case the inventory is moved and stored in support of global supply chain management objectives, not individual business objectives. Yet it is still the individual businesses that must perform these activities—and so the question of who incurs the cost and how the supply chain rewards individual entities for incurring those costs in practice frequently becomes the turning point at which integrated logistics management succeeds or fails.

What Are the Best Practice Methods and Techniques?

In my opinion, the first port of call when tasked with the design of best practice business processes should be to attend the conferences and meetings of professional organizations such as the Council of Supply Chain Management Professionals (CSCMP)—formerly called the Council of Logistics Management (CLM)—and the American Production and Inventory Control Society (APICS) and its national affiliates in other parts of the world such as British Production and Inventory Control Society (BPICS) and South African Production and Inventory Control Society (SAPICS). These organizations are set up—in many cases exclusively—to disseminate knowledge about current best practices and implementation experiences.

Major business system suppliers, such as enterprise resource planning (ERP) vendors and advanced planning and scheduling (APS), provide a very useful source of best practices. In designing their systems, these vendors usually perform extensive research and then code best practices into their system offerings. The better ones offer a wide range of configurable best practices with guidance on selection criteria.

There are also consulting practices that provide a service by analyzing the organizational entity, the supply chain strategy, the industry particulars, and the environment and then using that information to design appropriate best practice business processes for their clients.

What Are the Organization and People Issues?

Often significant opportunity for cost optimization exists by carefully designing a business process to streamline activities in such a way that fewer people can execute the required activities. In other cases, this is precisely what one does *not* wish to do. Best practices, as well as legislation in some countries (e.g., the Sarbanes-Oxley statute in the United States), call for separation of duties in specific areas. For example, purchasing processes are usually designed in such a way that the person authorizing a purchase order and the person paying the supplier must be different individuals.

What Are the Systems and Data Requirements?

In every instance of integrated logistics business process design, the decisions about the computer systems have far-reaching effects. Unfortunately, this can be good or bad. For every case where information technology (IT) played a major role in the success of integrating the logistics of a supply chain, there is another where the project degenerated into self-serving computer chaos without any business benefits.

A few self-evident truths are worth repeating. Organizations that are more comfortable following than being on the leading edge of technology should not implement integrated logistics management that depends on systems in an untested configuration for success. The strategic objectives and the business process design should drive the selection of business systems, not the other way round. There is no magic in computers; the systems cannot do what the people do not know how to do themselves. Inaccurate data is worse than no data because an illusion is created that you have knowledge.

On the other hand, there are some (e.g., Bowersox, Closs, and Cooper 2002) who argue that the very concept of integrated logistics management was only made possible by the acceleration in use of computer systems and the Internet in the last decade of the 20th century. This phenomenon is still accelerating, with technology such as radio-frequency identification clearly poised to even further revolutionize the way we manage our supply chains.

There is no way to escape the inevitable conclusion: anybody designing modern logistics business processes has to first come up to speed with the very latest in computer technology.

What Are the Local Modifiers?

Global supply chains by their very nature cut across many different countries and cultures and have to accommodate them all without sacrificing the overreaching goal of global supply chain management. This introduces many constraints, some "hard" (e.g., differing legal requirements) and some "soft" (e.g., language sensitivities).

Implementing Integrated Logistics Management

Global supply chains require integrated logistics management to work, and this is best illustrated with a few examples.

Luxury Goods

A business designing and selling luxury goods such as watches and wallets had the following supply chain. The products with their distinctive trademark were manufactured in Europe by independent manufacturers and delivered to the company warehouse near London. From there, product was dispatched by airfreight to regional warehouses around the globe, principally Hong Kong, Tokyo, and Dallas. From the regional warehouses, local stores were supplied. Since many countries in the world require a locally registered company to do business, different legal entities existed along this supply chain with local management in each country accountable for profit and return on investment. The assets were mostly inventory ordered from the London warehouse, and so each regional entity carefully manipulated the replenishment process to have just enough inventory to support the anticipated sales in its region.

From a global perspective, there were two problems. First, the purchasing function in London only had visibility of the replenishment orders coming through from the regional warehouses on which to base the purchasing of new products from the manufacturing suppliers. The lead time was too short and, furthermore, those replenishment orders were "filtered" through the inventory policies of the regions—for example, destocking close to financial year end and building inventory if a regional business perceived that a shortage might be coming, and it wanted to grab as much from the London warehouse as possible before its sister companies from other parts of the globe ordered the same products.

The other problem from a corporate perspective was that this way of moving products around the globe resulted in too much inventory in some regions and too little of the same products in others. Since import duties are very high on luxury goods and there were problems with claiming such import duties if the products were reexported, it was not really cost-effective to transship between regional companies.

Clearly, the solution was to keep the inventory in London as long as possible (since the regional warehouses were supplied by airfreight anyway) and for London to base purchasing decisions on global demand of the end consumers—not the replenishment to regional warehouses.

Who Takes the Lead?

The chief operations officer in London, to whom all the country managing directors reported, made the critical decision that the supply chain strategy would change from local to global optimization. He informed the countries, appointed a team to design and implement business processes to achieve this strategic objective, and chaired the steering committee for the length of the project.

Who Owns the Inventory?

Legal and financial ownership, as far as accounting goes, was retained by the regional companies. Decision-making authority on what products would go where and in what quantities was transferred to a centralized function in London. The agreement with the regional managing directors was that per country financial performance measures would take into consideration that levels of inventory were not under their control.

What Are the Best Practice Methods and Techniques?

The project established regional forecasting in a standardized format visible to London, so that the global demand could be collated to drive the purchasing process from the European manufacturers. It also established a business process to communicate planned replenishment of regional inventory beyond the lead time for the actual replenishment orders. From the collated planned replenishment, the centralized planning function in London could see shortages coming and make appropriate rationing decisions based on global strategic objectives.

What Are the Organization and People Issues?

The change from regional to global optimization meant a transfer of the power to make decisions about the distribution of inventory around the globe from the regions to the head office. Without sacrificing the reality—and necessity—of this organizational change, many "on-the-ground" compromises were made to soften the impact.

What Are the Systems and Data Requirements?

Global visibility of what was going to happen in the supply chain was the single most important requirement. The forecasting business processes in every region, the replenishment planning processes in every region, and the centralized collation of forecasts and replenishment plans as well as planned purchases were implemented on a single IT platform running on a server in London and operated via virtual private network technology around the globe. Anyone (with clearance) could now access the global logistics plans from anywhere.

What Are the Local Modifiers?

An interesting illustration of the importance of balancing the aspects of methods and techniques, organization and people, and systems and techniques became apparent during the design of the standardized forecasting process. The consulting team wanted to implement a sophisticated forecasting algorithm that required parameter management by local personnel. In the Far East regions, personnel pushed for simpler graphical methods and eventually prevailed. The forecasting software that was selected was strong on graphic inputs with only moderately strong forecasting algorithms—but the implementation took only a few weeks, and the new business process was well received. The project paid for itself within four months from reduced global inventory alone.

Global Pharmaceuticals

One of the top 10 pharmaceutical corporations in the world had to replace some of the planning and control computer systems in its manufacturing plants, many of them in Asia, Africa, and South America. A decision was made to simultaneously implement a strategy of "centers of excellence" where, instead of everybody making everything, the business unit in each country would specialize in manufacturing only a few products and import the rest from other companies in the corporation located in other countries.

The implication was that individual countries would become linked in a corporate supply chain and that the amount of intercompany trading would increase dramatically. To synchronize product flow from one country to the other on a global basis, and to do so better than when each country produced to meet its own requirements, would require integrated logistics management.

Who Takes the Lead?

It was clearly not practical to have each of the many in-country businesses devise its own way to deal with all the others. The corporate head office, therefore, commissioned a team to design standardized business processes and to configure these processes to run on the new computer systems it had selected as a global standard. Subsequently, all the in-country businesses were instructed to replace their current systems with the new systems and to replace current business processes with those designed by the central head office team.

Who Owns the Inventory?

The centers-of-excellence strategy meant that the business unit located in one country would manufacture and keep finished goods inventory in anticipation of demand in several other countries. The business process design called for the anticipated demand to be delivered in the form of forecasts to the manufacturing country—but in this industry demand is generally acknowledged to be fickle and forecasts inaccurate. The practicality of the new design came down to the question of who would pay for the cost of obsolete inventory produced to an inaccurate forecast.

This vexing problem was resolved with a corporate edict, "the demand side owns the inventory," and the development of appropriate financial processes to account for this principle. The incentive for more accurate forecasts was clearly tied to those most able to do something about them, and the incentive for the manufacturing plant not to second-guess the demand side was simultaneously established.

What Are the Best Practice Methods and Techniques?

The central head office design team took the current best practices applicable to manufacturing, distribution, and sales in the pharmaceutical industry and designed five major business processes: forecasting, demand management, production planning and control, inventory planning and management, and product movement. For each business process, the specific methods and techniques were documented in flow diagrams and procedures. Performance measurements used by each business unit to measure the performance of its supply chain partner were prescribed in detail.

What Are the Organization and People Issues?

A number of mandatory roles were designed to ensure that the global supply chain would have point contacts in every country. Each role had a specific job description and responsibilities. For example, every country had to have a demand manager who would be responsible for negotiating with either the supply manager in his or her own country or the supply manager of other supplying countries for delivery schedules.

What Are the Systems and Data Requirements?

The corporation elected to support the business processes with a suite of computer systems instead of a single platform. The systems were preconfigured by the central head office team to support the centrally designed business processes and to integrate with each other. The central head office team also designed data structures, numbering systems, and lot traceability schemes to facilitate communication up and down the supply chain.

What Are the Local Modifiers?

Although the business processes designed by the central head office team went into great detail for the corporation to standardize as much as possible, they still had to compromise during implementation on the ground. One small example: At that time it was illegal in India to distribute a consumer product without a recommended retail price prominently displayed, and it was also illegal in the United States to do so. The standardized global process had to be locally modified to meet both conditions.

Summary

Integrated logistics management enables supply chain management. It is achieved by integrating the logistics business processes of the partners in a supply chain to ensure the coordinated flow and storage of materials across the supply chain. The actual work of logistics is carried out in the functional areas of inventory management, transportation management, warehouse management, and so forth.

References

Bowersox, Donald J., David J. Closs, and M. Bixby Cooper (2002), *Supply Chain Logistics Management.* New York: McGraw-Hill.

Cox, J. F., J. H. Stone, and M. S. Spencer, eds. (1995), *APICS Dictionary,* 8th ed. Falls Church, VA: American Production and Inventory Control Society.

12

Inventory Management

Funda Sahin

E. Powell Robinson, Jr.

E ffective inventory management is a critical concern for firms in all industries and plays a major role in determining a firm's success. Consider, for example, the trade-offs experienced by a fashion goods retailer who is considering how many ski parkas to buy going into the winter sales season. On the one hand, a large order size provides high levels of product availability, which equates to high customer service levels and increased revenues. However, holding inventory is not free because it ties up working capital, is costly to maintain, and may require substantial price discounting to liquidate unsold items at the end of the sales season. Striking a balance between the economic benefits and the costs of inventory investment is critical for the retailer because having either too much or too little can seriously threaten the future of the business.

Inventory is held for a variety of reasons and should be viewed as an investment that provides an economic return. Companies such as Wal-Mart, Dell Computer, and Toyota exhibit exemplary financial performance because of their operational capabilities that yield superior inventory management practices.

The objective of this chapter is twofold. First, we review the most widely applied models for planning and controlling independent demand inventory, identify the environmental parameters driving each one, and indicate the appropriate application of each. Second, we discuss a variety of emerging supply chain inventory strategies that are being implemented by leading firms to tackle the complexities associated with increased product variety, the demand for higher levels of customer service, and the globally expanding marketplace.

Inventory Basics

Inventory is any item or resource stocked by an organization. The policies, procedures, and control measures that monitor the inventory levels and determine the timing and quantities of replenishment define an inventory system.

Independent Versus Dependent Demand Inventory

Selecting the right inventory control system requires distinguishing between the independent and dependent demand items. By definition, an item is considered to have independent demand if its sales rate is not influenced by the sales activity of another item. Consequently, inventory decisions for independent demand items can often be made separately for each item without worrying about interrelationships among items. Independent demand items are typically forecast where the demand is influenced by market conditions or other external factors. Retail and wholesale merchandise; maintenance, repair, and operation (MRO) items; and spare parts are examples of independent demand items. Dependent demand items, on the other hand, include components, parts, or subassemblies required to make a product. The demand for dependent demand items is directly related to the demand for the parent item. A simple example is the demand for bicycle tires in a production environment, where the number of tires is directly related to the number of bicycles produced. Distribution inventories may also exhibit dependent demand relationships, where demand at a plant warehouse is dependent on demand at a regional warehouse. Dependent demand item inventories are managed by requirements planning techniques such as material requirements planning (MRP) and distribution requirements planning (DRP). This chapter focuses on inventory management and control of independent demand items using statistical inventory control techniques.

Reasons for Inventory

All firms, including manufacturing and service firms, maintain inventories. Despite the misperception, even just-in-time (JIT) systems have inventories. Inventories can be held at the end-item, assembly, component, part, or raw material level. The following are some of the reasons for holding inventory:

1. *To maintain independence of operations*: Because of uncertain and varying processing rates at different operations, production processes often maintain a buffer stock of work-in-process inventories to ensure that a constant input of materials is available at the workstations. Buffer inventories also help to handle inflexibility due to capacity limitations in the processes. Potential interruptions in production and assembly processes due to quality problems can also be effectively handled or avoided by maintaining buffer inventories.

2. *To handle expected or unexpected variations in demand or supply and lead times*: Because of seasonal demand or lead-time variations in production or transportation, a firm may maintain inventories to handle the mismatch between supply and demand. Maintaining inventories becomes particularly important if the supply source is capacitated. Building inventories prior to the peak sales season is helpful in case of mismatch between demand and supply. Similarly, keeping safety stock to respond to unpredictable demand and lead times mitigates the adverse impact of shortages and helps to maintain the balance between demand and supply. Inventories also help to protect against shortages or delays that can occur when materials ordered from a vendor arrive late.

3. *To gain economies of batch replenishment*: Timely and expensive production setups, changeovers, and long-distance shipments favor longer production runs and larger shipment quantities. Reducing production or transportation costs (or both) in these cases can be achieved only by higher inventory levels. Similarly, there are fixed costs associated with placing an order. Therefore, the larger the order, the fewer the orders that will be handled, resulting in lower ordering costs but higher inventories.

Reasons Against Inventory

Despite the pressures to maintain high inventory levels for smooth operations and high customer service levels, management must also weigh the costs associated with maintaining inventories to determine the right amount of inventory to carry. Inventory represents a major monetary commitment. For every unit kept in stock, the firm incurs inventory-holding costs, which include the costs of storage facilities, handling, insurance, obsolescence, pilferage, deterioration, and taxes and the opportunity cost of capital. This unit cost typically ranges from 20% to 40% of the stocked item's unit value. The component costs associated with maintaining inventories are discussed below in more detail:

1. *Interest or opportunity cost of capital*: The major component of inventory carrying cost is the interest or opportunity cost required to finance the inventory. Roughly, this often represents 10% to 15% of the item's value.

2. *Storage and handling costs*: There is a cost associated with storing and moving items in and out of facilities. Storage costs occur when a firm leases space. There may also be an opportunity cost associated with the space if the building could be used productively in some other way.

3. *Taxes, insurance, and shrinkage*: Firms pay taxes on inventory assets. The higher the inventories, the higher the taxes. Similarly, the insurance cost increases with higher levels of inventory. The costs associated with shrinkage may also be considerable. Shrinkage costs occur because of pilferage, obsolescence, or deterioration. Obsolescence is a major expense for apparel firms because any unsold seasonal items must be discounted. Similarly, excess inventories of short-life-cycle

items such as computers may need to be discounted when faced with new model introductions.

Types of Inventory

Inventory may also be classified according to the motivation for holding it:

1. *Cycle stock*: By definition, cycle stock inventory is held to meet the average (expected) demand between replenishment periods. In determining cycle stock levels, cost plays a major role, where production lot sizes, shipment quantities, storage space limitations, and lead times are important factors to consider. To reduce cycle stock levels, firms need to figure out ways to reduce the lot size or the replenishment quantity. However, reducing the replenishment sizes requires more frequent setups or ordering with additional setup or ordering costs. Therefore, finding ways to reduce the fixed charges associated with equipment setups or placing orders are some of the tactics firms can use to reduce cycle stock.

2. *Safety stock*: Safety stock is held as a buffer to protect against shortages that may arise owing to uncertainties in demand, lead time, and supply. Improving forecast accuracy to reduce uncertainties in demand, reducing replenishment lead time, and working with more reliable suppliers are some of the approaches to reduce safety stock levels.

3. *Pipeline inventory*: Pipeline inventories result from items being in transit. The longer the transit lead time, the higher the pipeline inventories. In a manufacturing context, work-in-process inventories are pipeline inventories.

4. *Anticipation or speculation inventory*: Building inventory in anticipation of price increases (e.g., for precious materials such as copper or gold) leads to forward buys. Firms also build inventory prior to a new product introduction speculating that sales will materialize for the new item.

Inventory Control Systems

An inventory system includes the organizational structure, policies, and procedures to control the stock of goods. Inventory decision rules dictate the timing and quantities of replenishment orders. Inventory control systems are classified into single-period and multiple-period inventory systems representing the number of replenishment opportunities during the planning horizon. A single-period model implies that the replenishment decision involves a one-time purchase occasion with no recourse for reordering. Multiple-period systems assume an unlimited planning horizon with multiple ordering opportunities.

Single-Period Inventory Systems

The single-period model is often referred to as the news vendor problem, in which the issue is to determine how many newspapers to buy for the day's sales knowing that if the vendor does not stock enough papers he will miss sales and forgo revenue. However, if he stocks more than he sells, he will have to throw the excess away at the end of the day and lose his purchase price. To arrive at the optimal stocking quantity, the news vendor must assess his potential sales volume each day and balance his expected shortage and excess inventory costs.

Although it is conceptually simple, the news vendor model has a variety of applications in supply chain management, including the following:

- Setting order quantities for seasonal and short-life-cycle goods such as skiwear, lawn mowers, garden seeds, and so on, where the retailer or distributor has a single ordering opportunity prior to the selling season;
- Establishing overbooking rules for hotel or airline reservations in anticipation of last-minute cancellations and reservations; and
- Determining safety stock inventory levels when replenishment lead-time demand is uncertain because of delivery or demand uncertainty.

The single-period inventory model is an important modeling tool for analyzing "yield management" or "revenue management" problems.

The decision rule for determining the profit maximizing number of units to order is to increase the number of items stocked as long as the marginal understock (i.e., not enough inventory) cost is greater than or equal to the marginal overstock (i.e., too much inventory) cost. Mathematically, the incremental order quantity is increased if $PM \geq (1 - P)L$, where P is the probability of selling the incremental unit, M is the profit margin per unit (i.e., marginal revenue minus marginal cost), and L is the per-unit loss if the incremental item does not sell. Rearranging terms yields $P \geq L/(L + M)$, which indicates that the order quantity should be increased if management's estimate for the probability of selling the next incremental unit exceeds $L/(L + M)$.

Multiperiod Inventory Systems

Multiperiod inventory systems, which determine the order quantity and order release date, are grouped into two major categories: continuous review and periodic review systems. Continuous review systems monitor and control inventory after each inventory withdrawal, whereas periodic review systems monitor and control inventory only at regular, predetermined time intervals.

Continuous Review System

Continuous review systems, also known as fixed-order-quantity models and reorder point systems, are the workhorse of many end-item and spare parts

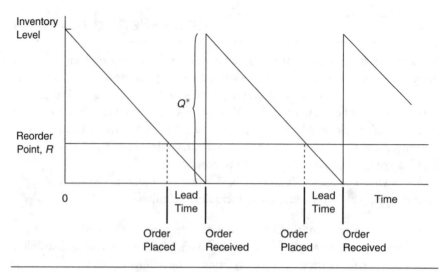

Figure 12.1   Continuous Review Inventory System

distribution and retail inventory systems. Continuous review systems are ideally suited for controlling the inventory of independent demand items whose demand is forecast. The controlling logic is easy to understand and implement, and the decision rules provide high-quality, robust solutions that are relatively insensitive to moderate errors in parameter estimation. The continuous review system controls each item individually, seeking to minimize the sum of its ordering and inventory-holding costs subject to prespecified in-stock service levels. Because the system monitors inventories at every inventory withdrawal, it allows for a quick response to potential shortages, making it ideally suited for managing both high-value items and critical items requiring high service levels. The continual monitoring requirement made the system cumbersome and time-consuming in the past; however, today's computerized systems automate these functions, making the systems economical to implement.

The continuous review inventory system hinges on answering two questions: how much to order, Q^*, and when to place an order, R. Figure 12.1 illustrates the relationships among Q^*, R, and inventory level moving through time. As noted, the system releases an order for Q units each time inventory position[1] falls to a specified quantity called the reorder point, R. The order cycle length is the time interval between successive order releases. The line depicting inventory position moving through time takes the shape of a sawtooth curve.

Basic (Q*, R) Continuous Review Inventory Model

The basic model for determining Q^*, the optimal economic order quantity (EOQ), was first proposed by Harris (1913). The EOQ model assumes the following parameters are constant and known with certainty: demand rate per unit time, replenishment lead time, per-unit purchase cost, per-unit inventory-holding cost,

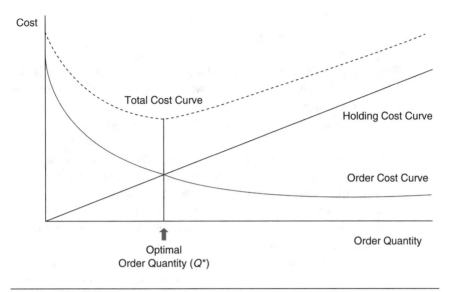

Figure 12.2   Determining How Much to Order

and ordering cost. In addition, the model assumes that all demand must be met and the complete order is delivered instantaneously. Hence, the basic EOQ model does not consider purchase quantity discounts, back orders, or inventory shortage costs.

The objective of the EOQ model is to minimize the expected annual total inventory policy costs as illustrated by the total cost expression in Equation (1). The two terms represent the expected annual ordering cost and the annual inventory-holding cost, respectively:

$$T = \frac{D}{Q}S + \frac{Q}{2}H \qquad (1)$$

where T is the total annual policy cost, D is the demand per time period, Q is the order quantity, S is the fixed ordering cost, and H is the per-unit inventory-carrying cost per time period. Finally, $H = iC$, where i is a fractional value (often called the percentage holding rate) and C is the item value. H and D are expressed in the same time units. Figure 12.2 graphically illustrates the cost trade-off, where the annual ordering costs decrease at a decreasing rate as Q increases, whereas annual inventory-holding costs increase linearly as Q increases. At the optimal order size, Q^*, the ordering and inventory-holding costs are equal.

The formula for determining the optimal value, Q^*, is derived, using calculus,[2] from the total cost formula:

$$\text{EOQ} = Q^* = \sqrt{\frac{2DS}{H}} \qquad (2)$$

The expected order cycle length, or the time between orders (TBO), is TBO = Q^*/D years. An order is placed when inventory position reaches the reorder point $R = dL$, where L is the length of the replenishment lead time and d is the expected demand per unit time. Under assumptions of the basic EOQ formula, the replenishment order arrives just as inventory falls to 0 (see Figure 12.1). Consequently, the average order cycle inventory level is $(Q^* + 0)/2 = Q^*/2$ units.

In addition to providing the optimal order quantity, the EOQ equation is also useful in understanding the relationships between the order quantity and changes in environmental parameters or managerial policy. These insights are often known as the "square root rule" of inventory control. Consider the following:

- *Demand increase*: If demand in the marketplace doubles, the optimal order quantity, and hence the average inventory level, increases only by the square root of 2 or by 41% over the original amount. Similarly, if demand triples, average inventory levels should increase by the square root of 3.
- *Warehouse consolidation*: The total average order cycle inventory required to maintain n identical regional warehouses is $n(Q^*/2)$. However, consolidating the regional warehouses into a central facility results in system order cycle inventory of only $\sqrt{n}\,(Q^*/2)$. Hence, a regional system requires $\sqrt{n}$ times as much inventory as a central system.
- *Product variety reduction*: The total average order cycle inventory required to stock three different colors of dishwashers (e.g., white, black, and almond) with identical demand in inventory is $3(Q^*/2)$. However, stocking only a white dishwasher with an interchangeable black/almond color panel results in system order cycle inventory of $\sqrt{3}(Q^*/2)$. Hence, again the square root rule applies.
- *Reduction in ordering costs*: Suppose an investment in an automated electronic ordering system reduces ordering costs (S) to only 25% of their former level. The optimal order cycle inventory reduces from $Q^*/2$ to $(1/\sqrt{4})$ $(Q^*/2)$ for a 50% reduction in inventory over the previous level of ordering cost.

Extensions of the Basic (Q*, R) Continuous Review Model

The basic continuous review model is often criticized because of its simplifying, and often unrealistic, assumptions. In this section, we discuss several variants of the basic model for which the limiting assumptions are removed.

Production Order Quantity (POQ) Model. The basic model assumes the replenishment order arrives instantaneously at the end of the order cycle. However, in a production environment, inventory may be replenished gradually over time with a periodic net addition to inventory equal to $(p - d)$, where p and d are the production and demand rates per unit time, respectively. Accounting for the gradual inventory buildup, the total cost equation for the POQ model is

$$T_{\text{POQ}} = \frac{H(p - d)Q}{2p} + \frac{DS}{Q} \tag{3}$$

where Q/p is the number of production periods for each order cycle and $(p - d)$ is the number of units added to inventory for each production time period. The optimal POQ order quantity is

$$POQ = Q_{POQ}^* = \sqrt{\frac{2DS}{H} \frac{(p)}{(p - d)}} \tag{4}$$

EOQ Model With Price Discounts (EOQ$_{DISC}$). The EOQ$_{DISC}$ model relaxes the constant per-unit purchase price assumption and determines the optimal order size when quantity discount price breaks are applicable. Let i be an index associated with one of N possible price breaks, where $i = 1, 2, \ldots, N$. The unit purchase price for price break i is C_i, where $C_1 > C_2, \ldots, C_N$, and the minimum purchase quantity to qualify for price break i is B_i. The nondiscounted price is C_1 with $B_1 = 1$. The total cost equation for price break i is

$$T_i = DC_i + \frac{H_i Q_i}{2} + \frac{DS}{Q_i} \tag{5}$$

The steps for solving the EOQ$_{DISC}$ model are as follows:

1. Starting with $i = N$, solve for Q_N^* using Equation (1) with $H = H_N$. If Q_N^* is feasible (i.e., $Q_N^* > B_N$), stop. Q_N^* is the optimal order quantity at unit cost C_N. Otherwise, go to Step 2.

2. Iteratively starting with $i = N - 1$ and decrementing at each iteration, continue solving for the optimal Q_i^* until a feasible value is found and then stop.

3. Using Equation (5), compute the total cost for the feasible Q_i^* and the total cost for the other lower-cost C_is at their price breaks. Compare the total costs. The quantity (Q_i^* or the price break) yielding the lowest total cost is the optimal order quantity.

The model determines the optimal replenishment quantity according to a given quantity discount schedule.

Continuous Review Model With Uncertain Demand During Replenishment Lead Time

Relaxing the constant demand and replenishment lead-time assumptions does not change the optimal order quantity, but it does alter the reorder point, R, indicating when the order should be placed. Given a constant demand rate per time period, d, and the replenishment lead time, L, the basic (Q^*, R) model's minimum cost reorder point is at $R = dL$ (i.e., the expected demand during replenishment lead time) with a 100% service level.[3] However, under conditions of uncertain demand or lead time, setting R at the expected sales level would result in 50% of the ordering cycles having insufficient stock to meet the customer's demand.

Consequently, in addition to holding inventory for covering the expected sales, a buffer or safety stock inventory is required to ensure that management's desired service level is met.

The quantity of safety stock is expressed as a safety factor Z, equating to management's desired service level[4] and the standard deviation of demand during replenishment lead time. When the demand per time period is variable and replenishment lead time is constant, the reorder point is calculated as follows:

$$R = dL + Z\sqrt{L\sigma_d^2} \tag{6}$$

In the equation, σ_d is the standard deviation of demand per time period, $\sqrt{L\sigma_d^2}$ is the standard deviation of demand during replenishment lead time, $Z\sqrt{L\sigma_d^2}$ is the safety stock, and dL is the expected sales during replenishment lead time.

If both demand and replenishment lead times are variable, Equation (7) is used to determine R, where σ_L is the standard deviation of lead time, $\sqrt{L\sigma_d^2 + d^2\sigma_L^2}$ is the standard deviation of demand during replenishment lead time, and $Z\sqrt{L\sigma_d^2 + d^2\sigma_L^2}$ is the safety stock inventory:

$$R = dL + Z\sqrt{L\sigma_d^2 + d^2\sigma_L^2} \tag{7}$$

As indicated in Equations (6) and (7) for a specified service level, the mean and standard deviation of replenishment lead time and the standard deviation of demand are the major drivers of safety stock, and it is worth management's attention to control them.

Periodic Review System

The periodic review system, also called a fixed interval reorder system or fixed time period model, reviews inventories at predetermined times such as every two days, every week, or every month and orders a sufficient quantity to attain a predetermined target inventory position. Because of the variability of demand, replenishment quantities may vary from order to order. The periodic review system is particularly advantageous over a continuous review system for these reasons:

- Controlling low sales value or usage items that do not warrant the extra effort associated with continuous inventory review
- Purchasing multiple items from the same vendor, where synchronizing orders permits the sharing of ordering and delivery costs, thereby lowering total system costs
- Balancing the workload of procurement processes by assigning different classes or families of inventory to different review time periods
- Implementing a vendor-managed inventory (VMI) system where the vendor periodically reviews on-site inventories

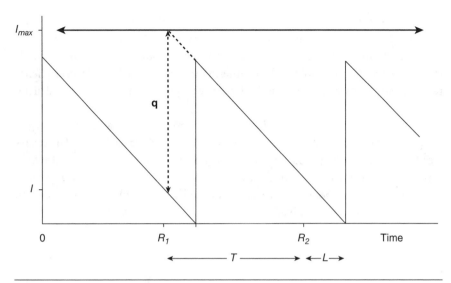

Figure 12.3   Periodic Review System

The major disadvantage of the periodic inventory system is that it requires higher safety stock inventory levels than a continuous review system to achieve the same in-stock customer service level. Figure 12.3 illustrates the mechanics of the periodic review inventory system, where T is the time interval between reviews, R_1 and R_2 are review points, I is the on-hand inventory, I_{max} is the target inventory position, q is the order quantity, and the other parameters are as defined earlier. At each review period, the inventory position is raised to I_{max}, which ensures sufficient inventory is available to cover demand until the next review period plus replenishment lead time (i.e., $T + L$ is the length of the uncertainty period). This is expressed mathematically in Equation (8), where the first term is the expected demand and the second term is the safety stock associated with the uncertainty period (the order quantity is $q = $ maximum$\{|I_{max} - I|, 0\}$):

$$Q = d(T + L) + z\sigma_d\sqrt{T + L} - I \qquad (8)$$

Implications and New Strategies in Inventory Management

Global marketplaces, higher product variety, shorter product life cycles, demand for more customized, yet affordable products, and premium customer service are increasing supply chain complexity and cost. To meet these challenges, supply chain inventory strategies are constantly evolving to find new ways to meet the customers' needs and to capitalize on new opportunities arising in the changing environment. Operating with substantially lower inventories while still meeting or exceeding customer expectations is one of the key dimensions of global competition. This is particularly the case for retail supply chains, where more integrated forecasting and inventory planning and control systems that are supported by increased supply chain speed and an automated data gathering system are enabling "rocket science retailing" to increase efficiency and effectiveness (Fisher, Raman, and McClelland 2000).

This section discusses several emerging supply chain inventory strategies designed to meet the challenges posed by the emerging global economy. The strategies take a variety of approaches in handling the supply problems caused by the expanding marketplace, high product variety, short product life cycles, long replenishment lead times, poor forecast accuracy, and the difficulties associated with securing supply chain coordination.

Postponement

Postponement strategies combat increasing fulfillment costs associated with both geographically dispersed markets and the expansion of product variety. Postponement in its most general sense involves delaying the commitment of resources to satisfy customer demand until the last possible minute. Geographic and product form postponement are increasingly applied in global supply chains.

Geographic postponement holds inventory centrally, delaying its commitment to particular market areas, often until after customer orders are received. The consolidation of end-item and spare parts inventories from regional warehouses into a central distribution center is a classic example. As discussed earlier, moving to a centralized inventory system can yield significant reductions in inventory investment and cost. However, holding inventories centrally instead of in the regions may increase delivery lead time, resulting in a deterioration of customer service. Leading third-party logistics providers, such as FedEx and UPS, recognize this trade-off and provide distribution services that combine geographic postponement, electronic order processing, and premium delivery service such that the inventory reduction benefits of postponement are obtained without sacrificing delivery lead time. Spare parts inventory and high-value end items with volatile demand are commonly distributed using geographic postponement.

Product form postponement delays the creation of product variety by stocking products in their most generic form. This allows the product to be inventoried in its least expensive form and promotes risk pooling, which maintains the flexibility of the item's application by stocking it in its most generic form and then performing final manufacturing or assembly once customers' exact demands are known. The food processing industry applies product form postponement when canned vegetables are stocked in "shiny," or unlabeled, cans, delaying the brand-labeling process until orders are received. Hence, instead of attempting to forecast and maintain inventories of a wide variety of product brands and labels, each vegetable is held in its generic form, thereby minimizing risk and reducing speculative inventory.

The earlier example of stocking only white dishwashers and including color panels is another example of form postponement. Here, color variety is delayed until the customer purchases the dishwasher, takes it home, and inserts the desired color panel. The associated reduction in end-item inventory more than offsets the added cost of providing extra color panels with each sold unit.

A third example of postponement is provided by Dell Computer in its direct sell and build strategy for supplying personal computers. In this scenario, Dell delays the commitment of computer modules to specific end items until the customer inputs his specifications over the company's Web site. Instead of attempting to stock all possible varieties of end items, Dell forecasts the demand for the modules, stores them in inventory, and, utilizing mass customization processes, pulls them as required to custom assemble end items matching the customer's exact specifications. Dell also practices geographic postponement, utilizing central manufacturing facilities to attain volume economies and air freight to provide fast product delivery. Dell's revolutionary application of postponement inventory strategy has redefined supply chain practices in the computer industry.

Reducing Seasonal and Short-Life-Cycle Inventory Costs With Quick Response (QR)

Quick resonse (QR) is a supply chain initiative that focuses on reducing inventory over- and understocking costs associated with supplying short-life-cycle and seasonal products with highly uncertain demand. Although the single-period, or news vendor, inventory model assumes a one-time supply of inventory is available at the start of a sales season without replenishment opportunities, QR alters supply chain processes such that multiple orders can be shipped during the sales season. QR hinges on shortening manufacturing and distribution lead times, which allows the supply chain to enter the seasonal sales cycle with a small initial inventory allocation at the retailers, observe early sales patterns, generate a posterior demand distribution, and choose the optimal replenishment quantity to maximize expected profits given the posterior distribution. The manufacturer (supplier) receives the early sales data, often in the form of point-of-sales data, and utilizes them to adjust production schedules to better match output with demand. QR began in the apparel industry as a response to JIT practices of the auto industry.

Sport Obermeyer, a manufacturer of fashion skiwear, provides an early QR success story (see Fisher and Raman 1996). The firm traditionally incurred high costs for both stockout and inventory obsolescence as it tried to anticipate the volatile seasonal demand of sportswear lines. The long production lead times, coupled with a concentrated selling season, forced production commitments several months prior to the sales season, when insufficient market information was available to accurately predict the new season's most popular styles, colors, and fabrics. Consequently, the firm experienced significant inventory shortages and markdowns as it attempted to guess future sales patterns. In the revised QR strategy, "speculative manufacturing capacity" provides the initial store inventories, and the majority of the season's production is postponed, often in the form of fabric type or styles later dyed to the hot selling colors, until after the early sales season is under way and data are collected with which to improve forecast accuracy. Based on the revised forecasts, the postponed products are completed using "reactive capacity" and a streamlined distribution process to quickly replenish the retailers with the season's hot sellers. Using the QR strategy, Sport Obermeyer reduced their stockout and markdown costs by 1.82% of sales for an estimated 60% profit improvement.

Zara, a Spanish clothier, developed a novel QR strategy that has provided it with a distinct competitive advantage in the fashion clothing industry. Its strategy is based on shortening the lead time from product design to store display. Instead of attempting to forecast individual item demand and maintain inventory of specific stock-keeping units over the sales season, Zara produces in small batch sizes, allocates the product to stores, and rapidly introduces new designs based on feedback from retailers. Because of small replenishment lot sizes and the extremely short product life cycles of the new designs, the customers know they had better buy the sweater they like when they see it because there may not be a follow-up production run. They also know to check back frequently with the retailer for new styles. In this manner, Zara's planned stock-outs become a marketing advantage, and they also avoid inventory obsolescence costs by quickly responding to changes in the marketplace. QR is also part of Zara's crisis management system. For example, after 9/11, clothing sales plummeted throughout the industry. However, Zara was able to utilize its QR capability to coordinate its designers, manufacturers, and supply chain partners to launch within two weeks a new clothing line in black that raised their sales significantly (see Beth et al. 2003).

Supply Chain Partnerships and Vendor-Managed Inventory

A supply chain is fully coordinated when all decisions are aligned to accomplish global system objectives. Lack of coordination occurs when decision makers have incomplete information or incentives that are not compatible with systemwide objectives. Even under conditions of full information availability, the performance of the supply chain can be suboptimal with major inefficiencies when each supply chain member acts independently (i.e., decentralized decision making) to optimize individual operations. Forrester (1958), in his study of industrial dynamics, observed the natural tendency of demand signals to amplify, delay, and oscillate moving upstream in the supply chain, thereby causing significant inventory inefficiencies. This phenomenon, known as the "Forrester" or the "bullwhip" effect, occurs in supply chains when final consumer sales data are not shared among all supply chain members and inventory decisions are not coordinated.

Potential causes of the bullwhip effect are artificially induced demand seasonality caused by forward buying actions prompted by marketing promotions and price discounts, order batching associated with production and transportation cost reduction, perceived product and capacity shortages that limit supply and encourage shortage gaming by retailers, long-order-cycle lead times that delay transmittal of timely demand information, and traditional purchasing and inventory policies that overreact to perceived changes in the demand pattern. To better manage the bullwhip, Forrester (1958) and Lee, Padhamanabhan, and Whang (1997) suggest shortening the order cycle lead time, sharing the retailers' point-of-sales data with all supply chain members, removing echelons from the supply chain, and altering inventory control procedures to provide a more gradual correction to changes in demand.

Information sharing between supply chain members is frequently suggested as a remedy to cure the ill effects associated with the bullwhip effect. The technology to share the data is readily available with enterprise information systems, automatic identification and data capture, and the Internet, thus making it possible to efficiently capture, process, and transmit sales data in real time throughout the supply chain. This allows each inventory stocking point to use actual customer demand information in the forecasting system versus the more highly variable orders from supply chain members. However, although information sharing mitigates demand uncertainty, research indicates that it does not fully eliminate the bullwhip effect if managerial incentives are not aligned with system objectives (Sahin and Robinson 2002, 2005).

One method gaining popularity for coordinating inventory decisions is described under the broad heading of VMI. Under VMI, the supplier is provided with point-of-sales data from the retailer or sell-through data from his immediate downstream supply chain member. The supplier then uses this information to plan economic replenishments, based on agreed-upon in-stock service levels, for his downstream supply chain member. Additional information, such as upcoming product promotions or new product introductions, is also communicated among supply chain members to aid in systemwide inventory management. VMI systems provide a win-win opportunity for all supply chain members. On the supply side, more timely demand data and the ability to set the timing and quantity of replenishments can yield significant savings through more efficient manufacturing and transportation processes. At the same time, the customer is relieved of the ordering process, is guaranteed high levels of service, and often shares the gains of increased supply chain efficiencies.

VMI is implemented under a variety of names. Since 1985, Wal-Mart's Retail Link Program has set the standard and provided the benchmark for the consumer goods (and other) industries. Under the program, certified manufacturers are provided with daily point-of-sales data and tasked with planning retail replenishments subject to specified product availability service levels. The manufacturer bypasses the distributor and ships a full truckload to Wal-Mart's cross-docking operations for break-bulk and consolidation shipment to individual retail stores. The Retail Link Program not only promotes manufacturing efficiency but also provides frequent delivery opportunities to the retailers, thereby enabling high in-stock service levels with minimal inventory investments. The system is mimicked by other leading consumer product retailers, including JC Penney, Sears, and Dilliard Department Stores. In the early 1990s, the grocery industry responded with its version of VMI, called efficient consumer response (ECR), with Campbell Soup, P&G,

and HEB Stores as early implementers. VMI has provided inventory savings ranging from 20% to 30% while increasing service levels. Kurt Salmon Associates estimated a potential $30 billion savings in supply chain costs from implementation of ECR in the grocery industry.

Conclusions

This chapter has reviewed the most widely applied inventory models for planning and controlling independent demand inventory. Although it is important to select the appropriate inventory model for the particular situation, it is equally important to recognize that the models provide optimal ordering decisions for specified environmental parameters and that these environmental parameters may be subject to change. In this chapter, we also discussed a variety of approaches taken in industry to alter the basic relationships among the model parameters. Postponement strategies illustrate that the form and location of stocked items can significantly affect inventory policy costs and often provide an effective approach to handling high product variety. The QR approach to inventory management looks at shortening replenishment lead times so that early sales data can be captured and used to improve forecast accuracy. Hence, the traditional single-period inventory model is modified to permit a secondary replenishment order under more certain demand conditions, resulting in better management of short-life-cycle inventories. Finally, the issues of information sharing and coordination are discussed along with the implications for VMI and ECR management, which targets improved systemwide inventory planning and control.

Although the 1950s and 1960s were the golden era for the development of statistical inventory models, today is the golden era for the development of integrated global supply chain strategies and the ideal time in which to effectively deploy them. The recent advances in information technology, the global expansion of the marketplace, and the outsourcing of manufacturing and distribution processes provide many challenges and opportunities for getting inventory management right. We are only scratching the surface of best practices for the application of computer and modeling technology to address these critical issues.

Notes

1. Inventory position is defined as the sum of on-hand inventory plus outstanding replenishment orders minus back orders.

2. EOQ is derived by taking the first derivative of the total cost equation, setting it equal to 0, and solving for the optimal Q. Mathematically, this is $\frac{\partial TC}{\partial Q} = -\frac{DS}{Q^2} + \frac{H}{2} = 0$, which yields $Q = \sqrt{\frac{2DS}{H}}$. The second derivative of the total cost function is also positive, indicating that a minimum is obtained.

3. In this chapter, service level is defined as the probability of not stocking out during replenishment lead time.

4. Assuming that demand is normally distributed during replenishment, the safety factor, Z, is obtained from the Standardized Normal Table, which indicates the required value of Z for a specified service level.

References

Beth, S., D. N. Burt, W. Copacino, C. Gopal, H. L. Lee, R. P. Lynch, and S. Morris (2003), "Supply Chain Challenges: Building Relationships," *Harvard Business Review*, July, 65–73.

Fisher, M. L. and A. Raman (1996), "Reducing the Cost of Demand Uncertainty Through Accurate Response to Early Sales," *Operations Research*, 44 (1), 87–99.

Fisher, M. L., A. Raman, and A. S. McClelland (2000), "Rocket Science Retailing Is Almost Here. Are You Ready?" *Harvard Business Review*, July–August, 115–124.

Forrester, J. W. (1958), "Industrial Dynamics," *Harvard Business Review*, July–August, 37–66.

Harris, F. W. (1913), "How Many Parts to Make at Once," *Factory, the Magazine of Management*, 10, 135–136, 152.

Lee, H. L., V. Padhamanabhan, and S. Whang (1997), "The Bullwhip Effect in Supply Chains," *Sloan Management Review*, Spring, 93–102.

Sahin, F. and E. P. Robinson (2002), "Flow Coordination and Information Sharing in Supply Chains: Review, Implications and Directions for Future Research," *Decision Sciences*, 33 (4), 505–536.

Sahin, F. and E. P. Robinson (2005), "Information Sharing and Coordination in Make-to-Order Supply Chains," *Journal of Operations Management*, 23 (6), 579–598.

13

Transportation Management

Thomas J. Goldsby

Michael R. Crum

Joel Sutherland

Transportation management is a critical element of global logistics and supply chain management for several important reasons. Transportation expense often represents one of the largest single costs faced by a company. U.S. companies spent an estimated $636 billion[1] on transportation alone in 2004, representing 63% of the total logistics cost or approximately 5.4% of the nation's gross domestic product (GDP) (Wilson 2005). Transportation expense can represent a significantly larger share of total logistics costs and GDP in settings outside the United States, where the system of roads and other important forms of infrastructure may not be as well developed and the "friction of distance" is considerably greater. In fact, the costs and difficulties associated with transportation often preclude the pursuit of optimal logistics and supply chain strategies where sufficient capabilities and capacity are lacking.

Not only does the cost of transportation represent a significant expense for the company, but the element of service provided by transportation operations is also a critical aspect of logistics service. Transit times for transportation often represent the largest component of order lead time, sometimes taking several weeks for long-distance overseas moves. Not only does transportation consume a large portion of lead time, on average, but it also contributes to lead time variance—or departures from the "normal" lead time. Variance can occur from circumstances as simple and minor as truck drivers getting lost to very severe complications associated with

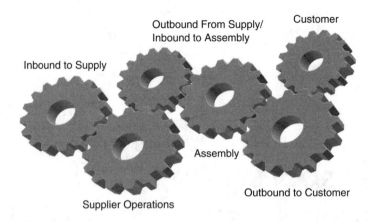

Figure 13.1 The Critical Workings of the Supply Chain

SOURCE: Stank and Goldsby (2000).

accidents, vehicle hijackings, carrier closures, or failures in the infrastructure. Many companies experienced significant failure of the transportation system following the events of 9/11 in 2001 and in late 2002 with the closure on ports in the U.S. West Coast. Unanticipated events happen every day throughout the world, causing substantial disruption to global logistics and supply chain operations.

In pointing to transportation disruptions that lead to broader disruptions in supply chain operations, we recognize an important attribute of transportation—it serves as the critical physical linkage among companies in the supply chain. Without transportation, the supply chain effectively stops. This critical dynamic is depicted in Figure 13.1, which illustrates that the workings of the supply chain "machine" halt with the failure of any one of the gears. In fact, the criticality of sound transportation management has only increased as a result of today's supply chains that routinely extend around the globe.

This chapter explores the global environment for transportation management, surveying the cost and service aspects of transportation operations, opportunities for collaboration among shippers and carriers, and key global transportation issues. It then reviews the decision scope of transportation-related decisions in logistics and supply chain management.

Transportation Decision Making

Transportation management is an activity that interfaces with many aspects of logistics, customer service, and supply chain management. Many interfaces inherently involve trade-offs with other logistics activities and the outcomes of delivered cost and service. One of the most common trade-offs faced by firms involves the costs of transportation and inventory. Ordinarily, a "lean" inventory strategy—where stocks of materials and goods are maintained at minimal levels—results in heightened transportation costs: Smaller volumes result in high-frequency shipments on both the inbound and the outbound sides of the operation. Although transportation cost is a significant expense for most companies, the total logistics cost of lean strategies may still be minimized because increased transportation costs are often more than offset by the savings in inventory carrying costs and warehousing expense. This recognition of cost trade-offs is central to the pursuit of least total cost in logistics and optimal service delivery in the supply chain.

Timeliness and certainty of delivery are important aspects of customer service. Promising damage-free delivery at a specific time often incurs a premium price for service but may be required to serve valued customers. Such guaranteed services are often required in the fulfillment of just-in-time (JIT) operations. Like the lean inventory strategy described above, there are instances where greater certainty in transit time and cargo safety results in justifiably higher transportation costs. The goal of transportation management is, therefore, not singularly focused on transportation cost reduction or guaranteed delivery but rather to fulfill the company's customer service commitment at the least total cost. As noted, higher levels of service typically involve higher costs. Therefore, the cost-service trade-offs found among logistics activities, as well as those involving the outside members of the supply chain, must be carefully considered and measured to optimize the role of transportation in global logistics and supply chain management.

Among the most fundamental decisions a company faces in its pursuit of the optimal transportation approach is whether to insource or outsource transportation. This decision, like so many involving outsourcing arrangements, may vary in form and degree. For instance, a company may elect to outsource the management of the transportation activity, the operations themselves, the administrative aspects of transportation, or some combination of the three. Operations and administrative aspects (e.g., freight bill auditing and payment) are among the most common outsourcing arrangements in transportation and logistics. Seeking for-hire common carriers has been the most pervasive form of transportation outsourcing, and this practice has grown considerably with the economic deregulation or liberalization of transportation that has transpired in many developed nations.

It was very common for shipper organizations to own and operate private forms of motor carriage in the United States prior to the Motor Carrier Act of 1980 (known as MCA-80). MCA-80 had a dramatic influence on the industry, allowing shippers to negotiate freely for services and rates with carriers, thereby reducing the incentives for owning and operating transportation assets given that competitive services could more readily be purchased in the marketplace. This phenomenon has been observed in many developed nations around the world as free market mechanisms allow shippers to buy heightened levels of service at competitive rates. Interestingly, the decision to outsource transportation operations has been revisited in recent years by U.S. and Canadian companies as trucking capacity has become tighter. The shortage of drivers in the long-haul trucking industry has made it difficult to find affordable and reliable service, especially during periods of peak demand. As a result, many companies that operated private fleets prior to MCA-80, and abandoned them soon afterward, have begun to rethink the decision and, in some cases, have reinstated a motor carrier fleet to ensure ready capacity and good service.

Table 13.1   Modal Service Characteristics

Operating Characteristics	Rail	Motor	Water	Air	Pipeline
Speed	3	2	4	1	5
Availability	2	1	4	3	5
Dependability	3	2	4	5	1
Capacity	2	3	1	4	5
Flexibility	3	1	4	2	5
Average score	2.6	1.8	3.4	3.0	4.2

SOURCE: Adapted from Bowersox, Closs, and Cooper (2002).

NOTE: 1 = best, 5 = worst.

Another critical decision in transportation management is mode and carrier selection. As illustrated by Table 13.1, each mode of transportation has its merits. A review of the table indicates why motor carriage is the pervasive form of transportation used by most companies. Although it may not rank as the fastest mode and has limited capacity, motor carriage is the best in terms of availability and flexibility, and it ranks near the top for each of the remaining criteria. This helps to explain why most products are moved by truck at some point in their distribution.

Apart from distinct modal options, there is the provision of intermodal transportation, or the combination of multiple modes of transport for a single shipment. By using intermodal means, a shipment may enjoy the respective benefits of different modes of transportation. This is the case for a shipment moving from Bonn, Germany, to Toronto, Canada, for example, where the shipment might move by truck from the Bonn shipping point to the port in Rotterdam, where the intermodal container is then loaded onto a ship for Montreal. On arrival in Montreal the container is transloaded onto rail for the trip to Toronto, where on arrival at the intermodal yard a truck collects the container for final delivery to the customer. Over the course of this intermodal movement, the shipment has enjoyed the best of what each mode has to offer: the speed, availability, dependability, and flexibility of motor transportation (in Europe and in Canada) as well as the economies of density and distance associated with both water and rail transportation. Although the shipment might have moved alternatively through a combination of truck-air-truck moves, the reduced transit time is unlikely to offset the premium paid for air transport, again reflecting the cost-service trade-off found with any shipment.

Sound transportation decision making, however, should involve a broader perspective than a single shipment. To optimize more completely the role of transportation in global logistics and supply chain management, the manager must comprehend the holistic picture of material flows into and within the business and the outbound flows to customers. Only with an understanding of these flows can managers identify and pursue opportunities for consolidation. A reality for many logistics and supply chain managers today, however, is that a company's logistics network need not be fixed. That is, through the advent of third-party relationships that offer to adapt the shipper's network to accommodate changing needs, the shipper is not required to settle for a less than ideal arrangement of storage and processing facilities. This is particularly important given the pace of change in business today. Outside providers of logistics services allow the shipper to keep up with these dynamics more easily. However, these prospects are feasible only with a ready supply of capable service providers. Unfortunately, this is not the case around the globe, forcing shippers to assume a fuller scope of responsibility for logistics network development and operations. To further recognize the opportunities inherent in managing transportation operations, one must understand the economics of service providers.

Transportation Cost Behavior

Carrier cost structures and cost behaviors affect carrier pricing and, thus, the transportation costs of shippers. On the other hand, shipper logistics strategies and practices and product characteristics affect carrier operating costs.

Carrier Cost Behavior and Efficiencies

Simply stated, carrier cost structure may be defined as the ratio of fixed costs to variable costs, and the cost structure is different across the modes of transportation. Cost behavior refers to how costs change with changes in the level of output. The two key cost categories for carriers are facility costs and vehicle costs. Most costs associated with facilities (e.g., freight terminals, railroad track, and land) are capital costs and other fixed costs (e.g., facility overhead costs and administrative costs). That is, most facility costs do not vary with the level of output or traffic volumes moved by the carrier and are often referred to as "time costs" (Boyer 1998). Vehicle costs comprise operating costs that vary with traffic volume (e.g., weight, distance, and number of shipments) and fixed costs that are mostly the costs associated with vehicle ownership (e.g., costs of financing and depreciation). Labor and fuel represent the two largest variable operating cost components for most carriers.

Carrier cost efficiencies may arise from a number of sources, including economies of scale, economies of density, and economies of scope. Economies of scale refer to decreasing average cost per unit as the size of the firm or operation increases. Most research indicates that transportation industries do not realize economies of scale with respect to firm size. That is, there is no evidence that large firms are more cost-efficient in the provision of transportation service than small firms. There are, however, economies of scale with respect to vehicle or vessel size. It should also be noted that large carriers may benefit from non-operating cost advantages. For example, large service providers often accommodate broader geographic areas, an attractive capability for shippers who prefer one-stop shopping for transportation. Furthermore, large carriers may be able to leverage their purchase volumes to achieve lower unit costs for factor inputs (e.g., bulk fuel, equipment, and parts). Also, the core carrier concept practiced by many shippers as a means for reducing transaction costs and establishing strategic partnerships with carriers may have the effect of creating larger carriers.

Transportation companies do experience economies of density and economies of scope. Economies of density refer to decreasing unit costs arising from greater utilization of existing capacity. That is, if the carrier does not need to expand its facility or vehicle capacity to serve increasing demand, its cost per unit will decrease. Economies of density are often referred to as economies of freight consolidation or economies of networking. Economies of scope arise when it is less costly to produce two services within the same firm than by different firms, and they are related to the prevalence of joint and common costs in transportation. Backhaul cost is an example of a joint cost. If a transportation lane is perfectly balanced (i.e., freight moving in both directions on the route), one carrier can provide the service more cost-efficiently than two different carriers.

Finally, product characteristics affect carrier costs and are thus reflected in carrier pricing structures and levels. Physical characteristics of the product, such as density, stowability, handling characteristics, and susceptibility to damage, directly affect carrier operating costs. Additionally, demand characteristics of the product (e.g., seasonality, variability, and predictability) may affect capacity utilization.

Carrier Implications

The aforementioned characteristics of carrier cost behavior have implications for both carriers and their shipper customers. Two key implications for carriers are (1) the need for costing methodologies that enable carriers to trace and allocate costs on a cause-effect basis and (2) the need for marketing and growth strategies more closely tied to operating efficiency and profitability. Activity-based costing (ABC) has increased in popularity among carriers of all modes. ABC involves determining cost-causing activities and processes performed in the transportation service for an individual shipper or shipment and using multiple appropriate units of measure to allocate these costs to the individual shipper or shipment. For example, vehicle or vessel capital or ownership costs are allocated on the basis of time in use to perform the service for a shipment or shipper, including time spent loading and unloading the freight and time spent waiting for it to be loaded or unloaded. Driver or operator costs may be allocated on the basis of time if wages are paid on a time basis (e.g., per hour) or on a distance basis if pay is based on distance covered (e.g., per kilometer). Order processing costs (e.g., order receiving, documentation preparation, and billing) may be allocated on a per-shipment basis. Although many factors and units of measure may be utilized in allocating costs to an individual shipment, carriers still typically utilize a one-factor pricing approach (e.g., price per kilometer or price per ton). A multifactor price approach may make more sense theoretically (e.g., x_1 euros per hour + x_2 euros per kilometer + x_3 euros per ton), but shippers prefer more certainty in price quotes.

One of the key benefits of ABC is that carriers gain a better understanding of their processes and costs. Such understanding is fundamental to continuous improvement efforts by both carriers and shippers and for ensuring that prices recoup costs. ABC is an important tool for determining the profitability of individual shippers, shipments, lanes, terminals, and types of freight. As carriers allocate costs more accurately, they are better able to differentiate between "good" and "bad" freight and become more selective in targeting customers.

ABC enables carriers to recognize and realize their network economies (economies of density). Generally, the more profitable carriers' organic growth occurs "in network," where the carriers can increase traffic and lane density and minimize deadhead (i.e., non-revenue) miles more readily because they already have an established operating and marketing/sales presence. Of course, carrier firms also continue to grow via merger and acquisition because it is often more efficient, and certainly faster, to acquire an entire network than to expand a network organically lane by lane. "Virtual networks" are another approach to network expansion. These are Web-based collaborative efforts where multiple carrier fleets are managed under the umbrella of one operational optimization model.

The fundamental underpinning of successful carrier growth strategies is a focus on freight and shippers that enables the firm to realize its economies of density and scope or, stated differently, to increase its capacity or asset utilization. Capacity utilization has two dimensions: (1) physical space on the vessel or vehicle and (2) time. Historically, one might argue that more emphasis was placed on the former. More recently, however, the time dimension has become a major issue and challenge as carriers strive to minimize vessel and vehicle downtime arising from unduly long waiting times and loading/unloading times at shipper and receiver facilities. Obviously, shipper logistics strategies and practices have an impact on both dimensions of capacity.

Shipper Implications

Freight shippers and receivers benefit from helping carriers to be more efficient. Operating efficiency gains resulting from collaborative efforts between carriers and shippers are generally shared, thus resulting in lower transportation costs and service improvements for the receivers. Additionally, attaining the status of "preferred shipper" or "shipper of choice" with a carrier because of carrier-friendly logistics practices often enables a shipper to obtain transportation capacity during periods of industrywide capacity shortages.

There are several practices that shippers may be able to implement to improve carrier capacity utilization. Leading practices include the following:

- Provide more advanced notice of the need for carrier service to facilitate improved carrier operations planning. With longer lead times, carriers are able to position equipment and labor geographically to meet shipper demands more efficiently and effectively.

- Consolidate shipments into larger loads to fill more vehicle or vessel space and to reduce the number of carrier trips. Though the focus on reducing inventories has resulted in smaller, more frequent shipments, there are still ample opportunities for most shippers to combine different shipments destined for the same receiver or the same geographic market.

• Establish regular routes and schedules. Some traffic volumes are repetitive and their regularity enhances carriers' capacity planning efforts. Also, there are operating cost and service efficiencies to be gained as vehicle operators develop a familiarity with the routes, customer facilities, and practices.

• Help carriers achieve lane balance by coordinating outbound and inbound shipments. It may be possible to coordinate inbound supply movements with outbound finished product movements or to synchronize interplant movements, and thus minimize the carrier's deadhead miles. Some firms have included the opportunity to create lane balance as a criterion in selecting vendors.

• Improve facility management loading practices to minimize carrier waiting time and loading/unloading time. Companies have implemented such practices as set appointment times, extended hours of facility operations, and the use of "drop" containers (i.e., the carrier delivers and leaves a container for the shipper/receiver to load/unload at its convenience) to ensure that carriers do not encounter unexpected delays. Additionally, shipment tracking and tracing capabilities and better communications of expected arrival times, in general, help reduce asset downtime for the carrier.

• Implement bidding and negotiation processes that enable the carrier to achieve economies of density and scope. Shippers are beginning to encourage multiple-lane bids rather than the traditional approach of having carriers bid on one lane at a time. Multiple-lane bid packages allow carriers to create lane balance and realize network economies.

These are just a few of the ways by which shippers can influence their carriers' cost and service performance. Clearly, communication, information sharing, and collaboration are essential to create opportunities for efficiency gains. Many of these opportunities for improved efficiency and service enhancements are found in an industry initiative called Collaborative Transportation Management (CTM).

Collaborative Transportation Management

CTM was conceived by the Logistics Committee of the Voluntary Interindustry Commerce Solutions (VICS) Association in the late 1990s. The VICS Association is made up of large and small companies that have proven that a timely and accurate flow of product and information between trading partners significantly improves the competitive position of all partners. It has been demonstrated that cross-industry commerce standards facilitate better customer service while reducing costs.

Defining the CTM Process

CTM is a holistic process that brings together supply chain trading partners and service providers to drive inefficiencies out of the transport planning and execution process. The objective of CTM is to facilitate interaction and collaboration between the principal parties to the transportation component of the supply chain—shippers, carriers, receivers, and secondary participants such as third-party logistics service providers (3PLs)—to improve operating performance by eliminating inefficiencies.

The CTM process is designed for application to both inbound and outbound transportation flows. As such, both the shipper and the receiver can perform some of the steps in the CTM business process, whereas other steps are performed individually by either the shipper or the receiver. Typically, the party that is ultimately responsible for the carrier relationship contract is responsible for the CTM steps. Participants collaborate by sharing key information about demand and supply (e.g., forecasts, event plans, and expected capacity), ideas and capabilities to improve the performance of the overall transport planning and execution process, and assets, where feasible (i.e., trucks and warehouses). CTM begins with an order or shipment forecast and includes capacity planning and scheduling, order generation, load tender, delivery execution, and carrier payment.

The CTM process comprises three distinct phases. First, the *strategic phase* defines the front-end agreement to collaborate. The front-end agreement formalizes the period of time during which the relationship is valid. The agreement also defines the scope of the relationship between the parties to determine which process steps are to be performed, what data will be shared, and how that information will be communicated among all parties. It should specify the goals of the relationship (e.g., reduce cost by X% or increase on-time delivery by Y%) and define freight terms, the geographic scope of the partnership, and the distribution strategies to be utilized. It should also specify the party that will manage the carrier or 3PL relationships (or both), delineating who is responsible for routing decisions and payment remittance, the freight terms (who pays for and controls the move), which products are included, the locations involved, the types of shipments that will be included, and the exception management protocol. Finally, the agreement should delineate the manner in which expected benefits will be shared.

Next, the *tactical phase* defines the process flow for planning purposes, beginning with the creation of a product/order forecast. The product/order forecast is rolled up and extended to a shipment forecast using predetermined load-building strategies (i.e., aggregation or consolidation). The shipment forecast should be shared with all parties to the relationship to provide an advanced look at anticipated shipping volume. On receipt, carriers review shipment forecasts and measure their ability to support the projected volumes with equipment. If a carrier is unable to meet a requirement, then all parties fall back to the exception management protocol defined in the strategic phase of the CTM process model (e.g., changing delivery requirements on some of the shipments, using alternative carriers, or using a public marketplace/exchange for coverage).

Finally, the *operational phase* defines the process flow for executing the logistics process for firm customer orders. This phase leverages previously agreed upon protocols to plan the orders into shipments using the agreed-upon distribution strategies (i.e., aggregation, pooling, cross-docking, load building, and continuous moves) and agreed-upon carrier assignments. Capacity-constrained carriers receive electronic load tenders, and if they are unable to provide equipment as planned, the

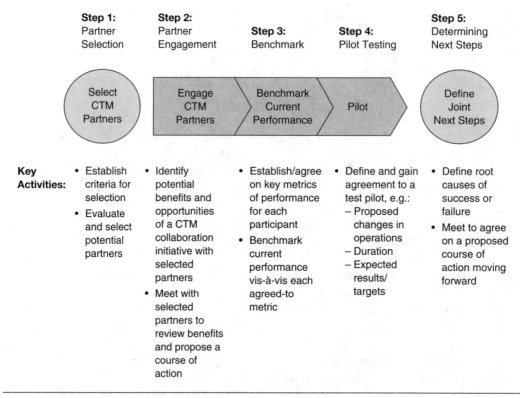

Figure 13.2 Five Steps to CTM Implementation

SOURCE: Collaborative Transportation Management (2004).

agreed-upon exception protocol is employed. As carriers accept the shipment tenders, appointments are scheduled and shipping/receiving resources are reserved. As the shipper prepares and ultimately ships an order, appropriate documentation and information (e.g., advance ship notice and shipment status) are generated and transmitted to all parties in the format agreed upon in the front-end agreement. When exceptions affecting the overall performance of the partnership occur (e.g., late delivery is anticipated), the appropriate exception protocol is referenced. Finally, the freight accounting process is activated to ensure that the carrier is paid per the terms of the front-end agreement or following the exception protocol to resolve any discrepancies. A five-step approach for implementation and the key activities associated with each step are illustrated in Figure 13.2.

Four areas that represent the key benefits of CTM include capacity procurement, inbound management, integrated movements, and transportation marketplaces. Capacity procurement enables carriers to anticipate demand much better than if they are left to guess where and when demands for service will surface. Improved planning also enables shippers to realize improved load consolidation, reduce administrative costs, and better leverage their carrier base nationwide. Participating carriers benefit from increased volume commitment, guaranteed lane assignments, process simplification, and reduced administrative costs. Inbound management refers to the proactive control of inbound goods flow and management of transportation by the receiver of the freight, enabling receivers to reduce transportation cost through inbound consolidation and vendor allowance and, thus, improve overall lead times and variances to generate greater sales with reduced levels of inventory.

Integrated movements aggregate volumes for multiple locations within a company, across divisions, or even across companies. Shippers and receivers benefit from reduced freight costs, an increased amount of dedicated usage, and improved service. Carriers improve asset utilization while reducing empty miles, labor cost, and sales and administrative expense. Transportation marketplaces refer to online venues for transportation capacity procurement to match supply and demand more accurately. Transportation marketplaces provide shippers with immediate access to capacity that is not normally visible, providing coverage for "unusual" load volumes and avoidance of premium freight costs. Carriers that make capacity available in transportation marketplaces enjoy opportunities for additional business, particularly for loaded backhauls and capacity, that might not otherwise be tapped.

CTM pilot initiatives implemented in various companies and settings in the United States since 1999 have demonstrated that the benefits of CTM are very real and substantial (Sutherland, Goldsby, and Stank 2004). Documented shipper benefits include the following:

- On-time service improvements of 35%
- Lead-time reductions of 75%
- Inventory reductions of 50%
- Sales increases of 23%
- Premium freight cost reductions of 20%
- Administrative cost reductions of 20%

Carriers have recorded equally dramatic benefits from CTM pilot projects:

- Deadhead mile reductions of 15%
- Dwell time reductions of 15%
- Fleet utilization improvements of 33%
- Driver turnover reductions of 15%

The potential benefits of CTM initiatives greatly affect return on assets and investment. Figure 13.3 illustrates how the benefits reported in CTM pilots translate into improved profitability and improved balance sheet performance. The increased sales potential and reduced costs result in improved profitability. Better utilization of transportation assets, inventory reductions, and the potential for reduced days' sales outstanding yield improved balance sheet performance.

Surprisingly, very little capital investment is required for CTM. Although a sufficient level of information system capability is required to capture and process the required information, physical assets are generally not required to bring about the results of CTM. Rather, the primary forms of investment involve people and time. Resources and commitment are required to build internal readiness for CTM and to create the collaborative culture within and between parties.

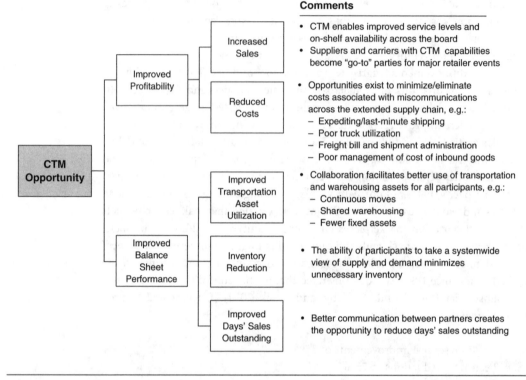

Figure 13.3 Possible CTM Benefits

SOURCE: Collaborative Transportation Management (2004).

Global Transportation Issues

As noted earlier, efficient supply chains rely on fast, responsive, and dependable transportation. Two key global issues have arisen, however, that threaten to lengthen transit times, create more frequent and unpredictable delays, and raise transportation costs. These issues are transportation capacity constraints and increased transportation security.

Capacity constraints arise when the demand for transportation exceeds the transport system's capability to meet the demand efficiently (i.e., at a higher cost or lower service level). Transportation capacity constraints, particularly at domestic points of entry, are afflicting several areas in the world with the practice of global sourcing increasing. For example, several European and U.S. seaports are currently operating at or near capacity. In a 2003 report, the National Chamber Foundation of the U.S. Chamber of Commerce projected that every major U.S. container port will double the volume of freight it handles by the year 2020, with some ports on the East Coast tripling in volume and some West Coast ports quadrupling in volume. Furthermore, economic "hot spots" such as China are putting pressure on ocean carriers' vessel capacity in specific trade lanes. The heightened security efforts that have been implemented since the terrorist attacks on the United States in 2001 also threaten to disrupt the smooth flow of freight and add to the congestion at critical points in the global transport network. The ability of global supply chains to continue operating in a lean and tightly synchronized manner depends on finding solutions to these difficult challenges.

Transportation Capacity Issues

Transportation capacity issues are complex because of the multiple dimensions and the integrated nature of transportation systems. Capacity constraints may occur at the "nodes" in the supply chain (e.g., freight terminals, seaports, and airports) or on the "links" in the supply chain (e.g., roads, railways, and waterways) (or both). These two components of transport networks, nodes and links, are obviously interdependent. For example, the land transport links that provide domestic inland distribution can compound seaport congestion problems when they do not pick up the imported freight in a timely manner. Conversely, inefficient port operations can increase the amount of time (and cost) required by land carriers to pick up their loads. The results of poor integration at the physical interface are clearly observed in the vast container yards at major seaports around the world.

Additionally, there are both physical-supply dimensions to capacity constraints and temporal-demand dimensions. Physical constraints to continuous, efficient freight flow may be due to shortages or inefficiencies in line-haul equipment, facilities (e.g., material handling equipment and storage or staging space), or labor. Regarding the temporal dimension, shipper facilities and public transportation facilities are frequently not operated at all hours of the day, creating artificial traffic peaks that strain facility, equipment, and labor capacities. The temporal dimension is often referred to as the peak-demand problem. The demand for transportation service is not evenly distributed over time, often resulting in transport system capacity constraints at high-demand times. Investing in additional capacity to meet peak-demand levels leads to underutilization of capacity during off-peak times. Differential pricing of transportation service (i.e., higher prices during peak times) may alleviate the problem by enticing some shippers to shift their demand to off-peak times, but it usually does not eliminate the problem. Also, when passengers and freight share facilities, peak passenger demand may affect freight movements (e.g., road congestion at peak commuter times).

Finally, the public sector has a very large and multifaceted impact on transportation capacity. The public sector's influence through government-funded infrastructure and government provision of transportation services is readily apparent. Government policies and regulations affecting transportation have a more subtle, but just as important, impact on capacity. Economic regulations and policies concerning carrier pricing and services have a direct impact on carrier financial performance and capacity to serve. Social regulations, such as those addressing safety, labor, environment, and energy issues, may also have a significant impact on transportation capacity, service levels, and cost. For example, hours of service regulations imposed on transportation equipment operators (truck drivers, railroad locomotive engineers, and airline pilots) enhance public safety by reducing the likelihood of operator fatigue, but they also restrict carriers' capacity utilization.

Port expansion is often constrained because it entails major landfill and channel deepening projects, which have significant environmental impacts. Local noise policies restricting aircraft landings and departures at night affect the service levels and capacity utilization of air cargo carriers. Engine emission controls, energy efficiency standards, hazardous materials regulations, speed limits, and numerous other rules and policies are necessary to protect the public or to promote social objectives, but they have an impact on transportation that must be considered.

Addressing Capacity Problems

The ways in which shippers can help carriers utilize their capacity more efficiently were discussed earlier in the sections on transportation cost behavior and CTM. Many of these same principles and concepts can be applied to public sector involvement in transportation. For example, improved government pricing of transportation infrastructure (e.g., congestion tolls or peak/off-peak price differentials) would result in more efficient utilization of existing transportation capacity. Extending the hours of operations for public transport facilities such as seaport terminals would help alleviate congestion by achieving a more even distribution of cargo volumes and, thus, effectively increase capacity. "Optimal" social regulation (i.e., balancing social and economic objectives) requires a better understanding of the ensuing economic impacts or ramifications of a stronger collaborative relationship between public authorities and the private sector—much like the CTM between shippers and carriers. In this regard, transportation companies, their customers, and labor need to work together to help define the issues and solutions for transport public policy makers.

Additionally, the U.S. Chamber of Commerce (2003), in its analysis of the U.S. seaport congestion problem, identified a number of needed improvements in national transportation public policy and planning, two of which are especially appropriate and applicable for most countries. Perhaps the most notable of its recommendations was the development of a national freight policy. The needs of freight transportation are frequently given lower priority than those of passenger transportation. This may be due to policymakers' general lack of understanding of supply chain management and its demands on the transportation sector, freight data availability problems (particularly for domestic transportation), or the greater visibility and political sensitivities of passenger transportation. Again, shippers and carriers may be able to elevate the priority of freight transportation by doing a better job of explaining their needs to public policy makers.

The integration of the various modes into cohesive and efficient national and global networks is a second area needing substantial improvement. Planning and funding are frequently targeted for the individual modes rather than from an intermodal perspective. Similarly, a broader geographic perspective often needs to be taken to improve the efficiency of the transportation system, that is, regional or national planning, rather than local.

Finally, technology plays a major role in alleviating capacity constraints. Technology that provides transportation asset visibility and equipment and shipment tracking capability is particularly important to improved capacity management.

Many transportation companies utilize global positioning system (GPS) technology and onboard computers and communications devices to achieve visibility and tracking. These are increasingly integrated with shippers' transportation management systems to enable improved vehicle routing and scheduling, establish more timely appointment schedules, and enhance event management capabilities.

Governments, too, are developing similar capabilities. Intelligent transportation systems (ITS) for road traffic management have been implemented by many countries. ITS integrates a wide range of information technologies based on wireless and wire line communications into the transportation system's infrastructure and in vehicles. These systems enable improved traffic flow and safety by providing travelers with information about roadwork, traffic congestion, weather, and other conditions that affect their travel. Also, ITS has freight and asset tracking capabilities that can provide information about the condition and location of goods and equipment en route, including verification that containerized cargo remains sealed within shipping containers. Finally, integrating ITS with customs automation systems provides faster and more efficient verification of cargo manifest information at border crossings, thus helping reduce delays.

Transportation Security Issues

Security has long been an important issue in transportation, as carriers are responsible for the safety of their employees, the public, and their customers' products. Although transportation has frequently been the target of terrorist attacks worldwide, the September 2001 terrorist attacks on the United States heightened security concerns and resulted in several new government security initiatives, particularly for international shipments. These initiatives are yet another example of social regulations that affect transportation capacity. The security issue, however, is even more pervasive and has broader impacts on transportation system flow, time variance, and cost.

Corporations, too, have increased their emphasis on supply chain security. Carrier security programs and practices have become a more important factor in shippers' carrier selection decisions. Supply chains typically have several potential points of vulnerability, but transportation arguably presents some of the greatest challenges. Relatively speaking, supply chain facilities are easier to secure because of their fixed location and the ability to establish controlled and limited access. Conversely, transportation has a greater risk of exposure as it often spans considerable distances and takes place in an operating environment that is more difficult to control.

Deterrence and detection are two key elements of transportation security programs. Deterrence refers to security practices, infrastructure, and technology that discourage or prevent theft and terrorism, whereas detection refers to the discovery of theft or product or shipment tampering during or after the fact. Fences around manufacturing plants and distribution centers, locks on containers and equipment, and employee identity verification are common methods of physical deterrents. Physical inspections of shipments and monitoring devices (e.g., surveillance cameras and satellite tracking of vehicles and containers) are common means of detecting security breaches. Real-time monitoring devices, in conjunction with quick response capabilities, may also be deterrents (i.e., by lessening the probability of success, they may discourage attempts at theft or terrorism).

Security Solutions

From a global supply chain perspective, the security practices of public authorities at border crossings or points of entry are a major issue. Countries are utilizing a two-pronged approach to increase security without impeding the efficient flow of international trade. First, there is an effort by many customs authorities to develop and apply better technologies for inspecting shipments (e.g., radiation or chemical detection sensors and improved X-ray technologies). These technologies increase both the speed and the accuracy of inspections. Second, customs authorities are attempting to reduce the number of inspections by targeting higher-risk shipments, shippers, and countries of origin for inspection. "Known shipper" policies, whereby frequent international shippers are less likely to have their shipments subject to physical inspection, fall within this approach. Another approach is providing incentives to importers who can demonstrate that they have effective security policies and practices in place within their supply chains. The U.S. Customs and Border Patrol's Customs-Trade Partnership Against Terrorism program (C-TPAT) takes this approach. C-TPAT-certified firms benefit from faster customs clearance at points of entry.

Security best practices for shippers and carriers involve organization and planning, employee education and training, and technology. An effective security plan, like any corporatewide strategic imperative, requires top management leadership and support, good fit with the organization's business model, integration across all functions and processes within the organization and with supply chain partners, and the ability to measure performance and attain continuous improvement. Security awareness and preparedness must become part of an organization's culture, and it is not accomplished without comprehensive and ongoing employee education and training.

Increasingly, companies are recognizing that technology is an important tool or enabler for security enhancement but is not by itself the solution. Fortunately, the technology applications that are highly important for successful supply chain management (including capacity management and utilization) also enhance security—specifically, those applications that enable shipment and equipment tracking, increase supply chain visibility, and facilitate interorganizational information sharing. For example, carriers' GPS applications enable detection of unplanned stops in transit, tampering with shipments en route, and vehicle departures from predesignated routes (i.e., "geo-fencing"). Advance notices of transportation-related delays are communicated to shippers and receivers and may be integrated with their event management systems. Supply chain disruptions can, thus, be managed efficiently. The "dual purpose" characteristic of many security initiatives (i.e., meeting both supply chain management and security objectives) is useful in building a business case for security investments.

The global transportation issues pertaining to capacity constraints and security highlight the need for comprehensive risk management by shippers and carriers.

Supply chain managers must understand where their systems are vulnerable to disruptions, assess the magnitude of the potential disruptions, and develop solutions and contingencies to avoid or mitigate the disruptions. This requires an understanding of processes and activities throughout the supply chain and, specifically with respect to transportation, knowledge of alternative carriers, routes, and sources of supply.

The future success of global supply chains depends on the ability of organizations to manage capacity and security issues. The requisite organizational and technological tools are already available. The challenge lies in integrating them throughout the global supply chain.

Conclusions

It should be clear that much of the "action" found in global logistics and supply chain management is associated with transportation. Transportation represents an area of substantial cost but also an important customer service component and physical linkage among companies in the global supply chain network. Although significant progress has been made with regard to transportation infrastructure, vehicle safety, information technologies, and relationships, there remains much more opportunity for individual companies as well as entire supply chains to reduce costs, improve service, and strengthen the global supply chain.

The problems and opportunities found with transportation management will only increase with further globalization. As supply chains continue to extend around the world, it will become increasingly important to ensure sound linkages among supply chain members in distant locations. The importance of international transportation intermediaries will increase as a result, making these specialized service providers an even more integral part of the global supply chain. Overarching security regulations added to the expanding scope of multinational companies will further underscore the importance of these intermediaries. Companies will continue to question whether transportation management and administrative activities should be performed in-house or outsourced to specialists whose core competency is to stay not only abreast but ahead of regulations and conventions for doing business in disparate locales.

The complexities of international transportation and logistics notwithstanding, managers must continue to recognize the importance of the trade-offs among logistics activities. As firms and entire supply chains pursue lean and agile strategies that promise higher levels of customer service with less on-hand inventory, greater emphasis and stress will be placed on the transportation system. These strategies depend completely on quick, reliable transportation services. Yet in fulfilling a rigorous service commitment, the firm must still keep transportation costs in check and, in fact, maintain the desired balance between total logistics cost and the service rendered to customers.

In this chapter, we have emphasized the movement among carriers to become more cognizant of the true costs of service provision. Only in understanding these costs can the carrier provide a service that is both valued by the customer and worthwhile for the service provider itself. When carriers better understand their costs, they can price their services more readily at sustainable levels, ensuring their own survival and also an ongoing service commitment to valued customers. Shippers today are placing more importance on the health of preferred carriers and the health of relationships formed with select carriers. This is particularly true in market settings where capacity is all but certain. A movement among shippers to become "shippers of choice" illustrates the concern among shippers seeking a constant commitment of excellent service and reasonable prices.

To take the concept of cooperation further, interest is growing in CTM where carriers are actively sought for collaboration among trading partners in the supply chain. The significance of these heightened relationships is noteworthy because service providers historically have not been privy to these collaborative efforts. Shippers and receivers are realizing, however, that much of the opportunity for cost reduction, efficiency improvement, and smooth supply chain operations rests in the links between companies. CTM is helping shippers, receivers, carriers, and entire supply chains recognize the opportunities and capture the benefits of broader collaboration.

Although much of the attention of supply chain management is directed toward the senior-level strategic direction of the companies involved, we must not forget the operations and activities that take place within and among companies. Transportation management is among the most critical of these activities. As the history of any economy illustrates, commercial development is closely tied to the development of the transportation system. Just as efficiencies associated with water, pipeline, rail, motor, and air transportation have resulted in greater commercial activity between distant trading partners within a single national setting, so too will commerce accelerate among nations as the friction of distance becomes less. Interestingly, nations that prove to be the most competitive in the global environment will be those that enjoy not only an advantage in assembly and product processing but also efficiencies within the domestic transportation setting. For those responsible for managing transportation, the challenges remain great, as do the rewards.

Note

1. This figure represents transportation expense in the U.S. commercial sector. When combined with public sector spending on transportation infrastructure and services, the United States spends more than $1 trillion on transportation-related activities, according to the Bureau of Transportation Statistics.

References

Bowersox, Donald J., David J. Closs, and M. Bixby Cooper (2002), *Supply Chain Logistics Management.* New York: McGraw-Hill.

Boyer, Kenneth D. (1998), *Principles of Transportation Economics.* New York: Addison-Wesley.

Collaborative Transportation Management (2004), White paper produced by the Logistics Committee of the Voluntary Interindustry Commerce Solutions (VICS).

National Chamber Foundation of the U.S. Chamber of Commerce (2003), *Trade and Transportation—A Study of North American Port and Intermodal Systems*. Author.

Stank, Theodore P. and Thomas J. Goldsby (2000), "A Framework for Transportation Decision-Making in an Integrated Supply Chain," *Supply Chain Management: An International Journal*, 5 (2), 71–77.

Sutherland, Joel, Thomas J. Goldsby, and Theodore P. Stank (2004), "Leveraging Collaborative Transportation Management (CTM) Principles to Achieve Superior Supply Chain Performance," in *Achieving Supply Chain Excellence Through Technology*, vol. 6. San Francisco: Montgomery Research, pp. 192–196.

Wilson, Rosalyn (2005), *The 16th Annual State of Logistics Report: Security Report Card—Not Making the Grade*, a report sponsored by the Council of Supply Chain Management Professionals, presented at the National Press Club, Washington, DC, June 27.

14

Warehouse Management

Thomas W. Speh

Every day several truckloads of paper towels, laundry detergent, potato chips, coffee, soap, toilet tissue, and several other items arrive at a third-party warehouse in Kansas City, KS. A third-party warehouse is a company that specializes in operating warehouses for firms and organizations that do not wish to manage their own warehouse operations. The products are all made by a large consumer goods company in its factories located in places like Green Bay, WI, Johnson City, TN, and Cincinnati, OH. Since many customers are unable to economically order a full truckload of each of these items, the Kansas City warehouse becomes a repository to collect the full line of the firm's brands, making it possible for customers to order the entire array of their products from one location, on one truck, with one order. Customers value this service because it simplifies their operations—it is much easier to place one order and receive one truck than to order each separate product line from each plant and then have to unload several different trucks, each with a less-than-truckload (LTL) quantity of paper towels, peanut butter, or coffee (which would definitely raise transportation costs!).

In addition to processing customer orders and managing the shipment of the manufacturer's full line of products, the warehouse in Kansas City makes it possible to combine the firm's products with other manufacturers' products that are moving to the same set of retail customers. This important function of the warehouse is referred to as consolidation and provides the opportunity to substantially reduce transportation costs for all the products that are combined on the shipment. As described above, the warehouse also performs the important functions of mixing and break bulk. Mixing involves creating a full array of the product line in one location, enabling customers to receive every item made by the company on one shipment, whereas break bulk is the process of receiving large, truckload shipments, which are transported over long distances, and then reshipping smaller quantities desired by retail customers over shorter distances. Break-bulk activities allow companies to reduce transportation costs by enabling the larger shipments to travel over greater distances and the smaller, more expensive shipments to travel much shorter distances. Figure 14.1 provides an illustration of the nature of warehouse consolidation, mixing, and break-bulk activities.

The Kansas City warehouse also performs an important storage function for products whose demand and supply are not constant. Thus, it serves as a mechanism to match demand and supply. A manufacturer can use the warehouse to build up a substantial inventory of a particular brand in advance of a large promotional program focused on that brand in the Midwest. Often, a manufacturer develops promotions of certain brands that require some type of display unit to be filled

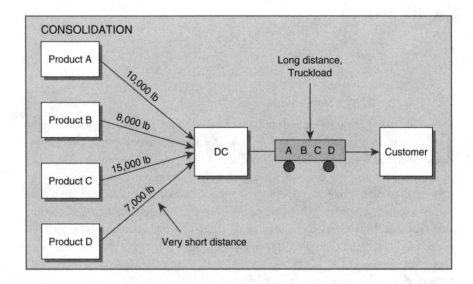

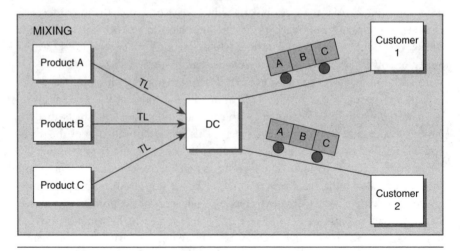

Figure 14.1
(Continued)

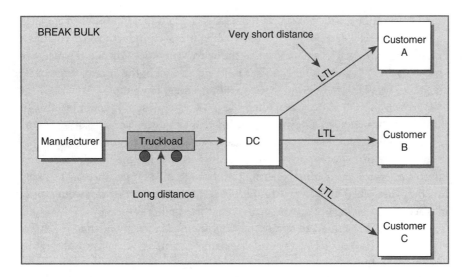

Figure 14.1   Consolidation, Mixing, and Break-Bulk Activities

Abbreviations: DC, distribution center; TL, truckload; LTL, less-than-truckload.

with product and placed at the end of an aisle in the grocery store to attract the consumer's attention more effectively. Here again, the Kansas City warehouse performs a value-added function by assembling store-ready display units of the promoted product. These are cardboard display units that are filled with product and shipped as a unit to the retail stores, thus reducing the effort required by the store in preparing the display. The display-ready unit is simply unloaded from the truck and taken right to its position on the retail floor.

In some instances, the warehouse assembles pallets of mixed products to meet the requirements of individual customers of the manufacturer. Some stores may not sell large quantities of certain brands, so the pallets are customized based on the nature of the volumes experienced by the store. In this way, the retailer's inventories of these items will be minimized, which provides a significant cost saving to them. Furthermore, the mixed pallet can be cross-docked (never placed into storage) at the retailer's distribution center and sent directly to individual stores. This again minimizes the retailer's handling and inventory cost. A final important service provided by the warehouse is to process any products that are returned by the retailers due to damage, being out-of-date, or due to overstocks. This reverse logistics process is costly and time-consuming because it often involves individual items rather than pallet loads, and it is labor-intensive because each returned item has to be inspected, and then something must be done with it.

The third-party warehouse in Kansas City is one of the several warehouses in the United States that the manufacturer uses for distributing its full product line to retail and wholesale customers. A significant advantage of having several strategically positioned warehouses is the fact that inventories of the manufacturer's products are carefully located within relatively close proximity to major markets. The warehouses actually help supplement transportation because the product is positioned closer to customers, thereby decreasing the time it takes to move product to the customer's distribution centers. The ability to speed the delivery of orders directly enhances the service level the manufacturer can offer to its customers. In this regard, warehouses are said to provide "transportation service at zero miles per hour."

Warehousing functions play a vital role in the overall supply chain process. In the past, the warehouse was generally regarded as simply a place to store goods. As supply chains have evolved, the warehouse has assumed a larger role in the global supply chain process because it allows reduced overall supply chain costs and improved service to the ultimate customer through the performance of the many functions described above. As a result, the term *distribution center* is often used in place of *warehouse* because it suggests that the facility is focused on distributing products, as opposed to simply holding them. The term *warehousing*, however, is quite entrenched in the supply chain lexicon, so we will use the terms interchangeably.

This chapter provides an overview of the role of the warehouse in the global supply chain process, describing the rationale for warehousing, activities performed in the warehouse, the relationship of warehousing to other supply chain functions, the technology applicable to warehousing operations, and key warehousing business issues.

The Role of Warehousing in Global Supply Chains

Not every supply chain requires the utilization of warehousing facilities in the network. Certain conditions indicate that warehousing operations are not necessary. When the typical order is large and the products are made at one location, the customer's requirements are effectively met by shipping product via truckload or (rail) carload directly from the plant. A firm selling tons of sugar to one customer every day to be used in the production of candy has little need for a warehouse in the supply chain network. Some very large manufacturers, although they use warehousing facilities extensively, have a program for shipments of truckload quantities of products directly to their retail customers' distribution centers. In fact, they may encourage customers to order in truckload quantities directly from the plant by offering a significant price break for doing so. Only the very largest customers are able to take advantage of this program.

Warehouses have little value when products are bought in bulk, and there is little or no time sensitivity associated with their use. Many raw materials, components, and manufactured items, such as steel, that are bought in bulk and shipped by rail do not benefit from moving through a warehouse.

When products are insensitive to transportation costs (i.e., transportation cost is a small percentage of product's value), typically, they move directly to customers. Many items sold from catalogs or over the Internet move directly from the factory to the customer because either the consumer is willing to bear the expense of the higher cost of transportation, or the product's value dictates that transportation costs are of little consequence. Expensive jewelry is a good example. It would be costly to keep expensive jewelry in inventory, and its high value suggests that direct shipment to customers is the best system.

Thus, there are a number of situations where warehousing simply would add cost to the supply chain. However, for the vast majority of companies, some type of warehousing is used in the supply chain process. The role of the warehouse is twofold. First, warehouses make the entire supply chain network more *efficient.* Here, the warehouse adds efficiency by storing product until it is demanded (e.g., lawn mowers and snowblowers that are produced year-round), reducing transportation costs by consolidating products for shipment to customers, or performing value-added activities like labeling and packaging. Generally, the warehouse adds to efficiency because it serves as a place to accumulate large quantities of a wide variety of goods, making it possible to ship in bulk into and out of the warehouse. Without the warehouse, many small shipments might be required from manufacturing sites to customer locations.

Second, warehouses make the entire supply chain network more *effective.* Strategic placement of warehouses allows a company to place product close to major markets and customers, thereby reducing the time to deliver orders. In addition, it often makes it possible for customers to pick up orders in their own trucks as the truck returns after making a delivery of the customer's finished product.

Product Type and Warehousing Operations

Certain types of products dictate the use of warehousing facilities in the supply chain network. The first characteristic to be considered is seasonality in either production or consumption. For example, the O. M. Scott Company, the largest manufacturer of lawn care products in the United States, operates its plants throughout the year, even though there is significant seasonality in the consumption of its grass seeds and fertilizers. Manufacturing economics dictate continuous production, which necessitates the utilization of large amounts of warehousing simply to store product until the spring and summer seasons. On the other hand, Vlasic Pickles must process cucumbers at the end of the growing season in July and August, and process enough to meet demand for the entire year. In this situation, warehousing is absolutely necessary to store pickles for sale throughout the year.

Products frequently sold through major promotions require warehousing so that enough supply is created to sustain sales volumes over the length of the promotion. For example, each year a major consumer goods firm runs a promotion with one mass merchandising chain for a two-week period in the fall. In anticipation of this promotion, the manufacturer begins strategically placing inventories at several warehouses across the United States in the spring so that they can accommodate the 1,100 extra truckloads of product that will be sold during the two-week promotion.

Transportation economies often dictate the use of warehousing in the supply chain network. There are literally hundreds of products that do not sell in very large volumes, and to reduce the significant penalty of shipping them long distances in small quantities, warehouses are introduced into the network to offset the transportation penalties associated with small shipments. In these situations, the cost of warehousing is more than offset by the savings in transportation cost. Figure 14.2 provides an illustration of the savings possible through moving the items in bulk to the warehouse and then shipping the smaller order quantities shorter distances to customers. Note in this example the significant savings that accrue when the product is shipped as part of a full truckload over the considerable distance from Chicago to Reno, and then only the smaller quantity is shipped from Reno to Los Angeles at the higher LTL rate.

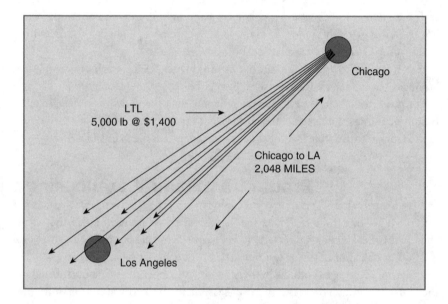

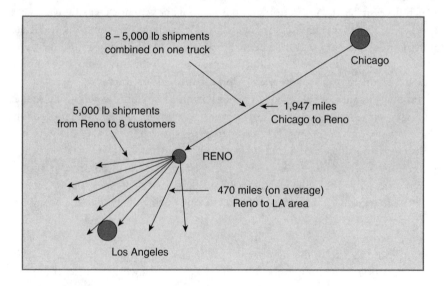

Figure 14.2

(Continued)

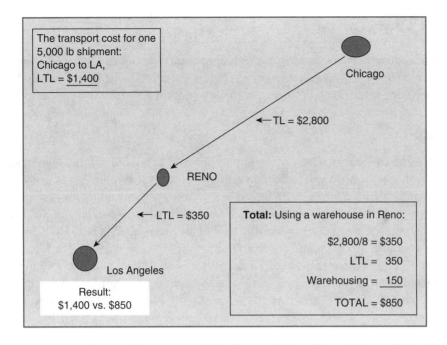

The transport cost for one 5,000 lb shipment:
Chicago to LA,
LTL = $1,400

Chicago

←TL = $2,800

RENO

←LTL = $350

Los Angeles

Total: Using a warehouse in Reno:

$2,800/8 = $350

LTL =   350

Warehousing =   150

TOTAL = $850

Result:
$1,400 vs. $850

Figure 14.2   Transportation Savings Through Warehousing

If products have extremely high service requirements from a time perspective, warehousing is often the solution to meet those requirements. For example, many distributors of industrial parts and industrial supply items have numerous small warehouses in their network to serve customers in all their major markets in a timely fashion. Replacement parts are very time sensitive because they affect the efficiency of a customer's operations, so companies that distribute parts for copiers and computers have warehouses in all major markets so that parts can be delivered within hours. In a similar vein, many automobile manufacturers have several warehouses located in close proximity to their plants so that subassemblies and other components can be put into "kits" in the order in which they enter the production process on any given day. These warehouses make it possible for major suppliers to provide just-in-time delivery to the auto manufacturer's assembly plant floor.

When demand is unpredictable, it often makes sense to wait until an order is received for the product and then assemble it in the warehouse. The benefits are significant because components can be shipped to the warehouse, oftentimes for less than it costs to ship the finished product, and the firm does not commit to products that may go unsold. Today, many computer resellers are following this practice, referred to as postponement, by keeping inventories of basic processors, connectors, ports, modems, and the like in strategically located warehouses. Then, when an order arrives, the computers are assembled in the warehouse and sent to the customer upon final assembly. This saves on inventory and transportation costs, reduces the chance of unsold product, and provides a high level of service to the customer.

Why Have a Warehouse?

The rationale for warehouses in the supply chain network has been well documented in the previous sections. However, it is worth recapping the major reasons for having a warehouse in the supply chain network.

Storage

Although a major goal of many supply chains is to minimize, if not eliminate, inventories for many products and situations, it is not always feasible or prudent to eliminate inventories. As indicated earlier, seasonal demand or seasonal production dictates that some products be stored to either secure manufacturing economies or meet seasonal demand. In addition, firms often need to store products because either demand or supply is unpredictable. For example, The Limited retail clothing chain keeps a certain number of days of sales in inventory simply because they cannot accurately estimate the demand for certain fashion merchandise. Similarly, many items they sell are produced in Asia and delivery schedules are often erratic, making it necessary to keep extra stock on hand in a warehouse.

Transportation Cost Savings

For many products, demand does not warrant ordering or shipping in truckload quantities. A-1 Sauce, made by Kraft, is a good example. It would be unusual for a grocery store to sell even one case a week of A-1 Sauce, so the retail grocer would almost never order an entire truckload. If they did, their inventory costs would be significantly high, with a real risk of the product becoming unsellable based on its freshness date. Thus, A-1 Sauce is shipped in large quantities from the factory to the warehouse, where it can be combined with many other items for distribution to the retailer's distribution center and, eventually, to the stores.

Product Assortments

Many manufacturers make several different products at a variety of plant locations, where each plant specializes in a specific element of the product line. However, the customer generally prefers to order the entire assortment of product on one order from one location and have it arrive on a single truck. The answer is to locate a warehouse or warehouses that are strategically placed in relation to plants and customers and create the full assortment in the warehouse where it can be shipped on one order to the customer on one truck. This is exactly the strategy pursued by Kraft Foods. They make many thousands of items in plants spread all over the United States, yet customers are served from a number of "mixing center" warehouses that each are supplied with a full line of products. The warehouses offer both transportation economies and the ability to provide the customer with the full product line on one order.

Postponement

Many firms that make private label merchandise that is sold to a wide array of retailers with the retailer's own brand ship product "in bright" from the factory to a market-positioned warehouse. *In bright* means the product is unlabeled. A labeling operation is set up in the warehouse so that when an order from Safeway grocery chain comes in, the product can be quickly labeled, packaged, and shipped to a Safeway distribution center. Labeling in the warehouse enables the manufacturer to position the inventory close to the customer and avoid the risk of labeling product that may not be sold. Postponement is also used in the industrial sector. One manufacturer of forklifts maintains a warehouse close to the seaport where they receive forklift parts, components, and frames from manufacturing sites all over the world. Inventories of all forklift parts, chassis, and forks are kept in the warehouse until orders are received. Once an order comes in, the specific forklift trucks are assembled and shipped.

Service

A critical role of the warehouse is to provide a local inventory of product that can be dispensed to the customer very rapidly. Many hospital supply distributors maintain a vast network of small warehouses throughout the country so that hospitals can be served rapidly—sometimes, deliveries are made twice per day to the same hospital by companies like Baxter Healthcare. In the industrial products field, W. W. Grainger, the huge industrial parts and hardware distributor, added warehouses to its network as its competitors were actually reducing their warehouse networks. Its rationale was that the additional warehouses provide a competitive advantage by placing inventories closer to their major customers.

Reverse Supply Chain

With the rapid growth of catalog selling, television marketing, and Internet marketing, companies have experienced a significant increase in the amount of return merchandise. In addition, there are several product categories for which technology changes, but the basic framework or skeleton of the product does not change (e.g., copying machines). These old skeletons need to be brought back to be refurbished with the latest technology. In both cases, there is a need for a supply chain that is outside the realm of the normal network. Most companies have solved the problem of reverse supply chain through the use of warehouses specifically organized to handle return goods. Handling return merchandise is quite different from the normal operations associated with forward supply chains, mainly due to the fact that we are dealing with individual items whose flow is somewhat unpredictable. In addition, when the goods come back, something usually has to be done to repair, recondition, or dispose of them. The warehouse has assumed a critical role in this process, and much of the work to recondition and repair products coming back through the system is now done in the warehouse.

The Location of Warehouses

Warehouses are positioned on the basis of many variables, and the importance of each variable depends on the situation confronting the particular company. Transportation cost and the cost of operating the warehouse dictate the location of the warehouse facilities. Considering transportation costs, warehouse location is determined on the basis of the combination of the location of major markets of customers, the location of supply points (plants or suppliers), the volume of product moving to or from supply points and customers, transportation rates from supply points and to markets, the level of service required, and finally the nature of the product. For example, when transportation costs are high and very small shipments are normally made to a customer, warehouses are positioned closer to the customer locations in order to control transportation cost. If, on the other hand, small quantities move out of each plant, and the customers buy fairly large quantities of the full product line, then the warehouse location moves closer to the plants to minimize the distance that the small, higher cost shipments travel. The more volume that moves to a particular market, the closer the warehouse location will be to that market because total transportation costs are reduced by locating where a majority of the volume is moving.

Local conditions also play a role in warehouse location. Hourly labor rates, construction costs, property values, taxes, and access to transportation have major impacts on the cost of operating the warehouse, and these factors must be weighed in relation to the transportation cost associated with a given location. In the end, the ultimate location of the warehouse is based on a combination of transportation costs, local operating costs, and the ability to achieve the desired level of service to the customer.

Warehouse Design and Operations

How the warehouse is designed—that is, the shape and layout of the building, how many dock doors are required, the way the product is stored, how the orders are selected, and the way shipping is organized—depend on the nature of the products, the way product comes into the facility, the nature of the typical order, the service levels required, and the typical mode of transportation. We now examine the important variables that determine the design (layout of the warehouse) and how the warehouse will be managed (how product will be handled). First, we discuss the major activities in the warehouse, then we look at the factors that affect how the warehouse is designed and work is performed, and finally we examine the different systems and procedures for managing the activities performed.

What Goes On in a Typical Warehouse?

Four tasks make up the majority of the activity that takes place in a typical warehouse: product handling, storage of products, value-added services, and cross-docking.

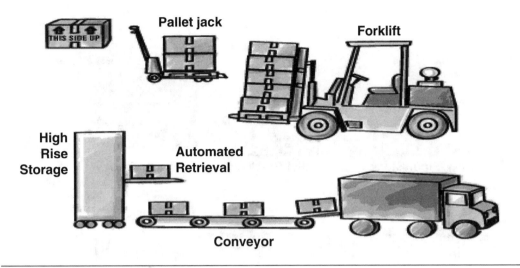

Figure 14.3 Product Handling Approaches

Product Handling

When product arrives at the warehouse, it must be unloaded and either placed in storage or shipped out. If placed in storage, it must then be handled again when customer orders are received for the product. When an order is processed, either the product is moved from its location in storage to a staging area, where it awaits loading into some transportation vehicle, or it is loaded directly onto a truck or railcar. The goal of the warehouse is to reduce the time handling product and to handle the product as little as possible. Products are handled with a variety of techniques ranging from a person carrying an item to forklift trucks that carry an entire pallet quantity of product at once, to highly automated systems where order selection is directed by computers and product moves by conveyor from truck to storage area and storage area to outbound truck. These different approaches to handling product are illustrated in Figure 14.3. The factors that determine the appropriate approach for handling products are discussed later in this chapter.

Storage of Products

The second major activity in a warehouse is storing the products once they are brought into the warehouse. A variety of approaches exist for storing product, including stacking items directly on the floor, stacking palletized products on top of each other, using steel racks to hold pallet quantities of product, bins, carrousels, and several very specialized approaches. These are illustrated in Figure 14.4. The goal in the storage of product is to maximize the use of warehouse space. Generally, space is used most efficiently when product is stacked to the ceiling, there are fewer aisles, and the aisles are narrow. Product that is packaged well and moved on

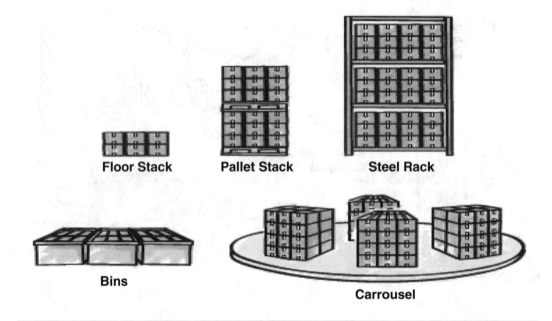

Floor Stack   **Pallet Stack**   **Steel Rack**

Bins

Carrousel

Figure 14.4   Storage Alternatives

pallets can be stacked effectively in the warehouse. On the other hand, if the package is weak or the product is fragile, racking can be used to obtain the necessary storage height. If the product does not have to meet demanding freshness code dates or if rotation of stock is not important, then items can be stacked three, four, or five pallets "deep" in the storage bays. This significantly reduces the number of aisles and frees up more space for storage. Aisles can be narrowed, allowing more storage space by using specialized forklift trucks that are able to operate in very narrow areas. Turret trucks are lift trucks on which the lift mechanism swivels rather than the entire truck. This allows aisles to be considerably narrower, but these trucks are more expensive than conventional trucks and more complex to operate.

Value-Added Services

A very important aspect of warehousing operations is the performance of a host of operations that "add value"; that is, these operations add to the efficiency and effectiveness of the entire supply chain process. Today, value-added services are becoming some of the most important aspects of warehousing operations because the warehouse is the best place in the supply chain network to perform these services, because of its efficiency, low labor cost, and proximity to the customer.

Most of the value-added services are focused on a concept termed postponement. Postponement simply means to wait until the last possible moment to create the final form of a product. In this way, components can be shipped in bulk very inexpensively, product can be finished once an order is received, and there is much less risk of having unsold product sitting around. The key postponement activities include the following:

A. *Branding and Labeling.* Product is not labeled until an order is received. The warehouse is equipped with machinery to perform the labeling and case-fill function.

B. *Packaging.* Many large retailers demand their own unique packing based on a certain number of items in the "normal" package. Thus, Wal-Mart may want four cans of Campbell's soup that are bound together by stretch wrap whereas Target Stores desires only two cans per pack. The warehouse is equipped with the proper packaging machinery to create any type of package on receipt of the order. For many industrial products, warehouses store bulk quantities of items like plastic pellets, and then package the pellets in containers ranging from 5-gallon cans to an entire tanker car load once an order is received.

C. *Final Assembly.* Many industries have moved toward assembling their final product in the warehouse once orders are received. This cuts down considerably on inventory costs since only inventories of basic components are maintained, and no inventory is kept of the huge array of finished product, each of which would need its own basic inventory plus safety stock. In addition, the company avoids keeping inventories of products that do not sell. Personal computers, forklift trucks, and industrial pumps are examples of products that are often assembled in the warehouse.

D. *Blending.* A variety of products require several ingredients blended together to create the final version of the product. Again, it is cost-effective to perform the blending operation in the warehouse after an order has been received. Chemstation, Inc., a distributor of industrial cleaning products, sells over 500 varieties of industrial soaps and cleansers. However, it keeps only a few basic chemicals and ingredients in the warehouse, and particular cleansers are custom blended from the basic ingredients for customers when their orders are received.

E. *Kitting.* Kitting is used in many industries that require several different components at the same time as the finished product is being assembled. A good example is the auto industry, where a certain color of interior is produced on a given day. Here, the warehouse assembles kits that might contain red dashboards, matching instrument panels, red seats, red carpets, and a red steering wheel. The kits are then delivered to the assembly line just as they are needed in the assembly process. This process is becoming more prevalent in industries that require several major components of a certain type—examples include electronics, personal computers, printers, and telephones.

F. *Reverse Supply Chain.* Reverse supply chain is another important value-added service. This process involves reversing the flow of product in the supply chain, that is, bringing items back to the manufacturer, disposing of them, or repairing or reconditioning them in the warehouse. This is a valuable service because reverse processes are outside the normal supply chain process and often require significant time and attention. Warehouse systems have to be programmed to have effective receiving operations and sometimes are required to perform maintenance and repair functions as well as disposal.

Cross-Docking

Cross-docking is a process that moves product from one transportation vehicle across the dock to another vehicle for ultimate shipment to the customer. Product is not put in storage and product flow is almost uninterrupted. Speed to market and reduced storage and inventory costs are the key benefits.

Now that we have reviewed the essential activities in the warehouse, we examine the critical factors that determine how the warehouse should be designed and how the handling process operates.

Factors That Determine Warehouse Design and Operation

As indicated above, the product, how it is received, the nature of customer orders, service levels, and transportation mode dictate warehouse design and operations.

Type of Product

Products that are fragile or whose packaging cannot withstand much weight usually require storage in racks. A rack is nothing more than a steel framework that is erected so that items can be stored on the rack rather than stacked on top of one another. Using racks allows the company to stack the product to the ceiling, thus maximizing utilization of space. On the other hand, product that is relatively dense, is packaged in strong cartons, and is palletized can usually be stacked several pallets high and does not require racking.

Products with short shelf lives are not able to use the storage space in the warehouse very effectively because they must be stored in a way that allows the oldest product to be selected first. Food, pharmaceuticals, and chocolate candies are some examples. In this case, these types of product cannot be stored in very deep bays in the warehouse, thus necessitating more aisle space. Products with no freshness issues can be stored in deep bays that tend to utilize space more effectively. Many food products and pharmaceuticals have relatively demanding requirements as far as the cleanliness of the warehouse is concerned. There are issues with rodent and insect infestation, which require that product not be stored next to a wall and that space be left for insect and rodent traps in those areas. In addition, warehousing design is constrained when certain products are affected by other products. For example, tires and appliances cannot be stored in the same warehouse because tires give off fumes that ruin the paint on appliances. Similarly, hazardous materials are subject to severe restrictions in the way they are stored and handled. Most hazardous items require a sprinkler system with significant space left between the tops of the stacks and the sprinklers. In addition, many hazardous products require a pond next to the facility to provide sufficient water in case of a spill or a fire.

How the Product Is Received

Product that is palletized can be taken right from the truck to the storage area and put away. Product that arrives "deadpile," that is, simply loaded on the floor of the truck, must usually be unloaded by hand and placed onto pallets so that it can be effectively stored. If the product is not palletized, then it is not possible to stack it very high, and valuable space is wasted in the warehouse. Products that are unpalletized or have an odd shape are very difficult to deal with in the warehouse, and they generally require more handling and do not use the full storage space of the warehouse very effectively.

Nature of the Orders

The types of orders that must be processed by the warehouse play a major role in determining how the warehouse is designed. If the typical order involves pallet quantities of products, then it is possible to store product efficiently because it can be stacked to the ceiling. If less-than-pallet quantities are the typical order, then it is necessary to keep a number of pallets on the floor so that the less-than-pallet quantities can be picked from them. This reduces the ability to stack the product and use space effectively. Firms often use racks if less-than-pallet quantities are picked so that these smaller quantities can be selected from the rack without destroying the integrity of the stack.

If the orders involve one or just a few cases of each item and there are many stock-keeping units (SKUs) in the warehouse, then warehouse design and operation become more complex. Orders that contain a few cases of each product may necessitate the use of racks, require that a separate picking area be established, or require that the warehouse be designed with shorter aisles and in other ways to facilitate the selection of orders. If the orders involve individual items, often referred to as *eaches*, then the entire nature of the warehouse changes. Here, firms may use a picking area, where the entire permanent storage area is duplicated, but only with one pallet of each item. This makes it fast and simple to select an order. In this case, the picking area is replenished from the permanent storage area as a full pallet of product is used up. In some cases, when the product line is long and orders involve eaches, it makes sense to automate the picking process. Here, product is kept in bins, the computer directs the selection of orders as a conveyor moves a carton down a line through each of the product bins. When a particular item is to be selected, and a computer directs the system to place that item into the carton as it moves along the conveyor. Usually, some type of device with an "arm" on it pushes an item into the moving carton. Avon, the distributor of cosmetics and personal care items, uses this type of system in its warehouses as its orders are generally composed of 10 to 20 very small individual items out of a total of thousands that are kept in the warehouse. A carton starts moving down a conveyor belt that moves past hundreds of bins of lipstick, makeup, and so on. As the carton passes a product on the order, an arm pushes the number of items into the carton. The cartons are then routed to a particular location based on the carton's label and are automatically moved by conveyor to the appropriate UPS truck for the carton's intended destination.

Service Levels Required

When speed is of the utmost importance, facilities are designed to move product through as rapidly as possible. In most cases, every warehouse hopes to select orders as rapidly as possible so as to reduce costs. To accomplish this, companies use a variety of techniques to speed up the order selection process. Many warehouses use bar code systems that allow the order picker to simply run a wand across the cases to be selected, which then tells him whether he has selected the correct item in the proper quantity. It also updates the inventory of the item, so that the inventory records show the proper quantity left in stock. Bar code systems are usually part of a more comprehensive set of software referred to as a warehouse management system (WMS). A WMS is a set of software that directs almost all activities in the warehouse, including receiving, put away, location of storage areas, order picking, bill of lading preparation, electronic data interchange with trading partners, and inventory tracking. The WMS enables the warehouse to operate at peak efficiency by reducing errors, improving accuracy, and increasing productivity (by directing workers to pick orders with minimum search time and reduced paperwork). The WMS improves space utilization by determining the optimal storage patterns.

Another technique to speed the order selection process is to place fast-moving items near the outbound dock spaces, thus minimizing the travel time through the warehouse. Some firms find it useful to utilize a zone system for selecting orders. Here, products are grouped in confined areas, and one person selects all the items in his or her area for a given order. In this way, the picker becomes an expert in his or her area, and the order selection process moves more quickly. The order is complete when the picker in each zone has completed his or her part of the order. This system works particularly well when the product line is extensive.

Another approach designed to speed the order selection process is called batch picking. Here, the order picker picks all the A, B, and C items for several orders and delivers them to an area where the entire order is reassembled. Other order pickers batch pick the remaining items on the order. This approach works well when you have many items in inventory and the same few are found on many orders. It tends to reduce travel time, but it does require a separate area to consolidate all the items for the entire order.

The ultimate in speed as it relates to the warehouse is the use of cross-docking, where product is received from a truck or rail car at one dock location, moved "across the dock" to another truck, and then delivered to the customer. The goal of cross-docking is to avoid placing the product in storage. This not only eliminates the storage cost and inventory-carrying costs but also eliminates handling the product multiple times. The products in a cross-dock operation are handled just once—out of the inbound truck or rail car and into the outgoing truck. In normal warehouse operations, the product would be unloaded, moved to a storage location, perhaps moved again to a picking area, and then moved from the picking area into a waiting truck for final shipment to the customer.

Cross-docking works well when the warehouse has perfect knowledge of the incoming merchandise and the outgoing orders are matched to known demand for a product. It is often used for products that are on a special promotion because the seller knows exactly how much product is to be sent to a given customer or store. For example, this would work if a food manufacturer were running a promotion on 12-oz bottles of ketchup, and each store in a food retailer's chain were expected to sell 10 extra cases during the promotion. Here, a truckload of ketchup would arrive at the grocer's distribution center and the ketchup could be cross-docked in 10-case units into the grocer's trucks being sent to the stores. The ketchup is handled only once and is never placed in storage. The major requirements for employing cross-docking are information and coordination: the shipper and receiver of the merchandise must carefully integrate their systems, and information must also be shared. The shipper has to know the order quantity for each receiving location, and the receiver must know when the shipper's truck will arrive so that they can plan the labor to unload it and coordinate the inbound products with the outbound shipments.

Cross-docking is most effective in buildings that are constructed for that purpose. The ideal cross-dock facility has many dock doors, and the building is relatively long and quite narrow. This facilitates the easy movement of product from the receiving docks on one side of the building to the shipping docks on the other side. If the products are moved out in case quantities or eaches, then there is a need for some type of conveyor system to facilitate the creation of the outbound shipment as well as an area to open the inbound cases and repack the outgoing cases.

Transportation Mode

If the warehouse receives or ships product by rail, the building usually is designed with an indoor "rail pit." The rail pit is simply an area inside the building where track is laid and boxcars are brought into the building so they can be unloaded in a controlled environment. If truck is the primary mode of transportation, then the warehouse must be constructed with sufficient dock space to accommodate the estimated volume of receipts and shipments. One way to minimize the number of dock doors is to alter the warehouse operations so that product might be received in the morning and shipped in the afternoon. In this way, the same set of doors can be used for both shipping and receiving. If shipping and receiving take place simultaneously all day, then there is need for enough doors to accommodate both. Warehouses with very heavy truck volume also require relatively large "yards" where trailers can be "dropped" by the trucking company and then picked up after they have been loaded. In this way, the driver is not required to remain at the warehouse while the truck is being loaded.

If the warehouse has considerable volume of small shipments by package express companies like UPS and Federal Express, then space will have to be set aside in the warehouse for assembling these small package orders. This entails an order assembly area, a packaging area, and a final packing area. Usually, a warehouse with heavy small-shipment volume is linked electronically with UPS, FedEx, or the Postal Service to print manifests and bills of lading and to determine and pay shipping charges.

The Role of Packaging and Unitization in Warehousing

Unitization refers to methods for increasing the amount of product that can be handled at one time. If there is no unitization, then individual products or cases of products are handled separately, which is more time-consuming and expensive. There are several levels of unitization. The first level is simply placing several items into a case or carton. This is the most common form of unitization used in all types of supply chains. Kellogg's packs cereal in cases of 12 or 24, whereas a case of Coast soap might contain upward of 100 bars of soap. Handling a case is obviously more effective than handling several individual bars of soap. The next level of unitization is the pallet, a wooden platform that typically measures 40 in. by 48 in. and may hold up to 120 cases or more of product (depending on the product, of course). The pallet is then moved as a unit, so that the warehouse worker is moving 120 cases of product in one movement, instead of 1 case 120 times. Pallet loads of product are often wrapped with stretch wrap, so that the pallet truly becomes a unit, and individual cases are held securely on the pallet. Sometimes, two pallets may be stacked together and stretch wrapped, creating an even larger "unit." The final level of unitization is a container in which product is placed and the container is sealed until it reaches its final destination. In this way, a very large unit that might contain 20 pallet loads is handled by itself. Containers are very important in ocean shipping and in some shipments by air, which simplifies the loading and unloading process immeasurably.

Unitization has a major effect on both the effective storage and handling of product in the warehouse. If product is palletized, it makes the unloading of transportation vehicles much faster than when it is simply loaded directly on the floor of the vehicle. A truck trailer typically holds 26 pallets of product, or 52 if it is possible to stack them two pallets high. A truck can be unloaded in a matter of minutes if the load is fully palletized. Palletized loads are also easier to store because in many cases the pallets can be stacked on top of each other. Some products can be stacked five pallets high, which effectively uses the cubic space available in the warehouse. In conclusion, unitization plays a pivotal role in both enhancing the effective use of space and permitting many items to be moved throughout the warehouse and out of and into transportation vehicles in an efficient manner.

Packaging also plays a major role in the efficient operation of a warehouse. Packaging has a dual role in that the package protects the product by providing the strength for the case to withstand other cases being stacked on top of it. To obtain the highest level of storage efficiency, it is necessary to use the full cubic capacity of the warehouse, and a poorly constructed and weak carton severely limits the amount of product that can be stacked within the storage space. If the upper 10 ft of the warehouse is unused, the cost per square foot of storage space significantly increases.

Second, the package contains written information or bar codes that identify what is in the case and any information about its freshness. If the package does not effectively identify the contents or if the writing is difficult to decipher, it dramatically slows down the put away and order selection processes. During the Gulf War of 1991, over $2 billion worth of supplies were left in the Saudi Arabian desert because the product could not be identified based on the information on the cartons. Bar code labels and crisp, clear writing simply make it possible for order pickers to select orders in the least amount of time.

Storage and Handling Trade-offs

Unfortunately, there is often a trade-off between storage efficiency and handling efficiency. When product is stacked to the ceiling and very deep in the storage bays, it is more difficult to pick an order rapidly. When the aisles are narrow in an effort to conserve storage space, it is difficult for the forklift trucks to negotiate through the warehouse. Having fewer aisles saves considerable space, but means that product is not as accessible as it is with more aisles. On the other hand, if product is not stacked very high and aisles are wide, product becomes more spread out and travel time through the warehouse to pick an order is lengthened considerably. An important element in managing warehouse activities is to strike the most effective balance between storage efficiency and handling efficiency. The decision on where to strike the balance depends on the nature of the products, how many items are stored in the warehouse, and the nature of the typical customer order.

Products that are storage intensive—bulky items, items that do not turn over very rapidly, and products that typically move in pallet quantities—should be managed to reduce the storage space that is used. Efforts should focus on stacking high and deep to curtail the use of space. On the other hand, items that by their nature do not require much space (computer chips, for example), products that turn rapidly, and items that move in case or eaches quantities should be managed to facilitate the put-away and order selection process. Here, we might create a separate picking area to speed up the picking process, or we might stack the product only one pallet high, so items can be easily reached. If the items are selling rapidly, it means they need less storage space, and the important issue is speed of the picking process.

If the warehouse has only five items in the entire facility, the picking process is straightforward and relatively simple. Therefore, the focus is on maximizing the use of storage space. On the other hand, a warehouse with 250,000 SKUs presents a huge challenge in terms of picking orders efficiently. In this case, the focus is on enhancing the picking process and perhaps conceding storage efficiency. Oreck Manufacturing, the company that markets the 8-lb high-powered vacuum through television and print media, has a goal of shipping every order on the day it is received. Its warehouse is oriented to maximize order picking efficiency to meet this service goal. In this case, space utilization is of secondary concern.

When order picking efficiency is the concern, aisles are wider, rapid turnover product is located closer to the dock doors, travel time through the warehouse is minimized, and a separate area, referred to as a pick area, is sometimes set up to allow rapid selection of orders in a very confined space. Although this area duplicates the permanent storage space, the extra cost is more than made up for in the reduction of time spent picking orders.

Warehousing in the Context of the Entire Supply Chain

Warehousing decisions should be made in the context of the entire supply chain. In other words, some decisions about warehousing may have significantly negative consequences on other elements of the supply chain, and these interactions must be carefully examined.

Warehousing and Transportation

Warehouses make it possible to reduce transportation cost because large shipments can be transported over long distances from plant to warehouse, with smaller shipments only traveling short distances. Overall costs are usually reduced because the long-haul LTL shipments are eliminated. However, there comes a point where once there are so many warehouses, the total cost of transportation increases—with so many facilities, the shipments to the warehouses become LTL shipments. Thus, there is some point at which adding more warehouses increases transportation costs. In addition, the extra warehouses cost money to operate and create more inventory costs.

Warehousing and Inventory

Generally, the more warehouses, the higher the total inventory-carrying costs. As warehouses are added to a supply chain, the amount of inventory increases in total but at a decreasing rate as shown in Figure 14.5. This phenomenon tends to occur as a result of the fact that each additional warehouse somewhat duplicates the safety stock maintained by other warehouses in the system. The supply chain manager must be mindful of this situation and continually evaluate the trade-off of smaller inventories versus more warehouses. A common supply chain strategy of many firms is to maintain one centralized warehouse for all slow-moving items and airfreight these items to customers as the need arises. The savings in inventory costs make up for the increased cost associated with airfreight, and the customer enjoys relatively good service with overnight delivery.

In addition to the increase in inventory costs, more warehouses mean additional investments in the buildings and additional costs to operate them. The key issue is the customer service level the company desires, and the level of inventory and warehousing cost they are willing to tolerate to achieve that level of service. More warehouses, located closer to key markets and customers, do indeed generate a higher level of service—but the extra cost must be justified by enhanced revenue or increased customer loyalty.

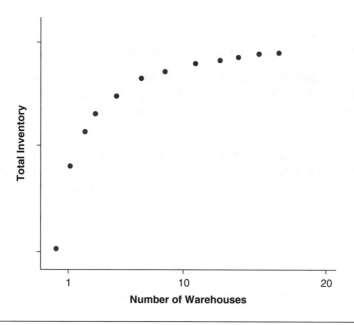

Figure 14.5   Relationship of Inventory and Number of Warehouses

Warehousing and Customer Service

As discussed above, more warehouses in the network mean better service to the customer. Customers tend to feel quite comfortable if they know the supplier has a warehouse near their operations. They do not feel as comfortable if the warehouse is 1,200 miles away. Again, the issue is the value of the better service versus the extra warehouse and inventory cost associated with providing it. Another dimension of service is the product mix—we may be willing to incur higher warehouse and inventory costs because it is so important to maintain a warehouse for the purpose of creating a full line of the firm's products. Customers perceive a strong benefit by ordering from one location and receiving only one shipment of the firm's entire product line. Thus, the additional costs may be justified by enhanced customer satisfaction that should translate into a high degree of customer loyalty.

Measuring Warehouse Performance

A relatively common set of metrics is used to evaluate the performance of the warehousing function. Looking back at the major activities in the warehouse, these metrics are centered on costs associated with moving products and storing products, order accuracy, on cycle time (how long it takes us to get the product to the customer once the warehouse has received the order), and product damage. The most common warehouse performance measures include handling productivity, space utilization, accuracy, damage, service, and macro measures.

Handling Productivity

1. "Units" (cases, pounds, barrels, bags, etc.) picked per man-hour.

2. "Lines" picked per man-hour. A line refers to one line on an order or one SKU, and may be a better indication of productivity than units because an order with 10 lines and only 12 units may be harder to pick than an order with 200 units but only one line or SKU.

3. Total handling cost per "unit." This includes the total cost associated with moving product into and out of the facility. It reflects not only the efficiency of the picking process but also the ability to manage costs—control equipment expense, labor, and supplies expense.

Space Utilization and Productivity

1. Percentage of total space available for storage. This measure provides an idea of how much space is allocated to nonstorage uses like aisles, work areas, and staging areas.

2. Percentage of usable storage space used for storage. This provides an indication of how effectively the warehouse is storing product and the extent to which space is being wasted. It is usually calculated as a monthly average, since usage of space varies as product moves into and out of the warehouse.

3. Storage cost per unit of product. This gives some idea of storage efficiency as well as the ability to manage all the costs associated with the building (such as rent, maintenance, utilities, and insurance).

Accuracy

1. Percentage of items picked correctly.

2. Percentage of orders picked correctly. This may be a better measure because one incorrect item makes the order incorrect. Thus, one incorrect item on a 100-item order is 99% accurate, yet the percentage of the orders correct is zero. The purpose of the measurement system is to spot problems, and an incorrect pick, even though just one item, suggests a problem.

Damage

1. Percentage of items picked that are undamaged when received by the customer.

2. Percentage of orders picked without damaged merchandise.

Service

1. Fill rate. The fill rate is the proportion of the total order that was in stock and could be shipped to the customer. The fill rate for the warehouse is measured

by looking at either the total number of cases that could be filled or the total number of orders that were filled completely. Usually, the measure based on total orders filled completely is a better measure, because if 10 cases out of 1,000 are unavailable, the fill rate looks impressive at 99%. However, if 10 orders were each short one item, it could mean 10 customers were unhappy with not receiving their full order. Thus, the measure based on orders is more revealing.

2. Order cycle time. This measures the elapsed time from when the warehouse received the order until the customer receives the product. Another way to measure this is to look at the time from order receipt by the warehouse to when the order was shipped. This is a better measure of the warehouse since the warehouse does not always have control over the transportation of the product, but the former is a better overall logistics process measure.

Macro Measures

1. Total warehouse cost per unit handled.

2. Warehousing cost as a percentage of sales. This is useful for benchmarking against industry standards to know whether your costs are out of line. The average for all industries is a little over 2%.

3. Inventory turnover. This is a measure of how often the average inventory is cycled through the warehouse. It is more a measure of the effectiveness of inventory managers than it is of warehouse management, unless the warehouse manager causes the firm to hold extra inventory or slows down the throughput of product in the facility.

The Role of Information in Warehouse Management

As for all elements of the supply chain, information is the critical driver for successful warehouse operations. There are several important types of information that drive warehousing operations. First, good forecasts of future volume are an absolute necessity, particularly estimates over a short time interval. This is not to say longer-term forecasts are not important. The long-term forecast is used to determine the size of the warehouse, the average size of the workforce, and the amount of equipment required to handle the volume. This sets the overall capacity for the longer term. But the warehouse manager needs to plan the warehouse operations on a daily basis, so he must be provided with an accurate estimate of product coming into the warehouse and orders to be shipped during a very small time window. If the warehouse expects 20 trucks to arrive on Monday, and 50 arrive, they will not have enough labor to handle the volume, or they may not have enough space to handle the inventory. Thus, accurate projections of receipts and orders are critical to running an effective warehousing operation.

In addition to forecasts, the warehouse needs information on exactly what products are on the trucks scheduled to arrive at the warehouse on a particular day.

In this way, they can again plan how to deal with that particular truck and where to store the merchandise that will arrive. Many firms now communicate this information through advanced shipping notices (ASNs), which are sent electronically when the shipment leaves the plant. In similar fashion, the warehouse must have accurate information about each specific order that is to be processed. Orders are often communicated electronically through electronic data interchange (EDI) systems that are set up between the shipper and receiver. Many firms now use the Internet for communicating orders. The orders must specify the products, their exact quantity, and where the order is to be shipped. Communications with transportation companies are also of special importance to the timely unloading of vehicles and the on-time shipment of orders. The warehouse has to know the availability of equipment to be used to ship orders, when the carrier is expected to arrive with inbound product, and whether the driver will unload the truck or unloading will be the responsibility of the warehouse.

Other forms of information are used internally in the warehouse. Many warehouses use locator systems, which is a computer software that directs where product should be stored. The software uses a host of information about the products, their movement, and physical characteristics to determine the optimal location to store the items. As indicated earlier, WMS systems are used for an array of functions in the warehouse to most effectively manage the key processes. An absolute necessity in the warehouse environment is an information system for tracking and monitoring inventory levels. Most WMS systems include inventory management software that permits the warehouse to have real-time information on the inventory status of all items in the warehouse. Much internal data gathering takes place so that the warehouse has the necessary information for calculating the performance metrics described earlier. Thus, the warehouse has procedures for capturing the total man-hours worked, the number of order picking errors, the number of accidents, the number of out-of-stocks, and so forth.

The modern warehouse cannot run effectively without the external sources of information regarding the product to be received and orders to be shipped. It can neither manage internal processes well nor understand their performance levels without a sophisticated internal information system.

Technology and Warehouse Operations

Throughout the discussion of warehousing operations, an array of technologies was discussed in the context of the role they play in enhancing warehouse productivity. Warehouses can be very simple, with no more technology than a few forklift trucks and personal computers. However, the current standard is to utilize as much technology as can be supported by the nature of the operation. A significant amount of technology has become relatively inexpensive, enhancing its application in the warehouse. At a minimum, most warehouses have computer systems assisting with management processes and database management. Many have instituted bar code systems to track product and record transactions. Another important technology associated with bar coding is radio frequency (RF) systems. An RF system is simply a radio frequency system whereby a portable computer used by an order picker communicates with a host computer from anywhere in the warehouse. This system greatly enhances productivity, as the host computer is able to direct all the activities of the warehouse workers, telling them where to find product and verifying that they picked the correct order.

WMS systems were mentioned several times in the earlier sections of this chapter. Today there are literally hundreds of companies supplying WMS systems, and the key issue is whether the warehouse should use an off-the-shelf system or develop a custom system. The choice is difficult because of the fast pace of change in the industry—a custom system designed today may be out-of-date by next year, and the extra cost of the customization may not be warranted. However, off-the-shelf versions tend to drive the processes in the warehouse rather than being tailored to the warehouse's existing processes. Thus, the firm loses some flexibility with these systems.

Warehouses sometimes approach a *Star Wars* level of sophistication through the application of high-level automation technology. The Nintendo warehouse in Washington employs a high level of automation because the products in question are high value and can "afford" the system. Products are received at the dock, a conveyor belt is run into the truck, and product is placed on the conveyor. From that moment on, humans do not intervene in the warehousing process. Automated guided vehicles (AGVs) take the product to its storage lane. At that point, product is transferred to an automated storage/retrieval system (AS/RS) where totes containing the items are automatically lifted to their storage bay high in the warehouse. When orders are selected, product is retrieved by the system and is once again brought back down to the AGV that takes it to a packing station. Once packed, the order moves by conveyor into a waiting truck. Systems of this complexity are not effective in all situations, and their application must be carefully evaluated because they are relatively unforgiving. That is, because they are automated they are built on the basis of a given set of specifications based on product size, density, and so on. If the product mix changes or product and case dimensions change from their original configuration, then the system may not accommodate them.

The Major Business Issues Confronting Warehousing Management

Like any business function, there are several major challenges that will confront the warehouse manager in the future. Some of these issues are quite unique to warehousing, whereas others are common to most business functions.

Human Resource Issues

Most warehouse operations are fairly labor-intensive as a result of the nature of the processes that take place. For the most part, the typical warehouse cannot justify the huge investment in automation and other labor-saving devices. In addition, the wages typically paid to warehouse workers are relatively low, which contributes to the issues associated with labor. The major current issue is simply the availability of a good pool of qualified hourly warehouse workers. Declining birthrates, higher high school drop out rates, the inability of potential workers to pass drug tests, and the rapidly growing economy have all combined to reduce the pool of labor available for warehouse jobs. In one instance, a company establishing a warehouse in Memphis, a city with almost no unemployment, interviewed 210 people, and only 9 were able to pass both the drug and literacy tests! Thus, a major challenge is finding good people, training them to be effective, and retaining them. Some warehouses now offer bounties to their current employees for finding a new hourly employee who stays with the company for six months. Added to the lack of a large labor pool is the fact that the new labor force is culturally quite diverse, making it imperative that the management recognizes and effectively deals with the different cultures and languages.

Outsourcing Issues

Most manufacturers and retailers face the decision of whether to operate the warehouse function or outsource it to a third-party firm, who then takes responsibility for all the activities associated with warehousing. There are compelling reasons to outsource:

1. The firm eliminates a large set of assets from its books.

2. Labor is no longer an issue. The third party relieves the company of involvement in labor contract issues and usually uses much cheaper nonunion hourly labor.

3. Third parties have a core competency in warehousing and are often able to run the operation more effectively than the client.

4. Third parties have several clients, which affords the opportunity to gain transportation consolidations to customers.

5. Third parties frequently have significant skills in the management information systems necessary in the warehouse and are able to effectively interface with the firm's customers.

Although the advantages of outsourcing are many and significant, outsourcing is no panacea. The single largest impediment is managing the relationship between the two companies. More often than not, the marriage between users and providers of third-party services is not made in heaven. The reason for this is that the firms have their own cultures, objectives, and strategic issues, and these are not always compatible. In many cases, top management of the client company does not understand the third-party business and places extreme demands on their performance. On the other hand, many third parties promise anything to win the business, yet are never able to deliver on their promises. On balance, the relationship between clients and third-party companies is neither easy nor stable, and the issue of whether to use a third party is one that must be very carefully researched and evaluated.

E-Commerce

The tremendous growth in e-commerce businesses has created a huge opportunity for warehousing. Most e-commerce firms that sell to final consumers have found that their success or failure is very much related to how effectively they can perform the warehousing function. The warehouse is really the linchpin in the e-commerce business model because it is a major cost center and has the greatest impact on whether the customer is satisfied with the experience.

E-commerce raises some interesting issues for the warehouse. First, consumers dealing with e-commerce firms tend to have very high expectations about the speed with which they will receive their merchandise. This puts pressure on the warehouse. Next, depending on how the e-commerce business is organized, there is a problem with what is referred to as *scalability*, which means that since the Internet is available to people all over the world, it is very difficult to predict daily volumes. This puts a huge strain on capacity when thousands of unexpected orders are received. The third key issue is returns. It is well-known that the return rate of merchandise is much higher for products not purchased in the typical retail store. This puts a premium on the e-commerce warehouse ability to handle the large volume of product coming back through the system. Finally, since many of the orders are very small, e-commerce warehouses must absolutely be skilled in order selection systems oriented to picking eaches.

Future Trends for Warehousing

There was a time when many were predicting the demise of the warehouse because it was looked upon as simply a repository for goods. The thinking held that all firms were striving to eliminate inventory, so warehouses could not possibly play much of a role in future global supply chain networks. As this chapter has shown, the warehouse is alive and flourishing, playing many key roles in traditional supply chain networks as well as assuming a pivotal place in most e-commerce operations. The future of the warehouse is bright indeed.

The future will probably witness a wider variety of types of warehouses. Some will be very different from the traditional buildings in that they will be long and narrow and have a multitude of dock doors to support cross-dock operations. Others will be 50 to 60 ft high and designed to accommodate AS/RS systems as that technology becomes more affordable and more widely applied. Still other facilities will be huge and serve larger segments of the country as a result of the application of technology in the trucking industry. And in some cases, other firms will opt to use many smaller facilities that are strategically positioned in key markets in response to the need to strategically increase service levels for a variety of market segments. Another segment will focus on the challenging demands of selecting small orders of individual items required in the e-business environment. Warehouses will be strategically important for controlling total supply chain cost and meeting service requirements in this environment.

The application of postponement will accelerate due to the increased emphasis on responding to individual consumer requirements and the significant savings in inventory, transportation, and the reduction of obsolete product associated with postponement strategies. The end result will be a blurring of warehousing, assembly, and retail operations, and the warehouse will be the place in which much final assembly, labeling, and packaging will take place. It is well positioned for this role as a result of low labor cost, closeness to markets, and effective systems for managing the processes associated with assembly, blending, labeling, and packaging. With more firms placing emphasis on "mass customization"—creating products for individual tastes in a cost-effective manner—the warehouse will become more involved in this strategy. The personal computer industry is a good example of the extent to which this concept has taken hold.

Significant emphasis will be placed on plant warehousing—that is, the warehousing activities associated with storing and handling all the materials, components, supplies, and subassemblies that are used in the manufacturing process. This has been a neglected area of warehousing, yet one that can have major cost and service impacts. Some progressive manufacturers are strategically using plant-positioned warehouses to stage incoming materials and components, and arranging them in the order in which they will be used in the production process. This not only frees up valuable floor space in the factory but also allows the production process to work on a just-in-time basis. As more firms explore the potentials of coordinating plant warehousing activities with key suppliers, this area should grow rapidly.

The warehouse will play an important role in bringing manufacturers together for the purpose of creating consolidated shipments into major markets. There are hundreds of firms that continue to ship in LTL quantities, paying a significant premium in the process. The third-party industry should be instrumental in bringing manufacturers to regional "campuses" of warehouses, where the small shipments of firms shipping to the same retail customers can be consolidated. The trend is only lately beginning to take hold. Similar warehousing systems may unfold in the distribution of products through e-commerce.

Finally, new technology in the form of RFID (radio-frequency identification) will facilitate the movement and location of product in the warehouse as soon as it becomes commercially viable. Currently, the "chips" that are embedded in products and pallets that are used to communicate product location to the computer are too expensive (in most cases) to make this form of automated information communication viable. Many experiments are being conducted in several supply chains to iron out difficulties and to create a workable scenario for using the technology.

Suggested Readings

Ackerman, Ken (2004), *Auditing Warehouse Performance*. Columbus, OH: K. B. Ackerman Company.

Frazelle, Edward H. (1996), *World-Class Warehousing*. Atlanta, GA: Logistics Resources International.

Frey, Stephan (1983), *Warehouse Operations: A Handbook*. Beaverton, OR: M/A Press.

Lynch, Clifford F. (2000), *Logistics Outsourcing: A Management Guide*. Oak Brook, IL: Council of Logistics Management.

Simchi-Levi, David, Phillip Kaminsky, and Edith Simchi-Levi (2003), *Designing and Managing the Supply Chain*, 2nd ed. New York: McGraw-Hill-Irwin.

Stock, James R. and Douglas M. Lambert (2001), *Strategic Logistics Management*, 4th ed. New York: McGraw-Hill-Irwin.

Tompkins, James A. and Jerry D. Smith (1988), *The Warehouse Management Handbook*. New York: McGraw-Hill.

15

Supply Management

Lisa M. Ellram

Paul Cousins

S upply management (SM) has undergone a significant transformation from a function responsible for placing purchase orders to a strategic process focusing on the management of goods and services. The role of SM is to create the maximum strategic advantage for the firm. This includes areas such as the management of technology and innovation, streamlining processes, insourcing and outsourcing, and managing complex relationships. Before the days of data warehousing and integrated information technology (IT), much of purchasing's activity involved dealing with myriad transactions, embroiled in minutiae. Because of the overwhelming level of activity involved in keeping track of orders and paperwork, it was extremely difficult for those in purchasing to rise above the day-to-day fray and make a significant, value-added contribution to the organization. The focus of SM was first on getting the lowest price, without regard to production, process, and design inefficiencies in suppliers or their own systems. Sometimes the focus ended there. In more enlightened organizations, purchasers were also responsible for selecting reliable suppliers to provide availability of purchased items. These organizations may have also moved to a more cost-focused, as opposed to price-focused, strategy. This involved examining where the key cost drivers are within and between organizations and then trying to reduce them.

SM has long been recognized as an important contributor to corporate profitability through price reduction. For example, for a firm with a 10% profit margin, a 1% saving from SM brings the same profit increase as roughly a 10% increase in sales. In other words, SM savings go directly to the bottom line of the organization, thereby increasing profitability. Although this direct savings effect has forced management to appreciate the potential impact of SM on short-term profit, it has not necessarily caused management to look at SM strategically.

Thus, a key question that we may pose is why SM should be seen as important (or strategic) to a business organization. There are several possible answers to this question. When analyzing the reasons for SM's importance to the firm, two distinct arguments emerge: economic and strategic congruence or alignment. The economic argument is relatively straightforward. Firms must compete globally and face continuing price reduction pressure from the market. Buyers could squeeze supplier profits in the short term to reach acceptable prices. Of course, this is not sustainable in the medium to long term, leaving only the option to reduce costs. Cost reduction could be achieved in two ways: examination of the organization's internal processes (with subsequent efficiency measures) and reduction in the input costs (materials and services). For many organizations, such as Honda of America Manufacturing, the value of materials and services acquired from outside, as a proportion of overall costs, is often quoted as 70% or higher. Reduction of input costs is a natural focus for organizations seeking to reduce their costs.

From a strategic perspective, with the emergence of supply chain management, most organizations now see managing their supply base as a key strategic issue. SM is often seen as the facilitator of this success of key supply strategies, such as outsourcing, supply base restructuring, and partnership development. Thus, there is a growing recognition that SM makes contributions beyond price savings to add value and generate profit for the organization. SM has gone from "purchasing," which was simply "the acquisition of required material, services, and equipment" (Dobler, Burt, and Lee 1990, p. 5), to SM, defined as "the identification, acquisition, access, positioning, and management of resources the organization needs or potentially needs in the attainment of its strategic objectives" (Duffy 2002). The issues surrounding the management of supply are illustrated in a model called the Supply Wheel (see Figure 15.1).

The model shows the range of key issues that are faced in strategic SM. First, in the center of the figure, all SM activities must be based on, and congruent with, the firm's corporate strategy. Increasingly, SM is represented at the board level (A.T. Kearney 2005). There are five other key elements to consider. First, there is a need for people with the appropriate skills and competencies to deliver the strategy. Second, firms require a portfolio of relationships, as presented below, to match their needs with supplier capabilities and market conditions. Third, cost-benefit analysis requires that the buying firm understands the relative costs and benefits of pursuing any given strategy. Amazingly, many companies do not determine the costs of doing business before and after improvements to their processes. Fourth, the organization structure considers whether SM should be centralized, decentralized, or conducted in commodity teams. This decision must support the needs of the business. Finally, strategic performance measures are extremely important in that they facilitate behavior and strategy implementation. Different strategies require different measurement systems and emphasis to drive success.

The Supply Wheel shows how integrated strategic supply fits within the business organization. Each element of this model needs to be considered when making

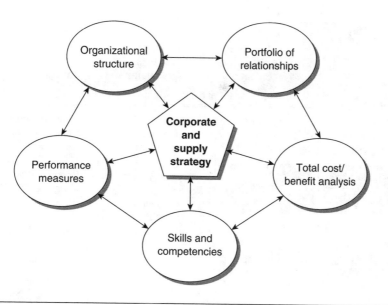

Figure 15.1   Supply Wheel

SOURCE: Cousins (2002).

important SM decisions because if one element within the model changes it affects all others.

With the professionalization of SM, standard processes have been developed that are used by many organizations. In the following sections, we introduce the standardized, step-by-step approach to strategic SM. As part of this process, we also present a classic approach to commodity segmentation. The chapter ends with a presentation of cutting-edge SM trends.

The Strategic Supply Management Process

The strategic SM process, as shown in Figure 15.2, is a five-step process. Many consulting firms have similar approaches, some consisting of seven steps (A.T. Kearney, Accenture) and others with six (McKinsey and Co.). However, most focus on the same issue—concentrating SM on improving its performance through portfolio management. These five steps are based on experience with many organizations throughout the world, such as the aforementioned consulting firms and Rolls-Royce, MoD, Tesco, Deere and Company, American Express, and many others.

Step 1: Analyze and Gather Data

Good information is necessary to get good results. The starting point of strategic sourcing is to develop an understanding of the organization's strategy, strengths, and weaknesses and assess the potential opportunities and problems in the

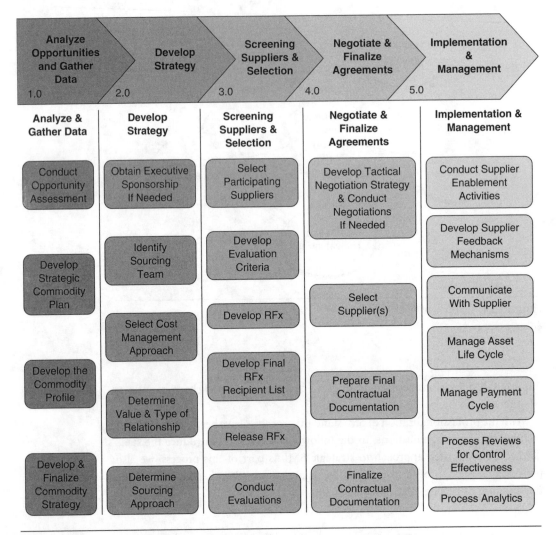

Figure 15.2   Strategic Supply Management Process

environment in which the firm operates. This can be done using a classic approach like Porter's strengths, weaknesses, opportunities, and threats (SWOT) analysis (Porter 1982). This supply opportunity assessment step may be conducted at a companywide level, on a regular basis, as part of the strategic planning process. It can be conducted on a continuous basis, founded on data received from the marketplace, changing competitive conditions, or changing strategy. It can also be conducted within a given commodity[1] area. Regardless, the process is basically the same. In this discussion we assume that strategic sourcing analysis is part of the annual planning process.

Five-forces (Porter 1975) analysis is a good tool to identify issues of concern in the external marketplace (Figure 15.3). We consider issues related to the power of buyers, the power of suppliers, the intensity of rivalry within the industry, the availability of substitute items, and the barriers to new entrants into the relevant

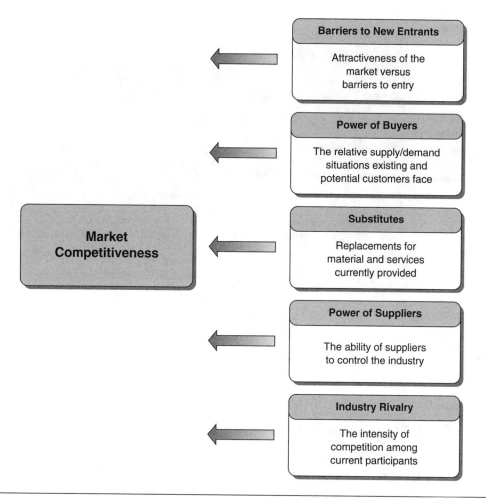

Figure 15.3   Five Forces Shaping Market Competitiveness

industries. These factors come together to help determine if there is a good opportunity to improve the current situation based on what is happening in the marketplace and to anticipate potential problems.

At the same time, we need to look internally to understand our current strategy with regard to the products that use the commodity. Is there willingness to change from our current supplier, use substitute items, or change the relationship with a current supplier? These would all bode well for support from internal customers. We also want to consider how much has been done internally to improve the management of this commodity. In general, the items that have not received as much attention may have greater potential return, provided there is internal support for change and the change is not very costly or time-consuming. After the data have been gathered and preliminary analysis has been conducted, we are ready to develop a commodity strategy.

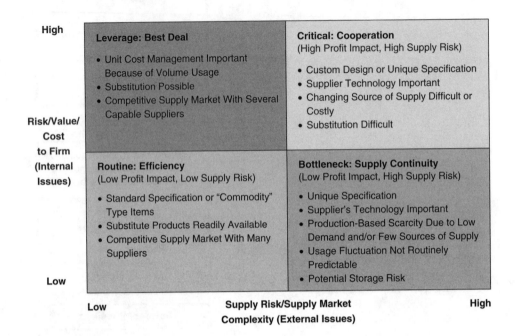

Figure 15.4 Classification of Purchase Items

SOURCE: Adapted from Kraljic (1983).

Step 2: Develop Sourcing Strategies

Understanding the marketplace and the criticality of purchases is a starting point in developing supply strategy. With a thorough understanding of the marketplace, as well as your organization's own strategy and goals, you can begin to classify your purchases to better manage them. For large expenditures or strategic commodities, a cross-functional team made up of key stakeholders may be used to develop strategies. You may also need executive sponsorship if the item you are analyzing is viewed as critical by the organization.

In the early 1980s, Kraljic (1983) developed a positioning matrix to help consider these and other factors to support buyers and suppliers in their sourcing and competitive positioning strategies. He identified four key purchasing approaches or strategies: routine, bottleneck, leverage, and critical. These strategies are positioned against the level of supply exposure or technical risk, compared with the strategic nature of the product or service, that is, the level of value or cost exposure to the buying firm. Figure 15.4 illustrates the basic positioning matrix in which buyers position the types of products and services they buy, otherwise known as *commodities*. This matrix is very simple but also very powerful and has proved invaluable to firms in enabling them to focus on their SM approaches. Because of its flexibility, this classification matrix can be used for any type of purchase, for any organization.

Technical or supply risk can be derived from a few key factors, all gathered in the five-forces analysis. For example, in the oil sector, supplier power is very high because there is a natural resource limitation to the supply; there are few viable, well-developed substitutes; and most organizations that use oil cannot do without it. Because each of the axes is a continuum, the buyer's judgment is required to determine where to place a particular item on the line. The horizontal axis refers to the level of impact the supplier's product or service has on the buyer's ability to deliver the final product. Value, risk, or cost are assessed as the item could be of relatively low cost but of high strategic value or risk to the buyer's product. For example, in the aerospace industry, the battery that powers the flight recorder serves as a beacon to help searchers recover the recorder in case of a crash. Although the battery is relatively inexpensive (compared with the other elements of the aircraft), it is of high strategic value and risk—without a good long-life battery that can withstand water and extreme heat and cold, the flight recorder may never be recovered, and the plane, survivors, and important safety information would be lost.

Keep in mind that the supply market is continuously changing, so what is classified as a leverage item today could be a bottleneck tomorrow. Think of electricity—a commodity and historically a leverage item. But in California in 2001, electricity was a strategic item, hard to come by and critical to operations. This was so pervasive that many companies created their own ability to generate power using fuel cells and other alternative energy sources. A variation of this matrix is used by John Deere and American Express. Where a commodity is placed in the matrix suggests the appropriate sourcing approaches, relationships, number of suppliers, and cost management tools to use.

Routine Items

The routine purchases are characterized by relatively low importance and relatively low market risk. This category is often described as the "insignificant many" and includes many maintenance, repair, and operating supplies. One-time buys and buys with relatively low cumulative dollar spending fit here. The overall supply strategy is in reducing the number of transactions and simplifying processes— perhaps by using purchasing cards or making online catalogs available. The value SM adds here is not in filling out paperwork to place an order but in finding good suppliers and setting up the contracts for ongoing buys. These should be sourced from the most efficient suppliers. In small, one-time buys, SM adds value by setting up easy-to-use self-service systems. On a tactical level, similar decisions that streamline operations with suppliers are part of the supply chain design.

The fact that these items are placed in the routine category does not mean they are not important and should be ignored. These items may still be important to a firm's continuing operations, as are office supplies purchased by a manufacturing firm. The objective is to get the most competitive price for the product, while maintaining delivery and quality standards. As switching costs are low and the market is highly competitive, buyers bid focusing on price.[2] Thus, single sourcing is a good approach in this low-risk quadrant to maximize leverage while reducing administrative burden. Multiple sourcing is also used here if there is concern about continuity of supply (certainly in the short term). Because suppliers are plentiful and only minimally differentiated in terms of value, lowest cost is still a driving selection factor. For very low dollar buys, the suppliers are often selected by contacting known suppliers and asking for prices. As the dollar value increases, an online reverse auction or request for quote may be appropriate.

Bottleneck Items

Bottleneck items are the bane of a supply manager's existence. These are items that no one notices when they are available but that create a minor crisis when not available. These are items where there are few suppliers and low, sporadic demand. This makes it difficult to get any kind of priority from the supplier. Things like repair parts fit here. The amount of money spent is not significant, but the harm from lack of availability could be great. The focus is on continuity of supply at a reasonable total cost. Liquidated damages clauses are often put in place in these sorts of contracts to maintain continuity of supply.

The best thing to do is to try to standardize what you are buying away from that item toward something readily available. If that is not possible, try to make yourself important to the supplier by using one of the volume concentration techniques discussed in the Leverage Items section or by giving the supplier something else it wants, like training, the chance for future business, additional business in an unrelated area, and so on. Although you do not want to devote a great deal of time to supplier relations for these minor items, good supplier relationships can make a difference in getting attention for your order. Because there are few qualified suppliers to choose from, selection is generally determined by contacting known suppliers directly to establish pricing and delivery. There may be a sole source, in which case a selection process is not required.

Leverage Items

Although concentrating purchase volume can help increase your power in any of the quadrants, it is essential to the approaches used to support the leverage quadrant. The aim of this approach is to increase bargaining power, thus establishing a much stronger negotiating position. To concentrate on leverage volume, volume can be pooled across business units, supply base can be reduced, items bought can be standardized, or even participation in a consortium can be initiated. The leverage category is the most favorable category from a buying standpoint because many viable options are available and the firm is in a good negotiating position. For example, a buyer of seats (illustrated in Figure 15.5), instead of sourcing Model A with Supplier 1 and Model B with Supplier 2, sources both models from the same supplier. This gives the buyer the advantage of economies of scale, thus allowing a stronger negotiating position from which to leverage. Firms that pursue a strategy of cost reduction consistently use leverage. This approach to SM can, and often does, change the nature of the supply market exposure.

This quadrant must be watched very closely. Although close supplier alliances are generally not required in this quadrant due to the plethora of available sources, if the market shifts and supply becomes scarce or if you begin to depend heavily on

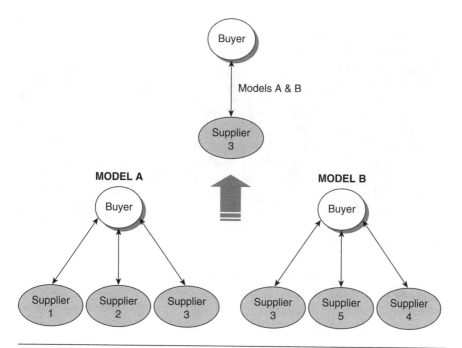

Figure 15.5   Leveraging Strategies

a supplier's expertise, the buy will start drifting into the strategic category where it will need to be managed differently. Do not let yourself be taken by surprise when this happens and the balance of power shifts between you and your suppliers, or you will be in a weaker bargaining position.

To get around this dependency and maintain competition while gaining leverage, Japanese firms have used the concept of dual or parallel sourcing. This involves splitting the supply over a variety of models. For example, Honda purchases the seats for an Accord from one supplier and for the Civic from another. This allows Honda to maintain competition across model groups and also facilitates price and performance benchmarking. This is a complex structure to manage but has the advantage of maintaining competition.

Alternatively, delegated sourcing involves making one supplier responsible for the delivery of an entire subassembly as opposed to its individual part.[3] The customer (buyer) delegates authority to a key supplier, known as a *first-tier* supplier. The principle is that the customer manages only one supplier and that supplier manages the other suppliers that provide parts to complete the product (see Case 15.1).

CASE 15.1   Automotive Industry Supply Delegation

A major car manufacturer was investigating how to reduce the number of suppliers to its business, while maintaining quality, cost, and delivery requirements. It decided to implement a tiered structure approach to SM.

This meant that it would work closely with one key or first-tier supplier, allowing for the exchange of learning and development of a clear integrated cost structure. The buyer firm would also not have to assemble the part by itself. It would arrive complete and be inserted directly onto the vehicle.

The buyer decided to choose a major product area, which was the wheel assembly. It looked closely at the suppliers and decided the bearing manufacturer should be the prime, or first-tier, supplier. It would now be the supplier's responsibility to provide the buyer with a completed wheel assembly. Thus, the buyer moved from a multiple source to a delegated sourcing strategy. The move significantly reduced the number of suppliers to the customer (95% reduction). It also enabled the manufacturer to focus its resources on the first-tier supplier.

Delegated sourcing gives the buyer the opportunity to work closely with one supply source instead of many, thus reducing day-to-day transaction costs. The increased mutual dependency results in the buyer and supplier exchanging more detailed information, particularly around technology and cost issues (implementing cost transparency techniques is commonplace; otherwise known as an *open book* approach). The risk is that the process of delegated sourcing tends to create "mega" suppliers. These suppliers, if not managed properly, can became very powerful and then exert their power over the buyer, usually in the form of price increases. It is vitally important for the buyer to make sure that when these arrangements are put in place the dependencies are well understood and managed. This strategy is often found initially in the "leverage" section of the matrix and in the medium term; because of the high dependency and high switching costs, it moves into the "critical" area (Figure 15.4, top right).

From a cost management standpoint, it is a good approach to gain leverage while bearing in mind the same total cost considerations as noncritical items. An online reverse auction or request for quote is generally appropriate for supplier selection. Relationships are important for continuity of supply and to be in touch with market trends. However, because there are many qualified sources available, close alliances are generally not beneficial in this quadrant.

Critical Items

This leads to the final quadrant, critical items, where there is high exposure to the supplier and high impact on the business (value or cost). These products or services are often seen as critical or strategic to the business, perhaps due to shortages, supplier's technical or quality superiority, regulatory requirements, or patent ownership. These tend to be high-value items. Also, sometimes mega suppliers inadvertently created criticality through leveraging strategies. Examples of these sorts of products include modular assembly suppliers (i.e., first-tier suppliers and key technology suppliers). In services, they could be major outsource providers such as key suppliers of IT or companies such as EDS, IBM, and CSC Index, who take over the operations of the entire IT network, resulting in a single-source relationship. These relationships tend to be single or sole sourced, mainly because of the large amount of investment required, high switching costs, and mutual dependencies. These relationships need to be managed carefully. They are seen as long term, with a strong relationship focus.

Be careful to avoid the tendency to classify too many items as critical. Many suppliers may want to be viewed as critical because they know that it gives them leverage. If you have established a good working relationship with a supplier in this quadrant, you may have long-term relationships that allow two-way sharing of cost data and joint continuous improvement efforts. These types of relationships are generally negotiated, often based on information gathered from responses to a request for information (RFI) solicitation.

Summary of Item Classification

From reviewing the approaches outlined in the previous paragraphs, it is clear that this classification scheme is not an easy "one size fits all." Not only do the classifications change as the market changes, they also change as your business or technology changes, and they vary by company and even strategic business unit within a company. Thus, supply strategy requires continuous review and updating, even more so in a rapidly changing environment. Clearly, the nature of buyer-supplier relationships varies among quadrants, as does the appropriate approach for analyzing the price or cost of the purchase.

Step 3: Screening and Selection

The next steps are reserved for higher-value or riskier purchases. During the screening and selection process, a cross-functional team develops a set of supplier selection criteria, weighted by importance. Some organizations have a standard set of selection criteria they apply to all decisions. Criteria may be added, and the criteria may receive different importance weights depending on the item. For example, Intuit, a software producer, uses standard supplier selection criteria of technology, quality, business ethics, responsiveness, delivery performance, cost competitiveness, and viability (Ellram and Tate 2004). There are more specific criteria under each of the major criteria. For example, "technology" is too vague to evaluate and might include specific factors such as the amount invested in R&D relative to sales revenue or the age of telecom systems.

The team has already gathered significant information on the key suppliers in the market, based on step 1, and is narrowing down the possible suppliers. If this item is not a high-value, critical item, the team might move right into sending out a request for quotation (RFQ) to be used as a prerequisite to participating in an online auction, bidding, or negotiations. If this is a more critical buy, or one for which the organization feels it needs to gather more information, it will ask the potential suppliers to provide data related to the supplier's ability to meet its needs. This is often called an RFI and usually does not include highly confidential information but focuses more on capacity and capability. Based on this information, the suppliers are screened further. Intuit notes it may screen 80% to 85% of suppliers out at this stage. Then, the organization approaches a small subset of suppliers and asks them to specifically respond to an RFQ. It often provides the supplier with specific information about contract terms and conditions to prevent misunderstandings as the process continues. Once the team reviews the information provided, depending on the importance of this purchase, it may make site visits to the most promising suppliers, further narrowing down the choices.

Supplier site visits are costly and time-consuming for both the supplier and the buyer, so these should generally be reserved for only a small set of suppliers that appear to hold much promise. Site visits have several purposes. These include verifying information the supplier has provided, getting answers to additional questions, meeting the supplier face-to-face to get a feeling for the culture and the openness of the supplier, and viewing the supplier's facilities and workforce. Such visits are generally made by a subset of the cross-functional team representing various areas of expertise, such as operations, SM, and finance. With all the information collected, sorted, and analyzed, the cross-functional team is now ready to enter into step 4 of this five-step process. The firm may now be in a position where it has identified one to three suppliers with which to engage in negotiations. If it has decided that the issues are relatively straightforward and addressed through the supplier's proposals, negotiations may be limited or nonexistent; the buying firm will simply present the winning suppliers a contract to approve.

Step 4: Negotiate and Finalize Agreements

During the negotiation process, all the data gathered in the previous steps come into play as the buyer works to develop a "fact-based negotiation brief" to identify its own areas of negotiation strengths and weakness, the "must have" and "nice to have" items, and develops an understanding of its alternatives if it cannot reach agreement with the supplier. It should also try to gauge its supplier's position on each of these issues. There are many negotiation techniques beyond the scope of this chapter, presented in excellent books (Harvard Business School 2004; Lewicki et al. 2004; Fisher, Ury, and Patton 1991).

The outcome of the negotiation process determines which supplier(s) are selected for business. Many of the contractual terms and conditions are finalized as part of the negotiation process. In the case of a large contract, legal representatives from both firms usually get involved in finalizing the contract. The contract includes all the terms and conditions of the agreement. There are usually also numerous addendums. If the contract deals with services, there are generally specific statements of work, clarifying the requirements, and service level agreements providing more details on performance levels and timing. If the contract deals with goods, it may include specifications and blueprints as well as volume requirements and schedules. As a matter of standard operating procedures, most contracts include confidentiality or nondisclosure agreements concerning the other party's operations. If there is any development of goods or services involved, it is a good practice to include agreements related to ownership of intellectual property developed. Once the contract and all the associated documents have been finalized and signed by all parties, implementation may begin.

Step 5: Implement and Manage

Implementing and managing the SM relationship involves many routine practices, such as getting access to each other's inventory and ordering and reporting systems and getting the supplier set up so it can receive payment as an active supplier. At an operating level, it involves establishing metrics to monitor the actual performance versus contractual commitments and communicating with the supplier. All these elements are important for effective supplier relationship management.

At a more strategic level, are there opportunities for the supplier to contribute to the firm's competitive advantage? SM is in a position to consider whether a supplier should be closely aligned with the firm, perhaps as an alliance partner, working together to develop new technologies, ideas, and even market opportunities. As part of the daily interaction with suppliers, and the five-forces analyses that supply managers conduct on key buys, the supply manager is often more aware of changes in the market than anyone else in the organization. Some of these may have strategic implications. See Case 15.2 for an example.

CASE 15.2   PC and Peripheral Company Counts on Supply for Innovation

A major PC and peripheral manufacturer relies on its supply managers to bring new supply ideas into the organization. At this organization, where product change is constant, supply managers are paired with engineers who are experts in that commodity area. This team of supply manager and engineer is completely responsible and empowered to make all decisions related to their commodity. This combined business and engineering organization represents a major evolution in SM duties, one that both engineers and supply managers agree works very well. The engineers provide the technical expertise, and the supply managers provide the cost expertise, understanding of intellectual property and contractual issues, and other business skills. They share common goals, and both report to the supply organization. This pairing of supply and engineering has allowed SM to take a much more active role in new product development, beginning with heavy involvement in the design phase. It is the supply manager-engineer team that actually selects and qualifies the suppliers, not R&D, as has traditionally been the case at this firm.

SM can play an important role in determining which suppliers are truly strategic, and cultivate appropriate relationships. SM is poised to make an important contribution to the success of the supply chain. Research advocates that SM be seen much more strategically. A.T. Kearney's *Assessment of Excellence in Procurement* surveys CEOs at 275 global companies. Two thirds of companies studied have at least one high-level SM executive on their management team, up from 40% in 1999. In addition, 60% noted that they specifically use SM expertise to help set strategy rather than simply to execute the decisions (A.T. Kearney 2005).

Trends in Supply Management

This section presents some of the significant trends in SM. It includes trends toward strategic involvement, customer focus, involvement in indirect and services spending, globalization and outsourcing, continuous improvement focus and involvement in payables, and environmentalism.

Strategic Involvement

The alignment of strategic goals and objectives is essential if SM is to be seen as strategic to the firm. Given that the term *strategic* means that the function or process is able to have a significant impact on the firm's business position, this means that SM needs to understand what having a "significant impact" means to the firm. The following model illustrates this point and argues the need for alignment (see Figure 15.6). This model was developed in a large-scale research project to understand how SM should function to be seen as strategic within the business organization (Cousins 2005). The horizontal axis defines the strategic focus of the business using Porter's (1982) generic strategies regarding whether the firm competes based on cost (low price) or differentiation (predominant focus on nonprice factors such as technology, speed, service, etc.). The vertical axis refers to the type of business outcome toward which SM can contribute. These range from short-term, tactical exchanges to much more long-term strategic exchanges.

Within each quadrant are the research findings of the various strategies that SM should follow if it is to be seen as strategic. For example, if the firm is cost focused, SM's short-term approach should be an "operational collaboration" strategy (Figure 15.6, quadrant A). This includes tactics focused on cost reduction through either improved efficiencies or process improvements. In quadrant B of Figure 15.6, market collaborations still have a cost reduction focus but concentrate more on product improvement.

Among firms pursuing differentiation, the research did not identify any short-term approaches. Rather, "strategic collaborations" prevailed (see Figure 15.6, quadrant C). If SM is to be seen as strategic (defined as important to the business), then it must deliver what the business wants. For example, if the firm is pursuing a cost-focused approach and SM concentrates on strategic collaboration tactics (identified with differentiated firms), then SM will not be seen as strategic to the business, even though it is doing things that are useful. Thus, we argue that the question that should be asked is what SM needs to do to be seen as strategic to the business. This strategic alignment also allows better portfolio management within the Kraljic matrix presented earlier.

Customer Focus

As stated above, to effectively support the goals of the organization, SM must understand what its customers—the internal businesses—want. This requires that SM go beyond its traditional duties of spending the organization's money well to truly understand the needs of its customers and even "sell" its services so that

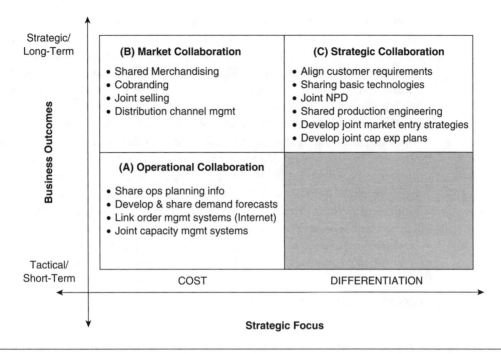

Figure 15.6   Strategic Purchasing Alignment Model.

SOURCE: Cousins (2005).

internal customers want to come to SM. This sort of philosophy has been used effectively by a variety of firms, such as American Express, GlaxoSmithKline, General Motors, and Energis (an international telecommunications company), to grow SM's reputation as a business partner. The business must appreciate the benefits that a strategically managed SM function can deliver. Energis set out to show the importance of supply to the firm. It has achieved significant cost savings through a focused strategy. Moreover, it now works with some of its customers (and their salespeople) to pass best practice up the supply chain, that is, the supplier educates the customer on SM "best practice."

By taking a customer service approach, SM gains greater awareness of strategic issues. It is still SM's responsibility to follow company SM processes and adhere to ethical standards. However, the customer focus should be at the forefront of the minds of supply managers.

Involvement in Indirect and Services Spending

For years, particularly in manufacturing organizations, the focus has been on establishing good systems and controls for purchasing raw materials, components, and goods for resale. Much less focus has been given to other spending categories, such as marketing, advertising, benefits, and supplies. Yet these can amount to 30% or more of revenues in service organizations. These items have in the past been purchased by end users, primarily based on preferences and the available budget rather than on following a rigorous SM process as presented above. This is changing rapidly in firms such as Whirlpool and Hewlett-Packard. Firms are constantly discovering massive areas of spending that are not controlled professionally. One large railway provider in the United Kingdom recently discovered that it was spending £10 million a year on consultancy work. None of this work was negotiated through SM; it was all conducted on informal contracts! In another, typical case, a very large U.K. bank had problems when its telecommunications lines went down for a day, paralyzing its commercial banking and brokerage arms. Although the losses were huge, it was entitled to only a £50,000 penalty, because the outsourcing contract had not been negotiated by SM and there were only very minor remedy clauses in place. Research indicates that there is a significant trend toward SM involvement in these categories (CAPS Research 2002, 2003). It is a challenge to become involved in areas of spending where people feel that they are experts and are accustomed to spending their budgets as they wish. Taking a positive, customer-service-oriented approach can help break down potential barriers to involvement.

Globalization and Outsourcing

During the 1990s, the adoption of outsourcing as a strategy to improve a firm's competitive position was followed by many major international firms. Outsourcing is the removal of a business process from within the boundaries of the firm to an external provider (supplier). The choice of what to outsource and what to insource is a key area of debate. In the early 1990s, much of the discussion was on outsourcing "peripheral" business processes such as catering, security, and information systems. The idea was that firms should focus on core competencies and outsource the rest. When these routine business processes were outsourced, frequently all the people and equipment associated with these processes were also transferred to the outsource provider, as was the case when Rolls-Royce Aero Engines outsourced its IT requirements to Electronic Data Systems (EDS). EDS then had the responsibility of supplying the IT needs of the firm. Moving resources to an outsourced provider also offers an instant improvement to a firm's liquidity and fixed cost structure as the costs of the assets are passed to the provider.

According to Fine (1998), identifying what to outsource is the most critical decision an organization faces. He argues that knowing what and how to outsource is an organization's ultimate core competency in these rapidly changing times. Do not outsource important knowledge, or your supplier could gain leverage against you and perhaps even become a competitor! Yet many organizations do not do a good job of analyzing the outsourcing decision and consequently end up insourcing, bringing outsourced activities back into the organization. There is a great risk when you outsource knowledge rather than just capacity (Leavy 2004; Fine 1998).

Outsourcing is also referred to as the make-or-buy decision. The critical steps in this process are illustrated in Figure 15.7. The decision of whether or not to outsource involves analyzing whether the organization should make an item in-house or buy it from a supplier. It applies also to services where an organization must

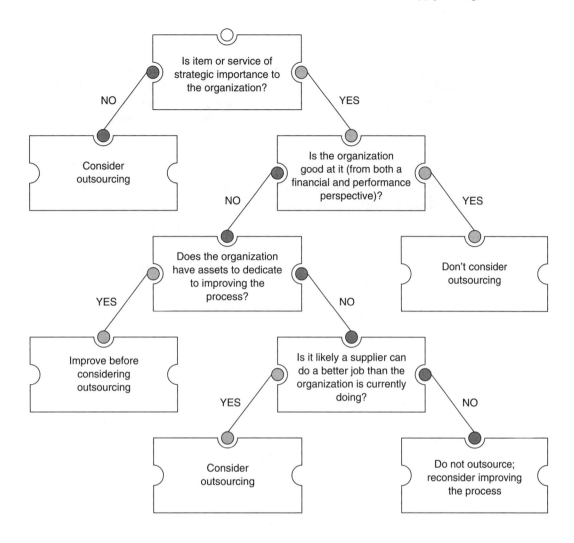

Figure 15.7   Make-or-Buy Decision-Making Process

decide whether to have necessary services such as janitorial and security services performed by its own employees or by an outside contractor.

Once the process of outsourcing is complete, the firm must then manage a buyer-supplier relationship, often conducted through the use of service level agreements (SLAs). SLAs define the level of service required from the provider, which is often difficult to define, such as an acceptable level of security. Thus, if one outsources a problem area, it will likely continue to be a problem. Only when you know how the system should work properly and what type and level of service you actually require can you properly specify an SLA.

This is critical today, because outsourcing is on the rise. SM is increasingly seen as a key player in outsourcing, called upon to bring rigor to the process using the five-step strategic SM process presented above. There is a huge amount of growth in global outsourcing, also referred to as offshoring, which further complicates management and decision making. For example, managing an Indian IT center from the United States presents challenges of significant time zone differences, differences in values and customs, and cultural differences. SM's analytical skills in total cost of ownership, cost management, and understanding business strategy are all important in these critical, often strategic, decisions.

Continuous Improvement Focus and Involvement in Payables

Although SM in many organizations has long had an emphasis on continuous improvement in its supply base, SM is now also looking internally. With the advent of business process outsourcing, no function is safe from outsourcing unless it can establish its strategic worth. For SM, this means heavy reliance on improved IT, automating routine processes, and outsourcing areas that can be better managed by another organization. SM is taking a "total quality" or "six sigma" view of its own process as part of its preemptive strategy to focus on value while delivering cost savings. Accounts payable has long been a weak process link because finance may like to stretch terms to improve cash flow, putting undue stress on supply relationships because suppliers are continually paid late. In addition, there has been conflict because contract terms set out by SM regarding payment are not always clear, particularly in the area of professional services. Thus, as part of creating excellent processes, many organizations have moved the payables area to SM, building in proper controls and segregation of duties. This allows greater visibility and more effective corrective action if payments are delayed and terms are unclear.

Environmental Issues

The rise of environmentalism has been one of the defining social movements of the last 30 years. Against the background of global environmental loss and degradation, environmental awareness in most industrialized countries has grown dramatically. The role of SM in mitigating and reducing the *environmental* exposure of the firm is becoming increasingly important. Cousins, Lamming, and Bowen (2005) discuss a range of strategies that firms can take, including "no choice," which is a basic compliance to the legislation approach. "Why bother" suggests the costs of noncompliance are not high enough, and therefore it is cheaper and easier to pollute than to look at ways to reduce emissions. "Go first" is a strategy of market leadership, that is, to be seen as a "first mover" in the marketplace, as a pioneer, as were, for example, Body Shop, IBM, Hewlett-Packard, and others.

These strategies require a strategic approach to SM, sophisticated performance measures, and the ability to achieve cost savings (through packaging reduction, reduction in emissions, etc.) so that the firm is viewed in the best possible light by its stakeholders. Environmental SM will become an increasingly important aspect of a firm's strategic market positioning. Firms need to consider these issues now to compete successfully in the future.

Concluding Thoughts

As the well-known curse and blessing states, "May you live in exciting times." These are indeed very exciting times for the SM area. The SM professional's role has been significantly elevated from one of a paper pusher to one of a strategic business partner. SM has developed professionalism as well as rigorous processes, such as strategic sourcing, to guide its actions. It is viewed as much more than simply a source of price savings; it is also a contributor to the firm's strategic success. But with power comes responsibility, so SM is held more accountable and brought in earlier and to more areas of the organization's spending, such as services, indirect spending, and outsourcing decisions. With increased globalization and competitive pressures, SM promises to continue to be an area of great promise and change.

Notes

1. We use the term commodity here to indicate a group of similar purchased items, whether these items are services, components, or any other type of item a firm may purchase. For example, nuts, bolts, and rivets are often referred to as a commodity.

2. Probably a reverse auction approach, where the buyer bids the price of the parts down sequentially, telling each supplier what the previous supplier bid. This short-term strategy is used to get low prices.

3. For a detailed discussion on this approach see Womack, Jones, and Roos (1990).

References

A.T. Kearney (2005), *Excellence in Procurement,* cited from "Procurement Seen as Strategic Player," *Inside Supply Management,* April, 6.

CAPS Research Benchmarking Study (2002), *Defining and Determining the "Services Spend" in Today's Services Economy.* Tempe, AZ: CAPS Research.

CAPS Research Purchasing Performance Benchmarking Study (2003), *Managing Your Services Spend in Today's Services Economy.* Tempe, AZ: CAPS Research.

Cousins, P. D. (2002), "A Conceptual Model for Managing Long-Term Inter-organizational Relationships," *European Journal of Purchasing & Supply Management,* 8 (3), 71–82.

Cousins, P. D. (2005), "The Alignment of Appropriate Firm and Supply Strategies for Competitive Advantage," *International Journal of Operations and Production Management,* 25 (5), 403–428.

Cousins, P. D., R. C. Lamming, and F. E. Bowen (2005), "The Role of Risk in Environmental-Related Supplier Initiatives," *International Journal of Operations and Production Management,* 24 (6), 554–565.

Dobler, Donald W., David N. Burt, and Lamar Lee, Jr. (1990), *Purchasing and Materials Management Text and Cases,* 5th ed. New York: McGraw-Hill.

Duffy, Roberta (2002), "New Frontiers: Defining Supply Management," *Inside Supply Management,* http://www.ism.ws/ResourceArticles/2002/010230.cfm, posted January 2002, accessed March 22, 2005.

Ellram, Lisa M. and Wendy Tate (2004), "Managing and Controlling the Services Supply Chain at Intuit," *PRACTIX: Best Practices in Purchasing and Supply Management,* 7 (4), 1–8.

Fine, Charles (1998), *Clockspeed.* New York: Perseus Books.

Fisher, Roger, William L. Ury, and Bruce Patton (1991), *Getting to Yes: Negotiating Agreement Without Giving In,* 2nd ed. New York: Penguin.

Harvard Business School (2004), *Winning Negotiations That Preserve Relationships: The Results-Driven Manager Series.* Cambridge, MA: Harvard Business School Press.

Kraljic, Peter (1983), "Purchasing Must Become Supply Management," *Harvard Business Review,* 61 (5), 109–117.

Leavy, Brian (2004), "Outsourcing Strategies: Opportunities and Risks," *Strategy and Leadership,* 32 (6), 20–25.

Lewicki, Roy J., Bruce Barry, David M. Saunders, and John W. Minton (2004), *Essentials of Negotiation,* 3rd ed. New York: Irwin/McGraw-Hill.

Porter, Michael (1975), *Note on the Structural Analysis of Industries.* Cambridge, MA: Harvard Business School Press.

Porter, Michael (1982), *Competitive Advantage.* Cambridge, MA: Harvard Business School Press.

Womack, James P., Daniel T. Jones, and Daniel Roos (1990), *The Machine That Changed the World.* New York: HarperPerennial.

16

Personnel

Scott Keller

istorically, logistics personnel rarely have been identified as strategic corporate resources. During the development of modern industry, transportation and warehouse labor was obtained from a pool of less educated, unskilled, and unemployed men. Logistics jobs required little more than the ability to manually lift boxes, operate unsophisticated lift equipment, drive a truck, and perform basic math and reading. Corporate value was obtained through scale economies in purchasing and manufacturing, and through the efforts of marketing and sales to push product to the customer and consumer. As such, logistics operations entailed the nuts and bolts, or nodes and links, for supporting the goals of other strategic functions of the firm.

Contemporary advances in customer demands, equipment, infrastructure, technology, and the economy have brought about competitive industry pressure to offer product and service assortments of higher quality, at lower cost, and at reduced lead times. Such strategic challenges brought together suppliers, manufacturers, and customers to perform marketing exchanges unlike in the past, ever evolving toward a unified integrated global supply chain. Global supply chain partners required coordinated information and efforts, reduced process duplicity, and elimination of errors throughout the many stages of processing an order. Clearly, advances in equipment, technology, and infrastructure have helped in achieving these initiatives. In addition, product and service industry leaders have recognized the supply chain value in pursuing advances in workforce development.

The goal of this chapter is to identify and discuss the core principles for developing and supporting employees in this new and dynamically competitive environment, with the ultimate aim to leverage human resources for their tangible and intangible supply chain value.

The Changing Nature of the Workplace

"The structure of logistics organizations today is not the structure of the past—or the structure of tomorrow. Logistics managers must create organizations that adapt quickly to rapid change and quickly add to the organizational knowledge base" (LeMay et al. 1999, p. 2). Early manufacturing and distribution functions often exchanged employee resources to temporarily shift capacity and improve the flow of production or distribution occurring at a bottleneck activity in a process. Redistribution of workers from the warehouse to the production line was a viable alternative, assuming the line jobs required little or no formal skills. Labor and physically intensive manufacturing production shortly gave way to automation-assisted tasks, job complexity, and process sophistication. Such changes required highly skilled production line employees. Low-skilled workers were no longer qualified to perform jobs outside the physical-type positions found in warehouse and distribution operations.

Further widening the gap between skilled and unskilled supply chain labor was the domestic corporate quality movement of the late 1970s and 1980s. In an effort to keep pace with foreign competition, U.S. manufacturers sought to adopt manufacturing quality initiatives. Production processes, tools, measurements, and employee knowledge were improved through investments in analysis, redesign, rationalization, and training. At the same time, logistics jobs remained relatively unchanged, requiring traditional physical ability, basic accountability, and, for some workers, the skill to operate materials handling equipment.

Following the initial U.S. quality movement and with the proliferation of 20th-century computerization, managers became captivated by the potential value of a highly accurate exchange of data and information within and between organizations. Businesses were now poised to satisfy the demands of well-informed customers and at a competitive level unseen before. Competition was waged between entire supply chains, and managers pursued every advantage available including exploiting the value potential of logistics services once seen only as support cost centers. The stage was set for a new logistics operating environment requiring employees trained and skilled in communications technology, data analysis, self-management and team management, and relationship building. For managers to guide the "new" employees in such a dynamic workplace requires advanced and highly disciplined leadership and relationship skills.

Creating a Customer-Focused Logistics Workforce

Supply chain initiatives often include the performance of logistics services, such as product movement, handling, storage, packaging, labeling, and other tangible and intangible service-related processes. Accordingly, frontline employees have an elevated impact on the quality of products and services delivered by the firm, and this influence should be fully leveraged by supervision (Hartline and Ferrell 1996). Emerging during the time of the quality movement within the United States, the concept of adapting traditional marketing tools to "market" jobs to employees was advocated. Throughout the next two decades, the concept became a reality for pioneering firms that considered employees to be crucial resources for accomplishing the service-marketing objectives of the firm.

Employees who are not directly responsible for sales, marketing, and formal customer service functions often provide the critical link where the order fulfillment process extends beyond the internal activities of the firm and affects product and service value (Berry 2002). Such frontline employees require support from their colleagues to meet customer needs; and the level of support must match that expected by employees who have direct impact on customers (Grönroos 1981; Gummesson 1987; Piercy and Morgan 1991). Thus, frontline service employees assume roles as internal customers, whereas support personnel function as internal suppliers.

Managers implementing the concept have tailored internal plans to support the workplace needs of frontline employees, who in turn provide exceptional levels of service to each other and their customers (Berry 2002; Heskett et al. 1994). Internal plans include a quality-driven agenda to support employees through fundamental exchange of information required to perform the job, knowledge development, assistance to employees, performance feedback, and workplace affirmation. Figure 16.1 illustrates the framework of core employee support competencies. Quantitative and qualitative field research documents the positive impact of a service environment where exercising competencies is commonplace (Piercy and Morgan 1991; Rafiq and Ahmed 1993; Kennedy, Lassk, and Goolsby 2002). Significant improvements in employee performance, safety, retention, attendance, communication, job satisfaction, and ultimately end-customer satisfaction result from successful internal efforts.

Fundamental Information Exchange

Successful plans for creating a quality- and customer-focused workforce include providing frontline employees with the information support needed to perform the basic tasks of the job. Managers and coworkers must be competent in providing such employees accurate and timely job information. Successful firms provide employees job information that is

- Specific and relevant to an employee's job
- Void of errors in calculation and description
- Frequently provided so that an employee knows exactly what to expect
- Concisely presented so that the information is easy to use while on the job

Most logistics service operations attempt to accomplish this through start-of-shift information meetings, where employees are informed of daily workloads and

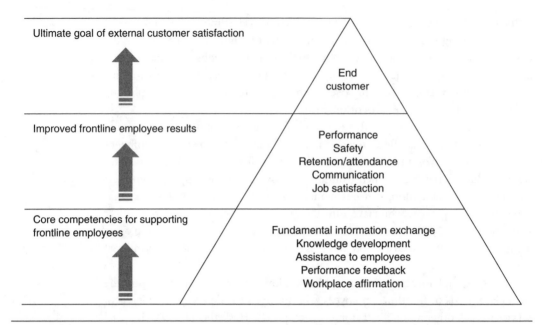

Figure 16.1 Competencies and Expectations of a Customer-Focused Workforce Plan

performance expectations and through informal face-to-face interactions through-out the workday. More progressive managers move beyond this and provide employees with informational support through the following:

- Co-location of internal customers and internal suppliers
- Computer kiosks situated throughout the facility for employee access to information
- Highly active and visual information boards
- Employee-led information and safety meetings

A walk-through of a cross-dock facility revealed that the department of customer service and traffic personnel was conspicuously absent. When asked, the general manager of the facility explained that, in the past, information disconnects occurred between the operations department, customer service, and transportation. As a result, the organization decided to colocate the three departments and reduce all information- and knowledge-sharing barriers. The same organization strategically placed computer terminals or kiosks near employee break rooms, locker rooms, and common areas for employee use. Each kiosk offered employees interactive information sharing with the Human Resource Department, whereby, for example, employees could formally request and schedule vacation leave, inquire on their sick days accumulated, and confidentially review their individual employee portfolio.

A final example comes from a manufacturing support warehouse facility. At the beginning of each shift, information meetings are conducted by the employees rather than by the managers. Then, in the presence of managers, employees present critical work plans and expectations, discuss safety issues and assign responsibility to coworkers for researching issues, and hold each other accountable.

Knowledge Development

Advanced employee knowledge and comprehension are equally important for creating frontline service employees who are focused on the customer and provide high-quality results. Employee knowledge is gained through fundamental training and experience, but there must also be more advanced plans to develop service-employee understanding of how their jobs affect the overall goals of operational processes and the broader objectives of corporate marketing. Most successful firms provide knowledge for the following:

- Performing the technical aspects of the job
- Understanding the employee's integrative role in the organization
- Through formal and informal means

On-the-job experience is the traditional means for training logistics service employees to perform job tasks. Lead personnel may be assigned to demonstrate job duties to a new recruit, and more technical training and certification of equipment operation may be required. Traditionally, logistics operations managers rarely have had luxury time to educate frontline employees beyond the basics. Most often, training was swift so that employees could quickly help in daily production. Today's quality-focused and service-oriented logistics responsibilities require more knowledgeable employees because of the need for self-managed process teams, decision making in the field, and the push for continuous improvement. To achieve knowledge competence in employees, managers must provide the following:

- Formal classroom instruction, including traditional reading and illustrative materials, realistic workplace scenarios and role playing, and testing through computer-simulated process activities
- Professionally trained trainers
- Employee team involvement
- Cross-training for employees in multiple process activities

One distributor of consumer-packaged goods floor-loads trailers to achieve higher capacity utilization of transport equipment. Improved utilization leads to significant reductions in operating costs and order cycle time. Technical training, for example, in efficient and safe trailer loading requires physical practice. However, prior to hands-on experience, employees hired to perform such tasks undergo five days of classroom instruction. Professionally skilled trainers provide instruction through verbal and written procedure reviews, process illustrations using visual blueprints to demonstrate who provides the employee inputs and how the employee's output affects the quantitative and qualitative goals of the process team, and computer simulations to test the load-building decisions of employees in a controlled environment. Trainees are required to demonstrate competence in load-building procedures by achieving a specified level of capacity utilization within a given time constraint prior to receiving on-the-job training.

Assistance to Employees

Highly customer-focused logistics organizations, through the adoption of a customer-focused internal plan, groom supervision attuned to continuous improvement of the workplace for the benefit of employees and their productivity. Efforts require proactive behaviors of management to eliminate barriers to employee satisfaction and success while on the job. Responsiveness is also required to demonstrate the willingness and put forth the effort to address and help resolve frontline employee issues once they occur. Assistance, whether proactive or responsive, must be timely and focused on the specific needs of the individual or employee group. Progressive assistance to employees is characterized as

- Proactive effort to reduce workplace barriers
- Responsive effort once problems arise
- Immediate and direct assistance to the employee in need

Assistance to employees may be as straightforward as assigning personnel for temporary production assistance in constrained activities of a critical process, thereby allowing for a better balance of the workload. To achieve a customer-centric workforce where managers and coworkers provide critical assistance to other employees of the firm, organizations must

- Direct employees in setting daily priorities that lead to goal attainment and employee advancement
- Trust employees with critical information, and train and encourage employees to use their own discretion to make disciplined decisions in the field
- Provide working supervision in the form of team leaders who are present on the work floor and are trained in responding to and resolving employee concerns
- Provide supervisors the time and resources necessary to lead and coach rather than to command and control employees

Today's supply chains require highly responsive people and processes. One high-speed flow-through facility manager has taken responsiveness to a new level as she visibly posts written explanations and solutions for all employees to review. Employees wishing to submit a written question, concern, or suggestion must do so with professionalism, and the manager provides a written response within two weeks. Employee feedback indicates that the "Ask Alice" assistance program works well because the facility manager, Alice, provides timely and straightforward responses that are posted for all employees to benefit from the assistance.

Performance Feedback

As can be seen, the core employee support competencies are not mutually exclusive of one another. However, each support competency has unique factors important for the development of service employees focused on providing high-level outputs to internal and external customers. As such, feedback specific to the performance of an individual employee is highly important for motivating employees. Performance feedback must focus on the individual contribution of the employee and offer the employee an understanding of how his or her efforts affect the logistics process and overall customer satisfaction. It is often the case that employees are rewarded on the basis of achieving individual performance goals; however, often employees are temporarily reassigned to assist coworkers, and such efforts are excluded from an employee's production tally. As such, customer-focused performance indicators are flexible in design to capture the entire employee effort and include planned and unplanned performance.

It is not enough, however, to capture performance. Successful logistics service organizations also provide employees ongoing and visual performance feedback, thereby unleashing the potential of immediate feedback at the most critical point where employees perform the work. The results include positive motivation and, if required, employee redirection of effort if they are falling behind expectations. Moreover, to enhance the motivating power of performance feedback, successful organizations offer employees comparisons of individual performance with respect to coworker performance. This offers a benchmark for frontline employees to compare their accomplishments meaningfully. In summary, customer-focused supply chain logistics performance must be

- Specific to individual employee efforts
- Inclusive of all planned and unplanned employee efforts
- Continuously updated and reported to employees
- Visually positioned at employee workstations
- Meaningfully comparative to coworker performance data

Supply chain logistics jobs vary and so too will tactics to achieve exchange of information and encourage performance of employees on the job. For example, employees responsible for the physical unloading of product from trailers, railcars, or aircraft may find motivation by knowing how many units have passed through their control during a shift. Employees performing such activities in one high-volume distribution center requested that information specific to their individual performance be provided throughout the workday. The employees' request was granted, and a healthy competition among the unloaders was facilitated when simple digital counters were openly displayed near the unloading dock. Exchange of the information was individual specific, accurate through radio-frequency barcode scanning, immediately upon scanning, and concisely displayed as a raw number. Similar digital displays convey information to employees throughout the workday in more sophisticated process environments, such as in automobile assembly.

Workplace Affirmation

The last core competency for creating an internal work environment that is focused on achieving internal and external customer satisfaction pertains to workplace affirmation—positive messages that instill productive employee attitudes, openness, and interest in the workplace. It is affirming communication and includes positive reinforcement with and between coworkers to influence customer-oriented behaviors throughout the organization and with external customers. Affirmative internal communication may be utilized to project a fair and nonthreatening work environment. Successful firms provide positive workplaces through

- Emphasizing fairness in work assignments
- Encouraging open communication pertaining to potential workplace issues
- Supporting team spirit
- Publicizing positive outcomes and praise for good work

Successful managers are well trained in displaying positive attitudes, even when facing adversity. Self-control and a focus on the employee are two critical behaviors that managers must pursue to provide an ongoing positive atmosphere for accomplishing daily work. Specifically, managers are encouraged to

- Explain how work assignments are determined
- Train employees in identifying potential concerns and communicating to management before concerns become fully developed problems
- Create a team atmosphere whereby employees offer frequent praise to each other for the successful accomplishment of even the most routine job duties

All too often, managers focus on problem issues without giving much attention to the multitude of workplace activities that are performed as planned. This is not unusual, and is expected. However, the complexity of performing logistics services routinely leads to difficulties. In essence, difficulties are a part of logistics operations and should neither become nor be perceived as the "norm" and replace all the daily accomplishments of the organization. Managers who desire to create a more positive attitude among employees are encouraged to

- Illustrate the current state of the firm compared with industry benchmarks
- Formally calculate and communicate the number of positive outcomes of employee issues resolved compared with the issues raised
- Educate supervisors and employees to openly praise others for good work
- Formally identify and praise employees who are advancing according to plans

Implementing a Customer-Focused Employee Plan

The first step in creating a supply chain logistics workforce that is highly customer focused and productive is to establish executive-level support for pursuing such a plan. Organizational cultures must be open to the core support competencies described in the previous sections. Many individual managers and some entire organizations presently pursue an "employee-sensitive" environment; however, much of the pursuit is left to the discretion and knowledge of the manager. As such, managerial efforts may not be as efficient and effective as efforts could be with a formal internal plan to create and maintain such an environment. Table 16.1 contains 12 steps for organizations to follow in creating a customer-focused workforce. The steps are meant to be logically intuitive; however, the level of success is influenced by the discipline achieved in pursuing the plan according to the prescribed stages.

Attention should also be given to potential barriers to creating and implementing a customer-focused workplace plan. Managers should evaluate the extent to which the organization, as a whole, believes that the environment of the workplace is in need of realignment. In one logistics group of a large department store chain, the executive manager of logistics explained, "I know when our employees are happy and successful by looking at the bottom line. If the bottom line is good, then the employees are happy." This is not an unexpected response from a manager who believes that change is only good when something is broken. In addition, more mechanistic and hierarchical cultures may not adapt to such an internal and external customer-focused environment. One third-party logistics provider

Table 16.1   Steps for Creating a Customer-Focused Workforce Plan

1. Establish executive-level support

2. Inform all employees at all levels of the internal customer-focused plan

3. Identify internal customers/employees closest to external customers

4. Identify internal suppliers/coworkers closest to internal customers

5. Survey internal customers to understand their perceptions

6. Identify the key support competencies where internal customers feel their needs are met

7. Document productive internal-supplier behavior and repeat and reward behavior

8. Provide positive feedback to internal customers

9. Identify the key support competencies where internal customers feel their needs are not met

10. Educate internal suppliers and improve processes pertaining to areas in need

11. Provide feedback about improvements to internal customers

12. Repeat the process beginning with surveying internal customers

traditionally hires former military officers to fill the firm's frontline supervisory positions. Former military personnel are highly disciplined and structured; however, the firm provides each supervisor with ongoing training and education on how to effectively develop and coach, rather than command, his or her subordinates. Training is accomplished through the firm's internal formal "university" education institution. Other barriers include

- Failure to achieve buy-in from all employees and managers
- Failure to accept, plan, train, implement, monitor, measure, and reward
- Failure to establish real costs of not employing an internal plan
- Low executive priority
- Failure to financially invest in programs

References

Berry, Leonard L. (2002), "Relationship Marketing of Services—Perspectives From 1983 and 2000," *Journal of Relationship Marketing,* 1 (1), 59–70.

Grönroos, Christian (1981), "Internal Marketing—An Integral Part of Marketing Theory," in *Marketing of Services,* James H. Donnelly and William R. George, eds. Chicago: American Marketing Association.

Gummesson, Evert (1987), "Using Internal Marketing to Create a New Culture: The Case of Ericsson Quality," *Journal of Business and Industrial Marketing,* 2 (3), 23–28.

Hartline, Michael D. and O. C. Ferrell (1996), "The Management of Customer-Contact Service Employees: An Empirical Investigation," *Journal of Marketing,* 60 (October), 52–70.

Heskett, James L., Thomas O. Jones, Gary W. Loveman, W. Earl Sasser, and Leonard A. Schlesinger (1994), "Putting the Service Profit Chain to Work," *Harvard Business Review,* 72 (2), 164–174.

Kennedy, Karen N., Felicia G. Lassk, and Jerry R. Goolsby (2002), "Customer Mind-set of Employees Throughout the Organization," *Journal of the Academy of Marketing Science,* 30 (2), 159–171.

LeMay, Stephen A., Jon C. Carr, Jeffery A. Periatt, Roger D. McMahon, and Kara A. Keller (1999), *The Growth and Development of Logistics Personnel.* Oak Brook, IL: Council of Logistics Management.

Piercy, Nigel and Neil Morgan (1991), "Internal Marketing—The Missing Half of the Marketing Programme," *Long Range Planning,* 24 (April), 82–93.

Rafiq, Mohammed and Pervaiz K. Ahmed (1993), "The Scope of Internal Marketing: Defining the Boundary Between Marketing and Human Resource Management," *Journal of Marketing Management,* 9 (January), 219–232.

PART III

Resource Management

17

The Lean Supply Chain

The Path to Excellence

Mandyam M. Srinivasan

James M. Reeve

S upply chains are not a recent phenomenon. They have been in existence for many centuries, starting with the trading supply chains dating back to the Phoenicians of 4500 BCE. Until late into the 20th century, most supply chains were able to operate under a traditional push model, as demand outstripped capacity and execution was measured in weeks.

The 21st-century supply chain operates in a vastly different environment. Capacity now outstrips demand for almost any product or service demanded by an end user, and the execution time is measured in days, hours, and, sometimes, minutes. Today's supply chain follows a demand-driven, customer-centric model that must respond quickly to rapidly changing customer demands. This model, in essence, is what we refer to as the lean supply chain.

Because the goal of the lean supply chain is to deliver products to the end user quickly and flexibly, its primary characteristic is, therefore, a quick response to customer demands. To establish contrast, we begin by reviewing traditionally managed supply chain operations to highlight where and how the process can be streamlined for lean operations.

Conventional Supply Chain Management

For the greater part of the 20th century, practically every supply chain operated in a batch production mode of operation. Scale economies drove the conceptual foundations of the supply chain. This worked well in a production-centric world where demand often outstripped supply and customers were willing to compromise their needs. This mode of operation resulted in unwieldy behemoths—organizations that produced their products in large lots. These large batches of products were transported in full truckloads to regional warehouses and distribution centers, from which they were delivered to retail stores or to other manufacturing facilities. A customer unwilling to buy the product had to place a special order and wait a long time for the product to be manufactured and delivered. The lead time, namely the elapsed time between order placement and product delivery, was usually measured in months. The suppliers to these manufacturing organizations, in turn, produced and delivered supplies in large lots. The manufacturers and the suppliers were able to coexist, blissfully unaware of any perceived threats to their operation, lumbering along in true behemothlike fashion. However, as we shall see later, the mating of two elephants does not produce a gazelle—at least, in a natural way.

To understand the hidden threats posed by such thinking, consider a bottling plant that uses weekly planning and execution cycles to respond to customer demand. The plant produces 40 different stock-keeping units (SKUs) consisting of a variety of flavors and container sizes. The process consists of two basic stages: mixing and packaging. The mixing room consists of a number of stainless steel vessels that mix concentrate with water and fructose to form the final beverage product. The product is released through a carbo-cooler, which adds carbonation to the beverage, prior to entering the head of the fill line. The fill line consists of a 60-head filling machine that receives the beverage and fills the containers. There are multiple fill lines.

The flow control system must be cleaned out prior to every flavor change, and the pack line needs to be staged with the appropriate containers prior to run. The aluminum cans must be staged in a cold state, or else the beverage will "boil over" upon filling. Thus, the bottling operation has flavor and container changeover issues. Both of these cause the plant manager to run the flavors and sizes in long run lengths. Indeed, the planned schedule is to run most SKUs once per week. However, it rarely turns out this way.

To see why, consider the demand management process. The business planning group does classic demand planning. Essentially, status information about existing inventories, order information from the field sales force, and estimated demand are combined to develop an executable forecast. Thus, the forecast is established as the master production schedule for the coming week and is eventually loaded into the actual bottling schedule. So, even though the demand plan is only an estimate of future demand, it completely drives execution. This is necessary under our scenario because the planning and execution cycles are not fast enough to respond to actual demand signals.

As the master production plan is loaded in the plant schedule, the materials requirement planning system issues the appropriate purchase orders upstream to the container supply base (cans and two-liter bottles). Thus, the upstream elements of the supply chain execute to an estimate that may or may not be realized. In addition, floor orders are released, identifying the appropriate products to be produced in the mix and bottling departments, again based on a weekly cycle.

The actual product shipped to the retail stores is a function of actual field orders and replenishment orders provided by the route salespeople. Notice the impact on the bottling plant. We now have a classic squeeze in the middle. That is, the production plan is based on best forecast, whereas the actual shipments from the bottling facility are based on actual demand. Any imbalance between the upstream production schedule and the actual shipments gives rise to speculation inventory. We have seen scenarios where the in-plant inventory continues to grow because the master production schedule is designed with an upward bias to prevent stock outs. If the planning group is incentivized by sales, without concern for inventory, this will be the likely result.

This inventory is evidence of misallocated capacity and materials relative to what was actually required at the time. These types of misallocations are classic symptoms of supply chains that respond more slowly than the rate of demand. Indeed, think of these misallocations as opportunity costs. For example, if a cola product was overproduced relative to the week's demand, then this means mixing room capacity and bottling line capacity were misallocated relative to what was actually required. This is significant, because the misallocation of the bottling line capacity could mean that what was actually required was never produced because the capacity was committed elsewhere. In addition, materials were overallocated to the cola product. This means that the cola cans from the supplier were oversupplied, causing the supplier to misallocate their can forming and labeling capacity. The misallocated capacity rolls all the way upstream, so that the whole supply chain is now out of sync with demand. Thus, we end up with the classic problems of having too much of the wrong thing and not enough of the right thing.

In addition, misallocated capacity in an unresponsive (time lagged) supply chain causes severe second-order effects. These effects cause the supply chain to move into exception modes to rebalance the supply chain with actual demand as it is being realized. Thus, the original weekly schedule becomes more dated as the week wears on. Consider the plight of the cola SKU, which is bottled on Monday every week. Since the cola is bottled on Monday, there is speculation built into the plan because we do not know what will actually be sold during the remainder of the week. If the week is hot and sunny, the demand for cola may exceed forecast, requiring the bottling plant to restart cola at midweek. Now the dominos begin to fall. The mixing and bottling areas now have an additional unplanned changeover, which consumes capacity. The flavor scheduled for midweek is now pushed back to make room for some additional cola. Because flavor #2 was delayed, its inventory now becomes dangerously low, and the chase is on.

Taiichi Ohno, the well-known originator of the Toyota production system, recognized the problems with the traditional mode of operation. He is reputed to have said, "the more inventory you have on hand the less likely you are to have the one item your customer actually wants." The changes he engendered in the automobile industry paved the way for lean thinking as we know it today.

It Is More Than "Just-in-Time"

When the Japanese automakers began to ship automobiles to the United States in the 1960s and 1970s, the U.S. industry found that the batch mode of operation was not able to cope satisfactorily with changing customer preferences. Because the Japanese automakers produced their products in small lot sizes, they were able to respond quickly to market signals compared with their North American counterparts.

How did the U.S. automakers react to the threat? The automakers studied the practices of their Japanese competitors and concluded that the secret to their gazellelike speed were just-in-time practices that allowed the supply chain to simultaneously operate with low inventories and fast response to customer demands.

The U.S. automakers instituted their conception of these practices. They instructed their first-tier suppliers to deliver material "just in time." However, they did not see the necessity of providing the suppliers with any visibility on their own production schedules primarily because they were, themselves, unable to estimate their customers' demands. Second, they were often unwilling to partner with their suppliers but were instead pitting one supplier against another, forcing suppliers to provide material at lower prices. In the absence of long-term partnerships and contracts, the automakers were, themselves, unable to estimate who would be their preferred supplier of a given part. Under pressure to supply parts just in time, suppliers simply stockpiled inventory and tried to pass on the higher inventory costs to the automakers. However, under continued pressure to provide year-over-year price reductions, these suppliers often buckled under pressure and either closed shop or stopped doing business with the automakers. The just-in-time concept was quickly losing favor, with both automakers and their suppliers.

Womack, Jones, and Roos (1990) introduced the underlying principles behind the practices of Japanese automakers, notably, Toyota. Their book resulted in a renewed interest in adopting the practices of the Japanese automakers. Thus, lean thinking was born. Lean thinking, in turn, paved the way for the next major development: the lean supply chain.

Lean Supply Chain Basics:
Flow and Pull Replenishment

The lean supply chain extends the concept of lean thinking to the entire supply chain. The essence of the lean supply chain is to create flow across the supply chain. Figure 17.1 conveys this idea. This figure shows a simple relationship between the manufacturer (*factory*), its customer, and its supplier. Briefly, the lean supply chain is designed to do the following (Greenwood 2005):

1. Start with the customer.

2. Deliver what is demanded.

3. Build what is sold.

4. Supply what is consumed.

5. Balance the flow.

These flow objectives are accomplished with high-frequency pull signals at each level of the supply chain. Thus, the vision of the lean supply chain is to have every upstream process react to a pull signal from its downstream customer and produce a product only when the customer demands it. Such a vision allows the members of the supply chain to delay commitment of their valuable resources and their raw material until there is a definite demand for their product or service. This delayed commitment is consistent with the familiar postponement design attribute that is key to most successful supply chain designs.

However, this pure conceptual vision must be adjusted for real-world imperatives. For example, in a retail environment, the consumer typically requires spontaneous fulfillment from stocked items. This requirement does not negate a lean approach to managing the supply chain. This is because the lean supply chain is not about zero inventories; it is about the strategic use of inventories. The question is how to ensure that the supply chain operates with minimal inventories at the right location.

To answer this question, let us replicate the Figure 17.1 model throughout the supply chain. That is, except for organizations that are producers of the basic raw material used in a process, practically every organization has a set of customers and a set of suppliers. We refer to this as a supply chain triad. Within this triad, for ease of exposition, we continue to maintain the terms customer, factory, and supplier.

Our objective of smooth flow with minimal inventories requires the supply chain triad to respond to a drumbeat. This drumbeat is based on customer demand, although, as we shall see later, it need not exactly match this demand. The customer demand itself could be either the actual customer demand where possible or a demand forecast. In either case, the customer demands might vary considerably from day to day. This demand produces what we refer to as the external *takt* time.[1] The factory tries to moderate this short-term variation by matching the external *takt* time to an internal *takt* time as shown in Figure 17.2. The internal *takt* time is an estimate of the average external *takt* time over a given span of time that will be used to set the operating rate. This has the immediate effect of smoothing out the demand and allows the factory to operate at a relatively steady rate instead of reacting to every little change in customer demand. As shown in the

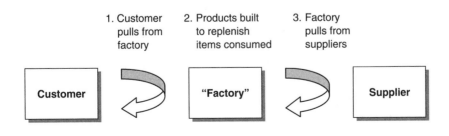

1. Customer pulls from factory 2. Products built to replenish items consumed 3. Factory pulls from suppliers

Customer   "Factory"   Supplier

Figure 17.1   Use Pull Signals to Create Flow Across the Supply Chain

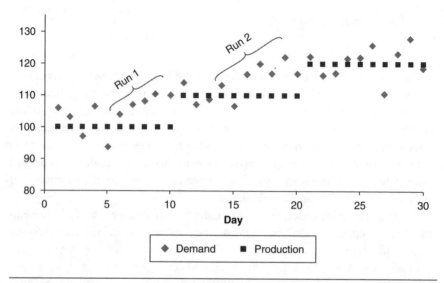

Figure 17.2   Recalibrating *Takt* Time

figure, the factory works according to the internal *takt* time while monitoring external *takt* time for adjustments. If there is a consistent trend displayed, then the internal *takt* time is recalibrated (Srinivasan 2004).

The internal *takt* time is used to establish the internal pace of work. Specifically, within the factory, one process, typically the constraint process, dictates this drumbeat to pace the flow of work. In the short term, the drumbeat process maintains a constant production rate and constant product mix. This creates a flat production and consumption pattern for the internal upstream processes and the external suppliers. A finished-goods inventory buffer or an order queue uncouples the drumbeat process from the short-term variation in customer demand. As noted earlier, the lean supply chain is not about zero inventories; it is about the strategic use of inventories. To decide on how much inventory to hold, we categorize the supply chain along two dimensions—one based on work flow and one based on the order fulfillment strategy.

Work Flow Characterization: V, A, and T Configurations

The flow of work through a production process has a direct impact on how the supply chain is designed, built, and managed. Practically every process can be categorized as belonging to one of three types of work flow, V, A, or T, or some combination of these three types.[2]

The V-Type Flow

A V-type flow occurs when a few basic raw materials are processed into a variety of end items. As shown in Figure 17.3, the product flow diagram resembles the

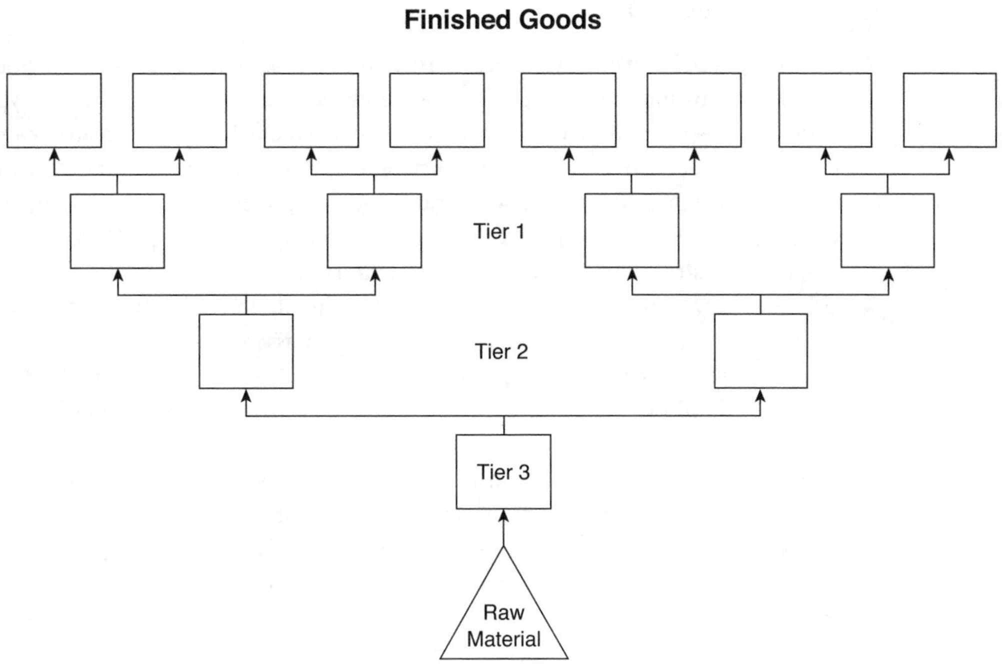

Finished Goods

Figure 17.3   The V-Type Flow

letter V, hence the name. V-type supply chains are characteristic of food processing, metals, chemicals, paper, and other continuous or batch processing supply chains.

In a V-type supply chain, the upstream elements are fairly uniform and simplified. As the product moves downstream, it is split into different specifications, product codes, or SKUs. In addition, V-type supply chains also split the product into geographic locations downstream. For example, in papermaking, a common chip stream can be split into either bleached or unbleached pulp. These two streams can diverge into a wide range of grades and colors on a paper machine. After the paper machine, the paper can be converted into an even wider variety of cut sizes and package counts. Thus, the downstream end of the supply chain presents the greatest opportunity for misallocation in a V-type supply chain. In fact, it is safe to say that each individual divergence point represents an opportunity for material misallocation.

The misallocations are exacerbated by the desire to enhance efficiency, resulting in material being released earlier than needed. These actions result in excess inventory of some products and a shortage of others as highlighted earlier. As Umble and Srikanth (1997) observed, managers of plants that have a V-type flow are often puzzled when, despite holding large finished-goods inventory, they have to scramble to meet market requirements. They level the blame on the customer, pointing to the constantly changing demand pattern. They do not recognize that while demand changes do occur, most of the problems are self-inflicted.

The A-Type Flow

A-type supply chains are characteristic of aerospace products, capital equipment, and consumer electronics. The A-type structure is the opposite of the V-type structure, as shown in Figure 17.4. A-type supply chains have their greatest complexity on the upstream end. The upstream is characterized by hundreds and maybe even thousands of individual parts and components that move through a variety of supply chain elements to a point of final assembly. After the product is assembled, distribution is often fairly straightforward. For example, a commercial airliner is very complex on the upstream end of the supply chain. Individual parts, such as flat pattern wing parts, are fabricated and assembled onto wings, which are then assembled to the fuselage. Complexity converges to final assembly. After assembly, the downstream distribution end of the A-type supply chain is very simple.

Thus, the A-type supply chain manager's focus is on upstream misallocation. Such misallocation occurs when upstream parts are produced for forecast product that is eventually not sold. The finished-goods inventory, in this case, represents the misallocated capacity and materials for every subcomponent and component in that finished item. These misallocations, of course, have domino impacts on other components that were not made (but should have been). A-type supply chains attempt to protect against assembly misallocation by committing to excess inventory of component parts. This, however, is an unattractive solution because it can lead to obsolescing parts, and hence forever losing the materials and capacity represented by those parts.

The A-type supply chain has the same problems experienced by V-type supply chains when products are processed in large batches. This causes a wavelike flow of material, further aggravated by the bullwhip effect. The use of large batches at one level in the supply chain causes downstream customers to receive material in an erratic fashion, while causing serious stress on upstream suppliers. Some of the solutions we discuss for the V-type supply chain apply equally well to the A-type.

The T-Type Flow

As the name implies, the T-type flow takes place when the flow across the supply chain resembles the letter T. It reflects a situation where a limited number of components are assembled into a wide variety of end items. T-type supply chains are commonly found in assemble-to-order environments, where customer lead times are relatively short. The T-type supply chain has elements of both the A and V types. The T-type and the V-type flows share the common characteristic of divergence, although the divergence is concentrated in the final stages for the T-type supply chain. With a T-type flow, it is thus relatively much easier to avoid misallocation by delaying commitment of resources and materials until receipt of a firm order. The T-type and A-type flows are similar in the sense that they are both dominated by many interactions that occur at the assembly stage.

Finished Goods

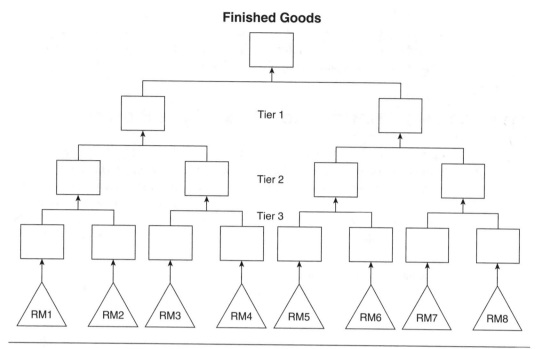

Figure 17.4   The A-Type Flow

Fulfillment Characterization: Build-to-Stock, Assemble-to-Order, Build-to-Order, and Engineer-to-Order

Whereas the nature of the product dictates the V-A-T workflow configuration, the requirements of the customer influence the demand fulfillment strategy. Supply chains can be characterized as build-to-stock (BTS), assemble-to-order (ATO), build-to-order (BTO), and engineer-to-order (ETO) (Reeve and Srinivasan 2005). The BTS supply chain provides the fastest response to the customer, but this response time is accomplished with prebuild end-item speculation. In contrast, BTO and ETO provide a long response time to the initial customer order but are accomplished with little prebuild speculation. The customer must wait for most of the parts and components to work through the supply chain as custom parts. The ATO configuration provides a middle ground where the response time to the customer is confined to the assembly time. This is accomplished with prebuild speculation of components and modules rather than end items.

In the ideal world, there is a marriage. As observed above, a supply chain that has the T-type flow is readily amenable to an ATO mode of operation. Similarly, it is tempting to conjecture that a supply chain with a V-type flow is amenable to a BTO operation, whereas a supply chain with an A-type flow is more amenable to a BTS mode of operation because of the relatively fewer products processed. Indeed, as noted by Schragenheim and Dettmer (2001), some authors have tried to link A-type flows with BTS and V-type flows with BTO. However, apart from the close relationship between the T-type flow and the ATO mode of operation, in practice there is little correlation between the type of flow and the demand fulfillment strategy. For example, an A-type supply chain may build to stock (automobiles) or build to order (construction equipment). Likewise, a V-type supply chain is used with a BTO strategy (specialty chemicals) as well as with a BTS strategy (paper).

Applying Lean Principles to a BTS V-Type Process

Let us return to the example of the beverage bottling facility. The customer demands bottled beverages instantaneously, and so the supply chain must be configured as BTS. In addition, the product and process streams are such that the process has a V configuration. That is, the scope of the product is the least on the upstream (flavors and containers) and becomes greater by moving downstream to SKUs (SKU flavor and package combinations) and locations. Under this design, the supply chain is most vulnerable to misallocating capacity and materials to downstream SKUs and locations because the product must be speculatively placed. Given this constraint, the supply chain responds best when the execution time interval is the least.

The objective of the beverage company supply chain is to build and deliver a product mix within a time interval that matches the demand mix. Thus, if all SKUs are sold every day from every location, then the optimal supply chain design attempts to produce and deliver every SKU to every location every day. This means the can supplier must produce every can specification every day, the plant must bottle every product every day, and distribution must deliver every product every day to every customer. These are the basics of achieving flow. Without this rapid execution cycle, the planning process must necessarily resort to more speculative placements. The design follows the basic principle of minimizing the impact of variation to very short time intervals. Alternatively stated, the longer the time intervals, the greater the forecast errors.

Once the upstream executes within the time interval of demand, the supply chain executes production and delivery from replenishment signals. That is, the actual sales of SKUs from the shelves provide the signals for upstream replenishment. These signals are generated by the route truck drivers, account representatives, or point-of-sale information. Thus, the complete supply chain is responding to demand rather than anticipating demand with production.

This design has significant implications for the bottling plant. The plant is no longer concerned with plant efficiency. Indeed, the bottling plant may be inefficient in the classic sense because its only responsibility is to replenish what was sold during the previous day, regardless of the available capacity. Rather, the plant's improvement focus is to maintain capacity for immediate activation from replenishment demand signals. In addition, the facility must achieve fast flavor and container changeovers. These changeovers must be drastically reduced for the plant to economically produce every SKU (or the Pareto 80%) every day.

Once the cycles are aligned in this manner, the supply chain can be designed to accommodate short-term daily variation in demand with capacity, as opposed to inventory. If actual demand is replenished with capacity, the opportunity for capacity misallocation becomes much less. The rapid execution supply chain uses planning to establish changes in the required capacities to satisfy demand. Thus, the planning function becomes focused on capacity management rather than inventory management. Thus, the demand for each SKU for each location, each day of the week, must be established.[3] To illustrate, assume the average daily demand for a two-liter cola SKU is 5,000 units, varying plus or minus 1,000 units per day from this average. This information is used to establish capacity "stream beds within the supply chain.[4]

To illustrate, demand information can be used to plan production capacity, which is expressed by the rate-based production schedule. Thus, because every product is made every day, the two-liter cola product could be established within the schedule according to the estimated daily demand. The actual amount to be produced is determined daily from replenishment signals. Thus, the production schedule is merely reserving capacity to be filled by actual consumption in the retail outlets. The amount of space required within the production schedule is the stream bed capacity made available for the production "river." The rate-based production schedule capacity is determined from the planning information as shown in Figure 17.5.

In the figure, the line rate is 2,500 cola liter units per hour (including change-overs). Thus, the production schedule reserves capacity for 2 hours of production at the beginning of each day for two-liter cola. The previous day's actual replenishment is the actual schedule for the day. Since the daily demand has historically varied from 4,000 to 6,000 units, the schedule varies from a low of 1 hour 36 minutes to a high of 2 hours 24 minutes. Thus, the schedule flexes from 9:36 a.m. to 10:24 a.m. The rate-based schedule for the remaining products is determined in a similar way. The production schedule repeats every day, maintaining the same order and approximate times.[5] This type of schedule facilitates learning, avoids confusion, and

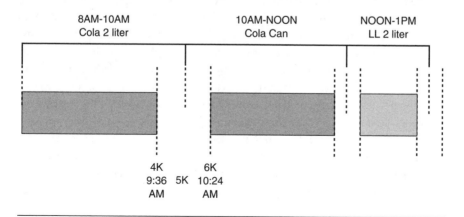

Figure 17.5   Partial Rate-Based Production Schedule

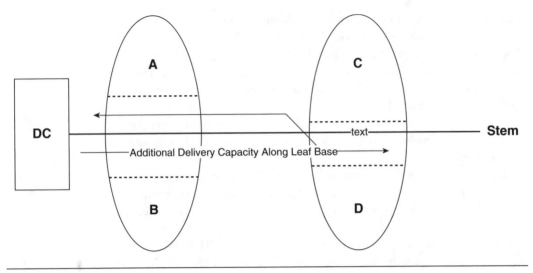

Figure 17.6 Stem and Leaf Route Plan

promotes process improvement because the production rhythms are repetitive and predictable.

In addition to the production resources, all elements of the supply chain are established according to the rate and expected variation of daily demand. Thus, the distribution center should reserve space for cola based on the rate and variation for the day (or more likely, the week). The distribution center holds safety stock inventory equal to three times the standard deviation of the daily demand, plus an amount to support the replenishment cycle, say one day. The flow through the distribution center is based on the daily replenishment signals. Each delivery truck's assortment plan is designed to reserve space for the daily rate and variation of demand for each SKU.

The delivery truck routes are established according to rate and variation using "stem and leaf" principles, as illustrated in Figure 17.6. The "leaves" in Figure 17.6 are the route zones A, B, C, and D. These zones are established to accommodate the lowest demand day for the route. That is, a route truck on a low demand day would be able to deliver the area of the city represented by the complete leaf. In the illustration, the zone C leaf was delivered almost completely to the dotted line. However, if demand increases, the route truck would be able to deliver only part of the leaf zone, such as with A, B, and D, leaving the base near the stem undelivered. Additional truck capacity could be released to deliver the bottom of the leaves along the stem, often a major road. The stem and leaf structure allows delivery capacity to flex up and down depending on the underlying demand in the leaf zone.

The supplier also reserves can-labeling capacity based on the SKU daily demand and variation. These relationships are communicated using a planning bill of materials. For example, the planning bill of materials for the two-liter cola may be as shown in Figure 17.7.

In this figure, the two-liter cola product has an estimated average daily demand of 5,000 units per day, plus or minus 1,000 units. The components of this product

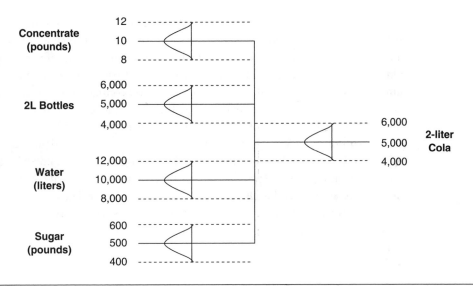

Figure 17.7   Planning Bill of Materials

include concentrate mix, two-liter bottles, water, and sugar. The relationship between the planned demand and the components is established by their underlying relationships in the bill of material. Thus, the number of two-liter bottles required from the blow molding supplier is also 5,000 units, plus or minus 1,000 units. The other units in the final product are estimated in a similar way. Thus, the two-liter bottle supplier must prepare to ship 4,000 to 6,000 labeled cola bottles every day.

Now the stream bed capacity is prepared and needs to be filled with actual execution requirements. The amount of beverage that is actually produced is determined from the actual consumption of product from the previous day. Thus, the retail outlets (POS data or drivers) broadcast these replenishment requirements simultaneously to the distribution center, the plant, and the bottle supplier. These are the actual demand signals that form the drumbeat of execution. The supplier ships bottles that were sold, the bottling plant schedules inside the established capacity boundaries the product that was sold, the distribution center prepares to stock and ship the amount that was sold the previous day, and the transportation department establishes the number of trucks required within the stem and leaf system. Thus, all elements of the supply chain move the same amount of product through the stream bed to the customer, based on the amount consumed the previous day. This is repeated every day so that the daily drumbeat is maintained. The result is a fast response supply chain that is flowing through the established capacity boundaries.

Conclusions

The lean supply chain is more than just-in-time, or doing more, faster. Rather, there are a number of basic principles applied in any supply chain configuration: begin with customer requirements, deliver what is demanded, build what is sold, supply what is consumed, and balance the flow. However, these basic principles must fit within the basic product-process supply chain structure, or V-A-T configurations. In addition, the basic principles must be applied within the strategic configuration required by the customer, or the BTS, ATO, BTO, or ETO configuration. Thus, there are two configuration dimensions that give rise to a variety of design combinations, none of which can be thought of as necessarily dominant. We have illustrated lean principles with the BTS, V-type supply chain. In this illustration, we identified the importance of matching the time interval for demanding the product mix with all upstream execution time intervals. Once this is accomplished, capacity rates and boundaries are established for all elements of the supply chain. The actual execution of flow fits within these planned capacities and flexes with short-term variation. With these principles in place, the supply chain is able to exhibit stable, repetitive, and predictive performance.

Notes

1. *Takt* is a German word that literally means cadence. It sets the demand rhythm for the upstream processes. *Takt* time represents the amount of time within which a product must be manufactured to satisfy customer demand.

2. Schragenheim and Dettmer (2001) identify a fourth type of flow—the I-type flow. We view this variant as a combination of the other three types of flows.

3. As noted previously, this demand is often expressed as external *takt* time. We will work with units of demand in this case to increase clarity.

4. When these boundaries are violated because of spikes in demand, such as a holiday or new store opening, there may be a requirement to prebuild inventory to satisfy the surge requirement.

5. The schedule would likely have unique daily estimated demands. For example, the Monday replenishment schedule would be planned at a higher rate than the Friday schedule because of weekend effects.

References

Greenwood, T. G. (2005), *The Lean Enterprise Systems Design Institute Workbook*. Knoxville: University of Tennessee.

Reeve, J. and M. M. Srinivasan (2005), "Which Supply Chain Design Is Right for You?" *Supply Chain Management Review,* May/June, 50–57.

Schragenheim, E. and H. W. Dettmer (2001), *Manufacturing at Warp Speed,* APICS Series on Constraints Management. Boca Raton, FL: St. Lucie Press.

Srinivasan, M. M. (2004), *Streamlined: 14 Principles for Building and Managing the Lean Supply Chain*. Mason, OH: Thomson.

Umble, M. and M. L. Srikanth (1997), *Synchronous Management,* vol. 2. Guilford, CT: Spectrum.

Womack, J. P., D. T. Jones, and D. Roos (1990), *The Machine That Changed the World*. New York: Rawson.

18

Financial Management

Stephen G. Timme

All companies compete against each other in the financial markets. Those companies offering a competitive return tend to prosper and grow. Those that do not are limited in their ability to grow and many times cease to exist. Providing a competitive return is becoming more complex because of increasingly demanding customers, heightened competition, and ever-changing technologies. CxOs (CEOs, CFOs, etc.) are seeking new solutions to meet this challenge.

Supply chain management (SCM) has the potential to provide these kinds of solutions. For example, a study exploring the financial benefits of collaborative planning, forecasting, and replenishment (CPFR) found that sales increased 12% on average from lower stock-out losses, improved promotional planning, and increased service levels. Inventory and related expenses decreased from 20% to 40% as a result of lower safety stock because of greater confidence in the forecasting and planning process, and there was a 3.5% to 7.5% decrease in production capital requirements as a result of better scheduling (Andraski and Haedicke 2003). Despite SCM potential to drive financial performance, and ultimately increase cash flow, relatively few companies use this effective tool.

There are three common impediments to companies making the financial-SCM connection. First, many executives view SCM as a tactical backroom cost-center activity and not a key tool for managing overall financial performance. Fortunately, this view appears to be changing. Second, most SCM professionals do not speak the language of finance. Hence, they lack the ability to link SCM to key financial metrics and articulate how SCM's drives financial performance. Third, SCM drives performance throughout the enterprise. Therefore, SCM strategic and tactical decisions cannot be made in a vacuum. Yet most SCM scorecards and analysis of SCM initiatives are incomplete since they are not from an enterprisewide perspective.

This chapter explores the connection between financial performance and SCM. In doing so, it addresses these three impediments and helps move SCM from the *back room* to the *boardroom*. It explores key financial metrics that are better managed by SCM. A three-step top-down approach is recommended to help make the financial-SCM connection.

Key Drivers of Financial Performance

As shown in Figure 18.1, the three key drivers of a company's financial performance are as follows:

- *Growth*—annual growth in revenue.
- *Profitability*—percentage of profits after deducting from revenue total operating expenses such as cost of goods sold and selling, general, and administrative expenses.
- *Capital utilization*—dollars of revenue generated relative to dollars invested in assets such as inventory, accounts receivable, warehouses, fleets, manufacturing, and stores; we like to refer to capital utilization as SPEED, with competing companies recording the highest average speed winning the race.

Return on capital (ROC) is net operating profits after taxes (NOPAT) as a percentage of capital. It is also useful to measure ROC as a combination of profitability and SPEED. For example, suppose a company has the following:

1. Revenue $100

2. NOPAT $6

3. Capital $50

ROC is 12% ($6/$50), which is also measured as

$$6\% \ (\$6/\$100) \times 2.00 \ (\$100/\$50) = 12\%$$

$$\text{Profitability} \qquad \text{SPEED} \qquad \text{ROC}$$

Figure 18.1   Key Drivers of Financial Performance and Value Creation

In this example, $1.00 of revenue results in $0.06 profit, and throughout the year, $1.00 invested in capital generates $2.00 in revenue. Therefore, $1.00 invested in capital produces $0.12 in profit and a 12% ROC.

Viewing ROC as a combination of profitability and SPEED highlights the benefits of SCM, improving both profitability and SPEED. The need for greater SCM SPEED is explored later in this chapter.

The value a company is creating for shareholders is determined by comparing ROC to the cost of capital. The cost of capital is a company's opportunity cost of money and is a weighted average of its cost of debt and cost of equity.

As an example, with a 12% ROC and 10% cost of capital, a company is creating value of 2% (12% − 10%) annually on a dollar invested in capital. For $50 invested in capital, $1 ($50 × 2%) is created annually in value. The $1 in annual value creation is the company's economic profit, which is also called economic value added.

Improved SCM has the potential for many companies to help better the three key drivers (1) growth, (2) profitability, and (3) SPEED and, in turn, increase ROC and ultimately value creation. However, different CxOs often have different views on how SCM helps achieve their goals. Table 18.1 provides examples of how the view of SCM often varies by CxO. It is imperative that in communicating the value of SCM, the views of different CxOs are incorporated to create a more meaningful motivating factor for change in SCM.

Need for SCM SPEED

Capital utilization or SPEED is an area with great potential for SCM solutions to improve the overall financial performance of many companies. As an example, Figure 18.2 shows inventory (a key SCM-related asset) as a percentage of net operating assets for a sample of companies from manufacturing, distribution, and retail. Inventory is almost 40% of net operating assets for manufacturing and approximately 60% for retail and wholesale distribution. Companies generally insist that their managers focus on results related to the profitability drivers like transportation and warehousing budgets but not on capital. Profitability-related measures are important but incomplete.

Research also suggests that many companies still have opportunities to significantly reduce inventory. Figure 18.3 shows days in inventory for the median and first quartile for the fabricated metals, motor vehicle parts and accessories, wholesale distribution industrial supply, and department store industries. Research shows similar results for many other industries. It is noted that some of the differences between the median and first quartile are due in part to unique company factors like product mix. But these differences also reflect differences in how effectively the underlying business processes are managed. The results show a substantial difference in days in inventory within industries. For motor vehicle parts as an example, the median company has 42 days in inventory compared with the first quartile of 26 days, indicating significant opportunities to better manage inventory, resulting in higher SPEED and ROC.

Many supply chain decisions involve trade-offs between capital and operating expense. For example, inventory levels generally can be lowered by upgrading

Table 18.1   CxO's View of Supply Chain Management (SCM)

CxO	View of Supply Chain Management
CEO	The CEO tends to primarily think about SCM from the perspective of delivering value-adding growing revenue. This includes items like product availability, new product speed to market, and customer service. The focus in recent years by executives and investors has been on growing the top line, but top-line growth needs to also deliver bottom-line results. See Manrodt, Gibson, and Rutner (2005) for more details on the CEO's view of SCM.
CFO	The CFO tends to think about SCM in terms of its ability to help better manage the balance sheet primarily in terms of inventory and fixed assets and the income statement in terms of better managing SCM-related expenses.
COO	The COO tends to touch multiple parts of a business, and thus tends to think about SCM from numerous vantage points including balancing supply with demand, sufficient levels of inventory to keep production flowing, adequate spare or warranty provisioning, efficient procurement operations including assuring that suppliers have adequate notice of current and future demand, and how distribution and logistics operations can be improved to enhance customer service.
VP of Supply Chain	The VP of supply chain or chief logistics officers tends to view SCM as a means to an end—how he or she can use SCM to better plan and fulfill the company's market demand for goods and services. The VP of supply chain typically looks at all aspects of the required SCM functionality including buy-side, sell-side, planning, and execution.
VP Sales	The VP of sales most often thinks of SCM in the context of customer serviceability. Are there sufficient quantities of the right products to sell? Operationally, he or she also recognizes an ongoing need to provide accurate and timely field forecasts.
VP of Procurement	The VP of procurement tends think about SCM in terms of its impact on suppliers. Is there the right level of visibility in current and future demand? That includes both quantities and required lead times or replenishment times.

modes of transportation. However, this upgrade typically results in increased transportation expense. A manager whose performance is measured on transportation expense is loath to spend more on transportation to lower inventories. Focusing managers' attention on profitability measures alone tends to create a

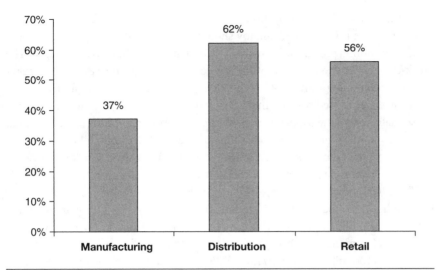

Figure 18.2   Inventory as a Percentage of Net Operating Assets

SOURCE: FinListics Solutions®.

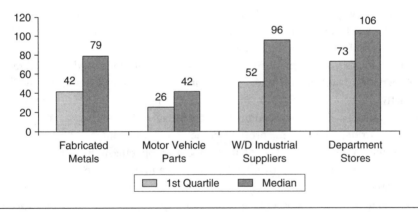

Figure 18.3   Days in Inventory

SOURCE: FinListics Solutions®.

mind-set that the responsibility for capital utilization lies with some corporate group. It is likely that SPEED is not optimized in these companies.

Think of SPEED as the average mileage per hour a race car records in completing one lap around a racecourse. The cars with the higher SPEED start at the front of the field. The car with the highest average SPEED wins the race. The business of all businesses is the efficient movement of cash. A company may manufacture, distribute, or create new products, but its real business is the generation and reinvestment of cash. The quicker the cash is generated, the quicker a business can grow, and the higher its financial performance and, ultimately, its return to shareholders.

The Economic Profit Break-Even Model in Figure 18.4 highlights the importance of SCM's impact on SPEED by showing the many different ways to earn a positive economic profit. In the analysis, a company has a 10% cost of capital. The break-even curve shows the combinations of profitability and SPEED that result in a zero economic profit (ROC = cost of capital). Pretax profitability (operating profit/revenue) is used because managers and investors often refer to a company's consolidated or segment operating profit margin. Anywhere along the break-even curve, economic profit is zero regardless of the level of profitability. Above the break-even curve, economic profit is positive and value is created; below the curve, economic profit is negative and value is destroyed.

The model shows that a company with a SPEED of 2.00 has an 8.3% break-even profitability. A company with $100 million in revenue has $8.3 million in operating profit ($100 million × 8.3%), which after taxes is $5.0 million in NOPAT ($8.3 million − $8.3 million × 40% tax rate). With a SPEED of 2.00, it has $50 million in capital ($100 million revenue/2.00 SPEED). The capital charge on the $50 million in capital is $5.0 million ($50 million capital × 10% cost of capital), which results in a zero economic profit ($5.0 million NOPAT − $5.0 million capital charge). Given a company's actual SPEED, the vertical distance from the break-even profitability and actual profitability is the pretax economic profit per dollar of revenue. For example, a company has revenue of $100 million, 10% profitability, and SPEED of 2.00. Its pretax economic profit is $1.7 million ($100 million × (10% actual profitability − 8.3% break-even profitability)).

The tool shows how increased SPEED resulting from improved SCM increases competitive advantage and economic profit. For the same profitability, any SCM initiative that increases SPEED increases economic profit. An increase in SPEED also creates a product market competitive advantage by letting a company generate the same or higher economic profit with the same profitability.

Suppose a company and all of its competitors operate in an ultracompetitive product market and have a profitability of 8.3% and a SPEED of 2.00. This combination of profitability and SPEED results in a break-even economic profit—the business returns just enough to pay the cost of capital. A SCM initiative is expected to increase SPEED to 3.00. At a SPEED of 3.00, as shown in Figure 18.4, the break-even profitability is 5.6%. If profitability remains at 8.3%, the company earns a positive economic profit. The pretax economic profit is 2.7% (8.3% − 5.6%) per dollar of revenue.

However, the increased SPEED provides a competitive advantage since the break-even profitability is now 5.6%. This advantage gives the company a variety of ways in which to capture market share. For example, it could lower prices, offer higher service levels, or spend more on advertising and promotions. Suppose the combination of these factors drives increased revenue (growth) and results in profitability of 7.0%. This runs counter to conventional wisdom that the goal is to increase profitability. The key element in this example is that the SCM initiative provides an infrastructure that lets the company operate in a lower profitability environment while earning more economic profit and providing higher returns to the shareholders.

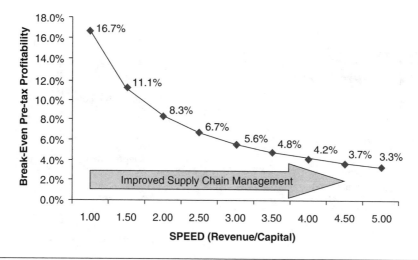

Figure 18.4   Economic Profit Breakeven

NOTE: Graph for 10% ROC = cost of capital.

SPEED is the key in this example. The company is passing along part of the benefits from increased capital utilization to its customers in the form of lower prices—the reduction in profitability from 8.3% to 7.0%. It captures the remaining benefits as increased economic profit and ultimately stock price. If the competitors do not experience a similar increase in SPEED, they can only follow the company's pricing, service, advertising, and other initiatives with a reduction in economic profit—and, in turn, stock price.

Measuring Financial Performance

Figure 18.5 is a financial driver tree and is a useful road map for exploring the connection between financial performance and SCM. The figure also provides for illustrative purposes values for Dell, Inc., for its fiscal year 2005 and the industry Electronic Computers. Table 18A in Appendix A provides the descriptions for each of the financial metrics.

Great care must be taken in comparing a company's financial metrics with those of its industry or other companies as they are affected by unique company factors like product mix, outsourcing, and accounting practices. Also, financial metrics are often interrelated as part of a company's strategy for maximizing overall financial performance. For example, a company may sacrifice gross profit margin (have a higher cost of goods sold as a percentage of revenue) to achieve higher revenue growth. Finally, caution must be used in assigning causation to individual company strategies and tactics. For example, Dell is recognized as highly focused on SCM, and this no doubt contributes to its overall performance. Nonetheless, not all of the difference between Dell's performance and that of its industry should be attributed to superior SCM.

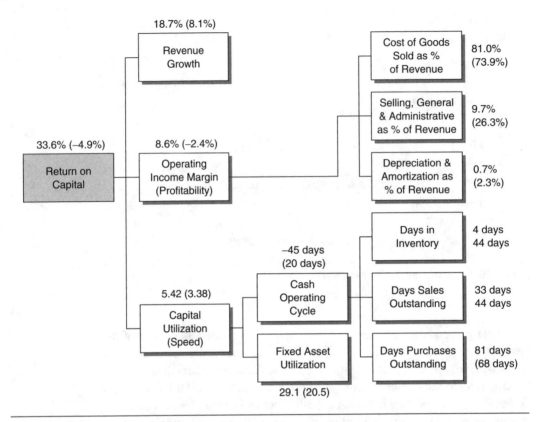

Figure 18.5   Financial Driver Tree

NOTE: Values shown for Dell, Inc., for fiscal year 2005. Values in parentheses are for industry SIC 3571 Electronic Computers, North America.

Figure 18.5 shows that Dell's ROC is 33.6% compared with the industry's, which is −4.9%. Decomposing Dell's ROC into growth, profitability, and capital utilization provides insights into its superior financial performance. Dell's revenue growth of 18.7% is more than double that of the industry (8.1%). Considering that Dell essentially operates in a commodity market, its higher revenue growth likely is explained in part by what customers perceive as an advantage in revenue-related business processes like ordering, fulfillment, and customer service. Dell's operating income margin is 8.6%, compared with the industry's (−2.4%). Dell generates $0.086 in operating income compared with an industry that lost $0.024. The difference in profitability reflects in part more efficient operations.

Dell's capital utilization of 5.42 is 60% higher than the industry's 3.38. For a dollar invested in capital, Dell generates $5.42 in revenue compared with $3.38 for the industry. Dell's higher capital utilization reflects its significantly higher fixed asset utilization and lower cash operating cycle. Dell's fixed asset utilization is 29.1, which means that a dollar invested in manufacturing, assembly, or distribution assets generates $29.10 in revenue compared with $20.50 for the industry.

Much attention has been given to Dell's cash operating cycle, which is also called the cash-to-cash cycle. The cash operating cycle is a measure of the net number of days invested in inventory, accounts receivable, and accounts payable. Dell's cash operating cycle of −44 days and the industry's 20 days are measured as shown in the following table:

	Dell	Industry
Days in inventory	4	44
+ Days sales outstanding	33	44
− Days purchases outstanding	81	68
= Cash operating cycle	−44 days	20 days

A cash operating cycle of −44 days means that Dell receives cash from the sale of inventories and collection of accounts receivable before it pays its suppliers.

Examination of Dell's cash operating cycle highlights the role played by days in inventory. Dell's days in inventory is 4 days compared with the industry average of 44 days. A company with fewer days in inventory has a strategic and financial performance advantage over competitors holding all other factors like fulfillment and services levels the same as it has less funds invested in capital per dollar of revenue.

Table 18.2 provides examples of how SCM-related activities are related to the key financial metrics. Table 18.2 shows that SCM affects the key financial metrics in many ways and as a result is receiving increasing interest by executives. A critical element, though, is that executives more fully understand the financial-SCM connection and how it can help improve overall financial performance.

Making the Financial-SCM Connection: A Top-Down Approach

It is recommended that a top-down approach be used to make the financial-SCM connection. The top-down approach as shown in Figure 18.6 comprises three steps.

Step 1: Calculate Value of Gaps in Key Financial Metrics

SCM drives key financial metrics such as revenue growth, percent cost of goods sold, and days in inventory. The values of the gaps may be based on benchmarks from competitors, industry aggregates, historical performance, or aspirations. The value of the gaps can be measured using a variety of value-based financial measures such as free cash flow, economic profit, and stock price (Meyers 1997). Whatever metric is used, it should be as follows:

- Used to reward senior managers
- Easily understood by many managers throughout the organization
- Related to shareholder value

Table 18.2   Financial Metrics—SCM Mapping

Financial Metric	Examples of How Supply Chain Management Adds Value	
Revenue Growth	• Fill rates • Forecasting • Customer service	• Lead times • New product speed to market
Cost of Goods Sold (COGS) as a Percentage of Revenue	• Transportation management • Warehouse management • Inventory management • Network design	• Procurement cost • Reverse logistics • Selective outsourcing
Selling, General, and Administrative (SG&A) as a Percentage of Revenue	• Customer service • Supply chain administration	• Information Technology
Days in Inventory (DII)	• Transportation management • Warehouse management • Network design	• Inventory visibility • Forecasting accuracy • Demand planning
Days Sales Outstanding (DSO)	• Shipment integrity • Fill rate • Proof of delivery	• Invoicing accuracy • Internal communications
Days Purchases Outstanding (DPO)	• Procurement terms	• Payment practices
Fixed Asset Utilization	• Warehouse management • Transportation management	• IT management • Selective outsourcing

The values of the gaps are an effective means to communicate to the organization the need for change and the potential value of improved SCM. For example, communicating that closing a 10-day gap in days in inventory is worth $100 million in cash flow and can potentially add $1 per share to stock price is likely to generate greater motivation for change compared with the strategy of simply announcing the need to reduce days in inventory.

Step 2: Link Gaps in Financial Metrics to SCM Business Processes and Strategies

The next step in the top-down approach is to link gaps in financial metrics to SCM-related business processes and strategies. A gap in profitability related to percent cost of goods sold, for example, can be mapped to a SCM-related process such as distribution and logistics, which, in turn, is linked to a key activity such as warehouse management. Warehouse management is related to tasks such as receive,

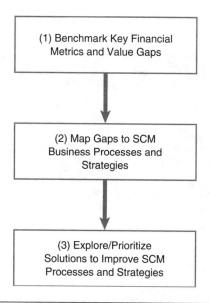

Figure 18.6   Top-Down Approach to Making the Financial-SCM Connection

put away, pick, pack, and ship and to key performance indicators (KPIs) such as labor costs, average time per pick, and pick accuracy. This mapping provides a better understanding of the cause-and-effect relationships between SCM business activities and financial performance.

Step 3: Map SCM Initiatives to Financial Performance Gaps

The information provided in steps 1 and 2 is used as the foundation for exploring SCM solutions that improve the SCM-related business processes and strategies underlying the gaps in the key financial metrics. This provides a logical methodology for identifying specific areas of opportunity. It also provides a disciplined approach for estimating the monetary benefits and understanding the critical success factors and risks of SCM solutions required for building a business case. Improvements in SCM business processes and strategies typically cannot completely close financial performance gaps, but for many companies, they can make a significant contribution.

Example of the Top-Down Approach

The following is an example of the top-down approach to making the financial-SCM connection. The results in Figure 18.7 are based on the consolidated operations for a publicly traded appliance manufacturer. The key financial metrics are compared with those of two competitors. Step 1 often provides the most powerful insights when applied to lines of business. A common impediment to analysis at the

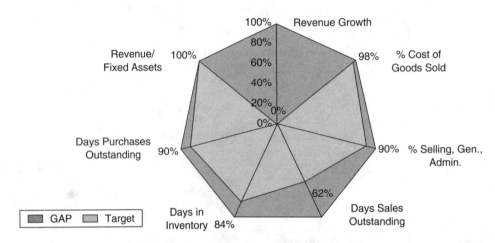

FinListics* Value Manager Financial Performance Gap Analysis					
Financial Metrics	**Target**	**Benchmark Value**	**Benchmark**	**1st Yr Cash Flow (Millions, USD)***	**LT Cash Flow (Millions, USD)***
Revenue Growth	−1.9%	1.8%	Comp 1	3.3	(57.5)
% Cost of Goods Sold	74.6%	73.1%	Comp 2	204.8	1,229.0
% Selling, Gen. & Admin.	17.6%	15.8%	Comp 2	224.9	1,349.6
Days Sales Outstanding	84	52	Comp 1	1,124.9	1,124.9
Days in Inventory	61	52	Comp 1	277.7	403.0
Days Purchases Outstanding	62	69	Comp 2	175.5	175.2
Revenue/Fixed Assets	6.03	6.03	Target		
Total 1st Year Cash Flow and LT Cash Flow Gaps				**2,010.1**	**4,224.1**
Target Actual Market Value					5,688.4
% Increase					74%
Total Price Per Share Gap					**23.07**
Target Actual Stock Price					31.07
*Present Value of Change in Annual Cash Flows					

Figure 18.7   Benchmark Key Financial Metrics and Value Gaps

line-of-business level is the lack of credible financial metrics. However, advanced cost accounting systems and business intelligence are making strides in providing more credible financial metrics and benchmarks.

The gaps in financial metrics are valued using first-year annual cash flow (before-tax) and the potential impact on shareholder value—present value of after-tax, long-term cash flow. The present value of the long-term cash flow gap is also expressed as a potential value per share. Again, it is recommended that the value of the gaps be expressed in terms of measures that are used to reward senior managers, are understood by many throughout the organization, and are linked to returns to shareholders. The differences in financial metrics are in part attributable to variations in sales mix, pricing strategies, outsourcing, accounting practices, and other factors not necessarily related to inefficiencies in business processes or effectiveness of business strategies.

Cost of goods sold as a percentage of revenue is 74.6% for the target company and 73.1% for the benchmark competitor. The chart shows that the company's percent cost of goods sold is 98% effective (73.1% divided by 74.6%) compared with the benchmark company. Focusing only on the percent effectiveness, which is a common practice in many benchmarking studies, provides limited motivation to explore solutions to reduce these expenses. However, valuing the gap provides different insights and motivation for change.

Reducing cost of goods sold as a percentage of revenue to the benchmark of 73.1% from 74.6% adds $205 million to first-year cash flow and $1.3 billion to market value, holding all other factors the same. To put this in perspective, the company's actual funds from operations and market value are $905 million (not shown in Figure 18.7) and $5,688 million, respectively. Consequently, even closing 10% of the total cost-of-goods-sold gap with improved SCM practices would make a significant contribution.

The results also indicate several other areas to explore for improvement with SCM initiatives. The company's selling, general, and administrative expense as a percentage of revenue is 17.6% compared with the benchmark of 15.8%. The chart shows that percent selling, general, and administrative expense is 90% effective. However, the valuation of the difference shows gaps of $225 million and $1,350 million in first-year cash flow and market value, respectively.

Days in inventory is 61 days for the company and 52 days for the benchmark. Completely closing the inventory gap would add $277 million to first-year cash flow and $403 million in market value. See Timme and Timme (2003) for more information on valuing a gap in days in inventory.

Days sales outstanding (DSO) is another area that warrants further investigation. DSO is 84 days for the target company and 52 days for the benchmark. Much of the difference in DSO is likely attributable to differences in credit and collection policies, which are not driven by SCM. However, SCM does affect DSO through fill rates, order completeness, shipment integrity, and proof of delivery. For the target company, an improvement in these areas that reduced DSO by only 1 day would add $35 million to cash flow and market value.

Having decided on what financial metric gaps to explore further, the next step in the top-down approach involves mapping the gaps to SCM-related business processes and the underlying activities and tasks. Figure 18.8 is an example of a mapping of days in inventory to key business processes and activities and tasks for industrial companies. This type of mapping provides a logical road map for better understanding the root cause of gaps in financial metrics. At this stage, the focus is more on understanding why a gap exists than on how much of the gap will be closed by better managing the business processes.

It is also recommended that the process of starting to better understand the root cause of a gap in a financial metric begin with discussions with the CxOs. The questions asked should be consistent with the CxOs' view of SCM as it relates to a specific financial metric. Table 18.3 provides examples of CxO-centric questions based on the inventory mapping in Figure 18.8. The questions are not exhaustive

Supply Chain Planning	Sales & Marketing	Procurement	Production	Warehouse Management

Supply Chain Planning

Develop Production & Supply Chain Strategy
- Design & Manage Network
- Make Strategic Sourcing Decisions
- Manage Compliance & Process Technology Strategy
- Manage Supply Chain Infrastructure

Manage Supply & Demand Planning
- Manage Demand Forecast
- Manage Supply Chain Capacity
- Manage Supply Chain Short-Term Planning
- Forecasting (Product Mix Optimization)

Manage Inventory
- Determine Inventory Strategy
- Evaluate Replenishment Requirements
- Optimize Inventory
- Manage MRO Inventory
- Collaborate With Suppliers
- Receive/Generate Inventory Replenishment Signal
- Collaborate With Supplier to Replenish Inventory
- Replenishment Inventory Plan

Sales & Marketing

Manage Customer & Partner Relationships
- Identify Partners
- Manage Relationships
- Manage Customer and Partner Requests

Manage Marketing Operations
- Develop & Distribute Marketing Collateral
- Develop Product/ Diseases Websites
- Manage Relationships With Key Opinion Leaders
- Manage Marketing Alliances
- Manage Industry Events, Trade Shows & Conferences
- Manage Internal Tools & Databases

Manage Sales Operations
- Develop Sales Objectives & Budgets
- Establish Sales Force Plan
- Manage & Distribute Sales Tools, E-detailing Programs, Internal Tools, & Databases
- Manage External Sales Relationships
- Analyze Sales Performance

Market and Sell Solutions
- Develop New Markets
- Bring New Products to Market
- Generate Demand (Marketing)
- Access/Manage New Opportunities
- Develop New Channels to Market
- Perform Sales Management
- Determine Pricing Rules and Dynamic Pricing
- Execute Sales

Procurement

- **Develop Strategy for Procurement**
- **Develop & Maintain Procurement Policies**
- **Quality Suppliers**
- **Establish Supplier Contracts & Manage Relationships**
- **Manage Purchase Requisitions/Orders**
- **Inventory Visibility**
- **Forecasting (Product Mix Optimization)**
- **Rebate Management**
- **Vendor-Managed Inventory**
- **Catalog Management**

Production

Production Support
- Develop Delivery Schedule
- Schedule Production Orders and Create Batch Paperwork
- Produce Bulk and Collect In-Process Samples
- Test & Release Bulk Material
- Develop and Maintain Production Processes/ Procedures
- Maintain & Repair Equipment

Production Performance
- Implement Changes to Production Processes
- Support Production Ramp & Volume Production
- Monitor Production Runs
- Identify Process/Equipment Configuration Changes
- Capture Production Improvements
- Send Feedback to Product Development Process
- Identify Production Process Performance Indicators
- Manage Quality Assurance

Finished Packaging Performance
- Produce Finished Products & Collect In-Process Samples
- Test & Release Finished Packaged Goods
- Maintain Batch Records and Manage Lot Traceability

Warehouse Management

Warehouse Internal Processes
- Value-Added Services
- Distribution Network Linkage
- Labor Management
- Pick, Pack, Ship
- Outsourcing
- Receiving/Put Away (Inbound)
- Staging (Load Analysis)
- Automated Processes
- Physical Layout
- Returns Process
- Union/Labor Relations

Transportation

Manage Inbound & Outbound Logistics
- Mode Optimization
- Carrier Management
- Loads, Routing, and Scheduling
- Distribution Center Optimization

Figure 18.8 Days in Inventory: Business Process and Activity and Tasks Mapping for Industrial Companies

Table 18.3   Examples of CxO-Centric Questions for Gap in Days in Inventory

CxO	View of Supply Chain Management
CEO	• Are you able to service your customers' needs adequately? • What is the average cycle time for customer request, and what is the percentage of demand not fulfilled due to stock-outs? • Are you able to drive the right number of new customers?
CFO	• Do you believe you have too much inventory in some categories (raw materials, work-in-process, and finished goods) and not enough in others? • How accurate are your physical and cycle count inventories compared with book inventory? • What is your annual inventory write-off as a percentage of sales? Is it acceptable?
COO	• Do you have sufficient raw material inventory to achieve your production and distribution goals? • Is your capacity utilization satisfactory? • What about your production and distribution cycle time? Are your product lead times competitive? • Do you believe you have sufficient visibility in the demand driving your suppliers including quantities and timing?
VP of Supply Chain	• Do you believe your inventory levels represent the appropriate balance between supply and demand? • How is your forecasting accuracy? Does your forecasting system have a built-in system bias? • Do you and your vendors have visibility into your production planning schedule and customer order system? • Are your customer deliveries often late or delayed? • Is your distribution network appropriately designed and optimized?
VP Sales	• Do you believe you have the right level of inventory to service your customers and achieve growth goals? • How is your field forecasting accuracy? Are you achieving your sales budget regularly? • How is the accuracy and timing of information coming from the field? • What is the average cycle time for customer requests? Are your customer satisfaction statistics satisfactory?
VP of Procurement	• Do you believe you have sufficient visibility in the demand driving your suppliers including quantities and timing? • How is your supplier quality? Is it affecting inventory levels? • How much of your procured goods and services are defective and must be returned?

(Continued)

Table 18.3 (Continued)

CxO	View of Supply Chain Management
	• Do you have the right number of suppliers? How well do your suppliers meet their promised delivery dates?
	• Are you satisfied with your overall procurement cycle time? Is your contracting cycle time also satisfactory? What about your replenishment cycle time?
	• How are your supplier order-fill rates?
	• What about your supplier lead times? Do you experience significant raw material inventory shrinkage and damage costs that are attributed to your suppliers?

and are provided for illustrative purposes. Again, the focus at this stage is to develop consensus on areas that should be explored further to help close a financial metric gap. Based on the results of the CxO interviews and others, it is useful to develop a prioritization plan focusing on those business processes identified as the likely root cause of the gap in the financial metric. Suppose, in the preceding example, the consensus is that the business process that should be explored further to help close the days in inventory gap is supply chain planning (see Figure 18.8). A useful framework to develop the prioritization plan is shown in Figure 18.9.

In Figure 18.9, CxOs and others are asked to rank KPIs related to the business process being explored. Those in Figure 18.9 are examples for supply chain planning. Each KPI is ranked in terms of financial benefit (high or low) if improved and time to benefit (less than 1 year or greater than 1 year). The definition for high or low for the financial benefit often varies by company. For example, $100,000 may be defined as the entry point to a high benefit for a company with $100 million in revenue, whereas a company with $1 billion in revenue may set $1 million as the minimum for high.

It is also noted that the assignment of financial benefit varies by company depending on its baseline efficiency for the KPI being ranked. For example, a company that has recently implemented a distribution network optimization initiative would likely assign a low financial benefit to further optimization. On the other hand, a company that has experienced growth through acquisition resulting in numerous distribution centers that have yet to be optimized would likely assign a high value to distribution network optimization.

The development of the prioritization plan is typically based on individuals' knowledge of the company and its business issues. At this stage, detailed financial analysis has often not been conducted. The prioritization plan is a useful tool for building consensus on which areas to explore further. In the prioritization plan in Figure 18.9, the KPIs in the northeast quadrant (fast time to benefit/high financial benefit) are explored first. Often the next areas to explore are those in the northwest quadrant (long time to benefit/high financial benefit). The areas in the southeast quadrant (fast time to benefit/low financial benefit) may be considered at a later date, but availability of resources (funds and people) often makes exploring these

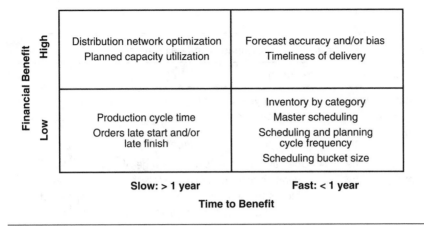

Figure 18.9   SCM Prioritization Plan—Supply Chain Planning Example

further impractical. Finally, it is recommended that the areas in the southwest quadrant (long time to benefit/low financial benefit) not be further explored since doing so would likely result in initiatives with a low return on investment and a lengthy payback period.

The final stage is to use the responses from the questions based on the mapping of the financial metrics to business processes and activities and tasks and the prioritization plan to explore SCM solutions that potentially help better manage the areas indicated as likely to be the root cause of the gap in the financial metric.

Conclusions

SCM has the potential to help provide higher returns to shareholders. Yet only a small percentage of companies use SCM to manage overall financial performance. There are three common impediments to companies making the financial-SCM connection. First, many executives view SCM from a tactical perspective and not as a powerful tool for managing overall financial performance. Second, most SCM professionals do not speak the language of finance and, therefore, are challenged in articulating how SCM drives financial performance. Third, SCM drives performance throughout the enterprise. However, many SCM scorecards and initiatives focus only on selected business processes and the entire enterprise.

It is recommended that companies make the financial-SCM connection using a three-step, top-down approach that benchmarks key financial metrics and values gaps, maps gaps to SCM business processes and activities, and uses this information to explore and prioritize initiatives to improve SCM business processes and strategies.

Appendix

Table 18.A   Financial Metrics Descriptions and Calculation

Financial Metric	Description
Revenue Growth	• Year-over-year percentage change in revenue. • Revenue is the value of products and services sold.
	Profitability
Operating Income Margin	• Operating income as a percentage of revenue. • Operating income is revenue less total operating expenses, which is the sum of the three components: (a) cost of goods sold; (b) selling, general, and administrative; and (c) depreciation and amortization.
Cost of Goods Sold (COGS) as % of Revenue	• Percentage of revenue absorbed by COGS. • COGS are expenses directly related to providing products and services.
Selling, General, and Administrative (SG&A) as % of Revenue	• Percentage of revenue absorbed by SG&A. • SG&A includes expenses indirectly related to sales activities, general, and administrative expenses.
	Capital Utilization
Capital Utilization	• Revenues generated per dollar invested in capital. • Capital is total assets less non-interest bearing current liabilities such as accounts payable, salaries and wages, and taxes.
Days in Inventory (DII)	• Number of days of operations held in inventory.· Inventory includes raw materials, work in process, and finished goods.
Days Sales Outstanding (DSO)	• Number of days on average that a company takes to collect credit sales from customers. • Accounts receivable are moneys owed to a company by its customers; they arise from the sale of products and provision of services for which they have not yet been paid.
Days Purchases Outstanding (DPO)	• Number of days on average that a company takes to pay vendors and suppliers. • Accounts payable are moneys a company owes vendors and suppliers for products and services bought and received but not yet paid for.
Cash Operating Cycle	• Number of days of operations invested in working capital (DII + DSO − DPO).
Fixed Asset Utilization	• Amount of revenue generated per dollar invested in net property, plant, and equipment. • Net property, plant, and equipment (PP&E) includes assets such as warehouses, fleets, manufacturing facilities, and stores.

References

Andraski, Joseph C. and Jack Haedicke (2003), "CPFR: Time for the Breakthrough," *Supply Chain Management Review*, 7 (3), 54–60.

Manrodt, Karl, Brian Gibson, and Stephen Rutner (2005), *Communicating the Value of Supply Chain Management to Your CEO*. Oak Brook, IL: Council of Supply Chain Management Professionals.

Meyers, Randy (1997), "Measure for Measure," *CFO Magazine*, 13 (November), 44–56.

Timme, Stephen and Christine Timme (2003), "The Real Cost of Holding Inventory," *Supply Chain Management Review*, July/August, 31–37.

19

Risk Management

Ila Manuj

J. Paul Dittmann

Barbara Gaudenzi

"On paper it looks like a great return on investment without the risk issue. With the risk, who knows?" said a former senior vice president for global outsourcing and supply chain management operations of a leading manufacturing firm. This chapter addresses the concerns reflected in this quote, which are shared by many supply chain managers today—understanding and managing the risks of global supply chain operations.

With the recent wave of outsourcing, managing risk in the supply chain has come to the forefront. Most firms are under extreme pressure to reduce cost. In addition to competitive pressure, boards of directors, shareholders, and other stakeholders are sending a clear message to management to become increasingly efficient and competitive. Today, offshoring (sourcing from across borders) and international marketing (i.e., marketing products abroad through exporting, licensing, franchising, joint ventures, or wholly owned subsidiaries) are seen more than ever as prime strategies. The pressures are so intense to leverage the opportunities of offshoring and international marketing that the management of risk is often pushed into the background.

For example, wage rates in China are roughly $100.00 per month for people working intensely for 60 to 70 hours per week. This is an overwhelming motivation to offshore to leverage this incredible pool of labor. The human resources available in Asia are being leveraged at a rapid pace. There is incredible activity in China and throughout Asia. It is estimated that by the year 2007, the Chinese middle-class market would be larger than the entire U.S. market. Other low-wage markets with a burgeoning middle class, such as Latin America and Eastern Europe, are also seeing great activity.

Ironically, within middle line management, there is a reluctance to enthusiastically embrace these global initiatives. There is an intuitive feeling that one is losing control, and taking on risks that are not fully understood. Also, there is the sentiment that global initiatives conflict with other proven concepts like the Lean and Six Sigma tools that have been sweeping the industry and are based on reducing average cycle times and variability.

In a nutshell, the dilemma faced by management is how to balance all these factors, and make the best decision for the future health and survival of the firm. Most firms have yet to fully understand how to identify and manage the risks associated with the complex trade-offs involved in making correct global decisions.

There is little debate that global supply chains are sources of considerable competitive advantage. The global configurations of firms provide access to cheap labor and raw materials, subsidized financing opportunities, larger product markets, arbitrage opportunities, and additional incentives such as tax rebates offered by foreign governments to attract foreign capital. These benefits are available to firms today because of the unprecedented transnational mobility of capital, information, people, products, and services; the tremendous leaps in information and communications technology; and the increased opportunities and willingness to engage in e-commerce. However, along with these benefits are the challenges that businesses need to overcome when operating globally. These challenges are related to foreign national economies, logistics, cultures, competition, and infrastructure. These challenges give rise to several risks in global supply chains. This chapter explores these global supply chain risks and ways to manage them.

What Is Risk?

In the corporate world, risks represent threats to the value the stakeholders or owners have in the business. Stakeholders include customers, stockholders, distributors, suppliers, creditors, competitors, industry, labor, government, and firm departments. There are several ways in which a risk can be defined. The most simple and common way to define risk is in terms of an expectation that an adverse event will occur that will be detrimental to the stakeholders in the supply chain. To explain the concept of risk, it is helpful to divide it into two components. The first component is the probability of an adverse event happening, and the second component is the sum of losses associated with an adverse event. For example, an adverse event in a global supply chain may be the appreciation of currency in the country where products are sourced. However, it is not possible to say with certainty that the currency will appreciate. Hence, there is a chance factor, called probability, of a risk event. The second factor is the losses associated with currency appreciation such as the increase in landed cost price or a decrease in sales due to increased cost to the customer. Risk to a company is the product of the probability and losses—that is,

$$R_{\text{Risk Event } n} = P_{\text{Event } n} X(L_1 + L_2 + L_3 + \cdots + L_m)_{\text{Event } n}$$

where R is the risk of Risk Event n; P is the probability of Event n happening; and $L_1, L_2, L_3, \ldots, L_m$ are the losses associated with Event n.

Therefore, to understand the significance of a risk event, we need to know the probability and losses. To illustrate, suppose a company manufactures product X abroad and imports it into the United States. Furthermore, it also imports some components and combines them with components procured in the domestic market to fabricate the finished product domestically. A risk on the horizon is a proposed regulation that could lead to container inspection rates at the U.S. ports increasing from 3 in 100 containers to, say, 25 in 100 containers. If this regulation is implemented, it will likely delay port clearance significantly. Hence, this potential regulation is a risk trigger that may lead to a risk event. Usually, the triggers are beyond the control of a single organization. The losses that may result from the event could be product stock-out and loss of sales, loss of customers, excess inventory when the product is actually cleared, damage to product while waiting for clearance, and product obsolescence. Furthermore, a manufacturing plant may need to be shut down or operated at a suboptimal capacity because of shortages of component parts. Some of these losses affect the supply side of the supply chain and some affect the demand side. Another example of risk is the possibility of losses due to violation of intellectual property rights if the process or products are proprietary and the legislation of the foreign country does not provide adequate protection. Such losses affect the information security of the supply chain. Given the wide range of possible risks, it is useful to classify them by their types.

Types of Risks in Global Supply Chains

An easy way to understand and categorize risks is to divide them into four categories: supply risk, operational risk, demand risk, and security risk (see Figure 19.1). Each of the four types of risks may be divided into subrisks for easier understanding. A subrisk is a major concern within the broad category of the risk.

Supply risk is the possibility of an event associated with inbound supply that may cause failures from the supplier(s) or the supply market, such that the outcome results in the inability of the focal firm to meet customer demand within anticipated costs or causes a threat to customer life and safety (Zsidisin et al. 2004). Supply risk resides in the course of movement of materials from supplier's suppliers to the focal firm, and it includes concerns (or subrisks) like reliability of suppliers (misrepresentation of a supplier's ability—quality or capacity issues), moral hazard (inadequate efforts by the selected supplier—quality or capacity issues), involuntary disruption of supply (events such as fire, bankruptcy, and changes in customs policies), price escalation (fluctuation in contract currency), inventory and schedule (suboptimal usage of capacity), technology access (failure to upgrade to new technology by suppliers), and quality issues. If manufacturing is offshored, the supply line gets extended with potential consequences that are much higher in magnitude than with a similar domestic outsourcing decision. For example, a critical component for a major appliance manufacturer was outsourced to China. When a quality problem was discovered by the major home appliance manufacturer, not

Figure 19.1   Risks in the Supply Chain

SOURCE: Adapted from Mentzer (2001).

only were there 60 days of inventory in the system, but the cost to airfreight good components also eliminated two years' worth of all offshoring-related anticipated savings. In addition, many thousands of units had been produced already and were in consumer homes, resulting in multi-million-dollar warranty issues for the company.

Operations risk is the possibility of an event affecting the focal firm's internal ability to produce goods and services, the quality and timeliness of production, and the profitability of the company. Sources of operational risk reside within the firm and may result from a breakdown in core operations, inadequate manufacturing or processing capability, limited flexibility in setting up operations, high levels of process variations, changes in technology that may render the current facilities obsolete, and changes in operating exposure due to currency fluctuations. For example, changes in operating exposure due to exchange rates may even affect companies that have no foreign operations or exports but face important foreign competition in the domestic market. The structure of markets in which the company and its competitors source labor and materials and sell products determines operating exposure. Hence, operating profit may not necessarily be linked to the currency in which prices are quoted and may vary with real exchange rates. For example, a major manufacturer recently completed an offshoring cost-benefit analysis study that indicated a 20% savings after total system costs were considered. The probability that the RMB (yuan) might strengthen by 20% was not taken into account. The foreign currency swing, therefore, could easily wipe out all savings associated with the project, wasting several person-years of effort to implement the new offshoring process and certify the new supplier, in addition to any capital investment. For this durable goods manufacturer, the potential loss was four person-years of effort and U.S.$10 million in investment. Operations risk may also arise because of supply risk such as shortage of, or defective, raw materials.

Demand risk is the possibility of an event associated with the outbound supply that may affect the likelihood of customers placing orders with the focal firm or with the variance in the volume and assortment desired by the customer. Sources of demand risk reside in the movement of goods from the focal firm to the customer's customers. Sources of demand risk could be delayed or inappropriate new product introductions (leading the firm to miss either market opportunities or inventory write-offs and stock-outs because of inaccurate forecasting), variations in demand (caused by fads, seasonality, and new product introductions by competitors), and chaos in the system (caused by overreactions, unnecessary interventions, and distorted information from the downstream supply chain members). Demand risks vary with the nature of the product, with functional products being less risky than innovative products (Fisher 1997). In the early 1990s, Whirlpool completed a study that showed how forecast accuracy declines over lead time. For a supply line that increases from 7 to 40 days because of an offshoring decision, it was shown that the forecast error more than tripled, causing a major increase in safety stock.

Security risk may manifest itself in several forms, including an adverse event affecting information, intellectual property, physical goods, and human resource security. A security risk is a threat from an unknown third party who may or may not be a member of the supply chain and whose motivation is to steal proprietary data or knowledge (i.e., intellectual property); tamper with sensitive and critical information; or destroy, upset, or disable a firm's operations by harming the goods or human resources. The sources of information security risk include individuals within the firm leaking vital information to competitors, system hackers, and weak security or firewalls of the members of the supply chain. Damage to physical goods can occur in the form of freight breaches—that is, violation of the integrity of cargoes and products leading to the loss or adulteration of goods. This may happen because of either theft or tampering for criminal purpose—for example, smuggling weapons inside containers—and poses a major supply chain security risk. Clearly, electronics firms like Sony and pharmaceutical firms like GlaxoSmithKline have a great need for security and must be careful to disguise the contents of their international shipments. As supply lines increase, opportunities for theft or tampering multiply.

One may argue that these four risks are present in domestic operations as well. Although this is a valid statement, these risks are much more difficult to manage in a global scenario because of physical and cultural distances, different time zones, long and variable lead times, infrastructural constraints such as telecommunications and internet access, availability of logistics resources such as transportation capacity and intermediaries, and most important, lower visibility in the supply chain. A company with a factory in Ohio, for example, might expect a maximum lead time of one week from its midwestern suppliers. But if the component is outsourced to China, a minimum lead time of 30 days exists. In addition, the variability inherent in this time period multiplies and poses a more serious problem. Furthermore, because of limited flexibility, Asian or Latin-American factories may not be as agile in responding to unexpected demand spikes, in turn extending the lead time further. In effect, this leads to a lower control of the entire process. The key points of this discussion are that compared with domestic operations, (1) some events do not affect the domestic operations at all (e.g., currency fluctuations) and (2) for those events that affect both domestic and international operations, the probability or the magnitude of losses may be significantly higher when operating globally.

A Risk Management Process Model

The proposed risk management process (see Figure 19.2) has the following steps:

Step 1: Identifying and profiling risks

Step 2: Assessing and evaluating risks

Step 3: Managing risks and risk management strategies

Step 4: Implementing risk management strategies

Step 5: Mitigating risks

The inputs to this process, and the expected outcomes, are guided by several risk management perspectives: enterprise risk management (ERM), business continuity

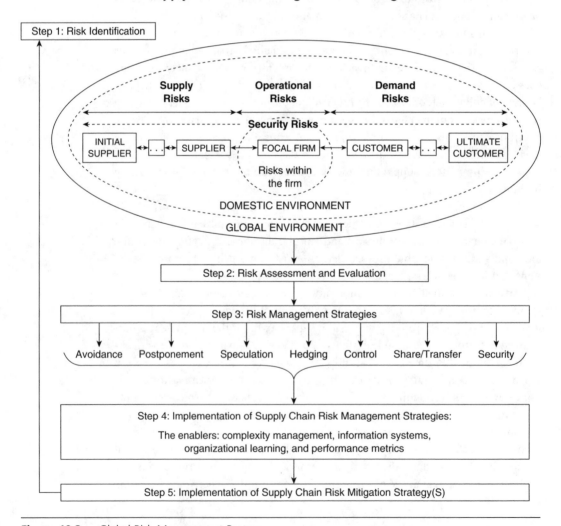

Global Supply Chain Risk Management and Mitigation Framework

Figure 19.2 Global Risk Management Process

and crisis management (BCCM), and integrated risk management (IRM). ERM is a holistic and enterprisewide approach that attempts to adapt traditional risk assessment tools and methods of financial risk management for operational and supply chain risk. In a purely financial management perspective, risks are defined as movements in exchange rates, commodity prices, interest rates, and stock prices. All the activities that affect revenue are assessed to define those that should be compensated with an insurance portfolio. For example, performance variation in a process is a chronic problem often addressed by Six Sigma techniques. As the supply time and distance from end customers increase, process variation also increases. The negative impact on overall business could be addressed with traditional risk assessment tools.

BCCM involves risks that are not always insurable (such as "service-drop" and reputation risk) and the activity of contingency planning. In this case, the management of supply chain risks should be focused on the exposure to serious business disruption along the whole chain to ensure continuity of all the processes.

In an IRM model, risk management is the result of three separate but overlapping processes: strategic management, risk management, and operations management.

All three perspectives have merit and, in fact, are more complementary than competing perspectives. The following discussion on managing risks is framed by these three perspectives.

Step 1: Identifying and Profiling Risks

The first step has two activities: identifying risks and profiling risks. There are several sources that may be used for identification of risk events. The best place to start is to get a cross-functional team involved early while formulating the global logistics and supply chain strategy. This is essential because it leverages the synergy and creativity inherent in a diverse group. Outside consultants and experts and peers in other noncompeting industries may also be consulted to facilitate the risk assessment process. As discussed earlier, it is important to look for subrisks (or concerns), risk events, and losses. Table 19.1 lists some subrisks (or concerns) for each of the four types of risk. For each type of subrisk, a potential event that might cause it and potential losses are also listed to work as a guide for filling in the table. The risk concern that is explored in detail is marked in italics.

As mentioned earlier, the objectives of the supply chain guide what risks are considered. For instance, for a firm like Sports Obermeyer, which faces unpredictable demand on a stock-keeping unit basis, visibility along the supply chain is an important objective. Lack of availability of reports and the absence of an integrated information system could represent a risk concern for such a firm. Similarly, for companies importing electronics or other components that may be misused, securing the supply chain may be an important security risk concern.

Once the risks have been identified, the second activity is to create a "profile" for each of the subrisks identified in Table 19.1. The risk profile contains elements of the specific risk within the broad category, whether the risk is atomistic or holistic and whether it affects domestic or global operations (see Table 19.2). Atomistic sources of risk signify that a selected and limited part of the supply chain is required

Table 19.1   Risks, Risk Concern, Risk Events, and Losses

Type of Risk	Risk Concern	Risk Event	Losses
Supply risk	*Economic shifts in wage rates* Price escalation by supplier Inadequate technology access Defective products Economic shifts in interest rates and exchange rates	Increase in wages by 20%	Higher cost of production, i.e., lower profitability or productivity; loss of sales due to increased prices
Operational risk	*Breakdown of machine* Changes in technology Changes in operating exposure	Defective raw material causing damage to machine	Production loss; repair or replacement cost
Demand risk	*Actions of national governments such as quota restrictions or sanctions* New product introduction Fads Seasonality Bullwhip Forecasting accuracy effect (demand distortion and demand amplification)	Inability to sell forecast product	Obsolete product or sales at lower price, i.e., loss of profits
Security risk	*Intellectual property violation* Information systems security Freight breaches Terrorism Vandalism Threat to human safety	Illegal duplication of a product	Loss of competitive advantage; inability to recover R&D costs

to assess risk. For example, the risk may be limited to border crossings, requiring only the experts in that specific process. The atomistic approach is suitable for low-value, noncomplex, and generally available components and materials. Holistic sources of risk signify that an overall analysis of the supply chain is required to assess risk. For example, the introduction of a completely new product by a firm requires an end-to-end, cross-functional assessment of risks. The holistic approach is preferable for high-value, complex, and rare or unique components or materials.

Apart from analyzing risks at the event level, an efficient way to assess and evaluate risks may be by ordering them according to a project or a process. For instance, in ordering risks according to a project, risks are identified and managed as threats to the success of the project or causes of the failure of the project.

Step 2: Risk Assessment and Evaluation

The next step is to determine which risks identified in Table 19.2 are important for the supply chain. Not all risks affect all supply chains. Weaknesses in a supply chain can make it vulnerable to certain risks, whereas a supply chain's strengths may

Table 19.2   Creating Risk Profiles

Broad Risk Category (1)	Subrisks (or Concerns) (2)	Specific Risk Event(s) (3)	Atomistic/ Holistic (4)	Domestic/ Global/Both (5)
Supply risk	Concern 1	Event 1		
		Event 2		
	Concern 2	Event 1		
		Event 2		
Operational risk	Concern 1	Event 1		
		Event 2		
	Concern 2			
Demand risk	Concern 1	Event 1		
		Event 2		
	Concern 2			
Security risk	Concern 1	Event 1		
		Event 2		
	Concern 2			

shield it from other risks. Those risks to which a supply chain is more vulnerable should be given more attention. Table 19.3 suggests a risk assessment and evaluation tool. The risk events from Table 19.2 are given in column 1 of Table 19.3. The probability of the event and dollar value of the total potential losses from a given risk event are assessed in columns 2 and 3, respectively. Significance (column 4) is calculated by multiplying columns 2 and 3. The worst possible scenario for an ongoing event or a frequent risk event is listed in column 5. For example, a one-time quality problem may not be a big issue, but frequent quality defects may eventually wipe out the profitability of global operations. The acceptability of the worst possible scenario can be yes or no (column 6). Other factors (usually judgmental rather than numeric) that may either aggravate or alleviate the significance of risk go in column 7. The final risk evaluation (column 8) may be insignificant, minor, major, or catastrophic depending on the objective of a global supply chain decision, the resources of the firm, and the risk aversiveness of the decision-making individual or team.

Several statistical tools that focus on potential failures to assess, prevent, and eliminate them as early as possible may also be combined with this stage of risk management. For example, failure modes and effects analysis (FMEA) is often used in engineering design analysis to identify and rank the potential failure modes of a design or manufacturing process and to determine the effects of failure modes on other components of the product or process to document and prioritize improvement actions. This principle can be used to analyze risk. For example, the potential

Table 19.3   Supply Risk Assessment and Evaluation

List of Risks (1)	Probability $(0 \leq p \leq 1^a)$ (2)	Potential Losses (3)	Significance (4)	Worst Possible Scenario (5)	Is the Worst Possible Scenario Acceptable (Yes/No) (6)	Other Considerations/ Factors, Especially Competitors' Exposure to Similar Risks (7)	Final Evaluation of Risk[b] (8)
Supply risk events							
Event 1: disruption of operations at supplier A	0.25	$10,000 per day	$2,500 per day	Loss of 10% of customers if supply disruption lasts over 3 weeks	No	Many competitors with no quality differences who can supply to our customers	Serious
Event 2							
Event 3							

a. $0 \leq p \leq 1$ (0 means no risk at all and 1 means a definite event).

b. Final evaluation of risk: insignificant, minor, serious, and catastrophic.

severity of a risk can be identified by multiplying three factors: the probability of occurrence of an event, how soon the event will be detected, and the total losses by the time the event is detected. Each of the three factors can be rated on a 1-to-10 scale and multiplied together to generate a ranking for the risks. The risks with the highest total then need to be addressed with the most robust prevention plan.

Table 19.3 is helpful when good estimates about probability and losses are available. There are several techniques that can be used to obtain these probability estimates. The probability distribution of a risk may follow some kind of distribution such as the normal distribution. However, in real life, the distributions may be skewed toward left or right or be leptokurtic (flatter than normal) and have "fat tails." The consequence of these characteristics is that extreme events occur much more frequently than indicated in calculations using normal probability distributions, and "most likely" events have a lower probability of occurrence. Sometimes a risk may increase exponentially with a parameter and hence is best understood by an exponential distribution. A detailed discussion on probability distributions for both discrete and random variables may be found in Ross (2003).

Historical data may be used to understand the behavior of risk probability distributions. In real life, however, there are many instances when historical data is inadequate, unreliable, or nonexistent. For example, a company may be considering offshoring manufacturing of some products to an Asian country and may not have much data. In such cases, techniques such as the Delphi methods, may be used to assign probabilities. The Delphi method is a technique that allows people to arrive at a consensus about an issue of interest. It consists of a series of repeated interrogations of individuals who are knowledgeable on the subject. After the initial interrogation of each individual, usually by means of questionnaires, each subsequent interrogation is accompanied by information about the preceding round of replies. Each participant is thus encouraged to reconsider and, if appropriate, change his or her previous reply in light of the replies of other members of the group.

Several problems may, however, crop up in this process. First, different managers in a firm may have different "risk appetites"—that is, a risk-averse manager weighs threats more heavily than his risk-taking colleagues. Second, the members of the supply chain should share data and information that could be an obstacle because of lack of confidence among members of the supply chain.

Once probability and loss estimates are available, they can be put into a user-friendly visual tool. One such tool is presented in Figure 19.3. Risks in the supply chain are divided according to severity of losses (insignificant, minor, serious, or catastrophic) and probability (very unlikely, improbable, probable, or very probable) of a given event. The radius of the circles approximately represents the significance of the risk (recall that risk = probability × loss). There are events for which clear estimates of probability and losses are either not available or impossible to ascertain a priori. For such events, the lines running across the circles represent the extent of uncertainty. For instance, for event 1, the probability estimate is very tight—that is, the event is probable, but the loss estimates range from medium almost up to catastrophic. For event 2, the loss is rather minor, but the probability estimates range from improbable to moderate. The radius of circle 1 is larger than that of circle 2 and signifies that event 1 should have a higher priority than event 2. Finally, an octagon is used to represent undesirable risks. General strategies to deal with risk, such as avoidance, transfer, and hedging, mentioned in Figure 19.3, are discussed later in this chapter. In any quadrant, a company may deliberately assume some risks.

The lines running across the circles are particularly useful when managers do not have hard data to build probabilistic models and have to go by the available business intelligence data and intuitive understanding of the business. For example, in the same industry, the risk of a customer finding competitive suppliers may be a serious and improbable risk for one company but a probable and insignificant risk for another based on the volume of business and relationships. Hence, both quantitative and qualitative risk events may be mapped onto this tool.

Step 3: Managing Risks and Risk Management Strategies

Usually some trigger—known or unknown—causes a risk event to occur. Triggers could be a port strike, economic issues resulting in a currency crisis, collapse of a competitor, an unexpected demand surge, and many other factors. As mentioned earlier, a single company is not in a position to control the triggers and prevent the event from happening. The risk event will occur with some probability and have losses associated with it. The significance of the risk event, as calculated by

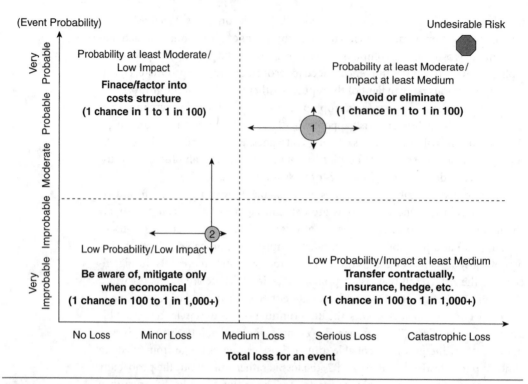

Figure 19.3   An Example of a Visual Tool for Risk Assessment

SOURCE: Adapted from Hallikas, Virolainen, and Tuominen (2002) and the Whirlpool Risk Evaluation and Management Framework. This is an example, and the details in the figure do not reflect how risk assessment is done at Whirlpool.

multiplying the probability and the sum of the losses, is what a company may in fact control through risk management. Risk management is defined as taking actions to reduce the probability of a risk event. In contrast to the assumption of a company not being able to control triggers and events, risk management assumes that an organization can influence the types and impact of losses that may happen and the probabilities of events causing those losses.

Seven primary strategies can be employed to manage risks: avoidance, postponement, speculation, hedging, control, sharing or transferring, and security. The strategies are different but closely related to each other. Furthermore, the use of one strategy may mandate the use of another strategy (e.g., hedging strategy entails avoiding some risks).

Avoidance

Avoidance strategy is used when the risks associated with operating in a given product or geographical market, or working with particular suppliers or customers, are considered unacceptable. In avoiding risks, managers are aware of the supply-demand and operating trade-offs associated with the options and choose to avoid or drop some of these risks. Avoidance may take the form of exiting through divestment of specialized assets, delay of entry into a market or market segment, or participating only in low-uncertainty markets. An example is Dell, which is building its next big factory in North Carolina. Many of the components are still offshored, but component outsourcing carries less risk than outsourcing final assembly if component standardization has been a priority. In effect, Dell has avoided the risks of offshoring assembly.

Postponement

Postponement entails delaying the actual commitment of resources to maintain flexibility and delay the incurring of costs. Postponement may lead to significant benefits in an uncertain environment. Form postponement includes labeling, packaging, assembly, and manufacturing. Time postponement refers to the movement of goods from the manufacturing plants only after customer orders are received. The extent of postponement depends on demand customization, component costs, product life cycle, and product modularity (Chiou, Wu, and Hsu 2002). One manufacturer had 20 varieties of a subassembly that it was to outsource to Asia. It found that it could reduce these to three if it did the final differentiation in the United States. There was a perceived higher cost, but after incorporating the expected costs of risk, the total cost was lower. Also, forecasts could be developed for only 3 items versus 20, greatly reducing forecast error. The end result was lower safety stock and a more reliable supply.

Speculation

Speculation (also called assumption or selective risk taking) is the opposite of postponement. In speculation, decisions are made on anticipated customer demand. In the business world where customer service standards are defined by the competitive environment and are customer driven, the resources in the supply chain are directed to those specific products and customers that provide the firm with a competitive advantage. This strategy would not be appropriate in an industry like the electronics industry where there is a high risk of obsolescence and high inventory carrying costs.

Hedging

The statistical approach and the economic approach are two ways to hedge risks (Chichilnisky and Heal 1998). The statistical approach (insurance) is based on the law of large numbers. With a large enough population, the number likely to be affected is known with considerable accuracy. The sample mean is highly predictable if the distribution for each person or group is known. Some companies pursue a global strategy with the capability of sourcing from multiple regions of the world. The theory is that not all regions will be negatively affected at the same time. The economic approach works when the same event may occur for many people all at once. For example, a drop in U.S. dollar value is the same for everyone in the U.S. economy. Most major appliance manufacturers, like Whirlpool, General Electric

(GE), and Maytag, have a strategy of procuring products from Mexico. If there are problems in Mexico, all are equally affected.

The ideal hedge is to combine these two approaches to achieve a position such that no financial catastrophe exposes the insurer to risks higher than can be afforded. In a supply chain context, hedging is undertaken by having a globally dispersed portfolio of suppliers, customers, and facilities such that a single event (like currency fluctuations or a natural disaster) does not affect all the entities at the same time and at the same level. For example, dual sourcing (or multiple contracting) is a hedge against risks of quality, quantity, disruption, price, and opportunism. Similarly, although the underlying cost structures in plant and technology acquisition and operating costs are specific to the industry, production risks can be offset by operating faster, more flexible plants rather than dedicated, efficient plants.

Control

There are several risks that provide incentives for firms to execute certain functions in-house rather than outsourcing or offshoring. It may be critical that the firm control more of its supply chain because of intellectual property considerations or the presence of powerful supplies who have other more important customers, or it may simply be corporate philosophy to fully control all supply chain assets. In the global environment, this could involve moving production offshore but retaining ownership and close control over the outsourced operation. This is a very common strategy employed by many global firms such as Procter & Gamble and GE. Vertical integration—that is, executing functions in-house—may increase control by reducing the risks of supply or demand failures in the supply chain but changes the variable costs into fixed costs. Hence, there is a strong incentive for an organization to satisfy high-probability demand internally and pass on the low-probability demand to other firms. This is called partial or tapered integration, which leads to full utilization of the equipment of the firm and allows the supplier to absorb the risks. Another mechanism to achieve control is to design flexible contracts with clauses that account for possible changes in the environment; associated risks also act as a control mechanism (Macneil 1978). Contracts with suppliers based in the home country, but having manufacturing facilities in low-cost countries, provide the benefit of low cost with better access to legal recourse.

Transferring or Sharing Risk

The transfer or sharing of risks in a supply chain can be achieved through outsourcing, offshoring, or contracting. Outsourcing in supply chains can take the form of domestic sourcing of services and products. In the context of global supply chain management, the term *offshoring* more effectively conveys the idea of sourcing across borders. Outsourcing or offshoring entails a transfer of risk by paying a premium to suppliers to absorb the risks in supply fluctuations. The collective risk of offshoring multiple pieces in the supply chain should be assessed against control.

International factoring, a form of offshoring treasury services, is used mainly by exporters to take care of cash flow concerns and concentrate on core activities such as design, manufacturing, and sales. Factors help exporters offer favorable buying terms by providing services such as collection and credit protection. Hence, exporters do not need to use expensive financial instruments such as letters of credit and are protected against payment delays and foreign exchange risks. The management of cash and working capital becomes exponentially more complex in a global environment. Firms need to consider the entire working capital and cash flow picture. When inventory increases, perhaps payment terms can be extended and payables can offset all or part of the increase.

If a company sells products in multiple countries and is susceptible to high fore-cast errors, a portfolio of contracts can be used to induce retailers with different levels of risk aversion to select unique contracts. In this strategy, a variety of contracts are offered to counter the inefficiencies created by the risk aversion of the retailers. For example, a manufacturer may offer discounted advance purchase contracts for quantities ordered in advance of the selling season and a regularly priced contract for replenishment during the selling season. Depending on the level of risk aversion, different retailers may choose quantities for the two prices. Assuming a normal distribution of risk aversion, the risk is transferred from the manufacturer to multiple members of the supply chain.

Security

Current technological research on sensors capable of identifying nuclear, chemical, and biological elements may help in identification of at-risk shipments. The ability to sort out what is moving, identify unusual or suspicious elements and concentrate on them, and deal with the rest of the movements through a sampling-based process may be a viable strategy. Efforts such as the Container Security Initiative, the Customs Trade Partnership Against Terrorism, and the overarching Operation Safe Commerce initiative provide directions that in the long term will enhance the security of global commerce.

Step 4: Supply Chain Risk Management Strategy Implementation

Adoption of a set of strategies for risk management requires certain fundamental structural and procedural changes in sync with the trends of globalization and increasingly customized product offerings. With customers and suppliers spread across the world, firms are forever expanding, consolidating, and experimenting with different configurations of upstream and downstream supply chain members. An increasing number of firms are offering customized products to customers spread out in different geographical locations. These trends, coupled with the dynamic international political, legal, and economic environments, give rise to complexity in global supply chains.

To manage the complexity of global supply chains, managers use four levers—flexibility, organizational learning, information systems, and performance metrics.

Flexibility is the ability to change or react with little penalty in time, effort, cost, or performance. Furthermore, in dynamic markets, a firm gains competitive advantage if it can devise ways to exercise its options faster than its competitors. Flexibility must be a key component of any global supply chain system configuration.

Firms are achieving flexibility in supply chains by procuring or manufacturing the same products from several regions of the world, standardizing product components and processes, reducing average cycle times and variations, employing postponement strategies, and embedding flexibility in the design of the product itself. In sum, supply chain flexibility provides for an inherent capacity to respond to emerging circumstances that cannot be fully anticipated in the planning cycle (Welch and Welch 1996).

The second lever is organizational learning. Organizational learning that promotes an ongoing stream of dialogue and inquiry, analyzing mistakes, seeking feedback, communicating, and questioning may be extremely valuable in the risk identification and assessment steps of the risk management process. Furthermore, the corporate organizational structure must have the capability to transfer knowledge and the skills required to succeed on a global basis to all national operations. It has been observed that the secret of the Toyota production system lies as much in the techniques as in the learning capacity of the organization, which is focused on continuous experimentation and improvement.

Information technology is critical to the implementation of all risk management strategies and for effective performance measurement. The process of risk management—from identifying risks, through selecting appropriate risk management strategies, and making necessary structural changes in the supply chain—is an information-intensive procedure. The challenge is to evaluate data and filter in the most important information. Unfortunately, global processes operate so differently that domestic firms have found that they need entirely new systems to support their international endeavors.

One dimension of the company culture—the performance metrics or the reward system—stands out as the most important contextual factor that affects several aspects of the risk management process, particularly the inclination of managers to look at risks proactively. Often, analyses are carried out without accounting for risk because of the reward system. If the incentive system is such that it rewards only those who achieve the objectives irrespective of giving due attention to risks, then the managers will focus only on the objectives. For instance, in a home appliance company, the major objectives are cutting costs, reducing inventory, and improving product availability. In this company, some senior managers perceive risk as something that slows down the process of achieving these objectives set up by the company. The following is an interesting quote from a former senior vice president for global outsourcing and supply chain management operations of a leading manufacturing firm with which many of the managers reading this chapter will empathize:

> They [company executives] probably figure, it's a low probability [event], probably won't happen and, frankly, my boss isn't asking me to look at it. So, why

should I be a hero and miss my objectives? Not too many people are willing to die for their company and, in effect, that's what you're really asking them to do, to really get in the risk. It [risk management] is the right thing to do but they aren't rewarded for doing it. Maybe that's at the heart of this, no one is compensated or incented in their day to day job to look at and evaluate the risks.

Step 5: Mitigating Supply Chain Risks

Even after devising risk management strategies, all the risk events cannot be covered. There may be risk events that have escaped identification. To address such risk events, it is important to plan for the unexpected. In some cases, contingency plans for risk events with unacceptable worst-case scenarios may be developed. For other risk events that cannot be identified a priori, speculation may identify several losses that may occur irrespective of what event causes them. For example, even though a company may not have historically seen any reason to use third-party transportation providers, it might be reasonable to have a backup service provider if delivery issues are critical. In another example, a company sourcing from overseas may plan for airfreight in case there are disturbances in using the low-cost waterways option. In these examples, the events that lead to the use of third-party transportation or airfreight may not be known, but the company can still plan for them. An approach used by some firms to speculate on losses is a war-gaming approach. Different scenarios are discussed and reactions planned. This provides a firm with a more mature decision-making process in facing any event, not only those anticipated.

Conclusions

It is critical that firms follow a disciplined process of risk management when significantly changing any aspect of their supply chains. Global supply chain decisions call for far more rigorous risk assessment and management than their domestic counterparts. Risks take many forms, including supply, demand, operations, and security risks. Each of the potential risks must be identified and profiled. This should be followed by an assessment and evaluation of the risks. Then, strategies must be developed for managing the most significant risks. Organizational levers of managing complexity, creating a learning organization, and effective use of information technology are key components in the development of risk management strategies. Finally, scenarios for mitigating risks, especially unforeseen risks, must be considered. This disciplined process often faces reluctance from managers who are usually compensated on the basis of short-term results. This process is time-consuming but in the end pays off by ensuring the long-term survival and profitability of the firm.

All stakeholders have a right to expect that major supply chain changes will be undertaken only when a highly disciplined risk management process is followed. Indeed, management cannot avoid this responsibility without putting the entire firm in jeopardy. Conversely, organizations that develop world-class risk management practices can expect to achieve major advantage in the incredibly dynamic global environment of the future.

References

Chichilnisky, Graciela and Geoffrey Heal (1998), "Managing Unknown Risks," *Journal of Portfolio Management,* 24 (4), 85–91.

Chiou, Jyh-Shen, Lei-Yu Wu, and Jason C. Hsu (2002), "The Adoption of Form Postponement Strategy in a Global Logistics System: The Case of Taiwanese Information Technology Industry," *Journal of Business Logistics,* 23 (1), 107–124.

Fisher, Marshall L. (1997), "What Is the Right Supply Chain for Your Product?" *Harvard Business Review,* 75 (2), 105–116.

Hallikas, Jukka, Veli-Matti Virolainen, and Veli-Matti Markku Tuominen (2002), "Risk Analysis and Assessment in Network Environments: A Dyadic Case Study," *International Journal of Production Economics,* 78 (1), 45–55.

Macneil, Ian R. (1978), "Contracts: Adjustment of Long-Term Economic Relations Under Classical, Neoclassical, and Relational Contract Law," *Northwestern University Law Review,* 72 (6), 854–905.

Mentzer, John T., ed. (2001), *Supply Chain Management.* Thousand Oaks, CA: Sage.

Ross, Sheldon M. (2003), *Introduction to Probability Models,* 8th ed. San Diego, CA: Elsevier.

Welch, Denice E. and Lawrence S. Welch (1996), "The Internationalization Process and Networks: A Strategic Management Perspective," *Journal of International Marketing,* 4 (3), 11–27.

Zsidisin, George A., Lisa M. Ellram, Joseph R. Carter, and Joseph L. Cavinato (2004), "An Analysis of Supply Risk Assessment Techniques," *International Journal of Physical Distribution & Logistics Management,* 34 (5), 397–413.

20

Interpretation Systems

Knowledge, Strategy, and Performance

G. Tomas M. Hult

David J. Ketchen, Jr.

S. Tamer Cavusgil

Roger J. Calantone

An evolving feature of modern competition is that rivalry is becoming less "firm versus firm" and more "supply chain versus supply chain" (Handfield and Nichols 2003; Ketchen and Guinipero 2004). Firms such as Wal-Mart, Toyota, and Dell have leveraged supply chain management skills into significant competitive advantages and strong performance, illustrating the importance of supply chain versus supply chain competition. A growing body of research suggests that information management is a key determinant of why some supply chains outperform others. Building on this research, our suggestion in this chapter is that a supply chain's ability to act as an interpretation system is strongly tied to its success or failure. Interpretation refers to the process of making sense of information that flows into and through a supply chain (Daft and Weick 1984). Simply put, chains that are able to manage information in ways that match their strategy

AUTHORS' NOTE: We appreciate the research assistance and support from the Council of Supply Chain Management Professionals, the Institute of Supply Management, and the Center for International Business Education and Research at Michigan State University. We are grateful for input provided by John T. Mentzer, Phil Carter, David J. Closs, and Charles C. Snow.

should prosper, whereas chains that fail to manage information in ways that match their strategy should struggle.

Our research is grounded in three prominent perspectives. The basic tenets of the resource-based view (RBV) (e.g., Barney 1991; Wernerfelt 1984) are used to identify knowledge elements that may serve as value creation vehicles within supply chains. Strategic choice theory (e.g., Miles and Snow 1978) is used to study knowledge elements within five supply chain strategies: prospectors, analyzers, low-cost defenders, differentiated defenders, and reactors. Configurational inquiry (e.g., Doty, Glick, and Huber 1993) is used as the theoretical foundation for the profile deviation method to examine how various types of supply chains leverage knowledge resources into superior performance.

Recent Research on Information Management Within Supply Chains

The dawn of the new century has seen the emergence of inquiry examining how supply chains manage information and how this management affects supply chain outcomes. This research on "strategic supply chain management" seeks to understand not just how supply chains move goods, but also how supply chain activities contribute to important strategic outcomes. In an initial effort, Hult, Ketchen, and Nichols (2002) shed light on learning's role in supply chains. As shown in Figure 20.1, these authors portrayed learning as one of three tangible indicators (along with innovativeness and entrepreneurship) that collectively reveal an intangible resource. This resource, cultural competitiveness, is defined as the "degree to which chains are predisposed to detect and fill gaps between what the market desires and what is currently offered" (p. 577). The extent to which chains possess cultural competitiveness in turn is expected to improve cycle time, a key measure of supply chain performance.

Data from 58 supply chains centered in one Fortune 500 firm demonstrated that learning is a significant indicator of cultural competitiveness, which in turn explains a significant portion of the variance in cycle time across different supply chains. From an information management perspective, these findings indicate that building knowledge through learning helps shape supply chain outcomes. However, the effect is not direct but rather is part of a complex milieu of relations, consistent with the RBV. Thus, understanding supply chains' information management activities is a necessary but not sufficient condition for diagnosing why some supply chains outperform others.

Hult et al. (2002) also focus on information management within supply chains from a resource-based perspective. Four orientations (team, systems, learning, and memory) are viewed as tangible indicators of "learning as an intangible resource that is deeply embedded within the fabric of the supply management system" (p. 582). In turn, learning is expected to positively influence a variety of outcomes, including relationship commitment, customer orientation, cycle time, and overall performance. The results revealed that the strategic resource (learning) had significant and positive links with relationship commitment, customer orientation,

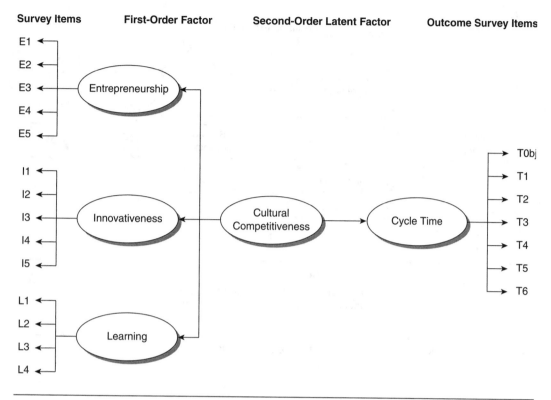

Figure 20.1   Cultural Competitiveness and Cycle Time in Supply Chains

cycle time, and overall performance but the individual orientations had very inconsistent relations with the outcomes. The overall conclusions indicate that information management activities influence an array of outcomes and that such effects are a function of complex rather than linear relations.

In recognition of the complexity surrounding the information management process, Hult, Ketchen, and Slater (2004) developed and tested a more elaborate model linking the overall knowledge development process within supply chains to cycle time. As shown in Figure 20.2, this process consists of memory and three elements of information processing: knowledge acquisition activities, information distribution activities, and shared meaning. As in the two previous studies, the RBV provided some of the conceptual basis for the study. To advance understanding, however, grounding was also provided by the knowledge-based view, the organizational learning literature, and information processing theory.

The results suggested that the four knowledge elements had varied relations with cycle time. Achieved memory had only indirect effects, through its influence on knowledge acquisition activities. Knowledge acquisition activities had a direct effect on cycle time and an indirect effect through their influence on information distribution activities. Information distribution activities had a direct, negative effect on cycle time and an indirect effect through their influence on shared meaning. Finally, shared meaning had a direct link with cycle time. Overall, this study advanced research on information management within supply chains by capturing a greater

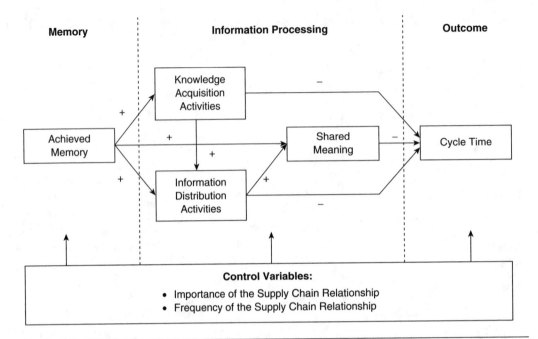

Figure 20.2   The Knowledge Development Process and Cycle Time in Supply Chains

array of dimensions than previous studies and by shedding light on the multifaceted ways in which different knowledge elements fit together to shape outcomes.

The Next Step: Fitting Supply Chain Knowledge and Strategy

Although the above studies all represent important steps, what is missing from the literature to date is attention to the role of strategy. Supply chain strategies differ, and it seems likely that these differences influence what approach should be taken to information management to enhance performance. As such, our research question is how knowledge elements and strategies are related to important supply chain outcomes. In addressing this question, we fill a gap in the literature by providing empirical support for theorized relations among knowledge elements, supply chain strategy, and performance. We also take a methodological step beyond previous studies. Hult et al. (2002, 2004) used one firm's supply chains. In contrast, we draw on supply chains centered in many different firms. We also take a step beyond Hult et al. (2002, 2004) by examining multiple outcomes. Perhaps more important, we also expand on the studies of Hult and colleagues by accounting for the role of supply chain strategy and by incorporating a broader set of knowledge elements.

One approach to understanding how concepts (such as knowledge, strategy, and performance) relate to each other is to search for linear relationships that apply across all members of a sample. A key disadvantage of this approach is that important relationships may be masked by data aggregation (Miller 1987). For example, if emphasizing knowledge intensity enhances performance for some supply chains and attenuates performance for others, these effects may "cancel out" in an aggregate analysis. As an alternative, we assess whether an array of supply chains' knowledge elements are organized to achieve the desired performance via a focus on configurations—the simultaneous consideration of multiple interwoven factors. In our study, a configuration refers to a constellation of knowledge resources and supply chain strategy. Configurational research contends that the closer a supply chain matches an ideal makeup, the better its performance. More broadly, a focus on such configurations avoids the aggregation problem identified by Miller (1987).

When the fit among multiple knowledge elements and strategy types is considered simultaneously and the impact on performance is assessed, as in our study, configuration should be conceptualized and measured via profile deviation analysis (Venkatraman 1990). This analysis assesses the fit between the knowledge elements and strategy as the degree to which the knowledge elements of a supply chain differ from those of an "ideal" profile for implementing a specific strategy. Below, we describe the conceptual background for the components of the profiles (knowledge elements and strategy), as well as our outcomes of interest.

Knowledge Elements

We used the RBV as a guide to selecting knowledge elements that are particularly important in the formation of strategic resources in supply chains. The RBV contends that a firm's resources shape performance. Resources are defined as physical assets, intangible assets, and organizational capabilities that are tied semipermanently to the firm (Wernerfelt 1984). Extending RBV logic to the supply chain context implies that chains that possess certain resources have competitive advantages over chains lacking such resources. Based on the RBV, we propose that knowledge can contribute to the emergence of an intangible strategic resource in supply chains.

Based on extant literature, eight knowledge elements can be delineated as critical in the formation of ideal profiles. Memory is defined as the level of knowledge, experience, and familiarity achieved regarding supply chain operations; it is the stored representation of the learning on which supply chain members can base their actions. Tacitness of knowledge is the degree of codifiability and teachability of the wisdom that exists in the supply chain. Accessibility of knowledge is the degree to which supply chain wisdom is easily available. Quality of knowledge refers to the relevance, accuracy, reliability, and timeliness of wisdom provided in the supply chain. Knowledge use refers to the application of wisdom to solve a particular supply chain problem or make a particular supply chain decision. Knowledge intensity is the extent to which a supply chain depends on the wisdom inherent in its operations as a source of competitive advantage. In our study, responsiveness is the tendency to act as a function of the knowledge that has been generated and disseminated in the supply chain. Learning capacity is the extent to which a supply chain continually increases its degree of usable knowledge to create a source of competitive advantage. Drawing on the RBV, our contention is that the fit between these knowledge elements and strategy exhibits the characteristics of being valuable, rare, and inimitable (Barney 1991).

Strategy Types

On the basis of Miles and Snow's (1978) seminal work, Walker and Ruekert (1987) propose five distinct strategic types centered on product-market strategy choices. Prospectors "take on an aggressive new product-market position within broadly defined markets and tend to be industry pioneers in the creation and development of new technologies" (Walker and Ruekert 1987, p. 16). As such, prospectors are frequently the first to adopt new supply chain concepts. They do not hesitate to use new supply chain tools when the opportunity arises, and they concentrate on using tools that push performance boundaries. Their aim is to always have the most innovative supply chain practices, whether based on substantial performance improvement or cost reduction. Analyzers "represent an intermediate form of strategy . . . [they] maintain a secure market position within a core market . . . but also seek new market positions" (Walker and Ruekert 1987, p. 16). As such, analyzers are seldom the first to implement new supply chain practices. However, by monitoring others' supply chain activities, they can be early followers using a "second but better" approach.

Miles and Snow's (1978) defender category includes both competitors that strive to maintain their positions in the marketplace via low costs and those that protect positions by providing high product quality or superior service. Successful implementation of these different defender strategies is likely to require very different knowledge processes and programs. Low-cost defenders attempt to maintain a relatively stable domain by aggressively protecting their niches, normally by avoiding disruptive change. They are rarely at the forefront of supply chain development. Instead, they focus on finding ways to lower the cost of their existing supply chain practices. As a main strategic focus, differentiated defenders attempt to maintain a relatively stable domain by aggressively protecting their niches, which are often peculiar to specialized customer needs. Like low-cost defenders, they are rarely at the forefront of supply chain development. Instead, they focus on exploiting the elements they do particularly well. The cost of their practices is typically higher than the industry average. Finally, reactors do not have a consistent strategy. Reactors primarily act in response to competitive or other short-term supply chain pressures.

Considering knowledge and strategy together, our first expectation in analyzing our data was that different arrays of knowledge elements are emphasized under different strategies. Our second expectation was that the closer a supply chain matched its ideal profile of knowledge elements given its strategy, the better the supply chain would perform.

Identification of Ideal Profiles

Following a series of pretests, we sent surveys on supply chain practices and strategy to supply chain professionals in 7,000 organizations (4,000 members of the

Council of Supply Chain Management Professionals and 3,000 members of the Institute of Supply Management). A total of 545 from the first group responded for an effective response rate of 16.9% (781 surveys were nondeliverable). A total of 368 from the second group responded for an effective response rate of 15.6% (642 were nondeliverable). Thus, our data come from 913 supply chains. A series of diagnostic tests suggested there was no evidence of nonresponse bias.

Measures

Strategy Types. We used previous work by Doty et al. (1993), Slater and Olson (2000), and Zajac and Shortell (1989) to operationalize strategy types via the paragraph descriptor approach. The appendix includes these paragraphs. Among our respondents, 162 (17.7%) characterized their supply chain strategy as prospector, 316 (34.6%) as analyzer, 288 (31.5%) as low-cost defender, 72 (7.9%) as differentiated defender, and 75 (8.2%) as reactor.

Knowledge Measures. As shown in the appendix, established scales were the basis for our measures of memory, tacitness of knowledge, accessibility of knowledge, quality of knowledge, knowledge use, knowledge intensity, and responsiveness. A new scale was developed to measure learning capacity, based on work by Grant (1996) and Hurley and Hult (1998).

Performance. Assessment of supply chain outcomes was grounded in the competitive priorities literature. According to this literature, four competitive priorities are directly tied to order fulfillment processes in supply: speed, quality, cost, and flexibility. The appendix lists the scales we used to assess these dimensions.

Analysis

Table 20.1a reports the correlations among the study variables. Table 20.1b reports the means, standard deviations, average variances extracted, composite reliabilities (and coefficient alphas), factor loadings, and fit indices. Prior to hypothesis testing, a six-step approach was used to assess the measures across the two samples and across the five strategy types. These steps included (1) conducting exploratory factor analyses in each of the logistics and supply management samples, (2) testing the robustness of each item across the samples, (3) testing the robustness of each item across the five strategy types, (4) conducting a confirmatory factor analysis using the full sample ($n = 913$), (5) assessing the reliability and validity of the scales, and (6) testing to ensure that common method bias does not inhibit the hypothesis testing. All these steps provided results that supported the validity of our design.

Next, we identified ideal supply chain profiles that could be used as the benchmark against which the fit of all members of a strategy type could be examined (e.g., Doty et al. 1993; Vorhies and Morgan 2003). To identify the ideal profiles, we examined the frequencies of the performance variables (speed, quality, cost, flexibility, and the combined effect of these four variables) and selected a cutoff within

Table 20.1a Correlations (*n* = 913)

	1	2	3	4	5	6	7	8	9	10	11	12	13
1. Memory													
2. Tacitness of knowledge	.44												
3. Accessibility of knowledge	.62	.52											
4. Quality of knowledge	.62	.48	.75										
5. Knowledge use	.48	.41	.53	.63									
6. Knowledge intensity	.66	.53	.63	.73	.58								
7. Responsiveness	.31	.36	.38	.41	.38	.35							
8. Learning capacity	.42	.43	.43	.48	.42	.50	.35						
9. Speed	.29	.36	.38	.41	.33	.39	.35	.36					
10. Quality	.35	.36	.37	.44	.38	.44	.42	.40	.67				
11. Cost	.35	.39	.41	.48	.35	.45	.35	.37	.62	.66			
12. Flexibility	.33	.39	.40	.44	.42	.44	.38	.42	.63	.66	.63		
13. Size (employees)	.01	.03	−.05	−.05	.01	.00	−.04	−.04	−.07	−.02	−.05	−.04	
14. Age (years)	−.09	−.05	−.04	−.04	−.00	−.12	−.03	−.07	−.10	.01	−.08	−.09	.23

NOTE: All correlations above .09 are significant at the $p < .05$ level.

Table 20.1b Basic Statistics and Confirmatory Factor Analysis Results (*n* = 913)

	Mean	Standard Deviation	Variance Extracted (%)	Composite Reliability	Coefficient Alpha	Range of Factor Loadings
Memory	5.22	1.25	74.5	.92	.90	.64 to .94
Tacitness of knowledge	3.65	1.28	59.3	.85	.83	.65 to .89
Accessibility of knowledge	4.77	1.38	82.3	.93	.92	.88 to .95
Quality of knowledge	4.93	1.20	78.0	.95	.94	.81 to .93
Knowledge use	5.27	1.02	65.4	.93	.89	.71 to .85
Knowledge intensity	4.58	1.52	82.7	.93	.94	.85 to .94
Responsiveness	5.51	1.04	79.5	.88	.84	.80 to .97
Learning capacity	4.64	1.35	80.3	.92	.91	.83 to .94
Speed	4.78	1.11	55.3	.78	.78	.51 to .84
Quality	4.80	1.13	66.0	.85	.86	.65 to .90
Cost	4.40	1.14	62.0	.83	.83	.58 to .90
Flexibility	4.52	1.16	69.0	.87	.88	.65 to .92

Fit Statistics

$\chi^2 = 6,141.2$ — RNI (relative noncentrality index) = .96

Degrees of freedom = 713 — CFI (comparative fit index) = .96

DELTA = 2.96 — TLI (Tucker-Lewis index) = .96

RMSEA (root mean square error of approximation) = .09

the top 10% of the performers, where a significant drop-off in performance was apparent. This resulted in a range of 4 to 17 cases included in each ideal profile. To examine whether supply chains' relative distance to an ideal profile was tied to performance, we first calculated the mean scores of the top performers for each segment (i.e., for each strategic type and performance variable) on the eight knowledge elements to form the ideal profiles (Vorhies and Morgan 2003). For the remaining cases, we calculated the Euclidean distance (ED) from the ideal profile for its supply chain strategy type across the eight knowledge elements (e.g., Drazin and Van de Ven 1985). The following formula was used:

$$ED = \sqrt{\sum_{j}^{N}(X_{sj} - \overline{X}_{ij})^2}$$

where X_{sj} is the score for a supply chain case on the jth element, $\overline{X}_{ij}$ is the mean for the ideal supply chain profile along the jth element, and j is the number of knowledge elements (i.e., 1, 2, 3, . . . , 8). These calculations resulted in a profile deviation score that represents the degree to which a supply chain's profile is similar to that of the ideal profile for each strategic type. Finally, the profile deviation score was regressed, using the ordinary least squares (OLS) method, on each of the performance variables. We also included firm size and age, indicated by the natural logarithm of the number of employees and years, respectively, as control variables.

Findings

Table 20.2 summarizes the ideal knowledge profiles based on strategy types that emerged from our analyses. As shown, different strategies call for emphasis of different knowledge elements. Table 20.3 reports the OLS regression results for the knowledge-based supply chain profile fit with strategic type and its effect on performance. As shown in Table 20.3, deviation from a supply chain's ideal knowledge profile was associated with decreased performance. Regarding prospectors, for example, deviation from the ideal profile had a significant, negative effect on speed ($\beta = -.47$), quality ($\beta = -.42$), cost ($\beta = -.38$), and flexibility ($\beta = -.35$). For analyzers and low-cost defenders, these relationships were also significant. For differentiated defenders, the results were significant for cost and flexibility, but the regression equation for the quality model was insignificant (F value = 1.34),

Table 20.2   The Ideal Profiles: Key Knowledge Elements Within the Strategic Types

	Prospectors	Analyzers	Low-Cost Defenders	Differentiated Defenders	Reactors
Memory	X		X		
Tacitness of knowledge					
Accessibility of knowledge	X				
Quality of knowledge	X			X	
Knowledge use		X	X		
Knowledge intensity	X				
Responsiveness	X	X	X	X	
Learning capability					

Table 20.3   Knowledge-Based Supply Chain Profile Fit With Strategic Type and Performance: Standardized Regression Results

	Competitive Priority (Criterion Variable)				
Predictor Variables	Speed	Quality	Cost	Flexibility	Σ (S,Q,C,F)[a]
Prospectors (n = 162)					
KB-SC Profile Deviation[b]	−.47***	−.42***	−.38***	−.35***	−.40***
Size (log)	.10	.08	.00	.01	.08
Age (log)	−.11	.08	−.02	.06	−.03
r^2	.23	.20	.15	.13	.14
F value	7.27***	6.33***	4.05***	3.71**	4.74***
Analyzers (n = 316)					
KB-SC profile deviation	−.32***	−.32***	−.27***	−.36***	−.37***
Size (log)	−.11	−.03	−.11	−.09	−.13
Age (log)	.17*	.12	.17*	.15*	.21**
r^2	.14	.12	.10	.16	.16
F value	7.16***	6.14***	5.18***	8.69***	9.31***
Low-Cost Defenders (n = 288)					
KB-SC profile deviation	−.20**	−.38***	−.40***	−.27***	−.45***
Size (log)	−.05	−.10	.06	.02	−.02
Age (log)	−.17*	−.12	−.22**	−.21**	−.21**
r^2	.06	.16	.17	.09	.22
F value	2.31*	7.20***	7.35***	3.52**	10.51***
Differentiated Defenders (n = 72)					
KB-SC profile deviation	−.24	−.35*	−.40**	−.63***	−.53***
Size (log)	.31*	.06	.15	−.09	.10
Age (log)	−.30	−.02	−.21	.08	−.17
r^2	.21	.13	.25	.38	.35
F value	2.58*	1.34	2.81*	5.92***	4.50**
Reactors (n = 75)					
KB-SC profile deviation	−.31*	−.40***	−.33*	−.11	−.42**
Size (log)	−.17	−.17	−.23	−.50***	−.29*
Age (log)	.01	.17	−.07	−.08	.02
r^2	.13	.21	.18	.25	.28
F value	1.86	3.33***	2.65*	4.06**	4.55***

a. Σ (S,Q,C,F) = summated scale of $\frac{1}{4}$ (speed + quality + cost + flexibility).

b. KB-SC profile deviation = knowledge-based supply chain profile deviation.

*$p < .10$; **$p < .05$; ***$p < .01$.

whereas deviation from the ideal profile was insignificant in the speed model. For reactors, the results regarding profile deviation and quality and cost were significant, but the regression equation for the speed model was insignificant (F value = 1.86). Finally, and perhaps most important, the results involving the summated outcomes were significant across all five groups: prospectors ($\beta = -.40$), analyzers

($\beta = -.37$), low-cost defenders ($\beta = -.45$), differentiated defenders ($\beta = -.53$), and reactors ($\beta = -.42$). For all the models, the variance inflation factors were lower than 1.30, indicating that multicollinearity did not inhibit the analysis.

Implications

Insights can be gleaned by considering both the vertical and the horizontal patterns revealed in Table 20.2. The vertical patterns reveal which knowledge elements matter most within each strategy. For four of the strategies, between zero and three elements were vital. For prospectors, however, five of the eight elements were keys to success. High-performing prospectors effectively managed memory, accessibility of knowledge, quality of knowledge, knowledge intensity, and responsiveness. In Miles and Snow's (1978) description of their typology, analyzers were portrayed as the most difficult firms to manage because they confronted the dual challenges of maintaining a stable core of products and seeking new market opportunities. Our findings suggest that in the supply chain context, prospectors may be the most difficult type to orchestrate. Managers of these supply chains must master more than twice as many knowledge elements as their counterparts in charge of analyzers, as well as more than both kinds of defenders. If our findings hold in future research for other aspects of the supply chain beyond knowledge, this represents an important step forward in understanding how the Miles and Snow typology applies to the supply chain context.

Successful analyzers in our sample were those that mastered knowledge use and responsiveness. Knowledge use is the application of wisdom to solve problems and make decisions (Deshpandé and Zaltman 1982). Interestingly, knowledge use was one of the few knowledge elements that were not vital to prospectors. One interpretation of these results is that the dual challenge faced by analyzer supply chains forces their managers to adopt a problem-solving orientation that draws extensively on knowledge embedded in the chain. In other words, whereas prospectors can rely on creativity and innovation, balancing the need for both stability and innovation requires analyzers to make hard choices grounded in existing wisdom.

Successful low-cost defenders relied on the same two knowledge elements as analyzers (knowledge use and responsiveness), but memory was also vital for them. Memory is the stored representation of the learning on which supply chain members can base their actions (Moorman and Miner 1997). Taken together, the three knowledge elements needed by low-cost defenders are very consistent with the emphasis on "efficiency" that Miles and Snow ascribed to defenders. When facing an issue, low-cost defender supply chains must find knowledge efficiently. Tapping existing knowledge (memory) is perhaps the most efficient option. Indeed, time-tested and fine-tuned practices are likely to be cost savers. This knowledge must be not merely elicited but also capitalized on in decision making (knowledge use) and ultimately put into action (responsiveness).

Like the three other viable types, the differentiated defenders that prospered relied heavily on responsiveness. However, this type of supply chain was alone in its emphasis on the quality of knowledge. We defined the quality of knowledge as the relevance, accuracy, reliability, and timeliness of wisdom provided in the supply chain (Low and Mohr 2001). Differentiated defenders walk a metaphorical tight-rope in that they try to protect a niche through aggression and specialization rather than the more traditional cost containment. In particular, such chains must make fast and sometimes dramatic adjustments as they attempt to keep their customers (Slater and Narver 1995). Given this need, it appears that the wisdom that forms the basis of decisions must be relevant, accurate, reliable, and timely. As noted previously, successful prospectors also need high-quality knowledge. Thus, there appears to be a consistent link between the aggressiveness of supply chain strategy and the need to have quality knowledge to support that aggression.

The horizontal patterns within Table 20.2 highlight the importance of certain knowledge elements across different ideal profiles. The most striking element here is that responsiveness was important to all four viable types (prospectors, analyzers, low-cost defenders, and differentiated defenders). Responsiveness was defined as the tendency to act as a function of the knowledge generated and disseminated with the supply chain (cf. Kohli, Jaworski, and Kumar 1993). The most direct implication of responsiveness playing a prominent role for all four types is straightforward—supply chains, regardless of their underlying strategy, are more successful to the extent that knowledge guides action. Viewed more broadly, however, a more interesting implication arises. Much of the empirical work that examines the RBV links resources (such as knowledge) directly to outcomes (e.g., Miller and Shamsie 1996). Our findings related to responsiveness indicate that models directly linking resources and outcomes create a "black box" problem. At the risk of sounding glib, customers do not send checks to a firm because the firm owns certain resources. Instead, the value of the resources emerges only when coupled with actions that capitalize on the resources (Sirmon, Hitt, and Ireland, in press), such as responsiveness.

In contrast to the viable strategies, responsiveness was not tightly linked to any ideal profile for reactors. This is a potentially important finding because most studies that build on the Miles and Snow typology ignore reactors. As a result, little is known about this group, including whether its members share some difficulties or whether *reactor* is simply a residual label that refers to all dysfunctional strategies. Our findings seem to support Miles and Snow's conceptualization of reactors as a distinct group in that our reactors were much less responsive than other supply chains (an average of below 5 out of 7 along the summated performance metric vs. 6 or above for the other groups—see Table 20.2). Whereas responsiveness seemed to be an imperative within all four viable supply chain configurations in our study, a consistent failure to take action to meet customers' needs appears to be the leading cause of being a reactor.

A second insight arising from the horizontal elements within Table 20.2 is that beyond their shared emphasis on responsiveness, the two types of defenders differed in terms of which knowledge elements were key. For low-cost defenders, memory and knowledge use were critical, whereas for differentiated defenders, quality of knowledge was vital. This has implications for the constitution of the defender type, which has been a source of disagreement between the management and marketing fields. Management research generally interprets Miles and Snow's original description of defenders as a fairly monolithic set of firms that carve out and protect niches through cost containment and modest innovations. Marketing research tends to rely on Walker and Ruekert's (1987) depiction of two distinct groups of defenders (cf. Slater and Olson 2000). Adherents of this approach build on assertions by Miles and Snow (1978) that there are two different ways to defend a niche.

If our two sets of defenders emphasized the same knowledge elements to be successful, this would lend credence to the notion that defenders are monolithic. Instead, our findings support Walker and Ruekert's interpretation of defenders, at least in the supply chain context. Viewed broadly, our results imply the need to reassess whether there is one type of defender or two, a notion supported by Slater and Olson's (2000) work on sales force management. This is an important question because the Miles and Snow typology continues to have a profound effect on both theory and practice (Ghoshal 2003; Hambrick 2003).

In examining the possibility that the closer a supply chain matches an ideal profile of knowledge elements and strategy, the better its performance, we sought to add value beyond extant research. Two recent articles considered the role of knowledge (Hult et al. 2004) and learning (Hult et al. 2002) in shaping the speed of supply chains centered in single organizations. Our examination takes steps forward by (1) including multiple performance dimensions, (2) tapping multiple organizations, (3) incorporating the concept of strategy, and (4) including a broader array of knowledge elements.

As shown in Table 20.3, the results were supportive of our prediction. We tested 25 relevant equations (five strategic types × five outcomes). In 23 of these equations, deviation from an ideal profile was negatively and significantly related to the outcome scrutinized. For three of the strategic types (prospectors, analyzers, and low-cost defenders), the equations for all five outcomes were significant and deviation from an ideal profile was negatively and significantly related to all outcomes. Thus, our level of confidence that knowledge and strategy are linked to supply chain outcomes is strongest for these three types. The results related to differentiated defenders and reactors were less consistent. In these cases, three out of five equations were both significant overall and included a significant and negative effect for profile deviation.

Of the five outcome measures we considered, the summated scale is the most comprehensive in that it incorporates the other four. Interestingly, the strongest results related to the summated scale of outcomes were associated with the two strategic types that had inconsistent findings across outcomes. The equation for differentiated defenders had an r^2 of .35, and reactors' r^2 was .28. The r^2 values for the other three types ranged between .14 and .22. Our interpretation of this pattern of results is that both the consistency and the potency of relations should be considered. Sticking close to an ideal profile is consistently beneficial to prospectors, analyzers, and low-cost defenders. Thus, managers of these supply chains can count on gains from approaching the ideal profile regardless of the outcome of interest. In some ways, however, differentiated defenders can benefit the most by approaching an ideal, especially in terms of flexibility (see Table 20.3). The results offer a similar conclusion about reactors; however, no clear ideal profile of reactors emerged.

Thus, for reactors, achieving strong outcomes may be a function of luck rather than skill.

Conclusions

Supply chains are an increasingly prominent element of organizational activity. Indeed, some authors have suggested that the main battles of modern competition are "supply chain versus supply chain" rather than "firm versus firm." Just as Daft and Weick's (1984) observation that organizations are interpretation systems inspired new ways of thinking about firms, we believe there are substantial benefits to augmenting the traditional view of supply chains as systems for moving goods. Indeed, our results suggest that managers can benefit from viewing supply chains as interpretation systems. Specifically, managers need to recognize that creating and maintaining fit across knowledge elements and strategy can help ensure supply chain success.

Appendix

Measures[1]

Strategy Types (based on work by Miles and Snow 1978 and Walker and Ruekert 1987; descriptions adapted from Doty et al. 1993 and Slater and Olson 2000). The word *logistics* in the statements below was replaced with *supply management* in the supply management survey.

This section of the survey deals with logistics strategies that an organization can adopt. Most organizations use a blend of strategies to be successful. Please read each of the short descriptions below. Then indicate which description seems to be the closest to your organization's logistics practices.

Prospector

These organizations are frequently the first to adopt new logistics concepts. They do not hesitate to use new logistics tools where there appears to be an opportunity. These organizations concentrate on logistics tools that push performance boundaries. Their proposition is to always have the most innovative logistics practices, whether based on substantial performance improvement or cost reduction.

Analyzer

These organizations are seldom first to implement new logistics practices or to adopt new logistics tools. However, by monitoring logistics activity, they can be early followers with a better logistics strategy, increased user benefits, or lower total costs.

Low-Cost Defender

These organizations attempt to maintain a relatively stable domain by aggressively protecting their logistics practices. They rarely are at the forefront of logistics development. Instead, they focus on implementing their current logistics activities as efficiently as possible. These organizations generally focus on lowering the cost of their existing logistics practices.

Differentiated Defender

These organizations attempt to maintain a relatively stable domain by aggressively protecting their logistics practices. They rarely are at the forefront of logistics development. Instead, they focus on implementing their current logistics activities by taking advantage of elements that they do particularly well. The cost of their logistics practices is typically higher than the industry average.

Reactor

These organizations do not seem to have a consistent logistics strategy. They primarily act in response to competitive or other logistics pressures in the short term.

Memory (adapted from Moorman and Miner 1997)

This section of the survey deals with your organizational memory with respect to logistics activities. Organizational memory refers to the achieved level of general knowledge, experience, and familiarity with logistics operations:

- We have a great deal of knowledge about logistics.
- We have a great deal of experience with logistics.
- We have a great deal of familiarity with logistics.
- We have invested a great deal of research and development related to logistics.

Tacitness of Knowledge (items 1–4 are adapted from Zander and Kogut 1995; item 5 is new, based on Simonin 1999)

This section of the survey deals with the inimitability (tacitness) of your organization's logistics knowledge. Tacitness of knowledge refers to the degree of codifiability and teachability of the knowledge that exists in the logistics function. The questions deal with the ease or toughness with which you would have to describe what you do to new employees.

- A useful manual describing our logistics activities can be written for new employees.
- We have extensive documentation describing our logistics activities for new employees.

- New personnel can easily learn our logistics activities by talking to skilled workers.[2]
- Training new logistics personnel is a quick and easy job.
- New personnel can easily identify the knowledge needed to perform our logistics activities.

Accessibility of Knowledge (based on O'Reilly 1982)

This section of the survey deals with the accessibility of logistics knowledge in your organization. Accessibility of knowledge refers to the degree to which knowledge that exists regarding logistics is easily available and obtainable. The questions deal with how the accessibility of knowledge affects your logistics activities.

- Knowledge that exists in our organization is readily available to assist in making our logistics decisions.
- Logistics knowledge contained in our organization is easily accessible when needed.
- On average, it is easy to obtain logistics knowledge from key people in this organization.

Quality of Knowledge (adapted from O'Reilly 1982)

This section of the survey deals with the quality of knowledge that your organization has with respect to logistics. Quality of knowledge refers to the relevance, accuracy, reliability, and timeliness of knowledge pertaining to logistics:

- The logistics knowledge we have is very accurate.
- The logistics knowledge we have is very reliable.
- The logistics knowledge we have is very relevant to our needs.
- The logistics knowledge we have is very specific to our needs.[2]
- The logistics knowledge we have is exactly what we need.
- The logistics knowledge we have is very useful.

Knowledge Use (adapted from Deshpandé and Zaltman 1982)

This section of the survey deals with your use of logistics knowledge. Knowledge use refers to the direct application of knowledge to solve a particular logistics problem or to make a particular logistics decision. The questions deal with your existing knowledge about logistics and how it affected your latest logistics activity:

- Our existing knowledge enriched the basic understanding of our latest logistics activity.
- Our latest logistics activity would have been very different if the existing knowledge had not been available.[3]
- Our existing knowledge reduced the uncertainty of our latest logistics activity.

- Our existing knowledge identified aspects of our latest logistics activity that would otherwise have gone unnoticed.
- We used our existing knowledge to make specific decisions for our latest logistics activity.
- Without our existing knowledge, our latest logistics decision would have been very different.

Knowledge Intensity (adapted from Autio, Sapienza, and Almeida 2000)

This section of the survey deals with the intensity of knowledge as it relates to logistics in your organization. Intensity of knowledge refers to the extent to which your logistics function depends on the knowledge inherent in its operations as a source of competitive advantage. The questions deal with the importance of up-to-date knowledge on logistics in your organization:

- We have a strong reputation for having cutting-edge knowledge about logistics.
- Knowledge intensity is a characteristic of our logistics practices.
- There is a strong knowledge component in our logistics practices.

Responsiveness (based on Kohli et al. 1993)

This section of the survey deals with your responsiveness to your customers' needs. Responsiveness refers to the product-specific action you take as a function of the knowledge that you have generated and disseminated in logistics operations:

- We respond effectively to changes in a competitor's product offerings.[2]
- We respond rapidly to changes in our customers' product needs.[2]
- We periodically review our products to ensure that they are in line with our customers' wants.[3]
- We rapidly attend to product complaints from our customers.
- When we find out that our customers are unhappy with a product, we take corrective action immediately.
- When we find out that our customers would like us to modify a product, we make a concerted effort to do so.[2]

Learning Capacity (new scale; item 1 is based on Hurley and Hult 1998; items 2–5 are adapted from Grant 1996)

This section of the survey has to do with "knowledge outcomes." As opposed to normal performance questions, these questions deal with a select set of knowledge-based performance issues. Knowledge outcomes refer to the extent to which the logistics function continually increases its degree of usable knowledge to create a source of competitive advantage.

- The number of logistics suggestions implemented in our organization is greater than last year.[2]
- The percentage of skilled logistics workers is greater than last year.[3]

- The number of logistics individuals learning new skills is greater than last year.
- The resources spent on learning have resulted in increased logistics productivity.
- Our learning activities have resulted in better logistics performance than last year.

Process Outcomes (Anderson, Cleveland, and Schroeder 1989; Boyer and Lewis 2002; Boyer and Pagell 2000; Hult et al. 2002; McKone, Schroeder, and Cua 2001; Ward et al. 1998; Youndt et al. 1996)

This section of the survey has to do with logistics outcomes. Based on current logistics practice, performance related to the order fulfillment process is typically assessed as a function of speed, quality, cost, and flexibility. The following questions address those issues as they relate to the order fulfillment process.

Speed

- The length of the order fulfillment process is getting shorter every time.
- We have seen an improvement in the cycle time of the order fulfillment process recently.
- We are satisfied with the speediness of the order fulfillment process.[4]
- Based on our knowledge of the order fulfillment process, we think it is short and efficient.
- The length of the order fulfillment process could not be much shorter than today.[4]

Quality

- The quality of the order fulfillment process is getting better every time.
- We have seen an improvement in the quality of the order fulfillment process recently.
- We are satisfied with the quality of the order fulfillment process.[4]
- Based on our knowledge of the order fulfillment process, we think it is of high quality.
- The quality of the order fulfillment process could not be much better than today.[4]

Cost

- The cost associated with the order fulfillment process is getting better every time.
- We have seen an improvement in the cost associated with the order fulfillment process recently.
- We are satisfied with the cost associated with the order fulfillment process.[4]

- Based on our knowledge of the order fulfillment process, we think it is cost-efficient.
- The cost associated with the order fulfillment process could not be much better than today.[4]

Flexibility

- The flexibility of the order fulfillment process is getting better every time.
- We have seen an improvement in the flexibility of the order fulfillment process recently.
- We are satisfied with the flexibility of the order fulfillment process.[4]
- Based on our knowledge of the order fulfillment process, we think it is flexible.
- The flexibility of the order fulfillment process could not be much better than today.[4]

Appendix Notes

1. All items used a 7-point Likert-type scale ranging from "strongly disagree" to "strongly agree." The word *logistics* was changed to *supply management* for the supply management sample (the term *supply management* was used instead of *purchasing* given that the sponsoring organization, which used to be named the National Association of Purchasing Management, recently changed its name to the Institute of Supply Management).

2. Item deleted after the item-level analysis across the logistics and supply management groups (i.e., an item was deleted if it was not robust across the logistics and supply management samples).

3. Item deleted after the item-level analysis across the five strategy types (i.e., an item was deleted if it was not robust across all five strategy types—prospectors, analyzers, low-cost defenders, differentiated defenders, and reactors).

4. Item deleted after the exploratory factor analysis.

References

Anderson, J. C., G. Cleveland, and R. G. Schroeder (1989), "Operations Strategy: A Literature Review," *Journal of Operations Management*, 8 (2), 133–158.

Autio, E., H. J. Sapienza, and J. G. Almeida (2000), "Effects of Age at Entry, Knowledge Intensity, and Imitability on International Growth," *Academy of Management Journal*, 43 (5), 909–924.

Barney, J. B. (1991), "Firm Resources and Sustained Competitive Advantage," *Journal of Management*, 17 (1), 99–120.

Boyer, K. K. and M. W. Lewis (2002), "Competitive Priorities: Investigating the Need for Trade-offs in Operations Strategy," *Production and Operations Management*, 11 (1), 9–20.

Boyer, K. K. and M. Pagell (2000), "Measurement Issues in Empirical Research: Improving Measures of Operations Strategy and Advanced Manufacturing Technology," *Journal of Operations Management*, 18 (3), 361–374.

Daft, R. L. and K. E. Weick (1984), "Toward a Model of Organizations as Interpretation Systems," *Academy of Management Review,* 9, 284–295.

Deshpandé, R. and G. Zaltman (1982), "Factors Affecting the Use of Market Research Information: A Path Analysis," *Journal of Marketing Research,* 19 (May), 14–31.

Doty, D. H., W. H. Glick, and G. P. Huber (1993), "Fit, Equifinality, and Organizational Effectiveness: A Test of Two Configurational Theories," *Academy of Management Journal,* 30 (December), 1196–1250.

Drazin, R. and A. H. Van de Ven (1985), "Alternative Forms of Fit in Contingency Theory," *Administrative Science Quarterly,* 30 (December), 514–539.

Ghoshal, S. (2003), "Miles and Snow: Enduring Insights for Managers," *Academy of Management Executive,* 17 (4), 109–114.

Grant, R. M. (1996), "Toward a Knowledge-Based Theory of the Firm," *Strategic Management Journal,* 17 (Winter Special Issue), 109–122.

Hambrick, D. C. (2003), "On the Staying Power of Defenders, Analyzers, and Prospectors," *Academy of Management Executive,* 17 (4), 115–118.

Handfield, R. B. and E. L. Nichols, Jr. (2003), *Supply Chain Redesign: Transforming Supply Chains Into Integrated Value Systems.* Upper Saddle River, NJ: Prentice Hall.

Hult, G. T. M., D. J. Ketchen, Jr., and E. L. Nichols, Jr. (2002), "An Examination of Cultural Competitiveness and Order Fulfillment Cycle Time Within Supply Chains," *Academy of Management Journal,* 45 (3), 577–586.

Hult, G. T. M., D. J. Ketchen, Jr., and S. F. Slater (2004), "Information Processing, Knowledge Development, and Strategic Supply Chain Performance," *Academy of Management Journal,* 47 (2), 241–253.

Hurley, R. F. and G. T. M. Hult (1998), "Innovation, Market Orientation, and Organizational Learning: An Integration and Empirical Examination," *Journal of Marketing,* 62 (July), 42–54.

Ketchen, D. J., Jr. and L. G. Guinipero (2004), "The Intersection of Strategic Management and Supply Chain Management," *Industrial Marketing Management,* 33 (1), 51–56.

Kohli, A. K., B. J. Jaworski, and A. Kumar (1993), "MARKOR: A Measure of Market Orientation," *Journal of Marketing Research,* 15 (November), 467–477.

Low, G. S. and J. J. Mohr (2001), "Factors Affecting the Use of Information in the Evaluation of Marketing Communication Productivity," *Journal of the Academy of Marketing Science,* 29 (1), 70–88.

McKone, K. E., R. G. Schroeder, and K. O. Cua (2001), "The Impact of Total Productive Maintenance Practices on Manufacturing Performance," *Journal of Operations Management,* 19 (1), 39–58.

Miles, R. E. and C. C. Snow (1978), *Organizational Strategy, Structure, and Process.* New York: McGraw-Hill.

Miller, D. (1987), "The Genesis of Configuration," *Academy of Management Review,* 12 (4), 686–701.

Miller, D. and J. Shamsie (1996), "The Resource-Based View of the Firm in Two Environments: The Hollywood Film Studios From 1936 to 1965," *Academy of Management Journal,* 39 (3), 519–543.

Moorman, C. and A. S. Miner (1997), "The Impact of Organizational Memory on New Product Performance and Creativity," *Journal of Marketing Research,* 34 (February), 91–106.

O'Reilly, C. A., III (1982), "Variations in Decision Makers' Use of Information Sources: The Impact of Quality and Accessibility of Information," *Academy of Management Journal,* 25 (4), 756–771.

Simonin, B. (1999), "Ambiguity and the Process of Knowledge Transfer in Strategic Alliances," *Strategic Management Journal,* 20 (7), 595–623.

Sirmon, D. G., M. A. Hitt, and R. D. Ireland (in press), "Managing Firm Resources in Dynamic Environments to Create Value: Looking Inside the Black Box," *Academy of Management Review.*

Slater, S. F. and J. C. Narver (1995), "Market Orientation and the Learning Organization," *Journal of Marketing,* 59 (July), 63–74.

Slater, S. F. and E. M. Olson (2000), "Strategy Type and Performance: The Influence of Sales Force Management," *Strategic Management Journal,* 21 (8), 813–830.

Venkatraman, N. (1990), "Performance Implications of Strategic Coalignment: A Methodological Perspective," *Journal of Management Studies,* 27 (1), 19–41.

Vorhies, D. W. and N. A. Morgan (2003), "A Configuration Theory Assessment of Marketing Organization Fit With Business Strategy and Its Relationship With Marketing Performance," *Journal of Marketing,* 67 (January), 100–115.

Walker, O. C. and R. W. Ruekert (1987), "Marketing's Role in the Implementation of Business Strategies: A Critical Review and Conceptual Framework," *Journal of Marketing,* 51 (3), 15–33.

Ward, P. T., J. K. McCreery, L. P. Ritzman, and D. Sharma (1998), "Competitive Priorities in Operations Management," *Decision Sciences,* 29 (4), 1035–1046.

Wernerfelt, B. (1984), "A Resource-Based View of the Firm," *Strategic Management Journal,* 5 (2), 171–180.

Youndt, M. A., S. A. Snell, J. W. Dean, and D. P. Lepak (1996), "Human Resource Management, Manufacturing Strategy, and Firm Performance," *Academy of Management Journal,* 39 (4), 836–866.

Zajac, E. J. and S. M. Shortell (1989), "Changing Generic Strategies: Likelihood, Direction, and Performance Implications," *Strategic Management Journal,* 10 (5), 413–430.

Zander, U. and B. Kogut (1995), "Knowledge and the Speed of the Transfer and Imitation of Organizational Capabilities: An Empirical Test," *Organization Science,* 6 (1), 76–92.

PART IV

Managing the Relations

21

Relationship Management

Jagdish N. Sheth

Arun Sharma

I n an increasingly global competitive marketplace, firms are seeking new methods of enhancing competitive advantage. Today, relationship management is becoming a strategic function and a key factor in competitive positioning. This chapter suggests that next-generation competitive advantage may come from an effective relationship with supply chain partners. The issue is already highlighted by research suggesting effective relationships with supply chain partners may be of strategic importance (Napolitano 1997; U.S. General Accounting Office [USGAO] 1994; Magnet 1994). The primary reasons for the emphasis on supply chain partners are changes in most market spaces that have witnessed consolidation of firms within industries, continuous product evolution, and constant pressure on costs. Supply chain partner relationships will become more critical in the future. Although relationship management is of strategic importance to a firm, good relationships between customers and suppliers are elusive. Firms realize that collaborative business relationships improve their ability to respond to the new business environment by allowing them to focus on their core businesses and to reduce costs in business processes. Firms, therefore, need to emphasize aspects that enhance supply chain partner relationships. This chapter discusses the emergence of supply chain relationships, and how this shift has and will change the role, processes, and strategies of firms.

Shift in Organizational Strategy

The reason for the emerging emphasis on supplier relationships is the shift in organizational buying strategies (Sheth and Sharma 1997). Organizational buying and purchasing strategies have been dramatically changing for four reasons. First, global competitiveness has caused firms to realize the competitive advantages of creating and managing supply chain relationships. The reason for competitive advantage is that in times of shortages, access to products becomes more critical. Second, the emergence of *reverse marketing*, starting with external customers and moving backward into procurement processes, has an impact. For example, demand-driven manufacturing, or flexible manufacturing and operations, has been instituted by firms to serve the diversity of demand with respect to form, place, and time value to customers. The role of suppliers is critical in this regard; demand-driven marketing requires access to supplies at the time of demand. Third, industry restructuring through mergers, acquisitions, and alliances on a global basis has reorganized the procurement function from a decentralized administrative function to a centralized strategic one. This is further intensified by outsourcing many support functions such as data processing and human resources. Therefore, access to supply becomes more important to the firm. Finally, uses of information technologies have restructured the buying philosophy, processes, and platforms by allowing firms to share market information and to use market information to better schedule design and manufacturing of products. Therefore, closer relationships with suppliers are critical.

Fundamentally, the consequence of changing paradigms of organizational strategy is likely to result in a two-dimensional shift. Organizational purchasing strategy shifts from a transaction-oriented to a relation-oriented philosophy, and from decentralized domestic sourcing to a centralized global sourcing process. Therefore, buyer-supplier relationships become more critical.

Relationship With Suppliers

The vendor management function is becoming more centralized, whereas the profit-and-loss responsibility of firms is becoming less centralized. In this context, heads of business units are examining the purchasing function, and more opportunities to partner with suppliers are available as firms attempt to capture critical supply resources. Taking advantage of these opportunities is increasingly important for several reasons:

1. *Shift in emphasis.* Vertically integrated companies—those that have complete internal capabilities and are self-sufficient—are becoming less prevalent as firms are outsourcing areas of nonexpertise. Therefore, products and services that were internally created are being outsourced. The supply function becomes more critical when companies outsource manufacturing to contract manufacturers and outsource warehousing to third-party logistics and warehousing.

2. *Sourcing.* With liberalization of markets and the emergence of the World Trade Organization (WTO), sourcing is becoming global. Free trade and investment among countries is becoming increasingly prevalent. Physical and temporal distances increase uncertainty, and supplier relationships are required to reduce these uncertainties.

3. *Global customers.* Customers are becoming global and, therefore, suppliers are asked to serve them on a global basis. This is particularly true for large global retailers such as Carrefour and Wal-Mart, as well as for global service industries such as banking, financial services, airlines, travel, and tourism. Global sourcing requires relationships at a global level.

4. *Cross-functional and cross-cultural emphasis.* Cross-functional and cross-cultural issues are becoming more important in global logistics and supply chain management. These issues are amplified in the context of integrated decision making across functions such as design, manufacturing, and marketing, along with finance, legal, and information technology. To manage these cross-functional and cross-cultural issues, firms need to develop relationships with supplier firms at these levels.

5. *Declining market prices.* Expectations of declining prices because of low inflation, especially in advanced countries, surplus manufacturing capacity, and low interest rates because of global savings rates exert greater pressure on firm margins. Thus, firms would like to obtain lower-cost products and services by working with suppliers.

6. *Rising competitive intensity.* Competitive intensity is increasing because of the restructuring of the world economy, as seen in the formation of the WTO, the rise of China and India, and the greater economic integration within and between regions. Global and regional consolidation is clearly taking place and is resulting in greater competition. Firms that have relationships with suppliers will be able to withstand competition better than firms that do not.

7. *Advanced technology enablers.* The Internet, electronic commerce, and networked computing have dramatically reduced cycle times and costs for firms. However, these technologies require both monetary and human asset investments. The process of partnering with suppliers increases these investments.

8. *Reverse marketing strategies.* The traditional process flow from R&D and sourcing to manufacturing, sales, and service is becoming a thing of the past. Today, market-focused organizations are organizing into reverse marketing—starting with the end users. Partnering with suppliers is critical to this strategy, as supply has to match the temporal requirements of demand.

9. *Strategic positioning.* In the past, companies partnered primarily for operational efficiency (i.e., just-in-time procedures or zero-inventory models). Today, intense competition is coming from existing rivals, new entrants, and the threat of substitutes. Partnering with suppliers is an increasingly important way to minimize the competition's negative impact on an industry and at the same time allow sharp strategic positioning.

Examples of Benefiting From Supplier Relationships

The major research regarding the advantage of supplier relationships comes from a study of the Japanese automotive component industry (Wasti and Liker 1997). This research found that the average length of the relationship between suppliers and buyers was 22 years. In addition, the major customer bought about half the output of the supplier firm. About 26% of the supplier's development effort was devoted to a single customer. Competition was restricted to two to four other suppliers. Finally, the quality of delivered product was very good. The data suggest that supplier relationship enhanced the design efforts of the buying company and reduced uncertainty and costs for the supplier company.

Eastman Kodak, Ford Motor Company, Levi Strauss, DuPont, McKesson, and Bose Corporation demonstrate that savings can be achieved by supplier relationships (USGAO 1994). These and other firms provide examples of the use of specific tactics to benefit from successful relationships.

Eastman Kodak outsourced its data and information processing system to IBM. Kodak achieved substantial cost savings through reducing personnel, assets, and capital expenditures in an area that is not its area of core competency. This shift toward asking data processing and systems management consultants to manage the information and data processing of a firm has accelerated, as most Fortune 500 firms have outsourced some aspects of their internal data processing systems.

Ford formed a relationship with one of its clutch suppliers. Ford examined the production process of the supplier and was able to reduce the cost of the clutch by 20%, benefiting both Ford and the clutch supplier. Similarly, based on its experience with Donnelly, Honda picked Donnelly as an exterior mirror supplier, although Donnelly had no experience in the area (Magnet 1994). Honda sent its engineers into Donnelly's plant, and Honda and Donnelly engineers reorganized the plant and reengineered the product process. Sales were $60 million in 1997 and costs are expected to decline by 2% annually, benefiting both Honda and Donnelly.

JC Penney and Levi Strauss are linked with an electronic data interchange (EDI) that allows Levi Strauss to obtain sales data. Levi Strauss obtains data on the exact size of jeans sold in individual stores. These data allow Levi Strauss to better plan the production process as well as better control inventory and delivery. This saving leads to a reduction in costs and prices, benefiting both JC Penney and Levi Strauss.

DuPont reduced the costs of each purchase transaction in the maintenance and repair supplies division from $120 to $16 by working with a smaller number of suppliers. The company selected one distributor in each region for a supplier relationship and then implemented a paperless order, receipt, and payment process. In addition to decreased costs of transaction, inventory at the maintenance and repair facilities dropped by 50%.

McKesson, a prominent drug distributor, developed a relationship with Johnson & Johnson, one of its major suppliers. Through a joint computer system development effort, both firms receive data on inventory, point-of-sale demand, and customer information. This enabled Johnson & Johnson to provide better service to McKesson, in turn increasing the level of service that McKesson provides to its customers. Owing to the success of the relationship, Johnson & Johnson gave a million dollars worth of business to McKesson.

Bose Corporation attempted to eliminate both purchasers and salespeople by bringing suppliers into the manufacturing process. Suppliers have access to Bose's data, employees, and processes. They work with Bose's engineers on present and future products. The reduction in personnel reduces costs for both sides, and a direct contact between the user and producer enhances quality and innovation.

Dimensions of Customer Relationships

Supply chain relationships have three dimensions: people, processes, and platforms. People deal with cultural aspects, especially the silent language of global business (time, friendship, agreements, possessions, and territory). There are strong cross-cultural differences in the people dimension of relationship management. Contrasts exist, particularly between Western societies (labeled low context) and Eastern societies (labeled high context). In high-context societies, social calculus that presumes loyalty in any relationship supplants rational calculus. In a contrast between low-context French society and high-context Japanese culture, Hall (1976) notes that for the latter "once a relationship is formed, loyalty is never questioned" (p. 113). Fundamental to the analysis of relationships in the United States and other Western contexts are the voluntary nature of the associations between the exchange partners and expectations of mutual gain from the relationship. Such expectations from the relationship are primary, and a certain degree of economic calculativeness is a precondition to forming and continuing relationships (Williamson 1992). In high-context cultures, many aspects of the relationships between individual employees and firms is governed by hierarchical norms and expectations, such as those of the lead bank in Japanese Keirestu relations, or those of close family ties, as in the relationships among business firms in India and China (Iyer 1999). Business groups in these regions render the relationship as one of forced compliance to norms and reputation sanctions rather than one of assumed voluntary and free associations between firms for the expectation of long-term mutual profits. Relationship continuity is assumed and never questioned, despite environmental changes affecting costs or profits. Indeed, the profit motive itself may be secondary because firms owe their primary allegiance to kinship, clan, or ethnic group and thus may forsake short-term profits for the fear of "losing face" within their business community (Iyer 1997, 1999).

The process dimension of relationship management deals with flow of activities, money, products, and materials, as well as information. Because firms are increasingly integrated, they need to establish relationships that enable better process integration. Relationships require special processes that transactional customers may not need.

Platforms deal with relationship infrastructure requirements. For example, Procter & Gamble (P&G) and Wal-Mart have a relationship where the Wal-Mart EDI system is critical for P&G's success. Infrastructures become more complex when crossing country boundaries, as there are physical, structural, and legal constraints. As stated earlier, relationships enhance the development of common platforms.

Both customer and supplier firms need to better align their firms for enhanced engagement. Alignment refers to the degree to which business units, departments, and teams work together efficiently to implement strategy (Weiss and Molinaro 2005). Engagement reflects the degree of commitment and investment in the success of an enterprise (Weiss and Molinaro 2005) (Figure 21.1).

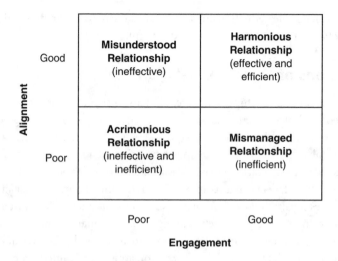

Figure 21.1   Alignment/Engagement Matrix

The good alignment/good engagement cell is labeled a harmonious relationship and is exemplified by the P&G and Wal-Mart relationship. The good alignment/poor engagement cell is labeled a misunderstood relationship. An example is the relationship between Kmart and OmniMedia, in which there was mistrust between the firms although they were good for each other. The poor alignment/good engagement cell is labeled a mismanaged relationship, and an example is the relationship between firms and suppliers in which buying firms have not been able to achieve the efficiencies promised by suppliers. The poor alignment/poor engagement cell is labeled an acrimonious relationship; an example is the relationship between auto manufacturers and auto parts suppliers.

It has been suggested by Weiss and Molinaro (2005) that firms can take three steps to enhance alignment and engagement of employees. First, employees need to develop a firm-level perspective and work in the interest of the entire firm. Additionally, firms need to work outside departmental boundaries and break down organizational silos. Second, employees need to build relationships with key stakeholders through both formal and informal methods. Third, employees need to increase collaboration and integration across the firm. This includes shared learning across firms and departments, joint planning, establishing common processes, collaboration on specific initiatives, and structural integration.

In summary, the objective of relationship management is to strive for a harmonious relationship because it results in both efficient and effective outcomes—doing the right thing and doing it right.

Establishing and Maintaining Supplier Relationships

Wilson (1995) suggests that the majority of alliances fail. Most of the failures are due to problems associated with selecting and maintaining relationships. Methods that enhance selection and maintenance of relationships, presented here, are based on findings from research, the USGAO (1994), and real-life experiences.

Establishing Supplier Relationships

Firms should be very selective in their criteria for establishing relationships. In addition to the normal criteria of competency and quality, the following additional factors should be taken into consideration:

1. *Trust and commitment to long-term goals.* Both suppliers and buyers need to demonstrate trust and commitment toward a long-term vision. Trust and commitment have been shown to be the major predictors of successful relationships.

2. *Mutual benefit.* The relationship should be of benefit to both the buyer and the seller. If the relationship has one-sided benefits, the relationship will not last, as firms will seek other suppliers or buyers.

3. *Top management support.* Most successful relationships are associated with support from the top managers of a firm. As examples, the success of Wal-Mart and Corning in forming relationships is because their CEOs have supported supplier relationships. Also, DuPont and Roadway Express have formed an Executive Board that meets at both companies to enhance their relationship (USGAO 1994).

4. *Compatible organizational culture.* The culture of firms should be compatible. This suggests that they share common values and common reward systems. A major relationship initiative between two telecommunication firms did not succeed because they did not share a common work philosophy. One firm was very intense, whereas the other firm was casual or laid-back. The relationship dissolved in six months.

5. *Sharing of information.* Relationships require sharing of information. The benefits of relationships arise from reducing the uncertainty associated with transaction-oriented exchanges. Information increases certainty and reduces needless interaction. As an example, the control systems manufacturer Bailey Controls shares data with two of its main electronics distributors, allowing Bailey to reduce inventory and costs (Magnet 1994).

6. *Strong and open communications.* Strong and open communications reduce misunderstanding and enhance the quality of relationships. Communication decreases conflict and enhances positive outcomes.

Maintaining Successful Relationships

Research suggests that the following aspects are important for the successful maintenance of relationships:

1. *Simple and flexible contracts.* Simple and flexible contracts enhance relationships, as they are used as guides rather than to specify all contingencies. For example, when Kodak outsourced its computer support services to IBM, they used an

11-page contract (USGAO 1994), in contrast to typical simple business contracts that run to about 30 pages.

2. *Intensive management involvement.* Cross-functional teams from both the supplier and buyer organizations that meet periodically enhance their relationships. For example, Ford uses salespeople to provide suppliers with consumer feedback (USGAO 1994).

3. *Periodic performance monitoring.* Performance monitoring is critical for relationships. As an example, Motorola evaluates and generates a scorecard for all its suppliers (Magnet 1994). The next order is based on that supplier's previous performance. Suppliers recognize the value of this knowledge and perform better as a result.

4. *Internal controls.* Companies need rigorous internal controls to protect access to and distribution of confidential information. With the advent of Internet communications and the ease of access to information, firms need to be more security conscious.

5. *Problem-solving procedures.* Companies need to establish problem-solving procedures that reduce or prevent conflicts. One of the simplest methods is to establish periodic meetings at all levels of the customer and supplier organizations.

Organizational Changes to Establish Supplier Relationships

As the business environment moves from a transaction and domestic orientation to a relationship and global orientation, firms need to emphasize the development of relationships. This relationship orientation leads to expertise in many aspects of business buying (Sheth and Sharma 1997).

1. *Supplier as a customer.* Firms need to treat suppliers as they have treated customers in the past. However, understanding in this area at the firm level is very limited. Firms need to develop commitment, trust, and cooperation with their suppliers. In addition, they need to invest in mutual goals, interdependence, structural bonds, adaptation, nonretrievable assets, shared technology, and social bonds to ensure successful relationships (Wilson 1995).

2. *Cross-functional supplier teams.* Marketers have used interdisciplinary teams to contact and maintain relationships with their customers. As individual supplier relationships become more important, there will likely be a similar thrust toward cross-functional teams that are dedicated to or focused on key suppliers. The importance of individual suppliers is expected to increase because of the emergence of sourcing on a global and relational basis with a few key suppliers. Thus, firms need to change goals, reward structure, and group norms of the purchasing function.

3. *Does partnering pay?* Firms need to monitor the return on investment in establishing relationships with suppliers. Therefore, firms need to develop performance metrics that analytically quantify supplier relationship equity. Ultimately, supplier partnering with smaller-share suppliers will not be economical. The cost-benefit analysis of supplier relationships should result in increased supplier selectivity.

4. *Supply experience curves.* Managing supply chain relationships is not an easy task. Particularly, the task of managing relationships on a global basis is more complex and not analogous to domestic supplier management, as most business customers have realized. Therefore, in industries where the supply function is a key strategic advantage, companies need to focus on creating core competency in supply side management and develop steeper experience curves.

5. *Hub and spokes organization.* Organizations can be expected to reduce the number of suppliers in each product or service category. In addition, reengineering has forced firms to outsource internal activities. The results of these two trends lead to a hub and spokes organization in which one or two suppliers in each product or service category are the spokes, and the procurement organization is the hub.

6. *Bonding with suppliers.* Marketers, specifically those that practice relationship marketing, have learned to bond with their customers. Bonding relates to the empathy that the marketing organizations feel toward their customer groups. With an increasing trend toward creating, managing, and enhancing ongoing relationships with suppliers on a global basis, organizations will need to invest in supplier bonding processes and philosophies.

7. *Global sourcing.* Global sourcing can be expected to become a source of strategic advantage. Although several global enterprises are establishing processes and platforms, especially in the automotive, high technology, and aerospace industries, global sourcing is still in its infancy in other industries. Firms have to develop expertise in global sourcing strategies as well as global logistics.

8. *Cross-cultural values.* Firms need to be more aware of cross-cultural values. These values may be in conflict with the firm's present value system. As an example, firms in the United States are accused of focusing on short-term profitability, whereas firms in Japan are concerned about long-term positioning. Similarly, in some cultures, reciprocity is declared illegal and unethical, whereas in other cultures it is the preferred way of doing business. What is considered an agency fee in one country is recognized in others as a bribe, subject to prosecution under anticorruption laws. Similarly, doing business with family members and politically connected individuals is presumed to provide a sense of trust and commitment in some cultures, whereas it is considered as nepotism and unethical behavior in others.

9. *Cross-national rules.* Firms also have to learn about cross-national rules. Specifically, the two-tier regulations (one for domestic and the other for foreign enterprises) are common with respect to ownership, management control, and

coproduction practices in countries such as China. With the rise of nationalism in recent years, this has become a key issue for global enterprises (McDonald's, Coca-Cola, and General Electric, as examples), particularly as they expand their market and supply scope in large emerging nations such as India, China, and Indonesia.

10. *Services procurement.* As organizations outsource more internal services, and as suppliers engage in providing value-added services to their customers, firms need to better understand and research services procurement. Additionally, because most advanced countries are service economies, service procurement will rise in prominence.

Emerging Issues in Relationship Management

As supply chain members develop better relationships, some issues will emerge that need more attention:

1. *Supplier dependence.* One of the key questions, specifically owing to Wal-Mart's operations, is whether suppliers should have "too many eggs in one basket." This is critical for firms whose majority sales come from one buyer. Except for analysis in the economics literature, this topic has not been examined in the supply chain or marketing literature. The conventional wisdom is to avoid putting too many eggs in one basket, but specificity is lacking.

2. *Limits of extending core competencies.* A key question is how many different products or services a supplier can offer with equally high levels of competency. For example, are banks really good in brokerage and insurance? Similarly, are consultants or lawyers capable of being everything to everyone? This is a problem, as firms do not want to see different salespeople from the same firm. An example is Hewlett-Packard, which has different sales forces for printing, PCs, storage, and consulting.

3. *Type of relationship.* Another key question that arises is whether multiplex relationships are superior to simple relationships. In other words, is the customer-supplier role, if extended to partnering and joint venture or coinvestment in R&D, really good for enhancing the relationship? It has been suggested by the popular press that the deeper the relationship, the bigger the breakup.

4. *Ideal relationship.* Finally, there is a need to determine optimal relationships. For example, how deep and wide can the relationship be? Should a firm have a relationship at only the top level or at all levels? There is no research in this area, and more work is needed.

Summary

This chapter suggests that collaborative buyer-supplier relationships improve a firm's ability to respond to the new business environment by allowing it to focus on its core businesses and to reduce costs in business processes. This chapter discusses the emergence of supply chain relationships and how this shift toward supply chain relationships has and will change the role, processes, and strategies of firms. The discussion addresses shifts in organizational strategy, relationship strategies, firm-level examples, dimensions of customer relationships, establishing and maintaining supplier relationships, and organizational changes needed to establish supply chain relationships, and it concludes with an overview of emerging issues in relationship management.

References

Hall, Edward T. (1976), *Beyond Culture*. New York: Anchor Books/Doubleday.

Iyer, Gopalkrishnan R. (1997), "Comparative Marketing: An Interdisciplinary Framework for Institutional Analysis," *Journal of International Business Studies*, 28 (Third Quarter), 531–561.

Iyer, Gopalkrishnan R. (1999), "The Impact of Religion and Reputation in the Organization of Indian Merchant Communities," *Journal of Business and Industrial Marketing*, 14 (2), 102–117.

Magnet, Myron (1994), "The New Golden Rule of Business," *Fortune*, February, 60–64.

Napolitano, Lisa (1997), "Customer-Supplier Partnering: A Strategy Whose Time Has Come," *Journal of Personal Selling and Sales Management*, 4 (Fall), 1–8.

Sheth, Jagdish N. and Arun Sharma (1997), "Supplier Relationships: Emerging Issues and Challenges," *Industrial Marketing Management*, 46 (4), 91–100.

U.S. General Accounting Office (1994), "Partnerships: Customer-Supplier Relationships Can Be Improved Through Partnering," Report Number 94–173, Washington, DC.

Wasti, S. Nazli and Jeffrey K. Liker (1997), "Risky Business or Competitive Power? Supplier Involvement in Japanese Product Design," *Journal of Product Innovation Management*, 14 (September), 337–355.

Weiss, David S. and Vince Molinaro (2005), *The Leadership Gap*. New York: Wiley.

Williamson, Oliver E. (1992), "Calculativeness, Trust, and Economic Organization," *Journal of Law and Economics*, 36 (April), 453–486.

Wilson, David T. (1995), "An Integrated Model of Buyer Seller Relationships," *Journal of the Academy of Marketing Science*, 23(4), 335–345.

22

Logistics Outsourcing

Clifford F. Lynch

Theodore P. Stank

Shay Scott

C orporate and business unit strategies determine the lines of business and markets in which a firm competes. The approach each business employs to implement strategies, however, is predicated on conditions in the firm's external environment. The trend of the external business environment in the last 30 years toward heightened global competitive pressure and availability of substitute products and services in such varied industries as automotive, electronics, consumer durables, and packaged goods has increased customer bargaining power and created a downward movement in pricing, forcing firms to focus on cost and risk reduction. In such circumstances, firms often seek to leverage the resources of other supply chain members to survive, saving scarce resources that are required to develop noncore in-house functions by contracting the function out to external service providers. Determining which activities should be carried out within a company and which should be contracted out is critical to business effectiveness. Such resource decisions have become central to ensuring long-term profitability and viability (Lynch 2004).

The logistics function, focused on movement and storage activities that must be performed by any firm regardless of strategic determination, has increasingly been targeted for outsourcing. Total revenue of outsourced logistics was estimated at US$ 333 billion in 2004 (Goodman 2005). Not coincidentally, the trend toward logistics outsourcing is highly correlated with increased global business. The heightened complexity and risk associated with coordination of processes across both firm and geographic boundaries increase the importance of seamless flows of product, service, information, and financial transactions, shifting the focus of logistics to movement and storage activities and processes that extend to integrated enterprises across the full range of supply chain participants. Although this complexity predicates a significant focus on trans-enterprise movement and storage activities, it does not necessarily dictate that a firm must invest resources to develop internal logistics expertise. If investment in logistics capabilities detracts from the development of expertise in core areas, logistics—although critical and significant—is best accomplished by outsourcing it to external service providers. For the purposes of this discussion, *logistics outsourcing* is defined as an arrangement whereby a logistics service provider performs services for a firm that could be, or have been, provided in-house.

Although increased logistics outsourcing volume has been beneficial for logistics service providers, it has not come without its costs, mostly because of the heightened expectations that logistics outsourcing clients have for the value delivered by service providers. Logistics service contracts have become more sophisticated and place more pressure on service providers to continually invest in process and cost improvements and to share these benefits with clients. Although success stories in this new environment are plentiful, logistics outsourcing also has been a victim of poor planning, lack of understanding, inadequate performance, and in some cases, abject failure. There are a number of reasons for this, but lack of understanding on the part of both client and provider, more often than not, is the major cause of difficulty and failure in logistics outsourcing relationships. This comment is even more poignant when made in relation to global logistics outsourcing. After years of discussing and writing about them, we finally have begun to see true global outsourcing arrangements. Until recently, although there were any number of firms that had operations in foreign countries, in most cases their logistics activities were confined to the countries in which they were located and to those in close proximity. Today, products are routinely moved back and forth throughout the world. To many firms, global logistics outsourcing has become more important than it is in their domestic markets.

This chapter highlights the business case for global logistics outsourcing and also provides a guide for the outsourcing process. The specific case of global logistics outsourcing is considered, and keys and barriers to success are identified.

Logistics Outsourcing History

Outsourcing of logistics services is not a new concept. Although it has gained renewed emphasis in recent years, the practice can be traced back almost as far as one would care to research it. In Europe, a number of logistics service providers can trace their origins back to the Middle Ages. The first commercial warehouse operations were built in Venice, Italy, in the 14th century. Merchants from across Europe used them as collection and distribution points (American Warehousemen's Association 1991). In the United States, the outsourcing of transportation and warehousing was common throughout the 1950s and 1960s. The relationships were primarily transactional and typically short term in nature. Although there were some long-term contracts involving large companies such as DuPont and Quaker Oats, these were the exception rather than the rule. Most warehousing transactions were standard 30-day public warehouse agreements. Contract motor carriage was available but not as we know it today.

During the 1970s, manufacturers throughout the industrialized world put heavy emphasis on cost reductions and improved productivity. Companies also began to realize that the real competitive edge was in enhanced customer service and relationships. The managerial resources and technological investment required to support both increased efficiency and customer effectiveness expanded significantly. As a result, there was an accelerated interest in outsourcing any function not directly related to a company's core business. This was particularly true of smaller companies that could contract with logistics service providers to offer service superior to what they could facilitate on their own. Many manufacturing firms, therefore, found logistics outsourcing to be an effective method of freeing resources to focus on the core business.

The movement toward logistics outsourcing was fueled by the deregulation of common transportation carriers of all modes throughout Europe and the United States in the late 1970s and early 1980s. These firms, newly freed from stifling regulation, were able to enter into innovative, long-term relationships with customers, and true logistics partnerships began to surface. The alliances quickly brought about major improvements in both customer service and logistics economies.

Longer-term relationships with logistics service providers became more common, particularly in the warehousing area. Single-tenant facilities were built and operated by warehouse companies in major markets. Consolidation of facilities into larger operations became more and more frequent. By the early 1980s, services offered by the outside firms expanded rapidly. The so-called value-added services included packaging, blending, systems support, inventory management, customized handling, and other offerings that had not been available previously. More users began to rely on their provider to handle complex technologies required to deliver such value-added service, including warehouse management systems, transportation management systems, and supply chain event management systems.

In Europe, the growth in outsourcing was sparked to an even greater degree by the creation of the European Union (EU) and the subsequent removal of requirements to hold inventory within each individual EU country. These changes brought with them a phenomenal number of mergers and acquisitions. In many cases, firms found themselves with more warehouses and distribution centers than any one company ever wanted, facilitating significant reanalysis of distribution systems to put centers where they really ought to be.

The changes that brought about increased logistics outsourcing also fostered a wave of consolidation in the logistics provider industry, and users of services found themselves dealing with different companies and individuals, as well as different cultures. The mergers of Deutsche Post/AEI/Danzas/Loomis/Airborne, Exel/Mark VII/Ocean Group, UTi Worldwide/Standard, UPS/Fritz/Menlo/Overnite, Kuehne & Nagel/USCO, APL Logistics/GATX Logistics, and others introduced larger and, in many cases, global entities into the outsourcing equation. In fact, many of these alliances were efforts to respond to the increasing global needs of outsourcing firms.

Today, there is still plenty of room for growth in logistics outsourcing. Only about 12% to 14% of the relevant logistics services in the United States are outsourced. In Europe, where outsourcing has a longer history, the percentage is more than twice that. As business continues to move into low-cost labor markets in relatively underdeveloped countries in Southeast Asia and Eastern Europe, the need for experienced logistics providers will spiral.

Why Outsource Logistics Activities?

There is no standard response to the question, "What should be outsourced?" Exactly what the firm should outsource depends on individual needs and strategies. Some choose to contract all extended supply chain logistics activities. More often than not, however, certain individual activities or combinations of activities or processes lend themselves to outsourcing better than others. A recent study identified the following most frequently subcontracted logistics activities and processes (Allen, Dale, and Langley 2004):

- Outbound transportation
- Inbound transportation
- Freight bill auditing and payment
- Rate negotiations
- Warehousing
- Shipment consolidation and distribution
- Cross-docking
- Order fulfillment
- Return or reverse logistics
- Product returns and repair
- Customs clearance
- Customs brokerage
- Information technology (IT)
- Consulting services
- Carrier selection
- Inventory management
- Procurement of logistics
- Selected manufacturing activities
- Product marking, labeling, packaging
- Fleet management
- Order entry and processing
- Product assembly and installation
- Customer service
- Inventory ownership

There are as many reasons for outsourcing as there are firms that do it. Many of these are unique to specific firms and industries, but in a broad sense there are several readily identifiable advantages to subcontracting logistics activities. No priority has been assigned to these because relative importance varies by firm and circumstance.

Return on Assets

Outsourcing reduces the substantial investment required in warehouse facilities, materials handling, order picking, transportation equipment, and information technology, and returns can be enhanced significantly. Although it is true that most firms capitalize leases, the fact of the matter is that the majority of logistics contracts are relatively short term and allow reasonable termination arrangements. Most important, the user firm does not have to make the capital outlay. This capital, in turn, can be invested in those ventures that fall into the core competencies or basic businesses of the user firms, whether they are in manufacturing, marketing, design, or other areas.

Flexibility

Flexibility is another key outsourcing driver for most firms. As new markets and new products are developed, many times it is impossible to predict future logistics needs accurately. Likewise, as existing market and product characteristics change, logistics needs change as well. New customer service requirements, ordering methods, and competitive offerings and services all influence a firm's logistics practices. The use of a contract provider greatly reduces the risk of misplaced or outdated facilities and equipment.

The benefits of flexibility are particularly potent in the case of capital investment, or the avoidance thereof. There are a number of empty buildings around the country located in markets for services or products that became obsolete. The building boom generated by the Internet bubble is a classic example. Several 500,000-plus-square-foot fully automated facilities were left empty after only a few months of operation. In the case of mergers and acquisitions, if the firms have outsourced logistics services, it is much easier to combine operations and take full advantage of logistics synergies. Often logistics cost reductions can be one of the major motivators of the transaction. This was effectively demonstrated by a major firm that had maintained 12 to 15 distribution centers for a number of years. After two acquisitions in quick succession, the company found itself with almost 200 warehouses, in some cases, two or more in the same city. Because the majority of these were contract warehouses, consolidation was greatly enhanced, and within two years, the total number of distribution locations was down to 20. Logistics costs were reduced by millions of dollars annually. If these facilities had been owned or operated by the firms themselves, it would have taken years to achieve the same savings if, in fact, they could ever have been realized at all.

Personnel Productivity

Utilization of personnel can be more effective because by emphasizing the core business, the productivity of the employees can be improved greatly. Often there are fewer people to train in fewer skills, thereby increasing the level of expertise. Take, for example, the case of a major grocery manufacturer that, a few years ago, operated a large manufacturing and distribution facility on the same site. For new employees, the entry-level route was through the distribution center as an order picker or forklift operator. All job openings in the facility were posted, and every time a higher-paying production position became available, those at the lower levels applied for it, often successfully. The end result was a warehouse that functioned more as a school for forklift operators than as a distribution center. Because the company never achieved true warehouse operations efficiency, the center was a prime candidate for outsourcing. The personnel productivity advantage is often difficult to measure but can be real, nonetheless.

Labor Considerations

Although labor issues can be somewhat delicate depending on the user firm's own labor environment, these considerations should not be ignored when considering outsourcing, particularly in the warehousing area. If you are operating in a union climate and your own facilities are organized, the advantages of utilizing a facility that is nonunion or even one that has a different union sometimes are obvious. The key word here is *caution*. All appropriate labor agreements should be evaluated carefully by a competent legal authority. Labor unions are well aware of outsourcing advantages and, in some cases, have taken measures to protect their members. With the outsourcing of hundreds of thousands of jobs to China, India, and other countries, the term *offshoring* (the movement of functional activities to a foreign location) has taken on a negative connotation to many. Although this is quite different from logistics outsourcing, the very mention of the word can raise a red flag. This caution is not intended as a deterrent but a reminder that thorough research will minimize the risks and protect the projected benefits.

Operating Expenses

To many firms considering outsourcing, operating costs are the most important consideration. In addition to capital savings, the outsourcer expects the outside facilities to operate at a lower cost or achieve savings that could not be generated internally. Obviously, this is important and is often the case; but the sophisticated firm sometimes finds this not to be true. If a company has an efficient, well-managed distribution system, outsourcing it may not reduce operating costs. Subcontracting, however, may add to the value of the system, and this should be the primary cost consideration. Although the absolute dollars spent may be more, the value received often can more than offset the premium based on the improved operational capability inherent in a good external logistics provider. It is most important, therefore, when comparing the cost of a firm's performance of a logistics activity with that of the provider, that the numbers compared capture the total cost associated with the level of service available or desired.

Management and Political Considerations

In the modern business environment, managing any function is difficult, particularly at the middle management level. More often than not, there is an ongoing pressure to reduce costs and improve productivity with fewer resources. People are more difficult to manage and some have work ethics that are often not compatible with the goals of the organization. Just as the firm wants to invest in its core competency, its managers should focus on it as well. Logistics and personnel issues require significant amounts of attention and resources; outsourcing facilitates managing the basic business and leaving the solution of distribution problems to others. It is far easier to manage one or a limited number of providers than to manage the individual functions internally. This is not intended to be a text on corporate politics, but one would be naive to ignore them. All too often, managers see their primary survival technique as recommending how others could manage their function better or, in some cases, how they themselves could manage it better than the incumbent. Outsourcing removes the logistics function from the corporate political spotlight and enables the logistics executive to manage it in a more orderly, less political, and more productive fashion.

Customer Service and Specialized Services

In today's environment of error-free, prompt deliveries and unique business and consumer requirements, customer service has to be the most important consideration for any firm. This focus on increased customer satisfaction in both the business-to-business and the business-to-consumer markets has resulted in many changes in logistics practices and service approaches. These changes are likely to continue and must be addressed in a timely fashion if the firm expects to remain competitive. Specialized services are becoming the rule rather than the exception. Although some logistics service providers have been able to serve the needs of various industries efficiently, a number of firms have gradually evolved into businesses that offer specialized services for specific industries. This, of course, shortens the learning curve, encourages expertise, and removes the inefficiencies from the system.

Just in Time

The automotive industry provides a good example of the potential for outsourcing. Just-in-time (JIT) techniques have been used in this industry for a number of years, and many of the associated functions have been performed by outside providers. One carrier-based contract logistics firm handles warehousing, transportation, and assembly for several major automobile manufacturers. The provider has the ability to acquire parts from hundreds of vendors in a myriad of geographic locations, move them into one warehouse, process the orders, and deliver to destination plants within two-hour time windows. Another warehouse-based provider has a similar arrangement. Through an electronic data interchange network, trucks are dispatched to suppliers of parts. Parts are collected and delivered to a cross-dock, where they are consolidated and shipped to 12 different assembly plants in North America. The parts are never warehoused or inventoried at the plants. This JIT delivery system schedules next-day arrival 15 to 30 minutes prior to the time the parts are needed for manufacturing. While they are en route, a sophisticated system monitors each part and its expected arrival time. Although JIT techniques have been utilized in the automotive industry for some time, the more recent introduction of the retailing and grocery industry's version has enhanced awareness of the outsourcing option.

Order Consolidation

Efficient consumer response (ECR), sometimes called quick response (QR) or continuous replenishment process (CRP), is designed to link all segments in the product pipeline into a smooth-flowing stream of products. Vendor-managed inventory (VMI) is another variation of the same theme, using a "pull" rather than a "push" inventory system. In the grocery industry, collaborative planning, forecasting, and replenishment (CPFR) links customer demand with replenishment scheduling. This joint planning, if successful, can lead to a smooth flow of products through the entire length of the pipeline. These techniques result in smaller, more frequent shipments all designed to reduce inventories in the system. Rather than handle small shipments from their own facilities, grocery manufacturers have turned to contract logistics companies. With a multiple client base and sophisticated systems, the providers are able to combine these shipments into truckloads, reducing freight and handling costs and even further enhancing the cost reductions in the ECR process. One food manufacturer eliminated its network of privately owned and operated distribution centers and outsourced the entire system to firms with sophisticated consolidation programs.

Although consolidation has been a factor in the food business since the 1960s, the early programs were very simplistic manual operations. Today, the leading logistics firms have systems that combine orders into truck or container loads by customer and requested arrival date, route the shipments, and electronically tender them to the appropriate carriers. One major logistics provider ships 500 to 1,000 trailers of consolidated product daily. Such consolidation programs, in addition to providing superior service, have produced consistent reductions in transportation costs ranging from 30% to 50%. Programs of this type would be virtually impossible without the logistics service providers.

Packaging

Logistics outsourcing also has facilitated the changing landscape of consumer goods retailing. Buying one of anything can be almost impossible in many of the "club" stores. In a high-volume manufacturing plant, combining two or three packages of the same item by banding or shrink-wrapping causes tremendous inefficiencies. Manufacturers are tooled up to put 12, 24, or 48 packages in a case, seal it, palletize it, and move it to storage or the dock, untouched by human hands. If the customer packaging requirements were all the same, the issue could be dealt with.

The difficulty arises when Wal-Mart wants three tubes of toothpaste shrink-wrapped together, Costco wants two tubes, and Target wants a toothbrush thrown in. Much of this labor-intensive work is outsourced. At the provider's facility, the original cases are opened, and inner packages are grouped together according to customer demands, using small shrink-wrap tunnels or other combining techniques. They then are placed back in the original case, or into some other form of display module and shipped. Although this is tedious, it is considerably less disruptive and less expensive than attempting to customize packages at the manufacturing plant.

Order Fulfillment and Electronic Commerce

It is an irrefutable fact that the Internet and electronic commerce have had an enormous impact on logistics service requirements. Although the concept of order fulfillment is not new (our grandmothers' Sears, Roebuck catalogs effectively demonstrate that), the direct consumer contact with manufacturers through the Internet resulted in more precise and critical communications, information, and customer service requirements. Residential deliveries are required more often than not, presenting an entirely new set of challenges. Many manufacturing firms simply do not have the expertise to establish and manage these delivery and communications systems as well as a dedicated outside firm and are turning to these providers for the necessary customer-focused services. In addition, an efficient order-picking facility is expensive to equip and maintain, and sales volumes can fluctuate wildly— a classic case for outsourcing. Here, selection of the best-qualified provider is critical. Sophisticated order fulfillment is not for the fainthearted. Be sure the providers are in the business for the long haul. There have been several conspicuous examples of those who were not. The most important thing to remember in electronic commerce is that there is direct exposure to the ultimate consumer at a number of stages in the process, and good rapport must be maintained. The selected provider must be one that will focus on, and nurture, customer relationships for its clients.

Information Technology

For firms engaged in electronic commerce and even those that are not, the increasing demands for new information systems and resources can often be met more efficiently and economically through outsourcing. When resources within the firm are scarce, or logistics systems development has a low priority, there can be significant advantages to utilizing a provider that has the necessary systems in place or the ability to develop them. Additionally, there are literally hundreds of firms that offer warehouse and transportation management systems as well as other supply chain management technology. Such firms can be included in outsourcing arrangements with transportation or warehousing specialists, assuming they add some value to the process. The technology available is quite impressive, and the outsourcing firm can acquire such capabilities as carrier selection, route optimization, order/shipment visibility, freight payment, load planning, and asset tracking, to name a few. Again, care should be taken to ensure that the provider is well capitalized and has the resources and expertise to maintain existing systems as well as to enhance them as needed. The important thing to remember about information technology is that, in and of itself, it has no value. Its real value is in the information and decision-making tools it enables. It must enable reporting metrics, operational efficiencies, visibility, and process integration. As Drucker (2004) said, "The computer can handle only things to which the answer is 'yes' or 'no.' It cannot handle maybe. It's not the computerization that's important then; it's the discipline you have to bring to your processes" (p. 118).

Global Capability

As firms seek to expand into worldwide markets, outsourcing can be an extremely effective method of establishing foreign distribution centers and arranging and making international shipments. There are a number of excellent freight forwarders, for example, that provide sophisticated logistics services throughout the pipeline. Many domestic-based logistics managers simply do not have the expertise necessary to be effective in the global logistics arena and therefore find outsourcing a valuable tool. Managing a domestic logistics network can be challenging enough. Combine these issues with customs, security, terrorism, foreign cultures, currency, and language, and the task becomes formidable indeed.

Expertise

Another important reason for outsourcing is the increasing maturity of the logistics service provider companies themselves. No longer is the industry characterized by smaller, unsophisticated companies. Today's successful integrated logistics service provider is a dynamic firm, using a combination of systems, facilities, transportation, and materials-handling techniques. It is managed and staffed with logistics professionals and, in many cases, has true global capabilities. Quite often, it is better qualified than its clients to perform the product distribution function and can contribute knowledge to the process that many logistics managers simply do not have. In "Has Outsourcing Gone Too Far?" (2001), outsourcing has been aptly referred to as moving from "economies of scale to economies of skill."

The Logistics Outsourcing Process

In spite of its impact on the logistics function, and often the entire corporation, outsourcing is frequently undertaken with little regard for overall logistics strategy. It is important to remember that outsourcing itself is not the strategy but rather a vehicle for achieving the strategy. Keep in mind that outsourcing may not be appropriate for every firm. Do not enter into an outsourcing arrangement simply because it is written or talked about frequently or because other firms in your industry are doing it. A sure recipe for disaster is to embark on a program that is not suitable, not understood clearly, or marred by unrealistic expectations. Major failures in outsourcing relationships occur when a firm outsources an activity that its own personnel do not totally comprehend and the provider promises to meet requirements that have not been fully defined, communicated, or understood.

As with any other significant undertaking in the firm, it is absolutely critical that the outsourcing project have senior management support. When all or part of the logistics function is turned over to an outside party, a number of other disciplines are affected. Some functional managers will be more supportive than others, and in a few cases, they may be totally opposed to the concept. If they view the outsourcing arrangement as a threat to their careers, they must be convinced of the benefits not only to the corporation but also to themselves. Usually, the logistics manager is the project leader or champion, but they must have the full weight of the organization behind them to be effective. Top-level management support is often achieved by communicating the potential return on assets emerging from the outsourcing initiative. For this reason, the CFO is often the key top-level supporter.

Once senior managers have committed to the project, it is important to have the commitment and participation of other departments or functions that will be affected by the decision. These, of course, vary by firm, but in addition to logistics, the groups most often affected are

- Information technology
- Production or manufacturing
- Quality
- Sales and marketing
- Merchandising
- Finance and accounting
- Purchasing
- Human resources

Ideally, some customer participation should be sought as well, either directly or through sales management. Representatives from these or other departments must be part of the process and should compose the study team. Not only is their input important to the success of the project; they must also support the decision, whatever it turns out to be. With most firms more aware of the need for internal integration, logistics managers who attempt to take major steps unilaterally are being naive and setting themselves up for failure. An outsourcing project can be a true test of how effective a logistics manager can be within an integrated environment. For the project to succeed, he or she must have a consensus of all the functions in the chain. Rarely will he or she have responsibility for them all, and a satisfactory result can be achieved only by exceptional negotiation and sensitivity toward other function heads.

One of the first tasks of the study team is to determine what the firm is attempting to accomplish through outsourcing. Objectives must be set, and many questions must be dealt with. They should go beyond "What will it cost?" and each question must be analyzed carefully. Some of the questions are the following:

- What problem are we trying to solve?
- What results do we expect?
- Is outsourcing consistent with the overall corporate strategy and mission?
- Will outsourcing be acceptable to other functional groups?

- Is the timing right?
- What is the competition doing?
- Is it working for them?
- How will it affect the organization?
- Are there identifiable managers who can implement and manage an outsourced function, and who are they?
- Will outsourcing enable us to concentrate better on our core competencies? How?
- Will it help maximize our strengths and avoid our weaknesses? How?
- What are our customer service requirements?
- How will the decision affect customer service?
- Do we understand what we are trying to outsource well enough to do it?
- Are we simply trying to outsource an activity we cannot manage efficiently?
- Will outsourcing expose us to innovative logistics techniques and information systems?
- What are the risks? Are they acceptable?

Once these and other questions have been answered, the objectives have been set, and the activities to be outsourced have been identified, it is necessary to establish a basis for comparison. For some managers, assessing current operations may be the most difficult part of the outsourcing process. To make an intelligent decision about providers, cost, and benefits, however, it is necessary to conduct this audit. The project team must have a clear picture of current logistics operations, their capabilities, limitations, and cost, as well as future needs. When this has been completed, a set of benchmarks against which to measure the various options can be established.

Outsourcing should not be evaluated strictly on the basis of various provider proposals but as an alternative to an internal solution as well. For most firms, the best way to develop the information is to flowchart the entire logistics process. Each function represented on the study team should be consulted to make sure the flow is accurate and properly reflects the impact on other parts of the company. Particular attention should be paid to the information technology requirements. It is necessary for the logistics provider to replicate the systems or, more appropriately, improve on them. The flowchart can be used to determine the strengths and weaknesses in the system. This helps determine what improvements can be made through outsourcing as well as which provider is more suitable.

It is important to remember that all costs must be captured: fixed, variable, direct, and indirect. It is quite possible that some logistics expenditures, such as those for order processing or management time, may be difficult to quantify, but they cannot be ignored if valid comparisons are to be made. If it is at all possible, it is much easier to compare internal and outsourced costs if corporate costs can be determined by activity. Activity-based costing (ABC) assigns costs to specific activities or products rather than traditional line item costing. The data collection task can be a formidable one, but it should be borne in mind that much of the information developed is necessary to define the scope of work for the potential service providers. In other words, the task is not optional. It is unavoidable.

Many outsourcing relationships have been developed by the interested firm preparing a request for proposal (RFP), which outlines the tasks to be performed and specifies the contents and format of the proposal. The RFP is presented to three or more providers who are asked to submit bids to perform precise tasks in precise ways. The contract is then awarded to the provider that demonstrates the best cost-to-benefit ratio. It is recommended that in anticipation of the RFP, a preliminary request for information (RFI) be used to gather information about potential providers that are known to have experience in the client industry. Not only will these responses aid in narrowing down the list of providers sent an RFP, but they will also help identify a qualified provider to include in the planning process.

The RFP makes providers' proposals easier to compare and evaluate but ignores the basic issue of determining the most cost- and service-effective logistics process. A true partnership or relationship suggests input by all parties, and the most successful ones are established through joint analysis and resolution of the logistics objective. This may require qualifying logistics providers before the cost of their services is known, but a more satisfactory relationship can result from bringing a potential provider into the planning process early. As a matter of principle, some logistics providers decline to respond to RFPs that they do not feel will maximize their assets, capabilities, and experience. They also avoid those that appear to be just "fishing expeditions." If a firm is going to enter into an outsourcing relationship, however, it makes good sense to leverage the provider's knowledge and expertise early in the process. After all, that is what the outsourcing process is all about.

The Challenges of Global Logistics Outsourcing

The globalization of the marketplace is now a reality for many firms that once competed only on a regional or national level, and this globalization has fueled rapid growth in global logistics. According to the World Trade Organization (WTO), in 2003 approximately 22% of all international services were logistics related, totaling over US $300 billion spent annually. As firms become more global in their operations, they may want to turn to one or more global logistics service firms to provide logistics services globally. To illustrate the prevalence of this issue, a survey by the Foundation for the Malcolm Baldrige National Quality Award revealed that 95% of the CEOs surveyed identified more globalization as their top challenge over a three- to five-year horizon. Eighty percent identified improving the performance of their global supply chains as a top challenge (Trent and Monczka 2003).

Services sought from global logistics providers may include coordinating inbound material shipments from suppliers; consolidating freight; securing ocean, air, or overland transportation; undertaking customs brokerage activities; delivering shipments to customers throughout the destination market; or even administering supply chain relationships in a particular geography or country. Although many of these services have traditionally been secured using transactional, spot-buy methods on an as-needed basis, the escalation of global business, in combination with the increasing shortage of global logistics capacity, is rapidly driving firms to seek longer-term relationships with service providers. In addition, customers themselves are becoming more global in nature, thereby demanding a relatively seamless presence across multiple countries or geographies. Once such longer-term arrangements are formed, shipping firms often form closer relationships with the logistics providers through information technology systems integration; colocation of logistics provider personnel or their customers at the shipping firm; and capital, infrastructure investment by the logistics provider to better meet the needs of the shipping firm.

There are many benefits associated with outsourcing global logistics processes. For example, many shipping firms possess neither the internal expertise nor licenses to execute global supply chain transactions themselves, and they do not wish to invest resources to develop them because of the dynamic nature of the environment. In addition, the trade volumes handled by logistics providers often afford considerably greater leverage than most shipping firms can generate on their own, enabling them to better secure superior services at competitive costs. Furthermore, using the services of a global logistics firm provides shippers with the ability to rapidly expand global sourcing without having to develop the logistics infrastructure to support such sources. Finally, careful selection of a global logistics provider can unlock the power of a worldwide information system that ensures full visibility of the supply chain from the point of international origin to the point of domestic delivery, improving control and enhancing reliability.

Significant challenges must be overcome to achieve these benefits. Many of these challenges are already familiar to the logistician engaging in domestic logistics outsourcing; however, taking an outsourced relationship to a global scope magnifies these familiar challenges. The physical distance between outsourcing parties as well as the legal or political and cultural differences inherent in varying degrees between any two countries only serve to further complicate the relationship between the shipping firm and the logistics provider (Zhang, Cavusgil, and Roath 2003). The physical distance between a shipping firm and the market where a global logistics provider is operating on the shipping firm's behalf enhances the need for clear, continuous communication and trust of the logistics provider. Communication occurs more naturally when a logistics provider can be closely monitored by the shipping firm, and language and time zone barriers do not hamper attempts to communicate. However, in a global logistics relationship separated by physical distance, conscious decisions must be made to ensure proper communication between the shipping firm and the logistics provider.

Extreme physical distance between outsourcing parties demands clearly defined and mutually agreed-upon objectives. In any multidivisional or multiparty effort, there are myriad opportunities to explore and ideas to evaluate. Clearly defined objectives provide a way to screen those opportunities and ideas to ensure that the logistics outsourcing arrangement focuses on what is important and unproductive behavior directed toward agendas that fall outside of the agreed-upon objectives is minimized. The scope of work to be performed by the logistics provider and the accompanying process maps should be formally completed and shared between the parties to remove any ambiguity surrounding the expectations of what is to be done through the relationship.

Organizations entering into global logistics outsourcing arrangements should know that a sharp managerial focus cannot be achieved without emphasizing a well-designed measurement system that eliminates ambiguity regarding objective achievement. A characteristic measurement system clearly and unequivocally tracks and simplifies reports and delivers results to the appropriate level of the firm to ensure that both parties stay focused on the objectives. For example, strategic planners should not be overburdened with operating data, and operations personnel do not need excessive information on strategic level metrics. The focus created by appropriate measurement can ensure that strategic planning meetings do not overly concentrate on operating data reviews and problem discussions but rather are centered on strategic decisions required to determine new avenues of cooperation. Experience clearly demonstrates that focus and measurement are intertwined and self-reinforcing. The separation of parties in a global arrangement further necessitates a deliberate effort to maintain focus and to maintain an unambiguous system of objective measurement.

Frequent, even repetitive, communication of objectives, measurements, and upcoming changes are also essential to keep all parties in the global outsourcing arrangement informed and focused. Periodic lapses in communication encourage participants to disassociate themselves from responsibility for relationship objectives and follow their own agendas. This is particularly true when anticipated results are negative and the logistics provider representative does not have to physically face the shipping firm personnel because of the physical distance and language barriers between them. One way this can be avoided is to begin all official communications with a list of events scheduled for the next six months to ensure that all parties are informed and there are no surprises. Regularly scheduled reviews of operational metrics should be a part of any global logistics outsourcing agreement. Metrics reviews should include participation of the logistics provider's managers in the destination countries as it cannot be assumed that domestic staffs are as prepared to report on the operations as those actually managing them on a daily basis. Frequent formal and informal communication can transform the arrangement from a transactional orientation to a longer-term relationship. When participants learn through frequent contact that both sides are making efforts to achieve relationship objectives, the focus of discussions concerning problems shifts from "Why did you . . . ?" to "How can we . . . ?" Communication builds a bridge between organizations. This can occur via telephone and e-mail; however, regular travel to the destination country and the face-to-face communication that ensues is essential to truly ensure continued progress in the relationship. Once this relational bridge is built, relationships based on trust can be further developed.

A final point in the discussion of how physical distance affects the logistics outsourcing relationship is that of trust in the logistics service provider. It is imperative that the logistics provider to which global business is given be trustworthy. Many times, shipping firms award domestic business solely based on cost. This practice is sound assuming the work is clearly specified and the chosen logistics provider can be closely monitored. However, the nuances of doing business in a different nation and culture, coupled with physical distance, preclude a shipping firm from having this "close watch" over a provider; therefore, a higher level of trust must be maintained. This point should be carefully considered during the provider qualification phase of any logistics outsourcing process. Finally, this trust should do nothing to minimize the focus and attention on measurement and regular communication discussed previously.

The legal and political differences between the shipping firm's country and the destination country represent a second major cause of complexity in global logistics outsourcing. Solutions to these differences manifest themselves at several levels. Beginning with the most straightforward, shipping firms should always be represented by a legal counsel who is knowledgeable about the laws of all countries in the outsourcing contract. The legal systems of countries vary greatly, and a shipping firm must ensure that they have the maximum amount of protection available in the event the relationship sours. Second, outsourcing firms should take the time to understand the legal customs of destination countries. For example, in many countries, written contracts do not necessarily overrule verbal agreements made between the parties. In others, foreign firms are treated differently than are local firms. One technique to mitigate this risk is to enter into a contract with the domestic division of a global logistics provider. This strategy, of course, works only in the limited cases where the logistics provider selected has a domestic division.

The political situation can also have a significant influence on global logistics outsourcing agreements. The rule of law and freedoms enjoyed by individuals and corporations in Western societies do not exist in many countries. Gaining an understanding of how the shipping firm will be treated politically by entering into an arrangement with a particular provider is important. For example, is one provider more respected locally, thus attracting less attention or trouble from the government? Does one provider keep more abreast of rapidly changing laws and customs to ensure continued flow of your products? These types of questions are important to consider when entering into global logistics outsourcing relationships.

The third, and possibly most ambiguous, category of additional complexity in global logistics outsourcing relationships is cultural differences (House and Stank 2001). These differences start simply enough with obstacles such as trying to manage communications across multiple systems, organizations, time zones, languages, and formats (e.g., March 10, 2006, in Europe is written 10/03/06, which in North America would be interpreted as October 3, 2006). These quickly intensify to include organizational culture and structure. Nothing should be taken for granted in the negotiation of a global outsourced relationship—shipping firms must be absolutely sure the logistics provider understands the business model and corporate values and is willing to abide by them. For example, if a shipping firm's business model depends on quick delivery to the customer, it must ensure that the chosen provider understands the delivery window and that there are no exceptions. "I didn't get to it today, but I will tomorrow" is not acceptable even though it may be to every other local client. In addition to an understanding of the business model, cultural differences must be accounted for in the management style and reporting relationship. We have previously discussed the importance of clearly defined goals and regular communication around those goals; however, this does no good if absolute candor is not present in these communications. Such candor is seen as disrespectful in many countries and cultures and therefore does not come naturally. Always be aware of how cultural differences can stymie the success of globally outsourced agreements.

Furthermore, firms have learned that many start-up problems in global logistics outsourcing can be avoided by starting small to work out process, communication, and measurement kinks. Unfortunately, necessity and short-term focus often dictate that such relationships commence during heavy traffic periods. It is during these periods, however, that there is the most opportunity for process glitches to occur—and the most to lose when inevitable start-up problems are encountered! Too often, the pressure to achieve dramatic cost reduction dictates the more risky path. Firms wishing to initiate long-term global logistics outsourcing relationships are cautioned to establish a pilot program to iron out operational difficulties or at least plan to change operational processes during slow points in the annual business cycle rather than peaks. Long-term success, for example, is more reliably ensured by initiating a program with a division that transports smaller volumes of imported product or starting during a slow season of the year. Lower volumes provide sufficient time for personnel to learn the issues associated with huge magnitude change without the stress of high-profile volumes. Experience has shown that going after the brass ring on the first trip around is an extremely risky strategy.

Finally, a few words of caution may help shipping firms avoid a common pitfall when choosing a logistics provider for global outsourcing. The global reach of a logistics provider does not mean an integrated company across the globe. Although hiring a single, global company to perform a variety of tasks across the globe has its benefits, namely a single point of accountability, it should be ensured that this company has the strength for each task. In other words, a shipping firm should hire a logistics provider based on his or her strength in each market where the scope of work is taking place and not by the number of countries in which he or she claims to have an office. For most businesses needing services more complex than parcel delivery to an address in a capital city, the logistics provider needs solid capabilities instead of just an address and a couple of trucks at the major national airport. Very few companies have excellent coverage in many countries and even fewer across regions or continents. If your intended scope of work requires broad delivery coverage or special infrastructure, take the time and effort to investigate the specifics of what the market has to offer in that country. Many times local companies offer the broadest and least expensive services. Consider the type of logistics service you are outsourcing and make decisions accordingly based on the success criteria needed for this service.

Some Concluding Examples

To deal with all the global complexities, outsourcing is almost "nonoptional." A case in point involved an American specialty chemicals firm with manufacturing facilities in the southern part of the country. As their volume grew in the European and Russian markets, they realized that their main focus had been on sales and product innovations with very little attention to the supply chain. As a result, they turned to UTi Worldwide, who conducted an analysis of their techniques and costs. As a result of improvements recommended by UTi, the company was able to reach these markets more effectively, and at the same time, savings of 30% of total supply chain costs were realized.

On the import side as well, global service providers can perform valuable services. A driving factor in Kuehne & Nagel's 2001 acquisition of USCO Logistics was the ability to gain full access to the North American contract logistics market. One important element was the company's network of multiclient distribution centers, which provides flexible logistics solutions for customers with changing distribution needs. Shared warehousing allows customers to pay only for the space and service they need, and as their business expands or contracts, logistics costs parallel the revenue stream. In addition, the new Kuehne & Nagel network throughout the United States allows foreign clients to position inventory closer to their customers. Kuehne & Nagel now is able to provide one-stop shopping for current or future customers looking to grow in the United States.

Minerva U.S.A., Inc., the North American subsidiary of one of the world's leading olive oil manufacturing and trading companies, had to move quickly when the company landed a major retail chain account at the end of 2002. The new account was expected to substantially increase the volume of Minerva, Fort Lee, NJ, a subsidiary of Minerva S.p.A., Genoa, Italy. The company had six months to procure the raw materials, manufacture the product, finalize packaging and labels, make all logistic arrangements, import the product, and begin shipping to the new account. Recognizing that its customer was taking a risk by using a single supplier to produce and deliver a large volume of private-label olive oil, Minerva sought to design a logistic solution that would deliver the highest levels of service at the lowest possible cost. The company examined all logistic possibilities, including shipping product direct to the chain account's distribution centers, and evaluated a range of distribution networks with different combinations of distribution centers. Minerva, which had historically worked with a freight forwarder, carrier, and multiple warehousing providers, knew that they had to make some dramatic changes and began thinking about an integrated solution. After evaluating several logistics providers, Minerva selected Kuehne & Nagel to manage storage, shipping, and delivery to the chain account's facilities via truckload and less-than-truckload distribution. Kuehne & Nagel was already managing all aspects of the import transportation, U.S. customs brokerage, and container delivery. All products arrive in ocean freight containers for storage at Kuehne & Nagel centers in Miami, Los Angeles, San Francisco, and Portland, Oregon. Working with a single provider helped streamline Minerva's logistics process. Vice President Stephane Picard, Minerva U.S.A., says, "Instead of talking with five companies with five systems and five cultures, I talk with one. It's very harmonized, and has saved us a lot of time and hassle."

References

Allen, Gary R., Thomas A. Dale, and C. John Langley, Jr. (2004), *Third Party Logistics: Results and Findings of the 2004 Ninth Annual Study*. Atlanta: Georgia Tech University.

American Warehousemen's Association (1991), *Traveling the Road of Logistics*. Chicago: Autor.

Drucker, Peter F. (2004), "Peter Drucker Sets Us Straight," *Fortune,* January 12, 118.

Goodman, Russel (2005, May), "Top 25 3PLs: A Great Club" [Editorial], *Global Logistics and Supply Chain Strategies,* 9 (54), 8.

"Has Outsourcing Gone Too Far?" (2001, December), *McKinsey Quarterly,* 4, 26–37.

House, Robert G. and Theodore P. Stank (2001). "Insights From a Logistics Partnership," *Supply Chain Management: An International Journal,* 6 (1), 16–20.

Lynch, Clifford F. (2004), *Logistics Outsourcing*. Memphis, TN: CFL Publishing.

Trent, Robert J. and Robert M. Monczka (2003), "Understanding Integrated Global Sourcing," *International Journal of Physical Distribution and Logistics Management,* 32 (7), 607.

Zhang, C., S. T. Cavusgil, and A. S. Roath (2003), "Manufacturer Governance of Foreign Distributor Relationships: Do Relational Norms Enhance Competitiveness in the Export Market?" *Journal of International Business Studies,* 34, 550–566.

23

International Sourcing

Redressing the Balance

Masaaki Kotabe

Michael J. Mol

The International Sourcing Phenomenon

The international sourcing (offshoring) strategy phenomenon continues to capture the public's mind, dividing observers into two opposite camps ("Rich World's Bangalore" 2004). There are those who loathe its effects, particularly in terms of the job losses it supposedly causes but sometimes also because of more general concerns over the effects of globalization or because it potentially undermines the long-term competitiveness of firms, and there are those who herald it as an efficiency-improving measure that helps support countries' competitiveness as well as the performance of firms. However, much of the debate on this topic has taken place without either substantial empirical or theoretical grounding.

We have now undertaken a range of studies on the international sourcing phenomenon.[1] In this chapter, we bring together the knowledge from our earlier publications and attempt to synthesize it. These studies have informed our understanding of the topic and, together with insights acquired through studying outsourcing decisions more generally, have enabled us to develop a more intricate understanding of how international sourcing decisions are made and their consequences, especially how they affect firm performance.

We offer some of these insights to provide a conceptually solid approach to this phenomenon. The key question we address is how much international sourcing firms should engage in to achieve the best results for overall firm performance. We start by offering an overview of how the phenomenon has developed over the past 15 to 20 years. We zoom in especially on the three major waves of international outsourcing the world has witnessed during this time period, the last one being the current offshoring wave. We then discuss the performance effects that have been suggested, both the advantages and the disadvantages, to develop a balanced view of international sourcing.

This chapter expressly focuses on international sourcing because this strategy adds many more complexities that do not apply in domestic sourcing. In developing viable international sourcing strategies, companies must consider not only manufacturing and delivery costs, the costs of various resources, and exchange rate fluctuations but also the availability of infrastructure (including transportation, communications, and energy), industrial and cultural environments, the ease of working with foreign host governments, and so on. Furthermore, the complex nature of sourcing strategy on a global scale spawns many barriers to its successful execution. In particular, logistics, inventory management, distance, nationalism, and lack of working knowledge about foreign business practices, among others, are major operational problems identified by both U.S. and foreign multinational companies engaging in international sourcing.

From a contractual point of view, the international sourcing of intermediate products such as components and services by companies takes place in two ways: (1) from the parent companies or their foreign subsidiaries on an "intrafirm" basis (i.e., internal sourcing) and (2) from independent suppliers on a "contractual" basis (i.e., external sourcing). We propose that there is a negative curvilinear relationship between the extent of international sourcing and the performance of the firm, such that firms should neither keep all their activities at home nor outsource everything to distant locations.

With this model in hand, we discuss what predicts the extent to which firms ought to engage in international sourcing. Finally, we examine some of the practical implications of our model.

Wave After Wave

International sourcing has been around for centuries, perhaps even millennia. It is, as the saying goes, as old as the hills. However, the type of international trade in the times of Adam Smith was qualitatively different from what we observe in modern times, primarily for two reasons, one technical and one social. First, there was limited, if any, trade in intermediate products such as components or services. Instead, there was mostly trade in either raw materials or final products. As the structure of the economy evolved and products themselves became more complicated, the grounds to engage in such trade increased. Second, the nature of supplier relations was not anything like the way we perceive them today. Buyer-supplier coordination and cooperation did not really exist and communications were normally limited to ordering processes. Thus, if we want to understand current practice, we should restrict ourselves to recent history in our analysis.

In recent history, say the last 15 to 20 years, we can distinguish between three waves of international sourcing. The first wave, starting in the mid-1980s and continuing to this day, was primarily focused on international sourcing of manufacturing activities. Research, therefore, focused primarily on manufacturing firms. Kotabe and Omura (1989) offered one of the first studies to address global sourcing in any detail. Large manufacturing firms were increasingly spreading their operations across the world and began to use suppliers from a variety of countries to exploit the so-called best-in-world sources (Quinn and Hilmer 1994). Supply chains, as a consequence, became more global and also much more complicated in nature. Products could now be created through a combination of inputs from perhaps 10 countries or more. In addition, some specialized suppliers, like Flextronics, emerged that could produce entire products including assembly operations.

A second wave started to occur in the early 1990s, when firms decided to start getting rid of their information technology (IT) departments, which had over time grown to a substantial size (Cross 1995). This IT outsourcing wave spawned the growth of specialist providers, such as EDS and Accenture. International sourcing mostly involved labor-intensive programming activities, which because of their relatively standardized nature could be sourced from locations like India with relative ease. IT itself had turned into more of a commodity and many firms started to show little interest in developing new information systems in-house. The rise of commercial applications for a wide range of firm activities, epitomized in enterprise resource planning (ERP) systems, also implied that a marketplace had developed where independent suppliers could make competitive offerings.

In recent years, we have seen the rise of business process outsourcing in what has become known as the offshoring movement. The object has now broadened from just IT services to a range of other services, including those in accounting, human resources management, finance, sales, and after-sales services such as call centers. India is still a primary target country and has now produced a range of strong local business process providers such as Infosys and Wipro, but competition from elsewhere is on the rise. It is this third wave of business process outsourcing that is now generating so much noise and so many media headlines, in part because it has been suggested that the foreign suppliers of such business processes may be moving up the knowledge chain more rapidly than buyers are expecting and such knowledge transfer could in the long run undermine buyers' ability to differentiate themselves from their foreign suppliers in the marketplace. Such concerns, of course, have previously been raised about outsourcing of manufacturing activities as well (Bettis, Bradley, and Hamel 1992; Markides and Berg 1988; Kotabe 1998). These recent waves of international sourcing are summarized in Table 23.1.

The Performance Rationale

It is widely suggested that international sourcing improves firms' performance, particularly their cost-effectiveness (e.g., Trent and Monczka 2003). Firms located in Organization for Economic Cooperation and Development (OECD) countries

Table 23.1   Recent Waves in International Sourcing

Time Period	First Wave (Since the 1980s)	Second Wave (Since the Early 1990s)	Third Wave (Since the Early 2000s)
Type of activity	Manufacturing	Information technology	Business processes
Destinations	China, Central and Eastern Europe, Mexico, and others	India, Ireland, and others	India, Pakistan, South Africa, and others
Type of firms	Manufacturing	Manufacturing, banks, and others	Financial services, more general services
Primary motives	Reduction in labor costs	Obtaining enough skilled programmers and cost reduction	Reduction in labor costs and round-the-clock service provision

often find the costs of labor excessive compared with the value added to their products. Although distant locations such as China lag behind in productivity, they make up for this lower productivity by providing much lower labor costs, sometimes even culminating in deautomation of tasks transferred to these locations. Indeed, we have seen some cases, such as the manufacture of a range of bicycle components, where the production cost differences are so large that it makes no sense to consider domestic sourcing. This labor cost advantage is of course most significant when labor costs actually make up a substantial part of overall production costs.

At the other extreme, we find some international sourcing that is motivated by knowledge concerns. Some inputs, such as aircraft parts and technical expertise, may be required that are available only in other countries, which makes international sourcing not so much a choice as an imperative. The source countries in these instances are mostly other OECD countries. Where sourcing of raw materials is concerned, a choice may not even be available to source them domestically. Similarly, for certain intermediate products, it makes sense to source them from locations near the raw materials source. Another argument in favor of international sourcing is that it may allow a firm to produce closer to sales markets, thereby increasing access. Japanese manufacturing firms have, for instance, over time replicated supply chains in North America and Europe to operate closer to these markets. Production and sourcing experience in these regions also allowed them to improve their product offerings. Another reason for international sourcing is that demand from various regions can be pooled, and hence maximum scale and bargaining power are achieved through single sourcing from a foreign supplier.

On the other hand, there are also disadvantages associated with international sourcing. Typically, the first type of problems managers and the popular press put forward is "cultural differences" between buyers and their foreign suppliers. Indeed, such differences may affect the relationship negatively, but we would also like to point out institutional and language problems as potential sources of problems in these relations. One Dutch manufacturer, for instance, mentioned how its Spanish supplier never appeared to respond to its faxes, which were written in English. When, however, the company had one of its employees translate the fax into Spanish, a response suddenly emerged. Cultural misunderstandings and other communication problems can lie at the heart of quality problems, although these can also be caused by differences in technical standards or even just different expectation patterns. Other sources of discontent over international sourcing are the long lead times and the supply chain uncertainty they often produce (Levy 1995). There are international trade rules that help determine the feasibility of international sourcing (Swamidass and Kotabe 1993). Finally, there is the possibility that foreign suppliers integrate forward into the buyers' market, sometimes by inventing around patents or ignoring them altogether.

This raises another layer of issues related to the long-term sustainability of firms' core competencies. There are two opposing views of the long-term implications of international sourcing. One school of thought argues that many successful companies have developed a dynamic organizational network through increased use of joint ventures, subcontracting, and licensing activities across international borders (Miles and Snow 1986). This flexible network system is frequently referred to as alliances. Such supply chain alliances allow each participant to pursue its particular competence. Therefore, each network participant can be seen as complementing rather than competing with the other participants for the common goals. Such alliances may even be formed by competing companies in the same industry in pursuit of complementary abilities (new technologies or skills) from each other. The other school of thought argues that although this may be true in gaining transitory advantages in the short run, there could also be negative long-term consequences resulting from a company's dependence on independent suppliers and subsequently the inherent difficulty for the company to sustain its long-term competitive advantages because it could not keep abreast of constantly evolving design and engineering technologies without engaging in those developmental activities (Kotabe 1998).

Over time, a firm's technical expertise and capability surplus vis-à-vis its foreign suppliers diminishes to the point that its value added is limited and it is little more than a trading company (Table 23.2). It seems fair to conclude that international sourcing provides both advantages and disadvantages.

On Balance

We, therefore, propose a more balanced view of how international sourcing is related to firm performance. Elsewhere, we have talked at length about the relationship between the degree of outsourcing across all activities of a firm and the performance of that firm (Kotabe and Mol 2004, 2006b). We proposed and empirically verified that firms are best off by outsourcing some but not all of their activities. The underlying argument is that firms that outsource all their activities run into a string of

Table 23.2   Some Advantages and Disadvantages of International Sourcing

Possible Advantages	Possible Disadvantages
Increased size of potential supply base	Having to deal with foreign institutions, which may, for example, give rise to legal differences
Lower production costs, especially for labor-intensive production and services	Having to deal with a foreign culture, which could affect communication
Increased technical expertise, especially for high-tech products from specialized locations	Having to deal with a foreign language, which could affect communication
More flexibility to switch between supply sources, whether internal or external	Need to pay import duties where applicable
Source closer to sales markets, experience in sourcing may be translated into sales	Transportation costs and supply chain uncertainty
Scale economies achieved through use of one global supply source	Forward integration by foreign suppliers, patent infractions possible
Source of intermediate products closer to source of raw materials	Quality problems
Raw materials available only from foreign sources	Can affect employee commitment and public relations
Focus on core competencies	Dependence on independent suppliers and decreased ability to keep abreast of emerging technical requirements

problems, such as lack of innovation and bargaining power and an inability to be distinct in the eyes of the customer. Firms that are completely vertically integrated, however, fail to use the powerful incentives supplied by markets and become bureaucratic and inefficient. Therefore, outsourcing some but not all activities provides the best solution overall, and there is an optimal degree of outsourcing. Deviations from that optimum are costly, and the greater the deviation, the more severe the performance penalty. Hence, there is a negative curvilinear relationship (inverted U-shape) between the degree of outsourcing and firm performance.

We believe a similar line of reasoning can be applied to the degree of internationalization of sourcing and how that affects performance. More specifically, there are advantages and disadvantages associated with international sourcing, as we highlighted earlier. As a firm does more international sourcing, the disadvantages become greater, to the point where they severely impede performance. If firms do no international sourcing at all, they cannot access any of the advantages of international sourcing, such as a wider supply base. This line of reasoning is consistent with research in the international business and neo-institutional economics traditions, particularly the transaction costs framework (Williamson 1985).

Williamson (1985) distinguishes between production costs and transaction costs, the former referring to the costs of actually producing a good or service, the latter to all those costs incurred as the product is transferred from one supply chain partner to the next. When firms use foreign suppliers, they potentially lower production costs, as discussed above. In some instances, of course, production costs of a local supplier are actually lower than those of any foreign supplier, but this is the exception and not the rule. Transaction costs, on the other hand, are invariably higher for international sourcing because there are all kinds of institutional, cultural, and language barriers to overcome. Rangan (2000) has discussed this in terms of the costs of "search and evaluation." Searching for supply sources abroad, whether internal or external, is somewhat more expensive than searching for local supply sources. Evaluating those foreign supply sources is much more expensive because the costs of evaluation are strongly related to the familiarity that decision makers have with the other party. Foreign firms are likely to be less familiar, and decision makers cannot draw on their networks so much to help them evaluate these sources, which induces substantial evaluation costs. Rangan (2000) uses this argument to explain why buying firms are much more likely to choose a domestic supplier than a foreign supplier, even when the physical distance between the buyer and each of these suppliers is the same.

International sourcing is therefore a balancing act between production and transaction costs. Firms need a proper balance between domestic and foreign supply sources if they wish to locate on the top of the curve and obtain the highest possible performance (Figure 23.1). They do this by using foreign sources for a part, but not all, of their sourcing. Sourcing everything from abroad produces poor performance results because the disadvantages of international sourcing become too great. Focusing all efforts on domestic supply sources, however, is a serious form of myopia with equally disastrous effects for firm performance, primarily because important opportunities to improve competitiveness are missed.

Redressing the Balance

If firms need to balance local and international sourcing, then what can we say about what their international sourcing strategies look like and what their international sourcing strategies ought to look like? For many firms, the sourcing location appears to be an afterthought, a decision that is a derivative of which internal or external source they wish to use. The process through which relocation takes place is often very discontinuous. No relocation takes place in an industry for quite a while, until all firms in an industry suddenly decide to relocate to one and the same location, say China. Kotabe and Mol (2006b) suggested the notion of bandwagoning, which implies leader-follower behavior in international sourcing decisions. There is much uncertainty surrounding international sourcing decisions in the form of currency fluctuations, political change, possible supply chain instability, and perhaps most important, uncertainty concerning the future development of relations with internal and external supply chain partners. In need of some reassurances, firms look for decision-making heuristics that allow them to avoid

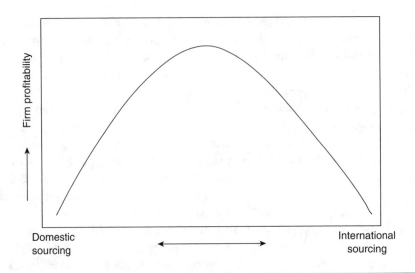

Figure 23.1   A Negative Curvilinear Relationship Between the Degree of
International Sourcing and Firm Performance

paralysis. Copying the behavior of competing firms can clearly be one such heuristic, which could be termed "competitive bandwagoning" (Abrahamson and Rosenkopf 1993) because it involves the perception that competitors improve their performance as a result of strategic decision making. Another heuristic can be to take the advice of external institutions, such as suppliers, consultants, media, and business school professors. This type is called "*institutional bandwagoning*" (Abrahamson and Rosenkopf 1993).

Bandwagon processes are not inherently bad, but there is no reason to believe they normally produce the best results. Bandwagoning can easily lead to too much international sourcing. On the other hand, periods preceding a wave of international sourcing caused by bandwagoning are normally characterized by inertia, implying there is too much domestic sourcing. In other words, if firms are led by bandwagoning in their international sourcing strategy, it is normally an indication that their international sourcing policies are not well-balanced. Furthermore, the firm's competitive advantage will not be raised if it merely copies other firms' behavior. The leaders of an international sourcing wave may appropriate some benefits early on, but for the followers this is normally not the case.

Tackling the second issue, what firms' international sourcing strategies ought to look like, we can take our negative curvilinear relationship as a base. Thus, firms should use some international sources but not rely on them exclusively. For purposes of simplification, we have up to this point discussed the curvilinear relationship and the top of the curve as if they were one and the same for every individual firm. This, of course, is not the case. Where the optimal point lies, in terms of what part of all sourcing should be international, varies widely depending on the context in which the firm operates. In addition, how high the top of the curve is—that is, what optimal performance is possible for a given firm—will equally vary from case to case. This does not mean, however, that we cannot provide any type of guidance as to what drives these outcomes. In fact, previous research has provided a range of possible guidelines for firms to follow. Essentially, these can be split into four types of predictors of international sourcing: country, industry and product, firm, and relationship (Kotabe and Mol 2006a).

At the country level, both the characteristics of the country the sourcing firm is located in and the differences between that country and the source country matter. Firms located in the United States are much more likely to find a proper domestic supply source than are firms in Denmark. In countries that are well integrated in a regional trade bloc, such as the North American Free Trade Agreement (NAFTA) or the European Union, it is easier to use foreign supply sources located in countries inside the trade bloc. If the country in which the sourcing firm is located has liberal policies concerning imports and exports, it helps promote various forms of international sourcing too. Tariff barriers negatively affect international sourcing.

In addition, there are several intercountry differences that matter. First, either the production cost differential or the knowledge differential between the sourcing country and the source country must be sufficient to overcome the costs of transacting across borders. By this we mean that either production in the other country must be a lot less expensive or sources in the other country must be able to produce a good or service that is far superior to what domestic sources can produce. This production cost or knowledge differential can therefore be seen as an enabler of international sourcing. On the other hand, there are several other intercountry differences that can act as inhibitors, invariably falling under the headings of culture, institutions, and language. They include written rules in the form of law, for instance, which may determine how safe it is to share intellectual property or other assets. They also include the costs that arise owing to the need to bring in translators or the costs that arise when no translators are brought in and ex post alterations must be made. They may include costs that come about because the habits of doing business vary from one place to another, for instance, because bribes can be perfectly acceptable in some countries but have been outlawed in others. As the magnitude of intercountry differences grows, they become more of an inhibitor and discourage international sourcing more.

At the industry and product level, several additional considerations arise. The type of product is perhaps the core consideration for determining the sourcing location. Many services, for example, require face-to-face contact, which simply makes international sourcing impossible. Some types of goods are so heavy compared with the value they represent that transportation costs become excessive even though for many other goods transportation costs have more or less become irrelevant. It may also be considerations of transportation time that drive a firm toward domestic sourcing. As noted earlier, for labor-intensive products the reverse is often true because labor intensity generally encourages international sourcing from low-cost source countries. Likewise, where many highly specialized inputs are needed to put a product together, international sourcing might be the only option. Airbus, for instance, sources different components from a range of European countries, where supplier firms have each developed their own area of specialization. Industry dynamics can be another factor driving the viability of international sourcing.

When there is much competition, especially competition to be the lowest-cost producer, firms not only tend to outsource more but are also pressed into looking for the lowest-cost supply sources worldwide. In highly uncertain environments, it may be helpful to source nearby because that improves response times. As discussed earlier, when many other firms in an industry source from abroad, a firm may feel bandwagon pressures to copy that behavior. There are, however, instances where this makes much sense, such as when foreign suppliers have managed to learn from other buyers and have now become more efficient or more effective producers as a consequence.

At the firm level, further explanations of international sourcing have been discovered. Large firms are much more prolific when it comes to international sourcing. There are two ways of explaining this. The literature has discussed the barriers that small firms face when they attempt to source internationally in the form of lack of knowledge of foreign supply markets, formal requirements for shipping goods, and the inability to force foreign suppliers to do their jobs well because of lower bargaining power. Unlike large firms, they are not able to build a dedicated international sourcing function. Large firms stand to benefit more from international sourcing. Because transaction costs are relatively, though not completely, independent of transaction volumes, they become smaller relative to production costs as production volume rises. In other words, large firms have much more of an incentive to source internationally because they stand to gain more in the form of production cost savings. Because large firms source larger volumes, they sometimes have to source internationally because it is the only way to find these volumes.

Multinational firms are also more adept at international sourcing. These firms have international experience and often have global networks that were built through other activities such as international sales or mergers and acquisitions across borders. Another way to look at this is to say that different forms of internationalization, inward and outward, are correlated simply because some firms' strategies and markets are more international. How multinational firms are organized internally is a further cause of differences in international sourcing. Those firms that are more tightly integrated between countries exchange more information between their various locations, which helps them to assess foreign suppliers more easily. In terms of the search and evaluation framework we discussed earlier, more tightly integrated firms are able to lower the costs of searching for and evaluating foreign supply sources because they can obtain more and more reliable information through their internal networks.

Another form of integration that has been shown to positively affect international sourcing is integration between the different functional areas of a firm (Kotabe 1992; Mol et al. 2004). Where there is much communication between operations, marketing, R&D, and other functions, it becomes easier to source abroad because sourcing needs can be defined less ambiguously.

The fourth level at which explanations of international sourcing can be invoked is the relational level. Outsourcing to a different business unit of the same company primarily relies on internal relations, between headquarters and subsidiaries or among subsidiaries. International outsourcing, on the other hand, primarily revolves around relations with external foreign suppliers. Because these two types are qualitatively different, we will discuss them separately. In the area of subsidiary relations, the focus has gradually shifted from how to control subsidiaries to how to best employ them for knowledge creation and knowledge transfer purposes. In sourcing terms, this implies that foreign subsidiaries are no longer used as just low-cost production bases, but they are also used to innovate and add value to products. Furthermore, all subsidiaries taken together are now viewed as the internal network of a firm. Because ties between network partners vary, outsourcing to another business unit is likely to depend on the strength of relational ties between the sourcing subsidiary and the source subsidiary. These relational ties may occur at both the personal and the organizational level. When subsidiary managers share previous experience with the managers of another subsidiary abroad, they are more likely to employ that subsidiary for sourcing inputs. Similarly, a previous sourcing relationship between two subsidiaries is a positive predictor for a future sourcing relationship. Where external suppliers are concerned, a similar argument holds: Previous experience increases the likelihood of future transactions, but some additional arguments apply. There is also an issue with the fit between the organizational cultures of the buyer and supplier firms. Moving beyond differences in national cultures, we can also look at how the company-specific cultures differ and how this affects international sourcing relationships. When one company values a perfect technical quality of services or goods, whereas the other is mostly interested in the timeliness of delivery, it negatively affects the likelihood of a future sourcing relation. Some firms are known to have a larger capacity for building supplier relations than others. Toyota is perhaps the best-known example of a firm that has managed to create strong relations with suppliers. Because building relations with foreign suppliers is generally harder than building relations with domestic suppliers, for reasons discussed earlier, this capacity is crucial in determining how effectively international sourcing can be undertaken and how much international sourcing can be undertaken effectively.

To complicate matters further, the optimal point in terms of how much international sourcing to engage in shifts over time. Over the past 15 to 20 years we have certainly seen it shift toward more international sourcing. Some underlying factors, discussed at length in the globalization literature, include new information and communication technology, lower transportation costs, more transparency, and perhaps even convergence across international markets. Of course, that a shift toward more international sourcing has occurred in recent years need not mean this trend will continue endlessly.

Riding the Waves

As we look over the landscape of international sourcing, there are several key points. First, research on this topic is scattered through a number of functional areas including marketing, operations management, international business and management, and supply chain management (for a more detailed discussion, see Kotabe and Mol 2006a). As a consequence, knowledge accumulation is not as effective as it could be. Rather than reinventing a wheel that has not yet been seen in their specific area of work, we encourage scholars and practitioners to explore other areas and find out how these can add to their understanding. Second, there is a clear lack of understanding of how the process of international sourcing develops over time. There are not many studies that follow the development trajectory a firm takes over time in international sourcing. Are capabilities to source across borders built over time? If so, does this happen in a more or less linear fashion or rather more through a set of discrete events? Is there a clear progression over time in terms of how different the source countries are? Is there perhaps a cyclical model where international sourcing is followed by disillusionment and a reversal of earlier decisions? Answering these questions requires process-based case studies.

Achieving the right balance is crucial in international sourcing. This implies that firms need to find mechanisms to adapt to changing circumstances without falling afoul of bandwagon pressures. Clearly an in-depth analysis of the advantages and disadvantages of international sourcing in every individual case benefits the quality of managerial decision making. The factors to analyze include those discussed above and probably some more. Formal evaluation tools might be developed based on these factors. An organization structure that could be of value to firms is an international sourcing center, where information on foreign sourcing opportunities is gathered and disseminated to local decision makers. A center like this could also aid in the development of formal evaluation tools. More generally, there clearly is an experimentation process involved in international sourcing, which requires firms to make mistakes in the form of episodes of too much domestic sourcing or too much international sourcing. Those firms that understand they are experimenting and are willing to learn from their mistakes are in a better position to improve future decisions on international sourcing.

Because there are bound to be further waves of international sourcing in the future, what matters is how to ride these waves. We believe that those firms that anticipate the wave and deal with it in a timely and effective manner will turn out to be winners. If, however, international sourcing is just a response to periods of inertia and sluggishness, there is unlikely to be much competitive value in it. The best wave riders understand how waves are shaped and as a consequence can predict their shapes and speed.

Note

1. See, for instance, Kotabe (1992, 1998); Kotabe and Mol (2006a); Kotabe and Omura (1989); Kotabe and Swan (1994); Mol et al. (2004); Mol, van Tulder, and Beije (2002); Murray, Kotabe, and Wildt (1995); and Swamidass and Kotabe (1993).

References

Abrahamson, E. and L. Rosenkopf (1993), "Institutional and Competitive Bandwagons: Using Mathematical Modeling as a Tool to Explore Innovation Diffusion," *Academy of Management Review*, 18 (3), 487–517.

Bettis, R., S. Bradley, and G. Hamel (1992), "Outsourcing and Industrial Decline," *Academy of Management Executive*, 6 (1), 7–16.

Cross, J. (1995). "IT Outsourcing: British Petrol," *Harvard Business Review*, 73 (3), 94–102.

Kotabe, M. (1992), *Global Sourcing Strategy: R&D, Manufacturing, and Marketing Interfaces.* New York: Quorum Books.

Kotabe, M. (1998), "Efficiency vs. Effectiveness Orientation of Global Sourcing Strategy: A Comparison of U.S. and Japanese Multinational Companies," *Academy of Management Executive*, 12 (4), 107–119.

Kotabe, M. and M. J. Mol (2004), "A New Perspective on Outsourcing and the Performance of the Firm," in *Global Corporate Evolution: Looking Inward or Looking Outward*, International Management Series: Volume 4, M. Trick, ed. Pittsburgh, PA: Carnegie Mellon University Press, pp. 331–340.

Kotabe, M. and M. J. Mol (2006a), "Outsourcing and Firm Profitability: A Negative Curvilinear Relationship," London Business School working paper, London.

Kotabe, M. and M. J. Mol, eds. (2006b), *Global Supply Chain Management,* Globalization of the World Economy Series. Cheltenham, UK: Edward Elgar.

Kotabe, M. and G. S. Omura (1989), "Sourcing Strategies of European and Japanese Multinationals: A Comparison," *Journal of International Business Studies,* 20 (1), 113–130.

Kotabe, M. and K. S. Swan (1994), "Offshore Sourcing: Reaction, Maturation and Consolidation of US Multinationals," *Journal of International Business Studies,* 25 (1), 115–140.

Levy, D. L. (1995), "International Sourcing and Supply Chain Stability," *Journal of International Business Studies,* 26 (2), 343–360.

Markides, C. and N. Berg (1988), "Manufacturing Offshore Is Bad Business," *Harvard Business Review*, 66 (September–October), 113–120.

Miles, R. E. and C. C. Snow (1986), "Organizations: New Concepts for New Forms," *California Management Review,* 28 (Spring), 62–73.

Mol, M. J., P. Pauwels, P. Matthyssens, and L. Quintens (2004), "A Technological Contingency Perspective on the Depth and Scope of International Outsourcing," *Journal of International Management*, 10 (2), 287–305.

Mol, M. J., R. J. M. van Tulder, and P. R. Beije (2002), "Global Sourcing: Fad or Fact?" Erasmus University Rotterdam working paper ERIM 2002-55-ORG, Rotterdam.

Murray, J. Y., M. Kotabe, and A. R. Wildt (1995), "Strategic and Financial Implications of Global Sourcing Strategy: A Contingency Analysis," *Journal of International Business Studies,* 26 (1), 181–202.

Quinn, J. B. and F. G. Hilmer (1994), "Strategic Outsourcing," *Sloan Management Review,* 35 (4), 43–55.

Rangan, S. (2000), "The Problem of Search and Deliberation in International Exchange: Microfoundations to Some Macro Patterns," *Journal of International Business Studies,* 31 (2), 205–222.

"Rich World's Bangalore" (2004), *Economist,* November 11.

Swamidass, P. M. and M. Kotabe (1993), "Component Sourcing Strategies of Multinationals: An Empirical Study of European and Japanese Multinationals," *Journal of International Business Studies,* 24 (1), 81–99.

Trent, R. J. and R. M. Monczka (2003), "International Purchasing and Global Sourcing: What Are the Differences?" *Journal of Supply Chain Management,* 39 (4), 26–37.

Williamson, O. E. (1985), *The Economic Institutions of Capitalism.* New York: Free Press.

24

Negotiating Throughout the Supply Chain

Lloyd M. Rinehart

Entry into the global supply chain environment has caused the need for increasing emphasis on managing relationships between suppliers and customers. This emphasis has highlighted several key elements that supplier and customer managers must understand to be effective in achieving their goals through the efforts of their suppliers or customers. The first element is understanding the process that organizations go through in creating the relationships (Rinehart, Cadotte, and Langley 1988). This process is based on negotiation activities that occur between the supplier and customer organizations as they attempt to achieve their strategic and operating goals by working with other organizations in the supply chain. The second element is the consideration of the strategic and operating elements that are negotiated to create these relationships. These elements are the foundation for the issues that are discussed during bargaining sessions. The third element is understanding the nature of the resulting relationship that is created between the supplier and customer. It becomes critically important to recognize that not all relationships are alike and that their differences have to be understood and managed. This chapter presents the elements of that negotiation process, links the process to marketing, purchasing, and operations concepts that affect the outcomes of the negotiations, and provides a structure for interpreting the types of relationships that exist between suppliers and customers.

Proper assessment of the activities that compose supplier-customer negotiation requires a definition of the content and boundaries of the process. The following definition has been developed for application to this process.

Negotiation is a management process involving the preparation for bargaining, the interaction of two or more parties in a bargaining situation, and the resolution

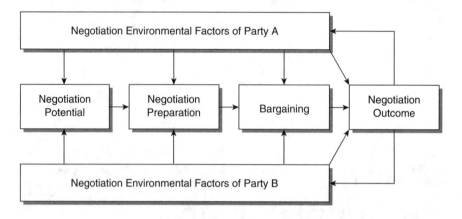

Figure 24.1   The Negotiation Process

or outcome of this interaction. Preparation includes the collection of information and the use of that information in the formulation of interactive strategies designed to achieve the firm's negotiation objectives. Bargaining includes the execution of these strategies and the give-and-take over individual issues, which is necessary to satisfy the parties. Outcome represents an agreement between the parties designed to accomplish mutual gain or the discontinuance of the negotiation process.

Using this definition, a conceptual model was developed that represents the process of supplier-customer negotiations (Figure 24.1). Because this model is designed to be a general model of the negotiation process, the interpretation of suppliers and customers can be very broad to include any individual or firm that supplies or buys a good or service located anywhere in a global supply chain setting.

The areas of the negotiation process include the environments that surround the parties to the negotiation (negotiation environmental factors), the nature of the relative relationship between the parties (negotiation potential), the activities of preparation that take place to ensure that necessary information is available for decision making during the interactions between the parties (negotiation preparation), the actual discussions that take place between the parties (bargaining), and the interpretation of the outcomes of the negotiation process (negotiation outcome). Understanding all these elements is critical to creating successful negotiation outcomes. The negotiation outcomes from Figure 24.1 result in one of seven types of supplier-customer relationships.

Relationship Types Resulting From Supplier-Customer Negotiations

The seven types of supplier-customer relationships that are the outcomes of the negotiation process result from relationship dynamics.

Relationship Dynamics

To fully understand supplier-customer relationships in the global supply chain, they should be characterized in terms of several different dynamics. These dynamics include the degree of trust that exists between the parties, the level of interaction that occurs between the parties, and the commitment of the parties to the relationship.

Trust is a concept that is critical to the foundation of supplier-customer relationships. The underlying elements of trust seem to be differentiated between personal characteristics and organizational dimensions. The personal level can be assessed by interpreting the character level of each party to the negotiation, whereas the organizational level addresses the capability of the organizations to meet the needs of each other through the relationship. These two dimensions can often be independent of one another. For instance, the customer may trust the sales representative of the supplier because of the weekly interaction that builds the relationship but not trust the company that the sales representative represents (or vice versa). This may be critical in a global context because the customer may not know the global supplier well but trusts that supplier's representative because of the personal relationship. This personal level interaction affects each party's perception of the value created by the other. At the organizational level, the success of the relationship is assessed through the amount of business the parties conduct. In many cases, large customers or suppliers are viewed as adding greater value to a relationship than small customers or suppliers. The added value can cause more frequent communication between the parties and result in greater volumes transacted.

Supplier-customer relationships are also the result of the level of commitment to the relationship by the parties. Commitment involves one party's perception of their dependence on the other party and the amount of investment they make in the relationship in terms of time and resources. For instance, efforts by companies to provide supplier training programs or attempts to acquire feedback from distributors through distributor advisory councils is evidence of a strong commitment to their supply and customer base. In other situations, commitment occurs in the form of specific investments in equipment and facilities to support manufacturing or distribution operations at various points around the globe, which enhances the value necessary to meet the market needs of unique global markets.

Relationship Types

Seven different types of supplier-customer relationships have recently been identified (Rinehart et al. 2004). Figure 24.2 represents a graphic structure for the seven types of relationships based on the trust in the other party, the interaction frequency, and the level of commitment to the relationship by the parties. The seven types of relationships range from basic transactions to highly complex relationships between global suppliers and customers, and they are differentiated by their levels of trust, interaction frequency, and commitment to the relationship. The following is a discussion of the characteristics of these relationships and the

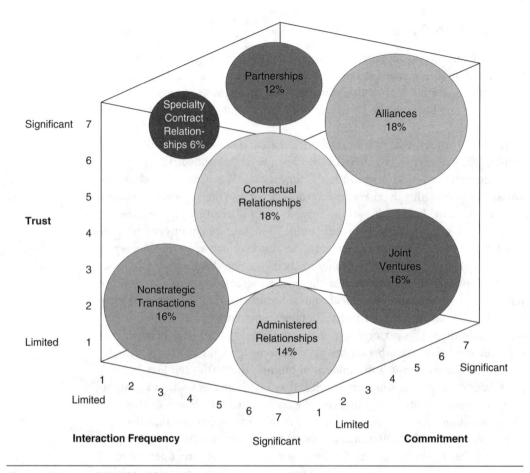

Figure 24.2   Relationship Characteristics

implications for global logistics, sourcing, and marketing managers responsible for the daily management of these relationships as well as executives setting strategic priorities for global supply chain operations.

Nonstrategic Transactions

The most basic situation is identified as a *nonstrategic transaction*. These situations can be one-time transactions or multiple transactions between parties over a period of time. The predominant characteristics of these situations include limited trust in the personal character of the other party; limited communication frequency between the parties; limited perceived dependence on the other party; limited capability of the other organization; limited volume conducted between the organizations; and very little investment in the other party.

Nonstrategic transactions require traditional interactive skills on the part of the boundary spanners (individuals who represent the organization to outside constituents) and executives responsible for working with the other party. There is significant need for defensive posturing when interacting with the other party to protect the organization's interests and objectives. The parties involved need to limit information exchange to pertinent issues and develop discussion positioning and concession strategies that optimize their opportunities relative to the other party.

Administered Relationship

Administered relationships are the most basic type that can be identified as a "relationship." These situations also can include one-time transactions, or multiple transactions between parties, but there is a stronger emphasis on attempting to manage the relationship through less formalized influence strategies. In these relationships trust is generally below average, but in some cases it may be significant. The communication frequency between the parties is higher than in nonstrategic transactions and perceived dependence and investment in the relationship are below average.

In contrast to nonstrategic transactions, administered relationships have a higher percentage of transactions over multiple products and services, which increases the level of dependence between the parties. Global logistics, sourcing, and marketing managers in these relationships must use significant tact when dealing with the other party, because their objectives must be attained through implementation of influence strategies that are not based on positive personal character traits of the other party. For example, a sales or sourcing representative of a firm must present himself or herself to the other party as an expert in some area of mutual need, such as merchandising expertise, inventory analysis, quality processes, or training capability. These services are critical to the demand volume objective of both parties and, ultimately, the long-term duration of the relationship. That expertise depends on presenting himself or herself in a personable and expert manner.

Contractual Relationship

Contractual relationships include typical levels of trust in the other party, average communication frequency and business volume between the parties, and average commitment to the other party. These relationships reflect the need for formalized control over business activity between global suppliers and customers. At the organizational level, there seems to be an increased need for the relationship based on the capability and volumes conducted with the other organization. This is indicative of the supply- or market-based need that exists between organizations that want to minimize investment and drive the relationship on transactional and economic elements. Personal level dynamics are stronger than in the situations and relationships previously discussed but not as strong as in other types of relationships. This may be due to the formal nature of the relationship. For example, in the administered relationship, the increased communication frequency and dependence between the parties may be due to the informal nature of the relationship.

However, in contractual relationships, the formalization of the contract dictated by the global exchange situation reduces the need for direct communication between boundary spanners and therefore increases the perceived dependence of one party on the other. In addition, global sourcing and marketing managers may have an improved impression of their counterpart through the recognition of the legal obligations of the formal contract that exists between the organizations.

Interactive skills used by managers and executives responsible for working with international suppliers or customers are critical for the successful performance of the relationship. At the same time, they must have knowledge of the contractual obligations between the firms to appropriately address the issues through managerial influence strategies, such as arbitration (which is becoming increasingly popular in business relationships), or through legal remedies in the court system. Obviously, the latter methods of dispute resolution are not desired but must be recognized as potentially important (when legal jurisdiction issues arise because of the diverse interests of suppliers and customers from different countries under different legal systems) if the contract is to be used for its ultimate intent of formalizing the bounds of the relationship.

Joint Venture

Another commonly used term to represent relationships between suppliers and customers is *joint venture*. Joint ventures are generally associated with some form of investment in the relationship to accommodate mutual benefits for the parties. For instance, two global manufacturers with complementary technologies might form a joint venture to produce a completely new product that is not currently available in other markets around the world.

The behavioral dimensions of joint ventures include below-average trust in the other party and above-average interaction frequency and commitment levels relative to other relationships. What differentiates joint ventures from contractual relationships is the perception of dependence of one party on the other. This implied commitment, associated with a lower level of trust in the other party, causes the firms to engage in greater levels of investment to ensure adequate performance and control over the relationship. In other words, the investment occurs because there is a lack of trust in the other party, and the former uses the investment as a mechanism to maintain control over the relationship.

Because the parties are tied by financial obligations of investment, the boundary-spanning personnel must possess managerial characteristics more closely associated with internal management assignments than external boundary-spanning responsibilities. This becomes a more substantial challenge when these internal managerial characteristics represent different business cultures and countries. Therefore, the parties may find emphasis placed on the exercise of legitimate and expert power (instead of referent power and reward power that may be more predominant in relationships with less formalization) created by investment and contractual terms, assuming that the legal structure can support the legitimate power being exercised.

Specialty Contract Relationship

Specialty contract relationships are unique contracts that exist for narrowly designed products or services that are exchanged between suppliers and customers. Trust at both the personal and organizational levels is highly prevalent in these relationships. Therefore, the relationship is significantly built on the personal relationship between the boundary spanners and the need for the relationship by the organizations. However, interaction frequency and commitment have limited importance to the relationship. The lack of importance of interaction frequency and commitment may be due to the specialized nature of the product, which may represent minor volumes of business relative to other parts of the organization for one of the parties but not the other and wider ranges of alternative sources of supply or market access for one party but not the other. This may reduce the perceived dependence and need for investment in the relationship by one of the parties.

Success in specialty contractual relationships requires strong personal relationships between supplier and customer representatives. There must be significant trust between the parties through their perceptions of honesty and integrity in the conduct of business. If the levels of trust are not maintained in these relationships, the customer party may feel less obligated to the supplier and find alternative sources of supply. The challenges identified here become even greater when the organizations represent different global competitive settings and different cultural situations because of the global exchange environment. In other words, it becomes critically important to match the right personality with the relationship.

Partnership

The term *partnership* is used frequently in industry. Partnerships here have more specific definitional characteristics that include above-average trust elements at both the personal characteristic level and the organizational level of capability, below-average interaction frequency at both the personal and organizational levels, and commitment of above-average dependence and investment. An example might be a relationship between a supplier providing a critical component part and a manufacturer that uses that part in the manufacturing of a final product. In this case, the relationship may be very close between the two parties because the manufacturer is dependent on the supplier owing to a sole sourcing supply strategy, and the supplier may also be just as dependent because of the relative amount of business that is conducted with this customer compared with other customers.

It is interesting that the elements of trust and commitment are high in partnerships, but elements of interaction frequency are significantly lower. This indicates that partnerships, like specialty contract relationships, require significant emphasis on the personnel involved in the relationship to allow the parties to accomplish their objectives. Therefore, the boundary spanners must possess the personal skills necessary to maintain the relationship, and they must have the authority to utilize organizational opportunities to demonstrate the necessary capability for success of the relationship. Unlike specialty contractual relationships, partnerships have greater levels of investment in the relationship to demonstrate the commitment to the other party. These investment factors may include the time that the organization is willing to invest in flying boundary spanners around the world to maintain the personal relationships of the parties in the global relationship and the willingness of personnel to learn languages (other than their primary language) for the benefit of conducting business with global supply chain partners.

Alliance

What differentiates an *alliance* from a joint venture is the above-average level of trust in the other party at both the personal and the organizational levels. This trust leads to greater levels of communication frequency between the parties and may contribute to increased investment in the relationship relative to other transactions and relationships (other than joint ventures). A good example is a supplier who provides a dedicated engineer to the global customer in a relationship, who works closely with the customer's new product development team in helping to design and develop a new product targeted at a new international market, which integrates the supplier's technology.

The resulting managerial dimensions for alliances require sourcing and marketing managers to influence and control the relationship through personal means of fostering joint cooperation between the parties. Emphasis must be placed on the use of reward and referent power, which is reflected by the limited use of formalized methods of documentation and increased use of verbal agreements or agreements that are designed by nonlegal personnel. These methods reinforce the "relationship" nature of alliances and provide the ultimate in desired relationships between global suppliers and customers.

Following the Negotiation Process in a Global Supply Chain Context

Negotiation comprises understanding the environments that surround the negotiation, understanding the existing and potential relationship between the parties, understanding the processes of using data and developing strategies in preparation for bargaining activities, the actual bargaining or interaction between the parties, and assessing the outcomes that have arisen from the negotiations.

Negotiation Environmental Factors

Global negotiation activities are influenced by the characteristics of the macroenvironment, the organization, and the participating individuals. In addition, the negotiator must distinguish between influences from different elements within the firm and those from outside the firm. These negotiation environmental factors have been classified into four groups: the external environment, the organizational environment, the departmental environment, and the personal environment.

External Environment

The external environment has variables over which the organization and negotiators have little or no control. These elements include the characteristics of competition, the state of the economy, technology, legislation and political decisions, and cultural factors. Competition influences the relationships between global suppliers and customers on a daily basis. This is a critical rationale as to why a local presence can be important in foreign markets. Firms competing in markets with which they are not familiar need supply chain relationships that have a stronger market understanding that results in a better competitive position.

Another important external element affecting global supplier-customer negotiations is the current state of each firm's domestic economy and the global economy. Economic conditions affect the stability of supplier and customer organizations, such as the effect of an increase or decrease in the rate of inflation or a change in the prime interest rate on a firm's ability to invest in facilities or technology. In addition, economic factors affect the cost of labor, which can be a significant contributing factor in the ultimate cost of the product or service being transacted.

Technology also influences negotiation activities. Computer technology offers global suppliers and customers immediate information pertaining to organizational factors, product characteristics, operational cost constraints, status of shipments in transit, and transaction cost parameters in a negotiation. Therefore, negotiators must view technology from three perspectives: the elements of technology that are built into the product or service, the use of operational technology that contributes to creation of the product or service, and the transaction technology used by boundary spanners to facilitate the transaction.

Legal elements are also critical to the success of supplier-customer negotiations. Strategies used by firms can affect how much power they may have in a negotiation relative to their counterpart. This relative power base may be affected by the legal interpretations of the relationships by policy initiatives of government regulators in various countries around the globe. Therefore, it becomes necessary to understand the implications of various relationship strategies on competitive conditions in various countries that have different antitrust policy structures.

Finally, each negotiator must understand the influence of cultural factors surrounding each negotiation. Cultural factors can be addressed from multiple perspectives. Three approaches to viewing cultural differences can be based on geographic location, gender, and age of the parties. Geographic locations give rise to cultural differences as companies around the world negotiate with each other. Gender differences are also important to consider in negotiations. Involvement of female negotiators may be received more positively in some parts of the world than in others. Finally, consideration must also be given to the effect of age on negotiation outcomes. Younger negotiators bring different cultural perspectives to a negotiation compared with older negotiators. Negotiators who fail to recognize these differences may find themselves struggling to work with negotiation counterparts representing different cultures.

Organizational and Departmental Environments of Negotiation

Each negotiator must carefully consider the elements of the organizations that can affect the outcomes of each negotiation. First, it is important to recognize that negotiations between global suppliers and customers may occur within domains of responsibility of particular units within each organization. For example, the selling firm may be represented by the sales or account management department of the organization, whereas the buying firm may be represented by the engineering unit. Each of these individual units has internal unit goals and objectives that may or may not be consistent with their respective organizations' goals. The commonality or differences between the corporate goals and the unit goals significantly affect the outcome of each negotiation. Therefore, it is critically important to differentiate between the organization and the unit when departments are representing an organization in a supplier-customer negotiation.

Second, each organization or department is affected by the contextual and climate elements of the organization. These include the mission and operating philosophies of the organization, as well as the size and financial and market positions of the firm. In addition, the organization and the department approach each negotiation differently based on the structural constraints that result from the specialization, formalization, and centralization that affect decision making by the boundary spanners.

Personal Environment

Each negotiation between a global supplier and customer occurs between the individuals that represent the organizations. These boundary spanners can be people who are in frontline positions on a daily basis (e.g., purchasing agent or sales representative) or senior executives who become involved in negotiations because of the strategic nature of the issues addressed in the negotiation. However, because of the competitive importance of the global transaction, there is a higher probability that more senior members of the management team will be involved, mainly because of the physical distances that may be involved in the resulting movements compared with a domestic relationship.

Regardless of who the boundary spanners are, consideration must be given to the personality characteristics of each of the parties. Another personal level of consideration is the personality that each party brings to the negotiation. Personality elements include the drive the individual possesses to accomplish his or her goals, the ability to structure information about the negotiation situation and use it in a meaningful manner, the individual's awareness of the environment that surrounds the negotiation, and his or her propensity for a cooperative relationship with the other party rather than a confrontational interaction. These personality elements provide the foundation for understanding how the other party will approach the negotiation and give a basis for direction to each negotiator as he or she builds strategy for each bargaining session.

Assessing the Negotiation Potential of the Relationship

Every negotiation requires effective assessment of the nature of the potential relationship prior to interaction between the parties. Negotiation potential is assessed when the parties understand the power and dependence positions of each other in the relationship (Emerson 1962). In the global context, each organization brings market and operational clout that affects each party's perceived need for the other in the relationship. In addition, one or more individuals may represent each organization in the negotiation. This brings a level of personal power to the relationship and negotiation. This level of personal power is reflected in the ability of one party to influence the other party when interacting in the bargaining environment. This influence may result from the type of power base that is implemented by the negotiators (French and Raven 1959). For example, a negotiator may use coercive power to influence the other party when he or she knows the other party is highly dependent on the relationship. In other situations, when the parties recognize a relative balance in their power and dependence, they may be more inclined to use referent power strategies to share information and work cooperatively to accomplish their objectives from the negotiation.

Therefore, it is critically important that the parties fully understand the nature of the potential relationship for a successful negotiation outcome. This assessment can occur through consideration of the dependence of the parties, the extent of global competition faced by the parties, the technology contributions of the parties, interpretations of past or potential future conflict, other behaviors of the parties, and financial constraints of the parties posed by global competitive conditions. These elements provide the foundation for the preparation and bargaining activities of the global supply chain negotiation process.

Negotiation Preparation

Initiation of the behavioral activities of the global supplier-customer negotiation process is based on the perception of the obtainable benefits relative to the costs incurred through the analysis of the potential relationship. Each party must assess the other's relative needs and capabilities. The negotiation preparation activities allow the parties to structure information in a manner that is meaningful during bargaining.

Negotiation preparation requires a detailed analysis of the situation. This includes the collection, organization, and evaluation of information about the participants, organizations, and external environments that may affect the bargaining activities. Negotiators use this information as a basis for developing goals and strategies to be implemented during the bargaining phase of the negotiation process.

Negotiators may collect information throughout the term of the negotiations, implying that the negotiation process is cyclical. This means the participants progress to a point of meeting with each other to initiate interaction, discuss each issue and proposal, reach some level of agreement on each proposal, and then reassess their positions and develop new strategies appropriate for the discussion of the next issue and proposal. Therefore, participants are continually collecting and analyzing pertinent information throughout the negotiation process. This may also include the time between meetings as well as during meetings.

Information Collection and Synthesis

Information collection and synthesis is the process of collecting, organizing, and evaluating the environmental information relevant to the global supplier-customer relationship. The information can be classified into two groups: the specific contract issues and the behaviors of the parties. The specific contract issues also fall into two categories: the transactional elements traditionally addressed by the marketing and purchasing elements of the organization and the operational elements that include the manufacturing and logistics elements of each organization (Rinehart, Cooper, and Wagenheim 1989).

These elements can be classified into five general categories for global supplier-customer negotiation purposes. They include consideration of the products and services transacted between the parties. The marketing and purchasing considerations include the characteristics of the product or service that are pertinent to the parties. These issues can include the variety and assortment in the product line, the quality of the products or services, and the warranty and support offered for the product. Associated with the marketing and purchasing considerations are the operational elements that ensure the product or service can be delivered within the agreed-upon terms of the negotiation. Operational elements include the inventory requirements of the production and distribution facilities that support the availability of the product in the marketplace.

The second area of specific contract issues discussed in a negotiation is the nature and location of the supply and market facilities and the operational elements of those facilities. Supply and market sources will be partly decided by their proximity to organizational facilities. The location of global suppliers and customers affects transportation costs for movements of materials and finished goods. Therefore, proximity of facilities may affect the outcome of these negotiations.

On the marketing and purchasing side is the ease of conducting business with one party over another. For example, a supplier may be physically close to the customer's plant but behaviorally be very difficult to work with in daily operational implementation circumstances. Although a second supplier is further away from the plant (causing increased transportation costs), the boundary spanners in the second organization may be easier to work with and consequently make the conduct of business worth the additional operational cost incurred through the more distant transportation movements. It is consideration of these trade-offs that offers justification for the use of global suppliers and customers to meet each other's needs.

The third decision area is the information structure that allows relationship decision making within each organization and between organizations. Historically, this has been reflected in the amount of promotion conducted to support sales of the product or service through boundary-spanning activities such as sales or account personnel on the marketing end of the organization and purchasing and sourcing personnel on the other end of the relationship. Operationally, information management systems are used to keep track of inventory, operations, and supplier-customer transaction activities. These costs include the personnel to support transactions and relationships between the parties and the information systems to allow effective information flows between the supplier and customer organizations.

Fourth, as previously mentioned, transportation costs are an important consideration in most negotiations that occur between suppliers and customers. The primary reason for consideration of transportation costs in these negotiations is that, on average, 20% of the cost of a material or good is attributed to the cost of moving goods between suppliers and customers.

Fifth, negotiation consideration must be given to price. Price negotiation is based on the elements built into the product, the supply and market strategies implemented, the transaction costs of managing the flow of information between the parties, the costs of moving the products or services between global suppliers and customers, and the exchange rates that affect fund transfers from one global economic arena to another. Therefore, pricing strategies are dependent on other issue outcomes in each negotiation.

Last, it must be recognized that every negotiation is affected by the cost constraints created by the administrative element of each organization. These costs include financial, accounting, and legal costs, as well as the cost of senior executives who provide strategic direction for the organization.

Once the issue characteristics have been investigated, each party must go through a process of determining the appropriate issues of consideration in the negotiation and structuring these issues for goal and strategy development during negotiation preparation. This process requires each party to take each issue of any level of importance and analyze it for subcomponents. Often, it is necessary to go through this evaluation process several times until the issues are subcategorized to their lowest level of specification, a process called "fractionation." When all the issues and subcategories are established, each party determines the importance of each issue relative to all other issues. Once the importance of each issue is established, consideration must be given to the nature of the potential discussion of that issue, along with an appropriate discussion range for the issue. For example, if, through this process, the acceptable range on the price of the product is $3.00 to $7.00, then that is identified as that party's "range of reasonableness" for the discussions. If the other party opens issue discussion with a price of $9.00, the former has already determined that their potential for achieving an agreement is less than had been anticipated, and therefore, the negotiation with the supplier or customer may not be worth the time investment. This circumstance of difference has a greater potential of occurring when the two parties come from different economic systems and cultures, as commonly exists in a global supply chain context.

In addition to the specific contract issues, consideration should be given to the management of information about the characteristics of the individuals and organizations that may be involved in the negotiation. This information must include an assessment of the personalities of the parties (including looking at your own personality) and the characteristics of the organizations involved. The combination of these behavioral issues and the specific contract issues provides the foundation for developing the goals necessary for a successful negotiation outcome.

Negotiation Goal Establishment

Negotiation goals occur at two levels. First, each issue must have a goal that falls within the issue discussion range previously introduced. These goals offer the target necessary for each negotiator to use to ensure potential attainment of their desired negotiation outcomes. In addition, each negotiator should be aware of the need to target a particular relationship with the other party. Therefore, a relationship goal is also necessary for a successful negotiation outcome. In some cases, the relationship goal may be the creation of an alliance that offers maximum exchange of information between the parties over the duration of the relationship, which in many cases is a significant period of time relative to other relationships. In other cases, the desired relationship may be very limited and may occur only through individual transactions in a nonstrategic transaction situation. These goals are a necessary foundation for each party's ability to develop strategy for the forthcoming discussions that occur in each bargaining situation.

Strategy Development

Negotiation strategy must be developed in several areas. First, consideration must be given to the roles and responsibilities of members of the negotiation team. Strategy concerning "who does what" can be critical for a successful outcome. If it is recognized that the other party is represented by a highly dominant individual, then you may want to build a strategy that counters that individual with a representative from your organization who has a more dominant personality (even at the expense of leadership by an individual who may be closer to the particular relationship and transaction). In other situations, the strategy may be just the opposite. When a serious attempt is made to create a partnership with a global supplier or customer, and your representative may be too driven to achieve the close relationship desired by the parties and in some cases mandated by the cultural expectations of the global partner, it may be necessary to involve a representative from your organization who can facilitate the desired partnership.

The second strategic consideration is the desired location of the bargaining sessions. Initially, it should be determined whether there is a need for face-to-face discussions of the issues or whether the discussions can occur over the telephone or by some other form of electronic interface. Obviously, global distance can incentivize the parties to use location strategies other than face-to-face because of cost considerations. However, in many cases, it is necessary for the parties to meet face-to-face to be able to fully understand the issues of concern and demonstrate the necessary commitment to the relationship. If face-to-face discussions are needed, then consideration must be given to the location. Most negotiators use one of three general strategies. The first is the "home territory" strategy, which gives the home party control of the facilities surrounding the discussions. The second is the "away" strategy. In this situation, the negotiator has little or no control over the bargaining environment and must depend on his or her individual self-confidence and skill to control the negotiation situation. The third is the "neutral" strategy, which is implemented at a location independent from both the parties. When a neutral strategy is employed, neither party has an opportunity to gain control over the specific bargaining environmental circumstances surrounding the negotiation.

Temporal strategy is the third component of negotiation strategy. It is critically important to know and understand the effect of time on the outcome of each negotiation. Two elements require consideration. The first is the total duration of each negotiation. Each negotiator must fully recognize what deadlines exist for the parties (i.e., the current contract expiration or an upcoming holiday that could cause the parties to break in the middle of the bargaining if agreement is not achieved or force one party to work through a holiday that the other does not observe). In addition, each negotiator must be aware of his or her daily strengths and routines, as well as the other party's strengths and routines. If your counterpart in a negotiation is an early riser and feels most productive in the morning, then you might schedule bargaining sessions early in the morning to catch the other party at his or her best. However, you may also use that information to schedule meetings in the afternoons, when you believe the other party would be most vulnerable if you are trying to achieve a nonstrategic transaction outcome.

Consideration must also be given to the appropriate discussion order for the issues involved. These issues include an assessment of the potential responses by the other party, how important each issue is relative to the other issues, and the level of difficulty that has been established by the goal set for each issue. These factors contribute to the strategy that will most likely create the right discussion order for each negotiation. An extension of the issue discussion order strategy is the implementation of the information exchange strategy. In some negotiations, significant information is exchanged between the parties (referred to as an integrative strategy); in other situations, the parties share some but not all information (referred to as a compromising strategy); and in still other situations, very little information is exchanged (called a distributive strategy). In these three circumstances, the parties approach the negotiation in a similar manner. However, in other circumstances, the parties may not approach the negotiation in a similar manner, which can lead to an accommodating strategy or a competing strategy in which one shares significant information, whereas the other does not. The implementation of these strategies is fundamental to the nature of the outcome of each negotiation. In addition, some negotiators who recognize their lack of power in a negotiation may attempt to undermine their counterpart's position by using others within the two organizations to influence the outcome of the negotiation. This strategy is called "politicking."

Consideration must also be given to two elements in the concession decision. The first is the starting position on each issue. Each negotiator must determine whether his or her opening position on an issue will be to ask for significantly more than he or she needs to achieve his or her objectives (referred to as a high starting position) or whether he or she opens with very little margin between his or her starting point and his or her bottom line (referred to as a low starting position). The second element of the concession decision is the concession strategy used. The concession strategy is the result of positioning on the issue over time. A negotiator who discusses an issue with the other party for a period of time and gives very little to the other party during that time is implementing a "hard-line" strategy. However, a negotiator who spends time discussing another issue and gives significant benefits to the other party at his or her expense is implementing a "concessionary" strategy.

These preparations are fundamental to the successful negotiation outcomes. However, consideration must also be given to the interactive nature of the bargaining environment.

Bargaining

The interaction phase of each negotiation is referred to as bargaining. Bargaining consists of three elements: position development, issue discussion, and finalization.

Position Development

Position development considers factors within the bargaining environment such as the arrangement of the room where discussions will take place, identification of the individuals present at each bargaining session, and establishment of the agenda for the discussions. The initial setting can substantially influence the attitudes of the negotiators during the issue discussion phase. The parties can use the location as a method of influencing and controlling the availability of information to the negotiators. For example, when negotiating in a foreign country, the traveling party may find they have limited access to external forms of communication that would be available if the bargaining sessions were conducted in the familiar confines of their corporate environment. Some parties will concede the advantage of the meeting at their location for the opportunity to observe activities at the other party's location. Consequently, the location can play a significant role in the establishment of information bases and access to that information as well as opportunities for "walk away" strategies by the visiting party. However, traveling firm representatives may find it more difficult to walk away from the bargaining table when significant sums have been invested in travel to get to the bargaining location and the cost of an "empty" return is not expected.

However, the party at their home location can control the environment of the room used for the bargaining sessions. Room environmental elements can include the particular room assignment (office vs. conference room), lighting in the room, and characteristics of the tables, chairs, telephones, and communications equipment. Control over the physical surroundings in the room can have a dramatic effect on the outcome of the negotiations.

As the bargaining sessions begin, the participants introduce their initial positions on the issues. The initial proceedings include the agreement by the parties about which issues will be discussed and in what order. These positions provide a basis for future discussions and therefore influence the eventual outcome of the negotiation.

Issue Discussion

Issue discussion involves consideration of the behavioral elements of interaction between the parties during bargaining. Consideration must be given to each party's behavioral posturing through body language, knowledge base for the negotiation, role performance, and activity performance. These behavioral elements can tell the negotiator about personal tendencies. However, these tendencies become more complex when the parties represent different countries and cultures.

Negotiators must also be aware of language posturing during issue discussion. Statements made by either party can have a substantial effect on either party's perception of the position taken by the other. Each statement made by a negotiator can affect the perceptions of power by the other party, especially when terminology in one language may have a different meaning in another language. Therefore, each negotiator must carefully assess the statements made for their impact on responding positions by the other party.

The quality of the information that is presented to the other party and the quality of information received by the focal party from the other party can be critical to the outcome of each negotiation. Therefore, introduction of information that can be substantiated through documentation in company records or other secondary sources (such as industry research reports) can carry significant weight in a bargaining session. When points are made with no documentation and are expected to be accepted on the faith of the other party, the perception of the quality of the information is much lower. The perception of the value of documentation may differ across cultures as well. For example, the presentation of support information that would be expected in one culture may be insulting to managers in another culture.

Issue discussion also includes an assessment of the actual concessions made during the bargaining sessions. The key elements of this activity are the same type of assessment of initial positioning implemented on each issue and the determination of the actual concessions made on the issues. This is the same basic process discussed during strategy development in negotiation preparation. The negotiator must also compare the actual positioning and concession strategies implemented with the intended strategies established during negotiation preparation. This comparison is necessary to assess the effectiveness of the concessions made and received during bargaining.

Finalization

Bargaining activity is a circular process moving from position development on each issue to discussion of the issues, finalization on each issue, and return to position development for the next issue to be discussed. Finalization is the part of the process when the parties reach agreement on one or all of the issues discussed during bargaining. This achievement of agreement depends on the complexities of the issues discussed. In addition, temporal constraints imposed by deadlines for achieving the agreement—such as expiration dates included on existing contracts, product introduction and operating system constraints, and market and supply base constraints such as holidays and other specified times that affect specific demands that occur in various markets—ultimately affect the success of the negotiation.

Negotiation Outcome

Negotiation outcome includes the elements that address the nature of the final agreement between the parties. The three elements considered at this stage of the process are verification, contract agreement, and negotiation breakdown.

Verification

Verification involves the specific characteristics of the agreement. Verification is important in situations in which the party responsible for the preparation of the final document includes provisions not previously agreed to by the parties. Therefore, negotiators must verify the contents of the contract according to their interpretation of the terms agreed to during the finalization stage of bargaining.

Some negotiations lead to verbal agreements between the parties. Under these circumstances, verification involves performance appraisal measures. Verbal agreements have differing levels of enforceability under legal expectations of different countries' legal systems. Therefore, knowledge of international law and the impact of legal jurisdiction can be critical to the interpretation of relationship expectations.

Verification might also take place prior to the signing of a written contract developed by one of the parties to the negotiation. In situations where the formal written contract represents the terms of the agreement, both parties must reach an agreement based on their notes and interpretations of the bargaining sessions. This agreement culminates in the "official" signing of the contract.

Agreement

When the parties can agree on the appropriate terms for a final document, agreement occurs as a negotiation outcome. This leads to one of four outcomes from the negotiation process: both parties benefit from the agreement (win-win), one party benefits from the agreement at the expense of the other (win-lose), the other party benefits from the agreement at the expense of the former (lose-win), or neither party benefits from the agreement (lose-lose). The nature of the agreement reached by the parties depends on the relative positions of the parties throughout the negotiation process, the amount of preparation, and the strategies used.

Negotiation Breakdown

A final possibility for a negotiation outcome is the decision by one or both parties that they should not conduct business. This occurs when the parties fail to agree on the key issues of the agreement and realization dawns that their mutual needs can be achieved more effectively through sources other than a mutual business relationship. This type of situation is not unusual in today's business environment where strategies such as niche marketing and supply base reduction are implemented as mechanisms to target specific customers or suppliers in the global market or supply base.

Conclusions

The circular nature of the negotiation process causes information from one negotiation to become a part of the next negotiation. For example, a firm that completes a negotiation with one supplier or customer will use information they gained in that negotiation for future negotiations with the same party. In addition, the party will use elements of the information base for future negotiations with other parties that have similar supplier-customer negotiation characteristics. This learning experience is critical to firms desiring market and supply base expansion in the global environments they are pursuing. This example of the "learning organization" helps negotiators learn from past successes and failures in global supply chain negotiations for the benefit of future negotiations.

In this chapter, the negotiation process is conceptualized to include the characteristics of the environments that surround each negotiation (negotiation environments), the assessment of the potential for the negotiation (negotiation potential), the activities necessary for the parties to prepare for the bargaining activities (negotiation preparation), the bargaining activities (bargaining), and the characteristics of the outcomes of the negotiation (negotiation outcome). In addition, definitional properties were developed for the types of relationship outcomes that evolve from supplier-customer negotiations: nonstrategic transactions, administered relationships, contractual relationships, joint ventures, specialty contract relationships, partnerships, and alliances. Understanding this process and the resulting relationships can assist global supply chain managers in creating successful relationships that support global market and supply objectives.

References

Emerson, Richard (1962), "Power-Dependence Relations," *American Sociology Review, 27,* 31–41.

French, J. and B. Raven (1959), "The Bases of Social Power," in *Studies in Social Power,* D. Cartwright, ed. Ann Arbor, MI: Institute for Social Research.

Rinehart, Lloyd M., Ernest Cadotte, and C. John Langley, Jr. (1988), "Shipper-Carrier Contract Negotiation: A Conceptual Foundation for Logistics Managers," *International Journal of Physical Distribution and Materials Management, 18* (6), 43–51.

Rinehart, Lloyd M., Bixby Cooper, and George Wagenheim (1989), "Furthering the Integration of Marketing and Logistics through Customer Service in the Channel," *Journal of the Academy of Marketing Science, 17* (1), 63–71.

Rinehart, Lloyd M., James Eckert, Robert Handfield, Thomas Page, and Thomas Atkin (2004), "An Assessment of Supplier-Customer Relationships," *Journal of Business Logistics, 25* (1), 25–62.

25

Interfunctional Coordination

Susan L. Golicic

Kate Vitasek

I n business today the pace of change is relentless, and business processes of global reach are ubiquitous. Increasingly, a company's competitive edge comes not from its unique products, its geographic spread, or its cost structure. Much of the traditional strategic advantages that have served companies so well can generally be reverse-engineered and often at a lesser cost.

The impact of this rapid evolution and broad geographic span is simply a smaller window through which competitiveness can be defined. The pace of change ensures there will quickly be the next best widget to replace the one launched just yesterday. The global reach of business processes ensures that the East Indian widget and the North American widget will have the opportunity to reach identical target audiences with products of limited differentiation.

Often, a competitive edge comes from the unique culture that the company creates and through which its changing product and thus customer value are delivered. Research has shown that continually collecting, analyzing, and coordinating information on the company's market, including customers, competitors, and other market influences contribute to value-creating capabilities (Slater and Narver 1994). Interfunctional coordination is an important component in this value creation process.

The reason for this should be obvious. First, functions that regularly communicate and cooperate reduce redundancies in tasks and improve process efficiencies. Greater efficiency translates to improved value creation and competitiveness. For example, a new product launch requires the input of multiple functions, specifically that these functions exchange information and plans. In these exchanges, the functions are increasing the chances of that product's success. Companies that successfully use interfunctional coordination to create customer value produce products and services that can be hard for competitors to duplicate, thus achieving a competitive advantage. But companies did not come to this conclusion quickly or easily. Herb Johnson, past president of the Council of Supply Chain Management Professionals and president of Summit Concept, a supply chain consulting firm, described the progression of interfunctional coordination in business (personal communication, April 13, 2005). Herb has worked in logistics and supply chain management with various firms for decades. In a conversation with the authors, he described the progression of firms from functional silos to interfunctional integration—a progression that took several years.

In the 1970s and 1980s, large organizations demonstrated resistance to any collaboration among functions. Companies did not have common goals but worked toward functional, separate, and sometimes conflicting goals. They were performing well and, therefore, did not see a need for change.

In the late 1980s, economic issues and increased competition caused companies to look for the golden goose that would help cut costs and increase productivity. This brought attention to logistics, which is, as Herb describes, "a compilation of prior functions working together in and of itself" (personal communication, April 13, 2005). One thing that was learned was that much more internal information sharing was required to do business. To improve business, technology was brought in, which facilitated this sharing, and management got more involved in making proactive decisions. This led to the realization that operating as separate functions often resulted in suboptimization of the business. Therefore, companies started to change this unsuccessful way of doing business by having the functions work together toward common goals. Herb noted results in levels of fulfillment, and customer service realized by some companies, such as soft goods and catalog retailers, will continue to drive others toward interfunctional coordination.

This chapter defines interfunctional coordination and its essential elements: communication, collaboration, and an organizational climate that supports the two. Once the groundwork has been laid, this chapter explores important axes for effective interfunctional coordination within the company. For example, the reliance and dependencies between sales and distribution is a key axis for interfunctional coordination. The mechanisms that can be used to drive coordination within a company are then discussed. Finally, we offer some examples of interfunctional coordination and the state of the art in business today. Throughout this chapter, we illustrate various points as well as the benefits and impact of coordination with real examples from companies within global supply chains.

What Is Interfunctional Coordination?

Interfunctional coordination (depicted in Figure 25.1) is defined as working together in close relationships across functions or departments to achieve common company goals (Min 2001). Narver and Slater (1990) equate this to a symphony

Figure 25.1   Interfunctional Coordination

SOURCE: From Mentzer et al. (2001).

orchestra. The common goal is a beautifully played piece of music. Each function (strings, percussion, horns, etc.) has its own individual responsibilities; however, all functions must work together and harmonize to successfully achieve the end goal.

Interfunctional coordination requires both interaction and collaboration to achieve high performance (Kahn and Mentzer 1998). Interaction emphasizes communication in the form of meetings and information flows between the different functions, whereas collaboration implies mutual understanding, a common vision, and shared resources. Both communication and collaboration promote close relationships among the functions. There must also be an environment within the company that supports frequent communication and collaboration among the functions (Kahn, Reizenstein, and Rentz 2004). The elements of effective interfunctional coordination, then, are as follows:

- Open communication
- Collaboration
- An organizational climate that supports these two

Communication: The Contact Rule

Frequent communication is vital for different functions to develop a basic understanding of what drives the other functions and the decisions they make.

Although communication is vital, it is important to understand that mere ease of communication will not ensure interfunctional coordination. Research shows that companies may have significant levels of communication and interaction but may, in fact, fall short of true coordination. This is because interaction and communication alone often lead to rule-making and turf-protecting behavior, which in turn breaks down collaboration. Increased interaction alone leads to greater rules and "standard operating procedures."

An office supply company practices interfunctional coordination in many of its daily operations. One employee in marketing noted that each week she e-mails about 50 different people in manufacturing, marketing, distribution, and customer service about promotion plans. In addition, when this company starts planning for heavy seasons, such as "Back to School," it conducts regular cross-functional meetings.

So the interfunctional communication rule is, "Limit contact to communication that is necessary for effective interfunctional coordination, open, and works toward collaboration."

Collaboration: The Key

Collaboration is a common understanding of what drives each function toward the company's overarching goals. Research shows that collaboration contributes more to effectiveness of interfunctional coordination than to ease of communication. It is important to remember that true collaboration is not just interaction through a series of interfunctional meetings and document exchanges (i.e., mutual goals, targets, and rewards); rather, it is associated with greater interdependence to succeed. Specifically, interfunctional collaboration reflects the degree of dependency between groups where the following exist:

- Mutual goals
- Mutual respect
- Mutual understanding of objectives
- Mutual reward systems
- Teamwork

Some companies, such as a petroleum products company, a transportation provider, and a consumer packaged goods company, set up formal cross-functional teams with specific titles and regular members to support business processes such as forecasting and supply management. It is the mutual dependency created by shared goals and vision supported by a mutual reward system that drives true collaboration.

Effective Collaboration Climate

What creates a climate primed for coordination? First, there must be trust and commitment among personnel from the different functions (Min 2001). A trust-embedded culture is at work when participants

- Attribute high levels of integrity, competence, reliability, loyalty, and openness to other participants
- View others as equal stakeholders in the product innovation process
- Define their own behaviors in light of these convictions

The more the members of one function perceive themselves as dependent on the resources, information, or performance of another function in successfully carrying out their jobs, the greater the amount of interaction and resource flows between the two departments (Min 2001). An environment that promotes coordination to accomplish daily tasks engrains this type of behavior in employees.

There must also be awareness and support for interfunctional coordination on the part of management—not just in words, but by example. Management must provide the motivation, empowerment, and organizational resources for the different functions to work together to create value (Kent 1996; Slater and Narver 1994). Management must also work to break down any walls that exist or obstacles that arise between functions.

A midlevel manager from a large, global company said that it helps their coordination efforts to have that feeling coming from the top down. He said that there is a definite push toward, and sense of reward for, a teamwork approach within their firm. "Everyone tries to help support each other."

Axes of Effective Interfunctional Coordination

Successful companies leverage several axes of relationships to help drive their interterfunctional coordination efforts. It is the effectiveness of coordination created along these axes that is difficult for competitors to duplicate. Table 25.1 provides some examples of these axes.

One way to look at these various axes of interfunctional coordination is to map the overlapping functions and their impact areas (Figure 25.2). This simplified view shows that the combined efforts of sales and operations affect measures related to customer retention and responsiveness; the combined efforts of sales and finance affect measures related to the cost of service and value added; and the combined efforts of operations and finance affect operational effectiveness (cash to cash and asset utilization, for example). As a whole, the combined efforts of the entire company contribute to the company's profitability, value creation, added; market share. This simplistic model effectively demonstrates the overlap and dependencies between any variety of organization axes around which improved performance spins.

Kahn and Mentzer (1998) examined the perception of interfunctional coordination outcomes in firms through interaction and collaboration between (1) marketing and manufacturing and (2) marketing and R&D. Their research found that marketing professionals felt collaboration with the other functions led to higher marketing performance, company performance, product development performance, product management performance, and satisfaction. R&D professionals also perceived similar outcomes from collaborating with marketing, whereas those in manufacturing felt they experienced higher product management performance

Table 25.1 Axes of Interfunctional Coordination

Axes		*Area Impact of Coordination*
Marketing	R&D	Innovation—new product development
Marketing	Manufacturing/ conversion of raw materials to finished goods	Product and market performance, postdevelopment and postlaunch activities
Sales	Distribution	Customer relationship management
Sales	Planning-procurement	Supply chain conditioning—supply and demand alignment
Sales	Finance	Cost of service, value added
Sales	Manufacturing operations	Customer retention and responsiveness
Product development	Manufacturing, procurement, distribution	Simultaneous engineering—product life cycle management
IT	All departments	Systems integration and scale

and satisfaction. The results concluded that collaboration among functions should be emphasized because it had a strong impact on performance success. A test between the sales and distribution functions of consumer products companies found similar results—interaction promoted greater effectiveness for distribution management, whereas collaboration promoted greater effectiveness for both functions (Kahn et al. 2004).

One method that many companies have started adopting to help create improved interfunctional coordination between multiple company functions is sales and operations planning (S&OP), highlighted in Chapter 5. S&OP is a process for matching supply to demand for the company. To do this effectively requires representative personnel from all functions who deal with supply or demand, which is nearly all functions but particularly the marketing, sales, operations, and finance functions. Representatives from the different functions attend regular meetings with the goal of achieving consensus on the resulting demand and supply plans (Lapide 2002). Because S&OP allows all functions a voice in the resulting plans, this process helps close any gaps between those that work on the demand side and those that work on the supply side. S&OP processes by their very nature are a means for achieving interfunctional coordination.

Mechanisms to Drive Coordination

Although communication, collaboration, and a climate that supports the two are critical elements of effective interfunctional coordination, many companies

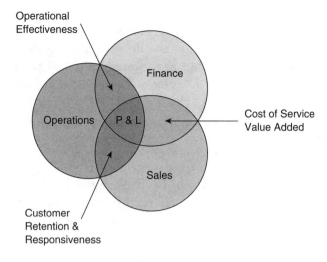

Figure 25.2 Axes of Coordination Map

struggle to implement these effectively. Some companies achieve innovation and competitiveness while failing to have effective interfunctional coordination. Although these companies do achieve degrees of success, they are not best in class and, given their inability to collaborate, often suffer slow product development cycles, excessive overruns and inventories with regular backorders at the same time, poor employee satisfaction, and low customer satisfaction. This section outlines five mechanisms that companies can use to implement improved interfunctional coordination: cooperative arrangements, management controls, standardization, functional expertise, and organizational structure (Min 2001).

Cooperative Arrangements

Cooperative arrangements are informal but regular communications, interactions, and collaborations among the functions encouraged through interdepartmental meetings, hall talk, and cross-functional or customer-focused teams (Kent 1996; Min 2001). These arrangements enable communication and collaboration among the lower layers of the company—employees from different functions responsible for daily operations. Cooperative arrangements can be started by the employees themselves and may be facilitated by upper management.

Following reorganization at one consumer products company, the forecasting group started conducting a series of informal "lunch and learns" with other departments. The purpose was to share information the different groups had on the various markets the company serves.

Management Controls

Management controls entail management promoting teamwork efforts by setting an example and working cross-functionally themselves. In addition, management can establish shared functional goals and performance measures to promote integration of their departments with others (Kent 1996; Min 2001). At one pharmaceutical company, the divisions in the company established joint service level targets and performance measurements, which resulted in improved communications and decreased time to market for new products. The concept of shared goals and measurements is explored in more detail later in this chapter.

Standardization

Standardization helps predetermine and formalize individual roles and behaviors and, thus, is another mechanism to implement interfunctional coordination. The output, skills, and norms of personnel can all be standardized (Min 2001). For instance, documented job descriptions and performance standards help determine appropriate output. Skills become standard through training and orientation, and norms are developed through the use of common policies and rules. If expectations are formalized, then meeting these expectations becomes second nature.

Functional Expertise

Although it is important for personnel to work cohesively with other functions, it is also important that the firm employs people with in-depth functional expertise (Min 2001). A company cannot survive with generalists in every position. It is important, however, that the functional experts have the ability to work cross-functionally as well. A cross-functional team will only be successful if they have members who possess not only depth of knowledge and skills in their functional area but also the ability to work with a breadth of others with varying expertise.

Organizational Structure

The organization should be designed to go beyond the functional silos (Min 2001; Tuominen, Rajala, and Moller 2000). Jassawalla and Sashittal (2003) found that organizations with functional silos breed paranoia because functional divisions of like-minded individuals lead to the distrust of others outside the function.

Going beyond functional silos does not necessarily mean that the organization has to be completely restructured. It can be accomplished through something as simple as short-term task forces or project groups. A matrix organization could be constructed with multiple reporting relationships within, as well as outside, an employee's function. Or the organization could be completely redesigned around integrated processes rather than functions. The organizational design, whether formal or informal, should influence how interfunctional coordination and its outcomes are managed.

At one consumer products company, an operational team (comprising directors from all functions) was created by executive management. This team meets every week to make joint decisions about business execution. A company employee noted, "The team has to focus on the business, not functions; there is no tolerance for 'he said/she said'—it is 'we.'"

Common Goals and Measures

As noted earlier, one of the mechanisms companies use to help foster interfunctional coordination is management controls. Although management controls are central to effective interfunctional coordination, best practice companies go far beyond simple management controls and insist on common goals or objectives and mutual rewards that help prevent suboptimization. It is the achievement of common goals that defines the purpose of interfunctional coordination in the first place.

Balanced Scorecard: The Basic Foundation

Many companies have adopted a balanced scorecard (BSC) to track progress toward strategic goals. The BSC is a performance measurement tool designed by Kaplan and Norton (1992) to help companies consider measurements from varying perspectives of a company (Figure 25.3). There are four key elements or quadrants in which metrics are grouped and on which balance hinges: financial,

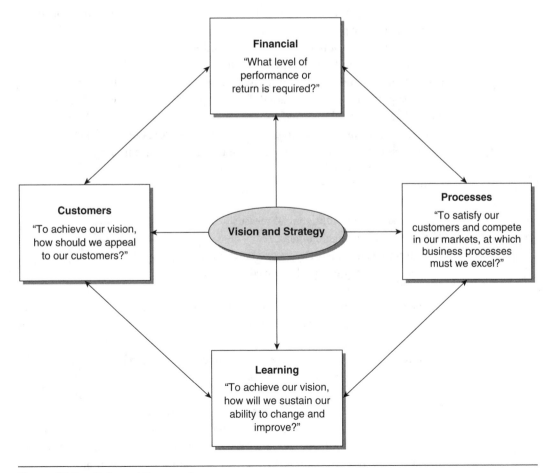

Figure 25.3   Balanced Scorecard

processes, customers, and learning. A key element in successful performance management is ensuring that what is measured is cross-functional and balanced. These together assure that the company remains focused on strategic outcomes and does not overlook key indicators of the health of the company.

Beyond Balance: Using Interfunctional Process Metrics

Although a BSC helps give management an overall understanding of the health of the organization, using cross-functional process metrics is an important tool in understanding the effectiveness of interfunctional coordination. If multiple functions are collaborating well toward common strategic objectives, then the cross-functional metrics will reflect that collaboration.

After the breakup of "Ma Bell," one telecommunications company found itself facing a brave new world of competition and informed customers. Its response was to develop a robust marketing effectiveness measurement program. The approach included collaboration of multiple functions across the supply chain to achieve broad, customer-oriented goals. Metrics were cross-functional process measurements.

Leading companies understand that optimal health of the company depends on the caliber of core processes and that core processes span multiple functional areas. Moreover, leading companies understand and value process measures to monitor their progress toward clearly defined strategic objectives. Process measures span the entire company and not just an individual function. This emphasis on measuring overall supply chain processes is a differentiator between leading and average companies in how they address performance management (Ledyard and Vitasek 2004).

One example of a measurement framework that addresses interfunctional coordination and process measurement is the integrated metric framework. It emphasizes measurement of process results (i.e., collaborative results) and employs balance in the following:

- Financial and nonfinancial measures
- Leading and lagging measures
- Internal and externally focused measures
- Measures capturing all involved stakeholders

The integrated metrics framework builds on the BSC concepts, with the Kaplan and Norton BSC quadrants (see Table 25.2) down the left providing balance across supply chain roles (bottom). Key functional roles (buy, design/make, store/distribute, move, and sell) are considered in the model. The researchers who created the integrated metrics framework populated the template shown in Table 25.2 for demonstration purposes.

Beginning at the top, financial metrics include traditional measures such as revenue, profit, return on investment (ROI), and cash flow. These metrics span all supply chain functional roles because they measure the sum total result of all processes that have occurred throughout the company. In addition to these more traditional measures of financial performance, economic value added (EVA) and return on

Table 25.2   Example of an Integrated Metrics Framework

Quadrants	*Performance Metrics*				
Financial	Net Profit				
	Economic Value Added (EVA) or Return on Capital Employed (ROCE)				
	Return on Investment (ROI)				
	Operating Ratio				
Processes					
Information Capability	Tracking Accuracy				
		Raw Material Inventory Accuracy	Inventory Accuracy		Inventory Accuracy
Order Fulfillment			Fill rate		
			Inventory Level		
Forecasting	Forecasting Accuracy (Demand Management)				
Planning/ Scheduling and Execution	Cost/Order	Cost/Product			
	Order Lead Time/Order	Order Lead Time/Product			
		Asset Utilization			
		Machine	Space	Trailer Space	
		Labor	Labor	Labor	
		Throughput			
		Response Time to Changes in Customer Orders			
		Set-Up/ Changeover Time			
		Productivity			
		Capital	Capital	Capital	
		Labor	Labor	Labor	
Customer	Perfect Order				
	Error-free Ordering	Defect Free On-Time Mfg.	Damage Free Filled on Time Lines Correct Quantity Correct	Damage Free On-Time Delivery	Document Accuracy
Learning & Growth		Design Process Time for New Product/ Feature			
	Training—Internal				
	Training—External				
	Buy	**Design/ Make**	**Store/ Distribute**	**Move**	**Sell**
	←- - - - - - - - - - - - - - - - - - - **Supply Chain Roles** -→				

SOURCE: Taken from Benton, Watson, and Love (2000).

capital employed (ROCE) (both more complete measures of operating cost and capital) are included.

Within the process quadrant, metrics of four core processes are identified: information capability, order fulfillment, forecasting, and planning or scheduling and execution. Information capability is the process by which the company tracks its assets. Order fulfillment is the process by which the company provides service given the appropriate capacity and inventory. Forecasting is the process by which the company determines the demand for orders. Planning is the process by which the company schedules the activities and assets required to fulfill these orders.

The overall objective of the framework is to provide sufficient metrics to tell the company how well it planned demand, scheduled to meet demand, fulfilled demand, and tracked all the related transactions in this long flow of integrated processes. Although there are some measures that are functionally oriented, many are cross-functional in nature.

Let's explore the example of the order fill rate metric under the processes quadrant. Order fill rate is generally a functional measure that identifies how often a company ships orders on a required date. How often a company ships orders on time is directly tied to how well the company forecasts the demand that drives the orders, and therefore, whether there is inventory on hand to fill the order. Demand forecasting and inventory planning are highly sophisticated, and finding a single measure of the effectiveness of these activities is often difficult. Often companies use a series of metrics that, together, create a picture of effectiveness. For example, comparing high inventory turns to low order fill rates should demonstrate that the company is efficiently managing inventory and keeping levels low, but it is doing so at the cost of responding quickly to customer demand. In other words, the company is likely missing the larger strategic objective of customer satisfaction while improving its inventory carrying costs and cash cycle time.

Note that within the customer quadrant, the integrated metrics framework recognizes the need for a perfect order metric. The perfect order metric measures how effectively a company gets the right product to the right customer at the right time. The perfect order metric includes key elements such as on-time delivery, complete, damage free, and accurate invoice. Achieving the perfect order relies on processes that span all core functions of the company. The metrics identified below perfect order within each discrete supply chain functional role, in fact, make up the measures across the company needed to create a perfect order metric. As such, looking at a functional metric-like order fill rate gives a functional perspective, whereas looking at an interfunctional metric like the perfect order metric gauges how well the functions work together to meet overall customer satisfaction.

Achieving Interfunctional Coordination

Leading companies actively incorporate the three key elements of effective interfunctional coordination (communication, collaboration, and an organization climate that fosters these between all departments) and utilize one or more of the drivers to implement interfunctional coordination. This section highlights some organizations that have had interfunctional coordination success as well as one that was not so successful.

S&OP in an Agricultural Products Company

Practices of a major agricultural products company were studied as part of a forecasting audit (Mentzer and Bienstock 1998). This company is considered to display characteristics of a world-class S&OP process by coordinating its forecasting and planning through several meetings between marketing, finance, production, distribution, sales, and forecasting during the course of a month.

The first is a demand planning meeting, during which various functional areas of the organization are represented, including the factory marketing managers, vice-president of sales, factory master schedulers, finance, demand planners, and order fulfillment. The purpose of the meeting is to arrive at a consensus on the forecast numbers. The second is the supply planning meeting, during which the master scheduler, supply management managers, and factory marketing managers discuss how the factories will adjust to the consensus estimate. A partnership meeting then occurs in which everyone involved in the previous meetings arrives at a general consensus on the forecast, production schedule, and shipment forecast. The final meeting is the executive review meeting during which final adjustments are made. The participants in this meeting include the vice president of marketing, the vice president of sales, the order fulfillment controller, and the director of marketing and sales. The partnership and executive review meetings provide a method for feedback to be provided to all participants in this process.

CPFR at a Major European Conglomerate

One major European conglomerate used a collaborative planning, forecasting, and replenishment (CPFR) model in two steps: first, it built collaborative internal processes for one of its businesses, and second, it built a collaborative partnership with its largest customer. In the first step, the company's goals were to eliminate internal glitches in forecasting and planning, including stock-outs, delivery errors, and invoicing complaints. Forecasts had to be synchronized with production at one end and consumer demand at the other. Purchasing and distribution, two of the corporate world's most notorious silos, had to be integrated. Sales and marketing had to be kept in the loop as well for access to key demand data.

The company undertook massive process redesign while also implementing a new demand planning system. As part of the process redesign, it built in solid key performance indicators (KPIs) in the areas of forecasting and promotions. But without improving the quality of input from its customers, the company would not likely reap optimum improvements in the forecasting and planning arena. In the second step, the company identified its largest customer as a potential partner in a CPFR effort. The company's sales forecasts had an average error of more than 50%. Stock-outs were common, especially on promotional items. Shipments frequently arrived late at the customer's central warehouse, which serviced 500 stores.

Using a common systems tool between them to network their collaborative efforts, the partners began exchanging information once a day, once a week, every 15 days, and every four months. With the help of the Internet, they developed common business and promotional plans; compared sales forecasts, order forecasts, and exceptions; and obtained information on changes in promotions and product availability relative to demand. Throughout their joint pilot program, the two companies closely monitored performance against select KPIs, including customer-service levels at the customer's central warehouse, number of stock-outs, number of promotions, stock rotation, forecast reliability, truck fill rates, pallet fill rates, and number of urgent orders.

The single most important hurdle to overcome was the deeply held, traditional business practices that, in any industry, need to be confronted and stopped if they prove detrimental to the long-term mutual and individual objectives. A "mentality change" was necessary in order for the partners to collaborate across the supply chain and tear down barriers between internal functions to encourage free flow of data.

With the CPFR pilot program in place, the quality of the company's sales forecasts improved steadily. In the period between October 1999 and March 2000, average forecast accuracy improved to 80%. Other KPIs showed similarly strong results: a 98% customer-service level, five days of supply, 2% stock-outs, better than 85% forecast reliability, 98% truck fill rates, and 99% pallet fills. Moreover, the company integrated new product forecasts into the ongoing forecast, further improving the planning process.

Interestingly, the company required its senior account manager responsible for this customer account to spearhead the collaboration that led to creation of a sales forecast, and the customer-service team was given responsibility for incorporating promotions into the forecast. The company recognized that although the sales and customer-service teams are not demand-planning experts, their market knowledge is too valuable not to incorporate into the planning and forecasting process.

Software Provider Customer Service

One consumer products company recognized that interfunctional coordination can contribute to the delivery of customer value while working with a large software firm to provide support in their six sigma initiatives. Several different contact points exist between the two firms. The customer noted that the software company is interfunctionally coordinated because working with them "is incredible. Interactions with contacts in different departments are seamless."

Functional Disconnects at an Automotive Supplier

Unfortunately, not all examples of interfunctional coordination are positive. Some companies find it incredibly hard to coordinate internal functions, despite the research and guidelines available. An automotive company faced major problems because of disconnects between all their functional areas, primarily those involved with the demand side (i.e., sales and marketing) and the supply side (i.e., manufacturing and logistics). As one company executive put it,

> There is a pervasive attitude on the part of the sales and marketing people that manufacturing does what it wants to do, regardless of what demand exists in the marketplace. The perception on the part of the field organization is that what gets forecast does not get manufactured, leaving them with an inability to ship what the customers want, leading to high levels of frustration for the demand side. At the same time, there is a feeling on the part of the supply side of the company that the field sales organization does not adequately understand its customer base. There is a general lack of trust between the demand and the supply sides of this company.

Individuals on both sides of the company indicated that the corporate culture did not encourage communication between the two sides of the business and that people tended to focus on their own silos. One individual in the company commented, "it's like there are two different companies—[Company Name] Manufacturing and [Company Name] Sales and Marketing."

Interfunctional Coordination: A Collaborative Climate for Success

The premise that effective interfunctional coordination leads to improved competitiveness is supported by research. Different functions working together harmoniously to create customer value can be hard for competitors to duplicate, thus leading to a competitive advantage (Kent 1996). Tuominen et al. (2000) further found that effective interfunctional coordination was a discriminator between high- and low-performing firms. Those firms that emphasize coordinated and committed organizational arrangements between functions experience higher operational excellence.

The most successful companies are taking steps to implement cross-functional process metrics to help them measure their performance and foster an environment for eliminating process suboptimization. If multiple functions are coordinating their efforts toward common strategic objectives, then the cross-functional metrics will reflect that collaboration. As the pace of business quickens, companies can no longer rely on their laurels of past successes. In business today, competitive advantage is more often than not coming from the unique culture that the company creates, and this unique culture is built around successful interfunctional coordination, which includes open communication, collaboration, and an organizational climate that supports these two. Effective interfunctional coordination can also be extended beyond the company to intercorporate integration, which is the topic of the following chapter. Both of these are important components for successfully managing relationships in a global supply chain.

References

Benton, Helen M., Julie Watson, and Doug M. Love (2000), "Research Agenda: Metrics for Evaluating Supply Chain Control Systems," *The Fourth International Conference on Managing Innovative Manufacturing, Responsive Production and the Agile Enterprise.* Bradford, UK: MCB University Press, pp. 118–126.

Jassawalla, Avan R. and Hemant C. Sashittal (2003), "The DNA of Cultures That Promote Product Innovation," *Ivey Business Journal,* 68 (November/December), 1–6.

Kahn, Kenneth B. and John T. Mentzer (1998), "Marketing's Integration with Other Departments," *Journal of Business Research,* 42 (1), 53–62.

Kahn, Kenneth B., Richard C. Reizenstein, and Joseph O. Rentz (2004), "Sales-Distribution Interfunctional Climate and Relationship Effectiveness," *Journal of Business Research,* 57 (10), 1085–1091.

Kaplan, Robert S. and David P. Norton (1992), "The Balanced Scorecard: Measures That Drive Performance," *Harvard Business Review,* 70 (January/February), 71–79.

Kent, John L. (1996), "Leverage: Interfunctional Co-ordination Between Logistics and Information Technology," *International Journal of Physical Distribution and Logistics Management,* 26 (8), 63–78.

Lapide, Larry (2002), "New Developments in Business Forecasting," *Journal of Business Forecasting,* 21 (2), 11–14.

Ledyard, Mike and Kate Vitasek (2004), "Is Your Metrics Program Measuring Up," *CLM Explores,* 1 (Spring/Summer), 8.

Mentzer, John T. and Carol C. Bienstock (1998), *Sales Forecasting Management.* Thousand Oaks, CA: Sage.

Mentzer, John T., William DeWitt, James S. Keebler, Soonhong Min, Nancy W. Nix, Carlo D. Smith, and Zach G. Zacharia (2001), "What Is Supply Chain Management?" in *Supply Chain Management,* John T. Mentzer, ed. Thousand Oaks, CA: Sage, pp. 1–24.

Min, Soonhong (2001), "Inter-functional Coordination in Supply Chain Management," in *Supply Chain Management,* John T. Mentzer, ed. Thousand Oaks, CA: Sage, pp. 371–390.

Narver, John C. and Stanley F. Slater (1990), "The Effect of a Market Orientation on Business Profitability," *Journal of Marketing,* 54 (4), 20–35.

Slater, Stanley F. and John C. Narver (1994), "Market Orientation, Customer Value and Superior Performance," *Business Horizons,* 37 (2), 22–28.

Tuominen, Matti, Arto Rajala, and Kristian Moller (2000), "Intraorganizational Relationships and Operational Performance," *Journal of Strategic Marketing,* 8, 136–160.

26

Intercorporate Coordination

Terry L. Esper

arket changes, such as electronic commerce, economic uncertainties, increased globalization, and hypercompetition, are causing firms to explore new strategic approaches to business operations. Such a competitive marketplace is placing more pressure on companies to be increasingly responsible and effective in meeting their customers' needs. Consequently, many firms have turned to coordination with supply chain partners as a way of facing the challenges of operating in the rapidly changing marketplace. Supply chain relationships have moved from adversarial exchanges to more collaborative ventures. Thus, instead of relationships based on opportunism and competition, many supply chain exchanges now put a greater emphasis on trust, interdependency, and coordination solutions to operational issues that benefit all parties involved.

The inefficiencies associated with not coordinating in supply chain exchange are well documented. One of the more prevalent concepts that illustrates the importance of coordinated supply chain processing is the bullwhip effect. Because of independent decision making in the supply chain caused by a lack of information sharing, demand information is amplified as it flows upstream in the supply chain. The result is forecast inaccuracy, poor utilization of assets, and ultimately, ineffective customer service. Coordination is considered the key to combating demand amplification and other operational inefficiencies in the global supply chain that are often associated with supply chain members focusing solely on the operations and performance of their respective firms.

One of the primary drivers of the increased coordination among supply chain organizations is the notion that focusing on systemwide operational efficiency yields much greater results than focusing solely on individual organizational units within the system. In fact, it has been suggested that the potential savings associated with increased coordination in the supply chain could be as high as 35% of total system costs (Sahin and Robinson 2002). Thus, what undergirds interorganizational coordination efforts is the promise of synergistic effects regarding supply chain cost management and customer service.

The increased focus on coordination in the global supply chain has resulted in many strategic initiatives aimed at bringing exchange partners closer through coordinated and synchronized operations. Examples include

- collaborative planning, forecasting, and replenishment—coordination of sales forecasting and replenishment between trading partners to improve inventory flows;
- quick response—coordination in the retail supply chain to shorten the retail order cycle and allow for lower necessary inventory levels;
- efficient consumer response—coordination in the grocery supply chain to support more efficient store assortment, replenishment, promotional events, and new product introductions;
- collaborative transportation management—managing distribution operations, such as mode/carrier selection, load tendering, tracking, scheduling, and payment, in a more integrative manner to support increased efficiencies in product transport; and
- vendor-managed inventory—supplier monitoring and management of retailer inventory to coordinate more efficient replenishment and lower inventory levels.

The commonality across these coordination initiatives is the focus on enhanced operational efficiencies through coordinated product, information, and resource exchange flows. The vast majority of coordination mechanisms in global supply chain management involve upstream and downstream flows. By focusing on integrated and synchronized flows, supply chain members stand to realize the enhanced efficiencies and performance that coordination promises.

In light of the nature of today's competitive marketplace, coordinated flows in the global supply chain are becoming a widely attempted strategic initiative. The potential benefits of interorganizational coordination are much too promising and appealing to ignore. The issue, then, is ensuring that coordination efforts are strategically managed in a manner that supports the ability to realize the potential benefits that served as a motivation for supply chain coordination in the beginning.

The key to flow coordination is the behavioral exchange of supply chain personnel. Without efforts to engage in behaviors that connote a willingness and desire to coordinate flows, the coordination effort will remain a dream that never progresses beyond the point of a great idea. The many behaviors involved in managing global supply chain coordination are therefore worthy of further discussion and delineation. This chapter addresses this issue by highlighting the various strategic behaviors involved in global supply chain coordination efforts and some environmental issues that support more effective global supply chain coordination.

The Managerial Behaviors of Interorganizational Coordination

The management behaviors associated with interorganizational coordination in the supply chain can be categorized by the underlying strategic focus of the exchange behavior (see Figure 26.1). Process-oriented exchange consists of behaviors that are concerned with managing the actual processes and flows associated with coordination efforts in the supply chain. Governance-related exchange consists of behaviors associated with managing the structural elements of the coordination-focused interorganizational relationship. Facilitative exchange involves behaviors that are concerned with facilitating the coordinated flows in the supply chain by maintaining a collaborative exchange environment among all participating parties in the coordination effort.

Process-Oriented Exchange

The essence of coordination in the supply chain involves the management of business processes and flows that are the basis for the coordination initiative.

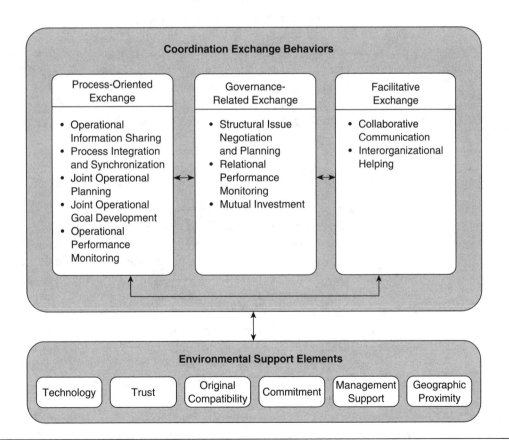

Figure 26.1 A Model of Interorganizational Coordination

Processes such as inventory management, replenishment, order processing, transportation, and returns are just a few of the flows that are at the core of coordination efforts. Process-oriented exchange behaviors are behaviors that are focused on managing these operational processes between coordinating parties. Such behaviors include operational information sharing, process integration and synchronization, joint operational planning, joint operational goal development, and operational performance monitoring.

Operational Information Sharing

The fundamental process-oriented exchange behavior is operational information sharing. To realize the benefits of supply chain coordination efforts, it is imperative that all parties have a common understanding of each other's operational constraints and issues. This is accomplished by sharing operational information across organizations involved in the coordination relationship. Behaviors associated with information sharing may include, for example, providing other organizations with inventory information, advance shipment notification, fluctuations in projected demand patterns, cost constraints, new product initiatives, and human resource adjustments.

In today's global supply chain-oriented marketplace, information sharing is quite prevalent. Now, more than ever, firms are willing to exchange information to provide smoother exchange flows. In the past, this most fundamental coordination behavior was the biggest impediment to effective efforts to coordinate flows in the supply chain. The adversarial and opportunistic undertones of the marketplace created resistance to engaging in significant levels of information sharing. In some industries the arm's-length approach is still a reality; however, in many cases the importance of information sharing is generally accepted and viewed as a necessity for effective organizational functioning.

Process Integration and Synchronization

Organizations engaging in coordination arrangements must share information, as discussed above. However, the reason for sharing information is to allow for process integration and synchronization. This is the actual process of coordinating flows. The touted benefits of supply chain coordination, as previously discussed, involve the exploitation of integrated processes, which allows for increased efficiencies and the resulting cost savings. It is therefore inherent in the coordination concept that supply chain personnel managing these exchanges exhibit behaviors that connote an attempt to integrate and synchronize processes across organizations. This behavior involves actually using information received from other parties in the coordination effort to influence the operational flows of the focal firm. In essence, this behavior is an extension of information-sharing behaviors and consists of any operational adjustments that are made to accommodate the operations of other coordinating parties, with the intent of creating efficiencies for all parties involved and maintaining seamless flows across participating organizations. The adjustments in replenishment and order cycles associated with coordination initiatives such as vendor-managed inventory and quick response are examples of such behavior.

Joint Operational Planning

Another extension of the operational information sharing dimension of process-oriented exchange behavior is joint operational planning. In the process of sharing information, coordinating parties must engage in planning for future operational challenges and opportunities that the collaborative effort faces. This includes the potential efficiencies of further operational synchronization and the operational implications of altering either the number or the extent of processes coordinated in the arrangement. Essentially, operational planning centers on proactively discussing the changes in information sharing and synchronization behaviors necessary to facilitate future coordination opportunities.

Joint Operational Goal Development

Joint operational planning focuses on the processes necessary to facilitate operational changes in the coordination effort. Joint operational goal development, on the other hand, is concerned with establishing mutual operational goals that each coordinating party understands and agrees with. Hence, this dimension of process-oriented behavior entails all exchanges that occur in the interorganizational coordination effort with the intent of developing mutual operational goals in a jointly established fashion. As such, information sharing is the foundation of joint goal development behaviors. In the process of sharing operational information, such information should be used to determine the operational goals of the respective organizations and then shared with other coordinating parties so that the goals of all parties are discussed and jointly understood. Although it is not necessary that all coordinating parties have exactly the same goals, what is important is that the organizations have a sense of the goals of all other parties involved, share their operational goals, discuss goals openly, allow other coordinating parties to suggest operational goals, and be willing to adjust accordingly.

Operational Performance Monitoring

Operational performance monitoring, in the context of supply chain coordination, involves both reactive and proactive elements. Proactive operational performance monitoring involves up-front development of performance management mechanisms and standards that define the operational expectations and boundaries inherent in the coordination process. This can be carried out by benchmarking against other supply chains and developing new performance monitoring structures from benchmarking these initiatives. Also, the joint operational planning behaviors discussed above can be translated to proactive performance monitoring measures. Reactive monitoring, on the other hand, entails behaviors that are associated with ensuring compliance with agreed-upon operational performance standards and measurement levels. These include operational cost analyses and reviewing of output measures.

Process-oriented exchange behaviors are coordination efforts centered on managing the actual processes of interorganizational integration. In today's global supply chain environment, appropriate relationships must be forged to support the coordination mechanisms in interorganizational exchange. Governance-related exchange behaviors are focused on this important component of interorganizational coordination.

Governance-Related Exchange

Interorganizational governance involves the maintenance of the structure and behavioral exchange of interorganizational relationships. The primary focus of governance structure management, particularly in the context of supply chain coordination, is to negate opportunistic behavior among the organizations participating in the coordination effort to ensure an exchange relationship where all participating firms stand to realize the increased efficiencies associated with the coordination venture. Opportunistic behavior by a party in a coordination-based relationship could erode the long-term gain potential for participating parties. Governance-related issues are therefore of primary importance to coordination arrangements, because monitoring and maintaining a collaborative structure provides all involved parties with the assurance of beneficial outcome potential. Although it is still a reality that benefits of coordination efforts can be "one-sided" in many interorganizational relationships, in today's global supply chain environment collaborative exchange to foster mutually beneficial coordination is becoming more of an adopted practice. Governance-related exchange behaviors include the following dimensions: structural issue negotiation and planning, performance monitoring, and mutual investment.

Structural Issue Negotiation and Planning

One important aspect of governance-related behavior is the behavior associated with discussing issues, planning accordingly, and making adjustments when applicable. Once the coordination effort has been agreed upon and implemented, supply chain personnel must periodically discuss structural issues as environmental events and circumstances present themselves. This is especially true when such circumstances can potentially alter the structure of the coordination effort. Examples of structural issues include the potential addition or reduction of coordinating parties, new technologies that could potentially change the operations of the coordination effort, and joint reaction to the competitive moves of other supply chains. In the context of interorganizational coordination, it is likely that the result of issue negotiation will be structural planning and mutual adjustment to maintain the coordinated nature of the relationship.

It is important to note that although issue negotiation is fundamental to behaviors associated with managing the structure of coordination efforts, negotiations can also have detrimental effects. This is especially true when the relationship surrounding the coordination initiative is collaborative in nature. Executives view annual negotiations as an impediment to collaboration in the supply chain because they often lead to time management inefficiencies and ultimately erode the trust and sharing that are the foundations of collaborative agreements (Mentzer, Foggin, and Golicic 2000). Consequently, issue negotiation in interorganizational coordination should perhaps be considered on a contingent basis, where environmental changes and process improvement opportunities drive the need for issue discussions and subsequent structural adjustment, instead of regularly scheduled annual negotiations.

Relational Performance Monitoring

In many cases it is not only important to monitor the operational performance of coordination-based exchanges (as discussed above); oftentimes performance appraisals should also include the degree to which coordinating parties effectively manage the structure of the relationship. As highlighted above, performance monitoring should involve both reactive and proactive components. Proactive performance monitoring, from a relational perspective, involves discussing up front how coordination outcomes will be shared and expressing the relationship management expectations of all participating parties (i.e., regular meetings, conference calls, and points of contact). Reactive relational performance monitoring, on the other hand, mainly involves behavioral assessments of the coordinating parties to ensure that the relationship is managed according to the plans and expectations outlined.

Mutual Investment

One key component of coordination efforts is idiosyncratic investment. Such investments are often nonfungible in nature, in that they are not easily transferred to other relationships, thus losing their value if the coordination-based relationship is terminated. They can be either tangible (i.e., systems, machinery, or facilities) or intangible (i.e., shared services, relationship-specific knowledge, or capabilities). Therefore, behaviors that are associated with investing in relationship-specific assets are considered a component of governance-related exchange behaviors in supply chain coordination. Examples include investigating the feasibility, applicability, and beneficial nature of potential investments, lobbying for support of investments within the respective organizations, and managing the implementation of idiosyncratic investments.

Governance-related exchange focuses specifically on managing the structure of relationships in which flow coordination takes place. In many cases, it is also necessary to ensure that the relational environment is conducive to closer integration and coordination among organizations in the global supply chain. This higher level of coordination often involves behaviors that are geared to creating such an environment—that is, facilitative exchange behaviors.

Facilitative Exchange

Facilitators of supply chain relationships represent the overarching conditions under which the interorganizational arrangement exists and serve as the "energy" and "motivation" to maintain the structure and exchange processes associated with the interorganizational relationship. Facilitative exchange behaviors engender perceptions of trust, commitment, and openness. Facilitative behaviors contribute to the effective functioning of the coordination-based relationship yet are not behaviors directly related to maintaining or managing the structure or processes at the core of the exchange.

Although facilitative behaviors are often difficult to distinguish, because they are often exhibited at the same time as governance-focused and process-oriented collaboration behaviors, they are inherently different. The primary distinguishing factor of facilitative behaviors is that they set the tone within which other exchange behaviors are carried out. Hence, facilitative behaviors maintain a collaborative atmosphere in the coordination effort, whereas the other exchange behaviors maintain coordinated structures and processes. Facilitative collaboration behaviors consist of collaborative communication and interorganizational helping.

Collaborative Communication

Communication is the glue that holds interorganizational relationships together. As implied by the previous discussion of governance-related and process-oriented collaboration behaviors, communication is at the heart of managing the structure and processes associated with coordination within the supply chain. Therefore, it is important that supply chain personnel managing interorganizational coordination efforts communicate and, in many instances, that they do so in a manner that sustains an environment conducive to coordination.

Collaborative communication represents a specific combination of communication elements that fosters an atmosphere of mutual support and respect and contributes to relationship building (Mohr and Nevin 1990). These elements of collaborative communication include frequency, bidirectionality, informality, and content (Mohr and Nevin 1990). Frequency refers to the amount of contact between persons managing the relationship. This considers different modes of communication (e.g., telephone, face-to-face, e-mail, and written letters). Bidirectionality is a measure of the amount of multidirectional communication flows that exist within the relationship. Informality refers to the extent to which communication is loose and unplanned.

The content dimension of collaborative communication involves the type of influence strategy embedded in the communication. Collaborative content is the extent to which noncoercive, indirect influence strategies are used when communicating. This involves, for example, requesting a behavioral change by communicating in a way that changes the other party's beliefs and attitudes about the desirability of the intended behavior, not coercing the other party to change their behavior by direct request. Collaborative content also refers to the extent to which coordinating parties communicate on a strategic, broad-focused, future-oriented level (Schultz and Evans 2002). In a global supply chain context, both perspectives of content are potentially important when engaging in coordination efforts and can contribute to the necessary environment that allows for facilitation of the coordinated structure and processes. Thus, collaborative communication content is considered multidimensional; it consists of indirect influence content and strategic content.

When exhibited in combination (i.e., communication that is frequent, informal, bidirectional, indirect, and strategic), this constellation of communication elements fosters a more collaborative environment and leads to synergistic outcomes, thus facilitating the coordination-focused exchange.

Interorganizational Helping

Interorganizational helping represents another category of facilitative exchange behavior in interorganizational coordination. Helping behaviors involve assisting exchange partners with work-related issues and showing altruism to one another, typically over and above what is generally required. Helping behaviors are a key facilitator of interorganizational collaboration (Mentzer et al. 2000). Moreover, the primary foundation of many coordination-based relationships is their win-win nature and sharing orientation. Interorganizational helping fosters this because supply chain personnel exhibit behaviors connoting that organizational boundaries within the relationship are "fuzzy" and that there is a vested interest in ensuring that other coordinating parties function effectively. Such behaviors are perhaps better reserved for coordination between organizations that is more collaborative in nature.

The aforementioned behaviors are at the heart of interorganizational coordination. Through process-oriented, governance-related, and facilitative behaviors, organizations in the global supply chain can build and manage effective coordinated exchange flows. However, it is also important to note that the nature of the environment within and between coordinating parties has a significant impact on the proclivity of supply chain members to exhibit and exchange these behaviors.

Environmental Characteristics for Effective Interorganizational Coordination

Although the behavioral dimensions of interorganizational coordination are the essence of coordinated exchange in the supply chain, there are other issues that must also be considered. Certain environmental elements should exist to support the exchange of coordination behavior. It is important that the contextual nature of the interorganizational relationship be conducive to coordinated exchange. Otherwise, attempts to coordinate flows may prove difficult, if not impossible, because of the lack of supporting environmental elements to drive the willingness and propensity to coordinate. Such environmental support mechanisms include technology, trust, organizational compatibility, commitment, managerial support, and geographic proximity (see Figure 26.1).

Technology

One of the keys to effectively implement and achieve the benefits of coordination in the supply chain lies in interorganizational information technology (IT). Such systems provide the foundation upon which coordination efforts can be developed and used to realize anticipated benefits. In fact, technology has been viewed as both an enabler and a supporter of coordination efforts (Kumar and van Dissel 1996).

IT has a significant impact on coordination effort formation by providing the necessary tools that make coordinated flows feasible. Functions of the enabling role of IT include, for example, real-time data transfer and automated communication. IT also plays a supporting role in coordination-focused interorganizational relationships. This role of IT involves, for example, the reduction of transaction costs and transaction risks that result from the automated coordination arrangement, thus supporting the perpetuation of the coordinated flow exchange.

It is important to note, however, that technology, in and of itself, is not enough to lead to successful coordination. IT only enables or supports the coordination effort. Firms must know how to effectively apply the technology to reap the benefits of coordinated processes (i.e., data analysis and automated communication). Therefore, the enabling and supporting role of IT in coordination efforts can be realized only if the technology is employed effectively.

Trust

Global supply chain members attempting to coordinate flows must trust that the other parties involved are willing to share both the rewards and the risks associated with the coordination effort. Otherwise, attempts at coordination would be limited in scope and potential benefits because the parties have not established a level of trust that ensures that the investment in coordination is worth the effort. Consequently, it is not advisable that organizations attempt to coordinate flows at the infancy of interorganizational exchange relationships. It is important that some degree of prior relationship history exists to foster the type of trust that will sufficiently support flow coordination.

Organizational Compatibility

Organizational compatibility refers to the extent to which coordinating organizations possess cultures, business objectives, managerial philosophies, and styles that are similar to, or complement, each other. The more similar or complementary are these areas in the firms, the more likely is the level of comfort that can support coordination of flows. Without organizational compatibility, the conflicting organizational artifacts may lead to a lack of trust and overall negative attitudes toward other coordinating parties. Issues such as employee empowerment and organizational structure may also impede some of the coordination efforts if the organizational representatives are not equally empowered or authorized to make strategic decisions related to the management of coordinated flows.

Commitment

It is important that all participating parties have a personal stake in the coordination effort and its operational outcomes. Entering one-sided flow coordination initiatives may lead to a lack of commitment to the ongoing continuous improvement and management of the coordinated exchange. Hence, firms should ensure that potential coordination opportunities involve parties that share some degree of interdependence. This can serve as an indication of the other parties' commitment to the exchange effort.

Managerial Support

Coordination of flows is not an easy task that can be accomplished overnight. The integration and synchronization of processes takes much time, effort, and investment. Furthermore, information sharing, which is such a fundamental feature of coordination efforts, requires a willingness to share sensitive information with supply chain exchange partners. It is, therefore, important that a level of managerial support exists in each coordinating firm to effectively invest the resources necessary to make coordinated flows a reality. This requires management that serves as a champion of the coordination effort and provides organizational representatives with the level of empowerment, flexibility, span of control, and resource allocation necessary to support the intricacies of coordination in the global supply chain.

Geographic Proximity

Geographic proximity is often suggested as an environmental component that can enhance integrated relationships (Lambert, Emmelhainz, and Gardner 1996). This issue is of significant importance when considering coordination in a global supply chain context. The ability to locate near each other is quite difficult when exchange partners are global. Technological innovations such as teleconferencing and simple e-mail communication have significantly reduced this barrier. However, close geographic proximity is still considered an important issue in coordinating flows with supply chain exchange partners. Many large organizations require key customers and suppliers to develop satellite locations in close proximity to their facilities. This allows more seamless coordination and exchange flows, as well as easy access to customer or supplier support personnel. Hence, geographic proximity is a major point of consideration where coordination is concerned, especially in the just-in-time and lean-focused market in which many global supply chains operate today.

In addition to managerial behaviors, it is also important for firms to consider the nature of the support environment that directly affects and influences the behavioral exchange in the coordination initiative. By ensuring that the necessary levels of trust, commitment, organizational compatibility, and managerial support exist to effectively support flow coordination with targeted supply chain partners, firms will more likely be successful in their attempts to streamline flows. Furthermore, taking the necessary actions to address geographic proximity issues, either through facility location or technological support, ensures the customer service and support that are necessary for smooth flow coordination.

Conclusions

With the appropriate levels of environmental support and the willingness to engage in the behavioral prescriptions discussed in this chapter, organizations interested in coordinated exchange will be well on their way to operational efficiencies and systemwide cost savings. The next steps involve assessing current flow coordination initiatives to ensure that they are operating at optimal effectiveness (e.g., assessing if there are certain exchange behaviors that are neglected or if there are environmental support elements that either can be enhanced or are currently lacking) and preparing for future coordination activities. This involves conducting an "environmental scan" to determine if the characteristics of the internal and exchange environment with potential coordination partners are conducive to flow integration. Furthermore, an assessment of the propensity and willingness of supply chain personnel to engage in the coordination behaviors discussed can also provide management with insights regarding their firm's level of preparedness when considering interorganizational coordination.

References

Kumar, K. and H. van Dissel (1996), "Sustainable Collaboration: Managing Conflict and Cooperation in Interorganizational Systems," *MIS Quarterly*, 20 (3), 279–300.

Lambert, Douglas, Margaret Emmelhainz, and John Gardner (1996), "So You Think You Want a Partner?" *Marketing Management*, 5 (2), 25–41.

Mentzer, John T., James Foggin, and Susan Golicic (2000), "Collaboration: The Enablers, Impediments, and Benefits," *Supply Chain Management Review*, September/October, 52–58.

Mohr, Jakki and John Nevin (1990), "Communication Strategies in Marketing Channels: A Theoretical Perspective," *Journal of Marketing*, 54 (4), 36–51.

Sahin, Funda and E. Powell Robinson (2002), "Flow Coordination and Information Sharing in Supply Chains: Review, Implications, and Directions for Future Research," *Decision Sciences*, 33 (4), 505–536.

Schultz, Roberta and Kenneth Evans (2002), "Strategic Collaborative Communication by Key Account Representatives," *Journal of Personal Selling and Sales Management*, 22 (1), 23–31.

27

Global Supply Chain Control

Daniel C. Bello

Meng Zhu

Although multinational corporations (MNCs) plan and develop supply chain strategies, the actual implementation of these plans is often conducted in conjunction with local partners in foreign markets. Strategies such as implementing continuous replenishment systems, automated warehousing, and other complex supply chain initiatives may involve a variety of sophisticated logistics, information technology, and distribution elements. Strategies require both the MNC and its foreign upstream suppliers or downstream distributors to engage in costly new tasks and invest in new resources to support the deployment of supply chain initiatives across various countries. From the MNC perspective, severe implementation problems occur when local partners do not comply with the strategy by failing to perform planned tasks or make required local investments. The lack of support by foreign partners is a major reason for the failure of initiatives in the global supply chain, largely accounting for the poor performance of otherwise technically excellent supply chain strategies (Bello, Lohtia, and Sangtani 2004).

The control literature attributes poor implementation of nominally good strategies to a failure to provide adequate guidance, ensure coordination, and exercise effective oversight over those delegated to execute a strategy (Weitz and Jap 1995). Referred to in this article as the strategy controller, an MNC attempting a global deployment of a supply chain initiative can influence and control the way foreign partners participate in a strategy. Such control stems from three oversight processes: monitoring, providing incentives, and enforcing agreements (Heide 1994). Furthermore, the magnitude and scope of an MNC's control effort necessary for a successful implementation vary with the governance and technical production characteristics of the supply chain strategy. Although some strategies are easily implemented and require little governance oversight by the controller, other supply chain initiatives possess performance and investment characteristics that create a variety of challenging governance and production problems. Exacerbating the implementation problems associated with complex strategies are the problems encountered by a controller that ventures into foreign markets characterized by very different legal regulations, normative beliefs, and cultural practices (Bello et al. 2004). Hence, an MNC attempting to deploy sophisticated supply chain programs across foreign markets with complex legal and other institutional environmental features faces a challenging control task to ensure successful implementation.

The purpose of this chapter is to specify the control processes associated with implementing a supply chain strategy across institutional arrangements (IAs) and institutional environments (IEs) in a global context. Figure 27.1 introduces a model detailing the connections between the characteristics of the supply chain strategy developed by an MNC, the magnitude and scope of the control requirements inherent in the strategy, and the impact of a foreign market's IE on implementation effectiveness. The chapter makes four contributions to our understanding of control in the global supply chain. First, the source of control and implementation problems in supply chains is identified as flowing from key characteristics of the MNC's strategy. By integrating the governance and production cost elements of transaction cost theory, the role of the strategy's exchange attributes and technical requirements are demonstrated to be the foundation of implementation difficulties. Second, the magnitude and scope of control requirements are shown to be inherent in the characteristics of a controller's supply chain strategy. Characteristics of the strategy's exchange attributes drive the magnitude of control, whereas technical requirements determine the scope of control required by a strategy. Third, the effectiveness of alternative forms of control is explained in terms of the efficacy of the IAs that function as forms of control in supply chains. The effectiveness of contractual, ownership, and social forms of control is evaluated. Fourth, the moderating role of institutional differences between the home country of the MNC controller and the foreign partner on the relative effectiveness of IAs in implementing global supply chain strategies is specified. The chapter proceeds by analyzing the characteristics of the controller's strategy, the dimensions of the strategy's control requirements, and the implications for implementation effectiveness from IAs and IEs.

Characteristics of the Controller's Strategy

Implementing a strategy requires participating firms to commit resources and perform the tasks necessary to support the new supply chain initiative. From a governance perspective, these tasks and resources have implications for attributes of the

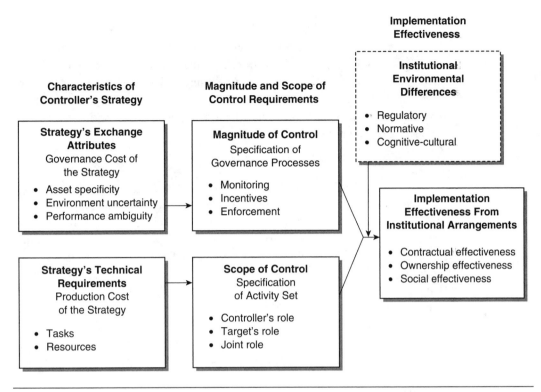

Figure 27.1   Global Supply Chain Control: Processes of Strategy Implementation Across Institutional Arrangements and Environments

exchanges that occur among supply chain partners as they execute the controller's strategy. Governance theory identifies several exchange attributes that can create such significant hazards for an investing party that unless these problems are addressed, the party is unlikely to participate in implementing the strategy. From a production perspective, a strategy involves certain technological principles and technical requirements that lead to the specification of activity sets across supply chain partners. For the strategy to be implemented successfully, optimal activity sets consisting of costly tasks and resource investments must be planned and fully accepted by each of the participating supply chain partners. Hence, inherent in a supply chain strategy are risky and costly production and governance issues that together generate transaction costs that may distort and otherwise impede successful implementation. As Williamson (1985) notes, the goal for a firm initiating a strategy is not to minimize the governance or production costs taken separately, but "to minimize the sum of production and governance cost," the strategy's overall transaction costs (p. 93). Consequently, both the governance and the production aspects of a supply chain strategy set in motion forces that must be organized and carefully managed by the controller if a strategy is to be implemented successfully by its partners in the supply chain.

Strategy's Exchange Attributes

Standard governance analysis focuses attention on the characteristics of a strategy in terms of its implications for three key attributes of exchange among supply chain partners: asset specificity, environment uncertainty, and performance ambiguity. Strategies involving unique assets, uncertainty, and ambiguous outcomes create the governance problems of safeguarding, adaptation, and measurement difficulties during implementation.

Asset Specificity

Asset specificity is the degree to which an asset cannot be redeployed to alternative uses without sacrificing productive value (Williamson 1991). Implementing a strategy efficiently and effectively may depend on the provision of unique assets that are highly specific to the tasks required but have little value in other applications. Specific physical assets such as specialized warehouses or materials handling equipment dedicated to a supply chain strategy represent sunk costs to the investing firm that are highly productive in the context of the strategy but cannot be redeployed to other uses without loss of value. Besides physical assets, other efficient but nontransferable assets can involve site specificity, human asset specificity, brand name capital, dedicated assets, or temporal specificity (Williamson 1991).

Although such assets are highly productive during implementation, they also expose the investing firm to opportunistic behavior by its partners. Having invested in highly unique supply chain assets, a firm is "locked in" because it is exposed to losses should its relationship end with other firms participating in the strategy. Such a lock-in situation may motivate the investing firm to tolerate opportunistic behavior by other members of the supply chain. Depending on the investment at risk, a firm may be forced to accept some blatant opportunism, a partner's failure to honor the explicit contract, as well as lawful opportunism, a partner's violation of the norms or shared understandings of the social or relational contract (Wathne and Heide 2000). Active blatant opportunism occurs if material facts are misrepresented or if actions expressly forbidden are performed or if required actions are not. However, contracts can also be passively violated by simply withholding critical information or effort implied by explicit agreements. Beyond contracts, relationships are governed by a variety of social norms and unwritten rules that an opportunistic partner can exploit to its advantage. Wathne and Heide (2000) state that "among the most central relational norms are (1) expectation of sharing benefits and burdens and (2) restraints on unilateral use of power" (p. 40) If these key norms are violated, a locked-in investor may be forced to tolerate deceptive cost or benefit shifting by an opportunistic partner as well as being forced to acquiesce to unfair demands. Thus, vulnerability due to specific investments "gives rise to a *safeguarding* problem, in the sense that mechanisms must be designed to minimize the risk of subsequent opportunistic exploitation" (Heide 1994, p. 73).

Environment Uncertainty

Defined as unanticipated changes in the circumstances surrounding transactions, environment uncertainty is another aspect of a strategy's exchange attributes that may give rise to potential governance problems. A supply chain strategy may be subject to two causes of uncertainty: volatility (unpredictable and rapid environmental change) and diversity (a complex environment characterized by multiple sources of uncertainty) (Klein, Frazier, and Roth 1990). While implementing a strategy, partners may face highly volatile and dynamic situations in which outcomes cannot be predicted because of the occurrence of unforeseen contingencies. Unexpected environmental disturbances create a volatile decision environment for supply chain members for reasons such as unpredictable volume or technological change (Heide and John 1990). Strategy involves volume unpredictability if the partners are unable to forecast their future volume requirements accurately. Such a strategy, for example, may focus on downstream markets that are so dynamic that the supply chain partners face a degree of demand volatility that precludes accurate forecasting. Likewise, future technological developments, industry standards, or product specifications associated with a strategy may change in rapid and unpredictable ways.

Besides volatility, a strategy may lead supply chain members into situations that are highly complex and heterogeneous in terms of suppliers, resellers, users, or competitors. Implementing a strategy in the face of a diverse task environment requires partners to obtain and process information about so many dissimilar entities that they are unable to address the multiplicity of demands and constraints effectively (Klein et al. 1990).

Unanticipated and highly complex circumstances provide opportunistically inclined partners with an opportunity to exploit situations requiring the partners to modify or otherwise adapt implementation plans. Rather than forgo taking advantage of an unexpected turn of events, an opportunistic partner uses the new circumstance to gain selfishly. Unanticipated circumstances pose two different types of opportunism (Wathne and Heide 2000). First, an opportunistic partner may improve its terms of trade by using a new situation to force renegotiations of an existing agreement. Forced renegotiation is active opportunism, whereby new circumstances are used to extract costly concessions from a firm. Second, a partner can engage in passive opportunism by refusing to adapt to changing circumstances. Such a partner may unfairly lower its costs or increase its revenue by being inflexible and unwilling to adapt to environmental change. Consequently, when "contingencies are too numerous or unpredictable to be specified ex ante in a contract, an *adaptation* problem exists . . . mechanisms must be put in place to permit adjustments to be made as events unfold" (Heide 1994, p. 73).

Performance Ambiguity

A partner's performance is ambiguous to the extent its resource investments or task performances are difficult to measure and verify. Measurement ambiguity is inherent in certain supply chain strategies because "strategic choices about markets and products profoundly affect the level of measurement difficulties" (Ghosh and John 1999, p. 135). A given strategy may call for investments that vary in measurability—a partner's investments in trucks and warehouses to serve customers are easy to assess, whereas its investments in employee training and quality processes are much less verifiable. Likewise, a strategy may require various tasks, efforts, or costly activities undertaken by the partner to serve targeted product markets. Carson et al. (1999) state, "More verifiable efforts are those matters for which an after-the-fact inspection of results or audits can reveal to a third-party referee that an action was undertaken at some level" (p. 122). For example, a partner's fulfillment of certain transportation tasks can be easily verified through on-time delivery, damaged goods, and other metrics. A partner's less verifiable tasks include "realigning its material handling procedures and equipment, and other 'invisible,' but costly, enhancements to its internal operations" (Bello et al. 2004, p. 59).

During implementation, a firm initiating a strategy may be subject to moral hazards in the sense that an opportunistic partner may exploit information asymmetry regarding its performance by underinvesting in key resources or performing tasks poorly. Such partners "have the motivation to undersupply quality, because quality reduction both provides immediate cost savings and is difficult to detect . . . [partners] have both the ability and the motivation to cheat" (Mishra, Heide, and Cort 1998, p. 279). Hence, when a partner's contribution to implementation is not easily verifiable by inspection of output, the strategy poses the *evaluation* problem of governance (Heide 1994). In the absence of control mechanisms to ascertain whether compliance with a strategy's requirements has taken place, the effectiveness of the implementation effort is put at risk.

Strategy's Technical Requirements

Whereas governance focuses on organizing and managing exchange, production concerns the conduct of exchange using various tasks and resources. For a supply chain strategy, "production costs are the costs of actually performing marketing-distribution functions" required for implementation (Klein et al. 1990, p. 198). At a technological level, implementing a strategy (such as a continuous replenishment system) has a variety of task and resource requirements involving ordering, transportation, warehousing, and other business functions. The key production cost question is, "Which supply chain partner is the low-cost producer for each aspect of the strategy?" Principles of economies of scale and labor specialization can be used to identify the firm best able to perform a task. A controller may find it economical to spin off to specialists those distributive functions that have a decreasing cost curve. Production cost theorists observe that tasks such as order processing and delivery may have declining cost curves as volume increases and, consequently, recommend assigning these scale-sensitive tasks to the firm best able to exploit the available economies of scale. Although functional spin-off reasoning generally holds for tasks employing easily measured, general assets in stable environments, departures from such "frictionless" settings lead to safeguarding, adaptation, and measurement problems that require governance oversight, as noted above.

Yet even in light of governance complications, a given supply chain strategy has inherent technical characteristics that drive the assignment of tasks and investments to those members best able to exploit economies of scale and labor specialization. To efficiently implement a strategy at the lowest cost, a controller must ensure that each strategy facet is conducted by the member best able to "(1) fully utilize human and capital resources, (2) employ scale-dependent process substitutions, and (3) achieve decreases in resource procurement costs" (Bello, Lohtia, and Dant 1999, p. 19). First, tasks such as operating a refrigerated warehouse are subject to economies of scale in the sense that specialized facilities and equipment lower costs only when efficient resources are intensively utilized across a high-throughput volume. A partner whose workload is low underutilizes the resource. As a result, supply chain costs fall as warehousing and other such tasks are performed by the partner able to operate nearest the optimal scale. Second, positive returns to scale occur when more efficient forms of resources are substituted for less efficient forms as workloads rise (e.g., automated vs. manual order picking). A supply chain task is "correctly" assigned to the partner whose overall operation possesses the scale and scope enabling it to cost-effectively employ the most efficient forms of capital and other resources during strategy implementation. Third, efficient task assignment occurs when the member achieves the lowest cost for supplies, services, and other resources because of the best quantity discounts and other economies in procurement. Beyond cost minimization, a strategy's technical requirements also hold implications for the interdependencies among the required tasks and resources. Because temporal and spatial dependencies exist among certain tasks and resources (i.e., order processing precedes and enables order picking and delivery), a controller must synchronize and otherwise coordinate tasks and resources across the supply chain (Bello et al. 2002). The optimal set of activities to be implemented by each partner must not only satisfy scale-related cost minimization criteria but also be highly coordinated within and across the partner firms (Crowston 1994).

Malone and Crowston (1994) define coordination as managing dependencies between task activities and resources, implying a range of dependencies that can be inherent in a supply chain strategy. In its simplest form, a dependency may exist between one firm's task (e.g., order processing) and another's resource (e.g., inventory investment)—a reseller's ability to process and fulfill an end user's order directly depends on its supplier's in-stock inventory levels. However, "more complex dependencies are analyzed by considering how a common resource is used by the two tasks or how one task can use multiple resources" (Crowston 1994, p. 15). Multiple task and resource dependencies across supply chain members become complicated because resources can be required, consumed, or created by tasks. For example, two tasks might share a common input resource—a controller performs one task (e.g., order processing) while an upstream partner performs a dependent task (e.g., order picking) and provides a joint input resource (e.g., refrigerated warehouse). If the partner opportunistically shirks its obligations for performance quality or investment, such poor role performance frustrates and defeats the controller's highly dependent order-processing activity. Likewise, one task might use multiple resources—a controller performs a task (e.g., order processing) and provides one input resource (e.g., warehouse) while a downstream partner provides a second input resource (e.g., truck fleet). A controller's ability to process and fulfill end-user orders from its warehouse in an on-time manner is highly dependent on the availability of its partner's trucks and related resources. Consequently, control processes must be put in place to ensure adequate coordination among global supply chain partners.

Magnitude and Scope of Control Requirements

The characteristics of a supply chain strategy may yield both governance problems requiring oversight actions and production problems requiring coordination actions to resolve interfirm dependencies. A controller attempting to implement a strategy may be highly dependent on a partner for tasks and resources required for strategy execution because the partner is the low-cost producer of certain tasks and the low-cost provider of certain resources. Yet other characteristics of the controller's strategy may expose it to significant risks of opportunism as supply chain members implement the strategy.

A controller addresses coordination and moral hazards by employing various forms of control over upstream and downstream partners. Using power, contractual terms, or relationship norms (Weitz and Jap 1995), the controller constrains a partner's degree of autonomy and influences decision making, greatly facilitating implementation efforts and goal achievements. The total amount of control required to implement a strategy is a function of both governance-driven magnitude of control and production-driven scope of control (Figure 27.2). Magnitude of control focuses on the exchange attributes of a strategy and its corresponding governance oversight requirements, and scope of control reflects the technical requirements of a strategy and the resultant specification and planning of the

	Governance-Driven Magnitude of Control Required	
	Low	**High**
Production-Driven Scope of Control Required **Low**	**Minimum Control Requirements** Narrow Scope and Low Magnitude	**Moderate Control Requirements** Narrow Scope and High Magnitude
High	**Moderate Control Requirements** Wide Scope and Low Magnitude	**Maximum Control Requirements** Wide Scope and High Magnitude

Figure 27.2   Magnitude and Scope of Control Requirements for Strategy Implementation

activity sets to be performed by each supply chain member. For the controller, magnitude of control involves the specification of certain governance and guidance processes, whereas scope of control reflects the allocation of the strategy's activity set to partners, specifying the content domain for controls.

Scope of Control

Technical production considerations lead to a joint profit-maximizing activity set, the optimum allocation of tasks and resources to supply chain members that maximizes the total profit available from a strategy (Carson et al. 1999). A supply chain's optimal activity set for a strategy best exploits the available economies of scale and scope while fully addressing interfirm dependencies for the tasks and resources required to implement the strategy. A key aspect of a controller's strategy development is the specification and planning of activity sets for itself and partners such that no other reallocation of tasks and resources increases the total supply chain profits derived from the strategy. From a planning perspective, such an ideal allocation of roles for supply chain members best exploits the profit potential inherent in a strategy.

The optimally efficient assignment of tasks and resources yields a controller's role, a partner's role, and a joint role. Given production considerations, the controller and partner autonomously self-perform their respective tasks and provide their assigned resources. Autonomous roles can be executed largely independently of other firms because the domains of relevant task-to-task and resource-to-task dependencies lie within the firm and are coordinated among the firm's employees (Bello et al. 2002). However, as noted previously, implementing a supply chain strategy involves many complex interfirm tasks and resource dependencies that lead to joint roles between partners.

Beyond managing its own employees' work, the scope of interfirm control facing a controller in the context of supply chain management depends on the partner's autonomous role and the joint role of both firms. A narrow scope of control faces a controller when it self-performs most of the tasks and provides most of the resources needed for strategy execution. Production requirements are such that the partner holds few technical advantages and is assigned a narrow activity set. That is, the content domain of controls is narrow because the partner engages in few strategy-relevant actions of interest to the controller. When partners perform only a few tasks or provide only a few resources, a strategy presents the controller with minimum-to-moderate control requirements (see Figure 27.2). In contrast, a controller faces a wide scope of control when a large number of tasks and resources needed to implement a supply chain strategy lie within the partner's and their joint role. Owing to the strategy's technical requirements, the partner is the low-cost producer of many key tasks and the low-cost provider of many important resources necessary for implementation. When the scope of control is wide, the controller has relatively few tasks and resources to manage in an autonomous fashion because most are conducted autonomously by the partner or are performed jointly by the supply chain members. Such a strategy presents a controller with a wide content domain to oversee, manifesting moderate-to-maximum control requirements.

Magnitude of Control

The magnitude of the interfirm control requirement facing a controller depends on the intensity of the safeguarding, adaptation, and measurement problems inherent in a supply chain strategy. As noted, these governance problems can impose considerable constraints on the implementation process and require oversight or control mechanisms to motivate, check procedures, and assess outcomes of partners. Monitoring, incentive systems, and enforcement means are the three most relevant governance processes employed to control strategy implementation (Heide 1994). The extent to which these governance oversight processes are required is determined by the level of asset specificity, environment uncertainty, and performance ambiguity inherent in a particular supply chain strategy.

As shown in Figure 27.2, the governance-driven magnitude of control required by a given strategy may be low. When the tasks and resources utilized during implementation involve only general assets, are not associated with environmental volatility or complexity, and are easily measured, a controller is faced with a minimum-to-moderate control requirement. In contrast, some strategies are characterized by highly specific assets that are unique to the strategy's supply chain requirements, and these assets lock in the investing party because of their loss of value in other applications. Likewise, a problematic strategy may also be subject to future uncertainty in terms of volume or technology that presents risks and adaptation problems to the partners. Finally, a given strategy may involve costly tasks or resource investments that—although crucial to successful implementation—are largely "invisible" to partnering firms in the supply chain. A strategy characterized by such challenging governance problems presents a controller with moderate-to-high control requirements.

As the magnitude of control requirements rises, a controller may unilaterally address governance problems through greater monitoring, incentive, and enforcement efforts. Control actions directly taken by the strategy owner, the controller managing the implementation process, is a unilateral form of governance (Heide 1994). Unilateral forms of governance are formally imposed by the controller, who establishes rules and sanctions to elicit compliance by partner firms to implementation requirements. However, a controller may also indirectly manage implementation through a shared consensus with partner firms. When implementation is controlled indirectly through informal, endogenously derived social arrangements between the partners, bilateral forms of control are employed. Firms cooperatively control aspects of implementation through less formal, less intrusive forms of monitoring, incentive, and enforcement efforts (social elements are discussed later as a separate form of IA).

Monitoring

Using information to identify whether the implemented actions have departed from strategy requirements, monitoring processes uncover deviations from the controller's plan. To address safeguarding problems, a controller monitors its partners to minimize the opportunistic exploitation of its specific asset investments.

Through forms of surveillance, a controller uncovers as well as discourages partners from violating explicit contract terms, exploiting its locked-in position. Likewise, adaptation problems can be better managed by obtaining information about partner adjustments to unfolding events. Surveillance can also address evaluation problems when a partner's investments and tasks are difficult to verify. Monitoring reduces information asymmetry by employing measurement systems to gather and evaluate information about partners. Systematic screening and examination across the supply chain greatly enhance the controller's ability to detect deviations and correct noncompliance.

Monitoring can be carried out using several different approaches: output monitoring, process monitoring, and normative monitoring. Unilaterally, a controller can explicitly monitor a partner's outputs such as sales performance, market penetration, or other performance indicators of the strategy (Bello and Gilliland 1997). Process monitoring emphasizes the assessment of behaviors; for example, the manufacturer can monitor a retailer's implementation of a strategy by directly supervising the manner in which in-store implementation efforts are conducted (Murry and Heide 1998). In contrast to a unilateral perspective, normative monitoring "deals with the measurement problem in a proactive fashion, through socialization processes that promote internal self-control" (Heide 1994, p. 77). For example, based on the extent to which beliefs, values, and expectations regarding the relationship are jointly held, shared goals among partners can ensure voluntary compliance to a supply chain strategy's task and resource requirements.

Incentive System

By providing motivations for partners to implement a strategy correctly, incentives compel required tasks and investments by rewarding appropriate actions. Incentive systems are typically necessary because involved supply chain partners may not be motivated to make resource commitments and fulfill mandated tasks in the absence of an inducement. Strategies characterized by high levels of environmental uncertainty and performance ambiguity tend to face implementation obstacles associated with a lack of motivation. An unexpected turn of events may lead to passive opportunism because a partner may inflexibly fail to adjust its behaviors in light of new circumstances. To control such behaviors, a controller's offer of a monetary inducement may motivate the desired task-specific adaptation in a partner's behavior. Likewise, evaluation problems may discourage a partner from investing in resources that are difficult to verify. By offering specific inducements, a controller can encourage investments that otherwise would not be undertaken by making them economically attractive. Thus, incentives can partly dissolve the adaptation and measurement difficulties confronted by the strategy owner. Without incentive systems, achieving coordinated implementation from supply chain partners in a joint profit maximization fashion may be unattainable.

Incentive systems can be crafted based on the size of the financial incentive and the manner in which the incentive is administered (Murry and Heide 1998). Three distinctive forms of incentive systems are typical: market, hierarchy, and purely bilateral reward systems. Market incentives are represented by resale profits or commission payments. Often combined with output measurement, market incentives are characterized by a short-term, pay-for-performance orientation. In contrast, an outcome-based hierarchical reward system is more long-term oriented and bureaucratically administered. Complementary to the two unilateral incentive forms, a purely bilateral incentive system promises long-run equity. As such, identification and expected future participation in the supply chain operates as a reward in its own right.

Enforcement

Referring to actions taken to realign behaviors with supply chain strategy requirements, enforcement supports implementation by ensuring that a partner's tasks and investments are consistent with prior agreements. Safeguarding problems can be partly addressed by enforcing contractual and other agreements to discourage a partner's blatant exploitation of a controller's specific investments. Similarly, a controller can rely on a source of authority to obtain a desirable adaptive response to environmental uncertainty. Legal and other appeals can be made by a controller, reminding a partner of its obligations regarding tasks and investments in the face of a highly volatile or complex environment. If compliance must be compelled, the strategy owner must offer a level of "disciplinary response" to enforce changes in deviant behaviors.

The controller can execute unilateral enforcement mechanisms through the legal system, rational rules, and contractual arrangements. More specifically, contractual enforcement relies on formalized agreements or terms to align task performance with prior promises (Gilliland and Bello 2002). Legal enforcement typically refers to the coercive power of an authoritative third party, in most cases, the judiciary and regulatory systems. Alternatively, the controller can resort to social norms, such as solidarity, flexibility, and information exchange, to achieve internalized self-enforcement and relational obligation.

Implementation Effectiveness From Institutional Arrangements

IAs are the rules of the game supply chain members deploy to control and facilitate upstream and downstream exchanges. "An IA can consist of various formal and informal components and will possess contractual, ownership, and social characteristics" (Carson et al. 1999, p. 115). IA elements such as contracts are the microlevel controls or specific tools of governance employed by the controller to decrease opportunism and increase coordination within the supply chain. IA elements are deployed to monitor, incentivize, and enforce aspects of the controller's strategy in a way that addresses task and resource dependencies occurring during implementation. As rules of exchange, IA elements are specific forms of control through which the governance oversight processes are legitimized and manifested. IAs legitimize the authority of the controller and the obligations of the partner regarding the monitoring, incentives, and enforcement that encompass the magnitude and scope of control required by a supply chain strategy. The particular ways the IA facets of contracting, ownership, and social elements support and control implementation are discussed briefly.

Contracting Arrangements

As a form of control, contracts can tightly bind supply chain partners to their activity sets by specifying obligations, compensation, and penalties. Through contractual commitments, a partner may be required to participate in a controller's monitoring program by periodically providing reports of its ongoing activities and output accomplishments. Explicit contract terms may also detail incentives that serve as a reward system to spur motivation, enhancing partner participation and performance during implementation. Likewise, a contract may have enforcement properties by specifying penalties for poor performance. Although a third-party logistics provider may be subjected to late-delivery fines or damaged goods penalties, not all required tasks and resources in a partner's activity set can be controlled through contracting (Carson et al. 1999). Summarizing contract difficulties, Bello et al. (2004) state:

> However, some activities are subject to serious contracting problems making them unsuited to this IA element. Activities where effort or output is difficult to measure or assess are not contractible since an objective third-party cannot verify compliance with contract terms. Verifiable effort or output is a key requirement for an activity to be contractible since this aspect of an IA consists of pay-for-performance. (p. 60)

Ownership Arrangements

For activities that are not contractible, Carson et al. (1999) suggest that ownership may be the IA that provides the control required by the controller to ensure successful implementation. The rights of ownership permit the controller to use more extensive monitoring and surveillance. The controller can "access whatever records, conduct whatever inspections, and request whatever reports it deems necessary to evaluate the behavior and outcomes" of the target (Brown, Dev, and Lee 2000, p. 52). Also, the controller can use a full system of incentives (e.g., wages) and sanctions (e.g., suspensions without pay) to gain coordination and implementation. Thus, a controller may decide to own an asset-specific refrigerated warehouse because performance ambiguity, as well as other measurement and quality verification problems, precludes easily drawing and enforcing a contract with a third-party warehouseman.

Social Arrangements

Depending almost entirely on a shared set of implicit principles, norms, and values (Weitz and Jap 1995), and minimally on legal aspects of the IE, social arrangements are the most complex and intangible part of IAs (Carson et al. 1999). As a bilateral form of control, these social norms support strategy implementation by promoting and cultivating internal motivation, and self-control as well as self-enforcement. For example, a strong information-sharing norm enables the strategy owner to access the partner's accounting records and marketing reports, which to a large extent reduces monitoring issues. Likewise, a strong solidarity norm implies a long-term orientation, which reduces safeguarding and enforcement risks of the strategy owner. Flexibility, defined as a willingness to adapt procedures, significantly mitigates the negative impacts of environmental uncertainty on the supply chain partner's strategy implementation performance.

To summarize, contracting, ownership, and social arrangements all potentially provide a great amount of support and control for the successful implementation of a supply chain strategy. Through these IAs, a controller can exert high levels of control and influence, increasing the likelihood that its supply chain strategy is implemented in an effective manner. However, the efficacy of the three IA elements in decreasing opportunism and enhancing coordination is likely to decrease somewhat as control requirements rise. As the magnitude and scope of control requirements increase for a supply chain strategy, the effectiveness of contracting, ownership, and social elements in eliminating implementation shortcomings tends to decline. That is, strategies facing the greatest governance and production challenges pose such substantial barriers to execution that some level of implementation difficulties persists despite the control efforts of the controller.

The Moderator Role of Institutional Environmental Differences

In a global context, a controller faces many additional challenges in establishing effective IAs to control the way supply chain partners implement strategy. Although controllers from industrialized countries find it relatively easy to deploy supply chain strategies in their domestic markets, they often confront many barriers to implementation in developing or transitional economies and other foreign markets (Bello et al. 2004). Why should a controller from North America or Western Europe encounter an especially large number of implementation problems with partners located in China, India, Vietnam, and other countries? Scott (2001) suggests that the explanation lies in the differences between the IEs of the controller and partner countries. Referring to the macrolevel aspects of a society, an IE consists of the building blocks of a national setting and context. Various forces within the partner's country may pressure the local firm in unique ways, resulting in an improper implementation of the controller's strategy (Grewal and Dharwadkar 2002). In particular, contracting, ownership, and social elements of IAs used by a controller may lose their effectiveness in controlling a partner's implementation activities. The regulatory, normative, and cultural-cognitive facets of an IE may weaken and otherwise interfere with control efforts.

Regulatory aspects refer to the demands of governments and regulatory bodies to comply with laws and other requirements. Two primary mechanisms of regulatory institutions that shape business conduct are imposition and inducement. Imposition refers to the coercive powers of rules, laws, or other authoritative sources that interpret social standards and impose constraints. Represented by subsidies, and tax, tariff, or trade barriers, inducements are strong monetary incentives provided by government bodies in exchange for conformity (Grewal and Dharwadkar 2002). Importantly, both the domain and the content of regulatory mechanisms may vary significantly in the home markets of two international partners, creating a serious regulatory misalignment within the global supply chain. The relative power of various regulatory bodies and the societal support generated by them may systematically differ across countries.

Confronted by regulatory misalignments relevant to the global supply chain, implementation effectiveness from contracting is significantly undermined. A mutually agreeable contract is difficult to establish because of contradictory definition and conceptualization of legal requirements and welfare and fair competition across international supply chain partners (Grewal and Dharwadkar 2002). More important, contractual compliance by a supply chain partner is at great risk as a result of conflicting legislative, executive, and judiciary systems. For example, in the absence of an easily enforceable contract, a Western controller would experience difficulty enforcing contractual safeguards with a partner in China (Bello et al. 2004).

Similarly, a controller is less able to control a strategy by exercising ownership because claims to property rights are not supported under the regulatory systems of many transitional economies and countries with strong centralized governments. Lacking effective legal devices and claims to property, a controller's nominal ownership of physical assets in certain foreign markets is vulnerable to opportunistic behavior by the partner and the local government. Thus, the expected superior control features of ownership of certain supply chain assets may not be realized in foreign markets possessing serious regulatory misalignments.

Normative aspects refer to a society's values and norms that direct behavior through social obligations and expectations (Scott 2001). Normative expectations prescribe how supply chain members are to behave in the context of a particular country, imposing constraints as well as empowering action. Through the mechanisms of authorizing and acquisition, normative elements influence exchange behavior by setting up standards for socially acceptable behaviors. Authorizing involves the development of socially appropriate codes of conduct, and acquisition refers to mimicking the behaviors of firms that are seen as legitimate (Grewal and Dharwadkar 2002). Normative elements affect strategy implementation because local firms adopt only certain modes of relational customs and mimic the business processes they consider legitimate.

Incompatible normative assumptions between supply chain partners give rise to contracting ineffectiveness. Shared business norms are the tacit assumptions for an explicit and a relational exchange contract. Ranging from "general ones such as trust, to the highly specific, such as assumptions about particular and precise trade usages" (Macneil 1980, p. 25), these assumptions may differ significantly across the global supply chain. For example, shared understandings of business ethics and fair competition serve as tacit assumptions in domestic contracts between U.S. partners. In contrast, collectivism, authoritarianism, and centralized planning are regarded as norms in some Eastern European business settings (Bello et al. 2004). Implementation effectiveness from contracting in countries with incompatible normative beliefs is limited.

Normative misalignments also challenge strategy implementation from social arrangements. Within a market characterized by low levels of trust and a short-term orientation, relying on social arrangements such as self-control and self-enforcement may impose substantial safeguarding issues on the strategy owner domiciled in a country with a long-term orientated normative environment. Likewise, a purely bilateral incentive system becomes impotent if a firm possessing the norm of flexibility is working in a country characterized by strong rules and rigid authoritarian beliefs.

Cultural-cognitive aspects are defined as a collective programming of the mind that distinguishes the members of one cultural group from another. As such, culture has rich implications for the effectiveness of IAs on strategy implementation across global supply chains. From an institutional perspective, cultural-cognitive elements of a society are the shared conceptions that constitute the nature of social reality and the frames of reference through which meaning is made (Scott 2001). Cultural-cognitive institutions habitualize behavior- and yield-programmed actions in a way that makes other types of behavior inconceivable to members of a culture.

Positioned as the most complex IA, social arrangements rely entirely on mutual understanding and shared values to achieve strategy implementation. Cultural-cognitive misalignments—namely, contradictory cognitive values and cultural frameworks—have a direct negative impact on implementation effectiveness from social arrangements. For example, in depending on self-control and other social elements, a risk-seeking strategy owner is unlikely to achieve effective implementation from a supply chain partner whose home market is not risk tolerant.

High levels of cultural-cognitive conflict also pose significant constraints on a controller's ownership arrangements. Intrafirm management requires high levels of coordination, otherwise inefficiency of the bureaucratic control mode reduces effectiveness. Cross-border supply chain integration through ownership involving significant cultural-cognitive misalignments typically results in poor internal control and coordination. For example, bypassing traditions such as the *keirestu* system in Japan, *guanxi* in China, or *blat* in Russia, to a large extent inhibits a Western strategy owner's ability to establish an effective ownership position in local supply chain enterprises.

Conclusion

An MNC deploying a sophisticated supply chain program across several countries may encounter severe implementation problems as foreign partners fail to perform their assigned tasks and make the required investments. This chapter specifies the nature of the control process that can be undertaken by a controller to implement a supply chain strategy across IAs and IEs in a global context. The linkages between the characteristics of the supply chain strategy and the magnitude and scope of the control requirements inherent in the controller's strategy are discussed and analyzed. Furthermore, the effectiveness of contractual, ownership, and social forms of control are evaluated, along with the moderating role of the institutional differences between countries on the relative effectiveness of the control forms.

References

Bello, Daniel C. and David I. Gilliland (1997), "The Effect of Output Controls, Process Controls, and Flexibility on Export Channel Performance," *Journal of Marketing,* 61 (1), 22–38.

Bello, Daniel C., David I. Gilliland, Talai Osmonbekov, and "Frank" Tian Xie (2002), "e-Business Technological Innovations: Impact on Channel Processes and Structure," *Journal of Marketing Channels,* 9 (3/4), 3–25.

Bello, Daniel C., Ritu Lohtia, and Shirish P. Dant (1999), "Collaborative Relationship for Component Development: The Role of Strategic Issues, Production Costs, and Transaction Costs," *Journal of Business Research,* 45 (1), 15–31.

Bello, Daniel C., Ritu Lohtia, and Vinita Sangtani (2004), "An Institutional Analysis of Supply Chain Innovations in Global Marketing Channels," *Industrial Marketing Management,* 33 (1), 57–64.

Brown, James R., Chekitan S. Dev, and Dong-Jin Lee (2000), "Managing Marketing Channel Opportunism: The Efficacy of Alternative Governance Mechanisms," *Journal of Marketing,* 64 (2), 51–64.

Carson, Stephen J., Timothy M. Devinney, Grahame R. Dowling, and George John (1999), "Understanding Institutional Designs Within Marketing Value Systems," *Journal of Marketing,* 63 (4), 115–130.

Crowston, Kevin (1994), "A Taxonomy of Organizational Dependencies and Coordination Mechanisms," Working Paper #174, MIT's Center for Coordination Science. Cambridge, MA: MIT Sloan School of Management.

Ghosh, Mrinal and George John (1999), "Governance Value Analysis and Marketing Strategy," *Journal of Marketing,* 63 (Special Issue), 131–145.

Gilliland, David I. and Daniel C. Bello (2002), "Two Sides to Attitudinal Commitment: The Effect of Calculative and Loyalty Commitment on Enforcement Mechanisms in Distribution Channels," *Journal of the Academy of Marketing Science,* 30 (1), 24–43.

Grewal, Rajdeep and Ravi Dharwadkar (2002), "The Role of the Institutional Environment in Marketing Channels," *Journal of Marketing,* 66 (3), 82–97.

Heide, Jan B. (1994), "Interorganizational Governance in Marketing Channels," *Journal of Marketing,* 58 (1), 71–85.

Heide, Jan B. and George John (1990), "Alliances in Industrial Purchasing: The Determinants of Joint Action in Buyer-Seller Relationships," *Journal of Marketing Research,* 27 (1), 24–36.

Klein, Saul, Gary L. Frazier, and Victor J. Roth (1990), "A Transaction Cost Analysis Model of Channel Integration," *Journal of Marketing Research,* 27 (2), 196–208.

Macneil, Ian R. (1980), *The New Social Contract: An Inquiry Into Modern Contractual Relations.* New Haven, CT: Yale University Press.

Malone, Thomas W. and Kevin Crowston (1994), "The Interdisciplinary Study of Coordination," *ACM Computing Surveys*, 26 (1), 87–120.

Mishra, Debi Prasad, Jan B. Heide, and Stanton G. Cort (1998), "Information Asymmetry and Levels of Agency Relationships," *Journal of Marketing Research*, 35 (3), 277–295.

Murry, John P. and Jan B. Heide (1998), "Managing Promotion Program Participation Within Manufacturer-Retailer Relationships," *Journal of Marketing*, 62 (1), 58–68.

Scott, Richard W. (2001), *Institutions and Organizations*, 2nd ed. Thousand Oaks, CA: Sage.

Wathne, Kenneth H. and Jan B. Heide (2000), "Opportunism in Interfirm Relationships: Forms, Outcomes, and Solutions," *Journal of Marketing*, 64 (4), 36–51.

Weitz, Barton A. and Sandy D. Jap (1995), "Relationship Marketing and Distribution Channels," *Journal of the Academy of Marketing Science*, 23 (4), 305–320.

Williamson, Oliver E. (1985), *The Economic Institutions of Capitalism*. New York: Free Press.

Williamson, Oliver E. (1991), "Comparative Economic Organization: The Analysis of Discrete Structural Alternatives," *Administrative Science Quarterly*, 36 (2), 269–296.

PART V

Making It Happen

28

Supply Chain Innovation

Daniel J. Flint

Everth Larsson

W hat is innovation and why do firms pursue it? We ought to address this question before discussing supply chain innovation specifically. Innovation can be viewed from a narrow or a broad perspective. Innovations can be radical and new to the world or incremental and innovative only to one user. The tendency is to think narrowly of only radical, new-to-the-world innovations—the first semiconductor, the Sony Walkman®, the iPod®, the first laptop computer, the Internet, a radical new vertical takeoff and landing (VTOL) jet military aircraft, FedEx services, and so on. We associate the first firm to launch the radical product as an innovator, but many innovations are not of the radical type and many are failures in the marketplace. In fact, many radical innovations that appear to arrive "overnight" took years to develop and market. The now ubiquitous Post-it® Notes took nearly 15 years to work their way out of corporate 3M and into the marketplace. At the other end of the spectrum, incremental innovations tend to be thought of not as innovations but as part of continuous improvement. And many innovations occur in what is called the "middle space"—that area between continuous improvement, incremental efforts, and radical new-to-the-world products and services. These are all innovations.

We adopt a very broad notion of innovation that refers to any aspect of a product or service that a focal audience evaluates as new and helpful in achieving its goal. Rogers (1995) states that innovation can involve an idea, practice, or object that is perceived as new by an individual or other unit of adoption. But why do firms pursue innovation? One reason is because they seek differentiation in the marketplace. Providing a new, and ideally superior, product or service helps a firm separate itself from its competitors and, if they are first, allows them to charge more for the innovation because of the lack of competitive offerings. Truly successful innovations either solve problems or create benefits that customers value and that no other firm has been able to develop to date. Sometimes, entire corporations are examples of innovations—that is, the entire bundle of services or products represents a completely new offering. Google and eBay each might qualify here. As the world's largest online auction company, eBay enables individuals to buy, sell, and barter directly with each other anywhere where there is internet access. Google pioneered online search technologies and went public as a corporation in the fall of 2004, its stock tripling in market value over 10 months. Not only did Google pioneer efficient search technology, they also demonstrated more successfully than any other firm the enormous amount of revenue that can be gained through advertising contracts connected to their search results.

For innovations to be successful on a large scale in the marketplace, they have to be available at a cost customers are willing to pay. For example, Sony displayed flat screen panel television sets in one of its Tokyo prototype showrooms a dozen years before they were purchased in any great numbers. The excessive costs to produce, and by extension to sell, the product did not at that time create a compelling value proposition for the average television consumer. Consumers were just as space challenged 12 years ago as they are now, but they were not and still are not willing to pay $60,000 for the convenience offered by a television or monitor that takes up less space. Eventually, the technology and manufacturing costs came down to a level where the value proposition began to make sense for consumers. This pattern of products that are technically viable yet not market viable has existed for many years across technologies. Just notice how economically friendlier hybrid fuel vehicles are only now beginning to sell well in the marketplace, with the Toyota Prius® and Honda Hybrid Accord® as recent U.S. standout brand examples, when various technologies have been available for many years.

On the radical end of innovation is discontinuous innovation, which focuses on entirely new technologies that disrupt current paradigms and processes. They completely change the rules of the game. In *The Innovator's Dilemma*, Christensen (1997) demonstrated how emergent technologies affect current industry standards and customers' expectations. Most supply chain innovations probably do not qualify as this radical, but some utilize technologies that are quite disruptive. Radio-frequency identification (RFID) technologies have been around for quite some time but have only recently disrupted supply chain relationships as suppliers scramble to comply with large retailer demands for RFID to increase product visibility within the supply chain. It is only recently that marketplace demand has viewed RFID as a viable solution to inventory visibility and control issues at (potentially) an acceptable cost.

In this chapter, we discuss the notion of innovation as strategy, innovation in supply chains, what constitute supply chain innovations, and processes for being innovative. We then discuss these concepts and implications within a global context.

Innovation as Strategy

Clearly, some firms adopt innovation as a strategy. As Treacy and Wiersema (1995) have discussed, successful firms often select one of the three central strategies on which to excel—product leadership and innovation, operational efficiency, or customer intimacy. They have the discipline to pursue superiority in that laser-focused strategy entirely, while remaining competent in the other two. The product leadership strategy is an innovator's strategy. For example, firms like IKEA, Dell, and Zara have found ways to differentiate themselves through continuous innovations; the way they compete is through innovations. Business strategy and supply chain strategy are intertwined. Think of IKEA's supply chain. By using rectangular packages and letting the consumers perform final assembly of the furniture they purchase, IKEA develops a supply chain that is completely different from that of its furniture competitors. For one thing, it is more efficient in its use of vehicle and storage capacity, effectively lowering costs and, subsequently, prices in the marketplace.

Similarly, Dell has proven over the years that the mastery of supply chain agility and postponement processes can serve as a differential advantage. Partially through the development of innovative information technology solutions and negotiating critical supply chain relationships, Dell is able to significantly beat competitors in many supply chain metrics in, for example, the areas of inventory turns, payment cycles, speed to market, inventory visibility, and (lower) capital investment requirements.

Zara, the Spanish apparel company, sells high-end fashion at prices affordable by middle-class consumers. They can develop new collections faster than many of their competitors. For example, within three weeks of the 9/11 attacks, Zara had a new collection of black clothes in its stores all over the world. In principle, stores get a few select consignments. Zara does not spend much on advertising. Consumers realize they must often check in stores to get updates on Zara merchandise. Customers visit Zara stores on average 17 times a year, compared with 3 or 4 times for Zara's competitors. Its ability to innovate faster than its competitors keeps customers loyal.

IKEA, Dell, and Zara do not rest on their laurels. They constantly innovate within their supply chains to operate faster, more agile product and information flows.

Supply Chain Innovation

So, what then constitutes supply chain innovation at the broadest level? Supply chain innovations represent innovations in products, services, and processes that affect supply chain management. At its most powerful level, supply chain innovation should be process innovation because processes are far more difficult to emulate by competitors than products, creating a more lasting differential advantage. Because supply chain management is largely about process management, it stands to reason that supply chain management innovations have the potential to create meaningful competitive advantages.

At a basic level, supply chain management involves at least these major interrelated management areas:

- Transportation
- Inventory
- Warehousing
- Packaging
- Forecasting
- Network design
- Ordering procedures
- Customer service
- Scheduling

There are many other management areas for supply chain management and alternative ways to envision supply chain management (e.g., interfunctional and interfirm processes for managing distribution, production, customer relationships, and so forth), but this list will serve our point. Let's consider just transportation. Transportation innovations can occur in the design of more environmentally friendly motor transport engines, more efficient trailers, more sophisticated tractors, and information systems contained in or on the tractor or trailer. The Swedish truck manufacturer Scania is well-known for its ability to use modularization and standardization of components. This makes it possible to offer a wide variety of vehicles at no extra cost and even at lower cost. Innovations can also be made in systems used for loading and unloading transport vehicles. Innovations can be made concerning the infrastructure that supports transportation or facilitates transfers from mode to mode. Innovations can also be made in terms of the processes for managing transportation or negotiating transportation contracts. For example, Transplace.com is an Internet-based company that brokers contracts between U.S. motor carriers and shippers by using an innovative proprietary network optimization software package. Changes in the transport vehicle itself can affect suppliers to the original equipment manufacturer (OEM) that produces the vehicle, either by new products or services suppliers must develop or by the emergence of entirely new suppliers.

Clearly, each area within supply chain management involves products and processes that offer opportunities for innovation. Some may be incremental and others may be radical, relying on disruptive technologies. One way to categorize such innovations is through a matrix similar to the one shown in Table 28.1.

Firms and supply chain partners must choose carefully the kinds of innovations they wish to pursue. Many innovations require extensive resources. Some require decades of investment. Some have a higher potential to create differential advantages than others. To pursue innovative products, services, solutions, or processes, they typically must have the potential to improve supply chain performance through

1. cost reductions,

2. revenue increases,

Table 28.1   Categorizing Supply Chain Management (SCM) Innovations

SCM Area	Products/Services			Processes		
	Incremental	Middle Space	Radical	Incremental	Middle Space	Radical
Transportation						
Warehousing						
Packaging						
Forecasting						
Network design						
Order reception						
Ordering procedures						
Customer service						
Flow scheduling						
Others						

3. decreased capital, or

4. all three of these.

Typical objectives of any corporate management structure include increases in profitability and market share. Reductions in cost without reductions in selling price increases profits. Increases in market share with no change in price increases revenue and, if each unit sold is profitable, also increases overall profitability. However, some markets demand price reductions. Two such markets are consumer electronics and automotive, specifically the automotive OEMs. Regarding consumer electronics, digital technology is innovating at such a rapid rate that the market price for "older" technologies (in many cases, only six months old) and products that rely on them falls at a rapid rate. As such, increases in profitability must come from either reducing costs at a faster rate than the rate of decline in market price or an increase in market share at a faster rate than the rate of decline in market price— that is, gaining more business faster than the rate of diminishing margins. Supply chain management can help in both respects—that is, help reduce costs through innovations and help serve new markets. Apart from affecting the return on investment (ROI) or other measures of profitability, less capital forces development of more effective and efficient (leaner) processes. The automotive marketplace is highly competitive and a supply chain context in which the OEM still retains a great deal of power (power has shifted toward the retailer in consumer goods). Powerful OEMs traditionally exerted significant influence over suppliers in demanding annual price reductions. Like the consumer electronics space, automotive suppliers (especially tier 1 suppliers) are forced to reduce costs at a faster rate than the annual reduction in price.

For some firms, simply changing account management teams to include supply chain management experts represents an innovation—in this case, an innovation in customer relationship management. From this innovation emerge additional supply chain innovations driven by the voice of the customer, such as new delivery methods, new package design, and new inventory management systems.

Supply chain management can be the location of innovation and can also play a role in facilitating innovations. Supply chain management processes play a supporting role to help launch and sustain research and development and new product introductions (Zacharia 2001). New products, often innovations, carry with them unique logistics and supply chain challenges.

Innovation Processes

Innovations emerge in a number of ways, but in business they usually grow out of standardized development processes. Not to be confused with innovations *in* processes, innovation processes refer to the methods firms use to develop innovations, whether product, service, or process innovations. Although much has been written about innovation and new product development, the general process is relatively straightforward. Specifically, new product development processes involve traditional stages as part of an often referenced Stage-Gate® process (Figure 28.1).

All stages of this model, from idea generation through to launch, have been extensively studied. Additionally, the importance of process owners, interpersonal dynamics of product development teams, fit between new products and corporate strategy, and innovation as an organizational culture have been explored. It is only recently that we have seen the growth of discussion concerning new service development. Given that supply chain management is significantly about processes that are service oriented—that is, supporting product movement, conducted either by

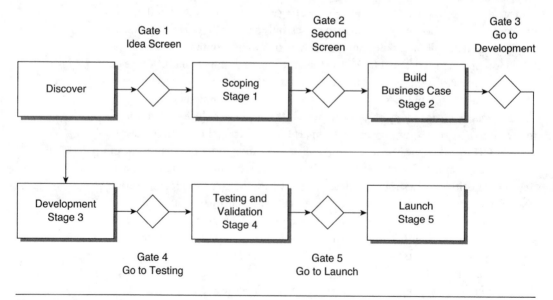

Figure 28.1   Typical Product Development Stage Model

SOURCE: From Cooper (1993).

manufacturing partners in a supply chain or by third-party logistics enterprises—many supply chain innovations are actually represented by new services. Just as product development involves formal processes, so too does service development (Kuczmarski and Johnston 2005). But services differ from traditional products. Services are

- Individualized to customers
- Intangible
- Instantaneous (produced and consumed at the same time)
- Inseparable among the individual components

As with the Stage-Gate® process, new service development processes begin with the identification of a customer need or problem; pass through to idea generation and screening; and then move on to conceptual, business, and actual development, testing, and launch. However, "the launch of a new service is never ending" (Kuczmarski and Johnston 2005, p. 103). Services are continually modified, adapting to emergent customer needs.

Consistent with this view, the idea generation phase of logistics innovation, an important component of supply chain innovation, is a continuous social process involving four components focused on uncovering customer opportunities:

- Setting a stage for capturing customer data
- Customer clue gathering
- Negotiation and clarification of customer and marketplace information
- Interorganizational learning (Figure 28.2)

The model applies equally well to broader supply chain management innovation.

Before discussing the components of this model, recognize that it is a customer-driven process. This means the marketplace needs drive the innovations. In some industries, technology *seems* to drive innovation. In these industries, many technological innovations are pursued simultaneously in the hope of finding commercial applications for some. When a new product representing a new technology application becomes viable, the tendency is to claim that a new market has been "created." Actually, what usually has happened is that new demand has been created for a particular product or product class that meets a previously unmet need or a currently met need better than competitive offerings by more effectively creating a benefit or removing some of the current sacrifices customers must make to receive the same benefits. In both cases—that is, meeting an unmet need or meeting a currently met need better—the need already exists. To be clear, the market need was not created by the innovator, but the demand (market) for specific new products that meet the need has been created. For example, inventory visibility has long been a desired customer benefit. Technologies like RFID are simply better ways of meeting the already existent need that many years ago was served through a phone call, visual sightings, and paper documentation. Similarly, innovative customer

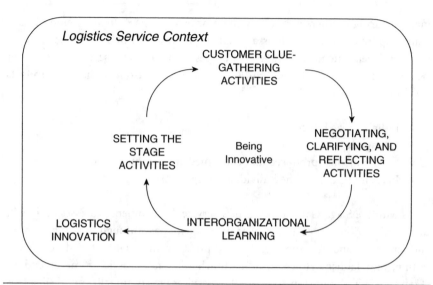

Figure 28.2   A Logistics Innovation Process

SOURCE: From Flint et al. (2005).

relationship management software systems are simply more sophisticated ways of staying in touch with customer-specific information that a hundred years ago managers maintained mentally or on a ledger.

Supply chain management is about coordination and collaboration across multiple organizations in a customer-focused manner. The services that support product and information flow through supply chains are often complex, requiring extensive development time and unique competencies. Companies such as Dell and Wal-Mart have found ways to leverage supply chain competencies, including supply relationships, to their competitive advantage. As such, supply chain innovation is often created in close coordination with customers, which brings us to the model in Figure 28.2.

Setting the Stage

Setting the stage refers to formal procedures for laying down a foundation to be innovative and customer oriented. Here, companies develop a culture of innovation by encouraging ideas from employees at all levels of the organization, hiring innovative thinkers, training employees in methods for collecting and analyzing customer and market data, and investing in facilities and equipment for interacting with customers and storing and analyzing customer data. For example, we know of one leading European third-party logistics firm that invested in creating an off-site location that encouraged deeper and more meaningful customer interactions. Other firms invest in training employees in customer satisfaction, survey, design, execution, and data analysis. These kinds of activities "set the stage" for seeing innovation opportunities.

Customer Clue Gathering

Customer clue gathering refers to the actual collection of customer data. It takes many forms across organizations and even within some organizations. Here are just a few examples we have found in organizations:

- Customer group meetings (multiple customers, multiple representatives from one customer)
- Customer one-on-one interviews
- Customer surveys (what-is-valued surveys, customer satisfaction surveys)
- Sales call reports
- Unsolicited customer comments and feedback
- Call center reports

Firms also gain part of the voice of the customer data from point-of-sale data, but this information is limited to what was purchased, not why it was purchased or under what circumstances. Customer insights must be inferred from these data.

Most firms collect voice-of-the-customer data to understand either what customers want now or how satisfied customers are with what they have already received or experienced. When it comes to innovation, firms must collect and analyze customer data with an eye toward unmet or emergent needs—that is, what customers will want. This is because it takes time to develop innovative solutions to customers' problems, and designing to today's needs may mean an obsolete product on launch.

We have heard managers say that customers do not know what they would want in the future, so it does not make sense to ask them. However, successful innovative firms do not ask customers what exact features or service attributes they would want in the future. They look at voice-of-the-customer data across time and try to understand where customers are trying to take themselves or their organizations and the benefits they want to realize. They interpret voice-of-the-customer data and do not simply respond to it. Armed with that knowledge, suppliers are able to develop innovative products and services that help customers reach their goals. This is why we term this stage "clue gathering," because it involves piecing together multiple kinds of customer data from multiple sources and interpreting what they mean about what might happen in the future. Doing so is much easier if it is done in close, regular contact with key, forward-looking customers. In the traditional product development space, these customers are sometimes called "lead users."

Negotiation and Clarification

Innovative firms do not simply respond to what customers request. They spend time trying to understand the data as well as the potential implications for their own organizations. Whereas the clue-gathering stage is about collecting voice-of-the-customer data, this stage is about making sense of the data and tying it to the supplier organizations collecting it. By carefully considering holistic projections of where customers are taking their organizations or where consumers are taking their lives, suppliers can choose to pursue innovations surgically, selecting opportunities carefully—that is, those with the highest market attractiveness and fit with their firms' internal capabilities. Many do this by negotiating within their organizations and supply chain relationships over the meaning of certain data and ownership responsibility for certain aspects of the innovation ideas emerging.

Interorganizational Learning

Out of the negotiation and clarification sessions emerge the early stages of actual product and service development. This often includes trial-and-error experimentation, sensitivity analyses, and joint sessions with supply chain partners that result in collective learning. Interorganizational learning takes organizational learning one step further. Whereas organizational learning traditionally focuses on creating and managing a learning enterprise, interorganizational learning extends the enterprise to groups that span organizations. Interfirm knowledge sharing helps create significant differential advantages (Adams, Day, and Dougherty 1998; Dyer and Singh 1998) as well as increased perceptions of the value in supply chain relationships (Cheung 2005). As supply chains continue to expand globally, interorganizational learning and knowledge sharing become increasingly critical for innovation.

The Importance of Organizational Culture and Processes

Supply chain innovation requires the coordination of idea generation, learning, development, and service launch across multiple organizations. During many innovation projects, people and organizational structures change, disrupting individual projects. As such, it is especially important to develop and nurture an innovative organizational culture, so that regardless of who becomes involved, their natural tendency will be to think innovatively. Additionally, successful innovative firms follow formalized processes for generating ideas and then bringing them through subsequent stages to the marketplace. There is no one standard process for being innovative, or for any other aspect of business for that matter. However, there is a standard way of being process oriented. Processes most often must be developed in-house by and for each firm or supply chain relationship. What works for one organization may not work as well for another. Organizational structures, cultures, people, strategies, and objectives vary significantly from organization to organization, demanding that firms develop unique processes for their own enterprises. At a minimum, management must be process oriented, meaning that they consider sequential methods of effectively and efficiently achieving solutions and demand that everyone follow established processes. Variation kills innovation as well as it does manufacturing. We want variation in ideas but not in how ideas are generated and processed toward development and launch.

Ramifications of Global Supply Chains

The opportunities for supply-chain-management-related product and process innovations are endless. At the basic level, the transference of a supply chain management process from one region of the globe to another might be quite innovative, even radical in its innovation. Conversely, exploring supply chain management's unmet needs in one region of the globe might help reveal similar unmet needs in other regions. So, from an innovation process standpoint, information must flow rapidly throughout supply chains globally to facilitate the knowledge sharing required for innovations to emerge and develop.

However, global supply chains do not equate to equivalent products and services globally and regionally. Regional economic strengths, regulations, infrastructures, technological sophistication, labor, cultures, preferences, and so forth all create unique challenges and opportunities for innovation. Different market segments value different kinds and levels of service (Mentzer, Flint, and Hult 2001). What is innovative and market viable for one market segment in one region of the globe may not be so in a similar market segment elsewhere. For example, dominant modes of transport differ globally, and within modes, capacity constraints, transfer requirements, lead times, operating procedures, and cost structures all vary widely around the globe. All these differences offer opportunities for innovation, either transferred from another region of the globe or developed from the ground up. Globalization adds considerably to complexity, and one of the main demands for the supply chain manager in the future will be to manage complexity.

Summary

Global supply chain innovation emerges from formal processes aimed at developing new supply chain strategies, services, processes, and relationships applied either regionally or globally that meet customers' unmet needs or meet currently met needs better than does the competition. The result of these innovations is competitive advantage. In trying to manage global supply chain innovation, firms should consider doing the following:

- Identifying opportunities to develop and strengthen supply chain partnerships with organizations also interested in seeking innovation
- Formalizing processes for being innovative *with* supply chain partners
- Identifying opportunities to transfer supply chain services from one region of the globe to another

- Recognizing the unique differences in customer desires from one region to another and innovating accordingly
- Looking at products, services, and processes when looking for innovation opportunities
- Identifying emergent technologies globally that offer supply chain innovation opportunities
- Keeping a customer focus when developing innovations

It is also very important to question and change strategies to adjust to new conditions. Innovative strategy development can create opportunities and solve problems in a way that can be said to be "out of the box."

References

Adams, M. E., G. S. Day, and D. Dougherty (1998), "Enhancing New Product Development Performance: An Organizational Learning Perspective," *Journal of Product Innovation Management*, 15 (5), 403–422.

Cheung, Mee-Shew (2005), *Inter-firm Knowledge Sharing and Its Effect on Relationship Value: A Global Supply Chain Perspective*, dissertation, University of Tennessee, Knoxville.

Christensen, Clayton M. (1997), *The Innovator's Dilemma*. Cambridge, MA: Harvard Business School Press.

Cooper, Robert G. (1993), *Winning at New Products: Accelerating the Process From Idea to Launch*. New York: Perseus.

Dyer, Jeffrey H. and Harbir Singh (1998), "The Relational View: Cooperative Strategy and Sources of Inter-organizational Competitive Advantage," *Academy of Management Review*, 23, 660–679.

Flint, Daniel J., Everth Larsson, Britta Gammelgaard, and John T. Mentzer (2005), "Logistics Innovation: A Customer Value-Oriented Social Process," *Journal of Business Logistics*, 26 (1), 113–148.

Kuczmarski, Thomas D. and Zachary T. Johnston (2005), "Service Development," in *The PDMA Handbook of New Product Development*, 2nd ed., Kenneth B. Kahn, ed. New York: Wiley, pp. 92–107.

Mentzer, John T., Daniel J. Flint, and G. Tomas M. Hult (2001), "Logistics Service Quality as a Segment-Customized Process," *Journal of Marketing*, 65 (4), 82–104.

Rogers, Everett M. (1995), *Diffusion of Innovations*, 4th ed. New York: Free Press.

Treacy, Michael and Fred Wiersema (1995), *The Discipline of Market Leaders*. Reading, MA: Addison-Wesley.

Zacharia, Zach G. (2001), "Research and Development in Supply Chain Management," in *Supply Chain Management*, John T. Mentzer, ed. Thousand Oaks, CA: Sage, pp. 127–152.

29

Global Supply
Chain Security

Omar Keith Helferich

Robert Lorin Cook

G lobal supply chains are critical enablers of world trade, which increased by 10.3% in 2004 after a 4.5% increase in 2003 (The World Bank Group 2005; World Trade Organization 2004). Despite their importance, these lengthy, complex global supply chains are especially vulnerable to disruptions caused by a myriad of major disasters such as terrorist attacks, electric power blackouts, and hurricanes. Such disruptions have significant negative impacts on supply chain effectiveness and efficiency that, in turn, devastate corporate performance and profitability (Hendricks and Singhal 2005). Consequently, global supply chain managers must have a basic understanding of disasters and their likely effects on the supply chain, plus knowledge regarding the process of disaster preparedness.

Disaster Classification and Vulnerability Assessment

The first step in global supply chain security involves the classification of disasters so that those who are responsible for security can assess supply chain vulnerability and allocate resources to defend the supply chain(s) effectively and efficiently. Major disasters are classified by cause, type, magnitude of impact, and supply chain resource impact.

Cause

The first order of classifications is the root cause of the disaster. The three primary causes of major disasters that can disrupt supply chain operations are intentional human acts (e.g., terrorism, product tampering, computer hacking), unintentional incidents (e.g., accidents resulting from equipment failures, power failures, human error), and abrupt natural occurrences (e.g., hurricanes, tsunamis, earthquakes).

The root cause of a disaster significantly affects the disaster management process. For example, the appropriate process for preventing a major fire from starting and then severely damaging a chemical production facility depends, to a large extent, on the cause: arson, old electrical wiring, or lightning strike. Clearly, the actions required to prevent arson differ from those required to maintain electrical wiring.

Type

The second order of classification is disaster type. The seven primary types of major disasters are (1) biological (e.g., bacteria, viruses), (2) chemical (e.g., matter that is flammable, poisonous, corrosive, or radioactive), (3) explosives (e.g., matter that explodes), (4) tampering and failures (e.g., product tampering, power failures, computer viruses), (5) temperature extremes (e.g., excessive heat or cold such as ice storms), (6) tremors (e.g., earthquakes), and (7) water and wind (e.g., floods, hurricanes). The type of agent involved in a supply chain disaster has a profound effect on every stage of the disaster management process. For instance, a biological virus disaster and a computer virus disaster differ regarding prevention, mitigation, detection efforts, response once released, and methods of supply chain recovery. Categorization of major disasters by cause and type is given in Table 29.1.

Magnitude of Impact

The total number of different potential disasters is almost unlimited, but the resources devoted to supply chain security are finite. As a result, security personnel must prioritize potential disaster classes. The *magnitude of impact* dimension provides planners with a tool to accomplish this task. Specifically, disaster impact is measured based on five factors: severity, duration, geographic scope, detectability, and frequency of occurrence. Severity measures the overall damage to supply chain capability. Duration estimates the length of time that the supply chain will be damaged. Geographic scope estimates the numbr of square miles affected by the disaster. Detectability measures the level of difficulty in detecting the disaster. Frequency measures the probability of disaster occurrence and is perhaps the most difficult to estimate. Some combination of historical data, future projections, and concern about a particular disaster should be blended to yield a probability of occurrence.

The disaster impact measurement factors, scales, and measures suggested for supply chain planner use are listed in Table 29.2. The scales for magnitude of impact

Table 29.1   Disaster Classification

Type	Cause		
	Intentional Human Acts	*Accidents*	*Natural—Abrupt*
Biological	Biological agent attack	Biological spills	Epidemic—plague
Chemical	Chemical agent attack Radioactive attack	Chemical spills	Poisons Radioactive material Corrosives
Explosives	Chemical explosion Nuclear explosion	Explosion	Volcanic eruption Asteroid—comet impact
Tampering and failures	Information Human Product Private infrastructure Public infrastructure Finances	Information Human Product Private infrastructure Public infrastructure	
Temperature extremes	Arson	Fire	Lightning fire Ice—snowstorm
Tremors	Avalanche triggered	Avalanche triggered by accident	Avalanche (snow, rock) Earthquake
Water and wind			Flood Hurricane—typhoon Tornado—water spout Tsunami Sandstorm

Table 29.2   Disaster Magnitude of Impact Measurement

Factor	Scale	Measure
Severity (level of supply chain damage)	1—Minor to 5—massive	Lives, injuries, dollars
Duration (time supply chain is damaged)	1—Days to 5—multiple years	Time
Geographical scope	1—Local (city) to 5—multiple	Square miles Countries (global)
Detectability	1—Easy (warning system in place) to 5—difficult (no warning system in place)	Human sensory and warning systems' capability of detecting
Frequency (of occurrence)	1—Low probability to 5—high probability	Historical frequency + forecasted frequency + level of concern

range from 1 to 5. Overall magnitude of impact is determined by totaling the first four factor scores and then multiplying this subtotal by the frequency score.

Supply Chain Resource Impact

Disasters are categorized by supply chain resource impact because disaster impacts on supply chains are likely to be dissimilar. For example, the actions required to recover from a bombing that destroys a facility are different from those required to recover from a computer virus. There are six specific supply chain resource categories that can be affected by a major disaster. Human resources can be severely affected by fates such as death, injury, illness, and so on. Obviously, significant man-hour losses of highly trained and experienced personnel disrupt supply chain operations. Product can be stolen, damaged, destroyed, or contaminated. Lack of product means stock-outs and lost sales. Private physical infrastructure such as plants, warehouses, vehicles, and equipment can be damaged or destroyed. Loss of critical production or logistical assets can cripple global supply chain operations. Public physical infrastructure that supports business, such as electrical, gas, and water utilities, bridges, ports, and airports, also can be severely damaged or completely destroyed. Such losses can paralyze some aspects of supply chain operations. Information systems disruption, tampering, and deletion can leave a supply chain blind or unable to transact business. Finally, financial disruption in the form of counterfeiting, theft, or illegal stock market manipulations can financially weaken a firm, thereby disrupting the necessary financing of supply chain operations.

The level of impact on these supply chain resources caused by a disaster may be estimated by using a scale of 1 (*minor impact*) to 5 (*massive impact*). Minor impact indicates the resource can be healed, repaired, or replaced quickly, and as a result, little supply chain disruption would occur. A score of 5 indicates the resource cannot be replaced for a long time, thus severely affecting supply chain operations and performance.

Figure 29.1 displays the complete disaster classification profile (Helferich and Cook 2002). After selecting the major disasters that pose the greatest threats to the supply chain(s) and understanding the impact each is likely to have on global supply chain resources, it is time for management to plan for these disasters.

Disaster Management Process

The disaster management process consists of five major stages: planning, mitigation, detection, response, and recovery. Planning involves preplanning for disasters, which may include major actions such as organizing a planning team, assessing supply chain vulnerability, and developing a long-range plan. Mitigation involves proactive steps (e.g., backup procedures, facilities) taken prior to a disaster to prevent or reduce supply chain disruption and damage. Detection consists of forecasting or warning mechanisms that signal that a disaster will occur or is occurring. Examples include weather satellites and bulletins and medical tests for bacterial infections. Response consists of initial response activities after a disaster occurs,

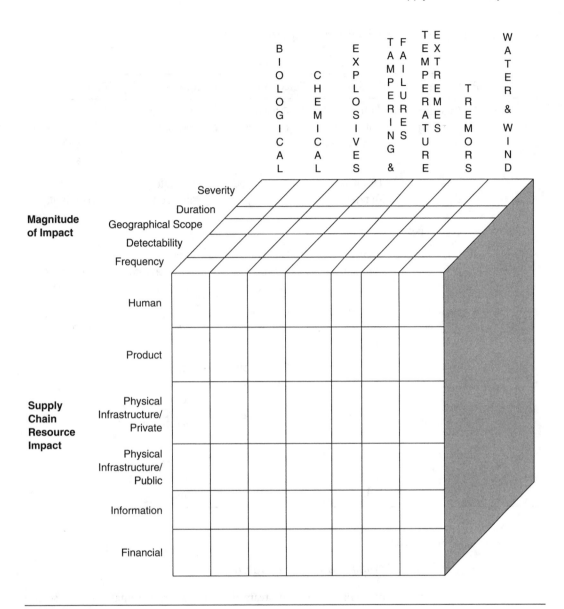

Figure 29.1   Disaster Classification Profile

such as first aid provided to the injured and to firefighters. Recovery involves longer-term response actions that include activities such as rebuilding a production facility and hiring new personnel.

Although the specific actions required during each stage of the disaster management process are determined by the cause type of disaster and its specific impact on the global supply chain, the major action steps required for each stage are generalizable. Table 29.3 provides an overview of the disaster management process.

Table 29.3   Disaster Management Process Overview

	Stages				
	Planning	*Mitigation*	*Detection*	*Response*	*Recovery*
Major steps	1. Establish a planning team	1. Define mitigation opportunities	1. Develop a detection plan	1. Implement a response plan	1. Develop and implement a recovery plan
	2. Analyze disasters and capabilities	2. Develop a mitigation plan	2. Acknowledge warnings	2. Evaluate direction and control	2. Ensure continuity of management
	3. Develop a plan	3. Implement the plan	3. Evaluate and act on observations	3. Evaluate communications	3. Maintain employee support
	4. Implement the plan	4. Continuous improvement program	4. Determine if further action is warranted	4. Evaluate life safety	4. Resume operations
			5. Continuous improvement	5. Evaluate property protection	
				6. Evaluate public services	
				7. Evaluate community outreach	

Planning

Step 1: Establish a Planning Team

Form a supply chain continuity team that includes representatives from senior and line management plus labor. The team should be cross-functional with representation from all critical supply chain functions. The team should establish its scope of authority, issue a written mission statement, and establish a schedule and budget.

Step 2: Analyze Disasters and Capabilities

For each disaster that poses a significant supply chain threat, estimate the likely impact on all global supply chain resources, including those provided by the firm, governments, emergency relief organizations, tier 1 suppliers, customers, and utilities that provide lifeline services (water, electricity, gas). Then, identify the current level of preparedness of supply chain resource providers. This analysis of current status includes an assessment of mitigation capabilities including backup inventory, transport, storage, communication, energy systems and building fortifications, fire, and security protection, among others; detection capabilities including forecasting systems, surveillance, and warning systems; response capabilities including direction and control, communications, evacuation, and first responders (police, military, fire, medical); and recovery capabilities such as insurance coverage, salvage processes, product and asset replacement, and infrastructure and utility restoration.

Step 3: Develop a Plan

The overall plan should contain a mitigation plan, detection plan, response plan, and recovery plan for each disaster-supply chain combination. The most critical part of the overall plan is the response plan, which should contain the core considerations for emergency management such as direction and control, communications, life safety, property protection, public services, and community outreach.

Direction and Control. Determine who will direct company resources, analyze information, and make decisions during an emergency. Establish a chain of command. Ensure that all relevant functions (safety, security, maintenance, human resources, logistics planning) report to the emergency director.

Communications. Develop a plan for communicating during a disaster. Communication is needed to report emergencies, warn personnel of danger, keep families and off-duty employees informed, coordinate corporate response actions, coordinate emergency response agency activities, and synchronize response actions with suppliers and customers.

Life Safety. Protecting life and health safety of supply chain personnel is the first priority during an emergency. Planning for life safety must include measures to protect supply chain personnel, evacuation procedures for each facility, sheltering services, and plans for liaison support with outside emergency agencies. Life safety includes training employees in the appropriate procedures.

Property Protection. Protecting facilities, equipment, and vital records is essential to restoring operations after an emergency. The assets covered include production, warehousing, transportation, inventory, and communications systems. Protection systems such as fire protection, lighting, automatic shutoffs, emergency power, and security should be considered. Procedures must be developed and personnel trained to properly shut down a facility, its systems, and processes. Records preservation should be a key consideration.

Public Services. Determine the public sources of disaster support. These sources may include multiple levels of government, global relief organizations such as the Red Cross, and other private corporations that provide public assistance during disasters.

Community Outreach. Community outreach is important because it influences the ability of a firm to protect personnel and property and return to normal operations. Develop a response plan that involves community leaders, first responders, community emergency response organizations, and utilities. The supply chain security team should participate in community emergency drills and develop mutual aid agreements such as providing assistance for cleanup activities and sharing assets, emergency power, or medical support.

Step 4: Implement the Plan

Ultimately, the approved plan must be distributed to all supply chain partners and public groups that are involved. Next, integrate the plan into company operations. Provide training to all parties involved in the plan. Test the plan using drills and exercises. Evaluate performance and modify the plan as necessary. A formal audit should be conducted annually.

Mitigation

Step 1: Define Mitigation Opportunities

Potential opportunities to mitigate global supply chain disruptions include disaster shelters; employee safety and security programs; safety stockpiles; duplicative inventory stocking locations; duplicate material sourcing; redundant production capabilities for critical products; contingency production capacity; preplanned alternate transport routes, carriers, and modes; contingency storage; backup computer systems; emergency power systems; preventive maintenance programs; upgrading facilities to current fire and building codes; supporting government efforts to improve security and protect citizens, utilities, and infrastructure; and conducting joint exercises with community and supply chain partners to assess disaster preparedness.

Step 2: Develop a Mitigation Plan

Mitigation opportunities should be prioritized and the highest-priority programs selected for implementation. Work with insurance providers to determine the impact of proposed programs on insurance rates. Define the organizations to be involved in each program. Investigate the mitigation programs of suppliers, customers, government, and relief agencies and identify opportunities for developing collaborative programs. Write the mitigation plan detailing the organizational roles and resources of each participant for all mitigation programs.

Step 3: Implement the Plan

Make the necessary changes to firm employee safety and security programs and retrain employees. Stockpile inventories and emergency supplies. Dedicate asset use for contingencies. Work with supply chain partners to implement emergency operating agreements. Install backup systems for essential computer and communication support. Modify facilities for disaster protection. Develop the necessary memorandums of understanding (MOUs) with government and relief agencies to assign mitigation roles and tasks to be performed.

Step 4: Continuous Improvement Program

Review the program on completion. Audit performance after a disaster and implement improvements.

Detection

Step 1: Develop a Detection Plan

Review current disaster detection sources, detection capabilities, and warning procedures for selected disasters. Natural disasters are detected primarily by the global scientific community using satellites and ground-sensing technologies. Most natural disasters are detected and the magnitude of the event measured. Early warning is common for many wind and water disasters and volcanic eruptions. In February 2005, 50 nations met to link their satellite observation systems (The Global Earth Observation System of Systems). Accidental disasters are detected and reported primarily by firm employees, citizen observers, or first responders. Although early warning is impossible, detection at the time of occurrence is possible with current communication capabilities. In controlled environments that are potentially hazardous, accidents are automatically sensed by computers, chemical devices, or heat-sensing devices, which trigger warnings, equipment shutdowns, or sprinkler systems. Disasters caused by terrorists are less easily detected, including those in progress (computer virus, biological or chemical attack). The U.S. government has taken the lead in providing a terrorist early warning system.

Determine who will be responsible for disaster detection to protect the supply chain and what detection methods should be used. A mixture of public and private detection systems is likely. Ensure that key stakeholders are properly trained to effectively use the detection methods deployed.

Step 2: Acknowledge Warnings

Implement procedures for receiving and acknowledging disaster warnings.

Step 3: Evaluate and Act on Observations

Develop procedures for evaluating disaster warnings (e.g., Is the warning credible, corroborated? Is the threat imminent? How grave is it?). Develop specific procedures for actions to be taken when early warnings are given. For each disaster, determine the level of magnitude that will activate the response plan.

Step 4: Determine if Further Action Is Warranted

If warranted, activate the response plan.

Step 5: Continuous Improvement

Periodically test and assess detection capabilities. After a disaster, reevaluate the detection plan. Monitor detection technology for improvements. Provide training updates to key stakeholders.

Response

Step 1: Implement a Response Plan

Activation of a formal response procedure with a known command structure drilled through mock exercises helps ensure minimum injury to personnel, quicker recovery time, and better cash flow and reduces the probability of future liability actions.

Step 2: Evaluate Direction and Control

Check that all critical tasks are initiated. Determine the need for backup resources and capabilities. Initiate contact with leaders of critical supply chain partners, governments, and relief providers.

Step 3: Evaluate Communications

Implement the communications plan. Provide information (e.g., facility maps, material specification data sheets) as needed, to first responders.

Step 4: Evaluate Life Safety

Implement the warning system as necessary for stakeholders. Implement safety procedures.

Step 5: Evaluate Property Protection

After assurance of personnel safety, assess potential disruption for all key processes, facilities, systems, data, and records. Follow plans for protection of the critical infrastructure and resources.

Step 6: Evaluate Public Services

Determine the need for resources. Initiate contact with the leaders and implement mutual aid agreements to ensure operational readiness.

Step 7: Evaluate Community Outreach

Maintain communications with community leaders, emergency management, government agencies, and first responders for up-to-date disaster information. Arrange for support from emergency response agencies.

Recovery

Step 1: Develop and Implement a Recovery Plan

Implementation of formal recovery procedures and contractual arrangements with supply chain partners helps control restoration costs and minimizes downtime for critical supply chain systems, processes, and facilities. At this stage, the emergency team is often the key unit in determining the long-term survivability of the firm.

Establish a recovery team and define priorities. Assess the impact of the disaster on corporate supply chain resources, supply chain partner resources, and community services and infrastructure. Determine the need for immediate support.

Meet with insurance providers and government officials to determine the sources and levels of available recovery funding. Business interruption insurance covers ongoing expenses and lost profits when the damage or loss of insured property disrupts a company's normal operations. Extra expense coverage provides for unanticipated expenses that occur during recovery from a disaster. More standard types of insurance may provide adequate coverage for employee and customer liability insurance, fire and property insurance, burglary insurance, and workers' compensation.

Step 2: Ensure Continuity of Management

Ensure the chain of command and maintain lines of succession for key personnel. Determine the need for alternate site operations.

Step 3: Maintain Employee Support

Meet immediate needs. Implement human resource recovery plans.

Step 4: Resume Operations

Implement recovery operations for all essential supply chain functions. Restore communications and life support systems (water, electricity, gas) as soon as possible. Coordinate the assessment of resource conditions after a disaster with proper authorities and experts. Inventory damaged property and resources. Conduct salvage operations. Restore supply chain infrastructure as soon as possible. Provide standard updates for key stakeholders. Maintain records of actions taken during recovery operations. Evaluate recovery plan performance and make improvements.

A list of information sources to assist in global supply chain disaster management preparedness is presented in Table 29.4. The table gives the organization providing the information, a brief description, and the source.

Table 29.4   Disaster Information Sources

Organization	Description	Source
FEMA	Information on ongoing disaster responses, Federal Response Plan, key emergency management officials, documents	http://www.fema.gov
U.S. EPA Chemical Emergency Preparedness & Prevention Office	Covers prevention, risk management, preparedness, emergency response, and counterterrorism; also covers regulations, software, publications, and links to related Web sites	http://www.rris.fema.gov
U.S. Geological Survey	Covers land-based natural disasters—earthquakes, floods, and volcanoes	http://www.epa.gov/ceppo
National Oceanographic and Atmospheric Administration/Office of Response and Restoration	Access tools, information, and software for responders to oil spills, chemical accidents, hazardous materials releases, and ship groundings	http://www.usgs.gov
U.S. Department of Health & Human Services Office of Emergency Preparedness	Information on Office's Counter-Terrorism Program, National Disaster Medical System, and Metropolitan Medical Response System	http://response.restoration.noaa.gov/index.html
U.S. Centers for Disease Control and Prevention	Health standards and statistics, fact sheets on health information and disease prevention	http://www.oep.dhhs.gov
United Nations Relief Web	Humanitarian emergencies and natural disasters	http://www.cdc.gov
United Nations International Strategy for Disaster Reduction	Creates disaster prevention strategies	http://www.reliefweb.int
United Nations Development Program	Partners with UN relief agencies and helps countries to prepare for and/or avoid disasters	http://www.unisdr.org
World Health Organization	Provides aid during emergencies	http://www.undp.org
American Red Cross (ARC) Disaster Services	Overview of ARC, including reports on Red Cross projects worldwide; coverage of disasters and relief efforts	

Organization	Description	Source
Extension Disaster Education Network (EDEN)	Links members from across the United States and various disciplines, so they can use and share resources to reduce the impact of disasters	http://www.eden.lsu.edu
European Community Humanitarian Office	Provides humanitarian aid in response to natural disasters and armed conflicts in countries outside the European Union	http://europa.eu.int/comm/ echo/en/index_en.html
Canadian Centre for Emergency Preparedness	Nonprofit organization dedicated to training and service to help government and industry; holds World Conference on Disaster Management	http://www.ccep.ca
Asian Disaster Preparedness Center	Training courses on urban disaster mitigation as part of Asian Disaster Mitigation Program	http://www.adpc.net
National Emergency Management Association (NEMA)	State-level emergency management officials; information on meetings of NEMA and contacts	http://www.nemaweb.org
International Association of Emergency Managers (IAEM)	Association of local (city and county) emergency management officials; IAEM activities	http://www.iaem.com
Disaster Relief, Sponsored by ARC	Features extensive collection of news on disasters back to 1996	http://disasterrelief.org
University of Colorado Natural Hazards Center	Articles and publications on hazardous materials; HazLit database	http://www.colorado .edu/hazards
University of Delaware/Disaster Research Center	Descriptions of disaster research, publications, and bibliographies	http://www.udel.edu/DRC
Disaster Resource Guide	Consolidates educational, organizational, and vendor resources in areas of emergency, crisis management, and business continuity	http://www.disaster- resource.com
Disaster Recovery Journal	Source of disaster preparedness research, articles, seminars, and hotlinks	www.drj.com

Disaster Preparedness: Current Status

Changing Disaster Profiles

As world trade has increased, national economic health has become increasingly dependent on the economic health of the major trading partners. Also, because global supply chains have developed in an integrated fashion across multiple business and governmental partners to facilitate world trade, corporate economic health has become increasingly dependent on the supply chain operational and security capabilities of all supply chain partners. As a consequence of the growing economic interdependency among nations and firms, the disruption of a global supply chain by a major disaster can result in economic catastrophe. For example, analysts estimate that a month-long disruption of U.S. West Coast ports would cost Asian economies 0.4% of their gross domestic product (GDP) and several Asian economies would lose as much as 1.1% of GDP.

Given the escalating costs of global supply chain disruption, it is alarming to note that major disasters caused by both nature and terrorists are increasing dramatically. Schirber (2004) reported that there were 3,535 global natural disasters from 1999 to 2003, up 66% in the past five years. A comparison of the global impact of natural disasters for 2003 and 2002 revealed a 300% increase in deaths and 100% increase in damage costs in 2003. A U.S. intelligence report (MSNBC 2004) revealed that major world terrorist attacks more than tripled in 2004 (from 175 in 2003 to 650 in 2004). A large percentage of these terrorist attacks occurred in Africa, the Middle East, South Asia, and Southeast Asia. As the cost of a supply chain disruption rises and the likelihood of a supply chain disruption increases, firms must improve global supply chain security.

Supply Chain Security Gaps

A broad assessment of supply chain disaster preparedness conducted by Helferich and Cook (2002) shortly after the terrorist attacks on the United States on September 11, 2001, revealed a number of gaps in supply chain security. First, most firms lacked adequate disaster preparedness programs, which include formal, tested plans covering all disaster management process stages.

Second, the scope of supply chain security planning efforts was too narrow. Specifically, firms planned to secure supply chain operations under their control but not those operations controlled by key suppliers, customers, and third-party providers. In addition, disaster planning efforts focused on protecting key corporate infrastructure (e.g., plants, vehicles) but ignored public infrastructure (e.g., airports, utilities) even when such infrastructures were critical aspects of supply chain continuity.

Third, some aspects of supply chain resources were well protected, whereas others were not. For example, product inventories were protected by packaging, fire protection devices, and antitheft technology. However, the protection afforded to intellectual property was limited. In fact, global losses from product counterfeiting amount to more than $350 billion, and counterfeit products account for 7% of world trade. Additionally, significant efforts were undertaken to improve air transport security, but few steps were taken to improve ocean transport security. As a result, global piracy continues to grow, and ocean containers and port facilities are not adequately secured.

Fourth, some stages of the disaster management process were not adequately represented in corporate disaster plans. Most corporate plans focused on response and recovery but did not adequately address disaster mitigation and detection. In fact, the 9/11 incident demonstrated a major gap in forecasting and detecting of disasters caused by terrorists.

Fifth, tactical response to a major disaster is too slow. Future supply chain security plans require dynamic replanning capabilities to enable quick reallocation of resources and smooth transition to backup resources to keep supply chains functioning.

Finally, security planners underestimate the scale, scope, and complexity of response needed to cope with a major disaster. Firms must develop collaborative plans involving key supply chain partners, governments, and global relief agencies.

A recent study regarding supply chain security (Crum 2005) confirmed that significant gaps still exist in disaster preparedness. Specifically, firms need to coordinate plans with suppliers and customers, integrate security features, benchmark security best practices, implement disaster plan performance measures, hire more security-conscious employees, and conduct more disaster-training exercises. Although gaps in disaster preparedness persist, significant government and corporate efforts are under way to close the gaps.

Recent and Emerging Developments

Global Developments

In 2005, the United Nations adopted a ten-year action plan for disaster reduction (Hyogo Framework for Action). A major aspect of this framework involves the establishment of the International Early Warning Program (IEWP), which will use a newly created web of surveillance satellites, the Global Earth Observation System of Systems (GEOSS) to detect natural disasters. GEOSS, which uses satellites from 50 nations, will support the United Nations' newest disaster reduction initiative: a tsunami early warning system.

The World Health Organization (WHO) established the Global Outbreak Alert and Response Network in 2000 to provide rapid identification of outbreak cause, issue global alerts, and provide global expertise for response. Additionally, WHO passed a specific Global Public Health Response Plan to be used for biological, chemical, and radio-nuclear material disasters. This plan provides information to guide preparation for, and response to, these disasters. Also, in 2005, WHO developed the Global Influenza Preparedness Plan to support nations struggling with influenza outbreaks.

To improve global shipment security, the World Customs Organization (WCO) developed a Framework of Standards to Secure and Facilitate General Trade. This framework includes (1) advanced electronic cargo information requirements, (2) a standardized risk management approach, (3) inspection of outbound containers and cargo, and (4) benefits to firms meeting the minimum standards spelled out in the framework. Additionally, a new world standard for ship and port security called the International Ship and Port Facility Security Code (ISPS) took effect on July 1, 2004. ISPS requires all nations to develop security plans with the aim of detecting and mitigating acts that threaten marine security.

Another effort in the planning stage to protect global shipments involves the development of an International Shippers and Freight Forwarders Security Code by the UN Centre for Trade Facilitation and Electronic Business (UN/CEFACT). The purpose of the Code is to provide a more holistic approach to supply chain security while facilitating world trade. The Code covers current national regulations and guidelines such as Customs-Trade Partnership Against Terrorism (C-TPAT) and StairSec®.

To reduce global intellectual property theft, more than 600 firms and organizations, including Interpol, the World Customs Organization (WCO), and the World Intellectual Property Organization, launched the Action to Stop Counterfeiting and Piracy in 2003. The initiative is coordinating efforts to thwart global product counterfeiting and piracy by sharing experiences, lessons learned, and intelligence. Examples of commonly counterfeited intellectual property include (based on enforcement incidents) entertainment and software, clothing and accessories, drugs and medical supplies, cigarettes, food, alcohol, and electronics equipment.

To date, significant security efforts have been made to provide improved security to global food supply chains. These efforts include the following: the International Association of Infant Food Manufacturers (IFM) has published a series of guidance documents online; the International Dairy Foods Association (IDFA) issues Voluntary Security Guidelines for Farms and Tankers; the International Association of Food Protection (IAFP) provides guidelines designed to reduce the risk of deliberate contamination of raw milk at various stages of processing and transportation; the Produce Marketing Association is promoting the Food Security Checklists; and guidelines have been created by the National Food Processors Association. In addition, CIES (International Committee of Food Retail Chains), an organization with more than 200 major food retailers and 200 suppliers in more than 50 countries, is developing a benchmark Guidance Document to help members improve security.

Also, China is addressing food supply chain security. A 2005 law requires all food manufacturers to obtain permission to produce food, and products that are produced must pass quality checks conducted by the State Administration for Quality Supervision and Inspection and Quarantine before they can be marketed. Food types covered include meat and dairy products, frozen foodstuffs, spices, beverages, rice, flour, edible oil, soy sauce, and vinegar. In addition, China implemented a Food Safety Credit Index. The index, published quarterly, monitors food brands sold in supermarkets and through wholesale channels.

Global supply chain security requires leading edge technology such as radio-frequency identification (RFID) and global positioning systems (GPS). Additionally, firms are experimenting with three-dimensional holographic imaging displays, radiation detection equipment, electronic seals using satellite GPS, and enhanced weighing and counting equipment. For example, Hewlett-Packard is starting to ship some RFID-tagged consumer products, such as notebook computers, directly from manufacturing facilities in China to Wal-Mart distribution centers.

U.S. Developments

It is necessary to focus on emerging developments in disaster management within the United States because that country is leading the attack on global terrorism. In addition, the United States is the largest exporter and importer of goods, and as a result, their disaster management policies affect a significant percentage of global supply chains.

In 2003, 22 federal agencies were merged into the Department of Homeland Security (DHS). DHS awarded $11 billion in security contracts in 2005 after awarding $9 billion in 2004. Notably, DHS has selected a program, the National Incident Management System (NIMS), that establishes standardized management processes, protocols, and procedures that all responders (federal, state, tribal, and local) will use to coordinate and conduct response actions for incidents. All responders will use the same standard procedures and a common language that will enable them to coordinate efforts more effectively when a disaster occurs.

Also, DHS has developed the National Response Plan (NRP). The NRP establishes a comprehensive all-disasters approach to enhance the ability of the United States to manage domestic disasters. The plan incorporates best practices and procedures from all disaster management disciplines—homeland security, emergency management, law enforcement, firefighting, public works, public health, emergency medical services, and the private sector—and integrates them into a unified structure.

DHS is currently creating centers of excellence to address critical issues of national security. For example, in 2004, the National Center for Food Protection and Defense was created at the University of Minnesota to address food supply chain security issues. Other centers will be created to address the consequences of catastrophic incidents, potential solution technologies, and issues concerning disease and toxicology.

U.S. shipment protection will be enhanced by the U.S. Customs' Automated Commercial Environment project. This project will enable U.S. Customs to more readily identify and intercept high-risk cargo, while at the same time reducing costs to firms through faster processing. Containers with tamper-evident electronic seals were deployed in 2005. Eventually, the technology could also indicate the container's location using a satellite tracing system, and a sensor within the container could monitor for radiological, biological, or chemical weapons. The system is estimated to save U.S. importers $22.2 billion and the U.S. government $4.4 billion in administrative costs over 20 years.

U.S. efforts to protect the food supply chain have been significant. The U.S. Department of Agriculture (USDA) through the Food Safety and Inspection Service (FSIS) has been very active in developing guidelines for processors, retailers, wholesalers, and logistics providers involved in meat, poultry, and egg product supply chains. Additional FSIS research targets include inspection procedures and policy recommendations, validated analytical methods to detect threat agents in food matrices, the development of a statistically valid sampling system for screening the food supply, operational risk management information to assist food security, the development of tamper-detection indicators for food packages, the development of methods to deactivate or neutralize threat-agent hazards in food and studies to determine the effects of these processes on food quality, and the development of decontamination technologies to safely clean food processing, distribution, and storage operations contaminated with threat agents.

The USDA is also working on a Common Computing Environment to establish a common network (Food Emergency Response Network) infrastructure to serve its consolidated service centers nationwide. Also, the USDA is expanding the unified network of public agricultural institutions to identify and respond to high-risk biopathogens in the food and agriculture system.

Private efforts to improve food supply chain security are progressing. For example, Grocery Manufacturers Association (GMA) has compiled a database of member firm executives in charge of food security processes so that they can be reached quickly by either GMA or the government in an emergency, conducted discussions with the Food and Drug Administration (FDA) and the USDA to keep the government informed of GMA's efforts, and identified experts in food security within GMA member firms for use by the FDA, USDA, and DHS.

U.S. government agencies are also planning to use RFID to enhance the visibility of material in the supply chain. For example, by 2007, the FDA anticipates the use of RFID tags at the case and pallet levels through the pharmaceutical supply chain. The National Association of Chain Drug Stores, key drug manufacturers, and distributors have announced their support as well. By tying each drug unit to a unique electronic serial number contained in an RFID tag, the industry will be able to track drugs effectively.

Conclusions

Efforts to protect global supply chains have been and will continue to be significant. These efforts aim to prevent or mitigate global supply chain disruption caused by intentional or unintentional disasters. In spite of the significant investments and planning efforts by economic regions, individual countries, and corporate partners, catastrophic disasters (e.g. the Katrina and Rita hurricanes in the United States in 2005) continue to threaten and disrupt private commerce and public life—some on a massive scale. Such disasters have resulted in massive casualties, destruction of infrastructure, disruption of commerce, and threats to public health.

The response to Hurricane Katrina demonstrated that even when a country has a National Response Plan and disaster management plans at each level of government in place, response to major disasters is still flawed. Greater disaster response effectiveness requires streamlined decision processes, improved communications within and between responding organizations, increased use of technology for field data collection, better definition of authority, improved and tested response plans at all levels of government, and a public that is better educated regarding their individual disaster preparation. Clearly, much more needs to be accomplished to effectively prevent, respond to, and recover from global supply chain disruptions caused by major disasters.

References

Crum, Michael (2005), "Managing Supply Chain Security," presented at the 2005 Distribution Business Management Association Conference, June 8, 2005.

Helferich, O. K. and Robert L. Cook (2002), *Securing the Supply Chain.* Oak Brook, IL: Council of Logistics Management.

Hendricks, Kevin B. and Vinod R. Singhal (2005), "An Empirical Analysis of the Effect of Supply Chain Disruptions on Long-Run Stock Price Performance and Equity Risk of the Firm," *Production and Operations Management,* 14 (1), 35–53.

MSNBC (2004), "Major Terror Attacks Triple in '04," retrieved July 4, 2005, from www.msnbc.msn.com

Schirber, Michael (2004), "Nature's Wrath: Global Deaths and Costs Swell," *Life Science Disaster Report,* 1.

The World Bank Group (2005), "Strong Growth in 2004," retrieved June 16, 2005, from http://worldbank.org

World Trade Organization (2004), "2004 Trade Growth to Exceed 2003 Despite Higher Oil Prices," *WTO News: 2004 Press Releases,* October 25.

30

Diagnosing the Supply Chain

James H. Foggin

Paola Signori

Carol L. Monroe

A supply chain has been defined as "three or more companies (suppliers, focal company, and customer) linked together by flows of products, services, information, and finance, which may include manufacturing" (Mentzer et al. 2001). In other words, a supply chain consists of multiple firms, with each firm engaging in multiple functions in a combined effort to meet common goals, while simultaneously coping with its individual needs to meet its own firm and functional goals. There are a multitude of processes, subprocesses, and activities in any supply chain, whether it is made up of large or of small firms. With these and perhaps other issues to deal with, one might ask, "What is the probability that everything will work according to plan in a supply chain?" Having posed this question, when something is not working correctly in a complex supply chain, how can management assess the problem and, equally important, determine a viable solution? Use of one or more of a number of supply chain diagnostic tools that have been developed may be the answer.

In this chapter, a variety of tools for diagnosing potential problems in a supply chain are reviewed and discussed. These diagnostic tools vary in terms of format,

AUTHORS' NOTE: The authors wish to thank Kate Vitasek of Supply Chain Visions for numerous helpful suggestions.

complexity, and cost. Quantitative approaches as well as some qualitative diagnostic tools are described. Some of these tools require less data gathering than others and are therefore less time-consuming. Discussion as to when one tool versus another might be used is also included. The tools listed are suitable for either self-assessment or assessment employing a small team of facilitators. Proprietary tools employed by consulting firms as part of a consulting contract have not been included.

Diagnosis

Diagnosis is defined as "the art or act of identifying a disease from its signs and symptoms" or the "investigation or analysis of the cause or nature of a condition, situation, or problem" (*Merriam-Webster's Collegiate Dictionary* 2005). For example, when a physician diagnoses a patient's illness, he or she begins the process by gathering information by taking notes of outward and visible signs, measuring vital signs, doing various tests, conducting patient interviews, and so on. This process involves both quantitative and qualitative measures. When the physician believes adequate data have been gathered, he or she determines the actual cause or causes of the illness. Only then can the physician prescribe a treatment with the goal of curing the illness.

By using as an example the definition of diagnosis and the medical process of diagnosis, we have a good model for supply chain problem diagnosis and problem resolution. This process may be summarized in three steps:

1. Identification of symptoms indicating the presence of supply chain problems (or, for the purposes of this study, pain points)

2. Identification of the cause(s) of adverse symptoms

3. Identification of viable solutions to the problems

The first two steps are the diagnosis. The third step is the process of bringing about a cure. The cure is unlikely to happen without performing the first two steps. Performing the diagnosis without performing the cure is a meaningless exercise. Thus, diagnosis and cure are codependent steps. Most of the tools described below consist of all three steps. Table 30.1 is a listing and comparison of the tools discussed below.

Benchmarking Approaches

A common way of identifying problems in a supply chain is through the use of a quantitative tool called benchmarking. Benchmarking relies heavily on performance measures. David T. Kearns, former chief executive officer of the Xerox Corporation, an early developer and user of benchmarking, defined benchmarking as "the continuous process of measuring our products, services and practices

Table 30.1   Table of Comparisons of Commercial and Academic Diagnostic Tools

Year	Title	Developers	Description	Time to Complete	Diagnostic Approach?
1996	Supply Chain Operations Reference Model (SCOR) (*Supply Chain* 2000)	The Supply Chain Council	Self-diagnostic tool	Extensive but unknown	Benchmarking
1998	The Customer-Centered Supply Chain Management Change Process (Kuglin 1998)	Kuglin	Self-assessment tool	Extensive but unknown	Mapping
1999	Supply Chain Management Benchmarking Series ("Web Based Tool" 1999)	Performance Measurement Group	Benchmarking tool	20 to 40 person-hours	Benchmarking
2002	Quick Scan (Naim et al. 2002)	Cardiff University	Supply chain analysis	9 person-days; 2 weeks start to finish	Cause and effect
2003	The Diagnostic Tool (Foggin, Mentzer, and Monroe 2004)	Foggin, Mentzer, and Monroe	Quick-time 3PL or self-assessment tool	< 2 hours	Cause and effect
2004	SCIMam, Supply Chain Integrated Management analysis method (Signori 2004)	Signori	Supply chain analysis	Extensive, 20 to 30 person-days	Mapping
2005	Supply Chain Visibility Roadmap (Borghesi et al. 2005)	Borghesi, Cavalieri, Meciani, Russo, and Signori	Quick-time diagnostic tool	2.5-day workshops	Mapping
2005	CSCMP/APQC Benchmarking Database (Gardner, Harrity, and Vitasek 2005)	CSCMP and APQC	Self-diagnostic tool	Extensive but unknown	Benchmarking

NOTE: CSCMP = Council of Supply Chain Management Professionals; APQC = American Productivity and Quality Center.

against our toughest competitors or those organizations recognized as leaders" (Camp 1989, p. 10).

Kearns' definition states clearly that benchmarking involves the use of measurements. A second definition of benchmarking is "the search for industry best practices that lead to superior performance" (Camp 1989, p. 12).

Camp describes this as a "working definition." In other words, Camp is advocating that benchmarking go beyond the simple assessment of one company's performance to identify best practices. Benchmarking is frequently used, and with success. Although it is an easy tool to use, there are some drawbacks. One is the considerable amount of time required for completion. A firm may not have that time, particularly when a quick initial assessment is needed for determining whether or not to enter into a relationship. Another drawback is the difficulty in ensuring that what is benchmarked is the same across all the firms in the database. Yet another drawback is the need for a preexisting database of benchmarked data from companies in similar industries or with similar supply chain strategies. For example, one would not expect to see similarities in the metrics of a firm that focuses on efficiency (i.e., cost) and another focusing on service effectiveness (and revenue generation).

Several tools that provide benchmarked databases are commercially available. Among the best-known and most widely used is one that is based on the Supply Chain Council's Supply Chain Operations Reference (SCOR) model. The SCOR model was developed in 1996 as a cross-industry standard diagnostic tool for supply chain management (*Supply Chain Operations Reference Model* 2000). The Supply Chain Council is an international organization of nearly 1,000 volunteer member companies that developed the SCOR model through their joint efforts. SCOR is a process reference model that links business processes, metrics, best practices, and technology. The Council implemented Version 7 of the SCOR model in 2005. The Supply Chain Council (*Supply Chain Operations Reference Model 2000*) describes the SCOR model as follows:

SCOR is used to describe, measure, and evaluate Supply-Chain configurations:

- Describe: Standard SCOR process definitions allow virtually any supply-chain to be configured.
- Measure: Standard SCOR metrics enable measurement and benchmarking of supply-chain performance.
- Evaluate: Supply-chain configurations may be evaluated to support continuous improvement and strategic planning. (p. 31)

Successful applications have been widely documented, both on the SCOR Web site and in trade literature.

The Performance Measurement Group (PMG) offers an online subscription service, called the Supply Chain Management Benchmark Series, that allows subscribers to compare their performance on SCOR model metrics with the performance of other participating companies. It takes a firm 20 to 40 person-hours to complete each of the survey installments ("SCOR Model Users" 1999). There are 10 overall measurement areas and 24 cost elements. Some of the measures used in PMG's Service Supply Chain Performance Scorecard—Spares Inventory area are given below (PMG 2005):

- Dollar value by stocking location
- Dollar value by warranty install base value
- Spares inventory write-off rules
- Record inventory accuracy

The analysis covers both a near term of 3 to 9 months and a medium term of 9 to 18 months. PMG claims that companies whose supply chains are in the top 20% on performance have costs that are half the costs of average performers (Keegan 2003).

The Council of Supply Chain Management Professionals (CSCMP) and the American Productivity and Quality Center (APQC) benchmarking database consists of 150 performance measures. Originally released in early 2005, the database was developed from the data contributions of 150 firms (Gardner et al. 2005). Users who participate by sharing their information with the CSCMP/APQC database have access to the database for free.

Companies use these databases to identify potential problems with their supply chains. They can compare their own performance measures with those of like companies in similar industries, provided enough similar companies have participated in developing the database. As is frequently the case, simply collecting and comparing data on performance is not enough. "Performance metrics alone are no guarantee of improved business results. While it is true that performance metrics are a necessary and irreplaceable element in performance management, it's essential to combine your business measurement efforts with qualitative process analysis and viable improvement efforts on core processes" (Supply Chain Visions 2004, p. 3).

Benchmarking[1] makes use of performance measurements to identify symptoms, but not all supply chain problems are revealed by benchmarking. For example, a firm may find that its inventory turns rate is significantly lower than that of its best in-class competitors. This is called a result metric. Benchmarking a single result metric, however, does not directly reveal the cause for low inventory turns. Put another way, a more detailed analysis must be conducted to discover root causes.

Benchmarking may identify root causes when result metrics and process metrics are used together. Like the physician who looks at a patient's different symptoms (e.g., elevated temperature as opposed to the norm of 98.6, swollen throat glands, etc.) to determine the cause of sickness, management must use a combination of metrics to determine the cause of a supply chain problem. For example, to find the cause or causes of slow inventory turns, management might take measurements of the various steps that are part of the inventory management process. If, for example, management were to find that only a small percentage of customers were able to submit point-of-sale (POS) information to the firm, and the inventory management process requires the use of POS data, one root cause has probably been identified. This example alone is sufficient to illustrate that no single metric from benchmarking will identify causes, but analysis of combinations of metrics may do so.

Mapping Approaches

Not all diagnostic tools use benchmarking to identify root causes. Some use a variety of mapping techniques. These mapping techniques often permit focusing on finding causes. An early qualitative approach to determining supply chain problems was offered by Kuglin (1998), who described a process for analyzing an existing ("as is") supply chain, followed by thoroughly redesigning the supply chain. Kuglin focused largely on the implementation of supply chain management in firms that do not have a supply chain orientation rather than on the diagnosis of supply chain problems. Nevertheless, he spent an entire chapter discussing how managers may understand what he calls the current (as-is) state of the supply chain. He advocates beginning the development process by the use of process mapping, followed by analysis of these maps, which ultimately leads to the development of "to-be" process maps.

The Supply Chain Integrated Management analysis method (SCIM*am*) (Signori 2001, 2002) is structured to help supply chain managers understand and evaluate the potential integration of the entire supply chain. This tool dates back to 1999 and has been tested and updated over the years. Diagnostics are performed before investing time and money in supply chain redesigns.

SCIM*am* was developed in Italy, where the distinguishing feature of businesses is the size of the firm—that is, small and medium-sized enterprises (SMEs) are predominant in the industrial fabric. Decentralization and international competitiveness mandated supply chain redesign for Italian SMEs, so a new tool geared specifically to the needs of these types of firms was needed. It needed to be easy to understand and use, inexpensive, flexible, and self-contained.

SCIM*am* scans the entire supply chain with both qualitative and quantitative approaches. The final report identifies the key members of the supply chain and what the critical paths of the supply chain processes are. It produces a supply chain dashboard of a few essential performance metrics. The scheme of work is composed of three levels, subdivided into different phases and steps (see Table 30.2). Each level provides report graphs that display the output of the analysis:

- The first level helps draw the supply chain map, a multidimensional graph showing the complexity of the system and the different kinds of relationships among firms.
- The second level outlines a simple supply chain process map of selected processes and metrics, as well as a dashboard consisting of the main supply chain key performance indicators.
- The third level is an evaluation of the organization's ability to manage the supply chain in different scenarios (as is and "what ifs") on radar charts.

Table 30.2   The SCIM*am* Scheme of Analysis

Level	Phase	Step	Report
I	1. Multidimensional map	A. Determine "actors" of the extended supply chain	Supply chain map
		B. Segment subjects (with logistics service criteria)	
		C. Select key subjects	
	2. Links	D. Study actual relationships	
		E. Identify potential relationships	
II	1. Process	F. Identify key processes	Supply chain process map
		G. Find critical points and bottlenecks	
	2. Metrics	H. Verify actual metrics	Dashboard
		I. Find performance data	
		J. Select or define a few supply chain metrics	
III	1. Organization	K. Verify integration requirements of each subject selected	Present radar chart ("as is")
		L. Define potential organization model of the supply chain (simulation—short term and medium term)	Potential radar charts ("what ifs")
Summary			Final report

SOURCE: Signori (2004).

NOTE: SCIM*am* = Supply Chain Integrated Management analysis method.

The first level of this method has been successfully implemented as a self-diagnostic tool to understand key relationships and critical links along the supply chain. The second level helps to discover the recurrent pain points and group strengths. The study of flows goes beyond the limit of the subjective point of view of one company. The third part discusses the perspective of supply chain management in terms of "what will happen" in different scenarios. This "as-is/what-if" approach is completely different from the Kuglin's and SCOR's "as-is/to-be" approach.

The SCIM*am* requires significant involvement and creativity on the part of the firm's management to achieve its full benefit. The main purpose of the analysis is to understand the potential of the supply chain network in dynamic scenarios. Benchmarking techniques are applied in this method to compare the current state with the potential goal. The goal is set as the maximum performance attainable by a defined supply chain system's capabilities. The comparison is internal to the supply chain. It is not used among supply chain partners or among supply chains. Supply chain benchmarking, as used in the United States, is not practical in Europe, because of poor industry data and the extraordinary variety of supply chain types.

Another approach is the Supply Chain Visibility Roadmap (SCVR) (Borghesi et al. 2005). It was originally developed by consultants to work with managers to determine how autoidentification technologies can support their operations (radio-frequency identification, bidimensional bar code, EPCglobal coding [Electronic Product Code is a new generation of product identification; EPCglobal is a joint venture between EAN International and the Uniform Code Council], Global Positioning Systems, real-time locating systems). It was derived from a similar Unisys assessment approach that was applied in the United States. The general purpose of the SCVR is to define the current and desired states of a company's operations. The process is designed to

- Clarify what visibility, or the lack thereof, means for the supply chain, helping managers better understand their supply chain operations
- Enable managers to share and confirm priority areas
- Identify symptoms that indicate the lack of visibility, and the causes of these symptoms
- Conceive practicable solutions to the problems and evaluate them in terms of importance (value, adherence to the strategic plan, and urgency) and feasibility (time, cost, and effort of adoption)

The tool allows managers to identify different areas of opportunity and the critical points of supply chain operations in a two-and-a-half-day workshop. A preliminary ramp-up stage is necessary to identify potential issues and provide a structure for the discussion. During the first meeting, the kickoff consists of introducing to the team the objectives and output of the diagnostic tool. The team should be composed of senior level business managers: COO, VP of supply chain, CIO, and business unit leaders, as well as supply chain, manufacturing, sales, and marketing leaders. Active participation of the team is required. For this reason the meetings are called *workshops*.

The first workshop identifies visibility opportunity areas and pain points of the supply chain. A supply chain map is drawn, pointing out where symptoms can be found. Causes of the symptoms are then highlighted on the map, having been deduced from their consequences.

The second workshop, using a group diagnostic technique, drafts a solution road map. It gives priorities to opportunity areas as well as explanations and leads to a discussion of potential solutions. The SCVR tool stresses practical "visibility" as a way to reach improvement in operations. In particular, the term *visibility* is applied to flows and contains multiple meanings: location (Where is what? When?), specificity (What is this exactly?), state (What environment has the object been in?), integrity (Has the object been tampered with?), authenticity (Is this exactly what it is supposed to be?), and productivity (data collection and identification processes). The visibility diagnostic leads to the identification of supply chain opportunity areas for increased visibility, the prioritization of potential solutions, and the scoping of improvement projects.

Means-Ends Approaches and Cause-and-Effect Diagrams

Another method for identifying symptoms is the use of questions that lead directly to the analysis step, the purpose of which is to identify root causes. Two tools are available that help develop cause-and-effect diagrams, which clearly show root causes. Elrod and Hubbard (1979) state that means-ends decision trees can be used to solve complex, ill-structured problems. Starting from the symptoms, the researcher can delve into the specifics of problem causes. Means-ends trees direct attention to a broad span of search, while leading to efficient diagnosis design.

Cardiff University's Logistics Systems Dynamics Group (LSDG) developed a tool called Quick Scan. Quick Scan is used at the start of a project to automate supply chain tasks. This, in turn, allows for the implementation or improvement of information and communication technologies. The Quick Scan process can be completed in a two-week period and requires three or four members of the firm to make up the Quick Scan team; thus, it is an on-site tool (Naim et al. 2002). LSDG has produced a handbook that "describes the Quick Scan methodology. It is designed to hand over the Quick Scan process to industry in conjunction with a training program run by the LSDG" (*The Quick Scan Handbook* n.d.).

LSDG describes Quick Scan as "a supply chain oriented business diagnostic. It is designed to take a snapshot of the present operation of the supply chain." Users develop a cause-and-effect diagram and then engage in the identification of the root causes. Users are provided with *The Quick Scan Handbook*, which helps them self-administer the diagnostic tool (*The Quick Scan Handbook* n.d.). Much of the data collected is attitudinal in nature and therefore permits the use of the judgment of the firm's managers.

The final tool discussed here differs from each of the above in that it was designed to produce a list of symptoms and likely causes as quickly as possible. All the various diagnostic approaches described above require a significant investment in time to complete, and some need detailed and precise quantitative data. Yet there are situations where a company in a supply chain may want to determine and address problems quickly and without significant expenditure of time or money. One example might be a small company with limited assets needing to fix problems. Another might be a situation in which when a third-party logistics provider (3PL) needs to make an initial assessment of a potential client to determine whether its services are a good fit for one or both parties. Or a larger company may want to make an initial assessment to determine if a deeper commitment is necessary or if it can be delayed for a period of time.

It becomes evident from this discussion that a different type of diagnostic tool is needed—one that is qualitative and free of the drawbacks inherent in the tools discussed above. To fill the void, the key characteristics of the tool should be as follows:

- It should not require large amounts of detailed data.
- The data should be readily available early on.
- The diagnosis should take only a short time to complete.
- It should be qualitative.
- It should not attempt to be all encompassing.

A tool meeting the above criteria, called the Diagnostic Tool, has been developed, which requires a relatively quick interview or workshop to complete the diagnosis. It was specifically designed for an outsider, such as a consultant or a 3PL, to provide critical information regarding the state of a client's supply chain operations in the small amount of time available (e.g., in a sales call). For the 3PL to make such an assessment, a qualitative approach to both the data-gathering process and the development of the diagnostic tool is necessary. So that it might cover a broad range of potential problems, while quickly focusing on the actual problems experienced by the potential client, the diagnostic tool takes the form of a cause-and-effect decision tree.

How can a 3PL get to know the client—its management, its product(s), its customers, and what is right and what is wrong about this strategic organizational function it manages? And how can this be accomplished in an initial contact visit so that the 3PL contact person can, at a minimum, take back enough information to those within the 3PL to decide whether or not this is a viable opportunity in terms of the needs and desires of the potential client and of their own capabilities?

An answer may lie in the use of a diagnostic tool by which the 3PL salesperson or other frontline personnel can audit the firm's supply chain operations. This tool could help determine if there are problems, inefficiencies, or needed improvements in a client's, or a potential client's, supply chain. Some methodology is needed for the 3PL to learn quickly what the nature and extent of the potential client's needs and problems are, so that the 3PL can decide early if it wishes to spend resources trying to win the contract. Developing contract proposals sufficiently detailed to win a long-term contract can be very expensive. Attempting to develop such a contract where the 3PL is unlikely to win the contract or be able to provide adequate service is wasteful. On the other hand, failing to develop a proposal where the likelihood of winning is high and where the relationship would be beneficial to both parties would cause the 3PL to incur high opportunity costs.

The situation is almost like a medical one involving triage. Here, a medical team is trying to determine where to focus its attention and limited resources to ensure that the greatest number of patients survive. Patients who are likely to survive without immediate attention are not treated. Patients who most likely will be lost are not treated either. Those most likely to be helped are treated.

The same sort of logic could be applied to a 3PL management decision. A "triage" tool—a diagnostic tool that separates those potential customers who do not need much help and those who cannot be helped from those with whom a viable relationship can be formed—could be beneficial in many ways and cost-effective as well. Making use of such a diagnostic tool during an early sales call could provide enough information to make an informed decision and thus prevent or alleviate the usual longer or, in some cases, "seat-of-the-pants" decisions firms are sometimes forced to make. This diagnostic tool could be used during an early sales call. Because sales calls are limited in time and usually involve a limited number of 3PL salespeople, this tool must be structured to (1) be completed quickly—probably within an hour—and (2) require data that are easily obtained from the client's representative and are thus most likely perceptual and qualitative in nature. The approach used to develop this diagnostic tool was to construct one or more means-end hierarchies describing the dimensions (attributes, conse-quences, and end states) of supply chain management and the links between them. The specific methodology used to develop the tool is described in Foggin et al. (2004).

During the course of the research, 33 major pain points were categorized into the following primary themes: customer service, inventory, product flow, organiza-tion, and systems. These five themes were not developed from any preconceived categories. They are, however, similar to existing strategic planning areas (Stock and Lambert 2001).

The Diagnostic Tool is a questionnaire in two parts (see Figure 30.1 for an example). One part consists of sets of means-ends hierarchies, on the left side of each page. These means-ends hierarchies show relationships of the dimensions of service from symptoms (at the top) to causes (below). The hierarchies are also deci-sion trees. The other part of the tool consists of a list of numbered questions on the right side of each page. Each dimension in the hierarchy has a number that matches a question.

There are a total of 140 questions. Some can be answered quickly, but many take time to answer. It would not be possible to cover all 140 in a short amount of time, but because of the decision tree structure, not all questions need to be asked. Positive responses to a question lead to one branch, and negative responses lead to another. The interviewer focuses on the hierarchies that are most appropriate for the client, based on their supply chain issues (wants, needs, and expectations). These hierarchies address pain points in the five major supply chain planning areas mentioned above.

Within a major supply chain area, questions typically begin at the top of a hier-archy, where one would expect to see symptoms of problems. The interviewer asks the client if that symptom is apparent in the client's supply chain. The response is the subjective opinion of the person being interviewed. In the Figure 30.1 example, the interviewer might ask if data and information flow efficiently and effectively. A "no" response indicates the presence of the symptom of poor infor-mation and data flows. If this symptom is present, then a series of questions follows. If this symptom is not present, the interviewer skips over that series of questions and moves on to another issue. In this manner, only those problems for which there are apparent symptoms in the supply chain are addressed. In areas where no appar-ent problem is detected, the questions are bypassed, allowing for quicker diagnosis.

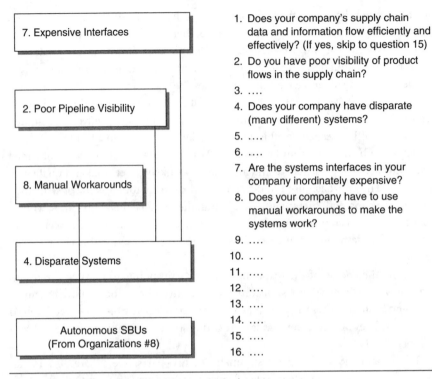

Figure 30.1   Example of the Diagnostic Tool

Furthermore, even within a series of questions addressing a particular symptom, skipping nonproblems is possible.

As suggested by Elrod and Hubbard (1979), means-ends decision trees can be used in both directions—from symptoms to root causes and from root causes to additional symptoms. A root cause may cause additional symptoms. Once found, the interviewer can search for these additional symptoms. The visual presence of the hierarchy with the questions helps the interviewer order the questions. The interviewer has both structure and flexibility in performing a preliminary diagnosis of a potential client's supply chain problems.

Making use of this diagnostic tool can be advantageous to a 3PL from both an economic and a relationship standpoint. The diagnostic tool not only focuses the 3PL's attention on the most apparent problem, but owing to its structure and breadth, it brings to light other supply chain problems as well. The diagnostic tool helps the 3PL avoid spending significant time and resources developing a formal proposal, only to realize later that, for various reasons, it must abandon the effort. Similarly, suppose that during a sales interview, a potential client focuses on one problem that the 3PL is well equipped to handle, but one that would provide little or no profit to them. Furthermore, if that same client neglects to mention other problems that are also within the 3PL's capabilities, the 3PL might make a "no-go" decision and significant revenue would be lost. Once again, using this diagnostic tool should clarify the potential opportunities for the 3PL.

By itself, the Diagnostic Tool does not provide a definitive assessment of a supply chain, and it is not a replacement for more detailed quantitative diagnostic tools. It is to business what triage is to medicine. This tool points to the cause of the problem but does not provide sufficient detail to tell the firm what the "treatment" should be to resolve the problem. Once the firm determines there is a potential problem in the supply chain, a more detailed assessment of the relevant supply chain issues must be carried out to diagnose problems and develop long-term solutions.

Used in conjunction with any of the various benchmarking or mapping approaches, the Diagnostic Tool offers a significant benefit. Benchmarking shows where symptoms exist. Benchmarking does not directly indicate root causes, particularly where these root causes may be identified by qualitative means or where the causes are complex. Means-ends approaches point to root causes very well.

Curing Problems and Eliminating the Pain Points

Referring again to the medical diagnosis analogy, once the physician knows the cause of the symptoms, he or she can begin treatment. Treatments may be simple ("take two aspirins and get bed rest") or complex (a hospital stay for a surgical procedure). Costs of remedies range from inexpensive to very expensive (the same two examples apply). It is the task of the physician to select the most appropriate treatment. Likewise, it is the task of the supply chain manager to select the appropriate means of fixing supply chain problems.

The most common approach to "curing" supply chain problems or pain points is through the application of best practices. The Supply Chain Council's SCOR model was one of the first to provide a comprehensive list of best practices for its members.

In 2004, CSCMP published its own comprehensive list of best practices for supply chain managers. These *Supply Chain Management Process Standards* have been published as six short volumes covering the topics of Planning, Sourcing, Making, Delivering, Returning, and Enabling. CSCMP developed both minimum standards and best practices. See Table 30.3 for examples of CSCMP's standards and best practices for the topic of Inventory Accuracy (Supply Chain Visions 2004, p. 12).

Other lists of supply chain best practices continue to be developed, some of which are comprehensive. Others focus on best practices that cover specific functional areas in supply chain management. For example, there are published descriptions of transportation best practices (Enslow 2005), collaboration best practices (Ireland and Crum 2005), and distribution of perishable products (Gentry 2005), to name a few.

With all the lists of best practices, it is obvious that the selection of best practices to implement first is critical. Vitasek and Manrodt (2005) advocate the use of a 2×2 table to assign a high priority to those processes that have a significant impact on both the customer and the firm. They also suggest that

Table 30.3 An Example of Minimum Standards and Best Practices

Standards	Best Practices
• Stock locations specified in system of records • Cycle counting with the minimum parameters – *A*, SKUs (high volume) counted weekly – *B*, SKUs (moderate volume) counted monthly – *C*, SKUs (low volume) counted quarterly • Pick (order picking) discrepancies trigger daily cycle count	• Cycle counting fully operational, feeding error prevention work groups, eliminating the need for annual physical inventory • System determines cycle counting frequencies from Pareto analysis of each SKU's volume • All SKUs counted with ASQL sampling standards • Six Sigma inventory accuracy maintained through correction of defective processes that generate inventory errors • Warehouse management using RFDC updates inventory balances and locations in real time

SOURCE: Supply Chain Visions (2004, p. 12).

NOTE: SKU = stock-keeping unit; ASQL = American Society for Quality; RFDC = radio-frequency data collection.

the overall improvement opportunity is determined by gauging the size of the gap, . . . the strategic importance of benchmarking and improvement, and the projected impact of a successful benchmarking effort. If, say, strategic importance is medium but impact and gap between current and best practice are significant, then the benchmarking initiative should be a "go." (Vitasek and Manrodt 2005, p. 57)

Using best practices to suggest cures rests on the assumption that the "sick" supply chain wants to be just like the "healthy" supply chain. This may not be the case. There may be "better" best practices that have yet to be discovered or put in place. Some of the tools mentioned above make use of creativity to find ways of improving on the current practices. For example, both SCIM*am* and SCVR make use of what-if approaches to find better ways of managing the supply chain.

This implies that several approaches might be used together. For example, a combination of best practices and what-if approaches might lead to a mix of practices that is superior to what is currently considered the best way to fix supply chain problems. Similarly, a combination of benchmarking and mapping or cause-and-effect diagrams (or both) may be a superior way to identify the root causes of symptoms.

Summary

In this chapter, a variety of tools have been discussed for diagnosing problems in a supply chain. These diagnostic tools vary in format, complexity, and cost. Both quantitative and qualitative diagnostic tools have been described. It was shown that benchmarking is one of the primary tools used to discover the symptoms of a problem, but other approaches, such as mapping, have also been used. How causes might be identified solely from a benchmarking approach or from a mapping or means-ends approach was also analyzed. Last, the use of best practices, as well as the use of other approaches to fix supply chain problems, was described.

Note

1. Another commercially available benchmarking tool was developed by Andersen Consulting (now Accenture), called the Supply Chain Performance Assessment. This tool is used as part of a consulting effort, not as a self-diagnostic tool, and will not be discussed here.

References

Borghesi, A., G. Cavalieri, P. Meciani, I. Russo, and P. Signori (2005), "Supply Chain Visibility Roadmap," Research paper, University of Verona, Italy.

Camp, Robert C. (1989), *Benchmarking: The Search for Industry Best Practices That Lead to Superior Performance.* Milwaukee, WI: ASQ Quality Press.

Elrod, Robert H. and Charles L. Hubbard (1979), "Applying Means Ends Decision Trees," *Business,* 29 (1), 17–25.

Enslow, Beth (2005), "Study Finds Leading Shippers Deploy New Set of Best Practices," *Logistics Management,* 44 (6), 17–18.

Foggin, James H., John T. Mentzer, and Carol L. Monroe (2004), "A Supply Chain Diagnostic Tool," *The International Journal of Physical Distribution and Logistics Management,* 34 (10), 827–855.

Gardner, Chris, Cheryl Harrity, and Kate Vitasek (2005), "A Better Way to Benchmark," *Supply Chain Management Review,* 9 (3), 20–28.

Gentry, Connie Roberts (2005), "Handle With Care," *Chain Store Age,* 81 (4), 55–56.

Ireland, Ronald K. and Colleen Crum (2005), *Supply Chain Collaboration: How to Implement CPFR and Other Best Collaborative Practices.* Ft. Lauderdale, FL: J. Ross Publishing/ APICS.

Keegan, Kevin (2003), "Modeling Total Supply Chain Costs," *World Trade,* 16 (9), 52–53.

Kuglin, F. A. (1998), *Customer-Centered Supply Chain Management: A Link-by-Link Guide.* New York: American Management Association.

Mentzer, John T., William DeWitt, James S. Keebler, Soonhong Min, Nancy W. Nix, Carlo D. Smith, et al. (2001), "What Is Supply Chain Management:" in *Supply Chain Management,* John T. Mentzer, ed. Thousand Oaks, CA: Sage.

Naim, M. M., P. Childerhouse, S. M. Disney, and D. R. Towill (2002), "A Supply Chain Diagnostic Methodology: Determining the Vector of Change," *Computers and Industrial Engineering,* 24 (1), 135–157.

Performance Measurement Group (PMG), LLC (2005), retrieved August 8, 2005, from www.pmgbenchmarking.com/public/product/scorecard/service_supply_chain/met rics.asp

The Quick Scan Handbook (n.d.), retrieved on August 8, 2005, from www.cf.ac.uk/carbs/ lom/lsdg/quickscanhand.html

"SCOR Model Users Get New Benchmarking Tool" (1999), *Purchasing,* 126 (5), 33–34.

Signori, P. (2001), "Valutando le Potenzialità di Integrazione di una Catena Estesa di Fornitura" [Evaluating the Potentiality of Integration of a Supply Chain], *Industria & Distribuzione*, 3, 61–76.

Signori, P. (2002), *SCIMam (Supply Chain Integrated Management Analysis Method): Un Metodo D'analisi per la Valutazione Delle Potenzialità D'integrazione Logistica di una Catena Estesa di Fornitura (SCIMam [Supply Chain Integrated Management Analysis Method): An Analysis Method to Evaluate the Potentiality of Logistics Integration of a Supply Chain]*, vol. 56. Verona, Italy: Sinergie.

Signori, P. (2004), *La Misurazione Dell'integrazione Logistica nel Supply Chain Integrated Management [The Measurement of Logistics Integration in the Supply Chain Integrated Management]*. Padua, Italy: Cedam.

Stock, James R. and Douglas M. Lambert (2001), *Strategic Logistics Management*, 4th ed. New York: McGraw-Hill.

Supply Chain Operations Reference Model: Overview of SCOR Version 5.0 (2000). Pittsburgh, PA: Supply Chain Council.

Supply Chain Visions (2004), *Supply Chain Management Process Standards: Plan Process*. Oak Brook, IL: Council of Supply Chain Management Professionals.

Vitasek, Kate and Karl B. Manrodt (2005), "Finding Best Practices in Your Own B.A.C.K.Y.A.R.D.," *Supply Chain Management Review*, 9 (1), 54–58.

"Web Based Tool to Help Evaluate Supply Chains" (1999), *Automatic ID News*, 15 (4), 14.

31

Change Management

J. Paul Dittmann

John E. Mello

Managing change is a constant in business today, and indeed the rate of change is accelerating. In the globally linked world with instantaneous information, change is occurring at an increasingly rapid rate. Major corporate decisions hinge daily on the effectiveness of change management. As Slone (2004) stated,

> Things would be very different today—for me, my colleagues, and my company—if the votes of Whirlpool's North American leadership team had swung in a different direction. . . . It was a move I hadn't expected; our executive vice president at the time decided to go around the table and ask each member of his staff for a thumbs-up or thumbs-down on the investment that I had just formally proposed. Did I look worried? I can't imagine I didn't, even though we'd spent hours in individual meetings with each of them, getting their ideas and buy-in. We thought we had everyone's support. But the facts remained: Our proposal had a bigger price tag than any supply chain investment in the company's history. We were asking for tens of millions during a period of general belt-tightening. (p. 114)

The story has a happy ending, as each functional head supported the change with enthusiasm. How was this degree of buy-in accomplished? The answer lies in following the disciplined change management process explained in this chapter.

Managing change is the primary activity of management. The penalty for a change management failure can be catastrophic. The Project Management Institute has determined that project failure is very common. In fact, only 63% of initiatives

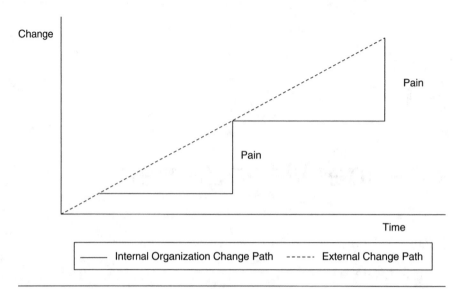

Figure 31.1   Internal and External Rate of Change

are completed on time, within budget, and delivering the targeted benefits; 53% are eventually completed with far less than the expected results; and 31% fail completely. In addition, 62% of companies report a catastrophic failure, with serious consequences for the firm. Burnes (2000) found that in various Institute of Management surveys, managers reported considerable levels of dissatisfaction with the change and that most organizations experience severe problems in managing change effectively.

A range of issues, such as excessive scope expansion, limited resources, and poor leadership, can cause the failure of projects. However, change management deficiency is at the root of many initiative failures. There are three major reasons for change management failures. First, some organizations fail to see that their environment is changing. Second, the wrong strategies are applied. Third, the implementation of the correct strategies goes wrong (Buelens and Devos 2004). A project can be beautifully designed and implemented, but if the organization is not ready for the change, it will reject it, wasting all the human effort and resources.

Project failures resulting from breakdowns in the change management process have resulted in wasting billions of dollars in cost and lost opportunities. Therefore, the constant management of changing external and internal environments is essential in all organizations. As depicted in Figure 31.1, it is clear that if the rate of change externally exceeds the rate of change internally, pain is a certainty and disaster a probability.

What Is Change Management?

Change management is defined as those strategies and action plans that support and maintain transition from the current state to a new outcome. Maintaining the transition is often more difficult than implementing initial change. Change management involves two very different critical processes: training and the buy-in process. Once an organization accepts the change, a well-designed and well-executed training plan is essential. Prior to that, the process of organizational buy-in sets the organization up for change, and this is arguably the most challenging aspect of any new initiative. The coming change must be embraced not only cross-functionally but also at all organizational levels. Achieving organizational support for change is thus critical to achieving the goals set forth in any change management initiative.

Developing the Change Management Strategy

Before developing the strategy, there must be an acknowledgement of the major time and resource commitment involved. One of the main reasons for change management failure is the lack of sufficient time and resources devoted to change. A good rule of thumb is that the project plan should show 50% of the time and effort devoted to the buy-in and training required to successfully implement the initiative. As Slone (2004) stated,

> We spent an enormous amount of time talking with the brand general managers and others who would be affected by the changes we were proposing. The Japanese call this kind of consensuses-building *nemawashi* (literally, "root building"), and it's impossible to overstate its importance. (p. 118)

Kotter (1995) states that the most basic lesson learned from successful change management is that it goes through a series of phases and usually requires a considerable length of time. Skipping steps only creates the illusion of speed and never produces a satisfying result. Three major areas consume management's time during change: aligning sponsorship, overcoming resistance, and conducting training.

Managing change requires alignment both up and down the organization. Senior management's sponsorship is especially critical. The organization must see senior management routinely involved throughout the project. This requires feeding upward key communication points to enable these extremely busy individuals to be heard at appropriate times to give the project the support it needs to be successful.

Watson (quoted in Gravenhorst and in 't Veld 2004) sees resistance to change as a natural reaction of individuals, originating from a need for stability. Resistance to change is a natural reaction of people to anything that upsets their status quo, which produces a loss of psychological equilibrium (Conner 1993). Kotter and Schlesinger (1979) list the four most common reasons for resisting change: when people focus on their own interests and not on those of the organization as a whole, when misunderstandings occur concerning the change and its implications for the organization and its individuals, when beliefs exist that change does not make sense for the organization, and when there is low tolerance to change within the organization.

Any change that excludes employees is a major cause of resistance (Gravenhorst and in 't Veld 2004). Employee involvement at many levels within the organization helps overcome resistance. It is axiomatic that when individuals feel they have some input and control over the coming change, resistance dissipates. This requires a massive communication effort and consumes a great deal of time and resources. Each stakeholder must be routinely involved throughout the change. This involves multiple meetings that need to be literally scheduled as tasks and tracked as rigorously as any technical task in the project plan. The communication process must be relentless. It is generally most efficient for the team members to divide the communication responsibility. This also should be structured into a set of precisely defined tasks in a project management framework, along with a process for feedback to the project leader.

Well-executed training for the ultimate users is critical not only for the flawless execution of the new initiative but also for the ownership process. Training should take place at multiple organization levels, from high-level overviews for management to detailed "how-to" training for the front line. Training for the front line must take place at the right time. True hands-on execution training must not occur too early and should take place just before "go-live."

The Change Management Plan

Once a full commitment is made to the level of effort involved, the change management plan can be structured into a disciplined set of tasks. This is a project in itself and should follow a rigorous project management process. The elements of a complete change management plan are shown in Table 31.1. Each requires a detailed written description. It is often helpful to develop a change management plan template as an aid for the change management leader.

The most significant component of the change management plan is the communication plan. It has been estimated that 2.4 million words are communicated to a typical employee in a quarter. A typical change management communication could include about 13,000 words. For example, it might comprise a 30-minute speech, a one-hour meeting, a 2,000-word memo, and a 600-word article in the company "newspaper." If these estimates are reasonable, they imply that change management has only about one-half of 1% of the total communication share. It is critical for a well-defined, carefully planned communication approach to be heard above the constant barrage of messages affecting the workplace.

The first step in change management involves identifying key stakeholders and assessing their ability to influence the outcome of a change initiative, either positively or negatively (Hayes 2002). The communication plan should identify those who can either support or sabotage the initiative and develop an appropriate communication approach for each. In general, the following can be used as a checklist for communicating change to an organization:

1. *Provide vision and strategy*: Articulate a clear and compelling vision of the future, as specifically as possible, supplemented with enough strategy to be credible to the listener.

Table 31.1   Change Management Plan Template

1. Describe the initiative and state the case for change.

2. State the specific objective and the desired business outcomes.

3. List the sponsor, owner, leader, and team members, along with the responsibilities of each.

4. Describe the scope of the change. What is in scope, and what is out of scope?

5. State the benefits of the change, both quantitative and qualitative.

6. Show the communication plan. List each stakeholder and mention who is accountable for the communication, frequency of the communication, and time-line.

7. List the detailed training plan by individual, including the specific content and dates.

2. *Explain why change is needed*: Present a clear and logical portrayal of the necessity for change due to internal or external factors (or both).

3. *Clearly communicate what is in it for the organization and individual employees*: Presenting individual benefits for each stakeholder is truly the essence of change management.

4. *Explain what is needed from each individual*: Outline the critical role each individual must play for the project to be successful.

5. *Provide regular progress reports on the project's status*: Include a record of successful progress and essential early wins by taking a large project and splitting it into multiple milestones, with progress toward each reported to the organization.

6. *Celebrate milestones*: This presents a clear message to the organization that progress is being made and the project is on its way to success.

People and Organizational Issues

"If the intent of organizational change is to have fundamental and long-lasting effects, the focus of the change agents will have to be on the more tangible and subjective aspects of organizational life" (Egri and Frost 1991, pp. 176–177). Change management can be summarized in one simple truth: "Each individual in an organization must see the individual benefit of the change," or put more simply, they must see "what's in it for them." The challenge is to align each individual's needs with the needs of the enterprise.

A simple approach to engage each key individual is to ask the following questions:

1. Do you understand the coming change and why it is needed?

2. Will you know what to do when this change is implemented?

3. Do you believe you will have the resources to do it?

4. Do you want to do it?

5. Will you be rewarded if you do it?

6. Do you believe your management truly supports doing it?

If there are any "No" answers, much more focus is needed to determine the source of the breakdown in the change management process.

Organizational Readiness for Change: The Change Management Survey

Clarke (1994) found that creating a culture for change means that change has to be part of the way things are done and cannot be "bolted on" to the existing culture. Therefore, the first step in embarking on a major project is assessing the readiness of the organization's culture for change. The results should guide the structuring of the change management plan. Areas to survey include the following:

- *Trust in leadership*: How much credibility does senior leadership have?
- *Work environment*: What are the current levels of organizational stress and of perceived instability in the work environment?
- *Shared vision*: How much of the future transformation is shared and understood by all employees?
- *"As-is" situation*: How much pain is present in the current situation?
- *"To-be" perception*: How attractive is the perceived future environment?
- *Involvement*: How involved do people feel with the change decision and direction?
- *People readiness*: How ready are employees to actually perform their jobs in the new environment?

The survey should be conducted with all stakeholders—that is, everyone involved in or affected by the change initiative. Another helpful survey technique is to ask each stakeholder to assess the change readiness culture of the organization. Dimensions, listed in Table 31.2, can be rated on a 1-to-10 scale for both actual and preferred dimensions. Gaps point to areas of focus for the change management plan. For example, one company saw scores on the dimension of "discipline" of actual = 3 and preferred = 5. This was of great concern given that the project was to install a process and software system requiring a great deal of discipline. Knowing this gap up front guides the focus of the change management plan.

Change Management Organizational Roles

After assessing organizational readiness, it is time to identify the range of necessary participants in the change process, each playing a key role. These participants should include the following individuals:

Table 31.2   Change Readiness Culture Survey

Dimension	Actual Situation Today	Preferred Situation in the Future
Teamwork		
Openness		
Management support		
Integrity		
Innovation		
Risk propensity		
Recognition		
Customer orientation		
Discipline		
Accountability		
Flexibility		
Goal alignment		

NOTE: Rate actual and preferred on a 1-to-10 scale, with 10 being the most desirable.

- *The sponsor:* The individual who legitimizes the change. This role cannot be delegated to others. The senior sponsor must be regularly visible, credible, and enthusiastic. Given that most senior sponsors have tremendous competing demands on their time, it is essential to formally schedule these activities on their calendars. Otherwise, the best of intentions can be overwhelmed by the "crisis of the day."
- *Change owners:* Individuals (often function heads) who reinforce the importance of the change throughout their area of responsibility. If there is a gap in support at this level, the problem cascades down the organization (Figure 31.2).
- *Change managers:* Individuals who are doing the hard work daily to make the change happen. The change manager is responsible for tracking the tasks in the project plan. If tasks fall behind schedule, the change manager must aggressively keep the task owners aware of the impact on the project.
- *Process owners:* Individuals who actually execute the details of the new system or process. These people are most likely to be the targets of detailed training on the unique skills necessary to implement and sustain the change.

Each of these roles must be addressed in a comprehensive change management plan, with each having clearly defined tasks, responsibilities, and associated timelines. It is critical that everyone understand and buy in to the critical component in the change process; without successful execution of each person's role, the change will fail. In the final analysis, *everyone* is a leader in a successful change process.

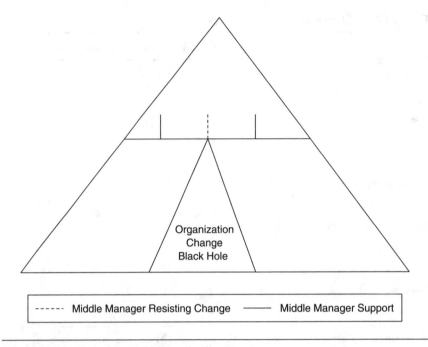

Figure 31.2 Typical Pyramid Organization Structure

The Initial Response to an Announced Change

At this point, it is time to launch the change. The initial response to an announced change will be very personal. "For change to occur, each individual must think, feel, or do something different. Leaders must win their followers one by one" (Duck 1993, p. 109). There are three possible initial reactions to an announced change: positive, negative, or no reaction. Of the three, the most disturbing is the last. This complacent attitude, addressed in detail later, implies the total breakdown in communicating the need for change. The imperative for change must be communicated with hope and intensity but should not be overdramatized (some people disengage if they feel they are caught in a hopeless plight).

If the change is initially viewed as positive, an individual must be managed through the five stages in Table 31.3 as quickly as possible. Each of these stages has clear danger if progress becomes stalled at that step.

If the change is initially viewed as negative, individuals must be taken as quickly as possible through the seven stages in Table 31.4. Again, it is critical that progress be rapid and continuous through all phases. Because each person tends to react differently, each key stakeholder should be individually assessed and a communication plan structured to deal with the stage-by-stage journey to acceptance.

Once an individual passes through the phases associated with the initial reaction, much work remains. It is then necessary to move from the phase of realistic acceptance to detailed understanding and finally to a total commitment to the new

Table 31.3   First Reaction Positive

Stage	Danger	Communication Focus
1. Optimism without facts	Expectations are set too high for the inevitable challenges that lie ahead	Manage expectations; focus on the challenge as well as the expected outcome
2. Pessimism as the challenge becomes apparent	Public resistance, and possibly an inclination to stand on the sidelines	A clear action plan showing the steps to success
3. Early sign of hope	A fragile stage, which if killed can lead to checking out	Encouragement; focus on the final outcome
4. Optimism based on facts	Early signs are not positive and there are no quick wins, causing a regression to Stage 2 or worse	Focus on the challenges and the eventual outcome; some setbacks are to be expected
5. Realistic acceptance of the change	We can now turn our focus to other things—launch and leave	We still have a lot of work to do

Table 31.4   First Reaction Negative

Stage	Danger	Communication Focus
1. Immobilization	This state could become permanent	Focus on the burning platform and the vision of the future
2. Denial	This is almost the same as "no reaction"	See above
3. Anger	This stage could eventually turn into sabotage if sustained	See above, with added firmness
4. Bargaining	The change could be compromised if concessions are made	See above, with a focus on the action plan
5. Depression	This stage could result in checking out of the process if sustained	See above, with a special focus on the successful outcome
6. Testing	No early wins cause a regression to earlier stages	Promote early wins
7. Acceptance of the coming change	We can now focus on other things	We still have a lot of work to do

Table 31.5   The Commitment Journey

Stage	Danger	Communication Focus
1. Acceptance	Support will fade, and other priorities will interfere	Vision of the future: the deliverables and the action plan
2. Involvement	Other priorities interfere	Task of involvement in the communication process
3. Commitment and ownership of the result	Inflexibility	Stay the course but constantly evaluate the changing environment

environment. Without full commitment, the journey will eventually stall and regress. Commitment goes far beyond involvement and involves active ownership of the change. The journey to commitment is shown in Table 31.5.

Complacency

As discussed above, complacency is a far more serious threat than outright resistance. "Companies today are full of change survivors, cynical people who have learned to live through change programs without really changing at all" (Duck 1993, pp. 111–112).

There are several sources of complacency:

- *A long history of only "happy talk" from management:* This conditions an organization to believe that a true crisis is really not possible.
- *A "kill the messenger" mentality:* Here, bad news is not tolerated, which instills a culture that is unable to react to an external threat.
- *The human nature of denial:* It is not unusual for some individuals to deny a threat even when it is clearly present.
- *Exclusively internal focus:* The organization never looks outside itself and therefore does not understand when the environment is dictating a need for change.
- *Poor metrics:* Internally focused metrics, with comparisons only to historical performance standards, can create a false sense of well-being.
- *A long history of success:* "If it ain't broke, why fix it?"

Complacency is devastating to the change process because it effectively neutralizes all the change effort under way. Complacent people need to be identified early and, if key to the eventual success, need to be involved in developing and even selling the case for change.

Resistance to Change

Once past the initial reaction, resistance will still be present to some degree. Indeed, it is in human nature to resist change. One way of overcoming resistance and changing the way people view change consists of three steps: (1) unfreezing the present level, (2) moving to the new level, and (3) refreezing the new level (Lewin 1947). Unfreezing usually involves reducing those forces maintaining the organization's behavior at its present level. Unfreezing requires confrontation with an organizational member or a re-education process. This might be achieved through meetings in which it is shown that a serious problem exists. The purpose of this is to enable those concerned to become convinced of the need for change. Moving involves acting on the results of the first step. Action is taken to develop new behaviors, values, and attitudes. Refreezing seeks to restabilize the organization at the desired state. It is frequently achieved through positively reinforcing new ways of working, including socialization processes such as recruitment, reward systems, and cultural reinforcement through the creation of new values and norms of behavior (Burnes 2000).

Resistance to Different Types of Change

Change can occur abruptly or slowly, with each having its own challenges. There are many examples of the dire effects of resistance to abrupt change, from Swiss watchmakers who refused to see the trend toward electric watches to U.S.-based electronics manufacturers who were unable to compete with low-cost producers in Asia. How many organizations are today facing the prospect of such an abrupt change? Andy Grove of Intel called such change "strategic inflection points." Failure to recognize the approach of such an inflection point has destroyed many enterprises. Figure 31.3 illustrates how a company may move along a path anticipated by management and suddenly be faced with drastic changes that must be recognized and dealt with in an effective manner.

Sometimes change happens quickly, as in the examples above. In other cases, it occurs in a slow, steady, insidious advance. There is the well-known analogy of "boiling a frog." Although a frog will jump out of boiling water if thrown in, it will sit and cook if the temperature is raised one degree at a time. A clear analogy exists in many businesses because the competitive fire is increased slowly and may not be recognized until it is too late. Slow change can in the long run be even more dangerous. However, whether fast or slow, change creates an environment of both danger and opportunity. The outcome depends on the change management culture in the enterprise (see Table 31.6).

A slow-response culture bogs down whether faced with slow or rapid change and has no opportunity for a successful outcome. On the other hand, a quick-response culture has a wonderful range of possibilities to pursue.

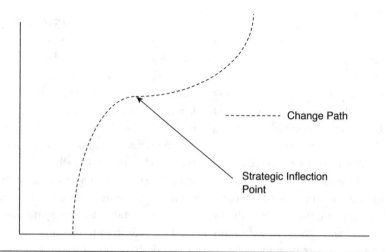

Figure 31.3   Strategic Inflection Point

Change Management Myths and Realities

A discussion of people and organizational change would not be complete without reviewing the numerous myths that experienced managers have faced:

Myth: Good change agents can force a group through change rapidly.

Reality: Change occurs at different rates for each individual. Each person must go through the gauntlet. Leadership is critical to moving each person steadily through the change process, but successful change depends on far more than dynamic leadership. Each individual must eventually accept the fact that he or she too is a leader in the change process. Communicating early and often while simultaneously seeking input is one effective way to speed up the eventual buy-in. Sam Walton was heard to remark that the most important words in the English language are "people support best that which they help create."

Myth: The best performers adapt to change the fastest.

Reality: Often the best performers are the most passionate about their work. They can therefore be the most vocal critics of change if they feel outside the process. But when managed carefully, these people can become incredibly influential supporters. High performers especially need to be involved early and often in the change process. Enlisting their help in communicating the change to others can ensure their buy-in.

Myth: Protecting people from bad news helps them not to fear change.

Reality: People have a tremendous capacity for change when involved early in the change process. In fact, some bad news can create the burning platform for change. As Samuel Johnson observed, "nothing so focuses a man's mind as the prospect of being hanged in the morning." This concept can, if carried too far,

Table 31.6   Impact of Different Change Management Cultures

	Rapid External Change	**Slow External Change**
Slow-Response Culture	Sudden death	Slow death
Quick-Response Culture	Breakthrough opportunity	Strategic opportunity

send an organization into a state of hopelessness. One factory manager painted a compelling picture of the "death spiral" that was engulfing the plant. The employees felt that there was no hope and stopped trying to make improvements. The communication of bad news involves walking the fine line between hope and despair.

Myth: The people who change easily are not resisting.

Reality: Some people assume that the best approach is to appear to simply go along, having an attitude of "this too shall pass." Indeed, having outlasted several administrations, history has taught them that senior management comes and goes with little lasting impact. These people can easily be the most difficult to really change.

Myth: People at lower levels in the organization exhibit greater resistance.

Reality: Middle managers often perceive a greater loss. When they are not participants in the change plan, they feel a loss of control over their environment. These are people who have a strong vested interest in the status quo when not involved in the future plans and can resist change in a multitude of creative ways.

Launching the Change

Once the change management plan is complete, including the all-important communication plan, and once an approach to dealing with individual reactions and resistance has been determined, it is time to begin executing the plan. A good summary of the task ahead is clear from Kotter's (1995) eight steps to transforming an organization, each of which requires significant effort:

1. *Establish a sense of urgency*. Clearly communicate the challenges facing the organization with a sense of hope, not panic.

2. *Form a powerful guiding coalition*. Ensure senior sponsorship and form a cohesive change team.

3. *Create a vision*: Develop a vision for the coming change along with high-level strategies to achieve the vision.

4. *Communicate the vision*: Use every vehicle possible to continuously communicate the vision. People need to hear about the vision repeatedly.

5. *Empower others to act*: Eliminate barriers and encourage risk taking.

6. *Plan for and create short-term wins*: Break projects into smaller releases and communicate success continuously. Do not declare victory too early, or it can kill momentum.

7. *Consolidate improvements and produce more change*: Hire the right people to sustain the change. Reinvigorate processes when appropriate.

8. *Institutionalize the new approach*: Ensure that leadership development and succession continue.

The sixth point above, creating short-term wins, is critical to sustaining momentum. One tactic used successfully in some companies is to divide a large project into multiple business releases and create a feeling of accomplishment and progress as each business release is successfully implemented.

Summary of Key Success Factors: The Change Equation

When engaged in the intensity of the change process, one should constantly keep in mind these six key requirements for success:

1. Always emphasize the *case for change*, the reason it is being done.

2. Constantly communicate the *vision*.

3. Involve the key stakeholders continuously in an intense *communication* plan.

4. Develop the *skills* needed at the end in a detailed training plan.

5. Remind all involved of the *incentives* to be successful.

6. Carefully manage the *resources* committed to change.

In other words, there is a change equation:

$$\text{Successful change} = \text{case for change} + \text{vision} + \text{communication} + \text{skills} + \text{incentives} + \text{resources} + \text{action plan}$$

If any one of these elements is subtracted, the result will be unacceptable, resulting in confusion, anxiety, frustration, false starts, or delays (Table 31.7).

Table 31.7   Necessary Conditions for Change

Change Element Subtracted	Impact
Pressure for change: "A burning platform"	Confusion: "Why are we doing this?"
Vision	Again confusion: "How does this change fit in the big picture?"
Communication	Loss of momentum, possibly stalling the change
Skills	Anxiety: "I haven't been trained; I don't know what to do."
Resources	"We don't have enough time and money to do this."
Incentives	Delays: "What gets rewarded gets done."
Action plan	False start: "ready-fire-aim"

Change Management in a Global Environment

Change management in a global environment holds an exponentially more difficult challenge. Time zones, language, and cultural differences create an entirely new set of challenges. As the degree of change required increases, it is necessary for the change team to be increasingly culturally competent. There are four stages of global cultural competence. Major change efforts require Stage 3 and 4 skills.

- *Stage 1*: an open mind
- *Stage 2*: a focused effort at awareness of the cultural differences
- *Stage 3*: a concerted effort to gain knowledge of the other culture
- *Stage 4*: the development of cross-cultural skills, including language skills

After years of implementing initiatives in a global environment, the authors have assembled a list of lessons learned:

- There must be a strong top-down commitment to global initiatives.
- Highly experienced project and change managers are essential. This is not a place for beginners.
- Projects should be expected to be exponentially more difficult, and the resources and timeline should reflect that degree of difficulty.
- Cultural differences must be respected and relationships must be initiated with each person.
- Communications must respect language barriers.
- It is definitely possible to be successful in implementing change in a global environment.

Language barriers are a huge challenge. Even nonverbal language can be a barrier if one is insensitive to it. The symptoms of communication breakdowns are clear: blank stares, non sequiturs, unnatural flows in the conversation, and a general sense of "not connecting." When faced with these language barriers, it is essential that much more time be taken in the communication process. The message needs to be explained in several ways, repeatedly. Simple visual aids are very important. Perhaps the most important requirement is to slow down speech, remembering that the other side is translating. Also, there is a need to keep any written communication very simple—remember that verbal fluency in the target audience does not imply written fluency.

If a translator is required, in-depth preparation of the translator is necessary. The translator needs to be prepared for the jargon and acronyms that inevitably occur. When translation takes place sequentially rather than simultaneously, the time required for communication at least doubles. Clearly, the additional time needs to be factored into the change management task plan.

People around the world view *time* differently, ranging from an obsession with meeting deadlines to completion of tasks based on the strength of the relationship. Communication styles also differ—from a task orientation to a relationship-based communication approach. Getting to the "bottom line" cannot occur too quickly in some cultures, without first focusing on building an awareness of each other as individuals.

It is instructive to reflect on the major difference in the U.S. and Chinese cultures as described by Kenna and Lacy (1994) and summarized in Table 31.8.

Table 31.8   Cultural Differences Between the United States and China

	United States	*China*
Face	You can learn from failure; need to admit mistakes; criticism should be done with tact	Very important never to put someone in the position of having to admit a mistake or failure; never admit a lack of understanding
Directness	Direct, to the point; uncomfortable with ambiguity	Politeness is more important than frankness; "Yes" means "I hear you"
Status	Power is more important than seniority and status; one's position in life is achieved through individual effort	Maturity is essential; status and titles are extremely important
Contracts	Direct, specific, legal	Agreements that can be adjusted later
Time	Impatient, punctual	Patient; use time as a weapon; very tough negotiators
Presentations	Hard sell, quick close	Soft sell

Table 31.9   Monochromic Versus Polychromic People

Monochromic People	Polychromic People
Do one thing at a time	Do many things at once
Concentrate on the job	Are subject to interruptions
Take deadlines very seriously	Time commitments, an objective to be achieved if possible
Are accustomed to short-term relationships	Lifelong relationships

A number of frameworks have been developed to better understand global cultural differences. There is the well-known distinction between monochromic and polychromic people of the world (Table 31.9). The traditional stereotype for a U.S. native is monochromic, whereas most of the rest of the world is more polychromic.

Another framework is the Hofstede (1991) model, which divides cultures based on the four variables of power distance, individualism versus collectivism, uncertainty avoidance, and masculinity:

- *Power distance*: Cultures are different in how they view extreme inequities of wealth and power.
- *Individualism versus collectivism*: Cultures differ in how they value individual versus group achievement and how strong relationships are between individuals.
- *Uncertainty avoidance*: Cultures differ in their comfort with risk and resistance to change.
- *Masculinity versus femininity*: Cultures are different in the role for women in society.

Although these comparisons are stereotypical by intent, the point is clear—major cultural differences exist that make the job of change management much more difficult.

Therefore, it is necessary to manage change fully respecting the global cultural differences at work (Dittmann 1999). In implementing a manufacturing planning system by Dittmann (1999), weekly meetings were held on alternating "sevens," 7 a.m. and 7 p.m., to respect the 12-hour time zone difference. Each of the 20 Chinese module leaders was asked to walk through the following five change management steps to overcome communication and cultural barriers in the Chinese environment:

1. Describe the old process.

2. Describe the new process.

3. Describe the differences.

4. Explain how you will implement the changes.

5. Sign off: "I agree to personally guarantee that the changes will be implemented."

This level of detail and rigor was needed in the Chinese environment, where an answer of "Yes" may only mean "I hear you."

Summary

Change management is a primary activity of management, but ironically, it is often not a priority. The time and effort required to successfully achieve organizational buy-in and execute a robust training plan are normally far greater than expected or planned. For any significant initiative, it is essential that a formal change management plan be developed. The communication component of the plan is critical and must focus on the key individuals. Communication tasks should be scheduled and monitored like any other task in the initiative. Skill development and training must also follow a well-defined plan with precise timing.

The case for change must be made in a compelling manner and must be continuously recommunicated. Leadership is essential in all organizational roles, not in senior management alone. Each individual has a critical role to play. It is vital to quickly establish beachheads of success and build on them. Finally, once a major initiative is successfully implemented, sustaining the change is the greatest challenge of all.

The economy is becoming increasingly globally interdependent. Change management in a global environment takes on a new dimension of complexity. In the environment of the 21st century, external change will accelerate at an increasing pace. The stars of the future will be those organizations that decide to proactively embrace the challenge of this rapidly changing environment.

References

Buelens, Marc and Geert Devos (2004), "Art and Wisdom in Choosing Change Strategies," in *Dynamics of Organizational Change and Learning*, Jaap J. Boonstra, ed. Cornwall, UK: TJ International, pp. 85–95.

Burnes, Bernard (2000), *Managing Change: A Strategic Approach to Organizational Dynamics*. Edinburgh Gate, UK: Pearson Education.

Clarke, Liz (1994), *The Essence of Change*. London: Prentice Hall.

Conner, Daryl R. (1993), *Managing at the Speed of Change: How Resilient Managers Succeed and Prosper Where Others Fail*. New York: Villard Books.

Dittmann, J. Paul (1999), "Project Culture in China: Different Strokes for Different Folks," *PM Network*, 13 (3), 45–51.

Duck, Jeanie Daniel (1993), "Managing Change: The Art of Balancing," *Harvard Business Review*, 71 (6), 109–188.

Egri, Carolyn P. and Peter J. Frost (1991), "Shamanism and Change: Bringing Back the Magic in Organizational Transformation," in *Research in Organizational Change and Development,* Richard W. Woodman and William A. Pasmore, eds. Greenwich, CT: JAI Press, pp. 175–221.

Gravenhorst, Kilian Bennebroek and Roeland in 't Veld (2004), "Power and Collaboration: Methodologies for Working Together in Change," in *Dynamics of Organizational Change and Learning,* Jaap J. Boonstra, ed. Cornwall, UK: TJ International, pp. 317–341.

Hayes, John (2002), *The Theory and Practice of Change Management.* Chippenham, UK: Antony Rowe.

Hofstede, Geert H. (1991), *Culture's Consequences : Comparing Values, Behaviors, Institutions, and Organizations Across Nations.* Newbury Park, CA: Sage.

Kenna, Peggy and Sondra Lacy (1994), *Business China.* Lincolnwood, IL: Passport Books.

Kotter, John P. (1995), "Leading Change: Why Transformation Efforts Fail," *Harvard Business Review,* 73 (2), 59–67.

Kotter, John P. and Leonard A. Schlesinger (1979), "Choosing Strategies for Change," *Harvard Business Review,* 57 (2), 106–114.

Lewin, Kurt (1947), "Frontiers in Group Dynamics: Concept, Method and Reality in Social Science; Social Equilibria and Social Change," *Human Relations,* 1, 5–41.

Slone, Reuben (2004), "Managing a Supply Chain Turnaround," *Harvard Business Review,* 82 (10), 114–121.

Name Index

Abernathy, William, 154
Abrahamson, E., 400
Achrol, Ravi S., 23, 28, 29
Adams, M. E., 484
Agarwal, Sanjeev, 26
Ahmed, Pervaiz K., 275
Allen, Gary R., 376
Almeida, J. G., 353
American Warehouseman's
    Association, 374
Anckar, Patrik, 44
Anderson, J. C., 354
Andraski, Joseph C., 299
Antia, K. D., 22
A. T. Kearney, 254, 265
Atkinson, A. A., 32
Attis, David, 40
Autio, E., 353

Baker, M., 137
Bardi, Edward J., 3
Barlow, Jim, 4
Barney, Jay, 20, 21, 338, 342
Beard, D. W., 23
Bello, Daniel C., 455–471, 545
Berg, N., 395
Berry, Leonard I., 275
Beth, S., 198
Bettis, R., 395
Bhawuk, Dharm P. S., 42
Biemans, W., 138
Bienstock, Carol C., 439
Bolton, R. N., 24
Borghesi, Antonio, 39–48, 514, 545
Bovet, David, 3
Bowen, F. E., 270
Bowersox, Donald J., 4, 22, 28, 41, 178
Boyer, K. K., 354
Bradley, S., 395

Brenchley, Richard, 31
Brett, M. Jeanne, 42
Brown, James R., 467
Bruce, Margaret, 135–146, 545–546
Bucklin, L. P., 25
Buelens, Marc, 524
Burnes, Bernard, 524
Burt, David N., 254

Cadotte, Ernest R., 31, 407
Calantone, Roger J., 41, 337–355, 546
Camp, Robert C., 510
CAPS Research, 268
Carson, Stephen, 460, 463, 466,
    467, 468
Cavusgil, S. Tamer, 337–355, 546
Chandler, Alfred D., Jr., 21, 22, 32
Chelariu, Cristian, 61
Chenneveau, Didier, 87–102, 546–547
Chetty, Sylvie, 21
Cheung, M. S., 24, 42, 484
Chichilnisky, Graciela, 331
Child, John, 20
Chiou, Jyh-Shen, 331
Choi, J., 23
Christensen, Clayton M., 476
Christie, Eilidh, 42, 43, 48
Christopher, M., 22, 33, 43, 109
Chryssochoidis, G., 138
Clark, Kim, 154
Clarke, Liz, 528
Cleveland, G., 354
Closs, David C., 4, 22, 28, 178
Commandeur, Harry R., 21
Conner, Datyl R., 525
Cook, Robert Lorin, 487–505, 547
Cooper, M. Bixby, 22, 178, 418
Cooper, M. C., 4, 25, 42
Cort, Stanton G., 460

Council of Supply Chain Management
    Professionals, 1, 4–5
Cousins, Paul, 253–271, 547
Coviello, Nicole, 131
Cox, J. F., 173
Coyle, John J., 3
Coyne, Kevin P., 20
Cron, William L., 119–134, 547
Crosby, Philip, 154
Cross, J., 395
Crowston, Kevin, 461
Crum, Colleen, 519
Crum, Michael R., 203–220, 501, 548
Cua, K. O., 354
Culbertson, Scott, 99

Dadzie, Kofi Q., 61
Daft, R. L., 337, 350
Dale, Thomas A., 376
Daly, Lucy, 135–146, 548
Dant, Shirish P., 461
Daugherty, P. J., 27, 28, 29
Davis, Donna F., 87–102, 548
Davis, J. Charlene, 26
Day, George S., 20, 21, 29, 484
DeCarlo, Thomas E., 119–134, 548
Deeter-Schmelz, D. R., 29
Deming, E. Edwards, 154
Deshpande, Rohit, 24, 347, 352
Dess, G. G., 23
Dettmer, H. W., 293
Dev, Chekitan S., 467
Devos, Geert, 524
Dharwadkar, Ravi, 468–469
Di Benedetto, A., 138, 139
Direct Marketing Educational
    Foundation, 125
Dittmann, J. Paul, 319–336, 523–540, 549
Dobler, Donald, 254
Doty, D. H., 338, 343, 350
Dougherty, D., 484
Drazin, R., 345
Droge, C., 28
Drucker, Peter, 382
Duck, Jeanie Daniel, 530, 532
Duffy, Roberta, 254
Dutta, Shantanu, 21
Dwyer, F. R., 23
Dyer, Jeffrey H., 484

Eckert, James A., 47
Egelhoff, William G., 20
Egri, Caarolyn P., 527
Eisenhardt, Kathleen M., 20

El-Ansary, Adel, 3
Ellram, Lisa M., 42, 253–271, 549
Elrod, Robert H., 515, 518
Emerson, Richard, 31, 417
Emmelhainz, Margaret, 453
Enslow, Beth, 519
Esper, Terry L., 443–454, 549–550
Estampe, Dominique, 65–84, 550
Evans, Kenneth, 451
Evans, Philip, 20
Evers, Philip T., 61

Fahey, Liam, 27
Farris, M. T., 28
Ferrell, O. C., 275
Fine, Charles, 268
Fisher, M. L., 196, 197, 323
Fisher, Roger, 264
Fliedner, G., 4
Flint, Daniel J., 26–27, 51–62,
    475–486, 550
Foggin, James H., 449, 507–521, 550
Forrester, J. W., 198, 199
Forte, M. J., 23
Frankel, R., 29
Frazier, G. L., 22, 24, 459
French, J., 417
Frost, Peter J., 527

Galbraith, Jay R., 20, 21, 22
Gale, Bradley T., 26, 57
Galunic, D. Charles, 20
Gammelgaard, Britta, 51–62, 551
Ganesan, Shankar, 30
Gantt, Henry, 153
Gardial, Sarah Fisher, 26, 57
Gardner, Chris, 511
Gardner, John, 453
Garrido-Rubio, A., 137, 138, 139, 146
Gassenheimer, Jule B., 26
Gatignon, H., 139
Gaudenzi, Barbara, 319–336, 551
Gentry, Connie Roberts, 519
Ghosh, Mrinal, 460
Ghoshal, Sumantra, 31, 349
Gilbreth, Frank, 153
Gilliland, David I., 465, 466
Glassman, M., 25
Glazer, R., 29
Glick, W. H., 338
Goldsby, Thomas J., 203–220, 551
Golicic, Susan L., 427–441, 449, 551
Goodman, Russel, 373
Goolsby, Jerry R., 275

Gordon, G. G., 25
Grant, R. M., 343, 353
Gravenhorst, Kilian Bennebroek, 525, 526
Greenwood, T. G., 288
Grewal, Rajdeep, 468–469
Griffith, David A., 42, 47, 48
Grönroos, Christian, 275
Gross, Barbara L., 26
Grove, Andy, 532
Gruen, Thomas W., 3
Guinipero, L. G., 337
Gulati, Ranjay, 58
Gummesson, Evert, 275

Habib, Mohammed M., 20
Haedicke, Jack, 299
Hall, Edward T., 365
Hambrick, D. C., 25, 349
Hamel, G., 395
Hamel, Gary, 20
Handfield, R. B., 337
Harland, Christine, 31
Harris, Ike, 99
Hart, S., 137–139
Hartline, Michael D., 275
Harvard Business School, 264
Harvey, Michael A., 48
Hauser, John R., 26
Hayes, John, 526
Hayes, Robert, 154, 162
Heal, Geoffrey, 331
Heck, R. H., 25
Heide, Jan, 31, 458, 459, 464, 465
Helferich, Omar Keith, 487–505, 552
Hendricks, O. K., 487
Heskett, James L., 275
Hilmer, F. G., 395
Hitt, Michael A., 4, 348
Hofer, Charles, 21, 32
Hofstede, Geert, 42, 539
Holbrook, Morris B., 26
Holcomb, Mary C., 59
Honeycutt, E. D., 25
Hoskisson, Robert E., 4, 20
Houston, Franklin S., 26
Hsu, Jason C., 331
Hubbard, Charles L., 515, 518
Huber, G. P., 338
Hult, G. Thomas M., 59, 485
Hult, G. Tomas M., 337–355, 552
Hultink, E. A., 137–138, 139
Hurley, R. F., 343
Hyogo Framework for Action, 501

Innis, Daniel E., 59
in 't Veld, Roeland, 525, 526
Ireland, Duane R., 4, 348, 519
Iyer, Gopalkrishnan R., 365

Jacobson, Robert, 26, 27
Jap, Sandy D., 455, 462, 467
Jassawalla, Avan R., 434
Jaworski, B. J., 348
Jayachandran, Satish, 21
Jayaram, J., 28
Jensen, Michael C., 93
John, George, 459, 460
Johnson, Herb, 428
Johnson, Samuel, 534
Johnston, Zachary T., 481
Jones, Daniel T., 52, 288
Juran, Joseph, 154

Kahn, K. B., 28, 135–146, 429, 431, 432, 552
Kaplan, Robert S., 435
Kazanjian, Robert K., 20, 21, 22
Kearns, David T., 508
Keller, Scott, 273–282, 552–553
Kenna, Peggy, 538
Kennedy, Karen N., 275
Kent, John L., 431, 434, 441
Ketchen, David J., Jr., 337–355, 553
Klein, Saul, 24, 459, 460
Kogut, B., 24, 47, 351
Kohli, A. K., 348, 353
Kohn, J. W., 27, 28
Konrad, B. P., 32
Kotabe, Masaaki, 393–404, 553
Kotler, Philip, 3, 4, 28, 29
Kotter, John P., 525, 535
Kraljic, Peter, 258
Kuczmarski, Thomas D., 481
Kuglin, F. A., 512
Kulatilaka, N., 24
Kumar, A., 348
Kurt Salmon Associates, 200

Lacy, Sondra, 538
LaLonde, Bernard J., 3–4, 59
Lambert, Douglas M., 4, 22, 25, 32, 42, 453, 517
Lamming, R. C., 270
Langley, C. John, Jr., 3, 376, 407
Langley, John C., 59
Lapide, Larry, 29, 72, 432
Lapierre, Jozee, 26
Larson, Paul D., 3

Larsson, Everth, 103–116, 475–486, 553
Lassk, Felicia G., 275
Laudicina, Paul, 40
Leavy, Brian, 268
Ledyard, Mike, 436
Lee, Dong-Jin, 467
Lee, H., 165
Lee, H. L., 199
Lee, Lamar, Jr., 254
LeMay, Stephen A., 274
Lengnick-Hall, C. A., 24
Lengnick-Hall, M. L., 24
Levitt, T., 150
Levy, D. L., 397
Lewicki, Roy J., 264
Lewin, Kurt, 533
Lewis, M. W., 354
Liker, Jeffrey K., 363
Liu, Peter C., 61
Ljungberg, Anders, 103–116, 554
Lohtia, Ritu, 455–456, 461
Low, G. S., 348
Lowson, Robert H., 21, 27
Lubatkin, Michael, 20
Lusch, Robert F., 3, 56
Lynch, Cifford F., 373–390, 554
Lynch, Daniel F., 43

Mabert, V. A., 29
Macneil, Ian R., 332, 470
Magnet, Myron, 361, 364, 367–368
Mahajan, V., 138
Malnight, Thomas W., 47
Malone, Thomas, 4, 461
Manrodt, Karl B., 519–520
Manuj, Ila, 319–336, 554
Marcoulides, G. A., 25
Margolis, Glen, 65–84, 554
Markides, C., 395
Marshall, Andrew, 42, 43, 48
Mason, P. A., 25
McAfee, R. B., 25
McCarthy, Teresa M., 74
McClelland, 196
McGinnis, M. A., 27, 28
McGuinness, Tony, 21
McKone, K. E., 354
Mello, John E., 523–540, 555
Mentzer, John T., 1–15, 19–33, 42,
    47, 58, 59, 60, 65–84, 429, 431,
    439, 449, 451, 485, 507, 543
Meyers, Randy, 307
Miles, Raymond, 20, 21, 22, 338, 342,
    347, 348, 349, 350, 397

Millar, V. E., 29
Miller, D., 341
Miller, D., 348
Min, S., 27
Min, Soonhong, 428, 431, 433, 434
Miner, A. S., 347, 351
Mishra, Debi Prasad, 460
Mitchell, Thomas, 121
Mizik, Natalie, 26, 27
Mohr, J. J., 348
Mohr, Jakki, 450
Mol, Michael J., 393–404, 555
Molinaro, Vince, 365–366
Moller, Kristian, 434
Monahan, Sean, 40
Monczka, Robert M., 385, 395
Monroe, Carol L., 507–521, 555
Moon, Mark A., 29, 65–84, 555
Moorman, C., 347, 351
Morgan, N. A., 343, 345
Morgan, Neil, 275
Morgan, Robert E., 21
MSNBC, 500
Murphy, D. J., 28
Murry, John P., 465
Myers, Matthew B., 1–15, 19–33,
    39–48, 543

Naim, M. M., 515
Napolitano, Lisa, 361
Narasimhan, Om, 21
Narver, John C., 26, 29, 348, 428, 431
Nathanson, Daniel A., 20
Nedungadi, Prakash, 21
Nevin, John, 450
Newman, Bruce I., 26
Nichols, E. L., Jr., 337, 338
Nonaka, Ikujiro, 87
Norton, David P., 435

Oakley, P., 138, 139
Okumura, Tetsushi, 42
Oldroyd, James B., 58
Olson, E. M., 349
Omura, G. S., 395
O'Reilly, C. A., III, 352
Orlicky, Joseph, 154

Padhamanabhan, V., 199
Pagell, M., 354
Pagh, Janus D., 4, 25, 42
Parsons, G. L., 29
Patterson, Andrea, 21
Patton, Bruce, 264

Peck, Helen, 43
Penton Media, 124
Picard, Stephane, 390
Pienaar, Abré, 169–182, 555–556
Piercy, Nigel, 275
Pine, B., 3
Pittman, P. H., 27, 28
Plossel, George, 154
PMG, 511
Pohlen, T. L., 22, 32
Polo-Redondo, Y., 137, 138, 139, 146
Porter, Michael E., 6, 20, 21, 29, 51,
    156, 157, 256, 266
Pothukuchi, Vijay, 42
Powers, Richard F., 3–4
Prahalad, C. K., 20

Quinn, J. B., 395

Rabinovich, Elliot, 61
Radosevich, Steve, 99
Rafiq, Mohammed, 275
Rajala, Arto, 434
Rajan, M., 23
Rajiv, Surendra, 21
Raman, A., 196, 197
Rangan, S., 399
Raven, B., 417
Rayport, J. F., 29
Reeve, James M., 285–298, 556
Reizenstein, Richard C., 429
Rentz, Joseph O., 429
Richey, R. G., 29
Rinehart, Lloyd M., 47, 407–425, 556
Robertson, T., 139
Robinson, E. Powell, Jr., 149–168,
    185–200, 444, 556–557
Rockart, John F., 4
Rodrigues, Alexandre M., 43
Rogers, Everett M., 475
Rogers, Ronald C., 20
Roos, Daniel, 52, 288
Rosenkopf, L., 400
Rosenzweig, P. M., 24
Ross, Sheldon M., 328
Roth, Victor J., 24, 459
Ruekert, Robert W., 21, 342, 349
Rumelt, Richard P., 20
Russo, Ivan, 39–48, 557
Ryals, L., 22, 33

Sahin, Funda, 149–168, 185–200,
    444, 557
Samiee, Saeed, 44

Sangtani, Vinita, 455–456
Sapienza, H. J., 353
Sashittal, Hemant C., 434
Schein, E. H., 24, 25
Schendel, Dan, 21, 32
Schirber, Michael, 500
Schlesinger, Leonard A., 525
Schonberger, Richard J., 3, 28
Schragenheim, E., 293
Schroeder, R. G., 354
Schroeter, Jon, 82
Schulman, Lawrence E., 20
Schultz, David P., 3
Schultz, Roberta, 451
Scott, Richard W., 468, 469, 470
Scott, Shay, 373–390, 557
Sengupta, S., 25
Setz, H. J., 138
Shamsie, J., 348
Sharma, Arun, 361–371, 557
Sheffi, Yossi, 3
Shervani, Tasadduq A., 27
Sheth, Jagdish, N., 26, 361–371, 558
Shewhart, Walter, 153
Shortell, S. M., 343
Signori, Paola, 507–521, 558
Simonin, B., 351
Simons, Robert, 32
Singh, Harbir, 484
Singh, J. V., 24
Singhal, Vinod R., 487
Sirmon, D. G., 348
Skinner, W., 154
Slater, Stanley F., 26, 29, 339, 348, 349,
    428, 431
Slone, Reuben, 523, 525
Snow, Charles C., 20, 21, 22, 338, 342,
    347, 348, 349, 350, 397
Speh, Thomas W., 223–250, 558–559
Spencer, M. S., 173
Sprague, L. G., 47
Srikanth, M. L., 291
Srinivasan, Mandyam M., 285–298, 559
Srivastava, Rajendra K., 27, 28
Stalk, George, 20, 21
Stank, Theodore P., 1–15, 19–33,
    43, 213, 373–390, 543–544
Stern, Louis W., 23, 31
Stock, James R., 42, 517
Stone, J. H., 173
Strong, Carolyn A., 21
Strout, Erin, 126
Stryker, J., 138
Sutherland, Joel, 203–220, 559

Sviokla, J. J., 29
Swamidass, P. M., 397

Tate, Wendy, 263
Teas, R., 26
The World Bank Group, 487
Timme, Christine, 311
Timme, Stephen G., 299–316, 559–560
Treacy, M., 21, 477
Trent, R. J., 24, 385
Triandis, Harry C., 42
Tuominen, Matti, 434, 441
Tzokas, N., 138, 139

Umble, M., 291
Urban, Glen, 26
Ury, William L., 264
U.S. Chamber of Commerce, 214, 217
U.S. General Accounting Office (USGAO), 361, 364, 367–368

Van de Ven, A. H., 345
Van Hoek, Remko I., 21, 28
Varadarajan, P., 21
Vargo, Stephen L., 56
Venkataramanan, M. A., 29
Venkatraman, N., 341
Vickery, S. K., 28
Victor, Bart, 20
Vitasek, Kate, 427–441, 519–520, 560
Vokurka, R. J., 4
Von Hippel, E., 138
Vorhies, D. W., 343, 345
Vos, Bart, 21

Waecker, J. G., 47
Wagenheim, George, 418
Walker, Helen, 31
Walker, Orville C., 21, 342, 349
Ward, P. T., 354

Wasti, S. Nazli, 363
Waterhouse, J. H., 32
Wathne, Kenneth H., 458, 459
Webster, Frederick E., Jr., 21, 24
Weick, K. E., 337, 350
Weiss, David S., 365–366
Weitz, Barton A., 455, 462, 467
Welch, Denice E., 334
Welch, Lawrence S., 334
Wells, R. B., 32
Welsh, M. A., 23
Wensley, Robin, 20
Wernerfelt, Birger, 21, 338, 341
Whang, S., 199
Whipple, J. M. R., 29
Wiersema, F., 21, 477
Wilding, Richard, 32
Williamson, Oliver E., 365, 398–399, 457, 458
Wilson, David T., 366, 368
Wilson, Rosalyn, 203
Wind, Y., 138
Winston, Evelyn, 61
Wolf, Joachim, 20
Womack, James P., 52, 288
Wong, V., 138
Woodruff, Robert B., 26, 57
World Trade Organization (WTO), 487
Wu, Lei-Yu, 331

Youndt, M. A., 354

Zacharia, Z. G., 27, 42, 480
Zajac, E. J., 343
Zaltman, G., 347, 352
Zander, U., 351
Zeithaml, Valerie, 26
Zhu, Meng, 455–471, 560
Zinn, Walter, 61
Zsidisin, George A., 32, 321

Subject Index

Activity-based costing (ABC), 208–209, 384
Administered relationship, 411
Advanced planning and scheduling
    (APS), 177
Advertising, 124
Alignment/engagement matrix, 365–366
Alliances, 127, 367, 397, 414
American Airlines, 133
American Express, 259
American Production and Inventory
    Control Society (APICS), 153, 177
American Productivity and Quality
    Center (APQC), 511
Analyzer strategy type, 342, 347, 350
Anticipation inventory, 188
Antitrust policy, 4–5
Assemble-to-order (ATO) supply chain, 293
Assembly, value-added warehousing
    functions, 229, 235
Assembly line, 153
Asset specificity, strategy implementation
    and, 458
Atomistic risk, 325–326
A-type flow, 292–293
Automated guided vehicles (AGVs), 247
Automated picking process, 237
Automatic replenishment programs
    (ARP), 40
Avon, 237

Bailey Controls, 367
Balanced scorecard (BCS), 435–436
Baldrige National Quality Award, 154
Bandwagoning, 399–400
Bar coding, 164, 238, 241, 246–247
Bargaining, 407, 422–424
    finalization, 423–424
    issue discussion, 423

    position development, 422
    See also Negotiation
Batch production-oriented supply chains,
    285–287
Baxter Healthcare, 231
Benchmarking, 508–512. *See also*
    Best practices
Best Buy, 52
Best practices, 153
    benchmarking, 510
    integrated business process design,
        173, 176, 177, 181–182
    lists and selection of, 519–520
Bill of materials (BOM) forecasting, 66
Bose Corporation, 364
Brand differentiation, 138
Break bulk, 223–224
British Production and Inventory
    Control Society (BPICS), 177
Build-to-order (BTO) supply
    chain, 293
Build-to-stock (BTS) supply chain,
    293, 294–297
Bullwhip effect, 198–199, 292, 443
Business continuity and crisis
    management (BCCM), 324–325
Business process design and integration,
    169–182
    best practices, 173, 176, 177, 180,
        181–182
    business process framework,
        172–173
    core processes, 107, 160–161
    implementation examples, 178–182
    inventory ownership, 177, 179–180, 181
    leadership, 176–177, 179, 181
    organization and people aspects,
        173–174, 177–178, 180, 182

systems and data, 174–176, 178, 180, 182
See also Process orientation
Business process offshoring.
    See International sourcing
Business-to-business telemarketing, 125

Campbell Soup, 199
Capacity planning, 29, 71
Capital utilization and financial
    performance, 300–305
Cash operating cycle, 306–307
Change management, 15, 523–540
    assessing readiness for change, 528
    causes of project failure, 523–524
    change equation, 536
    complacency, 532
    defining, 524–525
    global environment and, 537–540
    initial response, 530–532
    launch, 535–536
    myths and realities, 534–535
    organizational roles, 528–529
    people and organizational issues,
      527–528
    planning, 526–527
    resistance to change, 525–526, 533
    strategy development, 525–526
    success factors, 536
    time and resource commitment, 525
    training, 526
Change managers, 529
Change owners, 529
Chemstation, Inc., 235
China:
    cultural differences from U.S., 538–539
    food supply security, 502
    outsourcing advantages, 319, 396
    political economy, 44
    U.S. supply chains and, 40
Circuit City, 52
Cisco Systems, 121–122
Collaborative business relationships,
    28, 121. *See also* Relationship
    management
Collaborative forecast, 99
Collaborative planning, forecasting, and
    replenishment (CPFR), 380, 439, 444
Collaborative transportation management
    (CTM), 210–214, 444
Commitment to relationship, 31, 409
Communications technology.
    See Information technology
Competence center, 111
Competitive bandwagoning, 400

Computer-aided design/computer-aided
    manufacturing (CAD/CAM), 155
Computer-integrated manufacturing
    (CIM), 154–155
Computer numerical control (CNC), 155
Configurational research, 338, 341
Complacency, 532
Consolidation, 223
Consultative relationships, 131–132
Continuous replenishment process
    (CRP), 380
Continuous review inventory system,
    189–194
Contracts, 467
    enforcement, 466
    institutional environment and, 469
    logistics services, 374
    maintaining supplier relationships,
      367–368
    negotiation outcome, 424
    specific negotiation concerns, 418
    verbal agreements, 424
    verification, 424
    violation, 458
Contracts, negotiating. *See* Negotiation
Contractual relationships, 411–413
Control processes, 14, 456
    business process design, 176–177
    culture-based norm expectations, 42
    governance-related exchange and
      interorganizational coordination,
      445, 448–449
    interfunctional coordination and,
      433–434
    risk management strategy, 332
    See also Global supply chain control;
      Intercorporate coordination
Cooperative arrangements, 433
Core processes, 107, 160–161. *See also*
    Business process design and
    integration; Processes
Correlation analysis, 75
Council of Logistics Management, 1
Council of Supply Chain Management
    Professionals (CSCMP), 177, 343,
    428, 511, 519
Critical path method, 153
Cross-cultural issues, 41–43, 47–48, 365
    cultural-cognitive institutions, 470
    differences between U.S. and China,
      538–539
    establishing supplier relationships, 369
    global logistics outsourcing, 388–389
    governance issues, 42

international sourcing and, 396–397
language, 397, 538
monochromic and polychromic
    people, 539
negotiation and, 42, 388
norm expectations, 42–43, 469–470
supplier-customer negotiation
    influences, 415
supplier relationship trends and
    opportunities, 363
Cross-docking, 225, 236, 238–239, 249
Cross-functional teams, 100–101, 110,
    325, 368, 434
Cultural-cognitive institutions, 470
Cultural competitiveness, 338
Cultural differences. *See* Cross-cultural
    issues
Customer clue gathering, 483
Customer lifetime value, 57, 59
Customer relationship management
    (CRM) systems, 60
Customer relationships management.
    See Relationship management
Customer satisfaction, 3
Customer segments, 23–24, 122–123
Customer service management, 6, 52,
    59–61
    front-end contact quality, 60, 275
    logistics outsourcing and, 379
    online interactions, 61
    supply management and, 266–267
    transportation issues, 205
    value management and, 61–62
    warehousing and, 243
Customer value, 52–56. *See also* Value
    management
Customs-Trade Partnership Against
    Terrorism (C-TPAT), 218, 502
Cycle stock inventory, 188
Cycle time management, 27–28

Data, defined, 89
Data aggregation effects, 341
Data characteristics, 79–81
Data quality, 80–81
Defender strategy type, 342, 347–349, 351
Delegated sourcing, 261–262
Dell Computer, 51, 159, 185, 197, 306–307,
    331, 337, 477, 482
Delphi methods, 328–329
Demand:
    data characteristics, 79–81
    dependent, 6, 65–66, 186
    derived, 6, 30, 65

derived versus independent, 66–68
independent, 6, 30, 65, 66–68, 186
Demand forecasting. *See* Sales or demand
    forecasting
Demand management, 6–7, 29–30, 65–84
    batch-oriented production systems,
        285–287
    bill of materials (BOM) forecasting, 66
    bullwhip effect, 198–199, 443
    capacity planning, 71
    collaborative transportation
        management, 212
    CPFR, 380, 438, 444
    customer base and, 78
    data characteristics, 79–81
    definition, 68
    demand fulfillment strategies, 293–298
    demand planning, 30, 67, 71–72
    forecasts versus plans, 69–70
    iterative process, 84
    model, 69
    need for sales forecast, 72–73
    new products, 82–83
    sales and operations plan, 29, 70–72, 439
    sales targets and, 70
    supply chain relationship
        management, 68
    understanding demand types, 65–68
    warehouse functions, 224–225
    See also Inventory management;
        Lean supply chain; Sales or
        demand forecasting
Demand planning, 30, 67, 71–72. *See also*
    Demand management
Demand risk, 322–323
Dependency management, 461–462
Dependent demand, 6, 65–66, 186
Dependent relationship, 31
Derived demand, 6, 30, 65, 66–68
Diagnosing supply chain problems,
    15, 32, 507–521
    benchmarking approaches, 508–512
    comparing commercial and academic
        tools, 509
    mapping approaches, 512–515
    means-ends approaches, 515–519
    model, 508
    problem solving, 519–520
    SCOR model, 510–511, 519
    selecting best practices, 519–520
    Supply Chain Integrated Management
        analysis method (SCIM*am*), 512–514
    Supply Chain Visibility Roadmap
        (SCVR), 514–515

The Diagnostic Tool, 516–519
See also Performance measurement
Diagnosis, defined, 508
Differentiated defender, 342, 347–348, 349, 351
Disaster preparation and management, 14, 40
   business continuity and crisis management, 324–325
   classification and vulnerability assessment, 487–490
   global trends, 500
   global warning systems, 501–503
   information sources, 498–499
   mitigation, 494–495
   planning, 492–494
   process, 490–491
   quick response product management, 198
   recovery, 497
   response procedure, 496–497
   supply chain gaps, 500–501
   U.S. initiatives, 503–504
   warning and detection, 495–496
Distribution centers, 226. *See also* Warehousing
Distribution requirements planning (DRP), 186
Donnelly, 364
Dual sourcing, 261
DuPont, 364, 367, 375

Eastman Kodak, 364, 367
eBay, 476
E-commerce:
   customer service implications, 61
   go-to-market development, 125
   logistic service requirements, 381
   warehouse management, 249
Economic order quantity (EOQ) model, 190–193
Efficient consumer response (ECR) system, 199–200, 380
Electronic data interchange (EDI), 245–246, 364
Electronic Data Systems (EDS), 268
Electronic Product Code, 514
Employee training, 277–278, 526. *See also* Human resources
Engineer-to-order (ETO) supply chain, 293
Enterprise process model, 159–162
Enterprise resource planning (ERP), 154, 177, 395

Enterprise risk management (ERM), 324–325
Environmental capacity, 23
European Union (EU), 375
Executive management support:
   establishing supplier relationships, 367
   for information sharing and interorganizational coordination, 453
   knowledge management competence development and, 92
   logistics outsourcing and, 383
   strategic orientation and, 25
   See also Leadership
Executive management, view of SCM, 302, 311, 313–314
Explicit knowledge, 89, 96–97
Exponential smoothing, 74
External *takt* time, 289–290

Face-to-face sales, 126–127
Facilitative exchange, 445, 449–450
Failure modes and effects analysis (FMEA), 327
FedEx, 53, 150, 196, 240, 475
Feminine culture, 539
Fender Musical Instruments, 167
Financial performance management, 10–11, 32–33, 299–316
   capital utilization (SPEED), 300–305
   capital/operating expense tradeoff, 301–302
   drivers of financial performance, 300
   establishing supplier relationships, 368
   international factoring, 332–333
   linking financial metric gaps to business processes, 308–309, 311–314
   logistics outsourcing, 377
   mapping SCM to, 309, 311–314
   performance metrics, 305–307, 316
   supply management function and, 253–254
   top-down approach, 307–315
   transaction cost reduction approach, 24
   value management and, 26–27
   value of gaps in financial metrics, 307–308, 310–311
   See also Performance measurement; Value management; *specific supply chain activities and functions*
Five-forces analysis, 256
Flexibility, 333–334, 477
   environmental diversification, 24
   knowledge development, 91

order fulfillment processes,
343, 345, 355
outsourcing driver, 377
product form postponement, 196, 331
social norms, 468, 470
synchronizing demand and
supply, 165
transport modes, 206
Flexible manufacturing systems
(FMS), 155
Flextronics, 395
Flow and pull replenishment, 288–290
Ford, Henry, 153
Ford Motor Company, 364, 368
Forecasting. *See* Sales or demand
forecasting
Forecasting hierarchy, 80
Foreign exchange rates, 43–44
Fractionation, 419
Function-based silo, 104
Function-oriented organizations,
103–106, 110–111
SCM compatibility, 112–113

Gantt charts, 153
General Agreement on Tariffs and
Trade (GATT), Uruguay round, 46
General Electric (GE), 331
GlaxoSmithKline, 267, 323, 477
Global Earth Observation System of
Systems (GEOSS), 495, 501
Global environments, 6
change management and, 537–540
currency volatility, 43–44
differences between global and single
markets, 39
global SCM strategy and, 23–24
hypersecurity consciousness, 47
key global market characteristics, 23
munificence, 23
political economies, 44–45
risks and limitations of older SCM
models, 40–41
uncertainty in, 23
unfair trade practices, 45–46
See also Cross-cultural issues;
specific factors
Global logistics outsourcing, 12, 374, 382,
385–389. *See also* Logistics
outsourcing
Global market characteristics, 23
single markets versus, 2, 39
Global Outbreak Alert and Response
Network, 501

Global positioning system (GPS),
217, 502–503, 514
Global sourcing. *See* International
sourcing
Global supply chain control, 455–471
contracting arrangements, 467
dependency management, 461–462
enforcement, 466
environmental uncertainty and, 459
exchange attributes, 457–460
incentive systems, 465–466
institutional arrangements, 466–468
magnitude and scope of control
requirements, 462–466
moderator role of institutional
environmental differences,
468–470
monitoring, 464–465
opportunistic behavior versus,
458, 459, 460
ownership arrangements, 467
performance ambiguity, 459–460
social arrangements, 467–468
technical requirements and production
costs, 460–462
See also Control processes
Global supply chain management
strategy (GSCMS), 5–6, 19–33,
339–340
core capabilities, 25–32
culture-strategy fit, 42
demand management, 29–30
environmental and structural factors,
22–25, 459
global market characteristics and, 23–24
governance-related exchange attributes,
457–460
implementation effectiveness from
institutional arrangements,
466–468
integrated performance measures, 22
integrating into firm strategy, 33
magnitude of control, 464–466
organizational culture and, 24–25
performance implications, 32–33
product and service management, 27–29
relationship management, 30–31
resource management, 31–32
resource-based paradigm, 21–22
scope of control, 463
strategy-structure-performance (SSP)
paradigm, 20–22
technical requirements and production
costs, 460–462

top management support and, 25
transaction cost reduction approach, 24
understanding competition and
    competitive advantage, 20
value management, 26–27
See also Global supply chain control;
    Integrated logistics management;
    specific strategic activities, functions,
    or issues
Global supply chain risk management.
    See Risk management
Globalization, defining, 2–3, 39
Google, 476
Go-to-market strategy, 122–127
Governance-related exchange, 457–460
    interorganizational coordination and,
    445, 448–449
    See also Control processes; Global
        supply chain control;
        Intercorporate coordination
Government policies and regulation, 23
    global SCM strategy implementation
        and, 469
    offshoring decision-making and, 400
    security initiatives, 503–504
    transportation issues, 215–216
    unfair protectionist trade practices,
        45–46
Grocery Manufacturers Association
    (GMA), 504
Grundfos, 55

Hamburger University, 155
Hazardous materials handling and
    storage, 236–237
HEB Stores, 165, 200
Hedging, 331–332
Helping behaviors, 451
Hewlett-Packard (HP), 99, 121, 125, 268
Hierarchical function-oriented
    organizations, 103–106
Holistic risk sources, 326
Home Depot, 55
Honda, 254, 364, 476
Hospital supply distributors, 231
Human resources, 10, 273–282
    assistance to employees, 278
    creating customer-focused force,
        274–275
    customer-focused employee plan
        implementation, 281–282
    frontline employees, 60, 274
    information support, 275–277
    knowledge development, 277–278

logistics outsourcing and, 378
operations management function, 157
performance feedback, 279–280
quality movement and, 274
resource management, 31
sales forecasting personnel, 83
warehousing management issues,
    247–248
worker empowerment and knowledge
    management competence, 93–95
worker redistribution, 274
workplace affirmation, 280

IBM, 127, 133, 154, 367
IKEA, 477
Incentives and rewards:
    global SCM strategy implementation
        and, 465–466
    knowledge management competence
        development, 93
    risk management and, 334–335
Independent demand, 6, 30, 65,
    66–68, 186
India, 51, 182, 395
Individualism versus collectivism, 539
Informatics technology, 164
Information, defined, 89
Information management, 87, 337
    aggregation effects, 341
    fitting supply chain knowledge and
        strategy, 340–342
    recent research and models,
        338–340
    resource-based paradigm, 338
    supply chain as interpretation system,
        337–338
    See also Knowledge management
Information sharing, 29, 446
    bullwhip effect and, 199
    establishing supplier relationships, 367
    knowledge management competence,
        97–98
    managerial support, 453
    "need-to-know" basis, 97–98
    operations management and, 164–165
    value management and, 58
    See also Interfunctional coordination;
        Knowledge management
Information technology (IT), 3–4, 29
    business process design, 174–176,
        178, 180, 182
    interorganizational, 452
    knowledge management competence,
        98, 99–100

logistics outsourcing and, 381–382
operations management and, 164
outsourcing, 268, 395
risk management and, 334
transportation and, 216–217
warehouse functions and, 245–247
Infosys, 395
Innovation, 14, 475–486
  as strategy, 477
  customer clue gathering, 483
  customer relationship management
    and, 479
  global supply chains and, 485
  marketplace needs and, 481
  organizational culture and processes
    and, 484–485
  processes, 480–484
  profitability and, 479
  SCM and, 477–480
  service development process, 481
Institutional bandwagoning, 400
Institutional environment, 468–470.
    See also Government policies and
    regulation; Political economy
Institutional gatekeepers, 23
Integrated logistics management, 8, 167,
    169–182
  advantages and disadvantages, 396–398
  best practices, 173, 176, 177, 180,
    181–182
  business process design and integration,
    170–172
  designing integrated business processes,
    176–178
  implementation examples, 178–182
  inventory ownership, 177, 179–180, 181
  leadership, 176–177, 179, 181
  organization and people aspects,
    177–178, 180, 182
  systems and data, 178, 180, 182
    See also Business process design and
    integration
Integrated risk management (IRM), 325
Integration, general concepts, 28
Intellectual property protections, 502
Intelligent transportation systems
    (ITS), 217
Intercorporate coordination, 13–14,
    443–454
  associated management behaviors, 445
  collaborative communication, 450–451
  dependency management, 461–462
  environmental factors, 451–454
  facilitative exchange, 445, 449–450

governance-related exchange,
    445, 448–449
information technology, 452
interorganizational helping, 451
investing in relationship-specific
    assets, 449
joint operational planning, 447
knowledge management
    competence, 101
managerial support, 453
model, 445
operational information sharing, 446
operational performance monitoring,
    447–448
opportunistic behavior versus, 448
organizational compatibility, 452
process integration and
    synchronization, 446–447
process-oriented exchange, 445–448
relational performance monitoring, 449
    See also Control processes; Global
    supply chain control
Interfunctional coordination, 13, 427–441
  axes of relationships, 431–432
  collaborative climate for success,
    430, 441
  cooperative arrangements, 433
  core processes and, 107
  cross-functional teams, 100–101
  defined, 428
  functional expertise, 434
  implementation examples, 439–441
  integrated process metrics, 435–438
  knowledge creation and transfer, 95–96
  management controls, 433–434
  mechanisms driving, 432–434
  open communication, 429–430
  organizational climate and, 430–431
  organizational structure, 434
  standardization, 434
    See also Control processes; Information
    sharing; Knowledge management
Internal *takt* time, 290
International Early Warning Program
    (IEWP), 501
International factoring, 332–333
International Organization for
    Standardization (ISO), 154
International Ship and Port Facility
    Security Code (ISPS), 502
International sourcing (or offshoring),
    12–13, 164, 270, 378, 393–404
  core competencies versus, 397
  cross-cultural issues, 396–397

decision-making influencers, 399–403
dependencies, 397
establishing supplier relationships, 369
firm performance versus, 397–399
large versus small firms and, 402
lead times and, 40
leader-follower behavior, 399–400
logistics outsourcing issues,
374, 385–389
optimal degree of, 398, 400
organizational culture and, 403
performance rationale, 395–397
research needs, 403–404
risk management strategy, 332
trends, 394–395
Internet:
go-to-market development, 125
online consumer interactions, 61
warehousing services, 246
See also E-commerce:
Interorganizational information
technology, 452
Interorganizational learning, 483
Interorganizational relations.
See Intercorporate coordination;
Relationship management
Interpretation systems, 11, 337–338.
See also Knowledge management
Intuit, 263–264
Inventory, 186–188
costs of, 187, 204–205
defined, 186
ownership, integrated logistics
management issues,
177, 179–180, 181
reasons against holding, 187
reasons for holding, 186–187
types of, 188
Inventory control systems. *See* Inventory
management
Inventory management, 8, 185–200
basic inventory concepts, 186–188
bullwhip effect, 198–199
Business process design and integration,
170–172
continuous review system, 189–194
CPFR benefits, 299
economic order quantity (EOQ) model,
190–193
exchange rates and, 43–44
independent versus dependent demand
inventory, 186
inventory control systems, 188
lean strategy, 204–205

misallocated capacity, 287
multiple-period systems, 188, 189–195
news inventory model, 189
periodic review system, 189, 194–195
postponement strategies and,
196–197
production order quantity (POQ)
model, 192–193
quick response, 197–198
single-period systems, 188, 189
unplanned inventory, 171
valuing days in inventory gap,
311, 312
warehousing and, 242
See also Demand management;
Lean supply chain; Operations
management; Safety stock;
Warehousing
ISO 9000 standards, 108, 154

Japan:
dual sourcing model, 261
high-context culture, 365
supplier relationships, 363–364
supply chain replication overseas, 365
U.S. reactions to quality-associated
innovations, 154, 288
JC Penney, 364
John Deere, 259
Johnson & Johnson, 364
Joint venture relationships,
127, 397, 412
Just-in-time (JIT) methods, 40, 119, 154,
165, 187, 205, 288, 379–380

Kellogg's, 240
Kitting, 235
Kmart, 366
Knowledge:
accessibility of, 352
defined, 89
explicit, 89, 96–97
intensity, 341, 353
quality of, 341, 352
responsiveness, 347–348, 353
tacit, 89, 95–97, 341, 351
Knowledge management, 7, 87–102, 338
building competence, 88, 90
challenges to building competence,
101–102
cross-functional teams and, 100–101
demand data characteristics, 79–81
development as core competence, 7
executive commitment, 92

fitting supply chain knowledge and strategy, 340–342
holistic approach, 7, 88
identifying ideal knowledge profiles, 342–347
implications of ideal knowledge profiles, 347–350
in Korea, 92
information technology, 98, 99–100
infrastructure, 99–101
intellectual property, 90
interfirm teams, 101
knowledge creation and transfer, 95–97
knowledge development process and cycle time, 339–340
knowledge sharing, 97–98
knowledge use, 98–99
learning from mistakes, 99
memory, 341, 347, 348, 351
organizational climate and, 90–95
outcomes and, 338, 354–355
processes, 95–99
reasons for failure, 87
resource-based view, 338, 341, 348
reward alignment, 93
strategic types, 342–343
supply chain as interpretation system, 11, 337–338
terms and definitions, 89, 90, 341–342
vision statement, 92
worker empowerment, 93–95
See also Information sharing; Information technology; Interfunctional coordination; Organizational learning; Sales or demand forecasting
Kraft Foods, 230
Kuehne & Nagel, 390

Labor costs, 319, 396
Language issues, 397, 538
Leader-follower behavior, 399–400
Leadership:
  integrated business process design, 176–177, 179, 181
  process-oriented business model, 108
  team leaders, 110, 111
  See also Executive management support
Lean inventory strategy, 204–205
Lean production, 52
Lean supply chain, 10, 285–298
  application example, 294–297
  "conventional" SCM context, 285–287

demand fulfillment characterization, 293–298
flow and pull replenishment, 288–290
takt time, 289–290
work flow characterization, 290–293
See also Demand management; Postponement
Learning. *See* Organizational learning
Levi Strauss, 364
Lifetime value of customers, 57, 59
L.L. Bean, 51
Logistics management, 4–5
  defined, 4
  reverse logistics, 225, 231, 235–236
  SCM model, 169–170
  See also Integrated logistics management; Logistics outsourcing; Supply chain management; *specific logistics activities, functions, or issues*
Logistics outsourcing, 12, 162, 164, 373–390
  activities and processes, 376, 382–385
  communications issues, 387
  cultural differences and, 41, 388–389
  customer participation, 383
  customer service and, 379
  defined, 374
  e-commerce, 381
  European Union and, 375
  evaluation, 384
  examples, 389–390
  executive support for, 383
  expertise, 382
  flexibility, 377–378
  global capability, 382
  global outsourcing issues, 12, 374, 382, 385–389
  history, 374–376
  IT and, 381–382
  JIT and, 379–380
  labor issues, 378
  make-or-buy analysis, 56
  management and political considerations, 379
  objectives, 383–384
  operating expenses, 378
  order consolidation, 380
  packaging and, 380–381
  political economy and, 388
  productivity improvement, 377–378
  provider mergers, 375–376
  reasons for, 276–282
  return on assets, 377

start-up problems, 389
trust in service provider, 387–388
See also Vendor-managed inventory
Logistics Systems Dynamics Group
(LSDG), 515

Make-or-buy analysis, 56, 268–269
Management science, 151
Market segmentation, 23–24, 120–123
Market targeting, 121, 137–138
Marketing, 8, 29
    alliances, 127
    brand differentiation, 138
    decision-making model, 119–120
    demand management and, 68, 69
    global product launch, 137–140
    go-to-market strategy, 122–127
    interest creation, 123
    positioning, 121–122, 363
    postpurchase activities, 123
    prepurchase phase, 123
    product development
        management, 122
    product management and, 136–137
    purchase phase, 123
    reverse marketing strategies, 363
    SCM and, 122, 127–129
    strategies, 120–129
    tools, 124–126
    See also Demand management;
        Product management; Promotion;
        Sales management; Sales or
        demand forecasting
Masculine culture, 539
Mass customization, 3, 197, 250
Mass production, 153
Material requirements planning (MRP),
    174–176, 186, 286
Material resource planning (MRP),
    153–154
Maytag, 332
McDonald's, 150, 155, 166
McKesson, 364
Means-end chains, 26, 54–55
Means-ends diagnostic tools, 515–519
Meatpacking industry, 153
Memory, 341, 347, 348, 351
Minerva U.S.A., 390
Mixing, 223
Motor Carrier Act of 1980 (MCA-80), 205
Motorola, 158, 368
Multiple-period inventory systems,
    188, 189–195
Munificence in global environment, 23

Negotiation, 13, 407–425
    agreement verification, 424
    assessing relationship negotiation
        potential, 417
    bargaining, 407, 422–424
    breakdown, 424–425
    cross-cultural issues, 388, 415
    cultural differences and, 42
    detrimental effects, 449
    environmental factors, 414–416
    finalization, 423–424
    goals, 420
    innovation process, 483–484
    issue discussion, 448–449
    posturing, 423
    preparation for, 417–422
    process, 407–408
    strategic supply management
        process, 264
    strategy development, 420–422
    supplier-customer relationship types,
        408–414
    verbal agreements, 424
Nemawashi, 525
New product development or marketing.
    See Marketing; Product management
News vendor model, 189
Nintendo, 247
Noise, 74
Nonstrategic transactions relationship,
    410–411
Norfolk Southern, 53
Normative expectations, 469–470

Offshoring. *See* International sourcing
O.M. Scott Company, 227
OmniMedia, 366
Online consumer interactions, 61
Operating expenses, logistics outsourcing
    and, 378
Operational performance monitoring,
    447–448
Operations management, 8, 149–168
    creating adaptable processes, 166–167
    defining, 150
    evolution of, 152–153
    functional perspectives, 156–158
    global economy and, 162–165
    information sharing and, 164–165
    misconceptions about, 150–151
    process model, 158–162, 167
    process-oriented exchange and
        interorganizational coordination,
        445–448

promoting agility in supply chains, 165–166
services and, 150, 155
short life-cycle strategy, 166
standardized policies and procedures, 28
strategic decisions, 151–152
tactical plan, 152
technology advances and, 164
transformation processes, 150
value chain model, 156–158
See also Inventory management
Operations research, 151
Operations risk, 322
Opportunistic behavior, 448, 458, 459, 460
Order fulfillment process (OFP), 159, 160–162
logistic service requirements, 381
promoting agility in supply chains, 165–166
supply chain knowledge profile and, 354–355
See also Operations management
Organizational climate:
knowledge management competence, 90–95
support for organizational communication, 430–431
See also Executive management support; Organizational culture
Organizational culture:
assessing readiness for change, 528
customer-focused employee plan implementation, 281–282
establishing supplier relationships, 367
global SCM strategy and, 24–25
innovation process and, 484–485
national culture versus, 42–43
offshoring decision-making and, 403
process-oriented business model, 108–109
supplier-customer negotiation influences, 416
Organizational learning, 7, 88, 89, 90, 97, 338
cultural competitiveness, 338
innovation and interorganizational learning, 483
learning from mistakes, 99
memory, 341, 347, 348, 351
process-oriented business model, 108–109
risk management and, 334
supply chain learning capacity, 341, 343, 353–354

Organizational structure:
establishing supplier relationships, 369
function-oriented organizations, 103–105, 110–111
interfunctional coordination and, 434
process-oriented organizational design, 108, 110–112
supplier-customer negotiation influences, 416
supply management and, 254
Orlicky, Joseph, 154
Outsourcing, firm performance versus, 397–399
Outsourcing, logistics. *See* Logistics outsourcing
Outsourcing, make-or-buy analysis, 56, 268–269

Packaging:
logistics outsourcing and, 380–381
value-added warehousing functions, 231, 235
Parallel sourcing, 261
Parke-Davis, 127
Partnership, 413–414
Performance management. *See* Financial performance management
Performance measurement, 32, 435–438, 447–449
balanced scorecard, 435–436
benchmarking, 508–512
coordination role, 32
financial metrics, 305–307, 316
global SCM strategy and, 22, 32–33
interfunctional process metrics, 435–438
logistics outsourcing and, 384
operational performance monitoring, 447–448
personnel performance, 279–280
relational performance monitoring, 449
risk management and, 334
sales forecasts or plans, 70
strategy implementation monitoring, 465
supplier relationships and, 368, 369
supply management, 254
warehouse functions, 243–245
See also Diagnosing supply chain problems
Performance Measurement Group (PMG), 510
Periodic review inventory system, 189, 194–195

Personnel. *See* Human resources
Pfizer, 127
Pipeline inventory, 188
Plossel, George, 154
Point-of-sale (POS) data, 155, 495,
  511–512
  VMI and, 199
Political economy, 23, 44–45
  regional integration and SCM, 44, 45
  See also Government policies and
    regulations
Positioning strategy, 121–122, 363
Postponement, 27–28, 196–197, 289
  risk management strategy, 331
  value-added warehousing functions,
    229, 231, 234–236, 250, 375
Power distance, 539
Pricing strategies, 27, 89
  promotions versus "everyday low price"
    strategy, 165
  supplier-customer negotiation
    issues, 419
Process, defined, 103
Process orientation, 7, 103, 109–110
  enterprise process model, 159–162
  exchange and interorganizational
    coordination and, 445–448
  function-oriented organizations, 106
  knowledge management competence,
    95–99
  measurement systems, 114–116
  new organizational paradigm,
    109–110
  organizational design, 110–112
  process mapping, 114
  process owners, 110, 111, 113–114, 529
  standardization, 28, 113
  system-oriented business model,
    107–109
  See also Business process design and
    integration
Process owner, 110, 111, 113–114, 529
Processes, 106–107
  analysis, 114, 116
  business model, 108
  core processes, 107, 160–161
  creating adaptable processes, 166–167
  functions versus core processes, 107
  generic model, 159
  logistics supply chain model, 169–170
  mapping, 114
  operations management model, 150,
    158–162, 167
  types of, 107

value chain model, 159–162
  See also Business process design and
    integration; Process orientation
Procter & Gamble, 165, 199, 332,
  365–366
Procurement, 157. *See also* Supply
  management
Product form postponement. *See*
  Postponement
Product management, 8, 27–29, 135–146
  communications systems and, 28–29
  core processes, 160–161
  cycle time management, 27–28
  forecasting different numbers of
    products, 82
  global logistics considerations, 139, 140,
    142–143, 145
  global product launch, 137–140
  global product launch, case studies,
    140–145
  integration and, 28
  launch strategy influencers, 139
  market targeting, 137–138
  marketing support, 136–137
  positioning strategy, 121–122, 363
  quick response, 166, 198
  role of, 136–137
  services and, 137
  strategic implementation
    decisions, 122
  See also Postponement
Product returns, 225, 231, 235–236
Production costs, global SCM strategy
  implementation and, 460–462
Production order quantity (POQ)
  model, 192–193
Profitability, 10–11, 300
  innovation and, 479
  logistics outsourcing and, 377
  SPEED (capital utilization) and,
    300–305
  supply management function and,
    253–254
  value management and, 27
  See also Financial performance
    management
Project management, 153
Promotion, 124
  "everyday low price" strategy versus, 165
  value-added warehousing functions,
    224–225, 227, 239
Prospector strategy type, 342, 347, 350
Protectionist trade practices, 45–46
Purchasing. *See* Supply management

Quaker Oats, 375
Qualitative sales forecasting
    techniques, 75
Quality, 154, 288
    human resource issues, 274
    tradeoffs, 53
Quick response (QR), 197–198, 380
Quick Scan, 515

Radio-frequency identification (RFID)
    technology, 47, 100, 164, 235, 247,
    250, 476, 502–503, 504
Raw materials sourcing, 396
Reactor strategy type, 342, 348,
    349–350, 351
Regional economic integrations, 45
Regression analysis, 75
Relational performance monitoring, 449
Relationship management, 11–12, 30–31,
    361–371, 407
    alignment/engagement matrix,
        365–366
    consultative relationships, 131–132
    core processes, 160
    cross-cultural issues, 42–43, 365, 369
    customers and sales force, 130–134
    demand management and, 68
    emerging issues, 370
    enterprise relationships, 132–133
    establishing and maintaining supplier
        relationships, 366–370
    extending core competencies, 370
    innovation and, 479
    investing in relationship-specific
        assets, 449
    optimal relationships, 370
    organizational changes for relationship
        orientation, 368–370
    purchasing strategy shifts and, 361–362
    relationship dynamics, 409
    research showing advantages of supplier
        relationships, 363–364
    service level agreements, 269
    services procurement, 370
    supplier and customer relationship
        types, 408–414
    supplier relationship trends and
        opportunities, 362–363
    suppliers as customers, 368
    transactional relationships, 130, 131
    trust and, 30–31, 409
    value measurement, 31
    See also Intercorporate coordination;
        Negotiation; Supply management

Research & development (R&D),
    axes of interfunctional coordination,
        431–432
Resistance to change, 525–526, 533
Resource-based view (RBV), 21–22,
    338, 341, 348
Resource owners, 110, 111
Reverse logistics, 225, 231, 235–236
Reverse marketing strategies, 363
Reward alignment, 93
Rewards. *See* Incentives and rewards
Risk management, 32, 319–336
    assessment and evaluation, 326–329
    avoidance strategy, 330–331
    categorizing risks, 321–323
    control strategy, 332
    cross-functional teams and, 325
    defined, 330
    defining risk, 320–321
    disaster classification and vulnerability
        assessment, 487–490
    global versus domestic operations, 323
    hedging strategy, 331–332
    identifying and profiling risks,
        325–326
    IT and, 334
    management strategies, 329–333
    management strategy implementation,
        333–335
    mitigation, 335, 494–495
    organizational learning and, 334
    performance measures, 334
    postponement strategy, 331
    probability and loss estimates,
        328–329
    process model, 324–335
    resource management and, 31–32
    rewards and incentives, 334–335
    risk transfer or sharing strategy,
        332–333
    security issues, 333
    speculation strategy, 331
    triggers, 329
    See also Disaster preparation and
        management; Security
Roadway Express, 367
Rolls-Royce Aero Engines, 268

Safety stock, 188, 189
    continuous review systems, 194
    demand error and, 66–68
    periodic review system, 195
Sales and operations planning (S&OP),
    29, 70–72, 432, 439

Sales force adjustments, 76–77, 119
Sales management, 8, 29
  account relationship strategy,
    130–134
  decision-making model, 119–120
  face-to-face selling, 126–127
  go-to-market strategy, 122–127
  Internet and, 125
  joint venture alliances, 127
  sales force program decisions,
    129–134
  SCM and, 122, 127–129
  See also Demand management
Sales or demand forecasting,
    29, 65, 170
  accuracy, 84
  budget, 83
  bullwhip effect, 198–199, 443
  Business process design and integration,
    171–172
  collaborative forecast, 99
  CPFR models, 380, 438, 444
  definition, 84
  demand data characteristics, 79–81
  forecasting hierarchy, 80
  forms, 73
  inadvertent forecasts, 73
  iterative process, 84
  JIT implementation problems, 288
  lead time versus quality, 323
  management questions, 77–84
  narrow or broad customer base, 78
  need for, 72–73
  new products, 82–83
  number of forecasts, 81–82
  number of products, 82
  performance measures, 70
  personnel training, 83
  plans versus, 69–70
  regional differences, 83
  sales and operations plan and, 71
  sales goals versus, 73
  sales targets and, 70
  seasonality, 83
  short life-cycle strategy and, 166
  systems, 76–77
  time horizons or intervals, 73
  tools and techniques, 73–76
Sales targets, 70
Scientific management, 153, 155
SCOR, 113, 510–511, 519
Seasonality:
  bullwhip effect, 198–199
  demand forecasting, 83

inventory, 187
  quick response inventory approach,
    197–198
  sales forecasts and, 74
  tactical planning, 152
  warehouse functions, 227
Security, 6, 14, 47, 485
  business continuity and crisis
    management, 324–325
  global initiatives, 501–503
  global trends, 500
  risk, 323
  risk management, 333
  supply chain gaps, 500–501
  technology and, 502–503
  transportation issues, 217–219
  U.S. developments, 503–504
  See also Disaster preparation and
    management
Service level agreements (SLAs), 269
Single-period inventory systems,
    188, 189
Six Sigma, 270, 320, 325, 440, 520, 551
Sony, 52, 323, 475, 476
Sourcing, international. *See* International
  sourcing
South African Production and
  Inventory Control Society
  (SAPICS), 177
South Korea, 92
Specialty contract relationships, 413
Speculation inventory, 188, 287
Speculative risk management
  strategy, 331
SPEED (capital utilization), 300–305
Sport Obermeyer, 197–198, 325
Stage-Gate process, 480–481
Standardized policies and procedures,
    28, 113
  benchmarking, 508–512
  interfunctional coordination and, 434
  ISO 9000, 108, 154
  See also Best practices
Statistical quality management, 153
Stem and leaf, 296
Strategic choice theory, 338
Strategic management. *See* Global supply
  chain management strategy
Strategic planning, general concepts,
    20–21. *See also* Global supply chain
    management strategy
Strategic supply management process.
  See Supply management, strategic
  process

Strategy implementation control processes.
   See Control processes; Global supply
   chain control
Strategy-structure-performance (SSP)
   paradigm, 20–22
Strategy types, 342, 343, 350–351
   ideal supply chain knowledge profiles
   and, 342–350
Strengths, weaknesses, opportunities, and
   threats (SWOT) analysis, 256
Subjective sales forecasting techniques, 75
Summit Concept, 428
Supplier relationships, 361–371, 407
   alignment/engagement matrix, 365–366
   cross-cultural influences, 365, 369
   dependencies, 370, 397
   emerging issues, 370
   establishing and maintaining, 366–368
   historical trends, 394–395
   organizational changes to establish,
      368–370
   performance metrics, 368, 369
   relationship dynamics, 409
   research showing advantages of, 363–364
   services procurement, 370
   suppliers as customers, 368
   trends and opportunities, 362–363
   trust and commitment, 31, 409
   types of, 408–414
   See also Intercorporate coordination;
      Negotiation; Relationship
      management; Supply management
Supplier relationships, international.
   See International sourcing
Supply Chain Council, 510
Supply chain diagnostic tools. *See*
   Diagnosing supply chain problems
Supply chain innovation. *See* Innovation
Supply Chain Integrated Management
   analysis method (SCIM*am*), 512–514
Supply chain interfunctional coordination.
   See Interfunctional coordination
Supply chain knowledge profiles, 342–350
Supply chain management (SCM), 1,
   169–172, 478
   basic supply chain configuration, 10
   batch-oriented production systems,
      285–287
   definitions, 4, 19, 109–110
   executive management view, 302, 311,
      313–314
   flexibility, 334
   function-oriented organization
      compatibility, 112–113

innovation and, 477–480
logistics management, 4–5
sales and marketing involvement,
   122, 127–129
See also Global supply chain
   management strategy; Integrated
   logistics management; *specific
   activities, functions, or issues*
Supply Chain Management Benchmark
   Series, 510
*Supply Chain Management Process
   Standards*, 519
Supply chain management strategy.
   See Global supply chain management
   strategy
Supply Chain Operations Reference
   (SCOR), 113, 510–511, 519
Supply chain outsourcing. *See*
   International sourcing; Logistics
   outsourcing
Supply chain partner coordination.
   See Intercorporate coordination
Supply chain problems, diagnosing.
   See Diagnosing supply chain problems
Supply chain processes. *See* Business
   process design and integration;
   Process orientation; Processes
Supply Chain Visibility Roadmap (SCVR),
   514–515
Supply chains, 6, 51
   defined, 507
   promoting agility in, 165–166
   See also Value chains
Supply chains as interpretation systems,
   11, 337–338. *See also* Knowledge
   management
Supply management, 10, 29, 253–255
   accounts payable involvement, 270
   bottleneck items, 260
   continuous improvement, 270
   cost-benefit analysis, 254
   critical items, 262–263
   customer focus, 266–267
   defined, 254
   environmental issues, 271
   financial performance and, 253–254
   globalization and, 268
   indirect and services spending, 267–268
   leverage items, 260–262
   operations management function, 157
   organization structure and, 254
   outsourcing, 268–270
   purchasing strategy shifts and, 361–362
   routine purchases, 259–260

skills and competencies, 254
strategic involvement, 254, 265, 266
Supply Wheel model, 254–255
See also Relationship management
Supply management, strategic process,
    255–265
  commodities matrix, 258–259
  data collection and analysis, 255–258
  developing sourcing strategy, 258–263
  implementation and management, 265
  negotiation and contracting, 264
  performance measures, 254
  screening and selection, 263–264
Supply risk, 321–322
SWOT analysis, 256
System-oriented business process model,
    107–109

Tacit knowledge, 89, 341, 351
  knowledge creation and transfer, 95–97
Takt time, 289–290
Taylor, Frederic, 153
Team leaders, 110, 111
Telemarketing, 125
Time-series sales forecasting techniques, 74
Total quality control (TQC), 154
Total quality management (TQM), 154
Toyota, 154, 176–177, 287, 337, 476
Training, 277–278, 526
Transaction-based process mapping
    model, 114
Transaction cost reduction approach, 24
Transactional customer relations, 130, 131
Transition management. *See* Change
    management
Translation, 397, 538
Transplace.com, 478
Transport costs, 203–205
  carrier cost efficiencies, 207–210
  customer service and, 205
  products insensitive to, 226–227
  supplier-customer negotiation
    issues, 419
  warehouse functions and, 223–224,
    227–229, 230, 232, 242
Transportation management, 8, 203–220
  capacity constraints, 214–217
  carrier-shipper collaboration, 209–210
  collaborative transportation
    management, 210–214, 444
  global issues, 214–219
  global security initiatives, 501–502
  government policies and regulations,
    215–216

innovations, 478
lead time variance and, 203–204
mode and carrier decision, 205
online services, 213
outsourcing, 205, 374–375
replenishment demand signal flows, 296
security issues, 217–219, 503
technology and, 216–217
virtual networks, 209
warehouse design issues, 239
See also Transport costs
Trust:
  alliance relationships and, 414
  establishing supplier relationships, 367
  interfunctional coordination and,
    430–431
  interorganizational coordination
    and, 452
  logistics outsourcing and, 387–388
  relationship management and, 30–31
  supplier-customer relationships
    and, 409
T-type flow, 292

Uncertainty, 23
  avoidance strategy, 539
  competitive risks, 31
UPS, 196, 240
U.S. Department of Agriculture (USDA),
    503–504
U.S. Department of Homeland
    Security, 503
U.S. Food and Drug Administration
    (FDA), 504
U.S. National Cooperative Research Act, 4
U.S. Postal Service, 240
USCO Logistics, 390
UTi Worldwide, 390

Value chains, 6, 51, 156–158
  process model, 114, 159–162
  See also Supply chains; Value
    management
Value hierarchies, 26, 54–55
Value management, 6, 26–27, 51–59
  capturing voice of the customer, 57–58
  customer lifetime value, 57, 59
  customer service and, 61–62
  information sharing, 58
  integrated marketing
    communications, 27
  means-ends chains, 26, 54–55
  measurement systems, 27
  relationship management and, 31

trade-offs, 53–54
understanding customer value, 52–56
value appropriation, 56–57
See also Customer service management;
    Value chains
Vendor relationship management.
    See Relationship management
Vendor-managed inventory (VMI),
    40, 155, 194, 199–200, 380, 444
Vlasic, 227
Voice-of-the-customer data, 57–58, 483
Voluntary Industry Commerce Standards
    (VICS) Association, 210
V-type flow, 290–291

W. W. Grainger, 231
Wal-Mart, 119, 150, 155, 165, 185, 199,
    337, 365–366, 370, 482
Warehouse management systems (WMS),
    238, 246, 247
Warehousing, 8, 223–250, 239
    automated picking process, 237, 247
    break bulk, 223–224
    consolidation function, 223
    cross-docking, 225, 236, 238–239, 249
    customer service and, 243
    design issues, 236–240
    e-commerce, 249
    financial metrics and, 308–309
    future trends, 249–250
    human resource issues, 247–248
    information needs, 245–246
    inventory and, 242
    location, 232
    major functions and activities, 232–236
    marching supply and demand, 224–225
    mixing function, 223
    online services, 246

order types and, 237–238
outsourcing, 223, 248–249, 374–375
packaging and unitization, 240–241
palletized products, 237, 240
performance measurement, 243–245
product type and, 227–229, 236–237
rationale for, 230–231
returns and reverse logistics, 225, 231,
    235–236
storage and handling trade-offs, 241
supply chain process and, 226–227
technology and, 246–247, 250
total supply chain context, 242
transportation economies and, 223–224,
    227–229, 230, 232, 242
transportation mode and, 239
value-added activities (postponement),
    229, 231, 234–236, 250, 375
See also Inventory management
Web logs (blogs), 98
Whirlpool, 268, 323, 331, 523
Whitney, Eli, 153
Wipro, 395
Work flow, 290
    A-type flow, 292–293
    T-type flow, 292
    V-type flow, 290–291
Worker empowerment, 93–95
Work-in-process inventory, 188
World Customs Organization (WCO),
    501, 502
World Health Organization (WHO), 501
World Trade Organization (WTO),
    46, 362, 385–389

Xerox Corporation, 508

Zara, 166, 198, 477

About the Editors

John T. (Tom) Mentzer is the Harry J. and Vivienne R. Bruce Chair of Excellence in Business in the Department of Marketing and Logistics at the University of Tennessee. He has written more than 180 papers and articles and seven books. He was recognized in 1996 as one of the five most prolific authors in the *Journal of the Academy of Marketing Science* and in 1999 as the most prolific author in the *Journal of Business Logistics*. He was awarded the Academy of Marketing Science Outstanding Marketing Teacher Award in 2001. He serves on the editorial review boards of numerous journals and previously served as editor of the Systems Section of the *Journal of Business Logistics*. He is a past president of the Council of Logistics Management, a past president of the board of directors of the Sheth Foundation, and a former member of the board of directors of the American Marketing Association Foundation. He was formerly president, and is presently chair, of the board of governors of the Academy of Marketing Science and is a Distinguished Fellow of the Academy of Marketing Science—a distinction granted to fewer than 40 scholars worldwide. Dr. Mentzer was the 2004 recipient of the Council of Logistics Management Distinguished Service Award. He has served as a consultant for more than 100 corporations and government agencies, is on the boards of directors of several corporations, and previously worked for General Motors Corporation.

Matthew B. Myers is the Nestlé Professor of Marketing and Associate Professor, Marketing & Logistics, and the Director of the Global Business Institute at the College of Business Administration, University of Tennessee. He has studied, taught, and worked in Central America, South America, Europe, and Central and East Asia and has acted as a consultant to organizations in the global distribution, chemical, insurance, pharmaceutical, and marketing research industries. His research has been published in a number of outlets, including the *Journal of Marketing,* the *Journal of Retailing,* the *Journal of International Business Studies,* the *Journal of Business Research,* and the *Journal of Business Logistics.* He is a member of the editorial review boards of the *Journal of International Business Studies,* the *Journal of World Business,* the *Journal of International Management,* and the *Journal of International Marketing.*

Theodore P. Stank is the John H. Dove Distinguished Professor of Logistics and Department Head of Marketing and Logistics at the University of Tennessee. His research interests focus on the strategic implications associated with integrated logistics and supply chain management concepts, specifically related to integration, information exchange, and operational responsiveness. He is a coauthor of *21st Century Logistics: Making Supply Chain Integration a Reality* and has published more than 55 articles in academic and professional journals. He has worked for Abbott Laboratories, served as an officer in the U.S. Navy, and performed consulting and executive education services for numerous manufacturing and logistics firms.

About the Contributors

Daniel C. Bello (PhD, Michigan State University) is the Marketing Roundtable Research Professor in the Department of Marketing at Georgia State University in Atlanta. Previously, he was on the faculty at the University of Notre Dame and held management positions in the Product Development Group at Ford Motor Company. His research interests include distribution strategy in domestic and international channel systems. He has published widely in professional journals such as the *Journal of Marketing*, the *Journal of the Academy of Marketing Science*, the *Journal of International Business Studies*, and the *Journal of Business Research*, among others. Currently, he serves as Editor-in-Chief of the *Journal of International Marketing*, a scholarly journal focusing on international marketing and published by the American Marketing Association. He also serves or has served on the editorial review boards of the *Journal of Marketing*, the *Journal of the Academy of Marketing Science, the Journal of International Business Studies*, and the *Journal of Business Research*, among others.

Antonio Borghesi is Professor of Marketing Logistics in the Department of Business Economics in the College of Economics at the University of Verona. His research areas include the relationship between marketing and logistics, strategic management supply chain risk, and risk management. He has been Director of the Master in Integrated Logistics, Supply Chain Integrated Management of the University of Verona since 2001 and the Director of the Post-graduate course in Enterprise Risk Management since 1994. He has written 80 papers and articles and coauthored 12 books. From 1995 to 1998, he was President of the Province of Verona. He is a member of editorial board of the *Journal of Marketing Channels*, the Chairman of the CESRAS (Centre for Studies of Risk and Insurance), and a member of AIDEA (Italian Academy of Business Administration). He is also an Educational Member of the CSCMP (Council of Supply Chain Management Professionals, U.S.A.) and an Educational Member of RIMS (Risk and Insurance Management Society, U.K.).

Margaret Bruce, PhD, is the Director of the Centre for Business Research and Professor of Design Management and Marketing at the Manchester Business School (MBS), University of Manchester. Before joining MBS in 2003, she was Head of Textiles at UMIST (University of Manchester Institute of Science and Technology) and Professor of Design Management and Retailing at UMIST. She was responsible for establishing a retailing group at UMIST and for developing a new MSc program in International Retailing and five new undergraduate programs. She is the CEO of UMIST Ventures Limited (UVL), a strategic adviser to Hong Kong Polytechnic University, and a panel member of the AHRB (Arts and Humanities Research Board) and the Nesta Graduate Pioneer Programme. She holds an International Chair in strategic design management at ICN Graduate Business School, University of Nancy, France; a Chair in design management and fashion retailing at University of the Arts, London; and has an Honorary Professorship at Xi'an Institute of Science and Technology, China.

Roger J. Calantone is the Eli Broad Chaired University Professor of Business and is University Distinguished Faculty at Michigan State University. He is Program Director of the university specialization program in Information Technology Management and is also Adjunct Professor of Economics. He has published more than 250 journal and proceedings articles, five books, and several book chapters. His publications and research are mostly in the areas of product design and development processes, decision support systems, and organization process metrics and control. His publications appear in journals such as *Marketing Science, Management Science, Decision Sciences, IEEE Transactions on Engineering Management, Journal of Marketing, Journal of Marketing Research, Modeling Simulation & Control, R&D Management, Industrial Marketing Management, Journal of Product Innovation Management,* and *Journal of Business Logistics.* He has won numerous research and publication awards and research grants. He was previously associated with McGill University and the University of Kentucky in both academic and administrative roles and spent time visiting at Rutgers University, Bell Labs, the University of Florida, and the UCF Tourism Research Institute.

S. Tamer Cavusgil is University Distinguished Faculty and the John W. Byington Endowed Chair in Global Marketing at Michigan State University. He also serves as the Executive Director of MSU-CIBER (Center for International Business Education and Research). He specializes in international marketing strategy, early internationalization, and emerging markets. He is the author of several books and more than 100 refereed articles. *Doing Business in Emerging Markets* (Sage, 2002) is his most recent contribution. He is also the author of several computer-aided diagnostic tools for managers, including CORE V, COmpany Readiness to Export. He served as the inaugural Editor in Chief of the *Journal of International Marketing,* published by the American Marketing Association. He edits the Elsevier book series *Advances in International Marketing.*

Didier Chenneveau is Vice President of IPG Americas Operations, Hewlett-Packard Company (HP), and Vice President of Operations, Imaging & Printing Americas, Hewlett-Packard. As Vice President and General Manager of Operations for HP's imaging and printing business, he has responsibility for Americas manufacturing, product completion operations, distribution, reverse supply chain, order management, and all associated supply chain processes and developments. He joined HP in 1989 as Finance and Treasury Manager at its European headquarters in Geneva,

Switzerland. He moved to Santa Clara, California, in 1994 and was named Controller in 1996 and subsequently Worldwide IT Manager for HP's Home Product Division in Cupertino, makers of the Pavilion Home PC. In 1998, he was promoted to General Manager of Home PC's European operation and returned to France. He returned to the United States in 2001 as Vice President of Consumer Operations before moving to his current role. Prior to joining HP, he worked for Caterpillar. He is a native of France and has an MBA from EM-Lyon.

Robert Lorin Cook is Professor of Marketing and Logistics at Central Michigan University. He was recognized as one of the top five educators at Central Michigan University (CMU) twice, in 1999 and 1985, and has developed an undergraduate logistics program at CMU that graduates 125 majors per year. He has published in numerous prestigious journals, including the *International Journal of Logistics Management*, the *Journal of Business Logistics, Supply Chain Management Review*, the *Journal of Supply Chain Management*, the *International Journal of Physical Distribution and Logistics Management*, the *Journal of Marketing Education*, the *Journal of Advertising Research*, and *Production and Inventory Management Journal*. He is coauthor of *Securing the Supply Chain*. He has performed contract research for several Fortune 100 firms and has been actively involved in the Council of Supply Chain Management Professionals since 1984. In addition, he has served as Executive Committee Member and Chair of the Research Strategies Committee. He received a PhD in business administration (1980) and a master of business administration in logistics (1975) from Michigan State University.

Paul Cousins, PhD, is Professor of Operations Management and CIPS Professor of Supply Chain Management at Manchester Business School, University of Manchester. His career to date has spanned a range of business sectors from industry (Westland Helicopters & Sikorsky Aircraft) to consulting (A.T. Kearney) to academia (University of Bath, University of Melbourne, Australia and Queen's University Belfast). It has led him to work in various countries, including the United Kingdom, Europe, the United States, and Australia. He has obtained more than £1.5 million in research grants and has conducted research and consultancy work for numerous firms across a range of industrial sectors at the national and international levels. He has published several books and more than 40 journal and conference papers. His main research interests focus on the area of supply management: strategic supply management, environmental supply, and interorganizational relationship management.

William L. Cron, PhD, is Associate Dean for Graduate Education at the M. J. Neeley School of Business, Texas Christian University. He is also President-elect of the Academic Council of the American Marketing Association. His research interests are in the areas of sales and sales management, channels of distribution, and marketing and business research. His publications have appeared in the leading marketing and management journals, including the *Journal of Marketing*, the *Journal of Marketing Research*, and the *Academy of Management Journal*. He has been recognized as one of the top 10 researchers in sales and sales management and coauthors one of the leading sales management textbooks. His consulting is primarily focused on firms in the health care distribution and manufacturing industry.

Michael R. Crum is the John and Ruth DeVries Chair in Business and a Professor of Logistics and Supply Chain Management at Iowa State University. He has been a faculty member at Iowa State since 1980. He teaches business logistics, supply chain management, and transportation management and economics at both the graduate and undergraduate levels. His current research interests are in the areas of transportation management, transportation safety, and supply chain security. He has authored or coauthored more than 70 research publications, including three books. His publications appear in the leading journals in the field. Additionally, he has been a principal investigator on three U.S. Department of Transportation research projects. He earned DBA and MBA degrees from Indiana University. He was a Fulbright Scholar at the Warsaw School of Economics in Warsaw, Poland, from 1988 to 1989.

Lucy Daly, PhD, is the Business Manager of the Centre for Business Research (CBR) and a Lecturer in the Marketing area at the University of Manchester, Manchester Business School. She has worked on a variety of projects for CBR, including business and market research, strategy development, and product evaluation. She has extensive research experience in supply chain management and has been involved in the delivery of a number of programs for the Institute of Operations Management. She has published extensively and has a PhD in supply chain management in the textiles and apparel sector from the University of Manchester Institute of Science and Technology (UMIST).

Donna F. Davis is an Assistant Professor of Marketing in the Rawls College of Business at Texas Tech University. Her research interests are in supply chain relationships, brand management, and e-business. She has published research in the *International Journal of Physical Distribution & Logistics Management,* the *Journal of Business Forecasting,* the *Journal of Marketing Education,* and *Business Horizons.* She has also presented her research at several national and international conferences and business forums. She earned her PhD in marketing and information management from the University of Tennessee, Knoxville, before joining the faculty at Texas Tech.

Thomas E. DeCarlo is the Ben S. Weil Endowed Chair of Industrial Distribution and Professor of Marketing and Industrial Distribution at the University of Alabama at Birmingham. Previously, he was on the faculty at Iowa State University as Associate Professor. While at Iowa State, he served as the Faculty Scholar in the ISU Business Analysis Laboratory. The Laboratory, staffed by ISU faculty and students, performed various marketing research projects for companies such as 3M, Lockheed Martin, Andersen Windows and others. His primary research interests deal with strategic issues in sales force management, customer relationship management, and marketing communications. His research has been published in the *Journal of Marketing,* the *Journal of Consumer Psychology,* the *Journal of Personal Selling and Sales Management,* and the *Journal of International Business Studies,* among others. He is coauthor of *Sales Management,* a top-selling sales management textbook. He has had professional relationships with a number of Fortune 500 organizations in areas of market analysis and customer segmentation, sales force management, brand management, and new product development. He earned his PhD from the University of Georgia.

J. Paul Dittmann is the Director of the Office of Corporate Partnership and Managing Director of the Integrated Value Forums at the University of Tennessee. He also teaches logistics courses and takes sessions in the supply chain executive education programs. He joined the University of Tennessee after a 30-year career in industry. He has held Fortune 150 positions such as Vice President, Logistics for North America, and Vice President Global Logistics Systems, and most recently he has served as Vice President, Supply Chain Strategy, Projects, and Systems for the Whirlpool Corporation. In the latter capacity, he developed the global supply chain and manufacturing strategies for the Whirlpool Corporation, saving more than $600 million. He has been an instructor for the Project Management Institute, offering seminars around the United States in the areas of global project management and change management. He has also conducted numerous public seminars in the areas of lean manufacturing, global business, and supply chain excellence, and has spoken at more than 30 conferences on these and other topics. He has also served as a consultant for numerous firms.

Lisa M. Ellram, PhD, is Chairperson of Department of Management and Professor of Business at Colorado State University. Prior to that, she was the John and Barbara Bebbling Professor of Business at Arizona State University's W. P. Carey School of Business. She was named as a "purchasing practitioner to know" by *Supply and Demand Chain Executive,* 2004. She was also named as a member of the Dean's Council of 100 Distinguished Scholars at Arizona State University in 2001. Her research, teaching, and consulting interests include services purchasing and supply chain management, as well as strategic cost management, including cost/price analysis, total cost of ownership, and target costing. She has published more than 50 articles in a number of leading supply chain journals, has coauthored four books, and has received numerous research grants. She has served on the board of directors of CAPS research (2000–2003) and was chairperson of the Institute of Supply Management's Educational Resource Committee (2000–2003). She is a founding member of the Procurement Sciences Institute (2003–present). She currently serves on the editorial review board for the *Journal of Business Logistics,* the *Journal of Purchasing and Supply Management,* the *International Journal of Logistics Management,* and *Inside Supply Management.*

Terry L. Esper, PhD is Assistant Professor of Logistics in the Marketing and Logistics Department of the University of Tennessee. He is a three-time recipient of the Dwight D. Eisenhower Transportation Fellowship, an Eno Transportation Foundation Fellow, and a two-time participant in the Council of Logistics Management Doctoral Symposium. His research interests include supply chain collaboration, boundary spanner role perceptions and behavior, and interorganizational learning. His research has appeared in the *Journal of Business Logistics,* the *International Journal of Physical Distribution and Logistics Management,* the *Transportation Journal,* and several conference proceedings. His teaching specialties include purchasing/supply management and strategic transportation and logistics management. Prior to his graduate studies, he worked as a senior traffic administrator and logistics solutions strategic planner for Hallmark Cards, Inc., and Hallmark.com. He also conducted transportation research for the Arkansas State Highway and Transportation Department and the Federal Highway Administration. He received his PhD in Business Administration with emphasis in Logistics and Supply Chain Management from the Sam M. Walton College of Business at the University of Arkansas.

Dominique Estampe is currently Professor in Supply Chain Management and Director of the Institute for Supply Chain Excellence—ISLI, a Department of Bordeaux Business School. He is author of several publications on supply chain processes and performances. He is Editor in Chief of *Supply Chain Forum: An International Journal*, a refereed journal (www.supplychain-forum.com), and *Logistique & Management*, a French refereed journal. He was formerly Senior Consultant in reengineering processes and implementation of information systems for a nuclear engineering company, SGN. He has worked for many European companies as a consultant in operations management. He holds an Engineering Diploma from Bordeaux Electronic Engineering School in France.

Daniel J. Flint is the Proffitt's, Inc. Professor of Marketing and Associate Professor in the Department of Marketing and Logistics and Director of the Marketing PhD Concentration at the University of Tennessee, Knoxville. He has industry experience as an industrial sales engineer for the Aerospace/Commercial Rolled Products Division of Alcoa, is a former naval flight officer, and is a former aircraft maintenance division officer. He is well published in both marketing and logistics top-tier journals and regularly presents at global conferences. His expertise is in customer value management, specifically helping firms gain deeper insights into their customers. He is a member of the American Marketing Association, Academy of Marketing Science, and Council of Supply Chain Management professionals. He has worked with a wide range of industrial and consumer organizations as both a market researcher and trainer. He has a PhD in marketing and logistics from the University of Tennessee.

James H. Foggin is an Associate Professor of Business Logistics at the University of Tennessee. He teaches graduate and undergraduate courses in logistics strategy and logistics quantitative analysis. He teaches regularly in executive education courses and has designed and taught customized logistics short programs for large corporations. He has conducted research on customer value determination, inventory management, and relationship management in supply chains. He is a member of the Council of Supply Chain Management Professionals and the American Society of Transportation and Logistics. He serves on the editorial board of the *Transportation Journal*, is an occasional reviewer for the *Journal of Business Logistics*, and has been a reviewer for the annual Logistics Educators Conference since 1987. He is a graduate of the University of Tennessee, where he received his baccalaureate and his master's degree. He obtained his doctoral degree from Indiana University in Bloomington.

Britta Gammelgaard is Associate Professor at the Copenhagen Business School (CBS). Her research area is supply chain management (SCM), with special focus on learning and innovation in supply chains. Furthermore, she has a profound interest in methodologies in supply chain research and has played a leading role in the establishment of a Nordic PhD course program within that area. She is active on the international SCM research scene in networks such as the Nordic Logistics Research Network (NOFOMA) as well as the American-based Council of Supply Chain Management Professionals (CSCMP), where she has organized research tracks at their European conferences in 2005 and 2006. She has published in Danish and international journals such as the *Journal of Business Logistics* and the *International Journal of Physical Distribution and Logistics Management.* She earned her PhD from the Copenhagen Business School.

Barbara Gaudenzi is Assistant Professor at the University of Verona, Italy. Her areas of interest are marketing, supply chain management, and risk management. Her recent works are focused on the management of risks in supply chains. She has joined several projects and consulted on others in the areas of supply chain management and risk management. In 2004, she spent a period of time as visiting researcher at the Caledonian Business School, Caledonian University (Glasgow, U.K.) and at the Centre for Logistics and Supply Chain Management, Cranfield University (Cranfield, U.K.). She teaches at Verona University in postgraduate courses focused on supply chain management, risk management, and business management. She earned her PhD in 2004 from the University "Parthenope" in Naples, Italy.

Thomas J. Goldsby, PhD, is Associate Professor of supply chain management at the University of Kentucky. His research interests focus on logistics, customer service, and supply chain integration. He also has an interest in the theory and practice of lean and agile supply chain strategies. He has published several articles in academic and professional journals and serves as a frequent speaker at academic conferences, executive education seminars, and professional meetings. He is coauthor of *Lean Six Sigma Logistics: Strategic Development to Operational Success* (2005). He has twice received the Accenture Award for the best paper published each year in the *International Journal of Logistics Management* (1998 and 2002) and has received recognitions for excellence in teaching at Iowa State University and Ohio State University.

Susan L. Golicic is Assistant Professor in the Charles H. Lundquist College of Business at the University of Oregon, Eugene, where she teaches supply chain management and marketing strategy. Her research interests include supply chain management, interorganizational relationships, forecasting, and reverse logistics. She has experience in logistics at DaimlerChrysler and has more than 5 years experience in project management and environmental engineering. She has worked with numerous companies, including Bacardi, Continental Tire, Eastman Chemical Company, Michelin, Motorola, Sara Lee Intimate Apparel, Whirlpool, and Williamson-Dickie on sales forecasting reengineering. She has presented papers at numerous academic and practitioner conferences and has published in the *Journal of Business Logistics,* the *International Journal of Physical Distribution and Logistics*

Management, Transportation Journal, Supply Chain Management Review, and the *Journal of Business Forecasting.* She earned her PhD in logistics at the University of Tennessee, Knoxville, before joining the University of Oregon faculty.

Omar Keith Helferich, DBA, (Michigan State University; MSE and BSE, University of Michigan), is on the faculty at Central Michigan University in the Department of Marketing & Hospitality Services Administration and is involved in ongoing applied research for the Department of Homeland Security. He has more than 30 years experience of project consulting and management for Fortune 500 companies and the government. He has authored and coauthored articles in the *Journal of Distribution Management, Journal of Business Logistics* and for the Council of Logistics Management. As a 15 year American Red Cross volunteer in disaster logistics, he spent several weeks at the Oklahoma bombing and the World Trade Center 2001 incidents. In the fall of 2005, he served 15 days in Louisiana, volunteering with the Red Cross to help solve major logistics problems in caring for people after Hurricane Katrina devastated the Gulf Coast.

G. Tomas M. Hult, PhD, is Director of the Center for International Business Education and Research (MSU-CIBER) and Professor of Marketing and Supply Chain Management at Michigan State University (MSU). MSU-CIBER is the developer of globalEDGE (globalEDGE.msu.edu), the world's leading online source (based on a ranking by Google.com in February 2006 using the search term "international business") for international business information. He serves as Executive Director of the Academy of International Business (AIB), Deputy Editor in Chief of the *Journal of International Business Studies,* and Associate Editor of *Decision Sciences* and the *Journal of Operations Management* for the areas of international marketing and operations and supply chain management. He has published on global strategy and supply chain management in the *Academy of Management Journal, Strategic Management Journal,* the *Journal of Marketing,* the *Journal of Operations Management,* and *Decision Sciences,* among others. He is the founder of Hult Ketchen International Group, LLC, a firm specializing in international business strategy consulting services, and an Associate Member of the FedEx Center for Supply Chain Management. He has conducted executive seminars on global strategy and supply chain management for the University of California at Berkeley and has been an invited speaker by a number of institutions (e.g., University of Cambridge, University of Oxford, and Stockholm School of Economics). He has provided consulting services to a number of corporations (e.g., Avon, DaimlerChrysler, FedEx, Ford, General Motors, IBM, Masco, Raytheon, State Farm, and Textron).

Kenneth B. Kahn, PhD, is Associate Professor of Marketing in the Department of Marketing and Logistics at the University of Tennessee. His teaching and research interests concern product development, product management, and new product forecasting. He has published more than 30 articles, with recent publications in the *Journal of Product Innovation Management* and the *Journal of Business Logistics.* He is the author of the book *Product Planning Essentials* (Sage, 2000) and editor of the *PDMA Handbook on New Product Development* (2004). He is currently Vice President of Publications for the Product Development and Management Association (PDMA).

Scott Keller (PhD, University of Arkansas) is Associate Professor of Marketing and Logistics at the University of West Florida, where he has begun a new supply chain logistics management program. His research interests focus on faculty at Pennsylvania State University and Michigan State University. His research interests focus on the development of customer-focused logistics employees and the complexity and practice of internal marketing in service organizations. His research appears in leading transportation and logistics journals. His managerial experience is in motor carrier operations, large-scale distribution center management, foreign trade zone activation and operation, and ocean freight terminal operations. He was the recipient of multiple teaching and research awards while on the faculty at Michigan State University. Recently, he won the Distinguished Teaching Award at the University of West Florida.

David J. Ketchen, Jr. (PhD, Pennsylvania State University) is the Lowder Eminent Scholar and Executive Director of the Lowder Center for Family Business & Entrepreneurship at Auburn University. His research focuses on (1) uncovering the determinants of superior organizational performance, (2) strategic supply chain management, (3) entrepreneurship and franchising, and (4) methodological issues in management research. He has published articles in journals such as *the Strategic Management Journal, Academy of Management Journal,* the *Journal of Operations Management, Academy of Management Executive,* the *Journal of Business Venturing,* and the *Journal of Management.* He has served as an associate editor for the *Journal of Management, Organizational Research Methods,* the *Journal of International Business Studies,* and the *Journal of Operations Management.* He currently serves on the editorial boards of *Academy of Management Journal, Academy of Management Review,* and the *Journal of Management Studies.* He is the coeditor of an annual book series titled *Research Methodology in Strategy and Management.*

Masaaki (Mike) Kotabe holds the Washburn Chair Professorship in International Business and Marketing and is Director of Research at the Institute of Global Management Studies at the Fox School of Business and Management at Temple University. Prior to joining Temple University in 1998, he was Ambassador Edward Clark Centennial Endowed Fellow and Professor of Marketing and International Business at the University of Texas at Austin. He served as the Vice President of the Academy of International Business from 1997 to 1998. In 1998, he was elected a Fellow of the Academy of International Business for his significant contribution to international business research and education. He has written many scholarly publications, including *Global Sourcing Strategy: R&D, Manufacturing, Marketing Interfaces* (1992); *Anticompetitive Practices in Japan* (1996); *Market Revolution in Latin America: Beyond Mexico* (2001); *Global Marketing Management* (3rd ed., 2004); and *Global Supply Chain Management* (2006).

Everth Larsson is Associate Professor and Head of the Division of Engineering Logistics, Department of Industrial Management and Logistics at Lund University, Lund, Sweden. His current research is mainly in the areas of process-based business development and logistics innovation, and he has been and is the main supervisor of several PhD students. In addition to journal articles and research reports, he has also coauthored a book on process-based business development and has been codeveloper of Internet-based courses in this and other areas. Over the years, he has been active in academic leadership positions, such as Vice Dean at the School of Mechanical Engineering, and has served on a variety of boards. He is active in numerous international research networks and professional societies. He earned his degrees as Licentiate of Engineering and PhD at Lund University.

Anders Ljungberg is the founder of Trivector LogiQ AB (1996), a consultancy firm specializing in the field of process management and strategy realization. During its 10 years in business, Trivector LogiQ has worked closely with a broad range of firms in the industry as well as the public sector. He is the main author of the book *Processbaserad verksamhetsutveckling (Process Based Business Development),* used as a core text at a number of Scandinavian Universities, and he has also written a range of articles within the same field. In addition, he lectures at Lund University and frequently is an invited speaker at conferences. He has a PhD in process orientation from Lund University.

Clifford F. Lynch, of C. F. Lynch & Associates, has been in the logistics industry for 45 years. He was with the Quaker Oats Company for 29 years, the last 13 of those as Vice President, Logistics. He was president of Trammell Crow Distribution Corporation from 1987 to 1993 and has provided management advisory services in logistics for the past 12 years. He is a Certified Member of the American Society of Transportation and Logistics, Warehousing Education and Research Council, and serves on various editorial advisory boards. He is a member and past president of the Council of Supply Chain Management Professionals and has received numerous awards in the field of logistics. He is an Adjunct at the University of Memphis, a frequent lecturer at other colleges and universities, and the author of numerous articles on the subject of logistics and two books on logistics outsourcing. He is a director of the Memphis Food Bank and is licensed as an affiliate real estate broker in the State of Tennessee. He has consulted for clients in the United States, China, the Philippines, Mexico, and European countries.

Ila Manuj is currently pursuing a doctoral degree in logistics in the Department of Marketing and Logistics at the University of Tennessee. Her research interests are in the area of risk and complexity management in global supply chains. She worked with CARE, a not-for-profit social development organization, for 3 years. At CARE, she was involved with projects related to inventory management, streamlining information flows, disaster management, and coordination of global supply chains for donated food commodities and relief materials. She is a member of the Council for Supply Chain Management Professionals and Decision Sciences Institute. She earned her master's degree in international business from the Indian Institute of Foreign Trade, New Delhi.

Glen Margolis is the Founder and Chairman of the Board of Steelwedge Software, Inc. He also founded a contract manufacturing and logistics service provider with facilities across North America where he pioneered a collaborative demand management process. In addition, he served as a Senior Supply Chain Strategy Consultant with both Mercer Management Consulting and Ernst & Young, LLP, during which he led benchmarking and planning process improvement projects for more than a dozen Fortune 500 manufacturing companies. He is a frequent speaker and author on topics related to supply chain management, enterprise planning, and performance management. He holds a master's degree in public policy from Harvard University's John F. Kennedy School of Government and a bachelor of science degree in engineering from the Webb Institute.

John E. Mello is an Assistant Professor of Marketing at Arkansas State University. He is receiving his PhD in logistics in August, 2006 from the University of Tennessee. He earned a master's degree in management from Wilmington College in 2001 and a master's in public administration from the University of New Haven in 1985. He is also certified in production and inventory management by the American Production and Inventory Control Society. His business experience includes production supervision, inventory management, production planning, operations planning, materials management, and systems implementation. His research interests are supply chain management, organizational culture, and sales forecasting. He has published in the *Journal of Business Forecasting* and has forthcoming articles in the *International Journal of Physical Distribution and Logistics Management* and *Foresight: The International Journal of Applied Forecasting*.

Michael J. Mol is an Advanced Institute of Management research fellow at London Business School and a part-time Senior Lecturer in Strategic Management at the University of Reading, both in the United Kingdom. His main research interests are in the areas of sourcing strategy, in particular the causes and performance consequences of outsourcing and management innovation, especially how management innovations are created and can contribute to competitive advantage. His publications have appeared in, among other periodicals, *International Business Review*, the *Journal of International Management*, the *Journal of Purchasing and Supply Management*, *Research Policy*, and *Strategic Organization*, and in two forthcoming books. He serves on two editorial boards. He has been cited as an outsourcing expert by newspapers such as the *Financial Times*. He holds a PhD (2001) from RSM Erasmus University. He can be reached at mmol@london.edu and through www.michaelmol.com.

Carol L. Monroe is an independent marketing research consultant who specializes in customer value determination. Among her clients have been Procter & Gamble and USCO Logistics. Prior to earning an MBA at the University of Tennessee with a concentration in market research, she had a career in academic librarianship and holds a master of librarianship degree from Emory University.

Mark A. Moon is Associate Professor of Marketing at the University of Tennessee, Knoxville. His primary research interests are in buyer and seller relationships, demand management, and sales forecasting. He is coauthor, along with Dr. John T. (Tom) Mentzer, of *Sales Forecasting Management: A Demand Management Approach*. His professional experience includes positions in sales and marketing with IBM and Xerox. He teaches at the undergraduate, MBA, and executive MBA levels and teaches demand planning, forecasting, and marketing strategy in numerous executive programs offered at the University of Tennessee's Center for Executive Education. He has consulted with numerous companies, including Eastman Chemical, Hershey

Foods, Lucent Technologies, DuPont, Union Pacific Railroad, Motorola, Sony, and Sara Lee. He earned his PhD from the University of North Carolina at Chapel Hill and his MBA from the University of Michigan in Ann Arbor.

Abré Pienaar is Chief Executive of iPlan Industrial Engineers, a professional consulting firm based in South Africa but working on supply chain projects in many parts of the world (www.iplan.co.za). As Chief Executive, he coordinates iPlan's multiple international assignments. He serves on the Education Strategies Committee of the Council for Supply Chain Management Professionals (CSCMP) and teaches (part-time) supply chain management at the MBA School of the University of Pretoria. His work experience includes positions in production management, materials management, executive management, and project management for the implementation of globally integrated supply chains. He holds a doctoral degree in industrial engineering from the University of Pretoria, a bachelor's degree in mathematical statistics from the University of South Africa, and fellow level CPIM certification from the American Production and Inventory Control Society (APICS).

James M. Reeve, PhD, CPA, is Professor Emeritus of Accounting and Information Management, University of Tennessee-Knoxville and CEO Mahanaim Essentials LLC. He joined the faculty of the University of Tennessee in 1980 after completing his MBA from Drake University and PhD from Oklahoma State University. At the University of Tennessee, he was a member of the MBA and EMBA core faculty. He is also a member of the Lean Enterprise Institute and Supply Chain Certification faculty. He has won six teaching awards at the University of Tennessee. His research interests are in the areas of performance management, the lean enterprise, cost management, and supply chain management. He has published more than 40 articles in academic and professional journals, including *Supply Chain Management Review,* the *Journal of Cost Management,* the *Journal of Management Accounting Research,* and the *Accounting Review.* In addition, he has coauthored six books, including the market leading *Accounting* (South-Western Publishing). He has been a judge for the *USA Today*/RIT Quality Cup Competition. He has consulted or provided training around the world for a wide variety of organizations including, Boeing, Procter & Gamble, Philips Consumer Electronics, Freddie Mac, AMOCO, Lockheed Martin, Coca Cola, Sony, and Hershey Foods. He is presently taking his supply chain expertise and applying it to his own personal care products company.

Lloyd M. Rinehart is Director of the Logistics PhD Program and Associate Professor of Marketing and Logistics in the College of Business Administration at the University of Tennessee, Knoxville (UTK). His primary teaching responsibilities at UTK focus on graduate, undergraduate, and executive education instruction in negotiation processes between suppliers and customers, logistics operations at the undergraduate and MBA levels, and supply chain thought at the PhD level. His current research interests include theory and practical applications of the negotiation process used in creating transactions and managing relationships between procurement, marketing, and logistics personnel. The findings of these research efforts have led to numerous academic publications in leading academic journals, including the *Journal of Marketing,* the *Journal of the Academy of Marketing Science,* the

Journal of Marketing Channels, the *Journal of Marketing Education*, the *Journal of Business Logistics*, the *International Journal of Physical Distribution and Logistics Management*, *Transportation Journal*, and the *International Journal of Operations and Production Management*. He is also coauthor of *Creating Logistics Value: Themes for the Future*, published by the Council of Supply Chain Management Professionals.

E. Powell Robinson, Jr., is Professor in the Department of Information & Operations Management in the Mays Business School at Texas A&M. His specialty area is supply chain management, in which he has established an international reputation in the areas of production and distribution network design and inventory management. His work with Ashland Chemical Company received international recognition by the Decision Sciences Institute as the outstanding application of decision sciences to decision making in 1995. His current research explores interfaces between information technology and supply chain strategy. He received his PhD from the University of Texas, Austin, in 1986.

Ivan Russo is an Assistant Professor at the University of Verona, Vicenza Campus, Italy. He is involved in several projects and research efforts in the areas of supply chain management and internationalization. His research areas are the relationship between marketing and logistics, returns management and supply chain management, and the internationalization of small and medium-sized enterprises. In 2005, he spent a term at the University of Tennessee as a research scholar. He earned his PhD in business economics at the Department of Business Economics, College of Economics, University of Verona.

Funda Sahin is an Assistant Professor of Logistics in the College of Business, at the University of Tennessee. Her research and teaching interests are in logistics, operations and supply chain management, inventory planning and control, and information technology applications in supply chain management. Recently, she has been recognized as one of the outstanding young researchers by 2005 INFORMS Young Researcher Roundtable. Her publications have appeared in *Decision Sciences*, the *Journal of Operations Management*, the *Journal of Business Logistics and Production* and *Inventory Management Journal*. She is a member of CSCMP, DSI, and INFORMS. She received her PhD from Texas A&M University.

Shay Scott is Associate Pastor at Sevier Heights in Knoxville, Tennessee. Prior to this, he led the International Logistics team at Dell, Inc., and was a Research Associate with the University of Tennessee at Knoxville. During his tenure at Dell, he was responsible for shipment of product from Dell's domestic U.S. production facilities to more than 100 countries worldwide, and he has traveled and worked in more than 30 countries. In this position, he held responsibility for sourcing, transportation, and trade compliance activities. His primary research interests are logistics outsourcing and cross-cultural relationships. He holds an MBA and an MS in industrial engineering, both from the University of Tennessee.

Arun Sharma is Professor of Marketing at the School of Business Administration, University of Miami, where he was the Chairman of the Marketing Department

(2000–2004). Previously, he taught at the University of Illinois at Urbana-Champaign. Prior to joining the academic world, he worked for three years in a high-technology firm where he handled product management and sales management responsibilities. He has published extensively, is on the review board of major journals, and has received many excellence-in-research and excellence-in-teaching awards from the School of Business Administration at the University of Miami. He has consulted and conducted seminars for companies such as Accenture, American Express, AT&T, Exxon, Goodyear, HP, IBM, MasterCard, Motorola Siemens, Visa International, and Western Union. He received his PhD in marketing from the University of Illinois at Urbana-Champaign in 1988. He also has an MBA and a bachelor of engineering degree.

Jagdish (Jag) N. Sheth, PhD, is the Charles H. Kellstadt Professor of Marketing in the Goizueta Business School at Emory University. He is nationally and internationally known for his scholarly contributions in consumer behavior, relationship marketing, competitive strategy, and geopolitical analysis. He has worked for numerous industries and companies in the United States, Europe, and Asia, both as an adviser and as a seminar leader. His clients include AT&T, BellSouth, Cox Communications, Delta, Ernst & Young, Ford, GE, Lucent Technologies, Motorola, Nortel, Pillsbury, Sprint, Square D, 3M, Whirlpool, and many more. He has offered more than a thousand presentations in at least 20 countries. He is frequently quoted and interviewed by the *Wall Street Journal*, the *New York Times*, *Fortune*, the *Financial Times*, the *Economic Times*, and radio shows and television networks such as CNN, Lou Dobbs, and more. He is also on the board of directors of several public companies, including Cryo Cell International (NASDAQ) and Wipro Limited (NYSE). His many awards include Outstanding Marketing Educator (1989) from the Academy of Marketing Science, Outstanding Educator Award (1991, 1999) from the Sales and Marketing Executives International, the P. D. Converse Award (1992) from the American Marketing Association, Distinguished Fellow of the Academy of Marketing Science (1996), and the Distinguished Fellow Award (1997) from the International Engineering Consortium. He is also a Fellow of the American Psychological Association (APA). The year 2004 marked a stellar year for him as he was awarded both the Richard D. Irwin Distinguished Marketing Educator Award and the Charles Coolidge Parlin Award, the two highest awards given by the American Marketing Association. In 2000, along with Andrew Sobel, he published a best-seller, *Clients for Life*. His latest book, *The Rule of Three*, coauthored with Dr. Rajendra Sisodia, altered the current notions on competition in business. Published in 2002, it has been translated into German, Italian, Polish, Japanese, and Chinese. It was the subject of a seven-part television series by CNBC Asia and was a finalist for the 2004 Best Marketing Book Award from the American Marketing Association.

Paola Signori is Associate Professor at the Department of Business Economics, University of Verona, Italy. She has published more than 20 articles in academic publications on the subjects of marketing and logistics, and a monograph on a new supply chain diagnostic tool. Her areas of research interest include marketing, communication, logistics, and supply chain management (supply chain performance measurements). She has lectured at a number of colleges and universities in

Italy and has consulted for Italian manufacturing and service companies. She is a member of the editorial advisory board of the *International Journal of Physical Distribution & Logistics Management* and is a reviewer for the *Journal of Business Logistics*. Since 2000, she has been Executive Director of the Master in Supply Chain Management at the University of Verona. She obtained a PhD from the Naval Institute of Naples in 1999.

Thomas W. Speh, PhD, is the James Evans Rees Distinguished Professor of Distribution at the Richard T. Farmer School of Business, Miami University in Oxford, Ohio. He teaches courses in logistics management and supply chain management. He is coauthor of *Business Marketing Management: A Strategic View of Industrial and Organizational Markets* (9th ed.) and *Marketing: Best Practices* (3rd ed.). He was the Director of the Warehouse Research Center at Miami University from 1986 to 2000. He has published numerous articles in a variety of academic and professional journals, including the *Harvard Business Review, Supply Chain Management Review*, the *Journal of Marketing*, and the *Journal of Business Logistics*. He is a frequent speaker at logistics and supply chain conferences in the United States and many countries around the world. He was the President of the Council of Logistics Management for 2003 and is past president of the Warehousing Education and Research Council. He has conducted research and consulting projects in warehousing management, supply chain relationship management, warehousing cost analysis, logistics outsourcing, and marketing strategy planning.

Mandyam M. Srinivasan (Srini) is the Ball Corporation Distinguished Professor of Business at the University of Tennessee. He received his PhD from Northwestern University. He has worked in two leading automobile manufacturing organizations and has successfully installed materials planning and control systems in both of these organizations. He has consulted with and offered training programs for numerous organizations, including General Motors, IBM, Sony, Allied-Honeywell, Boeing, Cutler-Hammer, Carlisle, Woodward Aircraft Engine Systems, Delta Airlines, Robins Air Force Base, DeRoyal, and Pearson NCS. He is the author of the book *Streamlined: 14 Principles for Building and Managing the Lean Supply Chain* (2004). Journals he has published in include *Operations Research, Management Science, IIE Transactions*, and *IEEE Transactions on Communications* and *Queueing Systems*. He is the Editor for *IIE Transactions on Design and Manufacturing* and is an associate editor for the *International Journal of Flexible Manufacturing Systems*.

Joel Sutherland is the Industry Liaison Officer at Lehigh University's Center for Value Chain Research in Bethlehem, Pennsylvania, where he is responsible for building industry awareness of the center's initiatives while identifying potential research opportunities between the center and its corporate partners. From 2002 to 2005 he chaired the Collaborative Transportation Management (CTM) committee for the Voluntary Interindustry Commerce Standards Association (VICS), an industry association focused on improving the efficiency and effectiveness of the entire retail supply chain. He has more than 30 years of experience as a logistics and supply chain professional, having held executive-level positions in Fortune 500 companies such as International Paper, CSX Corporation, and Formica Corporation. He has also led logistics operations for global leaders in the automotive and pharmaceutical industries. He has taught logistics at the University of Southern California and is a frequent speaker at professional groups and universities. He has a number of published papers and has authored numerous logistics articles for various trade publications, receiving the Professional Achievement Award from *Logistics Management* magazine. He was recognized as one of the Top 20 Logistics Executives by *CLO* magazine and the *Logistics & Supply Chain Forum* and is a past president of the Council of Supply Chain Professionals (previously the Council of Logistics Management), a professional association with more than 10,000 members worldwide. He received his BS degree from the University of Southern California, with a focus in logistics and transportation management, and an MBA from Pepperdine University.

Stephen G. Timme is the President of FinListics® Solutions and is Adjunct Professor at the Georgia Institute of Technology in the School of Industrial and Systems Engineering. FinListics Solutions helps professionals link the financial impact of business process change with specific financial metrics. FinListics also works with solution providers who increase their revenues by using the FinListics ValueMANAGER ON-LINE® to gain an executive-level audience and demonstrate a tangible return on investment to their prospective clients. His and FinListics' services have been provided throughout the world for clients such as BellSouth, Coca-Cola, Colgate-Palmolive, Delta Air Lines, Disney, Eastman Kodak, Eli Lilly & Co., Exel Logistics, FedEx, Georgia-Pacific, Hershey Foods, Hewlett Packard, IBM, Lowe's, Manhattan Associates, Microsoft, PepsiCo, Siemens, United Parcel Service, Wal-Mart, and many other companies. He is often a keynote speaker at executive seminars sponsored by *CFO Magazine, BusinessWeek, Forbes,* and others.

Kate Vitasek is the founder and Managing Partner of Supply Chain Visions, a small consulting practice that specializes in supply chain strategy and education. She is a thought leader in the area of supply chain management. As a consultant, she brings a unique blend of consulting, practitioner, and general management experience to the firms she works with. This blend of skills ensures that solutions are both practical and cost-effective. Her approaches have been widely published; she has authored more than 50 articles, which have appeared in publications such as the *Journal of Business Logistics, Supply Chain Management Review, Inside Supply Management, Aviation Week, Distribution Business Management Journal, The Manufacturer,* and APICS *Performance Advantage.* She has been recognized for her leadership in the profession. Most recently, she was selected as a "Woman on the Move in Trade and Transportation" and was also recognized as a "Rainmaker" by *DC Velocity Magazine* for her efforts in helping to build the logistics and supply chain profession. She has also served on the board of directors for the Council of Supply Chain Management Professionals as well as on the Supply Chain Council's Deliver Committee.

Meng Zhu is a second-year doctoral student in the Department of Marketing at Georgia State University. Prior to pursuing her PhD, she spent one year in a master's program at the Andrew Young School of Policy Studies. Although her undergraduate major was comparative literature, her graduate studies were concentrated in applied statistics and public administration. Her primary research interests include channels of distribution and interorganizational relationships. She has published several articles in academic journals, books, and conference proceedings such as *Global Logistics and Supply Chain Management Handbook* (Sage) and INFORMS Marketing Science Conference. Currently, she serves as assistant to the editor in chief of the *Journal of International Marketing*, a professional marketing journal published by the American Marketing Association. She received her bachelor's degree from Nanjing University, China.